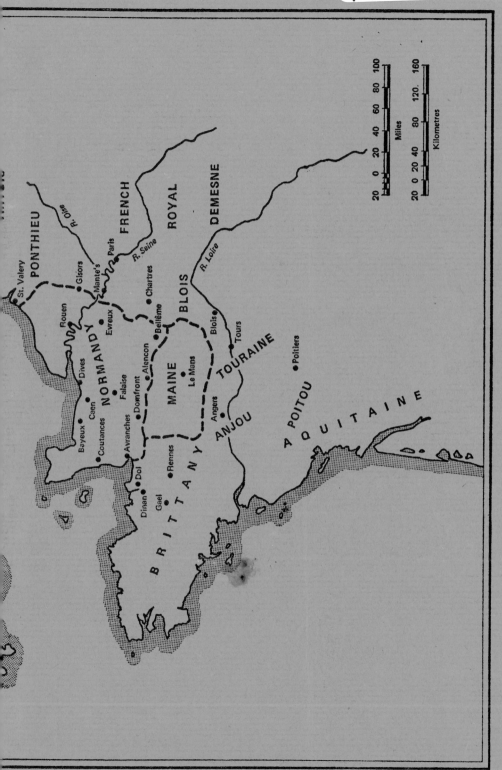

FLANDERS

PONTHIEU

St. Valery

R. Oise

FRENCH

ROYAL

DEMESNE

Paris

Gisors

Mante's

R. Seine

Rouen

Chartres

BLOIS

Evreux

Belême

R. Loire

NORMANDY

Dives

Blois

Tours

Caen

Falaise

Alençon

MAINE

TOURAINE

Bayeux

Domfront

Le Mans

Coutances

Poitiers

Avranches

Angers

POITOU

ANJOU

AQUITAINE

Dol

Rennes

Dinan

Gael

BRITTANY

20   0   20   40   60   80   100

Miles

20   0   20   40   80   120.   160

Kilometres

THE NORMANS AND THEIR WORLD

JACK LINDSAY

THE NORMANS AND THEIR WORLD

St. Martin's Press New York

CONTENTS

To Harry Chaplin

The light-spot shifts, with curious changes
and glints of sense, and then estranges;
a curtain slips and darkness falls.
Stare deeper still, stare from your centre
and suddenly you truly enter.
A comprehensive lustre seems
to pierce and flood the core of things—
till shadows of bewildering wings
disperse the scene with tottering walls
into malicious chaos where
the faces clot to iron masks
with eye-slots of mercurial dreams.
Then the slow light-shaft drills again,
the surfaces are neatly explored,
order fallaciously restored.

Thus, while at history we stare,
it opens out and all is plain,
then shuts and we are aliens there.
How break the circle of confusion,
delusion followed by exclusion,
unless we somehow learn to share
the struggles, the compulsive tasks,
the reckless joy, the sure despair,
the lonely vision that emerges,
the unpredictable wild surges?
We glimpse the body and spirit bare
in an apocalypse of pain
beyond which breaks the earth redeemed.

Still harder to communicate
the entangled whole, in words repeat
the onward movement, ring on ring
of dancers who advance, retreat,
advance again; freewill and fate
dictate the pattern that appears
obscurely from the hopes and fears,
the unifying circling sweep...
Something grows human at the core
in the dense night of evil's reign;
from blind recurrence born again
the wholly-free new forces leap;
and so the light breaks through once more.

Jack Lindsay

FOREWORD

This is a book about the Norman Conquest of England, but it seeks to cast its net far more widely than is usual in books on this theme. Firstly, it deals at some length with the Viking background of the Normans and with the general significance of the great Scandinavian expansion between the eighth and tenth centuries – the last large-scale movement of heathen peoples into the Christianized region of western Europe, with its roots in the Roman past. Secondly, it gives an account of the Norman irruption into south Italy, the conquest of Sicily, and the attempt to invade the Byzantine empire. These events had profound effects on the whole European situation in that they caused support to be given to the Papacy at the crucial moment of its self-assertion. Thirdly, while providing an account of Normandy, Anglo-Saxon England, and Norman England, it attempts to enlarge the focus by relating the events and developments to the whole pattern of medieval society, its structure and the deep conflicts which in the end led to its transformation. Fourthly, throughout the account, and particularly in chapters XIV-XV, an attempt is made to get inside the minds of the men of the period, to find what held them together and gave them a sense of identity.

So, though the book for the most part deals with the eleventh and twelfth centuries, it has been found necessary at moments to look backwards or forwards and to keep before the reader at all times a sense of what the society was moving out of, and what it was moving into. Both the Normans and the English of the eleventh century had very distinctive qualities. The merging of their contributions, after much stress and struggle, was what gave the English of later centuries their particular character and their important role in the full working out of the potentialities of the feudal world and in the creation of the new society that superseded it.

Jack Lindsay

PART I

THE NORMANS AND THE ENGLISH

CHAPTER I

THE NORMANS AND THE VIKING AGE

The Normans were Northmen or Norsemen. Their settlement in Normandy was part of the prolonged expansion by trade, piracy, raids, and colonization from Scandinavia (that 'womb of nations' as Jordanes called it) which went on in the early medieval period. This Viking movement was the last large-scale barbarian or pagan movement in the West, and it had important results in determining the shape and character that Europe was to take. A broad idea of the vast changes brought about by the Noresmen can be got by glancing at the Mediterranean world in 1000 AD and then in 1100. In 1000 that world was dominated by three powers: the Byzantine Christians carrying on the Roman Empire in parts of the east, and two Islamic caliphates: the Fatimite, centred on Cairo, whose control extended as far as Sicily; and the Spanish, centred on Cordova whose control extended over what is now Algeria and Morocco, and reached south through Mauritania towards Senegal. By 1100 that situation

was radically altered, with the Normans dominating south Italy and
Sicily, and crusaders advancing eastward. The Normans were not the
only factors in this change, which drew northern Europe into the
Mediterranean sphere with its ancient bases, its complex and rich
cultures; but they had been the most important. We cannot imagine
the swing occurring as and when it did without the Normans. Bloch
took 1050 as the date marking the decisive social changes 'trans-
forming the face of Europe'; it follows that those changes cannot be
conceived without the impact and expansion of the Normans.

The links between Scandinavia and Britain were formed much
earlier than the eighth century, when the raids began. For instance,
the finds at Sutton Hoo have shown that the East Anglian royal
house at around 650 was in touch with the Uppland region of
Sweden.[1] Too often historians have approached British history
largely from the Mediterranean angle, from that of the Romans or
the Roman Church. But we need also to see the Dark Ages and the
early medieval epoch in a Germanic perspective which includes
Scandinavia. Otherwise we get a very one-sided picture and fail to
grasp the entangled nature of the changes that went on. We must
regard the Norman Conquest of England as the last great Viking
expansion, linked with the developments going on in Italy and
Sicily. By adopting the Frankish language and the feudal system, to
which they gave their own stamp, the Norsemen of the eleventh
century changed themselves radically, but we can still see them as
Vikings making their own peculiar transformation of what they
took over from the Franks, the men of Anjou and Maine, or others.
Their irruption belongs generally to the same movement of peoples
that produced the Danelaw in England and brought about Cnut's
Anglo-Danish empire, and yet it introduced something quite new
into England and into the whole European situation.[2]

The first raid of Norsemen, according to the *Anglo-Saxon
Chronicle*, came late in the 780s, when they laid waste the Dorset
coast; then in 793 Lindisfarne, the cradle of Northumbrian Christianity, was pillaged; next year came an attack on Jarrow. After some
decades of quiet the raids were resumed on a larger scale.
Norwegians, looting in Cornwall, were defeated by Egbert of Wessex
at Hingston Down in 838; but such effective counter-action was
unusual. In the 840s Norsemen sacked London and ravaged Lincolnshire and Northumbria. 'Great slaughter at London...and at
Rochester,' says the *Chronicle*. Then in 851 there 'came 350 ships to
the mouth of the Thames, and the crews landed and took
Canterbury and London by storm'. Soon afterwards King Aethelwulf
of the West Saxons defeated them in Surrey. About this time they
dominated the Lower Thames and in 851 'the heathens for the first

time wintered in Thanet'. Four years later they wintered in Sheppey. Then a decade later 'the heathen army sat down in Thanet and made peace with the men of Kent, and the men of Kent promised them money for the peace'. They were beginning to settle. For years bands roved in central and northern England under Ivar the Boneless, whom the *Irish Annals* call 'Chief King of All the Northmen in Britain and Ireland'. Then came the wars with Alfred and his successors. From the late 860s the invaders had been settling in fair-sized groups. Healfdene took York and in 876 finally conquered the kingdom of Northumbria. Alfred's treaty with Guthrum in 886 gave the invaders the right to settle in the north and in the Five Boroughs (Nottingham, Lincoln, Stamford, Derby, Leicester). In the early tenth century warriors from Dublin and Norway added the north-west to the areas of Norse influence; but by mid-century English control had been nominally re-established all over the country.

From the early ninth century there were Norse settlements in Ireland, especially at seaports such as Dublin, until the decisive check at Clontarf in 1014. From 849 a new phase had developed. Instead of sailing round the north of Scotland, the invaders came round the south of England. These men, Danes, were called by the Irish the Black Heathen, as opposed to the White Heathen, the Norwegians. There was much settlement also in Wales, and a big attack in 915 that reached out to Archenfield on the borders of Herefordshire and Gloucestershire; a bishop was captured and had to be ransomed for £40. At last the Norsemen were driven off, but after 952 raids again became common. In 988 the two main monasteries of Glamorgan were ravaged, and in 997 came worse. Yet at the same time the Welsh kings were calling on Norse aid against rivals or the English; as late as 1088 Rhys ap Tedur used Norse and Irish mercenaries to regain his kingdom. The Norse settlements along the coast, of which Cardiff was one, had complete control of a thriving trade.[3]

We may note in passing that the *Anglo-Saxon Chronicle*, the *Irish Annals*, and the *Russian Chronicle* under the name of Nestor, were the only histories in the vernacular in Europe before 1200. Annalistic compilations in the monasteries derived from the custom of entering short historical notices on the pages of Easter Tables. In Alfred's time, perhaps at the instigation of the king or some noble of the south-west, a chronicle of events up to 891 was made, and copies were circulated to various centres of learning, where they were kept up to date with additions from bulletins of national events and items of local interest. Hence the *Anglo-Saxon Chronicle*.

The Scandinavians were the farthest north of the German-speaking peoples. They first made an impact on the Roman world in the late second century BC as the Teutones of northern Jutland and the Cimbri, their eastern neighbours. The Romans never reached Scandinavia; but in the early empire the Danish islands were a centre from which elements of Roman culture were carried northward. The Germanic tribes had been organized on a war basis when they began to encroach on the Roman world. Tacitus at the end of the first century AD wrote: 'The Germans have no taste for peace; renown is more easily won among dangers; and you cannot maintain a large body of Companions except by violence and war.' The war chief had not yet become the king. Tacitus mentions chiefs, *duces*, who owed their position to *virtus*, their qualities of war leadership. The *rex* and *dux* may have been related to different gods: the sacral ruler looking to Tiwaz (Tyr), sky god of order and law; the *dux* to Wodin (Odin, Othinn), god of the dead, lord of magic and spirit-possession, who became god of war. However that may be, *rex* and *dux* had merged by the time of the Germanic invasions of Britain.[4]

Warfare was endemic over these centuries. When the Norsemen come on the scene, we are in the early medieval period, and our information derives from the chroniclers, normally monks, who regarded the Vikings with particular horror. No doubt, one reason for this emotion was the fact that England had been free for some time from external attacks; but the main reason was that the raiders were heathens with no respect for church property. The sanctions that had some effect on Christians were disregarded by the Vikings, who found that monasteries with great accumulations of wealth were often built near the coast, in remote places open to attack, as at Lindisfarne. The new invaders were also terrible in the way they struck suddenly, without warning, from the sea. The chroniclers spoke of them with the sort of sheer dismay, as at utter abominations, that they kept otherwise for Christian rulers who despoiled the church of land and property: Charles Martel of Francia, Aethelbald of Mercia, William Rufus of England.

Already in Roman times the Northmen had looted temples. At Fycklinge in central Sweden a fine bronze vessel has been found, inlaid with silver and copper, and inscribed: 'To Apollo, the Benefactor of the Temple, Grannus Ammillus Constans offered this gift.' At Vang another bronze vessel was found, probably from a Gallic temple: 'Aprus and Libertinus gave this Vessel to the Temple.'[5] In 793 Alcuin wrote from Charlemagne's court:

Never before has such terror appeared in Britain as we have suffered from a pagan race, nor was it thought that such an inroad from the sea could be made. Behold the church of St

Cuthbert spattered with the blood of God's priests, despoiled of all its ornaments. A place more venerable than all in Britain is given as a prey to pagan peoples.

The *Annals of St Bertin* (composed at the abbey near what is now St Omer in the Pas de Calais) tell how Danish pirates raided Rouen: 'carrying everywhere a fury of rapine, fire and sword, they gave up the city, the monks, and the rest of the people to carnage and captivity. Some of the monasteries and other places near the Seine they devastated; the rest they left filled with terror, having received much money.' Abbo in his poem on the siege of Paris in 885–6 tells of the wild beasts going 'by horse and foot through hills and fields, forests, open plains, and villages, killing babies, children, young men, old men, fathers, sons and mothers'. He declared: 'They overthrow, they despoil, they destroy, they burn, they ravage, sinister cohort, fatal phalanx, cruel host.'[6] An Irishman of the twelfth century summoned up all his abusive rhetoric:

In a word, although there were an hundred hardsteeled iron heads on one neck and an hundred sharp ready cool never-rusting brazen tongues in each head and an hundred garrulous loud unceasing voices from each tongue, they could not recount or narrate, enumerate or tell, what all the Gaedhil suffered in common, both men and women, laity and clergy, old and young, noble and ignoble, of hardships and of injuring and oppression, in every house, from those valiant wrathful purely-pagan people.[7]

We have no accounts on the side of the Vikings for the earlier years; but we do have the runes from many of their graves. An early Swedish inscription at Rök in Östergotland gives us the Viking exultation over war loot and conjures up the heroic lays and legends that sustained the warriors:

For Væmod stand these runes. And Varin wrote them, the father for his dead son. I tell the ancient tale which the two war-booties were, twelve times taken as war-booty, both together from man to man. This I tell second who nine generations ago...with the Reidgoths; and he died with them, because of his guilt.
Theodoric the bold, king of sea-warriors, was the ruler over Reid-sea shores. Now sits he armed on his Gothic horse, shield-strapt, protector of Maerings.
This I tell in the twelfth instance where the Horse of the

Valkyrie sees food on the battlefield, where twenty kings lie.
This I tell in the thirteenth instance, which twenty kings sat on
Sjælland for four years, with four names, sons of four brothers:
five called Valke, sons of Radulv, five Reidulvs, sons of Rugulv,
five Haisls, sons of Harud, five Gunnunds, sons of Björn...I tell
the tale which of the Ingvaldings was revenged through a wife's
sacrifice. I tell the ancient tale to what young warrior a kinsman
is born. Vilin it is. He could kill a giant...I tell the ancient tale:
Thor. Sibbi, guardian of the sanctuary, ninety years of age, begot
a descendant.[8]

We cannot follow the references, but the phrases can still stir. The
alliterative opening, with its solemn rhythm, and the poetry in
many of the expressions, bring out the link with the exalted chant;
the italicized passage represents a complete verse-stanza.

The monks exaggerated, but beyond doubt the Vikings did much
damage – though the famous prayer, 'From the Fury of the Northmen, O Lord, deliver us', seems apocryphal.[9] Sometimes the monks
gathered what valuables they could and rushed off, then returned; if
too scared, they looked for safer areas. The monks of St Philibert
abandoned the island of Noirmouthier and after much roaming
settled inland at Tournus in Burgundy.[10] A few monks fled from
Fontanelles to Flanders, where they hung on till the revival of the
mid-tenth century there. At times the raids were less destructive. In
858 Vikings attacked St Germain des Près; but the monks, warned,
had removed the relics, treasures, library, and archives. The raiders
provisioned themselves, killed a few serfs, set fire to a store, and
withdrew; some lurking monks, with the aid of the Parisians, put
out the fire which was threatening the church. The *Chronicle of
Fontanelle* in the ninth century declares; 'The regions all around
bear witness that since the birth of the world never have such
ravages been known. So much has been wrought that none of the
wise [*prudentes*] chronographers can manage to relate it. So I have
been silent about much because I decided to be brief.' But the
appendix of the *Chronicle* in the eleventh century makes the
attempt to give some idea of the full blow.

Soon after the brutal army of the Barbarians, rising up out of
the waters, landed in this place. They found it deserted by the
inhabitants and they despoiled everything. They burned the
whole building and its sanctuary, levelled it, and went off. Then
they traversed the regions in all directions, installed themselves,
and carried out their general devastation of pillage and arson.
They destroyed the towns [*urbes*], threw down the forts [*castra*],

and razed the churches and the noble monastries which flourished more than elsewhere in this magnificent and populous province, which recalled Egypt. People were massacred without any distinction, all kinds of living creatures were wiped out. The finest of the young men were subjected to their lusts; the maidens were delivered up to the ravishing Pagans; and all the common folk, defenceless, were led off in captivity into foreign lands, to be shared out there among the Heathen [*Ethnici*]. For eighteen years this disaster went on unceasingly under the shock of repeated invasions, made under different chiefs. So the western coast of Gaul, lying broadly open on the British Sea, was transformed into a solitude and a desert.[11]

Things may well have been worse in this area than across the Channel in Britain, where there was better organized resistance as well as much bigger areas to be covered. The *Anglo-Saxon Chronicle* says of the *micel here* or army that invaded England in 892: 'By the grace of God the *here* had not on the whole afflicted the English people very greatly; but they were much more seriously afflicted in those three years by the mortality of cattle and men, and most of all in that many of the best royal thegns who were in the land died in those three years.' The writer does not link the deaths with the invasion, but perhaps the troubles were indirectly related to the war situation. Indeed, in another passage we find that it is the English army which most afflicted the people. Under 1006 we read: 'In spite of it all the Danish *here* went about as it pleased, and the English *fyrd* caused the people of the country every sort of harm, so that they profited neither from the native *here* nor from the foreign *here*.' (Their term *here* is used for both armies, though normally it was kept for the enemy.)[12]

The Danes have often been blamed for the breakdown of monasticism in England in the ninth and tenth centuries; but decay had set in without any attacks from outside.[13] The monastery of Much Wenlock in Shropshire was refounded after the Norman Conquest, and its failure has been attributed to a ninth-century Danish raid. But a charter of 901 shows the community still in existence.[14] Under Aethelred Unraed the raids were widespread, but seem to have had only a slight effect on monastic life. The houses in Devon first suffered; but Tavistock, burnt in 997, soon recovered – though Exeter and Bedford fade out of the records. In 1011 Aelfmaer, abbot of St Augustine's, Aelfheah, the archbishop of Canterbury, Godwin, bishop of Rochester, and Leofryn, abbess of St Mildred's, were taken prisoners; and in 1016 Wulsig, abbot of Ramsey, was killed at the

battle of Ashingdon, Kent.[15] But we find no general ravaging of
monasteries. Asser, in his *Life of Alfred*, thought the reason for
decay was the rise in the standard of living:

> At first he had no noble or freeman of his own nation who
> would of his own accord enter the monastic life, apart from
> children who by reason of their tender age could not choose
> good or refuse evil. For indeed for many years past the desire
> for the monastic life had been utterly lacking in all that people,
> and also in many other nations, though there still remain many
> monasteries founded in that land, but none properly observing
> the rule of this way of life, I know not why: whether on
> account of the onslaughts of foreigners, who very often invaded
> by land or sea, or on account of the nation's too great
> abundance of riches of every kind, which I am more inclined to
> think the reason for that contempt of the monastic life.[16]

And Alfred himself considered the raids the result rather than the
cause of religious laxity. The attacks were punishments: 'We possessed only the name of Christians and very few possessed the
virtue.' 'Before everything was ravaged and burnt, the churches
throughout all England stood filled with treasures and books, and
likewise there was a great multitude of the servants of God. And
they had very little benefit from those books, for they could not
understand anything in them, because they were not written in their
own language.'[17]

Certainly the Danish raids were one cause of the breakdown of the
Carolingian empire and the Mercian kingdom in the Midlands, but
only one cause; the full picture must include the inner conflicts of
the disrupted areas as well as other attacks from outside apart from
those of the Vikings. France was in a ceaseless state of civil war.
Arnulf in the mid tenth century built up a strong power in Flanders,
but his system broke down with his death. The Normans indeed
occupied Brittany in 921, but next year the Hungarians devastated
Italy and sacked the important town of Pavia. The Vikings went on
devastating Aquitaine and Auvergne. In 905 they had gone up the
Seine as far as Noyon. In 926 Robert of France beat a band in Artois,
while others invaded the valley of the Loire; and there were two
more Hungarian invasions. The terrible Hungarian raids went on in
933 and 935, and then on a vaster scale in 955. In Italy, after
devastation by Berengar, things were a little quieter, but bands of
Saracens watched over the Alpine passes where until 973 or 983 they
blocked the routes, killed travellers or held them to ransom, impeding the communication of Italy with the rest of Europe.[18]

Monks might denounce the heathen, but laymen were often ready
to collaborate with the Vikings. They helped them, called them in,
made alliances with them. Charlemagne's grandson treated them as
allies.[19] Charles the Bald in 858 was fighting hard against them, but
his brother seized the chance to invade his land and win over many
of his followers. Alfred's nephew deserted to the Danes, who accepted
him as king; and many of the Frankish royal family behaved in the
same sort of way. Old English poetry, celebrating the deeds of Danes,
Swedes, Burgundians, Franks and Frisians, shows a deep-rooted sense
of the common origin of all the Norse and Germanic peoples.[20]

After thus glancing at the sustained impact of the Norsemen on
England, Ireland, and France, we may return to the question of the
war basis and its effect on the Norse or Germanic freemen and their
leaders. The relationship of warrior and lord was throughout
western Europe crucial for the development of feudalism and of
medieval society. We saw how Tacitus stressed the need for plunder
if the war chief was to maintain his band of companions, his
comitatus. Through the Dark Ages and the medieval epoch a king or
lord was expected to be generous and open-handed; and this quality
was not a mere incidental virtue of the leader. It was something
essential to his whole being, his role, his function in society. He
had to be generous with hospitality and gifts: gifts that included
gold, other valuables, weapons, land. A letter from Theodoric the
Ostrogoth summoned the warriors settled in south Italy to attend his
court so as to enjoy his Royal Largesse; for a warrior 'is as one dead
who is unknown to his lord'. The Anglo-Saxon poem, The Wanderer,
tells of the exile, deprived of kinsmen, brooding on the 'Retainers in
Hall and the receiving of Treasure; of how in his youth his Gold-
friend was courteous to him at the Feast. It seems to him in his mind
that he clasps his Lord and lays hands and head on his knee, as when
once in past days he was near the Gift-Throne.' Beowulf's great
collar was a royal reward. Hrothgar, King of the Danes, is called the
Keeper of Ring-Treasures, an excellent Ring-Giver, the Treasure-
Guardian of Heroes. The young Wiglaf calls Beowulf himself: 'Our
Lord who gave us these Rings', to whom loyal battle-service is due.
For bard and warrior the stress was thus on gold, on the Fire of
Leifi's Road (a saga term). The lord was the one who gave swords,
byrnies, helmets, horses, rings, jewels, 'gracious giver of mighty
gifts', a gold-giver, 'a scatterer of the ice-of-the-hand'. The poet
Gunnlaug asked King Aethelred for permission to leave the court
reciting, 'I must go visit the house of three princes and two earls; I
have promised this to the possessors-of-land. I shall not return before
the gold-giver summons me. Give me the servant of the goddess of

the spearpoint, the Couch-of-the-Dragons, [gold] for his sleeves.'[21] It
is the possessors-of-land who can give gold; the lord is the 'lord of
land'. A scaldic singer praises a chief as 'the scorner of the fire of the
bow's seat', the gold rings of the hand. A poet of the court of Harald
Fairhair (c 860–933), the unifier of Norway, tells of the life led by his
warriors:

> They are favoured with wealth and finest swordblades, with
> metal from Hunland and maids from the East. Glad are they
> then when they guess battle's near, swift to leap up and lay
> hands on the oars, to snap off the grummets and splinter the
> tholes, and smite billows bravely at their lord's bidding.[22]

The bard or scald also relies on the lord's generosity:

> One may see by their gear and their golden rings, they are all
> comrades close to the king. Red are their cloaks with richly-
> wrought borders, swords bound with silver, corselets of ring-
> mail, belt-straps gilded and helmets graven. On their wrists are
> the rings which Harald gave them.[23]

But the gold that binds lord and man is also the cause of murder,
dissension, treachery. It is the dragon-hoard. Hence the central role
of the fatal Gold of the Nibelungs, as told in the tenth-century Eddic
poems and the prose *Völsunga Saga*, written down in Iceland in the
thirteenth century, but current orally throughout Europe much
earlier: a primitive version was known in England in the eighth
century. The *Saga* reflects the age of migrations also in its references
to various vast royal treasures which changed hands according to
the luck of war. Later we find the church, a hoarder of gold like the
dragons, seeking to guard its treasures with bans and curses. Abbot
Suger, recounting the treasures of St Denis in the 1140s, mentions
that the new gem-studded cross of gold was protected by a ban
which Pope Eugenius pronounced on the spot at Easter 1147; the
anathema was inscribed at the foot of the cross. 'Treasure, gold in
the ground, may easily madden many men, hide it who will,'
declares Beowulf.

In return for gold, arms, land, the Anglo-Saxon *gesithas*, the
companions, have to render a total loyalty to their lord. Beowulf in
the epic (probably composed in its existing form some time in the
eighth century) looks back on the services he performed for his lord,
King Hygelac (earlier sixth century): 'I repaid him in battle for the
treasure he gave me...Ever would I be before him in the troop, alone
in the van.' The lord can even take the honour of his companions'

exploits: Hygelac in *Beowulf* is called the Slayer of Ongentheow, though two of his thegns did the killing and he rewarded them. The retainer brings to his lord the spoils he has won. Beowulf gave Hygelac the gifts he gained through services in Denmark. Again, when killing the Frankish champion Daeghrefn, he was glad that he had prevented him from taking off to his lord the armour of Hygelac fallen in battle (apparently at Daeghrefn's hands). The poet Widsith, on returning home, gave his lord the ring which King Eormanric bestowed on him; he had been given land by his lord. The Anglo-Saxon lord presented armour and horses to the man entering his service, and this gift grew into a legal due, heriot (war-gear), paid on the man's death. The payment was remitted if the man fell on a campaign 'before his lord'. Until the end, heriot was paid in kind. Thus a twelfth-century ealdorman declares: 'And I bequeath to my royal lord as a heriot 4 armlets of 300 mancuses of gold and 4 swords and 8 horses, 4 with trappings, 4 without, and 4 helmets and 4 mailcoats and 8 spears and 8 shields.'

To fail one's lord was the ultimate disgrace. Beowulf's young kinsman Wiglaf felt only contempt for the men failing to come to their lord's support:

> He who wishes to speak the truth can say that the lord who gave you those treasures, that war-gear you stand up in – when he often gave to men on the ale-benches in the hall, as a prince to his thanes, the most splendid helmet and corselet that he could find, far and near – he wholly threw away this war-gear when battle befell him.

And he goes on to describe the life of dishonoured infamy that lay ahead of such men. On the other hand *Finnesburh* tells us that 'retainers never repaid better the bright mead than his young followers did to Hanef'. *The Wanderer* recounts the perils of the kinless man: 'Where is the mare? where is the young man? where is the treasure-giver? where are the banquet-benches? where, the joys of hall?'[24] Gifts had a ritual significance; they bound together the members of a group; they expressed and created the close bond of lord and man. A Norse proverb says: 'A gift always looks for a return'.[25]

This matter of the relation of king or lord to his retainers will continue to be of primary importance in our inquiry. As tribal brotherhood was eroded by differences in property and status, the war-bond constituted one of the key points at which new social formations could come about. Already in the breaking-up Roman empire of the West, the big landlords built up bodies of retainers, *bucellarii*; the tradition carried on through the gesiths and house-carles, the *antrustiones* and *gasindi,* to the bachelors of the high Middle Ages and the liveries of the fifteenth century; but a new force and significance was infused into the relationship as it emerged from tribal society.[26]

We must not however think of the war basis as the sole important factor at work in these centuries. The free warrior was generally also a farmer, and in Scandinavia he often combined farming with sea-voyages for trading purposes as well as for piracy. At times it is hard to draw a sharp line between marauding raids and the quest for new lands on which to settle. An important phase in the colonizing of Normandy seems linked with the dispersal of the Danish army in England in the summer of 896 after a campaign of four years. The *Chronicle* says: 'And those who were without money got them-selves ships and went south across the sea to the Seine.'[27] We see how plundering was often bound up with the wish to accumulate capital for settlement. And the traffic went on both ways. King Edward the Elder in the early tenth century encouraged his followers to buy land 'from the pagans'.[28] The Olaf sagas accepted raid and trade simply as alternative methods of gaining property.

> Loden was the name of a man from Vigg, rich and of good family. He went often on merchant voyages and sometimes on viking cruises. It happened one summer he went on a merchant voyage with much merchandise in a ship of his own. He directed his course first to Estonia and was there at a market in summer. Many trading goods were brought there, and also many thralls or sales for sale...
> He was a promising young man. In his earliest youth he had a desire to go abroad, and he soon gathered property and reputa-tion; and he was by turns a year abroad and a year with his father. Biarne was soon owner of a merchant ship of his own...
> There was a man called Eyvind Urarhorn, a great man of high birth, who had his descent from Easter Agder country. Every summer he went out on a viking cruise, sometimes in the West Sea, sometimes to the Baltic, sometimes south to Flanders, and had a well-armed *snaekke* of twenty benches of rowers.[29]

Few western European coins minted before 950 have been found in Scandinavia; money gained by looting was used for such purposes as buying land.[30]

We can now turn directly to the colonization of Normandy. Viking attacks on the coast of north-east France had been going on through the second half of the ninth century; and it was from Boulogne that the main army of Danes sailed in 893 for Lympne and Appledore. Already in the 840s Quentovic, Nantes and Rouen were sacked; and the port of Dorestad at the mouth of the Rhine was for a while controlled by Rorik, who in effect ruled the Lowlands. One result in France was the building of a large number of castles, often by royal agents, though in 864 Charles the Bald ordered the demolition of all raised without authority, as the lords of the castles were usurping his rights concerning justice, tolls, and the like.[31] Then in 911 the Viking founders of Normandy seem to come into the full light of history. The tradition ran that after being defeated at Chartres by the troops of Charles III, the Simple, their leader Rollo made a pact with the king at St Claire-sur-Epte, between two hills on the Paris-Rouen highway. Charles at the time was in a difficult position, striving to hold together the dwindled remnants of the Carolingian empire despite the anarchic pressures of his nobles; he was in league with Robert of Neustria, who was to supplant him. Rollo, advanced in years, is said to have agreed to be baptised by the archbishop of Rouen and to marry Charles's daughter; in return for his homage he was granted the area later called Upper Normandy.

William of Malmesbury records the tale that the people of Chartres had implored the aid of the Virgin Mary and flew her shift on the ramparts as a banner – Charles had brought this with other relics from Byzantion. 'At the sight the enemy burst out laughing and shot their arrows at it; but they didn't do so with impunity. Soon their eyes were dimmed and they couldn't advance or retreat.' The townsfolk rushed out and 'indulged in a plentiful slaughter of them, as far as fortune permitted'. Rollo, however, took Rouen soon afterwards. Charles, 'consulting his nobility, resolved it was advisable to make a show of royal munificence when unable to repel injury. So he sent for Rollo in a friendly manner.' But Rollo's 'inbred and untameable ferocity' was such that when bystanders suggested he should kiss his benefactor's foot, he disdained to kneel, grasped the foot and dragged it up to his mouth as he stood erect. Charles fell on his back, with the Normans laughing and the Franks indignant. Rollo passed off his rudeness by saying that he had acted according to the custom of his country. Then he returned to Rouen and died there. However Dudo, dean of St Quentin, in his *Praise of the Early Normans* (written a century after the event), stated that Rollo chose a follower to make the act of homage on his behalf, and it was this man who toppled the king over.

It seems clear that many legends grew up about Rollo and Charles, and that we cannot trust any of the accounts, as they were concerned to give a formal and definite basis to the acceptance of the Viking settlement. Still, we may accept as fact that some sort of accord was worked out around 911. About thirty years earlier Alfred had had to make a treaty with the Danish invaders under Guthrum, accepting and seeking to stabilize the situation in East Anglia.

The Northmen called Rouen Ruda or Rudaburg, so that the earls of Normandy were the Ruda-jarlar. There was as yet no idea of Normandy as a coherent district; the title was personal, not territorial in the feudal sense. Many of the Vikings led by Rollo into baptism are said to have been immersed ten or twelve times so as to get a good supply of the white garments given out for the rite. But for long any conversions were superficial. At Rollo's funeral, we are told that gifts were made to monasteries and a large number of captives were sacrificed. How summary and brutal the conversions of Norsemen by their lords could be may be read in the Olaf sagas. Thus Olaf behaved in the Uplands:

He inquired particularly how it stood with their Christianity, and, where improvement was needful, he taught them the right customs. If there were any who would not renounce heathen ways, he took the matter so zealously that he drove some out of the country, mutilated others of hands or feet, or gouged their eyes out; hanged up others, cut some down with the sword; but let none go unpunished who would not serve God. He went thus through the whole district, sparing neither great nor small.[32]

Charles was not giving much away, as part of the granted land lay in Robert's duchy or march of Neustria (from the Loire to beyond the Seine), and had anyway been overrun by the Normans; he probably meant to balance one vassal with another and use Rollo as a marcher-lord. Rollo's area seems composed of the counties of Rouen, Lisieux, Evreux, in the lower Seine basin, with a wooded plateau to the north-east between the rivers Bresle and Epte and the sea. The heart of the area was Rouen, which controlled the route to Paris along the Seine and was already the seat of a bishopric. In the late fourth century it had been the capital of a new province of Roman Gaul; then Saxon and Frankish invaders mingled with the Gallo-Roman population of Celts and Belgae, but did not impose their language. Under the Frankish kings old ecclesiastical boundaries became administrative units; what was to become Normandy was the Second Lyonnaise, the church province of Rouen; the Carolingian province of Neustria. But so far the region had evolved no distinctive political life of its own, and it might well have seemed that before long the Vikings too would be absorbed. Indeed in one sense that did happen. Rollo's followers adopted the French language and customs, but they stayed securely in control as a separate ruling class, unlike the Danish settlers in England who were being subjected to Alfred's successors.[33]

Dudo says that Charles, marrying Rollo to his daughter, granted 'a defined tract of land, as an alod and in proprietorship, from the Epte to the sea, from which he could draw sustenance'. Flodoard, more plausibly, says that Rollo got certain maritime districts and the city of Rouen; not till 924 did the Normans gain the Bessin. Dudo, in accord with Norman pretensions of his time, was trying to make out that Charles had given Rollo feudal rights over Brittany. We cannot however interpret his term *in alod* to mean that there were no close feudal ties between Charles and Rollo. From Norman charters of the eleventh century we see that *alodium* was used to mean, not land free from seigneurial services, but land held by hereditary right. (This usage must not, however, be carried back to earlier days, when to hold in alod would certainly have meant the same as in the Scandinavian homeland.) Rollo's status was certainly not precisely defined. Charles merely hoped to stop him being a nuisance and to use him to keep out further marauding Vikings.[34]

He seems to have pushed west into the districts of Bayeux and Sées by 924, his son into those of Avranches and Coutances in the next nine years. Lower Normandy was thus added and the general shape of the duchy established: a fertile region of pastures, orchards, woodland, and low hills, with a long coast and a dampish climate, a sort of extended beach-head.[35] The *Miracula Sancti Audoeni*, written before 1092 by the monk Fulbert (with additions made before the end of the century), uttered a panegyric to the area: 'We enjoy divine benefits: a temperate climate, fertile lands, gentle forests, an abundance of milk and cattle, an absolute peace, without fear of foreign incursions. And all this is given us by heaven, we proclaim, because of the merits of St Ouen of Rouen.' Lacking clearly defined geographical frontiers, the region was in fact not easily defended and its lords needed to be vigilant and well organized if they were to survive. The uplands on the west moved on into Brittany, while on the east the lowlands drifted into Picardy. The Seine valley led on to the Ile de France. Such a situation was liable to cause continual trouble in a feudal world; but for this reason it was likely to develop either anarchic conditions or very strong rulers ready to take action against weakening neighbours.

We can now look in more detail at what we know of Rollo's earlier career. His story, despite its confusions and uncertainties, illustrates well the hurlyburly of these years and the chance conglomeration of Vikings that led to the formation of the Norman state. He seems

certainly to be Rolf the Ganger, son of Rögnvald, Earl of Möre, and
of Hild, well-known in the saga world. He was called the Ganger
because no horse would bear his weight and he had to go on foot; but
Norwegian ponies were not very big so Rollo may not have been too
huge. He seems to have ridden during his Frankish raids. Rögnvald
was the man who cut Harald Fairhair's tousled locks, so that the
King was no longer called Lifa, Mophair. He played an important part
in the unification of Norway, and his brother Sigurd was Earl of
Orkney and Shetland. Another son of his, Hrollaug, according to the
Orkneyinga Saga, was one of the pioneers in colonizing Iceland. Rolf
took early to piracy and plundered in the Baltic, operating from an
island somewhere north of the mouth of the Namsen. Returning
(sometime after 864–5 if Snorre Sturlesson was right in his chronology) from an expedition that left him short of food, he landed in the
bay where Oslo now stands, on the coast of the Vik, and raided cattle.
The king was enraged, called a Thing, and had Rolf outlawed despite
the pleas of Hild.

Rolf sailed off to the Hebrides, ruled by Earl Ketil, and a daughter
he begot there was later married to a Scottish chieftain. (Dudo makes
Rollo come from Dacia where he and his brother quarrelled with the
king. Rollo, exiled, went to Scanza, or Scania, then to England. Rolf
did in fact go to Scania on a voyage of piracy and was banished by
his king.) Snorre says that he now went to Valland (western France);
Dudo says that he sailed up the Seine in 876, but the date seems too
early. Dudo, wanting to enhance his reputation, makes him a leader
in the many Viking campaigns; but no other writer mentions him,
though other leaders are named. He seems to have been a lesser chief.
Dudo recounts how the Norsemen, asked who commanded them,
replied that they were all equal and had no leader. Their reply was
true; Viking fleets or bands were made up of contingents under
leaders equal in rank, though for practical purposes someone of high
prestige must have taken charge at crucial times.

Dudo's date perhaps should have been 886. He tells us that Rollo
journeyed from the Hebrides to England where he was friendly with
the Most Christian King Alstemus. The name is probably not a corruption of Alfred, but stands for Guthrum who was baptised as
Athelstane. Dudo adds that Rollo went on to the land of the Walgri
(Walcheren); and names the opponents of the Vikings as the count
of Hainault and the duke of the Frisians, both historical characters.
Annals mention many raids on Flanders, 881–4. Next Rollo went on
to Rouen, where the *Annals of St Vedast* mention that Norsemen
defeated a French force under the count of Maine. In 886–7 Norsemen attacked Paris and Dudo says that Rollo was their leader; but
the accounts of the siege by Hincmar and Abbo (who was present in

Paris) name the leader as Sigfrid and ignore Rollo. The siege was raised; but the Norsemen, though defeated at Montfaucon, took and burned Méaux. A second attack on Paris, like a third in 830, was beaten off.

In 890 the Norsemen marched under Sigfrid into the Cotentin, and sacked and burned St. Lo. Dudo says that Rollo captured Bayeux. Popa, daughter of the city's defender, Count Berengar de Senlis, was claimed by Rollo in the Norse polygamous fashion; and he begot by her a son William who became the second count of Normandy. (A strong tie continued between the Norman ruling family and the De Senlis; we may accept the story of Popa.) Dudo then says that Rollo besieged Evreux, which the Rouen Chronicle says was taken in 892. William of Jumièges states that Rollo was not at Evreux, but took part in another siege of Paris with elaborate siege apparatus: a story that seems quite without foundation. Alstemus in England sent for help and Rollo went to him. Guthrum Athelstane had died in 890; Rollo, however, may have made another visit to England, though the fighting at the time was inland, in Mercia. William says that on his return he sent his commanders all over central France, to the Seine and the Loire, to the Gironde and to Burgundy. Probably this account was intended to fill in a gap, when no record of his activities had come down. The failures at Paris seem to have led to a splitting up of the Viking bands. We know almost nothing of what they did from 900 to 911. The decade was one of confused violence, civil war, ravages by Hungarians, Slavs and Saracens; no doubt the Vikings played their part in the killing and looting, but some seem to have settled down. We may assume that in these years Rollo and his men were colonizing the Rouen area and consolidating their hold. Otherwise it is hard to understand why the Frankish king was ready to accord them some sort of status in 911.

Rollo may have been killed at Eu in 925; he was clearly dead before the Breton wars of 933. Fresh bands of immigrants kept coming into Normandy. Rollo and his descendants did not act as mere marcher-lords barring out intruders; they welcomed reinforcements and extended their lordship over them, slowly welding a strong political structure. They were given, or assumed, the title of Count, which was gradually elevated into that of Duke. But the Franks for a long time looked on them as dubious outsiders. Till 1000 their region was the Land of the Northmen. A chronicler, recording Count Robert's death, calls him the Duke of the Pirates. Five counts or dukes appeared in four generations after Rollo: William I the Longsword, Richard I the Fearless, Richard II the Good, Robert the Magnificent, then William II the Bastard, who conquered England. These counts did not easily win or hold supremacy; each succession was challenged.

Rollo-Rolf was Norwegian; and the mixed band he led may well have included many Norwegians, from whom came his commanders or lords. In William's confirmation of the laws of King Edward after the Conquest we read that the Norman nobility who had accompanied him to England claimed descent from Norwegian ancestors. But the later immigrants, while no doubt comprising Norwegians and Swedes, seem mainly to have been Danes. These latter would have made up the lesser free peasantry. Of eighty-two Scandinavian names known in pre-1066 Normandy, only two are purely Norwegian, while twenty-six are purely Danish; the others could be Norwegian or Danish. Place names suggest Danish colonization and cluster mostly around Rouen, the Pays de Caux, the Roumois, the north and north-west of the Pays d'Auge, or of the Cotentin. The personal names even suggest a movement of Danes from the English Danelaw to Normandy, especially to the Cotentin and the Pays d'Auge.[36] It has been argued that the place names show an essentially aristocratic settlement in contrast with the peasant settlement of the English Danelaw. But the evidence has also been explained by the rapid disappearance of Scandinavian speech in Francia.[37]

The merging of the two peoples in England was made easier by the fact that Danes and English could understand one another. In Normandy we do not meet any such widely-used placename endings as the Danish -by, though a few Scandinavian endings such as -tot, -boeuf, -fleur, are found. The common -bec is also probably northern. Hybrids in which a personal name has -ville added (rare in England) suggest a new lord putting his name in place of a Frankish predecessor.[38]

We need not think of large hordes being involved in the raids, invasions, or settlements. We have noted the use of the term here in the Chronicle to express invading bands. It is usually translated as host or army; but the early seventh-century laws of Ine (preserved in a manuscript of Alfred's time) declare: 'We call up to seven men thieves; from 7 to 35 a band; above that it is a here.' We meet there an early definition; but we have no reason to think that at any time here meant more than a group of fighters big enough to cause trouble. And quite small detachments of well armed and resolute men could bring about astonishing results in those years. When in 865 the Chronicle speaks of a micel here, it hardly means the Great Danish Army, as it is usually rendered; it means only a larger than usual body of desperadoes. The army called up by a Norman count was probably quite small; not more than a few hundred would compose its ranks. The chronicler Hincmar tells how in September 866 Nor-

mans and Bretons rode from the Loire to Le Mans and devastated it;
on the way back they met Robert of Neustria, Rannulf of Poitou,
and two counts of Maine: an imposing group of potentates. In the
battle Robert was killed, Rannulf and another count were wounded,
Rannulf mortally. The Franks were defeated. Hincmar, who is not
likely to minimize the Norman strength, adds that it consisted of four
hundred men. Yet this small body could take Le Mans and rout a
force commanded by the leading nobles of western Francia.[39] When
a large campaign was intended, men would be got in from the surrounding areas (Brittany, Flanders, Auvergne, Aquitaine); William
II especially relied on Breton contingents. These mercenaries were
hired for a term, probably forty days, at so much a day, and they
expected a share in any plunder. They had to be watched or they
fired a town so as to be able to loot it thoroughly in the confusion.

The slight defences of the tenth century, which nevertheless baffled
attackers, are exemplified by those of Senlis, which defeated Louis
d'Outremer and Otto I in 946. The texts refer to a very strongly
fortified site; but the walls were Roman ones, some six centuries old.
Amiens too had its old Roman walls. In 950 Arnulf of Flanders fought
Herbert of Vermandois; the latter seized a tower which the bishop
had had built, and each of the belligerents was installed in a tower
that served as a miniature fortress.[40] Even if the story of the Norsemen using great catapults against Paris is a later invention, certainly
much ingenuity in attack had been developed over the years. Norse
writings give us some lively glimpses of the Norsemen tackling London in the early eleventh century. Even though the sagas, written
down, are imaginatively filled out, they come from a strongly maintained oral tradition and bring the scene to life. The *Sagas of St Olaf*
tell how Olaf and his men joined Aethelred on his return from exile
in Flanders in an attack on the Danes in London. Aethelred 'sent an
invitation to all the men who'd enter into his pay': who would serve
him as mercenaries.

Then many people flocked to him; and among others came king
Olaf with a great troop of Northmen to his aid. They steered
first to London and sailed into the Thames with their fleet; but
the Danes had a castle inside. On the other bank of the river
is a great trading-place, which is called Sudrviki [Southwark].
There the Danes had raised a great work, dug large ditches, and
inside had built a bulwark of stone, timber, and turf, where they
had stationed a strong army. King Aethelred ordered a great
assault; but the Danes defended themselves bravely and king
Aethelred could make nothing of it. Between the castle and
Southwark was a bridge, so broad that two wagons could pass

each other upon it. On the bridge were raised barricades, both towers and wooden parapets, in the direction of the river, which were nearly breast-high; and under the bridge were piles driven into the bottom of the river.

Now when the attack was made, the troops stood on the bridge everywhere and defended themselves. King Aethelred was very anxious to get hold of the bridge, and he called together all the chiefs to consult how they should get the bridge broken down. Then said king Olaf he would attempt to lay his fleet alongside of it, if the other ships would do the same. It was then resolved in this council that they should lay their war-forces under the bridge; and each made himself ready with ships and men.

King Olaf ordered great platforms of floating wood to be tied together with hazel bands, and for this he took down old houses. And with these, as a roof, he covered over his ships so widely that it reached over the ships' sides. Under this screen he set pillars so high and stout that there was room for swinging their swords and as well the roofs were strong enough to withstand the stones cast down upon them. Now when the fleet and men were ready, they rowed up along the river. But when they came near the bridge, there were cast down upon them so many stones and missiles, such as arrows and spears, that neither helmet nor shield could hold out against it, and the ships themselves were so greatly damaged that many retreated out of it.

But king Olaf and the Northmen's fleet with him rowed quite up under the bridge, laid their cables round the supporting piles, and then rowed off with all the ships as hard as they could down the stream. The piles were thus shaken in the bottom and loosened under the bridge. Now as the armed troops stood thick of men upon the bridge, and there were likewise many heaps of stones and other weapons upon it, and piles under it being loosened and broken, the bridge gave way, and a great part of the men upon it fell into the river, and all the others fled, some into the castle, some into Southwark. After that Southwark was stormed and taken.[41]

The poet Ottar Svarte made up a song that began, 'London Bridge is broken down'.

A more apocryphal tale is told in the *Jomsvikinga Saga*. We read how at the time of the midsummer fair armed Englishmen got under the covers of the market waggons. Thus they slipped into the city and massacred the Danes who were gathering unarmed for a church service at midnight, and only three Danish ships escaped. The story

perhaps derives from the fact of Aethelred's treacherous slaughter
of Danes ordered for St Brice's Day, 1002. Under 1016 the *Chronicle*
says that when Edmund was chosen king in London, 'then came the
ships to Greenwich, at Rogation Days'. They too found a defended
bridge in the way, but this time the lack of resistance from Southwark enabled the Danes to make a frontal attack. 'They dug a great
ditch on the south side and dragged their ships to the west side of the
bridge; and then afterwards they ditched the city round, so that no
one could go in or out. And they repeatedly fought against the city,
but the citizens strenuously withstood.' A second attempt later in the
year, by land and water, again failed. To attacks of this sort we may
ascribe the Viking axes, spears, and other implements found near
the site of Old London Bridge.[42]

Of placenames along the Lower Thames, Sheerness, Shoeburyness,
Thorpe, Northfleet, Greenwich, Woolwich, and perhaps Deptford
seem to be of Norse origin; and in London the dedications to St Olaf
on both sides of the river suggest a Norse connection. Stories describe
St Clement Danes in the Strand as a Danish burial ground. In the
twelfth century a monk at Crowland told about Siward Digri, a Norse
adventurer, who took service under the Confessor and was promised
the first vacancy in the ranks of the nobility. Siward created the
vacancy himself by killing Tosti, earl of Huntingdon, on a bridge
near Westminster. The followers of each man then fought; Tosti's
were beaten and buried in a field on which was erected a memorial
church still known as the Danes Church.[43] A legend, recorded in the
Chertsey Register of the thirteenth century, stated that the Danes
who destroyed Chertsey Abbey were later 'by the just judgement of
God all killed near London at the place called the Church of the
Danes'. There seems some genuine link between the site and the
Danes, and early in the thirteenth century the street in which the
church stood was called Dencheman's Street.[44] Again, William of
Malmesbury tells us that Harthacnut, 'at the instigation of Elfric,
archbishop of York, and others whom I'm loth to name, ordered the
dead body of [his brother] Harald to be dug up, the head to be cut
off and thrown into the Thames, a pitiable sight for men. But it was
dragged up by a fisherman's net and buried in the Cemetery of the
Danes in London.'[45] The runes tell of Norsemen dying in London. At
Valleberga (Skåne) the stone declares of two men, Manne and Svenne,
'May God help their souls well: and they lie in London'. Two stones
with runes have been found in London, one is in St Paul's church-
yard; both were parts of coffins of the first half of the eleventh century. More surprisingly a monument from Småland says of Gunnar:
'Helge laid him, his brother, in a stone coffin, in England, at Bath'.[46]

Such details make us feel how omnipresent was the Norseman in England in these centuries, how wide and deep his impact.

We have then made a brief survey of the Norse raids, invasions, and settlements, which did so much to transform western Europe between the ninth and eleventh centuries; the mingled aims of piracy and trade, war and colonization; the ethnic composition and the size of the bands. The emphasis has been largely on the destructive aspects: aspects stressed by the chroniclers in the monasteries which, because of their concentrations of treasure, were the main victims of raids. We have examined the bond between lord and companions which emerges as the central cohesive element in the Germanic tribal societies as they collide with the Roman world, and which provides the basis on which later the feudal system is to develop. Though there were similar elements in the Germanic tribes known to Tacitus and in the Norse societies exploding in the ninth century, we cannot equate the two. The Norsemen in their relatively isolated regions developed certain aspects of their way of life more than others, and the world on which they irrupted was very different from that of the Roman empire. We have looked at the Danes in their attacks on London and at the Norsemen who settled under Rollo-Rolf in the region that was to become Normandy. In the next chapter we shall explore more closely some of the specific characteristics of these Norsemen.

CHAPTER II

A CLOSER LOOK
AT THE VIKINGS

We have noted that the Norse expansion had its strongly constructive as well as its destructive side. The Vikings cannot be treated
merely as troublesome outsiders who were finally absorbed into a
superior culture. Indeed, the insiders, as the more direct inheritors
of the remnants of Roman civilization, could in certain aspects claim
superiority; but the conception of the Vikings as disruptive nuisances
crashing into an ordered world gives us a limited and misleading
idea of what happened. We must see both the pagan Norsemen and
the nominally Christian West as sections of a living whole, in which
many of the most valuable new impulsions come from the outsiders
– or at least in which the shocks and breakdowns they cause become
the basis of yet more vigorous integrations.

First, we must look at Norse society and its way of life, which
bred a strong spirit of initiative and independence. As with other
Germanic societies, Norse society had three levels, but it had a mobil-

ity that had been lost in England and Gaul. At the bottom were the slaves or *thraells*, war captives or men broken by debt; they could be sold and at times even sacrificed at a master's burial. The *karls* were free peasants; if they came of servile stock, they still owed services to the family of the man who had been their master. They could own land, but more often they held it in exchange for services or hired themselves out. Protected by law, they had a share in the administration, and they provided the soldiers, craftsmen, pedlars, even traders. On top were the *jarls* or nobles, with retainers, who had begun to fall into a sort of proto-feudal dependence on the king. In time merchant guilds grew up. The king imposed taxes and built up his own estate. Superficially the society was not unlike that developing in the West; but it was looser, less centralized, with many more opportunities for individual assertion and activity.[1]

A keystone was the system of land-holding. By the odal law the ancestral household was held jointly by the family. When the father died, the eldest son inherited, but had to pay compensation to his brothers for their shares. Such a system tended to encourage the younger sons to clear new ground, go on voyages of trade or piracy, or join in colonizing ventures. An owner could sell his land as long as he shared the price with the co-heirs. The younger sons got, as well as their compensation share, a share (defined by the law-codes) of any other lands, of chattels, and of silver; they thus had a basis on which to build up their own fortunes. Land was freehold without dues or duties to an overlord – though a man might accept a lord from need for protection in war or support in legal disputes and feuds. The tie was personal and could be transferred. A chief gave justice to his followers, rewards for services, support in disputes, and he shared out spoils and lands.

The *Rigsmal* thus vividly describes the three classes:

> Thrall was of swarthy skin, his hands wrinkled, his knuckles bent, his fingers thick, his face ugly, his back broad, his heels long. He began to put forth his strength, binding bast, making loads, and bearing home faggots the weary long day. His children busied themselves with building fences, dunging ploughland, tending swine, herding goats, and digging peat. Their names were Sooty and Cowherd, Clumsy and Lout and Laggard, and so on.
>
> Carl, or churl, was red and ruddy, with rolling eyes, and took to breaking oxen, building ploughs, timbering houses, and making carts.
>
> Earl, the noble, had yellow hair, his cheeks were rosy, his eyes were keen as a young serpent's. His occupation was shaping

the shield, bending the bow, hurling the javelin, shaking the lance, riding horses, throwing dice, fencing, and swimming. He began to waken war, redden the field, and fell the doomed.

Here the class divisions are more hardened than in the early days; but we see certain continuing characteristics.

Divorce was easy, and a woman could ask for it. The status of women was relatively high, and they could own land. An inscription from Hillersjö, Sweden, sets out a complicated case of inheritance:

Read these runes. Geirmund married Geirlaug, then a maiden. Later they had a son, before Geirmund was drowned. Afterwards the son died. Then she had Gudrik as husband...They had children, of whom only a girl survived. She was called Inga, and Rognvald of Snottsa married her.

Afterwards he died, and their son too; and the mother (Inga) inherited from her son. Inga later had Eirik as husband. Then she died. Then Geirlaug came into this inheritance after her daughter Inga. The poet Thorbjorn carved these runes.

Bastards were common, as men mostly did as they liked with female slaves. They had their lesser rights of sharing in property and blood-money; and they could gain full rights if adopted. The distinction between marriage and concubinage could become blurred; and we find illegitimate sons succeeding to the Norwegian throne.

Village settlements seem rare. There were many scattered farms, with agricultural methods growing more intensive and breeding more selective. The houses were of turf laid on two stone courses, with the main rooms wainscotted. A farm had a long hall with a hearth in the middle, benches along the walls, and various side-rooms, stores, kitchen, guestroom, dairies, haphazardly added. Almost everything went on in the hall, where at meals the master sat on a high seat near the middle and tables were brought in. A big feast might last several days, with songs, tales and games. If a man's *thraells* could not get in a harvest in time, he had the right to claim help from his neighbours; and it was the custom for crops and tools to be left out in the open, with severe penalties for thieving. The aim of the custom was to save time in the busy seasons; but it could only have grown up in a community with strong cooperative traditions. Youngsters were expected to work hard; despised was the charcoal-chewer, who hung round the cooking hearth. At twelve a boy was legally adult and might go on a Viking cruise. St Olaf embarked at that age and was a leader in his teens. At the Things or assemblies of free men the local chieftains dominated; but though any simple tribal democracy had been left far behind, the gatherings still did much to nourish the spirit of independence. Danish and Norwegian kings were bound to consult local or regional assemblies; and a striking expansion of the powers of the Thing occurred in Iceland where the colonists sturdily resisted any centralized forms of government and the courts functioned effectively without any basis in state force for carrying out their judgements.

The capacity for mingling extreme independence with strong discipline was shown by the Jomvikings established in Pomerania at the mouth of the Oder, a sort of military guild held together by a very strict rule and described in a thirteenth-century saga. Only men of proved courage, between the ages of eighteen and fifty, were admitted; no women were permitted in the castle; no man might be absent for more than three days at a time. Members assumed the duty of mutual support and revenge, and plunder was shared out by lot. The fact that the Jomvikings were set in a castle in the midst of Wendish foes helped to enforce the discipline; but the system is none the less remarkable. It helps us to understand how the Normans could hold together a compact front in England or in Italy in the early years of their invasions. The Icelandic Althing ruled without king from 930 to the thirteenth century.

The man of initiative, even of wilful and headstrong self-assertion, was the one respected. The saga writers are pleased to tell of someone: 'He was a difficult boy to deal with, strong-willed and quarrelsome.'

He [Gold Harald] went as usual to his friend Hakon and complained to him of his fate and asked for good advice and if he could help him to get his share of the kingdom, saying that he would rather try force and the chance of war than give it up.

Hakon advised him not to speak to any man so that this should be known. 'For,' said he, 'it concerns your life. And rather consider with yourself what you are man enough to undertake. For to accomplish such a purpose requires a bold and firm man, who will neither stick at good nor evil to do that which is intended. For to take up great resolutions and then to lay them aside would only end in dishonour.'[2]

In such a society not only the tie of man and lord but that of freeman and freeman was a deep concern. Hence the ceremonial swearing-in of blood-brotherhood (called foster-brotherhood), which created bonds similar to those of kinship. We have several accounts of the rite; thus the Saga of Gisli describes it:

They cut a neck-ring of turf from the ground and raised it up in such a way that the two ends were still fast, and under it they set an inlaid spear, tall enough for a man to lay his hand just on the rivers of the socket. The four of them were to pass underneath it...Now they drew blood and let their blood run together into earth scraped up from under the turf-ring. They mixed all this together, both earth and blood. After this they all fell on their knees and swore an oath that each would avenge the other like his own brother, and they called all the gods to witness this. And as they were about to clasp hands...[3]

The neck-ring of turf was a long strip cut so as to make a complete circle; the ceremony is a typical example of the passage-rite of a tribal initiation, a passage through the womb of mother-earth into a rebirth on a new level: here that of an enlarged brotherhood.

The kindreds too were strong. The laws dealing with wergild for murder have come down in a thirteenth-century form. The wergild is divided into three parts, one met by the killer, a second by his paternal kin, a third by his maternal kin. Each degree of kindred pays one half less than the nearer degree. The Jutland law, which restricts the kindred to the fourth man (the third cousin), insists that the king cannot let the killer buy peace from him unless he is reconciled to the kindred of the dead man. Clearly the laws were in force at the time they were recorded. The liability of the kindred for wergild was annulled by royal edict earlier in Denmark than elsewhere in Scandinavia; but a contemporary historian says that the edict of Knud VI for Skåne could not check manslaughter and that Valdemar II (1204–41) issued a more definite ordinance: the killer himself paid all the money, but it was still distributed to the whole kindred of the dead man. However, we still find kings in the sixteenth century complaining that wergild was collected from the killer's 'innocent kindred and friends [? connections by marriage], yes, the very babe in the cradle'. The kindreds were capable of acting corporately for nearly a century after the Reformation. Christian IV at last broke them, but only because of the backing he got from Protestantism.[4]

The Norse gods reflected the lives of their people, were linked with all human activities but did not intrude overmuch. There were spirits for every man, whether he lived by wisdom and statecraft, war and plunder, trade and seafaring, ploughing or pasturing. The functions of the gods overlapped so generously that Odin's man, Thor's man, Frey's man, and the rest, could expect to be looked after in all aspects or moments of life and death. The gods themselves lived in Asgard where each had his hall; here was Yggdrasil, the sacred world-tree, under which sat the three Norns spinning men's fates. There was a strong feeling of conflict and violence, of an attacking principle of evil. Ragnorök, world-end, was looming over both gods and men; all things would be consumed by fire and water in the midst of the battle against the dark forces led by Loki. Then a new world would arise; the gods would return, and happiness, wisdom, and fertility would reign. But there was no central organization of religion, no set doctrine, no uniform system of worship. The priests were not a separate caste, and often temples seem to have been served by the landowners. Much ritual took place in the open air, in woods, on mounds or stones, or at springs. There were many lesser deities, guardian spirits, heroes and divine kings. Some men revered the gods; others had a sort of partnership with one of them. Many enjoyed the feastings, but believed only in their good right hand and defiant self-reliance, with the gods perhaps as applauding spectators. When Christianity was imposed, it lay lightly on large numbers, as on Helgi the Lean who 'believed in Christ and yet made vows to Thor for sea-voyages or in tight corners and for everything that struck him as of real importance'.[5] These men could be ferociously cruel, cutting a bloodeagle by splaying out the ribs of a dead enemy; and the murder-spirit could descend on them in a berserk fury. The poet describing Harald Fairhair's court mentions a company of picked fighters on whom the king particularly relied, berserks, also known as wolfskins. The texts show that such men had an aura of mystery and horror; Snorre calls them devotees of Odin, filled with his power. 'They advanced without mailcoats and were as frenzied as dogs or wolves; they bit their shields; they were as strong as bears or boars; they struck men down, but neither fire nor steel could mark them. This was called the Berserk Rage.'[6] The term *berserk* means bear-shirt; and the possessed men were clad, at least in early times, in animal skins; they even became wildbeasts, werewolves. A pre-Viking Swedish relief shows two figures, one naked but for a horned helmet, the other wearing a wolfskin; they seem to be engaged in a ritual dance or combat. But in the sagas the skins seem to have been discarded. The *Saga of Grettir the Strong* tells us:

King Harald made for Thorir's ship, knowing him to be a terrible berserk, and very brave. The fighting was desperate on either side. Then the king ordered his berserks, two men named Ulf-hednar, forward. No iron could hurt them, and when they charged nothing could withstand them. The whole ship from stem to stern was cleared and her fastenings were cut, so that she dropped out of the line of battle.[7]

The battle-axe was the specifically Norse weapon, suited for such aggressively individual warriors. And challenges to single combat were naturally not uncommon.

It was the custom then in England, if two strove for anything to settle the matter by single combat; and now Alfin challenges Olaf Tryggvasson to fight. The time and place for the combat were settled, and that each should have twelve men with him. When they met, Olaf told his men to do exactly as they saw him do. He had a large axe; and when Alfin was going to cut at him with his sword, he hewed away the sword out of his hand and with the next blow struck down Alfin himself.[8]

But the war system could be used for collective action by the farmers against the king. When Olaf Tryggvasson was burning temples down, including the one at Lade where Earl Hakon had had a great gold ring hung on the door, 'as soon as the bonders heard of it, they sent out a war-arrow as a token through the whole district, ordering out a warlike force and meant to meet the king with it.'[9]

The sacral character of war appears in the imagery connecting it with Odin-Woden and merging the battle-fury with the tempests of nature:

The sword in the king's hand bit through the weeds-of-Woden [mail] as if it were whisked through water, the spear-points clashed, the shields were shattered, the axes rattled on the heads of the warriors. Targets and skulls were trodden under the Northmen's shield-fires [weapons] and the hard heels of their hilts. There was a din in the island, the kings dyed the shining rows of shields in the blood of men. The wound-fires [blades] burnt in the bloody wounds, the halberds bowed down to take the life of men, the ocean of blood dashed upon the swords' ness, the flood of the shafts fell on the beach of Stord. Halos of war mixed under the vault of the bucklers; the sword-tempest blew underneath the clouds of the targets, the lees of the sword-edges [blood] pattered in the gale of Woden. Many a man fell into the stream of the brand.[10]

The weapons assume a daemonic life of their own and the universe is constructed in the guise of their dynamic energies. The raven-flag also had its spirit-life. An interpolation in Asser tells us: 'They say further that in every battle, wherever that flag went before them, if they were to gain the victory, a live crow would appear flying in the midst of the flag; but if they were doomed to be defeated, it would hang down unmoving; and this was often proved.' In songs eagle and raven hover forever over the battlefield, thirsty for blood: 'the raven-friend in Odin's dress' (full armour) while the wolf, the Horse of the Valkyrie, roams about. The ravens were the steeds of the witch-wolves. *Beowulf* contains this imagery. Recounting the feuds between Geats and Swedes, the poet cries: 'Music of the harp will not awaken the heroes. But the black raven, flapping over the dead, will be garrulous and tell the eagle of its luck at dinner, when along with the wolf it plundered the dead.'[11]

Though the raven of battle is common in Anglo-Saxon poetry, it was essentially Norse in its sacral character. We noted its importance on the war-flag. The *Chronicle* records the capture of the Danish flag called the Raven under the year 878; the flag was said to have been woven by the two daughters of Ragnar Lothbrok, whose death shows signs of having been patterned on the victim-dedications to Woden. The *Saga of Olaf Tryggvasson* tells of the ravenflag made by Eithne, Jarl Hlödver's wife, which flapped above the Viking invaders of Ireland; at the battle of Clontarf Hrafn the Red called it the Devil because all its bearers were killed (as if victims to it). The raven (*corvus*) also appears as the devil or his emissary, stealing a page of script from Wilfrid when he was St Guthlac's guest; but a miracle recovered the page. The raven was an emblem or embodiment of Odin, who was known as Hrafnass or Ravengod; he had two other ravens (Thought and Mind) as his companions – names that suggest the bird's prophetic powers. A tale in the early *Life of St Gregory* shows a clear propaganda-effort to disprove these powers. One Sunday as King Edwin of Northumbria was on his way to church, a crow 'sang with an evil omen'. Everyone halted. Bishop Paulinus bade a servant take good aim and shoot an arrow; and he later brought bird and arrows into the hall and showed them to the heathen catechumens as proof that the bird could not prophesy, since it had failed to foresee its own death. Obviously then it could not prophesy to those 'baptised in the image of God'. (A crow on a tree prophesied to the king of the Warni, in about 500, that he would die within forty days.) A bird usually taken to be Odin's raven replaced the Roman winged Victory on Scandinavian gold bracteates of the sixth and seventh centuries. (We may note that the seal of the port-reeve at Colchester, which seems certainly pre-Norman, bears the design of a raven; the port-reeve was the chief official there before the bailiffs of Norman times. The town was occupied for a while by the Danes until in 912 it was retaken; but if the raven is Danish it probably derived from the presence of Danish traders there later on.)

There was a strong belief in an after life in which people carried on in much the same way as on earth. Sacrifices were made at funerals. An Arab geographer describes the funeral rites of a Swedish chief on the Volga. A third of the dead man's possessions were burned on the pyre, a third used at the feast, a third went to heirs. There was once a tradition that the wife was buried alive with the body. The *Saga of Olaf Tryggvasson* tells how Sigrithr the proud insisted on divorce from a Swedish king because a law stated that royal widows should be set beside their dead husbands in the barrow. The Arab geographer says that poorer men had a small boat made specially for their cremation, but chiefs were buried in their own vessels. The image of the dead journeying in a ship went back to Bronze-Age monuments in Gotland, and was carried on in ship-burials or by setting over a grave rows of stones in the outline of a ship.[12]

The idea of the death-journey appears in later runes, after the conversion to Christianity, when land-owners are praised for clearing roads and building bridges as well as establishing places for the Thing to meet in. The roads and bridges (mainly causeways over marshes or stone-laid fords over waterways) were encouraged by the missionary church so that people might attend church in all weathers. To construct them was thought to help the soul to pass through purgatory fires. 'Jarlabanke had these stones raised in memory of himself while he still lived; and he built this bridge for his soul', at Täby, Uppland. At Aby, brothers raised a stone to their father's memory and 'made the bridge to please God'. The soul-bridge was a very old image, here made to do Christian service. We may compare this effort to drive a roadway to the church, to heaven, with the efforts of Norman barons to found or endow a monastery – to buy a plot of land in heaven.[13]

Thus in a charter of Binham Priory under Stephen we read:

I have done this at the advice and with the approval of many wise men, moved above all by the exhortation, the request, and the counsel of the lord Theobald archbishop of Canterbury and primate of all England, who showed me by the most reasonable and unanswerable arguments that a noble gentlemen who has the fee of six knights should give not only the third part of a knight's land to God and Holy Church for the soul's health of himself and his kin, but the whole of a knight's land or more than that, adding also that if this man's heir should try to take away the alms which is interposed as a bridge between his father and Paradise, by which the father may not be able to pass over, the heir, so far as he may, is disinheriting his father from the Kingdom of Heaven, and therefore should not obtain

the inheritance which remains, since he who has killed his father
has proved himself no son.

Just as death was a sea-passage to a new world, so in the minds of
Vikings, as they listened to scaldic songs or drove into strange seas,
the dreams of piratic gold may well have merged with fantasies of
otherworld adventure, of journeys to paradise. When, coming from
their hard and rough northern world, they reached Byzantion, they
even felt that they had broken through to Asgard, the site of the gods,
and, returning home, they talked excitedly of this magnificent
otherworld. The urge for piratic or trading journeys shaded off into
the urge for pilgrimage, which was increasing in the early medieval
world. The *Chronicle* under 891 tells of three Scots (Irishmen) who
'came to king Alfred in a boat without any oars from Hibernia,
whence they stole away because they would go on a foreign pilgrimage for the love of God, they recked not where. The boat in which
they came was made of two hides and a half; and they took with
them food for seven days. And within seven days they came to land
in Cornwall, and soon afterwards went to king Alfred. They were
named Dubslane and Macbeth and Mawlinmun.' An Anglo-Norman
poet, Benedeit, patronized by Maud, Henry's queen, wrote a *Voyage
of St Brendan*, first in Latin, then (at Maud's request) in French. Here
the Irish tale of Brendan's voyage to paradise was vigorously
recounted, and paradise appears 'like a very royal palace to see, an
emperor's very rich fee'.

Linked with the free and impulsive character of the Vikings was
their readiness to undertake long and dangerous sea-voyages, in
which again their capacity under certain circumstances to combine
initiative with discipline was of great value. We have dealt with
their raids on Britain, Ireland and Gaul, but we must now add that
by the ninth century they had settled in the Shetlands and Orkneys,
and moved down the coasts of Scotland as far as Lincolnshire on the
east and the Isle of Man on the west. Though defeated in Ireland in
1014, their power there was not broken until the Anglo-Norman
attempt to conquer the island under Henry II; and Scotland did not
regain the Isle of Man and the Hebrides till 1266, the Shetlands till
1462. The Swedes largely turned east, to the Gulf of Finland and
the river-routes to the Black Sea. The Danes took the route down the
Channel, round Brittany and Cape Finisterre into the Mediterranean,
ravaging the coasts of Spain and even Italy. They burned Lisbon,
Cadiz, Seville, and sacked Pisa, and came near to locating and looting
Rome. The Arabs refer to their red-sailed ships and called the crews
'heathen wizards'. Few important rivers were not exploited. Besides

the Thames and the Seine, they sailed up the Loire and the Gironde. The Norwegians ventured on the ocean with a persistence and courage unknown to any previous people. About eight hundred Norsemen reached Iceland, where a few Irish monks seem to have preceded them; they colonized the wastes of Greenland from about 985 and may have finally merged with the natives to produce the Esquimaux; they even got to Labrador and Nova Scotia, perhaps sailing yet further south.[14] The *vik* of Viking has no link with the Latin *vicus*, village; it means a creek or inlet where ships could find a haven. In Iceland, which of all the Norse areas has kept most clearly the primitive form of placenames, many names end in *-vik*; later in Britain and on the continent it appears in connection with trading-points.

The long narrow clinker-built ships, sixteen-oared and masted, dragon-carved, could each hold some forty fighters. Lower in the middle and pointed at the ends, they were well devised to sail in open seas, yet were easily beached and could navigate far up rivers. On landing, the warriors often rounded up the horses nearby and turned into a mounted force which scoured the country. There was seldom any effective resistance and no navies to cut off retreats. At most a local levy might gather, with inadequate weapons and unlikely to catch the fast-moving riders; if they did catch them, they would be beaten. As raids were often made in summer or autumn when peasants were trying to get crops in, the result might be a winter of starvation.

The Norwegian raids, started in the last years of the eighth century, were earlier than the Danish. Why? There appears to have been a considerable population increase in Norway, to judge by the number of graves.[15] Placenames ending in *-setr, -bolstad, -land*, seem to mark the inner expansion, representing sites taken over by members of families who found the homesteads crowded and moved to outlying sheds or shielings. In the Shetlands and Orkneys the colonists again gave names to sites with these endings.[16] It was about this time that ships were developed which were able to cross to those islands with fair safety. In Denmark the local resources were used up to the limit. There was an expansion in Skåne, where in time the Danes had to compete with the Swedes.

Other theories to explain the emigrations have been propounded, such as the Frankish weakening of Frisian seapower. But the Frisians never dominated the seas by force; and the Franks, if anything, encouraged their trading. Charlemagne made some attempts to better the defences along the Frisian coast, but the Viking raids were not provoked by the Frankish conquest of Saxony. Nor did the dissensions in the Carolingian empire set the Danes on the move, though they made the raids easier and thus no doubt stimulated them. Both

Norwegians and Danes were essentially in search of land; and it was in Norway, with its harsh, rocky, mountainous country and its difficult communications, that the pressure of population was first felt. The age saw in general a steady expansion of populations in western Europe, to which people in many regions responded by what we may call internal colonization, a movement into wastelands and forests; but the Danes and Norwegians responded by turning to the sea.

The Swedes too turned to the sea, but their problem was not quite the same. They had much rich land, though the lowering of the water-level in middle Sweden slowly but steadily exposed the alluvium. The people, without neglecting piracy, were more concerned with trade than their Atlantic-facing neighbours. Already by 839 Norse warriors dominated the north of Russia, extorting tribute from the natives and using it for trade with Byzantion, Khazaria, and Bulghar on the Volga, where Moslem traders came. Their effect on placenames was limited to the river-routes and they did little settling – though the early princes in Kiev had Scandinavian names, Igor, Oleg (Helgi), Ingvar.[17] In 942, however, a son of the ruling dynasty had a Slavonic name, Sviatoslav; and even under Norse rule the town had little contact with the Baltic. The chiefs, who lived by the trading of tribute, may have made up quite a small group; in any event Kiev must have had a long history; traditions embodied in the *Povest*, such as that of a ferryman-king and his role in making Kiev a river-port, derive from the period when the Khazars were dominant in the area. The eastward move of the Vikings did not last for a long time; but it was very active while it lasted and it was of great importance in establishing links between northern (and so western) Europe and Russia, with the Moslem and the Byzantine east. It brings out sharply the way in which the Vikings in a short space of time expanded the whole horizon of western Europe.

The runes give us vivid glimpses of the men and their movements. One ninth-century inscription (Kälvesten, Ostergötland) tells how Öjvind 'fell eastward with Ejvisl'. But most of the stones date from the eleventh century. The land mainly named is Greece, *Grikkland*, *i Grikkum*, a term that includes all the north-eastern lands of the Byzantine empire. At Ed, north of Stockholm, on a huge boulder is the inscription set up by Rangvald for his mother, 'God help her soul'. As for the cutter, 'He was in Greece, he was leader of the host', perhaps a reference to the Varangian Guard. Such journeys were so common that the inheritance laws declare a man 'can receive no inheritance as long as he stays in Greece'. Rangvald had come home, but many warriors died afar. A stone of Ulanda says, 'He went boldly, he gained wealth, out in *Grikkland*, for his heir.' A stone brought to Oxford in the seventeenth century was cut by Torsten for his father and brother, 'They had gone out to Greece'. The stone raised by Ljut the skipper to one of his sons states that 'he steered the ship, he came to Greek harbours'.[19] He might have gone by the channels of the Neva to Ladoga, where trade-routes diverged, one to the south, one to the east. The usual route was by the Volkov down to Old Ladoga, the Norse Aldeigjuborn, where stood a trading-post from the ninth to the mid-eleventh century. If a man went down the Dneipr he had to face cataracts, sandbanks, dangerous shoal-waters, past Kiev on to the island of Berezanj. The wanderers had great experience of portage; for they usually preferred to drag a ship, if possible, over a promontory that lay right in their course. They thus avoided the difficult voyage round Jutland, carrying the ships from the river Eider to the Sli estuary in the Baltic. Here the water system at the time worked so that only a short haulage over land was needed. In the same way river-falls and rapids were evaded. The place name Drag, common in Norway, records a haulage-point. When a current ran too strongly, the ship was often pulled upstream from the banks by means of poles.[20]

Norsemen visited Byzantion which, as we saw, they even identified with Asgard. By 930 they served in the imperial army, and by the early eleventh century there was a special Norse regiment, the Varangians, whose men had a habit of spending their leave on a trip to Jerusalem. The first whom we know went there was Kolskeggr, in 992; Harald Hardrada, most famous of the Varangians, was there in 1034. Many men spent fifty or more years in the service, then made the pilgrimage before returning home. Friends, stirred by their tales, came south to see the same sights. The apostle to Iceland, Thorvald Kodransson Vidtförli, was in Jerusalem about 990. The half-Danish Sweyn, son of Godwin, set out with a company of Englishmen in 1051 to expiate a murder; he went barefoot in penance and died of exposure in the Anatolian mountains next autumn. Lagman Gudrodsson, Norse king of Man, who killed his brother, went on a similar penance-journey. Many pilgrims liked to make the round trip, coming by sea through the Straits of Gibraltar and then back overland via Russia.[21]

Other Norsemen did not go so far east or south. A boulder at Esta tells us, 'He fell in Holmgard [Novgorod], the ships captain with his crew'; a son raised the memorial. A rune from Sjusta, Uppland, states, 'He died in Holmgard in Olaf's church': the rune must date only a few decades after the death of the martyr-king Olaf Haraldsson at Sticklestad in 1030. A Mervalla stone says: 'He often sailed to Semgallen' in Latvia, 'in dear-prized knarr round Domesnäs', the northern tip of Kurland. The knarr was a roomy sea-going ship heavier and stronger than the long-ship. (*Cnearr* is the term in Old English, the verb *knarra* being cognate with our obsolete word *gnar* (*r*), to snarl or growl. The name thus refers to the creaking and groaning of the timbers in a big sea.) Domesnäs projected into the Gulf of Riga and carried on as a reef, a great danger point. Another man was 'killed in Vorland', the north-east part of Estonia on the southern shores of the Gulf of Finland. 'God and God's Mother help his soul.' Many personal names show the lure of the east: Est, Estulv, Estfare (Estonia-farer). Est was probably a slave-name. A rune in Vastergotland says of a 'young man active and able' that he was 'killed in Estonia'.[22] The saga tells how Olaf Tryggvasson and his mother were captured in the east Baltic. Her brother Sigurd had been long abroad in Russia with King Valdemar (Grand Duke in Novgorod at the time, 971), and was held there in high consideration.

Astrid now had a strong wish to travel to her brother there. Hakon the Old gave her good attendants and what was needful for the journey, and she set out with some merchants. She had been two years with Hakon and Olaf was three years old. As they sailed out into the Baltic they were captured by Vikings of Estonia, who made booty of the people as well as the goods, killing some and sharing out the others as slaves. Olaf was separated from his mother and an Estonian called Klerkon got him as his share along with Thoralf and Thorgils. Klerkon thought Thoralf too old for a slave and that not much work could be got out of him, so he killed him. But he took the boys and sold them to a man named Klerk for a stout and good ram. A third man, Reas, bought Olaf for a good cloak.[23]

An Uppland stone says of a man, 'He was killed in Finland.' One at Söderby tells of a man who fell in a remote Finnish province, Tavastland. Adam of Bremen, in his history of the metropolitan see of Hamburg-Bremen (about 1070–80), recounts how Anund, son of Emund the Old, 'sent by his father to extend his kingdom, came to the Land of Women, whom we think to be Amazons. There he died from a poison which they mixed in their water-springs.' Probably the legend came from a confusion between the Land of the Kväner (part of present Finland), where *kvan* is a tribal name, and *kvaen*, wife, cognate with English *quean* (a common woman) and related to queen.[24]

On the Turinge stone, Södermanland, Torsten and his dead brother are commemorated in verse by the rest of their family and their retainers. 'The brothers were best among men on land and out of the levy. They held their housemen well. He fell in action east in Gada-

rike [Russia], the levy's captain, of the land's men the best.' Near
the Dneipr's mouth, on the island of Berezanj, Grane buried his
comrade Karl. The isle with sheltered bays must have been much
frequented : several stones tell of men who went with Ingvar the
Far-traveller on his journey to Serkland, the Saracen Land (probably
the caliphate centred on Baghdad). Gripsholm records of Ingvar's
brother: 'They fared like men far after gold and in the East gave
food to the eagle. They died southward in Serkland.' One rune in
verse mentions a man dead in Italy: 'He to the eastward ploughed
with his prow and in Langobards Land met his end.'

Mainly as a result of the voyages into Russia and down into the
eastern Mediterranean, Sweden throughout this period was restlessly
trading.[25] Among the known ports was Skiringssal on the Oslo fiord,
a centre for the people of the Vik, also a market for furs and walrus-
hides from the far north (bartered for swords, amber and objects
from the East). Schleswig (Hedeby for the Danes) tapped most of the
trade between the Baltic and the North Sea across the neck of the
Danish peninsula. Birka on an island in Lake Mälar was the great
emporium of the Swedes and was perhaps linked with a chain of
other Birkas across the northern seas. Judging from the coins, it
reached its height in the later ninth century. Inside a semicircular
bank (which no doubt had wooden battlements) lay some twenty-
nine acres dominated by a fort built outside the line of the wall. The
beach was protected by stakes driven into the water; and in winter
men came on skis, skates and sledges. Local goods were antler-combs,
jewellery, leatherwork. Excavated objects include glass and rings.
One ring, set with amethysts, had an Arabic inscription and came
from lands south-east of the Caspian; a piece of fine silk had a gold
pattern like those made in China. Most imports seem to derive from
the eastern region of the caliphate; the line of communication was
probably by the Volga rather than the Dneipr; there are few signs of
links with Byzantion. Skiringssal (Kaupang) had a natural harbour
with a protecting string of islands and shoals, and a defence of hills
at the back; it flourished from the early ninth century to the early
tenth. It has revealed ornaments from the British Isles, pottery from
the Rhineland, glass from western Europe, various objects from the
eastern Baltic; of six coins, one was a Mercian penny, another a
denar of Louis the Pious, two were Kufic coins, one apparently
Abassid, the other minted at Birka. The hinterland, rich with graves
of the Viking period, shows the concentration of wealth. (Norway
had several Kaupangs; the name means market and is of the same
nature as the English *chipping*.) Hedeby was surrounded in the ninth
century by semicircular walls which were several times rebuilt. Iron
and glass were worked, and ornaments of bronze and silver; walrus

tusks came from Norway and stone for millstones from the Eifel; there are signs of clothmaking. Destroyed in mid-eleventh century, it was soon replaced by Schleswig, which deeper vessels could reach and which in turn was replaced by Lübeck. Late in the ninth century Hedeby had been occupied by a Swedish dynasty, then in 934 it was taken by the Emperor Henry I and stayed under the Germans for the middle years of the tenth century. Later in that century its contacts seem to have been with Slav lands east of the Elbe rather than with the eastern Baltic.[26]

There was no source of silver in Scandinavia. In the ninth and tenth centuries the main supply of minted silver was Moslem; some 85,000 Arab coins called Kufic (after the Mesopotamian city of Kufah, where the coins are usually dated which is useful for correlating finds) have been found.[27] Discoveries of hacksilver in a more or less uniform condition, in the area from central Russia to the Baltic, Germany and Scandinavia, suggest that silver was used as a means of exchange; the silver mines in the east and in south Russia doubtless provided one source.[28] There are also large numbers of coin-fragments, showing the need for small change. Kufic silver was carried to the British Isles; but export from the Baltic seems to end when Hedeby came under the Germans, though Birka kept up eastern contacts.

King Alfred has left us accounts of voyages which more than anything else help us to feel the impact of the Viking expansion on the minds of men in western Europe. We see in them a new sense of geography, of the unknown waiting to be tackled, of the interrelation of peoples; and we experience directly the bold character of these explorers. Also we see how other peoples, such as the English, were being stimulated to make their own ventures. Ohthere (Old Norse Ottarr) 'told his lord, King Alfred, that he lived furthest north of all Northmen'. The region was marked by the islands clustering about its shores broken into long narrow fiords, its valleys and great waterfalls roaring down cliffs in the southern section, and the far-stretching glacier, the Svartisen, the Field of Black Ice. This land was long but narrow; Ohthere could use for pasture or ploughland only that part near the sea, and even that was often rocky and bare. Further inland were wild mountains inhabited by Finns (Lapps). The land ran on northwards, inhabited only by a few Finns who hunted in winter and fished off the coast in summer. In Halgoland (Helgeland) there was such good whale-hunting that Ohthere and five others killed sixty whales in two days. Across the mountains of its more southerly section lay Sweden; and facing the more northerly section was Cwenaland (perhaps at the north end of the Gulf of Bothnia). The Cwenas now and then made raids across the mountains on the men of Norway carrying the small light boats which they used for ferrying over the big freshwater mountain lakes. (These Cwenas seem to have been Finns.) They in turn were raided by the Men of the North (the Halgolanders). Ohthere himself was a leading Halgolander, 'a very wealthy man in those possessions in which their wealth consists: that is, in the wilder animals. When he came to the king he had 600 tame deer unsold. They call these Reindeers. Of them, 6 were decoy-deer, very valuable among Finns, as with them they catch the wild-deer. He was among the first men of the land, though he had not more than 20 horned cattle, 20 sheep, and 20 swine; and the little that he ploughed, he ploughed with horses.' Another source of income was the tribute paid in kind to him and his neighbours by the Finns: furs, reindeer-skins, skins of bears, martens, otters, feathers, ships' rope from hides of whale and seal. The tribute was exacted from the Finns more or less according to an assessment of each man's rank and importance among his fellow-tribesmen. (Harald Fairhair finally won power through the battle of Hahrsfjord, probably in 885; he seems to have been taking the *finnskattr*, the Finn-tribute, as his royal prerogative, so that many men sailed from Norway in anger at what they held to be a usurpation – perhaps Ohthere was one of these.)

> He said that at a certain time he wished to find out how far the land went due north, or whether any man lived to the north of the waste. So he went due north along the coast. All the way he left wasteland on his starboard and on his larboard the open sea, for three days. Then he was as far as the whale-hunters ever go. He went yet due north as far as he could sail in the next three days.

He thus reached North Cape and found that 'the land bent due east'. He sailed on to the land of the Beormas on the White Sea. This region was more populated than the wastelands where there lived only a few fishers, fowlers, hunters, all Finns. He sailed into the Sea and went on for five days, along the southern coast of the peninsula till he reached the mouth of a great river. Now he and the few men he had taken along to help him saw that the land past the rivermouth was inhabited, and they were afraid of meeting some hostile tribe if they went on as before. (The river seems to have been the Varzuga, flowing through the south of the Kola Peninsula into the White Sea.) Ohthere turned his ship up the river and found more cultivated land. Again he feared attack and did not land; but he soon came on men who lived along the Kandalaskha Gulf. These were the Beormas. They must have been friendly as they told him 'many tales', which he had no means of testing. He had heard of the people in his own region. The Norwegians thought of them as the folk of Bjarmaland, a remote place of magic where the men confounded enemies by means of incantations that made the heavens burst open in time of battle and hurl down floods of rain and hail.

A second voyage, lasting more than a month, took him from Halgoland to Skiringssal. Then, when telling how he sailed on to Hedeby, he interested Alfred by remarking that some islands and Jutland, which he passed, were 'lands in which the Angles lived before they came to this country'.

Wulfstan seems to have been an English captain. He had taken a boat from Hedeby into the Baltic to the land at the mouth of the Wista (Vistula). There he met people living near the Zalew Wislany, the inlet now between Gdansk and Kaliningrad. They had many towns, each ruled by a king, and lived mainly on fish and honey. The master-class, a steppe-people, drank mares' milk while the poor and the slaves drank mead; no ale was brewed. A corpse lay in state among kinsfolk and friends for a month or two, sometimes even six months. The higher the man's rank had been, the longer his dead body was kept. All the time there was carousing round the bier, and funeral games were carried on. At last came the day for burial. The dead man's treasures which were portable were divided into five, six, or even more portions, depending on their number and value; the richest portion was set on the ground about a mile from the man's home, and the other portions at places in between – the portion of least value nearest the house. Men with the swiftest horses rode from a point five or six miles away to pick up the treasures, each portion falling to the man who reached it first. Next came the cremation of the dead man in his best clothes, girded with his weapons. As for the question of the long unburied corpses, certain men there knew the secret of refrigeration; even in summer they could keep water frozen into ice.

We see here the immemorial interest in travellers' tales, but also eager intellectual curiosity about the world, its peoples, geography, and history. Both Alfred and the captains share this attitude. Alfred indeed had translated Orosius's *History of the World* as an expression of the expanding perspectives of the later ninth century. What in particular gives a concrete basis for the intellectual awakening is the widening network of trade. Alfred sees that Orosius (a Spaniard of the early fourth century) is very inadequate in dealing with northern Europe, and he tries to get his bearings by taking as his fixed points the east Franks, who were in touch with Britain; the Old Saxons, distant kinsmen of his own people; the Moravians, who in this century had established a flourishing kingdom; and the south and the north Danes. Five of his 'middlepoints' lie round the Baltic.[29]

The runes tell us of the westward as well as eastward movements by Vikings, of men like the one mentioned on the Jula stone, who 'had been in the West, taken township and attacked'. An Uppland stone was raised by two sons to a father 'who in the West had his place in the Housecarles'. At Tjälve we meet a 'warrior who served with Cnut'. This stone was set up by a brother Väring, a Varangian. One brother had gone west, one east. An Yttergärde stone (1020–30) tells of a great yeoman farmer of Uppland who had three shares of tribute money. 'Ulv took in England three gelds. That was the first which Toste paid. Then Thorkel paid. Then Cnut paid.' Toste seems to be a chief mentioned by Snorre Sturlesson, whose son was Sigrid the Ambitious; Thorkel the Tall was chief of the Jomsvikings, involved in more than one attack on England in the early eleventh century; Cnut, king of England in 1017, paid in 1018 his last and biggest Danegeld to returning troops. Another Uppland farmer brought much money to his home in Väsby. 'He took Cnut's payment in England.' A Lingsberg stone tells of Gudve who went west to England and shared in the Danegeld; at Bjudby we are merely told, 'To England had the young warrior voyaged and later at home lamented died.' Cnut's son seems to be referred to on the Tuna stone, which tells of Assur, 'who was king Harald's seaman'. A Småland stone mentions a man who held the important post of marshall, *stallre*, under Håkon Jarl, probably Cnut's nephew who was drowned in 1029 in the Pentland Firth. An Uppland stone records a man to whom five brothers raised the monument: 'He died in Jutland; he was on his way to England.'[30] These men had profited from such levies as that William of Malmesbury mentions under Harthacnut:

> He imposed a rigid and intolerable tribute upon England, so as to pay, as he had promised, 20 marks to the soldiers of each of his ships. While this was harshly levied throughout the kingdom, two of the collectors discharging their office rather too strictly were killed by the citizens of Worcester. At which he burned and depopulated the city through his commanders, and plundered the citizens' property, so that he cast a blemish on his fame and diminished the love of his subjects.[31]

We get the English side of the picture in the poem on the Battle of Maldon, 991. The Vikings demand gold rings in return for peace. 'It's better for you to buy off our raid with gold than that we, famed for cruelty, should cut you down in battle...We'll take to the sea with the tribute you pay and keep our promise of peace.' Byrhtnoth replies:

> Can you hear, you pirate, what these people say? They will pay you a tribute of whistling spears, of deadly darts, and proven swords, weapons to pay you, pierce, slit and slay you in storming battle. Listen, messenger! Take back this reply: Tell your people the unpleasant tidings that over here stands a noble earl with his troop – guardians of the people and of the country, the home of Aethelred, my prince – who'll defend this land to the last ditch. We'll sever the heathen's head from their shoulders. It would be much to our shame if you took our tribute and embarked without battle since you've intruded so far and so rudely into this country. No, you'll not get your treasure so easily. The spear's point and the sword's edge, savage battle-play, must teach us first that we have to yield tribute.[32]

We see that loot or tribute was looked for in England more than trading gains; but though war here was continuous, trade must also have played a large part in the relationships of the North Sea and Baltic. In many Viking graves in Norway fragments of English metalwork adapted as ornaments for men and women have been found; some at least were torn from settings on books or shrines; and in Sweden more than 30,000 Anglo-Saxon coins in tenth and eleventh century hoards surely reflect the Danegeld. The eastern basis of Birka's trade had been made clear when the silver supply from Bulghar was held up, perhaps as a result of Kiev's growing power. Pirates of the Baltic's wealth then had to look elsewhere, and they found what they wanted in the west where silver had been accumulating, especially through exploitation of the Harz Mountains from the tenth century. England's wealth was manifested by the elaborate currency arrangements at the close of Eadgar's reign. Probably in 973 there was a major coinage reform, and new types were issued at regular intervals, at first of six years, then of three.[33] London was active in the early eleventh century in trade with the Rhine; and English wealth was largely dependent on the export of wool to the cloth-towns of Flanders which were now growing; and English as well as German silver was looted in the late tenth and early eleventh centuries. But trading also went on with the Danes. The Ely chronicler speaks of many moots held at Cambridge in the tenth century, and at one point mentions Irish traders with cloaks and other goods set out for sale. At an earlier date wares from Kent and even France reached the site, which as late as 1295 was considered a seaport. The Irish merchants we may take to be Danes from Dublin or Wexford;

they landed wares at one of the wharves or hythes in the quarter long known by the Danish name of the Holm, where now stands the church of St Clement, a favourite Danish saint. So Danish occupation, recorded in 875, left a trading as well as a military imprint.[34]

The role of the Vikings was to initiate Europe into the problems of deep sea sailing and the solutions of these problems. They integrated the whole Baltic and Atlantic side of the continent, from the Neva to Gibraltar, into a single navigation area. And they did so by their determined and adventurous sea exploits, which regarded raids, piracy and trade as different facets of the urge to acquire property and develop land-holdings at home and abroad. Some language points will bring out the way in which their ideas and methods pervaded European developments in shipping and sailing, and laid the basis for the whole future expansion. On their ships it was the custom for a small group of men to lay in a common stock of provisions. The custom, *motuneyti*, recognized in sea law, and the related term for mess-mates, *motunautar*, provided the word for seaman in several languages: *matroos* in Dutch, *matelot* in French. Indeed all French sea terminology is Norse, not only the words that define the constitutive elements of ship and sails, but also the words concerned with manoeuvring. Even the word for wave, *vague*, is Norse, And at Rouen was to be established the Royal Arsenal of the Marine called the Clos des Galées. Other debts to Norse sailors appear in our *keel*, German *Kiel*, French *quille*, all derived from *kjolr*; *heel*, in the nautical sense, with the verb *to heel*, comes from *háell*, the after-end of the keel.[35]

The *Saga of Olaf Tryggvasson*, under the year 1000, gives us a picture of his ships which were built in the later period:

The winter after King Olaf came from Halgoland, he had a great vessel built at Ladehammer [near Trondhjem], larger than any ship in the country, the beam-knees of which are still to be seen. The keel resting on the grass was seventy-four ells long. Thorberg Skafhogg was the name of the ship's masterbuilder; but there were many others as well, some to fell wood, some to shape it, some to make nails, some to carry timber; and all that was used was of the best. The ship was broad and long and highsided and strong-timbered. While they were planking the ship, Thorberg happened to have to go home to his farm on some urgent matter; and as he stayed there a long time, the ship was planked up on both sides at his return. In the evening the king went out, and Thorberg with him, to see how the ship looked, and everyone said they'd never seen so big and so beautiful a ship of war. Then the king went back to the town.

Early next morning the king comes again to the ship, and
Thorberg with him. The carpenters were there before them, but
all were standing idle with folded arms. The king asked, 'What's
the matter?' They said the ship was destroyed. Somebody had
gone from stem to stern and cut one deep notch after another
down one side of the planking. When the king came nearer, he
saw it was so, and he said with an oath, 'The man shall die who
thus destroyed the ship out of envy, if he can be found out,
and I'll bestow a great reward on whoever discovers him.'

'I can tell you that, king,' says Thorberg, 'who has done this
piece of work.'

'I don't think,' replies the king, 'anyone is so likely to find it
out as you are.'

Thorberg says, 'I'll tell you, king, who did it. I myself did it.'

The king says, 'You must restore it all to the same condition
as before, or your life shall pay for it.'

Then Thorberg went and chipped the planks till the deep
notches were all smoothed and evened with the rest, and the
king and all present declared the ship was much handsomer on
the side of the hull he had chipped, and bade him shape the other
side the same way, and gave him great thanks for the improvement. Afterwards Thorberg was the ship's master-builder till
she was quite finished. The ship was a dragon, built after the
one captured by the king in Halgoland, but far larger and more
carefully put together in all her parts. The king called it the
Long Serpent and the other the Short Serpent. The Long Serpent
had 34 benches for rowers. The head and the arched tail were
both gilt, and the bulwarks were as high as in a sea-going ship.[36]

The planks overlapped and were as wide as possible, to reduce the
number of seams; each part was made of a single piece of wood. They
were cut by wedge and adze, with which the carpenters could make
up to thirty-two planks from one oak trunk. The saw came into use
in the eleventh century. But the earlier planks were far stronger,
and sawn planks had to be made thicker. Thus a tendency to greater
weight and rigidity came about. The size of ships of the Gokstad
type was to some extent limited by the length of timber available
for the keel. Every ship had its captain, often the owner, though on
warships he was appointed by the king. At certain times the crew
gathered round him to get orders or information, or to discuss things.
A few words of command are known: more to starboard, more to
port, let the ship drift (that is, stop rowing), turn the ship, hold this
course. The crew took turns at all the jobs: working sail, tending
helm, rowing, baling, keeping watch. Much baling was needed; in

low-sided ships it was done with buckets, in high-sided ones by tubs raised on a spar. One man in the well saw to filling the tub, another on deck to the emptying. On land the water could be got out by removing a plug in the bottom. Watch had to be kept for hidden rocks or enemies; for the latter a man with a quick tongue was posted in the prow. Ohthere told Alfred that when he altered course he had to wait for the wind to change. The square sail was useful before the wind; otherwise oars had to be brought out. The ships could not tack or beat up into the wind.[37] (There may, however, have been attempts to tackle this problem. A Norse carving shows a number of ropes attached to the foot of a square-sail, which may thus have been compressed like a curtain drawn to one side. Such practices may have been leading on to the lateen sail.) Near the end of the epoch cooks were carried, but there was no fireplace on board; cooking was done ashore. Mostly the food was gruel; gruel vessels have been found in ships at Tune, Oseberg and Gokstad. Otherwise the men ate meal and butter, dried fish, at times bread. Water was drawn from big casks, but whey or beer might take its place. When a ship was short of food, the slaughter of strange cattle, *strandhogg*, was permitted. When Olaf Tryggvasson was in Ireland; 'as they needed to make a foray for provisions on the coast, some of his men landed and drove down a large herd of cattle to the beach. Now a peasant came up and begged Olaf to give him back the cows that belonged to him. Olaf told him to take his cows if he could distinguish them – but don't delay our march.' The man sent in his dog which quickly sorted out his cattle from the many hundred beasts. Olaf, impressed, offered to buy the dog, but the peasant said, 'I'd rather give him to you.' So Olaf at once 'presented him with a gold ring in return and promised him his friendship in future'.[38]

The men slept under deck. In harbour they also had a canvas cover spread over all or part of the ship and held up by a pole running the whole length of the ship, with the ends resting on two upright stanchions. Where pole and stanchions met, the pole supported two boards from the side, fitted together on it and crossing one another; the boards' lower ends were set in a socket on the gunwhale. On the Gokstad boat an oaken bed was found, constructed so that it could be taken apart; the length was seven feet five inches. This would have belonged to the skipper. The Old Norse *vængi* corresponds to modern Norwegian *veng*, sometimes used as a cabin at the back of the ship that can be set up or taken down; and the Lapps also have the word. There are less clear signs of a structure for the captain. Later warships had a *vida* behind the mast, used both as a bridge and castle (tower-of-vantage); *vida* must be a shortened form of *viduhus*, borrowed by the Irish as *idus*, castle. We hear of an *husasnotra* on merchant ships, a term that in modern Icelandic means an ornament-on-a-house-gable; and such a decoration suggests the existence of a *viduhus*.

In bad weather the mast was taken down or cut shorter, for fear that its movements would make the ship leak and force the timbers apart. On heavy merchant ships, boards were set up above the bulwarks, called *viggyrdill* or *vigi* – terms related to the Dutch *weger* and the French *vaigre*. On warships the terms denoted a strong breastwork, and the protective boards are called *hlyda* (O.E. *hliew*, protection). At times stays were also used, ropes thrown across the ship's middle, drawn under the keel, then tightened by means of spars of wood.

In coastal sailings the ship was steered by means of landmarks; there were also harbour beacons. The man of the crew who best knew the locality acted as pilot. For sailing in the open sea, the horizon was cut into eight equal portions. Four of the points between the divisions were the directions of north, south, east and west; the points midway between these were named from the relation to the mainland. Positions of sun and stars were observed; the steersman steered by the Pole Star. In the summer he had only the sun; and if that was obscured he had to trust his luck and often strayed. There is some evidence of bearing-dials and azimuth tables as well as of some notion of latitude, though none of longitude. The men probably used a method of reckoning by which they sailed to the latitude of the place they aimed at, then followed this parallel till they reached land. On familiar routes they sailed direct.[39] The rowing-spell, apparently about $7\frac{1}{2}$ miles, was the standard measure of distance; longer distances were measured in terms of a halfday's sail (twelve hours). Spring and autumn, when stars were visible, were best for long voyages; but storms, darkened skies and long nights prevented sailing in winter.

In autumn, as Gudleif was returning from the east, he met a contrary wind and lay for a long time at the island Oland. There came Thorgaut Skarde, who in autumn had heard of Gudleif's course, in a longship against him and gave him battle...

He sailed out to sea northwards in harvest, but encountered a tremendous storm, and they were in danger of being lost; but as they had a chosen crew and the king's luck with them, all went well...[40]

For wintering the ships were pulled up by ropes and rollers over a slipway and put under a shed, to be repaired and re-tarred. The laws dealt with the limited right of such laying-up of ships and with the obligatory help to be given by neighbouring farmers under certain conditions.[41]

The exultation of venturing into dark unknown seas, of sudden irruptions on strange lands, of sending people into helpless flight, of gathering all sorts of splendid plunder, of breaking through everyday bounds with a sense of stark power – all this is reflected in the saga names for the ships: Reindeer of the Sea-kings, Horse of the Gull's Track, White-winged Horse, Crane, Raven of the Wind. 'The blood ran down the Reindeer's flank of each Sea-king.' William of Malmesbury conjures up one of the ships in its full glory, in a note on Harthacnut:

> Looking wrathfully upon Godwin, he obliged him to clear himself by oath. But Godwin, to regain his favour entirely, added to his plighted oath a gift of the most rich and beautiful kind. It was a ship beaked with gold, having 80 soldiers aboard, each of them with two bracelets on either arm weighing 16 ounces of gold. On their heads were gilt helmets; on the left shoulder each man bore a Danish axe, with an iron spear in the right hand; and, to avoid enumerating everything, they were equipped with such arms that splendour vied with terror and hid the steel beneath the gold.[42]

There is one more aspect of Norse energy and discipline that we should glance at: their earthworks. In England such constructions are hard to find, though we know the Danes built fortifications in various places. When moving about, they preferred to camp on islands where they could beach their ships and were not open to attack.[43] But we learn that Harald Bluetooth built a sea castle on the isle of Wollin, which, in its inner port, could take three hundred longships; and Eirik, king of Upsal, built similar castles in Karelia, Estonia and Finland. In Normandy the Hague-Dicke was constructed, cutting off the north-west peninsula of the Cotentin. In Denmark the Danewirke cut off the peninsula in the south, running from the Schlei (Sli) on the east to the marshes of Treene in the valley of the Rehide in the west; where a marsh interrupted, a wooden bridge was built on the embankment.[44]

Also there are in Denmark the remains of four large earthworks, which reveal a remarkable organizing capacity. Together the four could take in some 6,000 warriors; they may have been built as winter barracks or as training camps for armies preparing to attack England. However, it may be relevant that the *Saga of the Jomsvikings* of the thirteenth century, which deals with a Norwegian war, tells of a community of warriors living under strict conditions in a fortress.[45] Archaeological material suggests the date 970–1120. The camps may have been in operation for housing mercenaries, at the time of Aethelred or of Cnut. The biggest camp, Aggersborg, is in the north of Jutland; Fyrkat lies a little further south; Bonne-bakken is on the island Fyn; Trelleborg on the island Sjaelland close to the Great Belt dividing it from Fyn. All the camps have circular ramparts, with four openings at regular intervals through which two roadways passed. The ramparts, probably about nine feet high, were made of timber filled in with earth or turves. In each quadrant a number of large houses were arranged in groups of four, all of the same design. The central area of each house was partitioned off from smaller rooms at the end. Building methods varied. Fyrkat houses were timber-framed with wattle and daub for the long curving sides and planks set horizontally at the gable-ends; Trelleborg houses had walls of vertical planks. Shingle roofs were held up by the walls, by an outer row of posts, and by large posts inside the buildings.

At Trelleborg a rectilinear extension of the outer ditch had a graveyard with 150 poorly furnished bodies; the sex of only forty could be made out – of these nine were women. Fyrkat graveyard had some richer furnishings and the camp was linked with the grave-yard by a wooden road. All the camps were laid out with great precision, using the Roman foot (11½ inches) as the unit of measure-ment. We get some idea of the organizing energy involved when we note that at Trelleborg alone some 10,000 oaks seem to have been used; each barrack could accommodate some seventy-five men sleeping in bunks along the sides of the hall. It is thus tempting to see each building as allotted to a ship's crew.[46]

It is hard to make out the origins of the camp-schemes. The quartering suggests Roman camps. We know the Vikings had many contacts with the Byzantine world, and Cnut visited Rome. But the form of the fortifications no doubt came from mounds, earth-works and stone circles of earlier times. A round camp (apparently of late Roman times or the early migration period) existed at Isman-torp, Öland; it was about 125 feet in diameter. There were nine gates in the heavy earthen walls that still stand to some thirteen feet. And there is a yet larger circular camp in the same area, at Gråborg. Both camps were used over a long period and were set in the barren limestone region of the island, far from sea or arable land. Gråborg, about 200 feet in diameter, was used on and off for over a thousand years, with its final re-fortification in the late Middle Ages. The camps were no doubt refuges for farmers during raids.[47]

But whatever traditions lay behind the four barrack-camps, the significance of the works is unchanged. We see what is for the period an unparalleled capacity for training and organization. In them, as in the sea-castles, we see evidence of the same sort of defensive and organizing energies as we see later in the Norman castles in England.

We have now looked at Norse society in its relative isolation, with its hard living conditions determined partly by climate and terrain; and we have seen how these conditions bred a particular quality of initiative and aggressiveness, which could at need be combined with strong self-discipline. Excluded from the Christian comity which had been growing up in western Europe, the Norse pagans, driven into expansion by mingled climatic and social forces, felt no compunction in raiding the other areas; but their raids were combined with trading activities which had no parallel anywhere else in Europe. They drove into Russia and into the Black Sea, made contact with Moslems and Byzantines, and bypassed the Moslem controls of the Mediterranean which had been in operation since Charlemagne's day. They sailed down the Atlantic coast into the western Mediterranean, and out across the ocean to Iceland, Greenland and Nova Scotia. They created deepsea shipping techniques for Europe; and though they caused considerable confusion, a much more farflung and closely cohesive system would emerge as a result of their impact and expansion.

CHAPTER III

NORMAN DUKES
AND ENGLISH KINGS

Legends painted Rollo's reign in Normandy as an age of pristine prosperity, in which a golden armlet, hung on a tree, was left untouched for years, and the old Norse customs of helping neighbours and respecting another man's crops or tools were brought to the new country. A farmer's wife at Lonpaon, it was said, hid the plough so as to claim compensation; Rollo found out the truth and hanged her for fraud, her husband for not controlling her better. North France indeed was quiet from 911 to 920; then conspirators, whom Rollo did not join, tried unsuccessfully to overthrow Charles the Simple. The Irish Viking Regnald from Waterford, who had made himself king of Northumbria but was defeated by Edward the Elder, came across the sea to join the Vikings on the Loire; he managed to dominate Brittany, Nantes and the Marshlands. When rebellion broke out again, Rollo backed Charles and drew Regnald in on the same side. But Charles was beaten at Soissons and Raoul of Burgundy gained the throne. He bought Rollo off with an offer of the Bessin and a large indemnity. However, Regnald was killed and Raoul did not pay up. Rollo went on fighting, took Amiens, ravaged the Artois, and invaded Flanders; then suffered a check at the fall of Eu. News came that Hungarians had crossed the Rhine and Raoul ratified the Normandy treaty. But about this time Rollo died or retired. At the request of his councillors – we see a suggestion of the procedure of the Thing – he nominated his son by Popa as successor. One story says he lived another five years; but in 927 it was William Longsword who did homage for Normandy. Rollo was buried in the sacristy of Notre Dame at Rouen, though Adhémar of Aquitaine later said that on his deathbed he ordered the sacrifice of several Christian slaves to Odin and Thor.

William Longsword was probably born at Rouen. Dudo stresses his French tastes, his friendship with the De Senlis, his preference for Christian and Gallicized Normans; but though Dudo (who had had much information from Richard I and his brother Raoul d'Ivri) was writing in good faith, we may doubt this picture. William had spent much time with his father, who certainly spoke Norse, was reared by a Norseman Botho (though this man was said to have been won over to French ways), and had later as his chief councillor Bernard the Dane. He took care to have his son taught to speak Norse. He carried on his father's policy of supporting Charles, till that king ended in a dungeon, starved to death, it is said. In 930, perhaps learning that a Saracenic threat had drawn away the forces of Burgundy and Paris to the south-east, the Loire Vikings began ravaging the countryside, but were defeated at Limoges. The Breton counts repudiated Norman supremacy; but with the aid of the Loire Vikings William overran the country. When he left, the Bretons rallied again and he had to devastate their region a second time. He annexed the Cotentin, the Channel Islands, and the Avranchin; and took a Breton concubine, Sprota. He settled down at Fécamp, where he and his successors restored and added to the Abbey.

Bayeux, whether or not set in an ancient Saxon area, seems to have been the centre of the Norse speakers, among whom malcontents found a leader in Riulf, a count set over the annexed Breton territories – though he was no Norman but uncle of Baldwin of Flanders and connected with the family of Charles the Simple. When he demanded some two-thirds of Normandy, the whole area west of the river Risle, William seems to have panicked, remained irresolute, and tried to buy off the rebels. However, when Riulf came up to Rouen, he led out the troops and won a victory. Riulf was captured and killed. Soon afterwards William heard that Sprota had borne him a son, Richard. He accepted Raoul of Burgundy as king of France and married Liutgarda, daughter of Herbert of Vermandois, a great French house; but he went on living with Sprota and recognized her child as his heir. He sent Richard to Bayeux under his own old tutor Botho to learn Norse. He may have wanted to placate the sections of his people who stuck to Norse traditions and resented French influences; or he may have thought it right for a Norman ruler at least to know and respect those traditions. In any event, Richard, the third ruler of Normandy, was bilingual like his father. Behind the circumspect narrative of Dudo we get the impression that William's rule was insecurely established and that it was still possible that the Norman state would be destroyed. We are told that in 933 he was so anxious that he meditated leaving Normandy and sent Sprota to Fécamp so that she could make an easy getaway to England.

Charles the Simple had married Eadgifu, daughter of Edward the Elder, who bore him a son, Louis. On his death, wife and son fled to Aethelstane in England. Dudo says that William took the lead in bringing about the restoration of the Carolingian line. But the Normans were unpopular at the English court as pirates and William is not likely to have cared much either way. Still he seems to have supported Louis, who in June 936 returned to France and was crowned at Laon. With English aid, Alan Barbe Torte, a fugitive Breton noble, landed in Brittany, drove out the pagan Danes and Normans, and established himself at Nantes. William did nothing and Alan became one of his supporters.

From 937 till his death in 943 William kept changing sides in the complex French situation. Out of hatred of his brother-in-law Arnulf of Flanders, he defied Louis, invaded Flanders and laid waste much land. He caused so much damage that he was excommunicated; but he still went on destroying. One of his aims was to get hold of Ponthieu, a small county between Flanders and Normandy. When conflict broke out between Louis and the new German ruler Otto, William once more supported Louis, who visited him at Rouen. Later, however, he made moves which can be interpreted as a turn to the Norse party in Normandy, but was coolly received. The Cotentin was said to have been depopulated by warfare and raids, and William seems to have asked for more immigrants from Denmark. Dudo and William of Jumièges tell a strange tale of King Harald Bluetooth coming with sixty ships to Cherbourg and occupying the country after being driven out by his rebel son. But the dates do not fit. Sweyn Forkbeard's revolt took place years later. Dudo was, we may assume, confusing some tale told him by Richard I who would have been a boy of eight at the time, being educated at Bayeux. Possibly Harald did pay a visit a few years later, or there may have been a leader named Harald among the immigrant Danes. In any event many pagan Danes did come in about this time.

William, alarmed by the whole situation, wanted to become a monk at Jumièges, but the abbot told him that his duty lay in the world – though he gave him a monk's habit, which William locked up in a box in his bedroom. On his return to Rouen he fell ill. He arranged a council of regency made up of seven lords, who took an oath of allegiance to Richard. A general assembly (suggesting a Thing) was called at Bayeux and its acceptance of the young ruler was secured. But not long after a group of conspirators, including Arnulf, Baldwin, and Thibault of Blois, managed to murder William at a meeting on an island in the Somme. Thibault later married his widow Liutgarda. Herbert of Vermandois died the same year and the powerful dominion he had built up promptly collapsed.

The earliest sample of Norman literature we possess is a *Complaint for William Longsword*, perhaps by a cleric of Jumièges, but clearly sung throughout the country, with a strong rhythm, returns of phrase, and refrain. It laments William's murder and states that his father (Rollo) remained a pagan, but that his mother was a Christian:

> *When his father died, then the unbelievers*
> *rose armed in revolt, rose to do him harm.*
> *Them he conquered, trusting in God's succour,*
> *them he defeated with his own right arm.*

But treachery did for him: 'Let all men weep for William, innocent yet done to death.' Something of the idea of a holy war of Christians against pagans is appearing. The second sample of early Norman literature, in rhythmic prose, tells of the return of St Ouen's relics to Rouen and shows the tendency to make Rollo respectable. To save his relics from theft, the saint appears to Richard 1.

Richard the Fearless had been accepted on 29 May 942; the recognition ceremony was carried out at Rouen. Throughout much of his reign the key figure was the loyal Bernard the Dane. King Louis granted investiture to Richard, who thus became his ward. But some Norman lords of the Évecin were indignant at homage being thus paid to the king and made contact with Hugh of Paris, who was an ambitious schemer and whose frontier adjoined theirs. Other sections had sworn fealty direct to Louis and favoured the close link with France, while yet others felt opposed to the whole direction that was being taken, and wanted to cling to Norse pagan ways. These latter, centred on Bayeux, broke into rebellion under one Thormod. The episode is obscure, since Dudo and William of Jumièges are reticent,

c

and we have to look to Flodoard and Richer (later chroniclers, both
of Rheims) for the facts. Somehow Thormod, reinforced by a Norse
fleet under Sihtric, got power over Richard, and proclaimed that he
had reverted to paganism. The rebels advanced southward with the
aim of occupying all Normandy. But against such an invasion both
Louis and Hugh of Paris combined. Hugh drove the rebels back, then
Louis routed them, killing Thormod, it is said, with his own hands.

In Rouen Louis reinstated Richard and condemned his father's
murder; but he was suspicious and did not mean to let Richard slip
out of his hands. After three days an insurrection broke out in the
town. Louis was unprepared and had to let Richard go free. Bernard
and the other leaders demanded that he should concede Normandy
to Richard, to be held by hereditary right, and should swear to defend
Normandy against its enemies. At a solemn ceremony Richard
renewed his homage and Louis took the required oath – as also,
reluctantly, did his vassals. But the pagan party was not yet crushed,
and the usual intrigues went on around Louis, Hugh of Paris, and
other great lords. Louis had promised to take vengeance on Arnulf of
Flanders, but instead he plotted with him to get rid of Richard, who
was at Laon.

One day when Richard and Osmund de Centeville came back from
a hawking expedition on which they had gone without leave, Louis
flew in a rage and imprisoned them. All Normandy soon knew, but
could do nothing. Osmund got in touch with Bernard de Senlis, who
lived not far off at Coucy, and gave out that Richard was dying.
While Louis was celebrating the news, he smuggled Richard out in a
truss of hay to Coucy. De Senlis decided to try to use Hugh of Paris
to oppose Louis; Hugh in turn felt that he could exploit the situation,
and offered troops to safeguard Richard's transfer from Coucy to
Senlis. (De Senlis was Hugh's vassal.) When Louis asked for Richard's
return, Hugh refused. Louis conferred with Arnulf, who advised him
to buy off Hugh, though the price would be high. Hugh agreed to
abandon Richard if he were given a lion's share in the partition of
Normandy.

Richard had two honest men on his side, Bernard de Senlis and
Bernard the Dane, the latter now an old man who had been a follower
of Rollo. To keep control of the situation, they agreed to pretend to
take different sides, the Dane turning to Louis, de Senlis to Hugh.
(Hugh had grown more ambitious than ever, as his third wife, sister
of the Emperor Otto, had borne him his first son.) Thibault of Blois,
a scoundrel who was now one of the great men of France, was
immobilized by a scheme that de Senlis put to him for the killing of
Louis; de Senlis knew it would start Thibault plotting how to betray
him (de Senlis). William of Jumièges, trying to explain Dudo's

account, says that Bernard the Dane sent to Harald king of the Danes, who was still at Cherbourg, asking him to raise a force from Bayeux and Coutances, and to launch a land-invasion of Normandy, while he himself attacked by sea. (Richer and Flodoard mention this Harald, Herald, Hagrald, but say he was the commander at Bayeux.) In any event civil war broke out in Brittany and Normandy was overrun by the Danes, who came in through Cherbourg. In this eventuality, Louis, Arnulf, and Hugh combined once more.

Bernard the Dane's aim all along was to split the enemy. So he did his best to hold the Danes back and offered submission to Louis, who then entered Rouen amid cheers. Louis now regretted his bargain with Hugh, and Bernard played on his regret, deploring the division of Normandy. He persuaded Louis to command Hugh to stop his operations around Bayeux. Hugh felt himself in danger, raised the siege of Bayeux, and returned to his own domains, where de Senlis urged him to take his revenge by supporting Richard. Louis appointed as his minister in Normandy Raoul Torta, a son of the French bishop of Paris, who had been an associate of Bernard the Dane under William. He imposed heavy levies, and William of Jumièges hated him for taking stones meant for his Abbey and using them to fortify Rouen. He may have made a secret agreement with Bernard, who wanted Rouen to be strong. The Normans were beginning to settle down afresh, but the French kept clamouring for the redistribution of Norman land and the dispossession of the Normans. De Senlis won Hugh over into making a sudden attack on Louis's dominions; he seized Compiègne and Montigny at Easter 945. Louis rushed off to defend the region and Danes swarmed into Normandy from Brittany. A fleet anchored in Barfleur. Louis hurried back. A conference was held on the Dive in July 945. What happened is unclear; but war broke out. Louis was routed and taken prisoner. His queen appealed to her brother Otto of Germany and to Edmund of England, without much effect, though Otto promised to intervene when he could. Louis gave way and accepted Richard as duke of Normandy and Richard made some slight acknowledgement of the king's precedence; a charter of 968 speaks of the *Princeps* of the Franks as the duke's *Senior*. Bernard kept Raoul in his office, but Raoul was so unpopular that he had to be dismissed after a while.

Richard heard of the beautiful wife of his forest-superintendent at Sècheville and decided to visit her; but she let her sister Gunnor take her place. Next day Richard found out the trick, but he liked Gunnor so well that he merely laughed. He made Gunnor his wife *more Dannico*, and she bore him several children, the eldest of whom succeeded him. The decisive change among the Normans seems to have begun now. The old allodial tenures became more like feudal tenures, and the freemen lost their independent status – though some allodial tenures remained. The changes were probably the work of Bernard the Dane, Osmund, and Ivo de Bellême, who seem to be the three foremost barons. Military service was organized more on the basis of feudal fealties and less by the old summons to all freemen. We hear no more of Bernard, though through his son Torf and grand-son Thorold he seems to have been the ancestor of many later noble families in Normandy and especially those of Harcourt and Beaumont.

Arnulf, Louis, and Otto now made an alliance against Richard and Hugh of Paris. They ravaged the two duchies, but Rouen held out and the allies began to quarrel among themselves. Finally in 950 peace was arranged, with Louis regaining Laon, but the duchies of Paris and Normandy were undefeated. For seven years Richard had peace. He was betrothed to Hugh's daughter Emma, but was in no haste to marry her. In 954 Louis died, succeeded by his son Lothaire; in 956 Hugh died, naming Richard as his son's guardian. Richard was now in a strong position. At last in 960 he married Emma, but she died in 962.

Lothaire got hold of Hugh's two sons and allotted them Paris and Poitou. Then a coalition against Richard seems to have been organized by Bruno, archbishop of Cologne and the duke of Lorraine, a brother of Otto; Richard was to have been murdered at Amiens in 960, but, according to Dudo, was warned. In 961 Lothaire called an assembly of his chief vassals at Soissons; the Normans tried to disperse the meeting by force, but failed. Next year Thibault seized Evreux. Driven out, he went to Lothaire, and war began between Lothaire and Richard. The latter succeeded in making his opponents give up their aggressive plans. Dudo tells us that he had called in Harald Bluetooth from Denmark, apparently while the issues were still doubtful. When the Danes came, says Dudo, they found Lothaire beaten. Harald at this time was master of the seas, overlord of Nor-way as well as king of Denmark, and it is possible that he went to Normandy to aid some further immigration and to equip his ships for a piratic expedition against the Moors of Spain.

Normandy seems generally uninvolved in the events of 978–87, when there was war between Lothaire and the Germans. (Otto had become emperor in 962.) Lothaire and then his son both died, and Hugh Capet became king of France. Richard seems to have played only a diplomatic role in the succession, as he had done in 965 when old Arnulf of Flanders died. In 996 he himself died after reigning more than fifty years.

Those years had been crucial in establishing the Normans as an integral part of the Frankish scene. Though their connections with

Norsemen persisted, it was no longer possible to call them an upstart pack of pirates who should be dispossessed. We cannot trace the details, but the Norman state now took definite form. We have two charters of Richard's reign, the first written documents of Norman history, but they tell us little except the names of Richard's chief advisers, the signatories. The number of baronies seems between 100 and 120, and there were a few counts. As yet there was no clearcut relation between land held and military services due. Normandy was much smaller than, say, the kingdom of Wessex, and the baronies were not large. Richard probably began the system of administration through viscounts, which was functioning in the next reign. The ecclesiastical system in early days had fallen into confusion, and the dukes held it firmly in their hands, with the viscounts controlling the bishoprics. Richard founded the abbeys of Mont St Michel and St Ouen, and did much for Fécamp. Mercantile activity was growing in the towns and at the fairs, and Richard seems to have been the first Norman duke to coin his own money. Tall, fair, handsome and energetic, in his later years he had a long beard and thick white hair; he was personally generous and easy-going. He it was who encouraged Dudo to write the history of the Normans.

Richard II (998–1026) soon had to face a challenge from the peasantry, who William of Jumièges says began to devise plans for their own self-government both on the coast and in the interior. Each local group elected two deputies for a central assembly which aimed at formulating general policy. Wace says that the peasants wanted to rise against their feudal oppressors and calculated that they outnumbered the latter by twenty to one. Raoul d'Ivri was put in charge of the forces for the destruction of the movement, and his well armed warriors soon crushed the peasants, who were cruelly punished. The deputies had their hands and feet cut off, and were then sent back to report to their electors. The monk William of Jumièges writes with delight at this treatment of a presumptuous peasantry.

The movement seems remarkably ahead of the times, suggesting as it does later communal movements or a peasant revolt like that in England in 1381. We know little of the composition of the small free farmers in Normandy at this time. It has been suggested that Norsemen filled the towns, while survivors of the earlier peasantry mostly carried on on the land. But we can understand such a movement for self-government in early eleventh-century Normandy only if we see the leaders as Norsemen remembering the Things and the odal systems of their homeland. Under Richard II the issue of paganism against Christianity seems to have faded out; but there was the one last effort to maintain and extend the system of government among the smaller free farmers which had nourished the spirit of independence, and which in more favourable conditions, in Iceland, produced a society without centralization or oppressive state-forms. The settlement of Norse farmers must have been helped by the depopulations caused by the early raids; but at the same time it is certain that considerable numbers of pre-Norman peasants carried on. One main argument for their persistence lies in the place-names; and on many large estates in the region continuity of tenure certainly went on without any large-scale break throughout the tenth century. But we can still argue that there were enough free Norsemen on the land to dominate the situation and to be the force behind the scheme for some sort of self-government. When Adhémar of Chabannes later wrote, 'They received the Christian faith, forsook the language of their fathers, and accustomed themselves to Latin speech', he was telescoping a process that took two or three generations; and the fact that by 1025 Norse speech was more or less obsolete in the Bayeux area does not disprove this comment.

The thwarted movement further suggests that a fairly high level of prosperity had been reached by the Norman peasants, whom we may take to be now a mixture of Norsemen and earlier stocks. One result of this whole development was to undermine systems of servile status. Soon the Normans were far more free from such systems than any other area in France.

The next trouble came from the nobles, led by the turbulent William count of Hiesme, a son of Richard I. Raoul d'Ivri crushed the revolt, and hunted down and hanged the rebels. William was imprisoned but escaped by making love to his jailer's daughter, who gave him a long rope; harried, he at last came on the duke hunting in the forest of Vernon, begged forgiveness, and was appointed count of Eu, with rights to hold his own courts.

Richard married Judith, sister of the count of Rennes. That count was recognized as duke of Brittany, and he married Richard's sister Hadwisa. Richard in his foreign policy carried on that of his father: good relations with Scandinavia and an alliance with Paris. But as usual troubles occurred. Flanders caused less anxiety; but there were threats from Chartres and Blois, and Anjou on the south, which was being built up by Black Fulk, needed more and more to be watched. Richard sent troops to help King Robert of France against the Burgundians in 1007; but tensions grew up between Normandy and France through Richard's friendship with Count Odo of Champagne and Chartres, who married his sister Maud with a dowry of half the county of Dreux – disputed land between Normandy and Chartres. Then when Maud died childless in 1015 and Odo refused to return her dowry, Richard attacked and defeated him and his allies of Maine and Meulan. However, Odo recovered, and Richard asked for Norse help. William of Jumièges tells of King Olaf of Norway and King Lacman of Sweden arriving with fleets in the Seine, come from piratic raids on Brittany. (In fact there was no Lacman; William probably confused the term *lagman*, lawman. But Olaf did visit Normandy.)

Saint Olaf's Saga gives us a valuable glimpse of the way in which Norsemen kept up their piratic voyages down the Atlantic coast, treating the Norse settlements as friends or enemies according to the needs of the moment. Normandy however seems to have been recognized as the place for wintering in or for disposing of plunder. In 1013 'Olaf sailed southwards out to sea' from England, 'and had a battle at Ringsfjord and took a castle on a hill to which Vikings resorted, and burned the castle', which Sigvat the Scald called 'a robber-nest hung in the air'. Then Olaf went westwards to Grislopol and fought there with Vikings at Williamspol. (These places must have all been in Valland, the western coast of France between the Seine and the Garonne; the hill-castle may be Mont St Michel; and Williamsby refers to the seat of William V, duke of Aquitaine (990–1030), who is said to have fought Vikings on the shores of Poitou. The names show that the various Norse settlements once had their own Norse names, which were later lost; we see also that Snorre is using scaldic poems for his account.) Olaf felt little sense of community with settled Norsemen if they offered a good chance of loot. He next sailed west to Fetlafjord and then south to Seliopol, fighting at both places. He was now somewhere in south-west France or north Spain. He took a castle Gunvaldsburg, very large and old, and made prisoner Geirfinn, the earl there. After a conference with the men of the castle, he laid a *scatt* on town and earl, a ransom of 12,000 gold shillings, which was paid. 'After that king Olaf steered with his fleet westward to Karlsa,' perhaps the Guadalquivir. 'He halted there and had a fight. And while he was lying in Karlsa river, waiting for a wind and meaning to sail up to Nörvasund,' the Straits of Gibraltar, and then on to the Land of Jerusalem, he had a dream: 'there came to him a great and important man, but of a terrible appearance, and spoke to him and told him to abandon his plan of going on to that land. "Go back to your odal, for you'll be king over Norway for ever." ' He interpreted this dream to mean that he'd be king over the country and his posterity after him, for a long time. After this apparition he turned about and came to Peitoland [Poitou]. Here he plundered and burned a merchant town Varrange, perhaps Guerande in south Brittany, north of the Loire mouth and not in Poitou; Snorre or the scalds may have confused the geography. The scald Ottar goes on, 'Poitou he plunders, Tuskland he burns. He fights and wins each way he turns.' Tuskland is the land of Tours on the Loire. Sigvat sings, 'The Norseman's king is up the Loire.'[1]

Icelandic written history had begun with the account by Are Totgilsson (soon after 1120); Eirik Oddson (1150–60) worked on contemporary events, questioning men with firsthand knowledge. An abbot of Tingöre, Karl Jonson, wrote on Norwegian history in the late twelfth century, and others carried on the work with varying reliability. Snorre Sturlesson wrote his *Sagas of the Kings* in the first half of the thirteenth century. For our purposes the attitudes and ideas preserved in Norse tradition are what mainly matter. After the tale of Olaf's voyages Snorre gives an account of the Norman dukes which ends:

From Ganger Rolf are descended the Earls of Rouen, who have long reckoned themselves of kin to the chiefs in Norway and held them in such respect that they always were the greatest friends of the Northmen; and every Northman found a friendly country in Normandy, if he required it. To Normandy King Olaf came in autumn, and he stayed all winter in the river Seine in good peace and quiet.[2]

An odd event that occurred during Olaf's visit was his conversion to Christianity. Clearly the religious impulsion was minimal; he must have been deeply impressed by the way in which his fellow Norsemen had advanced in Normandy, and have identified this advance with the Christianized feudalism that he found as their political system. He was baptised by Robert, the worldly archbishop of Rouen, who was Richard's brother. When he became king of Norway, he imposed Christianity with fire and sword and became the patron saint of the Scandinavian world. We see incidentally that men like Olaf had their scalds with them on their voyages; and such episodes as the sojourn of Olaf's fleet must have done much to revive traditional elements of culture among the Normans.

King Robert of France was sufficiently alarmed by events in Normandy to call a great council of his tenants-in-chief: a rare event in France with its unruly barons. Both Richard II and Odo appeared, and Robert settled their disputes. Chartres was to keep Dreux, Normandy was to keep Tillières, a strong fortress which Richard had built in Dreux. The last episode of the latter's reign was a campaign in support of Reginald of Burgundy.

We may now turn to England and the effects there of Norse invasions. After Alfred the kings of Wessex had steadily extended their power until Edward the Confessor became king of all England. Thus the resistance of Wessex to the Danes had ended in a rough unification of England under Alfred's line. Henceforth the old division into kingdoms gave way to one into large earldoms. Edward's son Athelstane was soon acknowledged by the princes of Strathclyde and Wales, and by the last semi-independent chief, Ealdred of Bamborough in Northumbria. There were the inevitable disorders and resistances; but Athelstane by his victory at Brunanburh in 937 consolidated his position. The bards sang of him in the same tones as those used of Beowulf and Hrothgar:

> In this year King Athelstane, Lord of Warriors, Ring-giver of Men, with his brother the prince Edmund, won deathless glory with the edge of swords in warfare round Brunanburh. With their hammered blades, the Sons of Edward clove the shieldwall and hacked the linden bucklers as was instinctive in them, from their ancestry, to defend their land, their treasure, and their homes, in frequent battle against the enemy.

Athelstane's son Edmund reigned five years. He and his brother had to fight hard against Eric Bloodaxe of Norway who had re-established Norse rule at York. Eadred, the next king, was weak; but after a year the Mercians and Northumbrians elected his brother Eadgar in his place. When Eadred died in 959, Eadgar ruled the south as well as the north, and was left in peace till his death in 975. His son Edward was only thirteen at his succession, and a conflict of magnates broke out. Edward was murdered in 978 when he visited his step-mother Aethelfrith at Corfe. No protests were made by the church dignitaries, who included Dunstan. Aethelfrith ruled in the name of her young son Aethelred II. The inadequately centralized kingdom had a strong tendency to break up into the main lay and ecclesiastical domains. Aethelred II Unraed failed to dominate the situation, and jeers at his incompetence even get into the *Chronicle*: 'When the enemy is in the west, our troops are kept in the east, and when he is in the south, they go to the north.'

William of Malmesbury mentions, without explanation, that Richard II of Normandy quarrelled with Aethelred in 991, apparently about the Norse raids, which had been resumed since 980 and had become serious by 988. Among the Norse leaders were Sweyn Forkbeard (son of Harald Bluetooth) and Olaf Tryggvasson. They were taking loot to Normandy, where they sold it in the markets. Pope John XV sent the Bishop of Trier to make peace between the rulers. But nine years later worse troubles broke out. Only William of Jumièges tells the story. He says that an English fleet attacked the Cotentin and landed an army, which Nigel de Coutances defeated. This year, the *Chronicle* states, the main Danish fleet had left England for Normandy; Aethelred took advantage of its absence to go north and ravage Cumberland. Possibly he left on guard over the south coast a Viking pirate, Palling, who was married to Sweyn's sister. In 1001 Palling deserted and joined the Vikings; and the raid on the Cotentin may have been his work. In any event the English had reason enough to resent the way in which Normandy sheltered and abetted the Norsemen.

In 1002 Aethelred's wife died and he at once married Emma, sister of Richard II. Perhaps he hoped by the union to get better treatment from the Normans. Later, in 1017, Emma, an ambitious woman, married Cnut. She was thus linked with the English, Danish, and Norman ruling families, and through her the Normans gained a dynastic claim to England. Her son Edward could set out a descent from both Cerdic, the remote ancestor of the Wessex royal family, and Rollo-Rolf the founder of Normandy.

Soon after his remarriage Aethelred ordered a massacre of all Danes in his realm. There was certainly killing on a large scale, and among the victims was Gunhild, Palling's wife and sister of Sweyn. The latter arrived from Denmark in 1003, captured Exeter (part of Emma's dowry), and then swept westwards, ravaging the land as he went. Emma fled to Normandy. But her brother had no wish to annoy Sweyn; he was growing ever more worried at the rise of Anjou. Emma went back to England. Perhaps about this time Sweyn made a treaty of perpetual alliance with Richard, under which the Danes were allowed to take English spoils to Norman ports, and sick or wounded Danes had the right of refuge there.

Danish attacks on England were renewed in 1004 and 1006. In 1007 Aethelred bought Sweyn off with a large sum; he tried to levy ship-money and raise a fleet, making a vain appeal to Richard. For three years the struggle went on, with Sweyn winning. In 1013 Emma again fled to Normandy, taking her two young sons. Next year Aethelred joined her, via the Isle of Wight, and was welcomed by Richard. Sweyn, acknowledged King of England at Bath, had died suddenly in 1013, succeeded by his son Cnut. Aethelred returned to fight, and for a while, with his son Edmund Ironside, had some success; he died in 1016 and Edmund did not long survive him. Emma submitted to Cnut and married him, no doubt to Richard's satisfaction.

As we have seen, we know little of the details of Norse settlement in Normandy, apart from the evidence for strong persistence of odal tenure and peasant independence and of pagan creeds, up till the early days of Richard II. We know relatively much more about the Danish settlements in England; and though the developments there were clearly very different from those in Normandy, they give us many pointers as to the way in which the Norse spirit and way of life asserted itself in colonizing groups in a strange land.

In the Danelaw we find an element of individual initiative and self-assertion that seems to have been largely lost in the Anglo-Saxon regions. The village, not the manor, provided the main basis on which men got together and organized their economic activities. Manorial ties were loose and many people were free, or almost free, from the burdens and restrictions of dependent tenure. The ways of culti-vating and holding the land were less rigid than in the areas of the open field system. There was less economic equality among the peas-ants; their holdings were less uniform, less symmetrically arranged. There were more smallholders, petty cottagers, and almost-landless men than elsewhere, though well-off peasants were not lacking.[3] We noted above how Rollo's men were said to have insisted on their equal social status. Benedict of St More in his *Chronicle of the Norman Dukes* elaborates their reply: 'Over us no prince or baron's known. We're all one of lordship alone. An equal and like life we share. Lord of himself is each man there; and each is faithful to the other.'[4] The men of the Danelaw, we feel, would have applauded these sentiments, despite their individual need to excel and make the most of things, despite their inability to make settled life a simple continuance of the rough brotherhood of the war expeditions.

In England as in Normandy there were no mass invasions. The Danes were usually in a minority in the areas where they settled, basing their power on towns like York, Lincoln, Nottingham, Derby and Cambridge, and at times taking over the lordship of villages inhabited by Englishmen (much the same must have happened in Normandy.) The Danelaw groups were mostly those who had come between 876 and 880, and in 896. However outnumbered by the English around them, they were dominant. At York they issued a coinage of their own, and, soon converted to Christianity, they set local craftsmen to carve stone crosses and gravestones in the styles they favoured. Norsemen cannot simply be identified with the soke-men of the Danelaw. Sokemen were few in Yorkshire, though making up half the population of Domesday Lincolnshire. If the latter group were all descendants of Danes, immigration must have been on a much larger scale than seems probable. So it has been suggested that the sokes of the Danelaw, as known in the eleventh century and later, were created by the government in an attempt to set up a system of jurisdiction and personal obligation to replace the tradi-tional bonds broken by the invasion. That may well be partly correct. But though we cannot identify Danish settler and sokeman, the total effect of the new settlements, together with the shake-up that earlier systems in the area suffered, was to give certain new characteristics to the sokemen, to the Danish regions in general, affecting both Anglo-Saxons and newcomers. The names of some towns were changed. Streoneshalh became Whitby, Northworthing became Derby. Other places kept the old names, but graves or memorials attest the Danish presence.

The Danes in some respects clung to their own terms and forms. We find the term *wapentake* for local units in the counties of Lincoln, Nottingham, Derby, Leicester, and in North and West Riding. It comes from Old Norse *vapnatae*: the flourish-of-arms at an assembly – a gesture made by free men. In the mid-tenth century it occurs in the Old English form *waepentac*, signifying an administrative unit with a court. An early law code of Aethelred, apparently laying down procedure for an area under Danish law, has a clause: 'And a court shall be held in every wapentake and the twelve leading thegns along with the reeve shall go out and swear on the relics given into their hands that they will not accuse any innocent man or shield any guilty one.'[5] Not that there seems any essential difference between wapentake and hundred.

The heart of the Norse area lay between the Welland and the Tees; but as far south as Peterborough Abbey, in a tenth century memorandum, the Norse term *festermen* is used for sureties to land transfers.[6] Many Norse turns of phrase and loan words, sometimes anglicized, appear in Aethelred's code for the Five Boroughs; and there are Norse ideas, such as that a man of bad fame must buy land to get a standing in the court. This principle is applied to suspects arrested by the twelve chief thegns of a wapentake and to money-makers believed to have struck bad coins.[7]

In Suffolk, Norfolk and Lincolnshire, the Danelaw took in the three richest and most populous counties; and many Danish settlers there were active in bringing new land under cultivation, the flat lands along the Norfolk broads, the Lincolnshire marshes, the forest of north-west Nottinghamshire. New settlements of the tenth and eleventh centuries are marked by names with the element *thorpe*. The speed and ease of assimilation were increased by the fact that Danes could understand English speech, and Englishmen could understand Danish; but the Norsemen kept to their own tongue long enough for many of their words to pass over into English, some in local usage, others in general currency, e.g. *toft*, used throughout the medieval period for building site, messuage, curtilage. A typical estate in the Five Boroughs in 1066 was a lord's house or *manerium*, with a home farm and unfree peasants, *villani* and *bordarii* living in the same village and doubtless helping in the cultivation of the lord's land. But there were also the *sochemanni*, sokemen. Though paying homage to a lord and rendering such payments and services as followed from that act, these were their own masters. They had a recognized place in the courts of the wapentake and shire; they could give away, sell, or exchange their land or any part of it; they paid their taxes (danegeld or sheriff's aid) directly to the royal officers or the sheriff, and were generally free from the villein's duty of working two or more days a week on the lord's land. (The *Liber Niger* of Peterborough, 1125, records twenty-nine sokemen at Scotter, Lincolnshire, owning a day's work each week, two days throughout August.) Sokemen were thus mostly free from the compulsions of manorial discipline, though they may have been expected to lend a hand at seasons like haytime or harvest.[8]

Thus at least some strong elements of the independent spirit of the sagas persisted in the Danelaw, preserved by individual ownership of land at peasant level. (We have noted that it is impossible to estimate just how much of this spirit was directly Danish, how much the result of Englishmen being relatively freed from lordships during the upheavals. No doubt both aspects were present and to some extent fused.) It is not by chance that our very word *law* comes from Old Norse, through O.E. *lagu*, the thing laid down. But we must not overstress the degree of freedom among peasants in the Danelaw; once the men were settled they could not but be subject to feudalizing pressures. Yet it would be equally wrong to underestimate the difference between the Danish areas and the old Anglo-Saxon ones. Thus, in England there are some ninety-five sites called Charlton (Carlton, Charleton, Chalton, Charlston, Chorlton), which represent places settled by groups of *ceorls* (Danish, *karls*). In the Charltons of the eastern shires we meet freemen (*liberi homines*) with a larger group of sokemen; on many estates the two classes coexist with the normal manorial population of villeins, cottagers and slaves, but generally they are set apart. The *liberi homines* are now not taken to be descended from the rank and file of the Danish armies that occupied East Anglia in the ninth century; but it is not easy to make out what distinguishes them from sokemen. Both groups were subject in some degree to signorial control, appearing in the lord's court, making him payments in money or kind, and working perhaps one day in seven on the demesne. But however we analyse the situation, it seems likely that these Charltons resulted mainly from the shocks inflicted on the older social structure by the Danes. Especially where a lord held villages at a fair distance from his centre, many peasants could be expected to take advantage of the upheavals to free themselves, by payments or simply by assuming a higher status. The extent to which they could grow independent would vary with time, place, circumstances. If this interpretation is correct, the Danish irruptions and settlements started off something like the decay that appears in villeinage in the fourteenth and fifteenth centuries. The process was not a simple one but it bore the seeds of a future society rather than an archaic return to tribal freedoms. We can understand why the Normans found the situation so hard to reduce to uniform terms and relations; we even find them calling villeins on their royal demesnes villein-sokemen.[9]

An example of the permeation of Danish attitudes appeared in 1049 when Sweyn murdered his cousin, the Danish earl Beorn. King Edward and his army (called *here* by the *Chronicle*) pronounced a Viking sentence of dishonour, calling him *nithing*.[10] An important instance of cultural penetration is again found on northern stone crosses. The theme of Sigurd the Volsung, dragon-slayer, appears at Halton, Lancashire, and three times in the Isle of Man. Perhaps the families who set up such crosses claimed descent from the royal Volsung line. A stone found at Winchester shows a wolf attacking a bound warrior who bites its tongue; the warrior here seems to be Sigurd's father, Sigmund. This stone was found in part of the Anglo-Saxon cathedral for which Cnut was responsible. A fourth Mancross, at Ramsey, shows Loki killing the otter with a stone: a tale linked by Snorre in the *Prose Edda* with that of Sigurd and the dragon. The moment of the Sigurd story which the artists depicted was that in which the hero roasts the dragon-heart, is inspired when the blood touches his tongue, and hears what the birds are saying. It is a moment of initiation, of deep change, of shamanist possession. Another group of stones deals with Ragnorök, the last battle between gods and monsters. Here the Christianization of the pagan theme is easier; Ragnorök becomes the end of the world and last judgement.[11]

We may then say that there were many similarities between Danelaw and Normandy, but also decisive differences. Above all the fact that the Normans had to adopt a new language and stop being a piratic enclave if they were to develop an effective state brought about a different orientation. Though a centralized state had developed far more in England than in Scandinavia, the Norsemen did not feel in a strange world when they settled beside Anglo-Saxons. To survive as part of a social and political system such as existed in France, the Normans had to accept the feudalizing pressure inherent in the system. With their vigour and thoroughness they developed what they took over, with more rigour and consistency than found in any Frankish region. Hence the way in which a split developed between pagan and Christian groups, between those who accepted feudalism and those who resisted it; a revolt of the free peasantry, we saw, was precipitated under Richard II. England lacked the pressures making for such sharp divisions. The danger was simply that the men of the Danelaw would support or join any invading

Danes. For there were groups of settlers who remained restless and liable to turn back to their old marauding habits. But probably such groups were those who now and then went off to settle in Normandy. We get a glimpse of such groups when we are told by the *Chronicle* how Edward the Elder lent his aid when Turketyl, earl of Bedford, 'fared overseas with such men as would follow him'.

Now back to Normandy. Under Richard I a baron's vassal held a *precarium;* he was a tenant-at-will and could lose his land if the lord so wished. Perhaps later in the same reign, certainly under Richard II, the *precarium* became a *beneficium* and the tenant had rights of a less precarious kind. The hereditary principle gained ground, and the *beneficium* gradually merged into the *feudum*, descending from father to son, while the lord gained the rights of wardship. Women could inherit land; but the lord held the right to choose a husband for a vassal's heiress; he claimed wardship over a minor heir and took a succession duty on his inheritance. Viscounts increased the scope of their powers. They commanded troops, collected revenue, administered justice, kept castles in order, but all in the duke's name. They were given no chance to become great men in their own right any more than the barons. Private war could not be outlawed, but was strictly limited. It needed a ducal licence; the duke set its rules and claimed the right to supervise campaigns. Devastation of opponents' property in land disputes was forbidden, as were assaults and ambushes in ducal forests. Arms, horses or property of a man captured in a bloodfeud might not be retained. A licence was needed for the building of a castle. We do not know the exact date at which many of these regulations came in, but they formed the system that was steadily extended from Richard II to William II.

The charters show the offices of chamberlain, constable, chancellor, *hostianus*; and probably the *dapifer* or seneschal already existed. We may assume that in early days the powers of the offices were very much limited and that they slowly grew. Richard II gave £100 from his *camera* to redeem lands of St Benigni; and he granted the tithes of the *camera* to Fécamp. But the financial system was doubtless still very primitive, and we may ignore Wace's tale that he shut himself up in the Rouen tower and went through the accounts with viscounts and provosts. We know little of the system of justice except that the duke kept a tight control of seigneurial jurisdictions. Criminal justice was early developed, though we do not hear of any method of compurgation such as was used by both Franks and Norsemen. Pirates did much to help the growth of trade, but regular systems for the exchange and sale of goods were developing, for example between Rouen and London. The fair at Caen was of some importance. Richard patronized the monasteries and so gained his name of the Good. He held his Easter assembly at Fécamp, where in a charter of 1006 he granted the abbey freedom of election according to the custom of Cluny.

Richard III, the first legitimate son of a duke to take his father's office, was invested at Rouen and went on to Paris to be instituted. There he was betrothed to the king's infant daughter. But his brother Robert, count of Hiesmes, resented not being granted the town of Falaise, and his resentment was fed by a Breton, Ermenold, suspected of black magic, who was killed, however, in a duel. A group of young malcontents gathered round Robert, and he seized Falaise. Richard then beseiged the town. Robert gave in, but still didn't get Falaise. The two brothers went to Rouen where Richard, taken ill during a feast, died. It was generally assumed that he had been poisoned; but medieval deaths in those circumstances always bred such tales.

Robert became duke in 1027, and was called both the Magnificent and the Devil. He began with some violent quarrels with leading churchmen. His uncle Robert, archbishop of Rouen, was also count of Evreux; and it was as count, not archbishop, says Ordericus, that he took a wife. Robert besieged him in Evreux. The archbishop-count fled to Paris, where he launched the church's anathema at his nephew and at Normandy. But he was reconciled with the duke, apparently through the French king, and later the two Roberts appear as good friends. Next, Hugh d'Ivri, bishop of Bayeux, went to France and sent home a garrison of knights for his castle. Robert blockaded the place and Hugh couldn't get in to join his knights.

William of Jumièges put these troubles down to evil councillors, but it seems more likely that the duke was resisting attempts by leading churchmen to achieve baronial status.

Falaise was set on a rocky height on the right bank of the Ante, a tributary of the Dive. The castle stood on a promontory jutting into the valley opposite the Mont Mirat. Robert is said to have seen a girl, Arletta or Herleva, paddling in the Ante or dancing in the roadway. He made her his mistress. Her father, Fulbert or Hulbert, was a tanner, a Walloon by origin, born at Chaumont near Lièges; his wife was Doda. He is said to have been unpopular because of the stink his trade made and because he added brewing to tanning. (The combination was forbidden in England.) Falaise was indeed the centre of the Norman leather trade. Herleva bore William, it is said, in the castle-keep. In a dream prophetic of the baby's greatness she beheld her own intestines stretched out all over Normandy and England. William of Malmesbury records the legend:

At the very moment also when the infant burst into life and

touched the ground, he filled both hands with the rushes strewn on the floor, firmly grasping what he had taken up. This prodigy was joyfully witnessed by the women gossiping on the occasion; and the midwife hailed the propitious omen, declaring that the boy would be a king.

Another prophecy made after the event may be read in the story that William Talvas of the ferociously cruel house of de Bellême chanced to call in and was shown the baby, whom he cursed: 'Shame! through you and your line mine will be greatly brought down.'

Though the Normans were used to alliances *more Dannico*, they seem to have been angered at the duke's union with Herleva, perhaps because of the connection with a tannery. William Talvas revolted. The de Bellêmes had wider territories and jurisdictions than any other Norman noble family. Robert promptly beseiged Alençon; and when Talvas surrendered, he forced him to come barefooted, with a saddle on his back, to make his submission, then gave him back his lands. There were four sons. The eldest, who had murdered a cousin come on a friendly visit, had been strangled, the tale ran, by the devil. Now the three surviving sons plotted and rose in revolt. They were defeated by local troops in the forest of Blason. One was killed, one badly wounded, and the third escaped to bring the news to their father, who died of sheer fury.

The putting-down of the ambitious clerics and of the de Bellêmes brought Robert some tranquil years during which he showed his capacities as a king-maker. Baldwin of Flanders had been driven out by his son; Robert restored him in a campaign remembered for its harshness. Then King Henry of France was driven out by his mother, who favoured a younger son; Robert invaded France and restored him to his throne. In Brittany the ruler Alan was a child. His father Geoffrey, married to a sister of Richard II, had been killed on a journey to Rome by an innkeeper's wife who, infuriated by one of his hawks attacking her chickens, threw a big pot at his head. In 1010 came a revolt of the Breton peasants, on the same lines, it is said, as that of the Norman peasants under Richard II. Alan, helped by his mother, put it down without Norman intervention. Then, after he had had the daughter of Odo of Chartres abducted for him by the count of Rennes, he began to feel too important to pay *homage en parage* to Robert of Normandy. (The latter paid the same homage to the French king.) To hold Brittany as a vassal region was a key part of Norman policy, and Robert at once invaded and defeated Alan, who gave in.

Now Robert had the two athelings, Edward and Alfred, sons of Emma and Aethelred, as fugitives from Cnut in his court. Emma

seems to have disliked them, or at least to have decided to put all
her hopes on her union with Cnut, discarding anything that interfered. Robert tried to get Cnut to agree to a partition on the lines of
the earlier agreement between Cnut and Edmund Ironside, but he
had no success. The story that he married Cnut's sister, Estritha, we
may ignore. But he was growing restless and eccentric. Perhaps the
old Viking wanderlust was asserting itself, forced to take odd forms.
He called a meeting of his vassals, made them do homage to his son
William, and announced that he was going to Jerusalem as a poor
pilgrim and a repentant sinner. To show how serious he was, he took
young William to Paris, surrendered the duchy in his favour, and
saw the boy do *homage en parage* to King Henry. Clearly he wanted
very much to ensure his acceptance, but he took no steps to marry
Herleva. Alan of Brittany was appointed regent.

Reaching Rome, he acted the fool, put a cloak on the statue of
Marcus Aurelius, and shod his mules with silver shoes that easily
fell off their one nail. At Byzantion he swaggered into the presence
of the Emperor Michael IV, bundled up his cloak, and sat on it.
Michael seems to have ignored his behaviour. On going, Robert was
offered his cloak by an attendant who picked it up, and rudely
replied, 'It's not the way in our land to carry our seats with us.'
Crossing Asia Minor, he had to be borne in a litter by Negro slaves;
and meeting a Norman pilgrim on the way home, he said, 'Tell them
you saw me being carried to paradise by devils.' In Jerusalem he
behaved with wild lavishness and died on his return journey at
Nicaea.

Why he didn't marry Herleva is unclear. He is said to have disposed
of her about 1034 by marrying her off to his vassal and servant
Herluin, vicomte of Conteville, to whom she bore Odo and Robert
(later of Mortain). By the twelfth century three types of union were
recognized among Norsemen: Christian marriage carrying full rights
of compensation and property for the wife; alliance with a free-
woman, *frilla*, also involving rights, though with some legal disabilities; and cohabitation with a concubine. The story of the Norman
dukes suggests that there was the same sort of system in Normandy.
Robert however may have married Herleva off over quickly to Herluin and later realized that he needed William as heir. William had
been born in 1027-8; and as Odo became bishop of Bayeux in 1049-
50, he was probably born in the early 1030s. Once Herleva was
married to Herluin, Robert could not undo the marriage and marry
her himself. In any event the ducal court did not rate Christian
marriage highly. What brought William such trouble was possibly
not so much his bastardy as his extreme youth on his succession. The
baronial unrest seized on the fact that he was *nothus*, *bastardus*, as

a stick to use against him. (Isidore's *Etymology* defines *nothus* as someone born of unlike or imperfectly matched stock.) *Herleva*, we may note, was a distinguished German dithematic name; Robert's archbishop uncle was also married to an Herleva. The looseness with which the Danes in general regarded the wedding tie is illustrated by a Durham tract dealing with the fate of six vills which bishop Aldhem (990–1018) gave from the episcopal estate with his daughter Egfrith when he married her to the son of a Northumbrian earl. A genealogy of six generations is set out. Egfrith had two husbands and was repudiated by both; her first husband made two later marriages; her daughter by the second marriage, Sigred, had three husbands in succession.[12]

Why Robert was later given the nickname of Devil we do not know. The name is linked with a tale-type about a great sinner who finally repents. In one episode the devil in the duke's likeness ravishes the wife in a wood, and she bears Robert the Devil.

Now let us turn again to England. When Sweyn Forkbeard died in 1014 at Gainsborough, the crews of Danish ships in the Trent gave their allegiance to Cnut, the younger of his two sons, who had been left in command as Sweyn went south. After yet another invasion, during which he harried the Danelaw, he became king at Edmund's death in November 1016. He rapidly built up a large empire, so that his full title was King of Englishmen, Danes, Norwegians, and part of the Swedes; but there is no sign that he attempted to work out any unifying system or to treat his dominions as a single organized state. He did not expect, it seems, that his empire would outlast him.

We saw how Emma hastened to marry him; and he for his part no doubt welcomed the union as strengthening his position. He kept his other wife Aelgifu, an English lady from Northampton, mother of Harold I, in a position of authority in the Danelaw.[13] Possibly in ancient Scandinavia and among pre-migration Germanic tribes the man who married a king's widow succeeded to his throne; the northern ruler had once been the husband of the goddess Freyja and the divine element was inherited through the woman.[14] That this sort of idea survived in weakened form is shown by texts suggesting that Cnut's marriage was in harmony with old Anglo-Saxon custom. Eadbald, son of the first Christian king in England, Aethelberht of Kent, married his stepmother at his father's death on ascending the throne; and Bede denounced him for the act. (Eadbald was a pagan.) St Augustine included among the questions to Pope Gregory the Great the problem of marriages with stepmothers in Anglo-Saxon society.[15] Queen Judith in ninth-century Wessex married her dead husband's son.[16]

Emma's marriage was accompanied by an attempt to deal with surviving members of the English royal family. Edmund's brother was taken out of a monastery at Tavistock and executed; his two young sons were deported to Scandinavia, whence they later went to Hungary. Emma's English daughter was later married to Dreux, count of Mantes; but the athelings, Edward and Alfred, as we saw, were safe from Cnut in Normandy. When Cnut died, Harold his son by Aelgifu was elected, mainly through the support of Earl Leofric, the seamen of London, and the thegns beyond the Thames. At first a regent, he was formally king by the end of 1037. During his short reign, however, his mother was probably the real power. It was natural, no doubt, in this situation for the athelings to attempt an assertion of their claim. Alfred crossed to England with a small force. He was hospitably received, then seized by Earl Godwin and handed over to Harold to be blinded and killed. This act left a heritage of suspicion and distrust of Godwin and his line; one of the ways that the Normans justified the slaughter at Hastings was as an avenging of the Anglo-Saxon Alfred. When Harold died on 17 March 1040, his brother Harthacnut invaded and took the crown. He seems to have regretted Alfred's murder; for he recalled Edward, adopted him as a member of his household, and almost certainly put him forward as heir. In June 1042 Harold collapsed and died 'as he stood at his drink' at the wedding feast of his father's retainer Tovi the Proud. Even before he was buried, Edward was elected king by popular acclamation in London, and was crowned at Winchester on Easter Day 1043. An invasion of Denmark by Magnus of Norway checked any Danish attack; but when Magnus took over most of the country, he claimed England by right of a treaty with Harthacnut which laid down that if either ruler died childless the other should inherit his dominions.

Through Emma we get the first intrusion of Normans into English affairs. We saw how Sweyn in 1003 began his campaign by taking Exeter; the *Chronicle* blames a Norman:

In this year Exeter was destroyed through Hugh the French fellow [*ceorl*] whom the Lady had appointed as her reeve. The host utterly laid waste the borough and seized much plunder there. Then great levies were assembled from Wiltshire and Hampshire, firmly resolved to march against the host, and it was ealdorman Aelfric's duty to lead the levies, but he was up to his old tricks. As soon as they were close enough for each host to see each other, he pretended to be ill and made violent efforts to vomit, saying he was taken ill, thus leaving in the lurch the men it was his duty to lead. As the saying goes: When the general grows faint-hearted, then the whole army suffers a severe check.

When Sweyn saw their lack of resolution and that they were all dispersing, he led his host into Wilton and sacked and burned down the borough, then went to Salisbury and from there back to the sea where he knew his Wave-stallions (ships) were.[17]

What were the errors or misdemeanours of Hugh is not made clear. We hear also of Matilda, a lady-in-waiting of Emma, who married Alfgar (Aelfgeard), a big man of Worcester; and there was Herluin, whom the bishop of Worcester took with him for the wedding of Emma's daughter Gunnhild with the future Henry III of Germany; on his return he was given by the bishop land at Lapworth in Warwickshire, and he and his son gained several estates in England.[18] Emma also did much to bring about the association of Norman monastic houses with England, though she did not start the process. From the early days of its restoration Fécamp had Englishmen among its monks. The Annals of Mabillon stated that Englishmen came there from across the sea. 'Among them was a man of the royal race named Clemens, who abandoned the pomps of the world and entered this monastery with the desire to serve God for the rest of his days. But, as his compatriots came too often to visit him and he was constantly forced to hear talk of the world's vanities, he retired to the monastery of Dijon.' Note that there was a continual stream of English visitors. A Life of St Aethelwold, who with Dunstan began the monastic revival in England, is found in a Fécamp manuscript, presumably reaching the monastery before the death of the author, Aelfric, in 1006. Mont St Michel was probably also a place where the two peoples met and mixed. When Aethelred in the late tenth century prepared his expedition against Normandy, he told his troops to spare the Mont: 'not to put fire to a place of such great sanctity'.[19] Again, at Winchester in the tenth century were composed or recited many poems, both hagiographical and epic, which were direct responses to the shock of events, and which often dealt abusively with the Danes; they reached the English court and perhaps crossed the sea. Dudo, it has been suggested, in dealing with Rollo, recalled the Anglo-Saxon poem about Brunanburh.[20]

Emma stimulated monastic developments in England as well as creating links with Normandy, and influenced Cnut in such matters. A grant of land at Brede near Winchelsea was made to Fécamp. She may have taken to Normandy in a moment of crisis the relics of St Valentine found at Winchester and not long afterwards claimed by the monks of Jumièges to be in their collection. According to William of Malmesbury, she brought back from Normandy the relics of St Ouen of Rouen. She persuaded the monk in charge of the treasury to sell them to her.[21] She may have helped to connect Winchester with

Mont St Michel, where we find the monks being affected by the
Winchester style of decorating manuscripts. She gave a gold cross to
the new Winchester minster; sent her brother, archbishop of Rouen,
an illuminated psalter; and entrusted a manuscript 'written in letters
of gold' to the embassy despatched yearly to her cousin William of
Aquitaine. In England she was patroness of Romsey nunnery and
Wilton, where her first husband's sister, St Edith, had been abbess;
and she arranged that a monastery of another saint of Edmund's
family (founded by Cnut and colonized from Ely) should have a
yearly gift of 4,000 eels. 'Merrily sang the monks in Ely, as Cnut
King rowed by.' Erwin, monk of Peterborough, offered her a psalter,
with a sacramentary for Cnut. Her piety influenced her husband,
who is said to have walked on bare feet five miles to St Cuthbert's
tomb at Durham. She honoured the tomb of St Elphege (martyred
by the Danes) whom she had known as bishop of Winchester and
archbishop of Canterbury; favoured St Bertin's monastery at St Omer,
long an important point for cultural exchanges between Flanders,
Lorraine, Normandy and England; and helped to rebuild St Hilaire's
at Poitiers.[22] Her exiled son Edward, wintering in Ghent in 1016,
had promised to restore St Bertin's English possessions if ever he
became king; in 1044 he carried out his promise, adding some London property.[23] In 1020 Cnut on his pilgrimage to Rome for the
emperor's coronation had visited St Bertin's and made rich gifts,
perhaps to offset the effects of Edward's visit; he clearly enjoyed
making these offerings there and at Chartres, amid scenes of excited
piety.[24] Through Emma, then, the English church and state gained
new links with the continent. She further encouraged missionaries to
go converting the Norwegians.

We may summarize by saying that in the tenth and earlier eleventh
centuries both England and northern France were powerfully affected by the Norse expansion. In both areas the invasions brought about
a considerable change in the population; but, largely because of the
closeness in language, the Norsemen were assimilated in England and
played their part finally in bringing about a relatively unified state,
while in France there was an enclave of newcomers who, after a
time learning to speak a new language, developed a state of their
own. That state played its part as one of many in France, but at
the same time modified and concentrated the feudal tendencies it
absorbed. Through warfare, piracy, trade, and (near the end) church
affairs, the two areas, England and Normandy, interacted on one
another. The connections came to a head with the marriage of Cnut
and Emma, which prefigured the way in which the fates of the two
areas were to be increasingly linked.

CHAPTER IV

EDWARD, HAROLD,
AND WILLIAM

Edward must have disliked Godwin as the betrayer of his brother
Alfred; but on becoming king his mother became the object of his
anger. Emma seems to have hated her first husband Aethelred; the
Encomiast in his account of her twice calls her *virgo* in contexts
which prove that he wanted to deceive his readers, and he must have
been following her attitudes. William of Malmesbury states that she
'had long mocked the needy condition of her son and never aided
him, transferring her hereditary hatred of the father to the child;
for she both loved Cnut more when living and commended him more
when dead.'[1] Edward himself had lost his English roots without fully
gaining any others. He had been dislocated from the English scene,
growing up in the Norman court where European issues impinged
more and more; yet, cut off from any participation in events, he had
seen the busy world of action all round him as something remote.
Now, as king, he could not simply settle down in the English world;

but he had no coherent idea of what he wanted to do if he were to introduce changes. He had a partiality for foreigners, as long as they were not Norsemen who reminded him of his early miseries and his mother's neglect; but his attitudes seem largely personal with little or no clear political colouring. Almost any foreigners were welcome at his court, Normans, Bretons, French, Flemish, Germans, Lotharingians. Because of the later importance of his link with Normandy, the Normans about him have been singled out; but even in his church there were more Germans than Normans. The only man to whom he gave an earldom was his nephew Ralph the Timid, son of his cousin and count of the Vexin. Lord of Hereford, Ralph built the first private or semi-private castle in England. *Chronicle D*, under 1052, says:

> Gruffydd the Welsh king harried Herefordshire, so that he came very near to Leominster; and men gathered against him, both the natives and the Frenchmen from the castle. And there were killed very many good Englishmen besides many from among the Frenchmen. This was the same day on which fourteen years ago Eadwin was killed with his companions.

Eustace of Boulogne, second husband of Edward's sister, paid him several visits. Two Bretons were granted estates in Essex and East Anglia; they were the only foreigners at his court with big English landholdings. In 1048 Robert of Jumièges, who seems to have been a Norman partisan, was brought from Normandy to be bishop of London; Edward liked him, but later he sacrificed him without apparent qualms. In 1049 Ulf, a Norman, was made bishop of Dorchester:

> but later he was expelled, because he did nothing worthy of a bishop while he occupied the see, so that it brings shame for us to speak further of it... The pope held a synod at Vercelli, which Bishop Ulf attended, and it was said that they were very near to breaking his staff if he had not given exceptionally costly gifts, for he did not know how to perform his offices as well as he ought to have done (*Chronicle*).

But Edward also had English favourites. In his later years he was much taken up with Tostig; and when he was forced to abandon him, his anxiety and grief seem to have contributed much to his death some ten weeks afterwards.

In essentials his court remained Anglo-Danish; and oddly the Norsemen kept a favourable memory of him. An addition to the *Saga of Olaf Tryggvasson* (probably thirteenth century) states that it was his custom to tell this saga 'to his great men and his bodyguard on the first day of Easter; and he chose that day above all others for the telling, saying that Olaf was as superior to other kings as Easter day was to the other days of the whole year.' Then one day, after recounting the saga, he announced that news of Olaf's death had come from Syria. There was also a saga about Edward himself; and his father Aethelred II was sung by the Icelandic Gunnor as a warrior king, a lord whom his men obeyed as a god.[2]

His reputation for piety came no doubt from his chastity and his oddities; but he showed little interest in church affairs or the reform movement, and seems to have been more concerned with hunting.

In the exaction of taxes he was sparing, and detested the insolence of the collectors. In food and drink he was free from the voluptuousness which his state allowed. On the more solemn festivals, though dressed in robes interwoven with gold, which the queen had most splendidly embroidered, yet still he had such forbearance as to be majestic enough without being haughty, considering in such matters more God's bounty than the pomp of the world. There was one earthly enjoyment in which he chiefly delighted: hunting with fast hounds whose opening in the woods he used with pleasure to encourage, and again the pouncing of birds, whose nature it is to prey on their kindred species. In these exercises, after hearing divine service in the morning, he employed himself whole days.

In other respects he was a man by choice devoted to God and lived the life of an angel in the administration of the kingdom. To the poor and the stranger, more especially to foreigners and men of religious orders, he was kind in invitation, munificent in presents, and constantly exciting the monks of his own country to imitate their holiness. He was of a becoming stature; his beard and hair milkwhite; his countenance florid, fair throughout his whole person; and his form of admirable proportion.

So William of Malmesbury records the legend, which had been enhanced by Edward's role as the last of Anglo-Saxon monarchs. His appearance, his red chubby cheeks, snowy hair, thin white hands and tapering transparent fingers, all perfectly embodied the medieval image of a saint. It has been suggested that he was in fact an albino. In character he seems to have been childish, suffering from arrested development, jesting with his courtiers, then, if crossed, exploding in a febrile fury.[3]

He exercised little control over the church and let ambitious ecclesiastics get hold of pluralities of several dioceses. Early in his reign he was accused of simony, but he didn't sell preferments. What he did was to give bishoprics to favoured clerics and promote a few monks. Near the end of his life he rebuilt Westminster Abbey to atone for his sins.[4] But we can find no system in his actions and views. Like many others of his age, indeed like his mother, he was a keen collector of relics; and was believed to have healing powers and prophetic gifts. Tales were told of his miraculous cures even while he was still in Normandy.[5] He could heal the blind and the scrofulous with the water in which he washed his hands. Such powers were considered signs of true Christian kingship. Robert the Pious in France also had them; and later the king's touch as a cure for the King's Evil was to become a hereditary royal gift.[6] But Edward's admirers claimed that his powers came from his sanctity, not his rank. However, they were simplifying things. Far back the Frankish King Guntram had cured ague by the touch of his royal mantle.[7] When the Danish Valdemar I travelled through Germany in 1164, mothers took babies and farmers took corn to him, believing that the royal touch would make them grow.

Edward's prophetic powers were thought to have developed on his widow Edith. When she saw Walcher consecrated bishop at Winchester, she was impressed by his snowy hair and ruddy face, which must have reminded her of the king, and she cried out, 'He'd make a lovely martyr!' A prophecy that came true.[8] As the Normans later tried to build up the fiction that they were the legitimate successors of Edward and his line, the first generation of Anglo-Norman historians took up the theme of English saints and heroes; lawyers collected the so-called Laws of King Edward; and thus in time the conquerors began to revere Edward. The first attempt to get him accepted as a saint was rejected by Pope Innocent on account of disorders in England; but on 7 February 1161 Alexander III issued a bull of canonization. Henry III rebuilt Westminster Abbey and named his eldest son Edward. But the wish for continuity did not go so far as to call the latter Edward II after his accession.[9]

One effect of the Danish invasions, the retort by Wessex and the final Danish conquest, was to break down the sharp particularism, the old tribal divisions of Northumbria, Mercia and Wessex. To deal with these large areas, earls were appointed where once there had been kings. They were not yet hereditary dignitaries with a fixed role; they were great landowners with an administration and officials of their own. Cnut's idea of the earldom as an office continued to have effect. The earls were representatives of the king, raising popular levies, not commanding hosts of private retainers; the courts where they presided were popular courts, not baronial jurisdictions; the organization over which they presided was based on the royal hundreds and the officer they used was the royal sheriff. In all these details we see the deep difference between England and the more feudalized areas of the continent. Here tribal kingship had reached its apex, creating a supra-tribal state in which many of the cohesive elements of earlier days persisted despite the enlarged form. In some ways the situation in England was archaic, driving tribal forms beyond the level at which they could effectively function, but it had aspects that looked far ahead of the more feudal systems operating in France and Normandy, towards the national state.

Edward was an odd mixture of strength and weakness, of sloth and energy, of dilatoriness and capacity to act with decision. He let things drift, but not too far. In the first years of his reign Earl Godwin quickly built himself up as the greatest magnate. He seems to have been the son of the thegn Wulfnoth who did well out of piracy in the Channel and who thus showed that not all the pirates were Norsemen. He attracted Cnut's notice and became earl of Wessex in 1018. Marrying Gytha, sister of Ulf of Denmark (Cnut's brother-in-law), he was a power in the land for some fifty years. He seems to have swung his crucial support behind Edward, who in 1045 agreed to marry his daughter Edith. The marriage was unconsummated; no grandson of Godwin was to take the crown as legitimate heir. But the union swelled the family's prestige; Edith got large estates as dowry and used her influence at court to advance her relations. Godwin and the two other earls, Leofric of Mercia and Siward of Northumbria, were with Edward when he rode to Winchester where Emma was living in luxurious retirement, in the summer of 1043. Edward took away all her property and confiscated her lands. One *Chronicle* text says that he was annoyed at being barred from a fair share of her wealth; another that she had done less than he wanted, before and after his accession. But Stigand, her chief confidant, recently made bishop of Elmham, lost his see at this point; and the author of the *Encomium*, who was in a position to know the facts, stated that she was intriguing with Magnus of Norway, inviting him to invade England and putting her treasure at his disposal. Caught out, she retired to Flanders.[10]

Sweyn, Godwin's eldest son, was made earl over the Severn valley; Harold ruled East Anglia; Beorn, nephew of Godwin's wife and brother of Sweyn of Denmark, held a region north of London. The family of Godwin dominated a great stretch of land which reached from the Wash to the south coast and along it, and which ran north to Hereford. But their prestige was damaged by Sweyn, who acted as wildly and recklessly as any Norseman. He ravished an abbess and murdered his cousin Beorn. And Edward either resented the extension of Godwin's power or clashed with him on a key-point of

policy. Perhaps he was nursing his anger at Alfred's death and biding
his time. Their disagreement came about over the empty see of
Canterbury. Godwin put forward a kinsman and won over the monks
of Christ's Church, who had the formal right of choice. But Edward
for once asserted himself and appointed Robert of Jumièges, the
Norman, who went off to Rome for papal confirmation. Then Robert
and Edward put another Norman into the see of London, blocking
out the bishop-elect, a friend of Godwin.

Next, conflict flared up on a secular issue, in which the count of
Boulogne played a part:

And then came Eustace from oversea shortly after the
bishop, and went to the king and talked over with him what he
wished, and then set off on his way home. When he came to
Canterbury, he and his men had a meal there and went to Dover.
When he was some miles or more this side of Dover, he put on
his mailcoat, and all his companions did the same, and went to
Dover. When they arrived, they wanted to lodge where they
pleased. Then one of his men came and wanted to lodge at the
house of a certain householder against his wish, and wounded
the householder, and the householder killed him. Then Eustace
got on his horse and his companions on theirs, and went to the
householder and killed him upon his own hearth. Then they
went up towards the town and killed both inside and outside it
more than twenty men; and the townsmen killed nineteen men
on the other side and wounded they didn't know how many.
And Eustace escaped with a few men and went back to the king
and gave a one-sided account of how they had fared; and the
king was greatly incensed against the townsmen and summoned Earl Godwin and ordered him to carry war into Kent to
Dover, because Eustace had told the king that it was more the
townsmen's fault than his, though it was not so. And the earl
could on no account agree to the foray because it was abhorrent
to him to injure the people of his own province (*Chronicle*
E).[11]

The troubles over the two sees and over the foray at Dover all concerned foreigners; it would seem that Edward was setting himself to
bring in Normans and others who might in time be able to outweigh
the power of Godwin and his sons. The *Chronicle* suggests that
tension had been mounting between English and Normans. 'At that
time the foreigners had built a castle in Herefordshire in Earl Sweyn's
territory and inflicted all the injuries and insults they possibly could
upon the king's men in that region.' It is even highly likely that,

under the influence of Robert of Jumièges and perhaps of Eustace, Edward was developing a pro-Norman attitude and had sent a message to William naming him as his heir. We see that he could act strongly if necessary, and for a year he was in control of policy. Foreigners were given places at court or appointed to offices in the country; the English attitude was that these men 'promoted injustice, gave unjust judgments, and counselled folly': which suggests perhaps that they created grievances not only through greed but also through ignorance of the running of the English system.

After the affair at Dover Edward called two councils, and finally Godwin and his sons were exiled. But the statement that their estates were granted to foreigners seems an extreme exaggeration. They made no resistance to the sentence. Godwin with his sons Sweyn, Tostig, and Gyrth, went to Flanders; Harold and Leofwin went to Ireland; and Queen Edith was put into a nunnery. Baldwin seems to have helped Godwin, perhaps resentful of the way in which Edward had gathered his fleet in 1049 and kept watch at Sandwich while the emperor attacked Flanders by land. Edward had been asked to prevent Baldwin from escaping by sea, though such a flight would have been very unlikely; no doubt the emperor wanted to divert Baldwin and stop him from massing troops for war in Lotharingia.[12]

Can we go further and find a pattern behind these events apart from a personal dislike of Godwin by Edward, and a liking for men of French culture? Edward had been lucky in gaining the throne without having to repel a Norse invasion. His mother seems certainly to have plotted for such an invasion, and the Danish threat continued. Edward and his councillors must have given much thought to it. Both Norman and Flemish ports had been used by Danes in the past; but the more recent provider of Danish bases had been Flanders. When it seemed that a bloody clash might come about between the king and Godwin, the *Chronicle* remarked: 'It was hateful to almost all to fight against men of their own race; for there were few men else of any consequence except Englishmen on either side. And besides they were unwilling to increase the danger of leaving this land wide open to the invasion of foreigners, if each side were to destroy the other.' Who were these feared foreigners? Not the Normans, whom no one at this stage could have seen as possible invaders; not the Flemish, however devious the policy of Baldwin. They could only be Danes and Norwegians; the leader most feared was Harald Hardrada. It is probable then that a strong section of the council, as well as the king, inclined to a policy of good relations with Normandy to offset the unreliability of Baldwin and the threat of Harald – while Godwin, with his strong Danish affiliations, opposed this attitude and was suspected of being likely to turn traitor if a Danish invasion was attempted and seemed to be succeeding. (The appointment of Herman to the see of Ramsbury in 1045 may have been an attempt by Godwin's group to bring in a cleric with Flemish links to balance Edward's French appointments.)

Whatever the reasons, the failure of Godwin to offer any resistance to Edward shows the strength of the English kingship, unparalleled in western Europe.

The Danish threat was kept alive over these years by such events as the attack in 1049 by Norsemen on Wales:

> Thirty-six ships came from Ireland up the Welsh Usk and did evil thereabouts, helped by Gruffydd, the Welsh king. Forces were gathered against them, and bishop Ealdred went with them, but there were too few troops and the enemy took them by surprise when it was quite early morning and killed many good men there, and the others escaped with the bishop (*Chronicle* D).

And in 1055 Aelfgar, son of the Mercian earl, exiled for unknown reasons, raised a force of eighteen ships from among the Vikings in Ireland, and then, in alliance with Gruffydd, invaded England, making for Herefordshire, where he defeated the local militia, who were getting ready to fight on horseback. The general fyrd was called out and an army led by Harold (now back from exile) came up. Aelfgar fell back into the Black Mountain and Harold negotiated terms with him; Aelfgar was restored to his rank and possessions. We see how easily Viking forces could become involved in any internal dissensions; and there could not but be a fear that warriors coming as allies of some English malcontent would turn into invaders on their own account.

Godwin was not a man likely to skulk idly in exile. In 1052, aided by Baldwin, he gathered a fleet and landed in the south of England. The people of the region welcomed him, especially the Londoners. But once more there was no recourse to civil war. Commonsense prevailed. The position of the foreigners had become untenable. Robert of Jumièges and Ulf fled overseas; Robert 'was declared an outlaw, together with all the Frenchmen, for they were the cause of all the ill-feeling which had arisen between him [Godwin] and the king'. However, Edward was allowed to keep the foreigners whom he favoured at court. But events of 1054 serve to show how easy it is to oversimplify the picture from the scanty records of the chronicles:

> In this year early Siward [of Northumbria] invaded Scotland with a great host both by sea and land, and fought against Scots.

He put to flight their king Macbeth and killed the noblest of the land, carrying off much plunder such as no one had previously won. But his son Osbern and Siward his sister's son and numbers of his housecarles as well as those of the king were killed there on the festival of the Seven Sleepers [27 July]. This same year Ealdred went oversea to Cologne on a mission for the king and was there received with great ceremony by the emperor. He stayed there almost a year and was entertained by both the bishop of Cologne and the emperor, and he gave permission to bishop Leofwin to consecrate the monastery church at Evesham on 10 October. In this same year Osgod died suddenly in his bed.

We learn that in Macbeth's army there died fighting many *Northmanni*, not chance Vikings but 'French castle-men' from Herefordshire under 'Osbern and Hugue, his ally'.[13] The mission of bishop Ealdred was connected with the negotiations for the return of Edward, son of Edmund Ironside, whom it had now been agreed should become heir to the throne and who arrived back in 1057. Such negotiations could only have gone on if there had been full agreement between the king and his council on the matter; whatever arrangements had been made with William of Normandy in 1051 would have been cancelled.

Godwin and his sons had a stronger position than ever after 1052. But in 1053 Godwin died and Harold took his place as head of the family. Sweyn had died in exile on his way back from a pilgrimage to Jerusalem. Harold seems to have been the most balanced of them all, courageous but careful, seeking conciliation where possible, generous, and without the violences of Sweyn or the hard, closed ambition of his father. Whether he had any outstanding political capacity, we cannot judge. He was a friend of Wulfstan, bishop of Worcester, who was pleased to act as his confessor; and he founded a community of secular canons at Waltham Cross in 1061. He also made a pilgrimage to Rome. But he was no doubt merely doing the things expected of a man in his position. He was shrewd enough not to marry in a church till he was king, so that he could use the offer of his hand as a political bargaining counter. In two campaigns, 1056 and 1063, he dealt efficiently with Gruffydd ap Llwelyn, who dominated Wales, and pacified the borderlands. And he carried on his father's policy of aggrandizing the family. He himself took over Wessex, which was expanded to bring in the Welsh marches of Gloucester and Hereford. When Siward's death in 1055 left the earldom of Northumbria vacant, Tostig was given it. Siward's son was a child and a strong hand was needed in the north where the Scottish king was brooding over his recent defeat and the Danes might attack at any time.

When Leofric of Mercia died, Aelfgar gave up East Anglia (which Harold had let him have on becoming Earl of Wessex) and took over his father's Mercia; East Anglia now went to Gyrth, while another brother, Leofwine, became earl of counties north and south of London, partly taken from Mercia. So the sons of Godwin held all England but the reduced Mercia, which in 1062 fell into the hands of young Edgar, son of Aelfgar. That king Edward, with his odd powers of adaptation, did not altogether resent the situation, was shown by his friendship with Tostig.

But Tostig was not popular in Northumbria. In late 1065 the people there rose against him, won the support of Edwin of Mercia and his brother Morcar, and chose the latter as their earl. (We have no evidence that Edwin or Morcar stimulated the revolt.) Neither Edward nor Harold made any attempt to resist. They accepted Morcar and agreed that Siward's son Waltheof should have an earldom made up out of lands in the midlands. Tostig went off with wife and followers into exile in Flanders and wintered at St Omer, welcomed by Baldwin. Edward moved to Westminster toward Christmas and the new abbey was consecrated on 28 December, Holy Innocents Day. He died on the Vigil of the Epiphany and was buried next day in the abbey, on 6 January 1066. On his deathbed he named Harold as his successor. Harold was the only man with anything like a princely status who was capable of defending the realm; he was Edward's brother-in-law and first cousin of the Danish king, though lacking any direct link with the Wessex royal line. He was clearly ready to accept the crown; and the magnates in council, assembled in unusual strength for the Christmas festivities and the abbey's consecration, seem to have given no sign whatever of disagreeing with Edward's choice. Edwin and Morcar must have been present, and their conduct in the following months proves that they fully accepted Harold's election. He on his part married their sister to consolidate his position. Probably he expected more trouble from Denmark than from Normandy over his accession.

Now let us look at how William had been getting on in Normandy. He seems to have spent his first years at Falaise, at his mother's house. When his father died, he was only seven or eight years old. Though there was no challenge to his accession, his reign was soon troubled. The leading lords, who were often counts, had distant ancestors in common with the rulers; and further mating among the nobles may well have increased the tangle of kinships.[14] There was even a son of Richard II, who avoided attention however, by becoming a monk. William's guardians were Alan of Brittany, Gilbert count of Brionne, a remote relation of the royal family, Osbern, seneschal, and Turold,

William's tutor; they were all to die violently. Meanwhile they put the lad in the strong castle of Vaudreuil. His education seems to have been neglected; and unlike his predecessors he is said to have been unable to read or write, though no doubt that is an exaggeration.

The various revolts may well have aimed at getting control of his person rather than at killing or demoting him. The temptation of a minor in charge seems to have been too much for the barons. The first revolt was led by William of Montgomery, who penetrated the ducal bedroom one night and killed the tutor and Osbern (son of Gunnor's brother); but Walter, Herleva's brother, saved the young duke. Next Gilbert de Brionne was murdered while out riding, and Alan of Brittany was poisoned in 1040. The second revolt was led by Hugh de Montfort, Roger de Toeny, and Raoul Wace, who had killed Gilbert. It failed, but as a compromise William accepted Wace as his tutor.

So far he had had no troubles from France; but now without warning King Henry invaded the Evrecin and demanded the castle of Tillières. After an uncertain campaign, William agreed to give up the castle if it were dismantled and not repaired for four years. But Henry, after gaining it, passed on to Argentan, which he burned; then went ahead at once with rebuilding Tillières. William established his court at Valognes. In 1042 came another revolt. Thurstan Goz seized Falaise, but was defeated by Wace.

William was now about sixteen, a fine rider, swordsman, and archer. In 1043–4 he was knighted. It was a moment, says William of Poitiers, which all France dreaded: 'a splendid sight, delightful yet terrible, to see him gripping the reins, girt about with his sword, shining under his buckler, menacing with his helmet and lance.'[15] Now he was no longer the more or less passive centre of a storm of intrigues and dangers. He tackled the situation as a soldier and triumphed. And a soldier he remained all his years, tough, callous, keen to scent threat and deceit, and quick to meet all challenges with complete ruthlessness. At the same time he was not rash or liable to be carried away by temper; he could prudently judge a situation, and, when advisable, build up his strength before striking. Distrustful, keeping his thoughts and plans to himself, he translated his struggle to overcome the anarchy of treachery and revolt in his early years into a creed of order at all costs. In so far as he had any political ideas, he had a belief that a ruler must rule as thoroughly and authoritatively as possible. His aim was simply to overcome insecurity and construct a strong basis of power and wealth; to achieve this end he pragmatically used any form or institution which he encountered and which he felt capable of moulding to his will. In the end, carrying the ideas learned in Normandy into England, he did much to construct a new

D

system, or at least one much more advanced than elsewhere in Europe.

In 1047 came the most serious revolt of all. This time the aim certainly was to kill or expel William and put in his place Guy, son of Renaud of Burgundy, with one of Richard II's five daughters, who had resided in Burgundy a lot as a boy and had had several lordships bestowed on him. The conspirators almost caught William at Valognes; but his jester is said to have rushed in and woken him in time. William slipped off across the Vire to Bayeux, but found that it would be too risky to enter the town. He rode round through a suburb to a supporter near Cherbourg, then was escorted to Falaise. Considering the situation, he decided that Henry of France would dislike Normandy falling into Burgundian hands. He rode on to Poiny, whence he appealed to the king, who promised him aid. The lords who opposed him included the vicomtes of the Bessin and the Cotentin, so it would seem that there was still something of a split between eastern and western Normandy, with the eastern section cherishing its Norse past and opposed to the inroads of Frankish feudalism.

Henry and William together advanced to meet the rebels at Val-ès-Dunes, south-east of Caen. They won a complete victory, though at one moment Henry, fighting the Cotentin contingent, was dismounted. William had the good sense not to take harsh reprisal against the defeated lords, apart from Grimoald du Plessis whom for some reason he would not forgive. He knew that he had now proved himself and could use his triumph to impose the sort of order he wanted. He insisted on all the rebels making submission; every lord must pay homage; castles without licence were destroyed.

He was soon able to pay his debt to Henry and gain much satisfaction from the payment. Henry quarrelled in 1048 with Geoffrey Martel of Anjou, whom William hated for having seized Alençon and Domfront, while becoming friendly with the Bellêmes. William attacked Alençon, where the townspeople hung out newly flayed skins on their walls. As the Normans came up, they beat the skins and shouted, 'Plenty of work for the tanner's son! plenty of work for the tanner!' William retorted with a fierce assault that took a number of prisoners – thirty-four, we are told. These men were paraded under the walls; their hands and feet were cut off and thrown into the town; their eyes were put out and they were left to crawl home if they could. Their fellow townsmen were threatened with the same fate when taken. The town at once surrendered. William built a frontier castle and withdrew. In the campaign he had showed his energy and initiative by leading his knights in scouting forays and raids; once in his ardour he nearly attacked the allied troops of

Theobald of Blois and Chartres. William of Poitiers in his eulogistic biography claims that he showed himself the world's chief knight, though guilty of rash scorn of danger. Exactly what title the Norman rulers had come to bear is unclear. William of Poitiers does not distinguish between William as *comes*, *dux*, and *princeps* (count, duke, and prince); Ordericus Vitalis, who completed his history by 1141, often calls him *marchio*, marquis. On documents he is often styled count, no doubt the correct title in his overlord's eyes; but writers dwelling on his prowess tend to call him *Dux Normanorum*, a term stressing his role as general. Duke, the title he most likely preferred, may then be used of him; and indeed it became for the historians the title accorded to all the counts back to Rollo.

After the war against Anjou, trouble at once broke out again. The son of William's uncle, archbishop of Rouen, conspired with other nobles, but was betrayed. He managed to slip off to south Italy. His county, Mortain, was given by William to his halfbrother Robert de Centeville. Meanwhile one of the rebel castles of 1047, Brionne, had continued to hold out and was not taken till perhaps late in 1049. It stood on an islet between two arms of a river. William had invested it, built rough castles round it, and then tried to starve or tire it out.

About this time he decided to marry and picked on Matilda, daughter of Baldwin of Flanders by Adela of France. But the emperor disliked the alliance, and so Pope Leo IX, an anti-Norman supporter of the Germans, forbade the marriage at the Council of Rheims, apparently on the grounds of consanguinity, which did not exist; Adela as a child had been betrothed to William's uncle, Richard II, but no marriage took place. William ignored the ban and married Matilda at Eu, in 1050–1, or at least before the end of 1053. A little earlier he had given his sister to Enguerrand, count of Ponthieu just over his northern frontier; he was clearly determined to strengthen his links with the regions to his north – whether or not he could as yet have envisaged an attack on England. It is more than doubtful if he had ever seen Matilda, and we can dismiss the story that he was passionately in love with her. He was not a man to be swept off his feet by any woman. What is more probable is that, once having decided on Matilda, he was too obstinate to submit to any bullying from the church. Mauger, together with Lanfranc the prior of Bec, told him that his marriage was null; and he in reply ravaged the lands of Lanfranc's abbey and banished him from the country. The story is told that William met him riding off on a poor nag and ordered him to get out more quickly; Lanfranc answered, 'Give me a decent horse and I'll go at a better pace.' William laughed and discussed the situation with him. Lanfranc agreed to urge William's case at Rome. (Later under Pope Nicholas II a compromise was reached; a dispensation was issued on condition that William founded an abbey for monks and Matilda one for nuns.) William of Jumièges insists that Matilda was beautiful as well as gifted with great abilities; certainly her husband seems to have respected her views. He had no concubine, or we should hear of her. Probably he was not interested in women apart from needing a wife to give him heirs.[16]

As part of his marriage-contract, says William of Poitiers, he exacted from his barons oaths of fidelity to himself and his unborn heir. He did not mean to leave any ambiguities as his father had done. In the course of sixteen years he begot four sons: Robert, Richard (who died young), William Rufus, Henry – and several daughters. Poitiers, piling up praises, says nothing of continence; William of Malmesbury tells us:

> Besides other virtues, he, especially in early youth, observed chastity; so that it was very commonly reported that he was impotent. However, marrying at the recommendation of his nobility, he behaved for many years in such a way as never to be suspected of criminal intercourse. He had many children by Matilda, whose wifely obedience and fertility in births excited in his mind the tenderest regard, though persons do not lack who chatter about his renouncing his former chastity, and say that after he acceded to the royal dignity he was connected with a certain priest's daughter whom the queen caused to be removed by having her hamstrung by one of her servants; for which he was exiled and Matilda was scourged to death with a bridle.
>
> But I consider it folly to believe this of so great a king, though I decidedly assert that a slight discord arose between them, in later days, through their son Robert, whom his mother was said to supply with a military force out of her revenues. Still, he proved that his conjugal affection was not in the least lessened thereby, as on her death he buried her with great magnificence, four years before his own death; and weeping profusely for many days, he showed how keenly he felt her loss. More, from that time, if we may credit report, he refrained from every gratification.

There was a strong homosexual streak in the Norman lords. But William seems wholly obsessed by issues of power; and with his suspicious brooding nature there may have been an element of ascetic withdrawal, a dislike of admitting any needs that disturbed his harsh self-discipline.[17]

A minor revolt by William Busac, son of the count d'Eu, was

easily put down. But Mauger was criticizing the duke's marriage, and his brother, count of Arques, William's uncle, joined in. William put troops into the count's castle, but they mutinied and went over to d'Arques. All the malcontents flocked to him. William moved from Valognes by forced marches, going so fast that he had only six men with him when he arrived at Arques, where however he found three hundred knights and their men waiting for him. He managed to catch his uncle in the open, and charged at him, despite his inferior force. The count, however, managed to get back into the castle and was beseiged there. Leaving Walter Giffard to carry on with the siege, William turned to oppose a strong army moving in from France. King Henry thought he at last had a chance to deal with Normandy, putting d'Arques over it as a puppet-duke. A body of troops under a grandson of Richard II ambushed the French at St Ubin near Dieppe, and Henry failed to raise the siege of Arques. The count surrendered and was allowed to go off to Eustace of Boulogne.

Then again in 1055 the king attacked Normandy. William now had the support of both eastern and western regions. By a dawn attack the Normans routed the French. (The Norman Roger de Mortemer took prisoner Montdidier, whose vassal he was, and then released him. William was said later, in his dying speech, to have praised Mortemer, but at the time he banished him.) There seems to have been peace till 1058, when again Henry of France, with the count of Anjou, made an attack. Western Normandy fell; but then the invaders tried to cross the Dive at Varaville. When only half the troops had crossed the tide began to flow in. William assaulted the rear and cut it to pieces. Henry decided that he had now had enough of meddling unprofitably with Normandy. He died in 1060; and his child-heir, Philip I, to whom William paid homage, had Baldwin as guardian. Geoffrey Martel, count of Anjou, had died in 1059, and was succeeded by a weak ruler who was taken up with the problems of a troublesome brother. William could now get on with subduing Maine, to which France, Anjou and Normandy all had unimpressive claims. William had worked out a story that the county had once been granted to the Norman rulers; in fact, since at least 1025, Angevin control had been effective there. William tried to buttress his claim by adding that the region had been bequeathed to him by its count Herbert II, whom, with mother and sister, he had taken in as an exile; Herbert had died in 1062. And he declared that he had married one of his daughters to Herbert before his death and his son Robert to the sister Margaret. So he now claimed Maine as Herbert's heir and Margaret's guardian. But Walter III of the Vexin, nephew of Edward of England, had married Biota, the dead count's aunt, and thus was a possible rival for both Maine and England.

By means of ferocious devastations William in 1063 took Le Mans, capital of Maine; then by firing the town he gained the fortress of Mayenns. William of Poitiers thus described the taking of Le Mans:

He had the skill and force available to set fire to it at once, destroy the whole town, and massacre the guilty. But with his usual restraint he preferred to spare men's blood, however culpable, and leave unharmed this strongly fortified city, the capital fortress of the land he had conquered. So he chose this way of subduing it: to sow terror by frequent assaults and by long soujourns in its neighbourhood, to devastate its vineyards, fields, and desmesnes, to capture all the castles round about, to set up garrisons wherever advisable, and finally to inflict without respite all possible hardships.

He captured Walter of Mantes and his wife, and shut them up at Falaise, where they died – poisoned according to Orderic. As Margaret had died before her marriage with Robert could be canonically celebrated, William himself took the title count of Maine. Now he could attack Brittany where Conan II, out of tutelage, was refusing homage and raiding the frontier. He marched round and about Brittany, but had to withdraw through lack of supplies and because Anjou threatened to come to Conan's aid. Harold, son of Godwin, was with him in this inconclusive campaign. However, William established contacts with some Bretons, notably the sons of Edo of Porhoet, who in 1066 supplied a large contingent for the attack on England.

Thus we see that for many years William had to suffer more revolts and treacheries than any other Norman ruler. The reason no doubt lay in the fact that Normandy was now experiencing a maximum tension between the old Norse bonds and the new feudal forms. The lords, with enhanced powers, wanted to show that they could achieve as much autonomy as the barons of France, Anjou, Maine and Burgundy; and against this increased assertion of the lords William had to mobilize both the old Norse ruthless initiative and those elements in the feudal forms which strengthened the hand of the prime overlord. The prolonged siege of Brionne must have involved very efficient organization of supplies, both of men and materials, the raising of funds and careful use of the available money. Many mercenaries must have been employed. It was probably round this time that William elaborated and systematized his methods of army service. He replaced the old type of barons, many of whom were related by blood to Richard I and II, with new men more willing to accept the fief-system. He allotted his two half-brothers their places. Odo became bishop of Bayeux and Robert, we saw, took over the county of Mortain. William was carrying on the policy begun by the two Richards of creating new counties, which were put into the hands of relatives whose tenures depended on their long military service and their loyal command of the ducal castles. At the same time he got his own garrisons into castles held by the magnates whom he considered to be too independent. He thus tightened up his controls and his administrative system in a way that few overlords elsewhere in France could have done in their own regions.

Not that we must look for any rigid application of a carefully devised system. In such a feudal world he had to act tentatively, continue trying to establish just what fealties could be demanded and held, and what delegations of power produced the best balance between a centralized overlordship and local forms of order, exploitation, and management. In a smaller way he was doing what he did later in England: building and controlling castles at strategic points, cutting fiefs out of his demesne and granting them on terms as definite and stringent as circumstances permitted, attempting to get a profitable coherence out of the various resources such as tolls, dues and feudal rights, always bearing in mind both central demands and local needs. The unifying aspect lay in the effort to build up effective military control over the whole duchy so that its resources in men, money and supplies could be tapped as required, both for the steady extension of his dominion and for meeting emergencies. But once again we must beware of thinking there were clearcut schemes or applications of policy. William's approach was based on a strong pragmatic sense of the realities of power. Thus, as part of his movement towards the greatest centralization possible in a situation with so many local and centrifugal elements, he had to avoid granting fiefs to vassals in areas where they were already too important.

In these comments we are dealing with tendencies rather than sharp policies. William was far from ending his problems; and, as we noted, he had the good sense to be cautious and even merciful in situations full of pitfalls and perils. He came to learn that a foreign policy strongly orientated towards expansion was useful in smothering opposition at home; but he knew that if he failed, internal envies, intrigues and ambitions would increase. In his later years he entered the general political scene of western Europe, where the main factor had become the Lotharingian rebellion against the Emperor Henry III. Baldwin and Henry of France had been drawn in, and Geoffrey of Anjou and Edward of England were allied with the emperor. William had to move from the problem of feudal stability inside Normandy to that of his duchy's role in the wider field.

We may now look at the use William tried to make of the Truce of God, which he instituted soon after Val-ès-Dunes as an important step in his struggle to pacify and control the duchy. The movement represented by the Truce tells us a great deal about the age. It arose earlier in the eleventh century, as an expression both of the increasing feudal anarchy and the possibilities of new centralized systems. It showed also the intrusion of the church into matters of war, an intrusion which in many ways had the opposite effect to that intended. Instead of halting or humanizing war, if such a thing were possible, it tended to draw war into the church's orbit and to lend it a Christian veil; it thus helped to build the idea of a holy war (such as William's invasion of England with papal banner and blessing) and to bring about the whole project of the crusade against the infidel.

Significantly the Truce had behind it a genuine popular movement, which had been aimed against the ruthless killing and looting indulged in by the warrior and knightly classes. This movement was that of the Peace of God, probably stimulated by fears that the world would end in 1000. At the council of Charroux, 989, the bishops of Aquitaine considered means of protecting the immunity of the clergy and creating guarantees that the poor would be left to live in peace. Next year at Le Puy the idea was taken up more strongly. At Poitiers in 1000 it was laid down that every dispute should be decided by recourse to justice alone; all men who refused to conform to the rule should be excommunicated. The duke of Guienne and his nobles accepted the proposals, and Robert the Pious of France followed their example. The church was mainly concerned to protect its property, and a number of councils took the matter up further. At Verdun-sur-le-Doubs in 1016 a formula was evolved whereby the nobility was to foreswear the impressing of clerics or peasants into their forces, the raiding of crops and the carrying off of beasts. The oath was widely taken through France with congregations shouting, 'Peace, peace, peace!' In 1038 the archbishop of Bourges ordered all Christians older than fifteen years to be ready to take up arms against the peace-breakers. Leagues of Peace were organized. The peasants, led by the lesser clergy, took the proposals seriously and attacked the castles of recalcitrant nobles. The authorities grew scared. After the League of Peace burned the village of Bénécy, Count Odo of Déols attacked and destroyed its members on the banks of the Cher, killing (we are told) some seven hundred clerics.[18]

The background of the movement lay in the fact that when in the ninth century the Carolingian state broke down, with a failure of royal authority and central organs, the local unit of administration, the *pagus*, functioned till the second half of the tenth century, when anarchy began with the swarms of lords building castles – a situation worst in the areas south of the Loire. The councils advocating the peace were the church's effort of self-preservation, supported by the *vulgaris plebs*.

From this crushed popular movement came the movement of the Truce, which was taken up and directed by strong rulers in the hopes of curbing internal anarchy. In 1027 a synod at Toulouse in Rousillon forbade all warfare on the Sabbath; in 1030 the bishops of Soissons and of Beauvais decided to 'imitate the Burgundian bishops'.[19] Behind the proposals was a strong Cluniac influence; Odilon of Cluny and Richard of St Vanne with their companions had done much to propagate the idea. In Flanders abbot Richard and his disciples won over the bishop of Cambrai, who had been the only bishop in the see of Rheims to resist such *novitates*. The French King Robert even thought of acting with the German emperor and Pope Benedict VIII to spread the idea over all Christendom.[20] In 1041 the bishops of Provençe, claiming to speak in the name of the whole church of Gaul, sent letters to the church of Italy demanding that the Truce be extended to include Good Friday, Holy Saturday and Ascension Day. Aquitaine had already taken this line; Burgundy went further and wanted the Truce to cover the whole week from Wednesday evening to Monday morning, plus the period from Advent to the first Sunday after Epiphany, and from the beginning of Lent through Holy Week to the Octave of Easter.

The idea did not fare well for a time in Normandy though churchmen like the Italo-Burgundian William of Volpiano would certainly have favoured it; and Richard of St Vanne was known at the ducal court. Richard II asked his advice; Richard III helped the pilgrimage he organized in 1026 to Jerusalem. Robert, grappling with a plot hatched by a lord of Breton origin, Ermenoldus, invoked his assistance: the abbot hurried to Rouen with his disciple Ermenfroi, archdeacon of Verdun, calmed the rebel, and took him to become a monk at St Vanne.[21] In Flanders, about 1030, Baldwin IV introduced the Truce. But the Norman dukes ignored it.

Perhaps they felt strong enough without it; perhaps they felt that such rules were impossible to impose on their lords. But William must have decided that anything which might curb anarchy was to be welcomed. Hugue de Flavigny says that in the first years of his rule he was often asking abbot Richard's advice. So in 1041–2 the idea was taken up. William probably addressed the bishops first, as he had done over the matter of monastic reform. But with the Truce, Hugue says, he met the opposition of 'certain persons of bad will who rejected his proposition as unheard of, saying that they didn't want to transgress the customs of their fathers by thus accepting unaccustomed novelties'. However, the *gens Neustriae*, who ignored the call, were struck with a cruel epidemic, 'a fire that tortured them', and famine made things worse. (*Ignis* is a term used in this period for various diseases, some attacking the skin, some the whole body, but mainly it seems to mean a gangrenous form of ergotism, caused by a mould on the damp corn. The modern drug L.S.D. is a form of ergot.)[22]

Then some five years later the Truce was adopted after all. This must have been before March 1048 when a provincial council sat near Caen. (Richard had died in June 1046.) A few weeks before the council the parish church of Rots (given by Duke Richard to the monastery, St Ouen of Rouen) had to be consecrated; and the relics of St Ouen were to be presented there. The procession was on its way from Caen when, about halfway (some two miles), a messenger galloped up and bade it wait for the duke, who had just finished some detaining business and who wanted to bear on his own shoulders the holy body for the rest of the way.[23] Fulbert mentions that among the crowd was a priest with a piece of linen he was going to sell at the *nundinae*, apparently the fair of the Pré; so the council must have met some time in October 1047. It was held no doubt on the right bank of the Orne, where are still the ruins of the church Sainte-Paix, chosen on account of the abundance of provisions and 'the *opportunitas* of the place'. The latter phrase seems to refer to the battlefield nearby, where the conspirators of 1046 were destroyed. (It may however mean that William had already noticed the suitability of the site for a town, or merely that the land belonged to the monastery of St Ouen.) The vast crowd included bishops and abbots of the province of Rouen; and St Ouen was kept busy miraculously exposing the many thieves.

The council lasted two days, dealing with the peace of Normandy. Persons who profited through disorders opposed the proceedings; but the other side won and the oath was taken. We are not told if the dissenters were forced to take it, as often happened at such gatherings. Fulbert mentions no lay lords; but the duke was there and the main opponents must surely have been laity, though doubtless aided by some bishops. And even here, in the midst of the discussion about peace, some usurpations were attempted. A Préaux cartulary remarked with irony, 'The same year, when was held for the first time a Council of Peace at Caen, in presence of the Relics, the bishop Hugues of Bayeux made an attempt on the lands of the abbey St Pierre of Préaux...'

The later tradition, probably correct, was that William initiated the movement; the choice of Caen also suggests his hand.[24] The texts make the Truce run from Wednesday to Monday, and define the forbidden acts in terms of individuals and groups, with penalties for offenders or accomplices. The sanctity applied to both moveable and immoveable goods, with less severe penalties for offences against them. A reservation was made in favour of the king or of a territorial prince, who was free to carry on war at any times. Then came a brief clause bidding diocesans assure peace to traders and strangers. A fifth article came back to the days when fighting was to cease. Priests should pray on Sundays and feast days for men who kept the Truce, and should curse the breakers. Any persons who pleaded that they broke the Truce involuntarily must justify themselves by oath and the ordeal of hot iron. (One manuscript differentiates between freemen and serfs.)[25] The reservation about king and prince is not found elsewhere in France at this time. A synod of 1080, presided over by William, confirmed the rulings about the Truce; and in the Coutumier of Bec, in the early thirteenth century, it is mentioned that at the end of the liturgic periods 'Peace was sounded'. In general by the mid-eleventh century the idea of the Truce was well established; and in 1054 the great council of Narbonne tried to link it with that of the Peace of God, the protection of the church and the poor, and to lay down that no Christian should kill another, 'for he that kills a Christian sheds the blood of Christ'.[26] At the council of Clermont in November 1095, which was concerned with the Truce of God, Pope Urban II launched the idea of the crusade to free the Holy Land.

We thus see an interesting sequence: a popular movement against feudal barbarity, which in a severely modified form is taken over by rulers as an instrument against feuds and violences that disrupt feudal order. To the extent that it helps to promote order at home, it ends by diverting and directing many of the impulses of greed, hatred and envy into war abroad against the infidels – or against Christian groups which can be construed as heretical or refractory to papal controls. Now the land and loot are to come from the alien or denounced groups.[27] William had used the Truce to assert ducal power over the church and the nobles, and to build ducal control of criminal justice. Other rulers of comital or ducal standing followed his example, as in the Spanish March of Catalonia; then in the twelth century the Capetians of France and Henry VI of Germany. We may note also that Roger I established a peace of his own just before he assumed the Sicilian crown in 1130.

The princes had no intention of obeying the Truce themselves. William fought Harold on a Saturday. Anna Comnena noted that the Byzantine church did its best to halt warfare on holy days; but the western knights attacked Byzantion itself in Holy Week, with their contingents full of armed and fighting priests, and with no attention

paid to the ban on looting churches.[28] England, whose system of law
and order was so much in advance of the continent, never knew the
Truce. The difference between the two societies is shown by the
comparison of the Truce with the peaceguild set up at London under
Aethelstane; member bishops and reeves were to carry out previously
issued royal decrees. Its members were divided into groups of ten,
each of which had a headman; and these groups were linked in
sections of a hundred. The group-headman and the headman of the
hundred formed a committee administering the common fund to
which each member contributed. Once a month the committee met
to take account of the guild's affairs, then to feast. This was no
merchant guild but a voluntary association to maintain peace and
security in daily life by catching thieves and recovering stolen goods,
while, like all organizations of the time, providing religious services.[29]

The episodes of the Peace and the Truce of God give us much
insight into the minds and hearts of men of the eleventh century.
Old sanctions and systems that held men together were breaking
down under the feudalizing movement which involved both anarchy
and a struggle for centralization. Men turned to the religion which
was said to hold the key to salvation and a good life; they sought to
find new forms of organization defined in religious terms which
seemed to promise a way out, a new basis of harmony. But the great
men of the world, lay and ecclesiastical, struck them down in the
name of the religion invoked; and tried to use for their own benefit
some of the very terms thrown up by the commoners. In a dark and
desperate way the terms of protest, seeking a new unity, and the
terms used for the consolidation of power, came together in the
transports and exaltations, in the brutal self-seeking of the Crusades.
Uprooted or fettered peasants, and landless younger sons of the
nobility contributed their contradictory hopes and fears to the total
situation. Dreams of a more fraternal system merged with a ruthless
determination to gain land and property by any means from the
enemy: the alien who exists outside the Christian comity. And the
ways in which wild dream and ruthless quest combined in any
individual were endlessly varied.

Now the question of William and the English crown, his relations
with Edward and Harold, son of Godwin. We possess only the Norman version of much of these matters, together with some hints from
works like the *Encomium* of Emma. The Norman version was worked
up with the utmost care to make William appear the champion
of feudal ethics against the perjurer Harold. A tractate was probably
compiled in 1066 to impress the pope and other princes with his
claim and to blacken Harold as a disloyal usurper; William of Poitiers

and others used this work. The thesis ran that the childless Edward appointed William as his heir because of kinship, gratitude for benefits that he and his family had received, and recognition of William's suitable qualities as ally and successor. The English Council or Witan had agreed and sworn to support William; the earl of Wessex, Godwin, had given William hostages as the final ratification. Robert of Jumièges, the Norman who became archbishop of Canterbury, was named as Edward's representative in the affair; so the date must have been 1051-2. Robert had been translated to the see in early 1051; and he visited Normandy on his way to get the pallium at Rome – some time before 21 June. One text of the *Anglo-Saxon Chronicle* mentions that after the discord between Godwin and Edward in 1051:

> Then soon came duke William from beyond the sea with a great retinue of Frenchmen, and the king received him and as many of his companions as it pleased him, and let him go again. In the same year William the priest was given the bishopric of London, which had been given to Spearhafoc.

We can disregard this statement, which has no support from the other texts or from other sources; it probably represents some confused account of Robert's journeys, which may in turn have been conflated with accounts of the visit paid by Eustace of Boulogne in 1051. Godwin's third son, Tostig, about this time married Baldwin's sister.[30]

The improbability of a visit by William is increased by the fact that at this time he was taken up with the siege of Domfront. But it is quite likely that Edward, in the midst of his conflict with Godwin, did agree to suggestions made by Robert of Jumièges and came to some agreement about accepting William as his heir. He would thus have gained Normandy as an ally if he were driven to a prolonged war with Godwin. William's attempts to build up a sort of northern maritime league fits in with such a conjecture. The emperor had won English naval aid against Flanders in 1049; and though William may not have had any clear hopes at this date of winning the English throne, he may well have hoped to get much benefit for himself from an accord between Normandy, Boulogne, Flanders, and England, which would have freed him for his self-aggrandizing policy on the continent.

Edward owed Normandy a debt of gratitude for having been allowed to use it as a refuge; but in early years his hope of becoming king must have seemed slender, and the Normans seem to have made no serious attempt to back him. The rapid breakdown of the Danish

line in Harold and Harthacnut must have come as a surprise. While
the two Danish claimants were quarrelling in Denmark and then
diverted by the invasion under Magnus of Norway, Edward was
elected in London as the result of a strong sudden movement in
favour of the ancient native dynasty; he was elected by acclamation
even before Harthacnut was buried. He owed nothing for his accession to William, who was a boy of about fourteen at the time,
though his long stay at Rouen had made him feel at home with Normans. Whether or not he dangled before William the bait of the
English throne in the early 1050s for diplomatic reasons, he certainly
did not hold to the plan of a Norman succession; for after 1054 he
took strong steps in Germany and Hungary for the return of the
English princes exiled by Cnut. It would indeed have been odd if a
man carried to the throne on a wave of English feeling had not
wanted to perpetuate the English line. As he seems to have been too
ascetic to beget a son, he had no choice but to turn to the exiles.

In the early 1050s, moreover, William was too entangled in local
politics to have given much thought to what was then so remote a
possibility as the English throne. But it is very likely that the
suggestions made at this time planted the seed which lay quiet in his
mind for some years, then germinated in the early 1060s as his power
increased and the uncertainties of the situation in England grew more
obvious. Edward had no right in any event to will his kingdom away,
however important his wishes might have been in affecting his
council and the people. But it seems highly probable that what turned
William's thoughts firmly towards England was the remarkable
chance that put Harold in his control in 1064.

For this event an important early testimony is that of the Bayeux
Tapestry. The traditional view that it was made for Odo bishop of
Bayeux is probably correct in view of its connection with Bayeux
cathedral and Odo's prominence in its scenes; even the three insignificant persons mentioned on it (Vital, Wadard and Thorold) all seem
to be retainers from the Bayeux area.[31] Further it is the only document which sets Harold's oath-taking at Bayeux. In addition, the
existence of an earlier tapestry in Bayeux cathedral suggests that Odo
probably had the tapestry made for one of his residences; we hear
that the palace he built in Rome was remarkable for its luxury and
splendid decorations.[32]

The designer seems to have been of the fine Canterbury school,
with a keen interest in factual detail; the needlewomen are far more
likely to have been English than French. For fifteen years Odo was
Earl of Kent and gave lands near Canterbury to the three vassals
mentioned above. William of Poitiers, telling of the spoils of the
Conquest, mentions how William's new robes excited wonder in

Normandy. William of Malmesbury knew of a long line of famous needlewomen, which included King Edward's wife and Margaret, sister of Edgar the Aetheling. Matilda of Flanders employed English seamstresses and *Domesday Book* says that in Edward's time Alwid or Aelfgyth the Maid held two hides in the hundred of Ashendon (Bucks), 'which Godric the sheriff granted her as long as he was sheriff, on condition of her teaching his daughter embroidery work'. She may have been the widow Leviet of Leofgyth, who held land in Wiltshire in 1086; she 'made and still makes the gold fringe for the King and Queen'.[33] The English character of the Tapestry is put beyond doubt by the form used for Hastings: *at Hestenga Caestra* – by the crossed D (turning *d* into *th*), and by the dot over the y in the name *Gyrd*.

On the Tapestry we see Edward speaking with his attendants, one of whom is probably Harold. Harold then rides with his knights to Bosham, prays and feasts, and goes aboard ship. Reaching the land of Count Gui of Ponthieu, he is held in prison at Beaurain. He confers with Gui till messengers come from William of Normandy. Another messenger, perhaps an Englishman asking for help, is received by William, and Gui conducts Harold to the latter. William leads Harold to the palace (where an English lady Aegifu gestures towards a clerk, who has been taken as her accomplice in some scandal). The next scenes show William marching with Harold against Conan in Brittany. They reach Mont St Michel, and cross to Dol, where Harold uses his strength to pull two Norman soldiers out of the quicksands. Conan flees; his castle of Dinan is invested until he offers up the keys on his lance-point. Harold, who has been shown, it seems, rendering the two primary services of a vassal, *consilium* and *auxilium*, receives arms from William as a sign of knighthood. (He must in fact have laughed at William's inconclusive campaign and compared it with his own efficient wars in Wales.) William and Harold leave for Bayeux. There Harold, laying his hands on some sacred relics, takes an oath before William. The text runs: 'William came to Bayeux where Harold took an oath to duke William.' We see Harold standing in William's presence between two reliquaries, with an outstretched hand on each. He then sails back to England and gloomily approaches Edward.[34]

On the tapestry the reasons for the departure and the capture by Gui – crucial points for the interpretation of the voyage – are not explained. We merely see Harold going off with hounds and falcons; and they stay with him till he reaches Rouen, where he gives them to William, so that it appears these highly valued gifts were intended for the duke. (They are common as costly gifts in the *chansons de geste*; Wace mentions in another context that Edward gave William

dogs and birds and 'whatever other good and fair gifts' he could find
that suited a man of high degree.)[35] No writer gives a plausible
reason for the voyage; and the *Anglo-Saxon Chronicle* is unaware
that it happened at all. Eadmer, an Englishman devoted to Anselm,
who should have known the English tradition, says that Harold asked
for leave 'to go to Normandy and set free his brother and his nephew
who were being held there as hostages'. Edward agreed, though with
forebodings of disaster. Harold, trusting his own judgment, put to
sea with 'a lordly provision of gold and silver, and costly raiment'.
A storm came up and the ship was driven into the river Maye of
Ponthieu, where Harold was arrested. He bribed a man to report the
event to William, who then demanded the prisoner under threat of
war. Harold was received in Normandy 'with all honour'. After
a while William asked him to support his claim to the English throne,
saying that Edward had promised it when they were both young.
Harold in fear swore on relics to support William if he were still
alive. On his return Edward reminded him of the prophecy that the
journey 'might bring untold calamity upon this kingdom'.[36]

A son and a grandson of Godwin, Wulfnoth and Hakon, had indeed
been brought up at the Norman court. How they got there is an
enigma. It is hard to find any moment when Godwin might have
agreed to let William have them as hostages. In 1051 he was at
loggerheads with Edward and Robert of Jumièges; after his return
from exile he would certainly not have sent them to Normandy. We
may conjecture that the pair had been left behind in England during
the exile of Godwin and his sons, and that Edward had handed them
over during his year of independence. Their existence is by far the
strongest point in the case for some deal having been made between
Edward and William in 1051-2. But no writer of the period or later
on gives any explanation; and there may have been reasons quite
unknown to us for their presence in Normandy. Eadmer's statement
that Harold's voyage was connected with them has however a certain
plausibility.

William of Malmesbury makes the whole thing an accident.
'Harold was at his country-seat of Bosham; he went for sport aboard
a fishing-boat, and to prolong the entertainment put out to sea. A
sudden storm came up and drove him and his companions on to the
Ponthieu coast.' Then he was captured by a crowd that gathered
from all quarters, 'as was their native custom' – presumably to repel
sea-raiders. Harold craftily pretended that he had been sent with a
message for William. In Brittany, 'Harold, well proved in both ability
and courage, won the Norman's heart, and, still more to ingratiate
himself, of his own accord, confirmed to him by oath the Coast of
Dover, which was under his jurisdiction, and the Kingdom of Eng-

land on Edward's death.'[37] Henry of Huntingdon declares, 'Harold was crossing the sea to Flanders when he was driven by storm on the Ponthieu coast.' Brought to William, he 'took a solemn oath on the most holy relics of the saints that he would marry his daughter and King Edward's death would aid his designs upon England'. But how confused traditions could become is shown by the tales Henry then proceeds to tell of the next year:

In the royal palace at Winchester Tostig seized his brother Harold by the hair in the king's presence while he was serving the king with wine. It had been a source of envy and hatred that the king showed a higher regard for Harold though Tostig was the elder brother. So, in a sudden paroxysm of passion, he could not hold back from this sudden attack on his brother. But the king predicted that their ruin was at hand and the Almighty's vengeance would no longer be deferred. Such was the cruelty of these brothers that on seeing a well-ordered farm they ordered the owner and all his family to be killed in the night and took possession of the dead man's property. And these were the justiciars of the realm.

Tostig went off from the king and his brother in great wrath and made for Hereford, where Harold had purveyed large supplies for the king's use. There he butchered all his brother's servants and enclosed a head or an arm in each of the vessels holding wine, mead, ale, pigment, mulberry wine, and cider, sending a message to the king that when he came to the farm he would find plenty of salt meat and that he would bring more with him. For this horrible crime the king commanded him to be banished and outlawed.

The tale about the arms and legs has been transferred from Caradoc, son of Gruffyd, who, according to Florence of Worcester (under the year 1065), was guilty of the butchery.

There is thus surprisingly little light to be got from the chroniclers. Eadmer's remark about the hostages and Huntingdon's about Flanders are plausible; and Malmesbury's remark about a prolonged sporting trip fits in with the hounds and birds of the Tapestry. But the one point common to all the tales is that a storm came up and Harold was driven off course. The notion then that Harold had been sent by Edward to confirm his position as heir gains no support from any version and is highly unlikely from every angle. What would Harold have been thinking about the accession in 1063-4? He well knew his own strong position; he knew that both Normandy and Denmark would claim the throne as soon as it was vacant. Edward the Aetheling, who would have provided a rallying point for the English cause, was dead. He had been treated in Hungary as a royal prince and had married a lady of the imperial house. He must have hesitated before leaving his assured rank in the empire for the uncertainties of England, for he postponed his return at least two years after it had been negotiated. Soon after he landed in England, before he had reached the court, he died. The *Chronicler* under 1057 complains that 'we do not know why it was so arranged that he could not see king Edward his kinsman'. Clearly he and his cause had enemies in England, but we cannot identify them, unless they were the Normans and other foreigners in Edward's entourage.[38] Harold does not appear to have been unfriendly; his visit to Flanders late in 1056 seems to have been connected with the preparation for the prince's welcome; and he took no action against his son Edgar, who was, however, too young in 1064–6 to be considered as the king in the dangerous situation of that time. The last step, surely, that Harold would have taken of his own accord in 1064 was to put himself at the mercy of William in Normandy.

The Tapestry provides by far the most coherent and likely account of Harold's misadventure. Though putting a Norman viewpoint, it portrays Harold as heroic and does not try to belittle him. Various difficulties are raised. The Tapestry describes the oath as taken at Bayeux; William of Poitiers puts it at Bonneville (a site he knew), and Orderic (well-informed, though writing in the twelfth century) mentions Rouen. Commentators have tried to explain the discrepancy away: William could have made a detour to Bayeux from the road between Mont St Michel and Rouen; or relics from Bayeux might have been taken to Bonneville. But the divergences in tradition remain.[39] The intrusive episode of the Cleric and the Lady may represent the designer who prepared the cartoon for embroidery work and perhaps transferred it to the material; the lady would then be the woman in charge of the embroiderers – we noted an Aelfgyth who taught embroidery in the very year of the Conquest. We can then amend the text to read: 'Here Duke William comes with Harold to his Palace where [are] a certain Clerk and Aelfgiva.' The latter may be introduced as eye-witnesses; or there may be an *oratio obliqua* illustrating what Harold is telling William and his court. (Later, the reason why the deathbed scene follows the funeral may be that two officials are telling Harold that he has been named successor by the dying Edward, who is represented. Hence the use of the term *defunctus*: Edward has ended his term as king and Harold is to take over.)[40]

If the Tapestry was made for Odo, as seems fairly certain, we should expect a version of the events close to that current in

William's court. William of Poitiers is explicit about Harold's pledge:

> First to be the *vicarius* of the duke at King Edward's court; second to use all his influence and wealth to confirm the duke in possession of the kingdom after Edward's death, third to set a garrison of the duke's knights in Dover castle at his own charge, and fourth to maintain and supply garrisons in other parts of England at the duke's will and his own charge.

In return Harold, after paying homage to the duke, was to be confirmed in all his lands and dignities.

It has been claimed that all this rings true in detail, though William and Harold may not have understood the compact in the same way. As here stated, Harold placed himself under oath in the position of an executor in Roman law.[41] But we might more cogently argue that the formulation is suspect because it is all too carefully precise, and that it represents rather the way in which Norman lawyers tried to fabricate a binding oath. Harold certainly did nothing about the garrisons he was supposed to have bound himself to provide. Any steps in such a direction, or any protests by William that they had not been carried out, could hardly have failed to get into the *Chronicle*; nor did the Normans even claim that protests were made. It seems certain that Edward had long dropped any ideas of a Norman succession and that he expected or wished Harold to succeed him. On this important point William of Poitiers several times makes Edward turn to Harold: the last thing he would have done if there were any chance of denying it. Thus, after telling of Harold's burial, he utters a final word: 'Your doom proves how lawfully you were raised up by Edward's dying gift.' That is, Harold had been proved a villain in God's eyes. The Anon of the *Life of Aedward* and later the English chroniclers agree that Harold received the king's bequest; and in the Tapestry Harold crowned has the central position, with the words *Haroldus Rex*. The Normans essentially based their whole case on Harold's perjury.

The misadventure of Harold, then, in being driven by a storm or some accident across the Channel in 1064 was crucial for the Norman Conquest of England.

CHAPTER V

THE NORMANS IN
THE SOUTH

As the Viking raids and invasions had been a movement of
'barbarians' from outside into the Christian pale of western Europe, so
the holy wars, following on the episodes of the Peace and Truce of
God, were an outwards movement, of the same restless sort, mainly
but not wholly into the infidel regions surrounding the papal west.
They had already been foreshadowed in the early tenth century, and
the area where the outwards movement began was Spain. Here the
enemy were the Moslems who controlled the western Mediterranean
from Tunis to Catalonia and threatened Italy, where they sacked St
Peter's in Rome in 846. Pope John in 915, with the Byzantines, helped
to form a league of Christian princes for the purpose of ousting the
Moslems from their castle on the Garigliano; in 941 the Byzantines
joined Hugh of Provence to attack their castle at Fréjus. Hugh let
the expedition down, but in 972 a league of Provençal and Italian
princes took the castle. In the tenth century the Moslems in Spain

were masters of almost the whole peninsular and the main Christian region, Leon, was being battered. The vizier named al-Manzur, the Victorious (known to the Spaniards as Almanzor), sacked Leon in 991, and in 997 he burned the city of St James of Compostella, a pilgrim centre ranking next to Jerusalem and Rome, though he left the shrine standing. In 986 he took Barcelona and was expected to cross the Pyrenees, when he died in 1002. Piratic attacks went on. Corsairs from Africa plundered Antibes in 1003, Pisa in 1005 and 1016, Narbonne in 1020. But largescale hostilities had slackened.

A counter-attack was planned by Sancho III of Navarre. The effort in 1014 to form a league against the infidels failed through the deaf ear turned by Robert of France. But Sancho won the support of the abbey of Cluny, which as the centre of the monastic reform movement was ready to take up the cause of pilgrims. Cluniac influence may have brought the Normans in, or the latter may have been ready to rush in anywhere where loot and land were to be won. Roger of 'Tosni went with a strong force to the aid of the Countess Erseline of Barcelona in 1018, only a few years after Normans had started riding to Apulia. William of Gascony joined Sancho in an attack on the emir of Saragossa. Blessings from Rome as well as from Cluny had gone with the fighters, so the war assumed the character of a crusade. In 1063 the king of Aragon, about to launch a big offensive, was murdered by a Moslem, to the vast indignation of the Christian West. Pope Alexander II promised an indulgence for all who fought in Spain, and began gathering an army. William of Montreuil recruited in north Italy. (Thus the same pope organized a crusade in Spain, blessed the Norman invasion of Sicily, and made William's invasion of England a sort of avenging crusade.) A brother of the Aragonese queen recruited men in north France. Geoffrey of Aquitaine, bringing the largest contingent, was given command. The crusade did little but sack a town which provided considerable plunder. But the signal had been given. French and Norman knights continued to cross the Pyrenees to kill and loot. Pope Gregory VII called on all Christian princes to lend a hand. Reminding them that the Spanish realm belonged to the papal see, he announced that Christian knights might keep any land they won from the infidels. Expeditions were organized in 1078, under the duke of Burgundy, and in 1080, under the count of Aquitaine. William of Normandy in his deathbed speech is said to have pardoned Baudri fitz Nicholas whom he had imprisoned for foolishly going to Spain 'without permission'; he admired Baudri's courage but objected to his wanderlust. (In fact Baudri on returning from Spain had taken advantage of dislocations in Normandy to encroach on his neighbours; and he was said to have remarked that no bastard would ever rule over Normans.)

The expeditions went on till 1085, when Toledo was captured. This city remained a strong seat of Islamic scientific culture; a school of Christian translators was formed there and their works were of the utmost importance in transmitting texts to the West and stimulating scientific interests and activities. After 1085 came something of a Moslem revival, but knights from northern France, including Normandy, kept roaming into Spain. Pope Gregory VII gave absolution to those dying in battle. According to the papacy, the conquered land was to be held under ultimate papal suzerainty; and this principle was held by the pope to apply to the Norman war against Harold of England.[1]

In the early eleventh century Norman knights began to go off to south Italy as adventurers and freebooters. These men were very different from their ancestors of a few generations back who had irrupted into Normandy. The tribal element had quite gone. Moving with a few retainers, they were fully feudalized in outlook. It seems that Normans going on a pilgrimage to Jerusalem kept a piratic eye open for regions that could be plundered or seized. One tale says that in 1016 such a group (forty men according to William of Apulia) was at the pilgrim shrine of Monte Sant'Angelo (Monte Gargano) and was met by a Lombard noble from Bari, Meles. The Normans had a special veneration for the fighting archangel Michael and may well have frequented this shrine. Meles had led a revolt in 1009 against the Byzantines; the revolt was not crushed till 1018, but after some success Meles had to leave Bari. Now he asked the Normans for help; they promised to return with reinforcements next spring. Another tale says that homing pilgrims in 999 were at Salerno when a Saracen raid occurred; they rallied the people and defeated the raiders. Gaimar II, the ruler, asked them to stay, and they too said that they would soon return, with friends. (We know of no raid in 999, but there was one in 1016.)

Certainly round 1017 a body of Normans was in south Italy. They joined Meles at Capua and by early 1018 had driven the Byzantines from a wide area; but in June the central government had organized its forces and the Normans were badly defeated near Canne by the catapan Basil Boiannes. Meles escaped, wandered about, and soon died at Bamberg, at the German emperor's court. Gilbert, the Norman leader, was killed and his brother Rainulf was elected in his place. The Normans had lost Meles and his cause; but that was a minor matter. They could always find or make more causes. The first site they chose as headquarters was plagued with frogs; they found a better place, but soon moved on. Some sources attribute their migration to other reasons than a wish to help Meles. Leo of Ostia (writing near the end of the century, with earlier material at his disposal in the monastery of Monte Cassino) declares that forty Normans came to Capua: 'They had fled from the anger of the count of Normandy; and they were now with many of their fellows wandering about the countryside in the hope of finding someone ready to employ them.' Adémar of Chabannes merely says they came to Rome under Rodulf, 'and afterwards with the encouragement of pope Benedict [VIII, 1212–34] they attacked Apulia and laid everything waste.' Glaber states that Rodulf 'had incurred the displeasure of count Richard [II]' and 'came to Rome to state his case before pope Benedict'. The pope complained of 'the invasion of the Roman empire by the Greeks' and Rodulf offered to attack the latter 'as long as he had the support of the Italians'. So the pope 'addressed himself to the magnates of the region of Benevento, bidding them put themselves under Rodulf's orders'. Rodulf then attacked the Byzantines, 'killed many of them and took much booty'.[2] Rodulf was apparently Rodulf II of Tosny, head of a leading family in central Normandy. It seems clear that whether or not other Norman adventurers had come into south Italy to fight for Meles or on the mere chance of loot, the invasion began seriously with Rodulf and was instigated by the papacy for the purpose of upsetting the Byzantine dominion in the south.

But the Norman adventurers were always ready to change sides or allegiances according to the fortunes of war and the lures of loot. For many years they were involved in all sorts of petty conflicts and robberies as well as playing their part in the major struggles of the region. They entered the services of the princes of Salerno, Capua, Naples, Amalfi, Gaeta; some even served under the Byzantines. They thus helped to worsen the disorder and confusion of south Italy until the time came when they could change from mere mercenaries into the ruling lords.[3]

The region was torn by many conflicting forces: the various local princes, the Lombards and the Byzantines, and soon the Papacy and the Germans. The Lombards invaded north Italy and settled extensively in the mid-sixth century, with Pavia their capital; but some went south and set up dukedoms there. After Charlemagne took Pavia, the Lombard centre shifted south; and by 1000 there were three strong rulers: at Capua, Benevento and Salerno. The dominating power was the eastern empire, which claimed to control Italy south of Rome (south of a line running roughly from Termoli to Terracina); but inside this area were the Lombard principalities, and sea-based city-states had grown up at Naples, Gaeta and Amalfi. The

main Byzantine official, a catapan, was located at Bari; and in Calabria and the area round Otranto Greek was normally spoken. Even
the Lombard cities were saturated with Byzantine culture. In the
half-century before 1025 the Byzantines had made the Adriatic fairly
safe for Christian ships, and thus had made possible the rise of the
mercantile city-states. They were challenged however by Islam. The
Byzantines had failed to retake Sicily, and Sardinia and Corsica also
remained in Moslem hands. And to the north they had to face
continual pressure from Rome. The Latin rite prevailed in most of
Apulia, among the Lombards, and in city-states like Naples, Gaeta and
Amalfi; and there were the two important pilgrim sites of the Latin
church, Monte Cassino, the home of Benedictine monasticism, and
Monte Sant'Angelo. Soon the German emperors, often at odds with
the papacy and attempting to control it, were to become another
important political force in Italy. Otto the Great claimed south Italy
as part of the dowry of his wife, a Greek princess, but was thwarted
by Moslems and Byzantines.

The papacy had long been in a degraded condition, with disputed
elections and puppet-popes fighting one another. But the reform
movement had been gathering strength. Reform had two ecclesiastical meanings. For the monasteries it meant the ending of many
abuses, a revival of ascetic self-dedication; for the papacy it meant
the throwing off of secular controls and the elevation of the pope
above all kings and princes. The assertion of papal power centered
on the question of investiture, with the popes fighting to take from
secular rulers the right to invest church-dignitaries. The new energies
and demands of the church came from the general productive
advances of the last few centuries. The forces that built up the secular
state had also strengthened the church, with its great landed estates
and treasures, its virtual monopoly of literacy and all the organizing
possibilities that went with that. The theocratic compromise which
had carried on since Charlemagne was nearing its end. By that compromise the ruler had defended the Christian faith as a sort of semi-
divine or priestly figure anointed by the church, while the church
accepted his role as long as he gave support to its privileges and
properties. But now the church was beginning to react against some
of the rulers' controls and their tendency to equate lay barons and
high ecclesiastics as vassals. It was the revived and jealous church that
was now seeking to assert itself all over Italy.

In explaining the exodus of knights from Normandy to Italy,
Amatus says that at home 'the people had increased so greatly that
the fields and forests were not long enough to provide for them'.[4]
The younger sons of large families were tempted by the chance to
seize land and valuables. There was certainly some truth in that;

and it clearly applied to a man like Tancred of Hauteville in the Cotentin, a small landlord with at least twelve sons and several daughters. But as well as economic pressures there were the bitter political struggles going on in Normandy. Many of the first migrants to Italy seem to have belonged to families who had suffered in the redistribution of landed estates that went on as feudal tenures and relationships grew stronger. Discontented lords or knights of this kind must have supplied many of the rebels who increased as the years went on; others of them, like Rodulf, 'fled from the anger of the duke' which their recalcitrancy had aroused. In Italy they watched for every local embroilment in which they might play a part. Thus in February 1027 the death of Gaimar IV produced disputes over the succession at Salerno; and later that year Pandulf III of Capua attacked Sergius IV of Naples and forced him into exile. Sergius apparently got help from a Norman, Rainulf, and won back Naples in 1029. Besides whatever wages had been paid during the war, Sergius in 1030 gave Rainulf and his comrades the hill-fortress of Aversa with its dependencies. Now at last some of the Normans had land and lordship in south Italy; and Aversa was well situated for warriors who wanted to play a part in the affairs of Naples, Capua, even Benevento and Salerno. The services of the Normans were ever more in demand, and they sold themselves to the highest bidder. Rainulf left Naples and went over to Capua, then left Capua for Salerno. In 1040 the Emperor Conrad II, who had come down into Italy, combined the territories of Capua and Salerno, giving a stronger position to Rainulf, who was count of Aversa and duke of Gaeta when he died in 1045. Before long his nephew Richard was to be accepted as prince of Capua.

Rodulf had given a clear political basis for the Norman irruption by making his agreement with the pope; Rainulf showed the way in which an astute, unscrupulous and daring Norman could reach baronial status. Normans flocked to Aversa, and the sons of Tancred of Hauteville began to ride southward. About 1035 William, Drogo (Dreux) and Humphrey, sons of Tancred's first wife, Muriella, set out. (Muriella bore two more sons; the second wife, Fressenda, bore seven.) In 1038 the Normans had their attention drawn to Sicily. The Byzantines took advantage of the civil war there among the emirs to send an expedition led by the giant general George Maniakes; in the ships were Varangians under Harold Hardrada. Some three hundred of the wilder Normans joined in, with Italians and Lombards; among them were the three Hautevilles. Norsemen who had come along the east routes were in the same host as Northmanni from the west. Maniakes took Syracuse. William de Hauteville saw the city's emir ride out on sortie; he charged and unhorsed him, leaving

him dead on the ground and earning the name of Bras de Fer. But
Maniakes was recalled. The Normans, anyhow, seem already to have
gone off after a dispute about Syracusan loot; Maniakes probably
repressed their exuberant rapine in a liberated Greek city.

Meles' son, Argyrus, in 1040 raised another revolt in Apulia. He
offered the Normans Melfi, a hill town on the Byzantine borders, as
their headquarters while they drove out the Greeks and shared the
land. Amatus cites him as saying: 'You still occupy the land given
to you, you live in it like mice in skirting.' From Melfi the Normans
went out raiding, killing, raping, devastating. Twice the Byzantines
were beaten. At the second battle Bras de Fer led them. In a state of
high fever he meant to watch from a hill, but was so stirred by the
sight of fighting that he jumped from his litter, charged down the
slopes, and led his men to victory. In September 1041 the Normans
captured the new catapan. The Apulian princes were jealous, and the
Normans were themselves torn by rivalries – the older men, settled
some twenty years before at Troia, refused to take orders from the
reckless upstarts of Melfi. Then Maniakes came back in favour with
the Byzantines; in the summer of 1042 he marched through the land,
burning and slaughtering even children, monks and nuns. But again
he found himself the victim of palace intrigues, revolted, and fell as
he defeated an imperial army in Bulgaria. The Normans had meanwhile invested Trani, a town loyal to the Byzantines; but Argyrus
betrayed them. He seems belatedly to have realized that they were a
far worse danger to his people than the Byzantines.

The Normans decided to set up their own chief and selected Bras
de Fer as count in September 1042. Needing an overlord, he turned
to Gaimar of Salerno, whom the Normans acclaimed as duke of
Apulia and Calabria. Gaimar gave William his niece in marriage and
divided the land won from the Greeks or yet to be won among twelve
leading Normans. The Lombard movement was at an end. More and
more Normans came riding in. They went on fighting the Byzantines
while robbing and wrecking peasants or anyone else who might
provide loot. In June 1045 Rannulf died and Gaimar invested Drogo
as count of Apulia, giving him his daughter as wife. At the moment
there were three popes competing for Rome, one in St Peter's, one in
the Lateran, one at S. Maria Maggiore. The Emperor Henry III, drawn
into Italy, held a synod at which all three popes were deposed and
Henry nominated a friend, the bishop of Bamberg, who, as Clement
I, crowned the emperor and his wife. For a while Henry repressed the
anarchy in Italy and invested Drogo as Duke and Magister of Italy
and Count of the Normans of All Apulia and Calabria.

Round this time, perhaps in 1047, there came to Italy Robert de
Hauteville, soon to be called the Guiscard, the Crafty. He was a man

of fine stature who rode a horse 'so small that his feet nearly touched the ground'. Anna Comnena, princess of Byzantion, described Robert with a frank admiration tempered by scorn for an upstart:

This Robert was Norman by descent, of insignificant origin, in temper tyrannical, in mind most cunning, brave in action, very clever in attacking the wealth and substance of magnates, most obstinate in achievement, for he did not allow any obstacle to prevent his executing his desire. His stature was so lofty that he surpassed even the tallest, his complexion was ruddy, his hair flaxen, his shoulders were broad, his eyes all but emitted sparks of fire, and in frame he was well-built where nature required breadth, and was neatly and gracefully formed where less width was necessary. So from tip to toe this man was well-proportioned, as I have repeatedly heard many say. Now Homer says of Achilles that when he shouted his voice gave his hearers the impression of a multitude in an uproar, but this man's cry is said to have put thousands to flight. Thus equipped by fortune, physique, and character, he was naturally indomitable and subordinate to nobody in the world. Powerful characters are ever like this, people say, even though they be of somewhat obscure descent.[5]

Malaterra, who knew him better, added that 'his gay and open manner was controlled by calculating prudence', and that he set about trying with lavish gifts and favours 'to collect a party of adherents who'd be devoted to furthering his fortunes'. No wonder that William of Normandy was fascinated by the tales that came back of Robert, and modelled himself on his bold and resolute character. William of Malmesbury says that he was in the habit of stimulating his own courage by reflecting on the Guiscard; for he thought it a dishonour 'if he yielded in valour to a man whom he excelled in rank', Robert being 'born in Normandy of middling parentage' and having gone off 'with fifteen knights to Apulia to rectify their penury in the pay of spiritless people. Not many years went by before he had established his dominions throughout the land by the amazing favour of God, for where his forces were inadequate he made up the deficiency by his wits.' Thus, by stimulating the ambitions of William and enlarging his whole horizon, men like Guiscard did much to bring about the invasion of England.[6]

Perhaps Drogo didn't like to enfeoff his brother Robert at once for fear of annoying fellow Normans who had served longer in the south. Robert went off on a career of endless skirmishes and small devastations, lurking in hill-caves and carrying on highway robbery until he joined Pandulf of Capua, but left him (says Amatus) when the promise of a castle and a daughter fell through. Pandulf, long a source of discord and trouble, died in February 1049. Robert returned to Drogo, who gave him command of a garrison in a hot malarial valley. But he soon moved on to healthier territory, becoming famed for his tricks. Once he got into an impregnable hilltop monastery by pretending to be dead in a coffin which his men brought up for a requiem mass. About this time he married Alberada, who seems to have been aunt of the Apulian baron of Buonalbergo.

Richard, son of Ascletin, unable to get a free hand at Aversa from Rainulf II, also turned to brigandage and grew in power. Challenging Rainulf, he was beaten and imprisoned. But in 1048, when Rainulf died and his infant son needed a regent, Richard was finally chosen and freed; for a while he governed in the child's name, then nothing more is heard of the child. Pope Clement lasted less than a year, the new pope whom Henry appointed lasted only twenty-three days. In December 1048 a council at Worms elected a tall red-haired Alsatian, Bruno, bishop of Toul, who had commanded an army at the time of Conrad I's expedition into Italy; he became pope as Leo IX. The Church was in a bad way; its appointments were put up to auction; priests usually didn't marry but had large families; tithes were unpaid; religious houses were lucky if they kept their treasures intact; monks and pilgrims to Monte Cassino were robbed by the Normans who systematically slashed vines and burned harvests. The people hated these brigands more than the Saracens and were provoked to reprisals. John, abbot of Fécamp, who had a narrow escape from death on a pilgrimage, wrote to the pope: 'Italian hatred of the Normans has now become so great that it's nearly impossible for a Norman, even if he's a pilgrim, to travel through the cities of Italy without being set upon, abducted, stript of all he has, beaten and chained up: all this if he doesn't give up the ghost in some fetid prison.'[7] (We can now see why, when the question of William of Normandy's marriage with Matilda came up around this time, the papacy tried to foil him.) All the while the Normans were extending their domains. Against them was the pro-Byzantine party led by Argyrus, the adherents of the pope, and the independents who saw the Normans as mere pests and wanted the old Italo-Lombard nobles back. Drogo, who had been one of the wilder leaders, was murdered on 10 August 1051 as he entered a chapel at Monte Ilaro. The pope went on raising an army; but Gaimar V said he would join the Normans if they were attacked. Then in June 1052 he was himself killed in Salerno by his four brothers-in-law. He was the last of the great Lombard princes of the south, a man of honour indeed compared with the Normans.

The pope had decided that the Normans must be driven out; he was particularly worried by the threat to Benevento, which had recently become a papal town. Argyrus, as representative of the Byzantines, promised support. Leo proclaimed the anti-Norman cause a holy one, and collected a large body of Lombard and Italian troops, plus German mercenaries from Swabia. At last he moved south, meaning to join up with the Byzantines. In early June 1053 he reached Benevento, with almost all the non-Norman nobles joining him. But the Normans, their left wing under the Guiscard, caught up with him at Civitate, and they routed his army, while he watched from the town ramparts. Escorted back to Benevento, he was in fact their prisoner. For nine months negotiations dragged on. Leo held out, hoping somehow to see 'this enemy nation expelled from the Church of Christ and Christianity avenged'. Then, worn out, he left in March 1054 and died on 18 April in the Lateran. Now the pope as well as the German emperor had to ratify the Norman gains.

This was the crucial moment of change in Norman fortunes. In the years 1054–7 those in Aversa moved northwards for Gaeta and Aquino; in June 1058 Richard captured Capua and overthrew the Lombard dynasty. To the south the Guiscard was steadily extending his conquests in Calabria; after the death of his brother Humphrey he commanded the Norman advance into Apulia. In 1058 Gisulf II of Salerno, his main obstacle to the west, agreed to treat with him. He gave his sister Sigelgaita to Robert, who repudiated his Norman wife. Sigelgaita was a big, stentorian-voiced woman, whose prowess on the battlefield became legendary. She was to bear Robert a son; but it was the son Mark by the first wife who inherited his energies, a great burly swashbuckling character, nicknamed Bohemond after the giant of that name.

The union of papacy and Byzantines against the Normans could not last. An embassy soon made things worse. Cardinal Humbert, who led it from Rome, ended by delivering a manifesto denouncing the eastern church for simony, priests' marriages, jettisoning the Law of Moses, refusing any communion with men who shaved, encouraging castration, insisting on rebaptizing Latins and baptizing women in labour even in their death-throes. Most of the charges were false; where correct, as regards castration, they applied equally to the papacy. The papacy remained as hostile as ever to the Normans; but a party was growing which urged conciliation. How could the popes stand up against both the eastern and the western emperors if they had the terrible Normans threatening them from the south? The Normans, as the strongest power in Italy, were indispensable for a papacy that sought to assert itself against secular domination.

Robert had been made guardian of the infant son of Humphrey, a cruel and jealous man. He was now marked out as the leader of the

Normans. His elder brother Geoffrey had not distinguished himself; William and Mauger were new arrivals and younger. By August 1057 Robert had seized all the lands of his ward and was formally acclaimed his brother's successor. In a few years he had become the biggest landowner and most stalwart warrior in the south, with only Richard of Capua as a rival. An eighth brother now turned up, Roger, twenty-six years old, who followed the usual practice of going first to Melfi. In 1057, however, we find him in Calabria with Robert, learning the freebooter's trade. Much of west Calabria had been subdued; but soon there was a break between the two brothers, probably Robert's fault. Though often generous, he seems to have been stingy with Roger, who couldn't pay his retinue. Early in 1058 Roger left him angrily, turned to his brother William, and was given a castle at Scalea, well situated for horse-thieving and highway robbery. Out of the loot gained by one attack on merchants (says Malaterra, who wrote his chronicle later at Robert's own request) he was able to engage a hundred more soldiers. In 1058 came a bad famine. The Norman depredations, we are told, had not left an olive-tree or cornfield; men had to sell their children into slavery and to make bread from river-weeds, bark, acorn and chestnuts. At last they rose in desperate revolt. Roger and Robert had to join in hunting them down.

In 1059 the papal party which supported a union with the Normans had its way. Things had been going badly. For a year there had been no pope. A struggle went on between the adherents of reform and the old aristocratic Roman families who looked on the papacy as their property. After nominating one of his councillors, who became Victor VII, the emperor died in October 1056, to be succeeded by a five-year-old son, Henry IV. Victor died in July 1057 and the party taking his body back to Germany was ambushed and robbed at Ravenna, where they hastily buried him. Archdeacon Hildebrand of the reform group now dominated the papal curia. His anti-Norman candidate was elected, but died in less than eight months. Conflicts with the Roman nobles led to open war. Hildebrand's next choice, a Burgundian, became Nicholas II. His party was admitted to Rome by a baptized Jew, who opened the gates of Trastevere. They stormed the Lateran, and the Roman candidate, Benedict X, fled to Galeria. Now it was that the Hildebrandines, hard put, called in the Normans, who were delighted. A large body advanced north, camped before Galeria, pillaged the regions, and stormed the walls. Benedict was publicly defrocked.

Hildebrand, with Norman backing, was in a strong position, and helped by the fact that a child was now on the imperial throne. He set up his own system of election, which has carried on until our day.

Since Lothair I (824) a pope had been chosen by the entire clergy and nobles of the Roman people, but was consecrated only after taking the oath to the emperor. In April 1059 a Lateran synod handed the election over to the cardinals; after they had chosen a pope, they might allow the rest of the clergy and people to give their assent. The throwing off of secular controls was glossed over by a vague phrase about 'the honour and respect due to Henry'. This turning point in papal history had been made possible by the Normans, a few years earlier damned as devilish brigands. The alliance was ratified in August at a synod held at Melfi. Pope Nicholas II received Richard and the Guiscard there as his vassals: Richard was hailed as prince of Capua and Robert as 'Duke of Apulia and Calabria by the grace of God and St Peter, and, with their help in the future, Duke of Sicily'. Robert in return swore to protect the person and status of the pope and 'to support the Holy Roman Church everywhere and against all men, in holding and acquiring the possession of St Peter'.[8] Further, he swore to support the new method of electing a pope. A lesser issue at the synod was the marriage of priests; the condemnation had no effect, though the bishop of Trani was defrocked.

The break between the papacy and Byzantion was intensified, and the Normans played their part by renewed attacks on the Greek areas. (The Byzantine government over these years was very pre-occupied with the Turks and the Pechenegs.) Robert went on making inroads into Calabria, gaining Reggio, Gerace and other areas, as well as Otranto in the south of Apulia. Apart from the vassals of Richard of Capua, all the Normans in Italy were now subject to him; and though he had to deal with the inevitable rebellions of unruly and ambitious vassals, he was able to prepare for the decisive attack on Bari, centre of Byzantine administration. By August 1068 the siege by sea and land was beginning; and after two years and eight months the city surrendered. Guiscard entered on 16 April 1071.

But meanwhile an important new field of operations had been opened up. Robert turned to Sicily and the pope blessed his expedition. The emirs of the island were disunited and the country population was largely Christian; but the conquest was to take thirty-one years, partly because the Normans could not give it their undivided attention. Their mainland rear was continually disturbed by revolts or Byzantine intrusions. Robert was at Mileto in February 1061 when one of the emirs asked his help. He ravaged the coast, took Milazzo, and got a good deal of plunder, but he failed at Messina and was harried home to Reggio by a Saracen fleet. In May Roger used the night of a new moon to cross and land five miles south of Messina. Before Robert set sail with the bulk of the army, he had taken the town. Marching inland, the Normans gained a victory at Enna, but couldn't take the stronghold. In autumn they built their first Sicilian castle near the ruins of ancient Aluntium not far from the north coast. After returning to the mainland, Roger was back in December. The stronghold Troina surrendered and he spent Christmas there.

Judith of Evreux, whom he had wooed in Normandy, had now arrived in Calabria. She was the daughter of a first cousin of Duke William, and at home Roger would have had slight chance of winning her. Now things were changed. But what brought Judith was a quarrel between the duke and her half-brother guardian, abbot of St-Evroul-sur-Ouche. The abbot fled south with Judith, her brother and sister, and eleven monks. Robert welcomed him; he was already encouraging the settlement of Latin monks in Calabria to offset the influence of the Greek houses. Now he founded the house of St Eufemia with the liturgic and musical tradition of St Evroul, and the place became the mother-house of many Sicilian foundations.

The year 1062 started well, but failed to live up to its promise. Roger, married, had in correct Norman style to enfeoff his wife and family in a way befitting their station; and Robert still shrank from fulfilling his promise to share conquests. Now, irritated with Roger's demands, he besieged him in Mileto. Malaterra tells a tale that brings out the odd combination of reckless behaviour with shrewd calculation in these men, the mixture of the chivalric with their too often cold and ruthless violences. One night Roger slipped out to seek aid from near Gerace. Robert hotly pursued, but had the gates slammed in his face. So he hid under a cowl, got inside the town, and made his way to a friend, Basil, who with his wife Melita asked him to stay and dine. A servant, recognizing him, gave the alarm; the house was surrounded by a raging crowd. Basil was struck down before he could reach the nearest church; Melita was impaled on a stake. Robert shouted for silence and gave a speech. For their own sakes let his enemies not lose their heads at finding the duke of Apulia in their power or they might see a reversal of fortune; he had come with no hostile aim; they had sworn him fealty and he had never played them false; it would be shameful if a whole city, forgetting its oath, hurled itself on a single unarmed man; let them remember that his death would bring down the lasting hostility of the Normans and would be mercilessly avenged. The crowd was calmed. Robert was taken to a place of safety. His followers outside the town heard what had happened and rushed to ask aid of Roger who was encamped a few miles away. He rode to Gerace in full state, called the elders into the open space before the gates, and angrily asked why they had not at once handed Robert over to him; he, not they, had suffered from Robert's duplicity; if they didn't hand him over, the town's farms and vineyards would be razed before morning. Robert was delivered up. Roger dropped his show of anger and the brothers embraced with tears of joy. Robert granted Roger all he asked, and they rode off together to Mileto. But, once secure, Robert regretted his concession. There was more fighting before Roger got what he wanted.

So Roger didn't return to Sicily until high summer of 1062, taking Judith with him. He garrisoned Troina and left her there. Meanwhile the local Greeks, finding the Normans worse oppressors than the Saracens, rose and tried to get Judith as a hostage; all day there was fighting in the streets. Roger left Nicosia which he was investing, and hurried back, to find the Saracens had joined the Greeks. He ordered a retreat to the area round the citadel and barricaded the approaches. For four months the siege went on; winter arrived early; Norman supplies were low. Troina, 4000 feet above the sea, was chilly, and there was little fuel. Judith and Roger had a single woollen cloak, worn by day and used as blanket by night. But one day early in 1063 Robert learned that the Moslems were drunk with the region's red wine. The Normans attacked in the windy night, moving on deep soundless snow, and took the beseiging lines. Harsh reprisals and a great feast followed.

Roger's main problem was manpower for extended campaigns. The Saracens were beginning to unite and the Normans in Apulia were too entangled with endless small wars to spare many reinforcements. Roger had to return to the mainland for more horses. Judith, in command of Troina, made regular day and night rounds. But Roger soon returned and with his nephew Serlo went on harassing the Saracens. In the summer he had to turn to the east and meet the main enemy force, swollen by new recruits from Africa, under the Prophet's green banner. The Normans were vastly outnumbered and for three days at Cerami the two armies watched one another. Then, says Malaterra, 'our men, unable any longer to bear seeing the enemy so near without attacking them, confessed themselves with the utmost piety, made their penances and then, trusting in God's mercy and sure of his aid, rode off into battle'. After a daylong fight they routed the Saracens and looted their camp.

They seized their camels and all else they found there. Next day they left to seek out all those 20,000 footsoldiers who had run off into the mountains for refuge. Many of these they killed. The rest they took captive and sold as slaves, getting a great price for each man. But after a short while the contagion that rose from the corpses rotting on the battlefield drove them away and they went back to Troina.[9]

E

Now they held securely the whole area from Troina to Messina. Malaterra tells of St George coming in person to join the Normans as they rode into battle. A section of the splendid booty, including four camels, was sent to Pope Alexander II.

Once again there was trouble at Rome. Alexander had been chosen by Hildebrand and the cardinals; Honorius II was set up by the Empress-regent Agnes and supported by the Lombard bishops. Agnes was soon deposed but her pope held out till 1064. Alexander was in bad need of allies. Once again the papacy reform group had to lean on Norman aid. Alexander sent Roger a papal banner and proclaimed absolution for all who joined him in the holy work of freeing Sicily from the heathen. Now the invasion was a crusade in the eyes of Europe – a point that Duke William did not forget when soon afterwards he wanted all possible sanctification for his attack on another island, England.

In August 1063 the people of Pisa sent a fleet to help capture Palermo; but Roger, while keen for controllable reinforcements, had no wish for allies who would claim an important share of his gains. He refused the aid and the Pisans failed. In early 1064 Robert, with five hundred knights and some thousand footmen, came down into Calabria, and Roger met him in Cosenza. They planned their own assault on Palermo. But when Robert reached the city's outskirts by land, he encamped on a hill swarming with tarantulas. Malaterra says their bites caused 'a most poisonous wind' with thunderous farts; unless hot compresses or the like were applied to the bites, 'it is said that their very lives were in peril'. Robert hastily moved camp, but the nerves of the Normans had been shaken. After three months' seige nothing was achieved. The Norman forces were insufficient for anything like a quick victory. Roger moved his headquarters on to Petralia, taken in 1062, a rocky site from which he could swoop down on the region round Palermo and keep the Saracens on the defensive. Once more the latter began to succumb to internal dissensions. But for a few years there was a stalemate. Robert could do little to help his brother; in 1064 he had to meet a serious revolt of his Apulian vassals, which the Byzantines aided. Then the threat of the Seljuk Turks in the east of the Byzantine empire eased things for the Normans. In Byzantion a Cappadocian, Romanos Diogenes, was acclaimed emperor on the first day of 1068; he concentrated all his forces against the Turks. Robert's rebellious vassals lost heart. Robert suborned an officer of the sole remaining rebel, Geoffrey of Conversano, and took his town; the traitor was given the fief.

All these events in Italy and Sicily were closely followed in Normandy. During the years when William was struggling for survival, Richard of Capua and Robert Guiscard had become important men in an area more spectacular than north-west France. They had been honoured by pope and emperor, and in the 1060s they began the conquest of Sicily with all its riches. William of Normandy was deeply stirred by these achievements of men who at home had only been members of lesser baronial families; the thought of what they had done nerved him for his attack on England and he drew on their experience for dealing with the technical problems of invasion. Only by becoming king of England could he equal, let alone surpass, these men who had begun as mere knights. Further, he was ensured of papal backing because of the dependence of the reform-popes on the Normans of the South – because of the lucky chance that had turned them from moral pariahs into the supporters of Hildebrand. The same decade saw the invasions of Sicily and of England; in each case the invasion was turned by papal blessing into a sort of crusade.

Between 1059 and 1085 the papacy, confident in a new political and theological militancy, was eager to draw the western nobles into wars which it saw as furthering the Christian cause. It promised beatitude for death in battle and provided consecrated banners. Earlier, such a banner could be taken to signify a papal investiture and St Peter's Soldiers were papal vassals rather than fighters for the faith. But with the Hildebrandine reforms the Holy War became a definite and effective means of strengthening the papacy and drawing together the west under its leadership. Christ's Soldiers were no longer monks or hermits; now the term 'had come to denote the armed might of the west mobilized for war under papal leadership' (Douglas). Here we touch on one of the reasons for the rapid decline of the monks from their central position in the Christian scheme of the west after 1100. Christ's Soldier was now not so much fighting an inner battle in solitude against the devils of the spirit; he was an armed knight fighting an actual infidel or heretic. What he gained was now not so much treasure in heaven as loot and land on earth, of which a due share must be handed over to mother church.

It was ironic that the great strengthening of the Hildebrandine papacy and the creation of the concept of the Holy War should have been made possible by the support of the Normans who had been papally condemned as anti-Christian murderers and marauders. The anti-Christian robbers became the most Christian vassals and servants of the pope. Leo IX had made an attempt to build his own army, but the Normans frustrated it; after that Rome's only hope lay in the Normans if it was to throw off the domination of the German emperor. In view of the important results of the revival of the idea of the Holy War we may glance at its past history. The roots go far back, reaching to the days when Constantine the Great was said to have had his victory at the Milvian Gate in 312 presaged by the sign

of the cross in the sky: that is, the acceptance of war by Christians
arose out of the crucial event which was soon to result in the incor-
poration of the church in the state structure. The acceptance of
the church by the state was as much the acceptance of the state by
the church. The Christian repudiation of war was finally corroded.
Augustine provided the rationalizations, arguing that there might
be occasions when war could be condoned if not sanctified. But
through the troubled centuries ahead most prelates were all too
aware of the dangers to the church of endemic warfare and tended
to condemn it. In the east, where Byzantion continued as a bulwark
against wave after wave of attacking non-Christians, the acceptance
of war was inevitable and the relative subservience of church to
state ensured that there were no dissentient voices. In the west the
change began under Charlemagne. His power was at root secular, but
he acted with the papacy as the militant representative of Christianity against the Moslems and the Saxon pagans. He saw himself as
having a special duty to defend the church against its enemies. The
Norse and Hungarian onslaughts strengthened the sense of a be-
leaguered Christendom waiting for the end of the world; and the
idea of righteous war was furthered by the fact that victories often
led to the conversion of pagans.

But the eleventh century saw a new aspect of the situation, with
a converted St Olaf forcing the Norwegians bloodily into the Christian
fold, and St Stephen ruling in Hungary. The Christian west had
made great economic and political advances; and despite the existing
anarchy it was increasingly aware of an underlying unity, which
found its ideological expression through the church – which in turn
began to assert itself with a new confidence, both at the monastic and
the papal level. Pilgrimages expressed both the restless spirit born of
the breakdown of old limits, and the desire to learn more of the
forces creating the new sense of unity. Men from diverse areas came
together on pilgrimages and found a deep satisfaction in reaching the
shrine of a saint who embodied the creed that was uniting them. The
saints themselves changed in the new climate of unrest and aggres-
sion. St James of Compostella in Spain, whose tomb was one of the
greatest pilgrim centres, had once been a figure of peace; by the
eleventh century he had become Santiago Matamoros, Killer of the
Moors. There was much enthusiasm for the warrior St Michael and
for St Gabriel, Chief of the Angelic Guards. Sword-blessings were
common; liturgical prayers for victory increased. *Chansons de geste*
gave a vigorous expression to the idea of the Holy War, especially the
Chanson de Roland, which depicts Charlemagne as the ideal king,
tireless in waging the Holy War, a priestly warrior who uses the sign
of the cross and can grant absolution. Roland, faithful vassal, is also

the ideal Christian hero, wielding a sword studded with relics; and with him is the warrior-prelate Turpin who promises salvation to the comrades who die with him. St Peter Damiani (died 1072) saw Christ as a war-lord who in the heavenly city gave his faithful largesse in the way of the feudal lord: 'Christ, palm of warriors, bring me into the city after my girdle of knighthood has been loosened; make me share the reward (*donativum*) of its blessed citizens.'

In defeating Pope Leo IX in 1053 the Normans dealt a temporary blow to the idea of the Holy War; but by becoming the militant agents of the papacy some six years later they more than compensated for this damage. They lifted the idea on to a new comprehensive level, leading quickly to the invasions of Sicily and England, and soon afterwards to the launching of the crusades.[10] The Holy War ceased to be a general concept of Christian resistance to a non-Christian world; its aims were identified with the carrying out of papal policy. Thus anyone who defied that policy and its enunciations, whether he was Harold in 1066 or the later Albigensian heretics of southern France, was as culpable as were irreconcilable pagans.

Ordericus Vitalis, writing in the first half of the twelfth century, shows clearly how the exploits in the South passed into the whole Norman tradition. Born on the banks of the Severn to a French father and an English mother, he knew only English when at the age of seven he was sent to the reformed monastery of St Évroult in the forest of Ouche. He saw the Norman nobility as first of all the founders and benefactors of St Évroult, but also as the 'mighty helpers of Robert Guiscard, Duke of Calabria, in Apulia and Sicily'. He depicts them travelling to southern Italy and back, then to England, Syria and Spain, establishing monasteries and lordships. He is delighted that the same chants are heard at Venosa and Sant' Eufemia and Mileto as at Évroul. From the seven sons and four daughters of Giroy of Montreuil and Échaffour and his wife Gisela there came 'a fighting clan of sons and grandsons, who struck terror into the barbarians of England and Apulia, Thrace and Syria'.[11] (For him peoples of a far higher culture than that of the Normans are mere 'barbarians'.) Orderic feels the unity of the Norman world all the more because he sees the expansion as the work of his friends from the valley of the Risle. Robert de Grandmesnil, son of Hadwisa Giroy, turned from war to become abbot of St Évroult, which he had helped to refound; then he went off south through Rome to rule Sant' Eufemia. This was the journey that Judith took to marry Roger de Hauteville. Another emigrant was her cousin, William of Montreuil, called in Apulia the Good Norman. He became duke of Gaeta; and at one time he commanded the army of Pope Alexander. What most interests Orderic are the gifts this William got ready to send from Italy to St Évroul if a trusty messenger came to fetch them. His own father, blind William Giroy, offered to go, and the abbot was 'glad to see such devotion and sad to lose his company'. The old man crossed the Alps with twelve companions and stayed awhile with his son, pleased at meeting many friends and kinsmen in the south. But as he was returning with a huge sum of money, he fell ill at Gaeta and died. He was buried there in the cathedral that was being built.[12] Among the kinsmen he might have met was William of Eschaffour (de Escalfo), the son of his son Arnold, of whom Orderic tells us that after many wanderings he joined Robert of Loritello (nephew of the Guiscard), was given thirty *castella*, and married a Lombard wife, begetting a large family. For nearly forty years he lived among the Lombards, forgetting his own people. He turns up again in 1095 when at Chieti in the Abruzzi, as William of Scalfo, he witnessed a donation of Robert of Loritello to the bishop of Chieti. (Orderic's tale of his great position is thus verified.) Some fifty years later in the same region a son or grandson still held many fiefs and served there as royal constable. Other persons of the house of Giroy, still bearing the name, are found in the records of the Terra di Bari.[13]

The importance of the Italian conquests and the part played by the memory of them in Norman tradition in England is brought out by the speeches put in the mouths of generals long after 1066. Aelred of Rievaulx, telling of the Battle of the Standard in 1138 against the Scots, makes the veteran Walter Espec stir his men's courage by conjuring up Norman glories. The very name of Gaul, he cries, has been wiped out from that part of the land taken by their ancestors. 'It was our father who conquered this island and imposed our laws upon it...and who was it but your Normans who overran far kingdoms, Apulia, Calabria, Sicily?' Henry of Huntingdon gives a similar speech to Ralph, bishop of the Orkneys: 'Magnates of England, illustrious sons of Normandy, there is none who can resist you with impunity. Bold France made trial and was reduced to second place. Fierce England fell captive before you. Sumptuous Apulia in your hands flourished anew. Far-famed Jerusalem and noble Antioch both made surrender to you.'

Interest in the different areas of Norman settlement and activity was kept alive by the many families which had members scattered about in those areas: Mowbray, Barneville, de Aquila (l'Aigle), de Say, Avenal, Taillebois, Cantelupe, Creun, d'Arques, Blosseville, and so on. Norman clerks, monks and bishops also moved continually from one Norman land to another.[14] The spoils of the south went on enriching Norman monasteries. The cathedral of Coutances was largely paid for by Robert Guiscard; that of Sées by other Apulian

Normans or adventurers in the Byzantine service. Similarly, after the conquest of England, the treasures of the abbey of St Martin were swollen by spoils from the Anglo-Welsh borders and the abbeys of Caen rose fast because of the confiscations imposed on Waltham.[15]

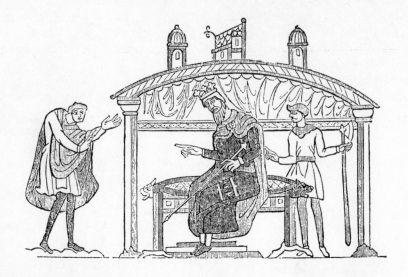

CHAPTER VI

THE NORMAN SYSTEM

Throughout the medieval world the primary source of wealth lay in land and its products. We must look then at the systems of land-ownership to assess the stages through which a society was moving. Norman society was military in a pervasive way that Anglo-Saxon society was not; and this fact was expressed in a closer link between military service and land-ownership. Far back in late Roman times cavalry men had been given land in return for their service, and their sons tended to go into the army; the Romans distinguished land held outright and land held on conditions. The Frankish church often got control of revocable land called a *beneficium*; and through this form of ownership it was able to circumvent the rule that church lands could not be alienated. The same term was used for the fief, *feudum*, granted to warriors in the Carolingian empire, especially between the Loire and the Rhine. A free man, putting himself into subjection to a lord, became a vassal holding land as a benefice from the latter. This relationship, based on an act of commendation by which a man placed himself under the protection or *mund* of a lord, was to be found in all Germanic societies, including England. The English terms *thegn* and *cniht* were similar in meaning (youth, servant) to the Celtic *gwas*, from which came the low-Latin *vassus*, vassal. In the mid-eleventh century Gospatrick, lord of Allerdale and Dalston, addressed a writ to his *wassenas* in Cumbria.[1] The act of homage consisted of a ceremony in which the vassal knelt and set his hands between those of his lord, swearing an oath of fealty. In Gaul the lord usually gave the vassal the right to hold for life a property which still belonged to the lord. Here was the *beneficium*. The benefice was thus a Roman institution adopted and adapted by the Franks. Roman law had the concept of *precarium*, land granted at someone's prayer and revocable at the granter's will. The precarious nature of the grant had lessened and by the ninth century the land was generally considered to be hereditary.

It took a long time for a vassal's duties to be clearly defined, but certain aspects of mutual obligation and abstention from doing any harm to the lord were present throughout. Thus Bishop Fulbert of Chartres tried to define a vassal to Duke William V of Aquitaine:

> He who swears fealty to his lord should always have these six words present to his memory: safe-and-sound, sure, honest, useful, easy, possible. Safe-and-sound, because he must cause no injury to his lord's body. Sure, because he must not injure his lord by giving up his secrets or his castles, which are the guarantees of his security. Honest, because he must do nothing to injure the rights of justice of his lord or other such prerogatives as belong to his wellbeing. Useful, because he must do no wrong to his lord's possessions. Easy and possible, because he must not make difficult for his lord anything the latter may wish to do, and because he must not make impossible to his lord that which his lord might otherwise accomplish.
>
> It is only right the vassal should abstain from injuring his lord in any of these ways. But it's not because of such abstention that he deserves to hold his fief. It's not enough to abstain from doing wrong; it's necessary to do right. So it's necessary that in the six matters aforesaid, the vassal shall faithfully give to his lord his counsel and support, if he wants to appear worthy of his benefice and carry out faithfully the fealty he has sworn. The lord must also in all things do similarly to the vassal who has sworn fealty to him. If he fails to do so, he will be rightly accused of bad faith, just as a vassal who has been found lacking

these qualities, whether by positive action or simply by consent, is guilty of perfidy and perjury.[2]

The papal reform movement tried to make the king the vassal of God, which in effect put him under God's representative on earth, the pope. Archbishop Langton told the barons under John that kings were thus God's vassals with obligations to him not unlike those of the barons to king or liege lord.[3]

What differentiated such land-holding from the holding of estates by soldiers of the late Roman empire were the immunities that inevitably became associated with it as central controls broke down. Delegation of power proved from the outset the only way of governing wide areas; and in such a situation there was little or no method of supervising and limiting the local lords who held delegated power. Border-lands in particular created difficult situations where lords needed strong forces and free hands. The policy of Charlemagne with regard to the marches helped to develop the fief, just as both in Anglo-Saxon and Norman England the Welsh marches produced especially warlike and consolidated earldoms. For the Anon of *Aedward's Life* Harold and Tostig were march-lords: 'The one drove back the enemy from the south and the other scared them off from the north.'[4] New fighting methods were needed to deal with swift raiders, Vikings with their ships or mounted Hungarians; the large heavy armies that had faced early barbarian invasions were no longer effective.

To hold up the fissiparous tendencies a Frankish king might send a count, *comes*, to each city; but in the conditions of the ninth century all local powers tended to grow autonomous. The magnates assumed the right to levy troops or taxes, to exercise police and law administration. Not that they needed any formal grant of such powers; they simply took them over, found them in their hands. Thus the kings kept some system of government in existence by not attempting to apply any system. The magnates wanted as much profit and power as they could conveniently take, but they did not want a state of endless private war and usurpation. They needed the king's sanction to hold the power structure together and in the last resort to legalize or maintain their positions. Things could still collapse into considerable anarchy at moments, but in varying states of tension a mixture of accord and conflict between king and lords continued throughout all the phases of the medieval period. The king was the lord of lords whose overlordship gave the individual lord his rights of control and profit, of exacting rents and fines from his tenants. The kingship had its prerogative as a final weapon, however little it could use it in any broad or consistent way during the more anarchic phases.

What ultimately prevented sheer anarchy and breakdown was the personal relation of lord and man, for the strengthening of which every possible religious and social sanction was brought to bear. The man, *homo*, made his solemn act of homage; by accepting it the lord bound himself to a set of obligations as well. However many infringements in fact occurred in feudal society, the lord and man relationship did make sense of the society, provided its deepest moral values and a cohesive force counteracting the many centrifugal ones. To withdraw from the relationship another solemn ceremony, *diffidatio*, was required.[5] The magnate's estate tended to become a miniature state in which the tenants acted the part which the king's subjects acted for the king; and the magnate in turn enjoyed on a smaller scale the rights of the king, military, fiscal, judicial, and policing. But we must not think the magnate's estate was a self-contained entity. There was enough interaction between the many miniature systems, and enough links with the royal system itself, to check disintegration without bringing the units together in an integrated whole. The medieval epoch in effect was the working out of this conflict through a long series of balances and imbalances till the relative triumph of the centralized state in the absolutist monarchies of the sixteenth and seventeenth centuries.

In pre-1066 Normandy the magnates and older churches already held land by military tenure from the duke; and the knights whose services they had to provide were generally grouped in units of five or ten. Much of what was to grow familiar later in England had appeared in great households. The duke or barons could take aids or reliefs from their military tenants, assume guardianship of heirs under age, hand out heiresses in marriage. They held the honour, with its rights and its court.[6] But Normandy did not have such a fully developed system of military tenures as was imposed in England. There are few signs of such a system before 1047. That is, it seems largely to have been the creation of William in his struggle to impose order on his duchy and gain a firm hold on the loyalties of all free tenants. As late as the twelfth and thirteenth centuries the feudal inquests of Champagne and France made no attempts to specify the number of knights to be supplied by a lord; and in earlier days the conditions of service were left rather vague, no doubt in part deliberately. The considerable orderliness of Anglo-Norman feudalism was thus the result of working out and applying a particular aspect of the feudal system under which land was the prime source of value and the extraction of profit from it (and from other value-creating sources) was done by non-economic methods: that is, through the

lord's physical power to evict, kill and damage. The special circumstances which produced this were first William's protracted struggle
for order in a situation where ducal administration was threatened
by local immunities, and his need to dominate England as an alien
ruler imposing an alien ruling class. In the early medieval world,
where money forces were only partially operative, a ruler needed to
combine control of the land (the source of wealth) with a military
system linked with land-holdings. Only thus could his military and
his administrative systems be brought effectively together. Hence
throughout the period the shifting methods of getting wealth from
the land through the peasants, and for combining with this wealth-
extraction a method of controlling and drawing together the available
number of warriors. Above all it was the low level of economic
activity and the ramshackle administrative systems that compelled
the development of the fief; and as soon as there was a considerable
economic advance, military service based on land tenure began to
give way to service based on wages.

In the transfer and the imposition of Norman methods on the
different society of England, things were both simplified and made
more complex. Some aspects of the previous system at once disappeared; others became mere survivals; others took on a new
strength. A rapid process of transformation was at once evident.

Now let us look more specifically at the Norman scene. A document
like the Bayeux Inquest of 1133 may contain developments since
1066, but it seems to give us the essentials of William's system before
that date. For the land's defence the duke could summon every man
holding a knight's fee; for less serious war inside the duchy, or for
service due to the French overlord, he could call up only some of the
men holding land by military tenures. From the fief of the bishop of
Bayeux one man in five had to come for service in the *marchis
Normannie*, one in ten for service due to the French king. On such
an occasion forty days' service was required. We know also that in
times of extreme danger the *arrière-ban* was summoned. This was an
emergency levy that reached out beyond the system based on military
tenures and applied to all free tenants, although it stressed the obligations of the most prosperous landowners (those with knights' fees
and vavasours who held more than fifty acres).[7]

The system was thus far more precisely organized than that in
England with its stress on the fyrd and the local levies. Apart from
the *ban* there were three sorts of armed gatherings: the duke's forces
proper, his retainers with some groups of friends and adherents; the
host which had been duly summoned; and an army recruited in
various ways according to circumstances for long or large-scale

campaigns. The first sort was made up of horsemen who were expert fighters. We do not know a great deal of the second sort, its quota and the length or conditions of service. William seems to have used new enfeoffments of knights and new appointments in the church to tighten up and regularize the system. For the third sort of army the duke had to look beyond the duchy. Thus, he freed the captured count of Ponthieu on condition that he became a vassal providing a hundred soldiers for yearly service when called on; and he paid the count of Flanders a yearly sum of money (a money-fief), presumably on condition that he provided on demand a certain number of soldiers. Probably most of the men whom a vassal brought along were mounted, but such a contingent as that of Ponthieu would doubtless include foot-soldiers. However, in pre-1066 Normandy we cannot expect any precise and uniform system: rather a conglomeration of customs which the duke kept trying to develop into a coherent unity. He seems to have expected the ducal host to keep together till the end of a campaign; he was furious when the count of Arques left during the Domfront fighting of 1051–2.[8]

We saw that the dukes had tried to control private wars; but even William set himself only to limit their range and to impose rules – the defeated were not to be ransomed or pillaged, nor their houses and mills burned. He tried to persuade his barons to bring their quarrels to his court. But a man was expected to fight in his lord's disputes; he was obliged to guard his castle and pay him sums called incidents, which included a relief when he, the tenant, entered on his inheritance, and contributions when the lord's eldest son was knighted or his eldest daughter married.

The barons or tenants-in-chief held direct from the duke and were his vassals with fiefs. They in turn granted sections of their land to under-tenants in a process of sub-infeudation. The resulting pattern could be complicated: one man holding land from several lords and owning fractions of a knight's fee. A baron might owe the duke five tenants, but he might grant his land so that he had ten at his disposal; he then had five left over for himself. The bishop of Bayeux is said to have had the service of some 120 knights for his own use, while he owed the duke twenty knights for the ducal and ten for the royal army. Between 1050–7 Wiliam made the abbey of St Évroult a barony and fixed the abbot's military service at two knight's fees, which were granted to two knights with the duke's consent. Grimoald du Plessis, imprisoned after Val-ès-Dunes, seems to have owed the service of ten knights for his fief. The principle of a fixed rate of knight service was doubtless inherited by William, but he certainly did much to regularize and extend it. We meet ecclesiastical decrees later condemning the bishops who converted church lands into lay fees for their relatives.

Except for churchmen, all men of any consequence bore arms, while the humbler folk tilled the soil. At the lowest level were the *villani* or villeins tied to the land and giving the lord special services such as work on his demesne, the land he reserved for his own support. In Richard II's time there was a slightly superior section of peasants, *hospites*, who performed occasional services, but were not bound to regular labour. Above them were the vavasours or smaller freeholders, bound to military service, mostly as footmen. Above them came the knightly class – though the line between vavasour and knight was often not clear cut. At first the military classes of north-east France and the counties bordering the North Sea and Channel were often of lowly and even unfree origin, and they held very small fiefs and rents. About 1050, however, knighthood grew in status and knights became more wealthy.[9] A decade or so before 1066 Normandy had many knights with small holdings. One charter deals with an estate and its appurtenances: 'a church, land for 3 plough-teams, 5 free knights, and a mill'. Knights of the superior type acted as witnesses.[10] Though Normandy had few serfs, in a document issued shortly before the Conquest William found it necessary to specify that he spoke to free knights. Before 1000 it was rare to find a simple knight witnessing acts of his lord, much less acting as adviser or judge in his court. Witnesses and judges were all of higher status, members of a count's own family, bishops or abbots (almost all of whom were members of the great families), vicomtes, castellans. Only with the fragmentation of power during the eleventh century did the lords find it necessary to call in knights for help in making judgments.[11] The vavasours were the lowest grade among the holders of military fiefs: their type of grant was half-fief, half villein-tene-ment. A knight, Ralf, in the decade after 1066, gave the abbey of Préaux his land, 'namely that of a vavasour', with the consent of William I and of his own lord in whose demesne lay the land.[12] Such early knights may be compared with the drengs of Norman England, who lay on the borderline of the noble class, ministerial in character, with their typical holding a single plough-gate, a small township, an outlying dependency of a village, often with lordship over villeins and bordars. Mercenary knights in the twelfth century were often given land in knight's fee which had been previously held in thegnage or drengage.[13]

The degree to which estates were inheritable is not clear; but it is more than unlikely that a society so feudalized as Normandy in the eleventh century would not have rigorously applied an hereditary principle. The tenth and eleventh centuries saw the emergence of the new sense of lineage in the use of family names, often toponymic in form. The family was identified with the chief seat of its property, and so toponymic names give us a rough but good measure of the increase of inherited estates. Among the great families before 1066 we meet Montgomery, Bellême, Tosny, Beaumont, Ferrières, Grand-mesnil, l'Aigle, Warenne, Montfort, Mandeville, Gournay, Bully, Port, Mowbray, Tracy, Sai and St John; and among the lesser, Aunou, Drincurt, Granville, Le Mesnil, Limesy, Luvetot, Planches and Vernon. Most of the great Norman families established in England used Norman toponymic names. Patronymics were still common, and some of them developed into family names, e.g. fitz-Walter. There were also a few family surnames (Malet, Martel, Giffard, Bigod), and a few tenants-in-chief took English toponyms: Essex, Berkeley, Gloucester, Salisbury, Tonbridge, Tornes, Stafford. It is possible that the Normans, finding themselves in an alien world, wanted to identify themselves by their relation to French localities, but it is much more likely that they were carrying on a custom learned in Normandy, and that among the great tenants of the duke hereditary tenures were the rule by the third quarter of the eleventh century.

We may also note that with the revival of the Norman church under Richard II grants were made to abbeys and cathedral churches of land or rights to be held *iure hereditario* or *in perpetuam hereditatem*. The terms were meant to indicate a perpetual benefaction, but are strange since the church did not die or have heirs. Probably we see the influence of Roman law, and an ecclesiastical wish to use terms which the laymen would comprehend. The same terms are used in documents concerned with laymen before 1066, and always refer to the fact that the property has been or is now being inherited.

Normandy was one of the most advanced areas where the close link between land-holding and military service had developed; only a few other areas such as Flanders or Barcelona could be compared with it. It has even been called the cradle of feudalism: a term which is applicable enough if we take it to mean that in it the full logical conclusions of military tenures were first worked out in precise terms. The system tended to produce a series of layers, the members of each of which had relatively equal status. Each layer was interlinked with those above and below it by the right to demand services or the obligation to give them. In such a world there could be nothing like the national state that emerged in the last stages of feudalism; for a man felt more solidarity with men of his own layer than with the men above or below him. While in theory the various layers and all the men in them were firmly locked in a set system of fealties and

homages, in practice the groupings were often very fluid (apart from
the labourers tied to the soil). The ethic of loyalty and the practice of
treachery made up much of the everyday scene of feudalism. In
one aspect the system brought to a climax the way of life of the
comitatus, the companions who had discarded the bonds of kin and
attached themselves body and soul to a war lord; but at the same time
it was in decay, corroded by manifold lusts after power and profit.
Its operations were too complex and wide-ranging for the old solidarities and bonds to work consistently. Extremes of loyalty and
disloyalty continued to mark feudal man.

The aim of a strong ruler was to make himself as much as possible
the centre of the whole network of loyalties. We saw how vassalages
could lead to problems of divided fealties, as when William resented
Roger of Mortemer letting go his captured lord, Ralf of Montdidier,
exiled him, then later gave him back his fief – though keeping
Mortemer castle which he granted to a kinsman of the count. We
see that he did not like to go too far against a man who had been
true to his immediate feudal duty, but wanted to emphasize his
own overriding claim. He acted in the same way with the church. A
kinsman, Robert of Grandmesnil, during a revolt that involved members of his family, made some remarks that William considered disloyal; he at once deprived Robert of his position as abbot of St
Évroult. Robert went to Rome and returned with papal legates and
letters of restitution. William met him at Lillebonne, and replied that
he would welcome the legates on any matter of faith or religion,
but he would hang from the highest oak in the wood nearby any
monk who falsely accused him.[14]

The advanced state of feudalism in Normandy can be gauged by
the extent to which the bonds of kindred had been weakened. After
a killing, reconciliation was required, but perhaps only with near
relatives of the dead man; and such a reconciliation was of no use
without the duke's pardon. We find the claims of kinship expressly
set aside. No oath-helpers of the kindred were invoked; on the contrary the jurors who most nearly corresponded to such oath-helpers
could not be related to either party. Remarkable is the anti-kindred
bias in such a statement as the following about wardship:

Who shall take charge of the orphan heir whom it is incumbent
to put in another's care? The mother shall not take charge of
him. Why? Because if she took a husband and had children by
him, those children for envy of the heritage would kill their
elder brother and be heirs, or the husband would himself kill his
stepson to give the heritage to his sons. Who then shall have
charge? His cousins? No. Why? Lest they perhaps should

ardently desire his death and covet his heritage, for that cause killing off the innocent. To avoid then such treachery and to eschew such cruelty, it was established that the orphan should be in charge of him to whom his father was bound in homage.

The exact date of such sections of the Custumal is not clear; but the passage shows the acute Norman sense of property. It is assumed that anyone is likely to murder children if he can thereby get land. But what matters here is the way in which the argument is used to demolish the claims of the kindred and to hand over to the lord what had previously been theirs. Such attitudes certainly go back to William's time and even earlier.

Incidentally we may note that the extreme length to which the idea of incest was stretched in the Christian west was certainly connected with the strength of the kindreds. The early Fathers, in denouncing incest, dealt only with close relationships such as brother and sister, uncle and niece, man and daughter-in-law; but with the early medieval penitentials we enter a world in which relationships are worked out for many degrees. If a man and woman become one flesh, then the relations on either side were brought into a consanguineous connection and the prohibited degrees stretched more and more. Spiritual kinship was added to the list of incestuous taboos. Relations created at baptism were considered similar to, and in some ways more significant than, those between child and parents. The kin-systems linked with the blood feud tended to become identical with the taboo-systems of relationship; Beaumanoir, as late as 1285 in his Coutumes de Beauvais on the customs of the country and the decisions of the court of Clermont, declared:

It used to be the custom that one could take revenge by right of feud as far as the 7th degree of kinship and this was not strange in the days of old, for marriages could not be made within the 7th degree [Laws of Charlemagne and Pope Gregory]. But as the degree for marriage has been made closer, beyond the 4th degree, so also one should not attack in feud anyone further removed from the kindred than the 4th degree, because the kindred stops there in all cases, since matters have been relaxed so that marriages can be made; except in claiming inheritances, for one can still claim inheritance on the score of kindred as far as the 7th degree.[15]

The extent of the turmoils we have noted in Norman society may be estimated from the fact that few of the families who had come to the fore by 1066, and who became great landlords in England, were able to trace their line back beyond the reign of Richard II. The great families were mostly descended from the ducal house and consorts of the dukes. They had grown through grants from the ducal estates or by alienation of old church lands. The highest title used in Normandy – that of count, equivalent to the English earl – was reserved for the ruler up to the eleventh century; and even in the last years before 1066 it was extended only to a few members of the ducal family. It had not become hereditary.

The governmental system was still rather rudimentary, though ahead of other such systems in France. There was a curia or ducal court, made up mostly of kinsmen and personal friends. Few bishops were regularly present, and there was no Norman class at all corresponding to the English thegns. The most important officials included the duke's steward or seneschal and the chamberlain; constables and marshals as yet had lesser roles. Sometimes the duke appointed delegates (often bishops) to hear judicial cases; but there were no chancellors and no seals. The duke couldn't issue writs or charters; the chaplains had to be called in for drawing up documents. William's diplomas were, however, mostly drawn up by the beneficiary and were authenticated by holographic crosses. Documents thus issued were merely the written records of gifts made by word of mouth; sealed writs like those issued by the English kings to the shire courts were unknown on the continent. A personal aspect was indeed prominent in all feudal relations, connected with the idea of reciprocal rights and obligations in lordship and vassaldom – though in fact the relations were continually viewed and expressed in the crudest terms of property and profit. A feudal prince expressed his domination in personal terms, even if he did so within the confines of custom that dictated a complex set of rules and determined the lines of thought and emotion. His curia or household was made up of close personal associates who were there to help him make decisions and carry them out – his own servants and churchmen, his own officials and retainers. One of the duties of the magnates was to advise him. But there was only an embryonic bureaucracy, so that the ruler's relations to anyone with whom he had business, large or small, tended to be direct. There was no class of ministerial nobility like the English thegnhood.

Besides the meetings of the household *curia*, there were councils composed of barons come to court for the great church festivals or to discuss some critical matter. Here were threshed out any disputes between duke and baron, or between the barons themselves. To wage a war the duke needed the assent of his barons. William would have brought up the project of invading England at such a gathering, just as it was at such a gathering that his father had proclaimed him his heir. Charters were issued at such times so as to have a maximum of publicity; trials by ordeal were held. There were no set rules of procedure; anything that deeply concerned duke or baron could be raised; but we do not hear of any judicial activities. Vicomtes and bishops as well as important household officers could attend. In size the council must have been smaller than the English *witan*; like the household it had originated in imitation of the French king's court. It was essentially a festive occasion when the barons could relax, get to know one another, eat and drink. But William was not a ruler who liked spending money on festivities; we hear little of his council before 1066.

The duke knew the lay-out of all Normandy, a region small enough for him to have ridden over many times; little of significance could happen without his knowledge. He could store in his mind the whole network of duties and obligations; and it did not matter much if he were more or less illiterate. In one sense government was centralized, but in the duke's person; in another sense it was extremely decentralized, with a minimum of interference from above in the workings of the complex system of dues and obligations. Slowness in the growth of an administrative machine derived ultimately from the low general level of literacy and of economic or social life; but no doubt it was also the result of a Norse preference for direct orders and communications; the duke and his lords, imperfectly literate or not literate at all, could not help being suspicious of systems set down in writing and dependent on a class of clerics.

The duke was overlord of all landowners, but ruled only his own demesne, his household, his own estates, and the barons or churchmen who held land directly from him. Finance was bound up with administration, and indeed the dividing line between such matters and the military or judicial sphere was thin. As we noted, in comparison with the rulers of the rest of France the dukes kept a great deal of administrative and judicial control in their own hands. *Vicaria* — the term that had come to be applied to a bundle of rights taken over by barons and transformed into seigneurial prerogatives – were being regained by the dukes at the end of the tenth century. The dukes appointed as their main officials vicomtes, with prévôts to collect the revenue. Leading barons at times held *vicomtés*, and the office tended to become hereditary. William's hardest task was to assert full control of the *vicomtés*; and he may have increased the number, in order to break down concentrations of power. But even at the height of the *vicomtés*, the holders, like the English sheriffs, never altogether lost their aspect of public functionaries. They were at times unruly; but, mastered where necessary by William, they remained the local agents of his authority. They dealt with almost anything that turned up, but especially with military, financial, and juridical matters; and they had charge of ducal castles.

The building and control of castles was indeed an important part of ducal policy. Feudal castles were prominent in other areas such as Anjou, and all too often became centres of baronial unrest and self-assertion. But though this did occur in Normandy, the dukes did their best to curb it, demanding licences for all non-ducal castles and using their own castles as centres of intimidation, as key-points in the organization and consolidation of their own grip on the duchy. The castle was used in this way in conquered lands such as England or South Italy.

In early days immunities had been granted or regranted to the great abbeys; but the practice stopped after the death of Robert the Magnificent. William made no such grants, not even to his own foundations at Caen. Counts, we noted, were rare and late; only one or two comital dynasties established themselves, at Eu and at Evreux. So the great cases in law, those dealing with murder, assault, arson, rape, and the like, stayed in ducal hands. Cessions of justice or any mention of such cases are unusual in charters; anything granted away was almost always on the fiscal and economic side.[16] True, we do find some monasteries exercising full ducal rights, even if we allow for forgeries. But it seems likely that the lay lords did not get the same concessions and that they exercised justice over tenants in their own courts without special grants allowing them to deal with the reserved cases. (By 1091 those cases included murder, assault on men journeying to and from the ducal court, attacks on pilgrims, violation of the currency. Arson, rape, and attacks on houses were lesser crimes left to the barons.)

We find the dukes administering justice in the early eleventh century. What was needed was knowledge of custom, not learning or eloquence; and justice was expected to be open to all, great or small. Defendants often had to pass an ordeal to test the truth of their case. Women held red hot iron, which was thought to blister their hands if they were guilty; men were often tied up and thrown into consecrated water, where if innocent they sank. But the warlike Normans often preferred ordeal by battle, a new form. There is no evidence of their using a jury; but Frankish kings used to summon groups of neighbours to declare on oath what they knew of the rights to a piece of land, and the Normans may have taken over this practice, though not inclined to judicial oaths. They had no written law of any kind; their first legal treatise, the *Très Ancien Coutumier*, as we have it, cannot date before the start of the thirteenth century, though it seems to hold earlier elements. Before 1066 they had not gone beyond the notion of ancient custom known to all and reasserted by king and lords.

The vicomtes paid a fixed rent for their office, and made their own profit out of what extra they could collect.[17] By thus farming out the revenues the duke knew just what the returns would be, and could grant definite sums of money out of a certain area's revenue. We see this system in action in the mid-eleventh century. A chamberlain was in charge of the *camera* or chamber where the revenues were kept in coffers. But the office is not clearly differentiated; the same title was given to various officials at the same time. The chamberlain of the *camera* probably had the task of merely guarding the money. In thus owning clearly defined cash revenues Normandy was ahead of the rest of France, even though we can make out no definite method of accounting or allocating money. Usually in early medieval times a prince could grant an income only by a gift in kind or by assigning it from some specific feudal source.

Coins of the ducal era are very rare inside Normandy or outside it, but documentary evidence shows that a large quantity of money was often in circulation. We see from the records of Fécamp that abbot John of Ravenna could pay out in mid-century sums of £80, £50, even £312, to defend certain domains against lords anxious to found new priories: large sums for the day. Coins and metal increased under Richard II; then again after 1066 – a regression covering the second third of the century. At times men preferred to pay in horses rather than in coins. But even so, compared with other regions (such as Burgundy), Normandy was rich in money.[18]

The collectors of the *graverie*, the direct money tax, can be clearly identified from the middle of the century. They were inevitably considered avaricious. One of them, Herbert, in the Vexin, rose in the world; his son-in-law gave three acres to the abbey of the Trinité, while a nephew held a benefice at Verclives and gave its tithes to the same abbey. Collectors of ducal or seigneurial market tolls had high enough status to witness charters; they often acted as general financial agents for their lords, while the ducal collectors had to handle large amounts of cash, as when they delivered alms to church-establishments. These men could become land-owners. The texts enable us to pick three of them out: Raoul, Eudes, Renouf. Raoul lived in a suburb of Rouen and his son had a miraculous cure. An inscription found in the chapel of St Nicholas in the cathedral addresses him: 'You dead, thieves and false money live again.' And, 'You gone, the people [*plebs*] are mourning, the city moans.' He had been murdered by thieves. Eudes, son of one of William's cooks, held land near Clères which he sold to the abbey of the Mont du Rouen for £25.

Renouf turns up a little after 1035, and some time before 1048 was engaged in business with the Italian abbot Suppo of Mont St Michel; there was trouble and he seized the mill of the count at Vains (donated by Robert the Magnificent to the abbey); between 1058 and 1066 the new abbey had to buy the mill back 'at no small price' from Renouf's son. Duke William had to intervene to see the matter settled. Renouf appears as witness in a document of St Amand of Roune. On 18 June 1066:

At Caen the Countess [Matilda] has bought from Waleran son of the moneyer Renouf a land of one plough, and at Amblie a mill and the land that his brother Conan had held in *allodium* in this locality, for 20 pounds and a gold mark, with the Count's assent.

The son Waleran emerges as a well known member of the nobility, in continual contact with the abbeys of Fécamp, the Trinity, St Etienne and Caen. He was very shrewd, as his success in lawsuits attests. A case at the royal court ended with Matilda having to indemnify him in hard cash. Driving a severe bargain with the abbey of Mont St Michel and getting away with it, he was generous to the Trinity of Caen. We see from his largesse how he profited from the conquest of England. In 1066–77 he gave the abbey a house that had belonged to the Englishman Liefred, west of the city of London, in Wood Street, not far from the church of St Peter in Westcheap. Soon after that he conceded to the abbey the church of St Mary of Bury, Suffolk, and important rural lordships including the manor of Panfield, Essex, and various dependencies in Cambridgeshire and Hertfordshire. By the third generation the family seems to be recognized as one of knightly rank; its landed estates became vast lordships. The son Waleran kept up his connections with the trading centres (Rouen, and doubtless London and Caen) while becoming a big landlord in Normandy and England.[19]

Ecclesiastics dealing with money also had a chance to build up big fortunes. We know of several, Ernauld and Odo Saillultra, who were ducal chaplains, Conan who was treasurer of the church of Bayeux, Ebremar who ended by becoming a monk and leaving his property to the same church. We see in the shadow of duke and church a rich group rising up and often merging with the nobility. The most likely to make such advances were the moneyers, ducal chaplains, and episcopal treasurers, who by purchases or by pledges acquired big urban and rural properties, gaining seigneurial and ecclesiastical rights. They built town houses of worked stone or installed themselves in strong towers, treated as equals with the great abbeys, and entered into the vassaldom of barons or bishops. There was still greater range for their activities after 1066. But no new class was thus created. Individuals merly rose up and became part of the ruling class. (After 1066 there was a steady abandonment of coining in Normandy with more governmental control of the workshops.)

The increase in the circulation of coins must have habituated increasing numbers of people to dealing with cash or money contracts; and one reason for the increase in such transactions was the continual emigration, especially to Italy. The emigrants sold their property for ready cash. They took away the money and to that extent weakened the economy, but they helped to make money dealings familiar. Trade, however, was the main factor in getting money into circulation. Between 1049 and 1093 the bishop of Coutances saw the product of his market tolls at St Lo rise by fourteen per cent. The duke also profited, as did certain *milites* of his entourage and certain abbeys. The presence of a great port at Rouen was very important. Its traders dealt in wine and large fish with the London of Aethelred II and had their own wharf at Dowgate under Edward. The best wine came from further south, but much fishing was done off the Norman coast. The big fish were called whales, and they may have been whales but were more likely lesser cetacea like porpoises, whose oil was much prized. Rouen was famed for its tanners, one of which was working under the protection of the eastern ramparts in William's time. But William felt also the need of a large and thriving town in the west (where the revolt of the early eleventh century and many of the events of 1046–7 had occurred). Hence his building up of Caen. Here he proclaimed the Truce of God in 1047; and when in 1066 he gathered his fleet, it was not in the Seine estuary, Fécamp, or Tréport; it was more to the west at Dives, though there he was further away from the shorter channel crossings. Caen no doubt was the base from which he planned and organized.[20]

The growth in trade and money transactions was accompanied, as in Flanders, with a considerable swelling of the population in the eleventh century. Lords were drawn to build up agglomerations and to accord them privileges so as to attract settlers. The term *bourg* is met for the first time in 1024 in a concession made by Richard II to Fécamp of the tithe of the toll of the Bourg named Caen.[21] Before 1066 some eleven *bourgs* are attested: Rouen, Sées, St James de Beuvron, Caen, Arganchy, Trun, St Sylvain, Alençon, Dives, Etouvy and Cherbourg. There must have been more, but they were still not numerous. After 1066 the references to the *bourg* of Caen and to *bourgs* in general grow more common.[22]

The new agglomerations were founded, not on ancient sites or near old towns, but away from these enclosures. Some were made round castles, some round or near abbeys. Of the first group were Alençon, Domfront, Verneuil; of the second, Caen, Montebourg, Bernay. The sole foundations with ancient bases were Lire, Dieppe, Exêmes and Lillebonne. But only the latter and Sées could be called old towns whose past prosperity continued. In the eleventh century we know the *bourgs* through the valuable rights they yielded to their lords.[23] Only after 1066 do we find urban customs mentioned: those of Cormeilles and of Breteuil. And we know these only from the traces left in the organization of certain towns founded by Normans in the Welsh marches – towns that it was necessary to fill quickly with people.[24] To meet franchises announcing *tenure en bourgage* we must wait for the reign of King Henry I with its big urban expansion, when castles like Verneuil saw settlements growing up around them and it was useful for the lord to make the place attractive, to draw people in by the concession of privileges. Not till 1080 did the word *bourgage* appear – and probably with it the reality that it expressed. It seems certain that these post-1066 developments were influenced by English forms.[25]

We saw how the dukes after Rollo began slowly rebuilding or building abbeys and organizing the shattered life of the church. The monks came back to Jumièges and to Fontenelles, where a new house was founded. Richard I put monks into the former sanctuary of the Mont St Michel; then established another house, Ouen, in Rouen. By 990 the old bishopric had come together again; and secular canons, not bound by a common rule like the monks, were settling at Fécamp, another pre-Viking site. Richard II took the important step of linking Normandy with Cluny in Burgundy, which followed the rule of the black-cowled Benedictines, the only regular order yet known in the west. Cluny was the centre of monastic reform, which sought to make monasteries independent of the secular clergy – to revive the whole monastic tradition on a new level adequate to the era and to ensure that it remained an essential part of the church. Cluny ended by developing a system in which its monks lived a wholly liturgical life, occupied unbrokenly in grandly conceived ceremonies of praise and prayer. The services were so extended that men said a Cluniac monk had hardly half an hour of his own, even on midsummer day. Cluny tried to make its buildings as grandiose as the liturgy, which was embellished with every musical device.

William of Volpane, a Piedmontese who was abbot of the Cluniac house at Dijon, was invited in 1001 to Fécamp, where he at once substituted monks for the canons. He went on reforming other Norman houses. Interested in music, medicine, geometry, architecture and art, he founded schools for youths who wanted to become monks. Laymen or people who wanted to enter the secular clergy could also attend. Out of twenty-eight or so monastic houses it seems that twenty-one derived directly from his work. In addition to the demand for a revival of monastic ways of life, at once both ascetic and deeply aesthetic, the century saw a growing attempt to formulate and apply ecclesiastical law, to grasp with a new fullness the issues involved in Christian theology, and to spread education more effectively.

Cluniac influence appeared in the increasing number of nobles going on pilgrimages to the East. The two leading dynasties of northern France, those of Anjou and Normandy, were linked with Cluny, and despite their rivalries patronized the pilgrimages. Fulk Nerra of Anjou, a terrifying character, went to Jerusalem in 1002, and returned there twice. The count of Angoulême went off in October 1026. Richard II of Normandy sent alms and Robert led a huge company away in 1035. All such pilgrimages were carefully recorded by Glaber of Cluny. In general the monasteries did well out of them, as later out of the crusades. Men mortgaged land to them to raise ready money for the journeys, or sold it. The monks seized mortgaged lands at once if the loan was not repaid on the stated day; and at the council of Tours, in the middle of the twelfth century, Pope Alexander III felt it necessary to stigmatize such practices as usury.[26]

William of Poitiers depicted the duke as regular in attending mass, open to the counsels of his clergy, and especially favourably disposed towards monks. The Anon, probably a monk of Caen, who told of his end, copied out a few phrases from Einhard's *Life of Charlemagne* Chapter 26, to praise him as addicted to churchgoing. But the Normans, apart from needing to use the church politically, seem to have been pious only in the fear of death. The warrior class had little moral respect for the secular clergy who enjoyed power and wealth if of high status, or who lived much as everyone else if of humbler rank, and yet were always ready to rebuke sin. Monks were different, however: the Militia of Christ who were making an effort to live according to the Gospels. By William's time the barons had begun to compete in endowing houses that would save their souls by prayer and even ensure good fortune in this world. William took a crowd of clerics and monks in his invading army, with two bishops, Odo of Bayeux and Geoffrey of Coutances. They were to fight with prayers, Poitiers comments. Gratefully William despoiled the English church after victory to enrich the Norman monasteries.

In the Bayeux Tapestry no stress is laid on William being a religious character. Poitiers says that he wore round his neck at Hastings the relics on which Harold swore his oath, but we do not see them.

However, the flag shown at his ship's masthead seems to be the gonfalon presented by the pope, as is shown by the cross-headed staff and the method of mounting the standard from a crossbar.[27] (For a masthead light we should expect open cressets like those that soldiers used in setting fire to the palisades of Dijon.) To defeat the contrary winds that kept his fleet from sailing, William 'fought with his prayers' by having the relics of the local St Valéry carried in procession; but this episode does not appear on the Tapestry. The chroniclers tell of his prayers before Hastings; the Tapestry shows a feast. Odo too is depicted as what he was, a feudal baron with benefit of clergy. He does not even say grace at the feast and does not appear in his vestments, but acts as fighter and councillor.[28]

William was shrewd enough to use his role as head of the Norman church to learn something of its organizing methods. Watching how it legislated in council, had begun using written records, and had devised administrative forms, he could not but ponder how to build up the same sort of apparatus. The intellectual and moral ferment at work now in the ecclesiastical world passed over his head; but he was ready to protect the church while it supported him and allowed him a free hand in his own affairs, which in his view included making church appointments. At Lillebonne in 1080, setting out the positions he had taken all his life, he showed that he accepted ecclesiastical courts as long as they behaved themselves. He sharply regulated ecclesiastical jurisdiction, while encouraging it when he approved of its aims: for example in moral matters, especially when attempts were made to discipline the lower clergy. He punished ecclesiastical judges whom he considered to have erred. Archdeacons, responsible to bishops, supervised the clergy within defined areas; priests serving cathedrals were organized in chapters with their own endowments and duties. The bishop dealt with offences committed in churches or churchyards; he fined clerks and members of his own household, but how far he could deal with laymen is unclear. A priest was subject to his lord for his secular holding; and the church had no concern with forest offences. As with all strong rulers of the century, the duke appointed prelates, or if he desired, had them deposed; no bishop could exercise comital powers within his own city.

In Normandy, as in Edward's England, men from other countries came in to take up high places. Germans were made abbots at Holy Trinity (Rouen), St Pierre-sur-Dive, St Wandrille; an Angevin was abbot of Grestain; there were also Burgundians and Italians such as Lanfranc.

Just as the ducal family had many blood-ties with the barons, so members of it took up the most important church seats, especially the see of Rouen which they held from 987 to 1087 (apart from 1055–67), and that of Bayeux (1015–99), Lisieux (1049–77), Avranches (1060–7).[29] Some were unashamedly worldly; but others took their vocation seriously – for instance, John of Avranches who was at Rouen 1067–87 and wrote a work on the liturgy. The bishops were in general more subservient to the duke than the barons; William controlled all preferments and demanded military services from his prelates.[30] He expected the synods presided over by the archbishop to keep order in the church, and was reluctant to let in influences from outside. The church magnates had vassals and at times many knights, and some of them were ready enough to fight in battle; but as a whole they needed the duke and his law for protection more than the lay barons did. He presided over their councils and they could feel he was committed to their policies. From about 1042, however, encouraged by the duke's youth and the reform movement, they had begun to assert themselves more. Archbishop Mauger's council, about 1042, not only attacked simony (the selling of church offices and sacraments) but also made some criticism of William, Mauger's nephew. That, however, may have been merely the result of the politics of the moment. Archbishop Maurilius, a papal man who had been in monasteries at Florence and Fécamp, held councils at Rouen and Lisieux, and made a strong attack on priestly marriage or concubinage. But so far, despite the church courts, there was nothing remotely like a clash between church and state, with the powers of the pope asserted against the temporal ruler.

Already by the end of the tenth century or early in the eleventh there seems to have been a school at Rouen. Dudo addressed his *History* to the *Northmannica Gymnasia*; and a satirist, Garnier, writing in Latin verse, reproaches his adversary Moriuht for having fraudulently introduced himself as one of the professors, *grammatici*, of Rouen, and takes up the defences of one of the masters against Franbald, whom he advises to leave Rouen, where his wretched talents should not be employed. In the second satire he also mentions the grammarian Donatus of the fourth century, showing that a methodical system of teaching was practised. The first satire is worth summarizing. The poet opens by celebrating the archbishop Robert, son of Richard II, and his mother Gunnor, mentioning also Robert of France. Moriuht comes from Scottia (Ireland), an island fertile but dishonoured by its inhabitants; a proper Irishman, he claims to be a grammarian, but is simply a he-goat. His wife had been carried off by Danes. He too is captured in his turn, and the crew of the ship use him as their plaything. Taken ashore at Corbric, he is sold to a nunnery for three deniers, where, bragging that he is a poet, he is well received and rampages sexually among the nuns. The people catch him at his fornications, put him in a boat, and let the sea carry him off. Pirates catch him again, and he, who sacrifices to the gods like a pagan, is brought into a Saxon port. A widow buys him up cheap and pays the price in forged money. He again rampages and the people are glad to let him go. In a rite of black magic, he learns from a Demon that his wife is a slave at Rouen and is about to marry a Dane. He rushes to Rouen in his Irish clothes and begs the countess (Gunnor) for aid; she promises to buy out his wife if he can find her. He discovers her somewhere working as a weaver. (The poet warns him of the woman's lubricity.) Getting the right to remove his wife, Moriuht carries her off on his shoulders all the way to Rouen; and he also recovers his daughter. At court he boasts of his poetic powers, but unhappily he makes an error in versification. The poet launches into an account of prosody, corrects Moriuht, and dismisses him to his lewd games. In the second satire, Garnier declares that true wisdom lies in the monastic state, with its stability and its poverty; he bids Franbald go back to his monastery. 'Theoretician, yes, but your voice is like a crow's, it makes the fishes flee, it's even put St Michael to flight. Return to silence: then you yourself can return to the Mont.' Franbald has come to Rouen out of cupidity to teach music.

Whatever the facts behind these works, the accounts are none the less instructive. Garnier has some classical knowledge; he shows much respect for Virgil, recalls the lessons of Horace, and seems to know Juvenal and Persius well. The picture of Moriuht's wife, 'Poor woman with bare shoulder, bare, with lovely breasts', for instance, is based on a line of Juvenal. An anonymous satire on Jezebel has the same qualities of pedantry, liking for abuse and scatology, and interest in magic. Its Jezebel does not seem to be an historical character, but merely a symbol of lascivious woman. Pre-1066 Normandy, besides chronicles, also had hagiographical works, and the *History* of Dudo, which was much more than a chronicle. Here is a definite literary effort, looking back to Boethius for its mixture of verse and prose, and seeking out-of-the-way terms or Greek words as did Liutprand of Cremona; it uses a circuitous approach as did Gumpold, bishop of Mantua (late tenth century), and displays great erudition. But there is something of a Norse fury about Dudo's way of attacking the themes, his accumulation of effects, his personal vanity, and his great need to flatter and to shine, by using whatever methods were available, however tawdry.

At William's accession there were nine abbeys and one nunnery; he himself built two houses in Caen to expiate his allegedly incestuous marriage – that is, to placate the church. He later built Battle abbey

in England to atone for the deaths at Hastings, and an abbey at
Montebourg in Normandy: not much, considering his resources.
Indeed he seems even to have stolen the land on which St Stephen's
was built at Caen; for when he came to be buried there, Ascelin
fitzArthur, with supporters present, declared that he had illegally
taken the land from his father, and had to be bought off so that the
burial might go on. William did not attend the dedication of the new
abbey at Bec though he and his wife were in Normandy at the time
and the event was of some importance. But he did not interfere when
his barons began founding monasteries instead of using their
resources for purposes of war. He was always ready to give someone
else's lands to the church, for example the six parishes in Guernsey
owned by Niel de Saint-Sauver, who, as vicomte of the Cotentin, had
been a leader in the 1047 revolt. William gave the estate to the abbey
of Marmoutier in Tours; later Niel confirmed the monks' title for a
payment of £30. Certainly monastic life in this period made many
advances in Normandy, but these were no doubt linked with the
general developments going on all over the west. William Calculus,
of Jumièges, soon after 1070 wrote his confused history of the
Norman dukes; Durand of St Wandrille, pupil of the German Isem-
bert and later abbot of Troarn, composed a theological treatise
against Berengar of Tours. But one of the best Norman writers was
William of Poitiers, a secular clerk and archdeacon, not a monk.
Three important scholars came from south of the Alps: John of
Ravenna at Fécamp, Lanfranc of Pavia at Caen, Anselm of Aosta at
Bec.

We know most about Bec because one of its monks, Gilbert
Crispin, later abbot of Westminster, wrote of Herluin and Lanfranc,
both his masters. Herluin was one of the members of the Norman
nobility who renounced the world of violence and greed. A knight of
William's uncle, count of Brionne, he gave his hereditary estates to
the church, with ducal permission, and in about 1034 built with his
own hands a chapel, on his lands at Bonneville, learning to read the
psalter at night. He visited monasteries to study their rules, which
disappointed him. Pulling down his old home, he built a monastery
there. The bishop of Lisieux consecrated it, accepted Herluin and
two retainers as monks, and later made him a priest, then, as the
community grew, an abbot. The monks worked the land, and Herluin's mother washed and cooked for them. The place was barren, the
nearest water two miles away, so they all moved to another part of
Herluin's land, Bec, on a stream in a wooded valley. A wooden church
and cloister were raised; but the site was unhealthy and some monks
couldn't bear it. Then Lanfranc stopped there and was won over to
Herluin's way of life. He stayed on and after three years resumed his

teaching, to raise funds. He became prior and urged a change of site. In 1060 Anselm joined them and Herluin agreed on a move. In June 1063 Lanfranc became abbot of St Stephen's, Caen; in 1067 he refused the see of Rouen, but in 1070 he was persuaded to become archbishop of Canterbury. In October 1077 he returned to dedicate the new church at Bec amid such a huge crowd that many of the monks were pushed out of the ceremony. Herluin died at eighty-four in 1078, succeeded as abbot by Anselm. Through Lanfranc Bec had come to conform more and more to the rule of the other Norman houses, and grew strongly Benedictine.

Lanfranc had studied letters and civil law in the Italian schools, and had roamed about till he settled in Normandy with his own school at Avranches. He had won fame for his skill in argument, in dialectic. But as a monk he rejected secular learning, gave up the pagan writers, and set faith and doctrine, with dialectical skill, beyond the range of the dialectician. He also took up study of the Bible and of canon law; but though his work in the latter sphere had some effects in England, his writings on such matters were soon outmoded. At first he was in conflict with William over his marriage. He attended Pope Leo's reforming councils at Rome and Vercelli, and took over the negotiations about Matilda, as we said.

He attacked the views of his old master Berengar on the Eucharist, and thus won much attention, partly through the new method of logical argument he had developed. The attack pleased William. Berengar was protected by Anjou and William gladly persecuted his followers. But Lanfranc's main importance was as a teacher. When he left Bec in 1063 among his pupils had been the reigning pope, Alexander II, and others who rose to prominence; Anselm, William of Bona Anima (later in the see of Rouen), and two future bishops of Rochester.[31] He sympathized with the moral aspects of the reform movement and was zealous for the dignity of the church; at the cost of a certain amount of strain, he managed to harmonize the claims of the papacy and of William in his attitudes and pronouncements, never quite admitting to himself how far William's rigid control of the church was already beginning to jar with the positions taken by the reform movement.[32] But William, as we saw, benefited greatly from the alliance with the Normans of south Italy which Hildebrand was forced to make. In the 1060s he was assured of every possible papal support in his ventures; and he was able to call on that support when he turned to England.

One of the themes of this book is the way in which men kept or regained a sense of personal and social identity in the confused and uprooted world of the period between the tenth and the twelfth centuries. It was a period when the tribal elements carried into the Roman west by the Germanic tribes were in many ways breaking down; the system of matured feudalism was making new demands on people, allotting them new roles in society; money was appearing as an active force, though we have far to go before there was anything like a cash nexus controlling men. Some elements of tribal society, such as the kindred, were being dislocated, yet were finding new forms; certain aspects of village life carried on despite all the changes in land-ownership and social status. At the same time men felt a deep need to adapt themselves to the new structures, not only socially and economically, but also emotionally and psychologically. A complex network of strains and stresses was at work; and one important issue was the way in which men responded to the dominant ideological insitution, the Catholic Church, either accepting it and finding ways of connecting their lives with it, or rejecting it in favour of heresies or the underworld of magical practices, in which many elements of paganism persisted, for instance in the witch-cults.

Often it was very hard for the man of this epoch to harmonize his secular way of life with the creeds and ethics of the church; he tended to swing violently one way or another. There seems to have been no halfway between a surrender to greed and violence, and a total rejection of the world and a turn to the monastic creed. The nephew of Geoffrey of Anjou, one of William's great rivals, has left us a brief biography of his uncle, which brings out well how a man who seemed irredeemably identified with violence and agression could hope at the end to turn suddenly into the opposite of what he had always been.

My uncle Geoffrey became a knight in his father's lifetime and began his knighthood by wars against his neighbours, one against the Poitevins, whose count he captured at Mont Couër, and another against the people of Maine, whose count, named Herbert Bacon, he likewise took. He also carried on war against his own father, in the course of which he committed many of the evil deeds of which he afterwards bitterly repented. After his father died on his return from Jerusalem, Geoffrey possessed his lands and the city of Angers, and fought count Thibaut of Blois, son of count Odo, and by gift of king Henry received the city of Tours, which led to another war with count Thibaut, in the course of which, at a battle between Tours and Amboise, Thibaut was captured with a thousand of his knights. And so, besides the part of Touraine inherited from his father, he acquired Tours and the castles round about – Chinon, I'lle-Bouchard, Château-renault, and Saint-Aignan. After this he had a war with William, count of the Normans, who later acquired the kingdom of England and was a magnificent king, and with the people of France and of Bourges, and with William count of Poitou and Aimeri viscount of Thouars and Hoel count of Nantes and the Breton counts of Rennes and with Hugh count of Maine, who had thrown off his fealty. Because of all these wars and the prowess he showed therein he was rightly called the Hammer, as one who hammered down his enemies.

In the last year of his life he made me his nephew a knight at the age of seventeen in the city of Angers, at the feast of Pentecost, in the year of the incarnation 1060, and granted me Saintonge and the city of Saintes because of a quarrel he had with Peter of Didonne. In the same year king Henry died on the nativity of St John, and my uncle Geoffrey on the third day after Martinmas came to a good end. For in the night which preceded his death, laying aside all care of knighthood and secular things, he became a monk in the monastery of St Nicholas, which his father and he had built with much devotion and endowed with their goods.[33]

There was deep fear and superstition in such an act, but more than that: a sort of dream transition from one pole of the strangely cloven world to the other pole. The same sort of dream transition appears in the pilgrimages that so many of the nobles and rulers made. On the corpse of the murdered William Longsword was found the key of the box which held his treasure; we can imagine the mingled disappointment, anger, and bewildered respect in the men who opened the box and found a monk's gown there. Some individuals in this world could build and rationalize a bridge between the two poles. Herluin did so, in order to return to simple productive labour, outside the tangle of exploitations, without degrading himself in the eyes of the world, substituting God's watchful eye for that of the manor lord. Lanfranc again did so, so as to be in a position in which he could effectively take in the intellectual tradition and transform it according to his understanding of the world's needs.

Finally some words on warfare and weapons. The rise of cavalry in the Dark Ages was connected in part with the need in the eighth century to meet Saracenic horsemen. We see the knights of the eleventh century on the Bayeux Tapestry, horsemen with mailshirts of interlined iron rings covering the body, upper arms and thighs; and when there is a coif, the neck. The head too might be covered. Gaiters were available for the legs, but wrists, hands and feet were unguarded. The iron helmets were conical with an extension across the nose. 'Thorstein Midlang cut at Bue across his nose, so that the nose-piece was cut in two and he got a great wound.' Footmen had garments of boiled leather. Horses were unarmoured. The rider had a kite-shaped shield rounded at the top, made of leather over a wooden frame with metal strengthening. War-horses or destriers were much prized, and Normandy had good pastures for them. The knight's weapons were a long, straight, broad-bladed sword for slashing, a lance or spear, and probably a knife or dagger. Cudgels or maces, often with metal heads, might be used, especially by churchmen, who could thus kill without drawing blood! (Turpin in the *Chanson de Roland* appears as a baron in council and encourages or leads troops; he cuts the pagans in half and disposes of a host. 'No tonsured clerk ever sung mass, who bodily so valiant was.' He preaches, 'A good vassal is never untrue.' Odo of Bayeux may have taken him as an example.) Shields were decorated, but not yet with heraldic devices. William probably had many shields with different designs; dragons and geometrical patterns were favoured. Commanders flew flags, gonfalons, from spear staffs.

The Normans in the South were no doubt much the same as those shown on the Tapestry. Anna Comnena states that 'their chief weapon of defence is a coat of mail, ring plaited into ring, and the iron fabric is so excellent that it repels arrows and keeps the wearer's flesh intact. A further weapon of defence is a shield which isn't round, but a long shield very broad at the top and running out to a point, hollowed out slightly on the inner side, but externally smooth and gleaming with a brilliant boss of brass.' She was writing about 1145 at the end of a long life; the boss may be a twelfth century addition. The charge of Norman cavalry was said to be almost totally irresistable, with an impact that 'might make a hole in the walls of Babylon'.

Some of the retainers, especially those of the duke, may have been highly trained and disciplined, but it is hard to imagine any large body of Normans acting in a steadily concerted way in battle. Initiative, fury, and determination would soon take the place of any regular tactics. True, we hear of Gilbert du Pin as the *magister militiae* of Roger of Beaumont; presumably he was in charge of any training of Roger's retainers, would ensure their effective presence, and give some orders. But probably it was the shock of the first massive attack, plus the resolute way that individuals or small groups then carried on, which gave the Normans their reputation as warriors. Generally the horsemen were in squadrons under their own feudal lords and captains in a line; they charged, with the general often posted in the rear with a select reserve. Archers might be used first to weaken or demoralize the enemy. William was an expert archer, and there are signs that he built up a contingent of reliable bowmen.

F

As the horseman came up, they threw spears, then engaged in hand-to-hand fight. The side with the most coherence and vigour ended by making the other give way and turn. After that came a helter-skelter pursuit. The rider faced what was perhaps the worst moment: he might be thrown, driven into a river, or knocked down at a tightly-packed bridge. William spent most of his days riding in the open; if there were no wars, he hunted in one of the wide forests under special jurisdiction dating from Frankish times. The Normans were clean-shaven with cropped hair. Though they were little given to learning, Malaterra described them in Italy as greedy but eloquent, hardworking, apt at war, and successful because of their imitative capacities; they showed ceaseless enterprise combined with lawlessness. William of Poitiers says that William tried to bridle the wilder impulses of his troops. No doubt he disliked indiscipline, but for military rather than humanitarian reasons.

Strategy was mainly based on castles or towns. The commander sought to hold his own and capture those of others. Castles could not normally halt an invader, but he moved on at the risk of sorties, ambushes and attacks from the rear. He could still devastate and loot, however, and loot was the aim of many wars. If the aim was the conquest of territory, then castles or towns would have to be taken and garrisoned. William had no siege engines and few engineers for mining or sapping. The first hope before a defended site was a surprise attack; if that failed, the defenders might be worn down, starved out, or bribed – treachery might let the besiegers in. A town that did not surrender on negotiated terms was sacked. Fire was a possible weapon if there were wooden buildings close inside the walls. In general warfare there were many skirmishes, a few large-scale battles. For the latter a challenge should first be sent and accepted. But customs varied. A defiance might be sent to an enemy about to be attacked.[34]

ET ҺIC: DEFVNCTVS EST

CHAPTER VII

ANGLO-SAXON ENGLAND

England had many unique characteristics in the eleventh century, while sharing in the general development of western Europe. Here alone had the Germanic invaders of late Roman times and early Dark Ages been able to develop largely on their own bases. They were pagans, as later the Vikings were. There had been no merging with a Romanized provincial aristocracy. Also the settlements were probably denser than in Gaul. All that is not to say that the Anglo-Saxons were unaffected by what went on on the continent, especially after their conversion; there can have been no period when the ruling classes on both sides of the channel were not in contact with one another to some extent; and there was trade through ports like Quentovic. The chiefs who started governing regions of Britain in the fifth and sixth centuries called themselves kings and must have been acquainted, as were the Franks in Gaul, with the *tributum*, the later empire's land tax. With the Romans the unit for assessing this tax had been a *caput* or *jugum*; but the provinces used various local terms. In Gaul the unit became the *mansus* and its occupants were *manentes*; and the Roman term for the tax was still being used at the end of the seventh century. Since Diocletian the *tributum* had been paid, part in money, part in kind. With the invasions the cash payments would have ended among the Britons, and systems of food-rent (met later in Welsh custom) would have been general. Food-rents, *feorm*, carried on through the Anglo-Saxon era into the Norman. The Anglo-Saxons had a unit of assessment, the hide, but when a king's grant of land was put into writing, the terms used by the post-Roman successor states were used; and the occupants became *manentes, cassati, tributarii*.[1]

Still, the English kingdoms had marked differences from the barbarian kingdoms on the mainland as well as affinities with them. There was an organic element in the society, a strong binding element, which was not to be found elsewhere. Despite tribal divisions, which finally took a large-scale form in the provinces of Northumbria, Mercia and Wessex, there was a movement towards unification, a slow, shifting and complex process largely brought about by wars, though sustained by other forces, social and economic. The church facilitated but did not initiate this movement. Already when Augustine landed, the king had the function of interpreting tribal custom or folk-law in consultation with the witan. Probably influences from Merovingian Gaul furthered the process, which came to a head in the period of Mercian supremacy in the eighth century when Aethelbald called himself *Rex Britanniae*. His cousin Offa deposed or executed kings of neighbouring states, degraded sub-kings to the status of royal officials, and incorporated newly gained areas into his *Regnum Anglorum*. This was a premature development, though none the less significant. The idea was not lost and was later taken up by the Wessex kings. The church's role was to make propaganda for authority, help in the breakdown of kindred groups, give kingship a semi-divine aura, and afford some sort of a model of centralized government by its own system, which most of the time monopolized literacy. As early as 787 Offa's son was anointed as king while his father was still alive.[2]

The king was seeking to transfer to himself all the old bonds and loyalties, those developed in tribal days through the *comitatus* and the kindred, and the new forms developed through commendation. The *fyrd* or host was essentially a royal force, and the ideal was expressed in a doom of King Edmund (942–6) which commands that:

all in the name of God shall swear fealty to king Edmund as a man should be faithful to his lord with neither objection nor treachery, both publicly and privately, loving what he loves and shunning what he shuns, and henceforth no one shall evade this oath for the sake of his brother or kinsman any more than for the sake of a stranger.[3]

Fealty to the king was thus conceived as fealty to the lord raised to a new level; the lesser sets of bonds were seen as merging harmoniously to create the great unifying bond of fidelity to the king. The peace of the king (his person and residence) was a basic feature of English law and contained elements of the old ideas about the sacrificial priest-king.[4]

In the earliest code, that of Aethelberht of Kent, a double compensation is assessed for an offence committed at a gathering of the ruler's *leod* summoned by the king or at a feast where he is present.[5] Early west Saxon laws consider violence against the king's person in connection with fights in his house or hall; later laws, reflecting the extension of royal jurisdiction, grow less localized and deal with plots against the king. The king's peace spread beyond his immediate neighbourhood to wider areas of jurisdiction, embracing the whole realm.[6]

But there was still a vital link with the sacral character of the kingship, stressed as it was afresh in the tenth century. This link appears further in the dooms concerning asylum; and indeed it affected the whole relationship of lord and man, strengthening its sanctions and the whole emotional nexus surrounding it. The first law that explicitly mentions plots is one from Alfred's reign. 'If anyone plots against the king's life, on his own account or by harbouring outlaws or men belonging to the king himself, he shall forfeit his life and all he possesses.' Death, unless the accused is cleared 'by the most solemn oath determined upon by the authorities', is also the penalty under Aethelred for plotting against the king. It appears again in another law of Aethelred and in Cnut's laws.[7] The king had been thought to descend from a god, and we find the pagan system adapted to fit in with Christian idioms. The Welsh prince Howel the Good was descended from 'Amalech, who was the son of Beli the Great and his mother Anna, who was the sister of the Virgin Mary'. Anna is Danu the Celtic earthmother and Beli the god Belinus. The *Chronicle* under 855 traces King Aethelwulf's ancestry back to Baeldaeg son of Woden and on to 'Sceldwea, son of Heremod, son of Itermon, son of Hrathra who was born in the Ark: Noah, Lamech, Methuselah, Enoch, Jared, Mahalaleel, Cainan, Enos, Seth, Adam the first man, and our father who is Christ. Amen.' Another version has '...Hathra, son of Hwala, son of Bedwig, son of Sceaf, who is son of

Noah was was born in Noah's Ark...' A passage from William of Malmesbury shows how the Sceaf-Noah connection came about:

> Sceaf, as they say, was brought as a child in a ship without oars to Scandza, a certain island in Germany...He was asleep and a corn-sheaf lay beside his head. He was therefore called Sceaf and was received as a prodigy by the people of that country and carefully fostered.

Sceaf, we see, is both an incarnation of the sheaf (perhaps the last one in harvest ritual) and a culture-hero making the spirit-journey from the other world with an important food-product.

Eight genealogies survive. Of these, seven (those of Kent, Wessex, East Anglia, Mercia, Bernicia, Deira and Lindsey) trace the kingly lines back to Woden. Essex starts the line with Seaxnet, a god known among the continental Saxons as Saxnet and identified as both a son of Woden and as the god Tiw (Tyr); his name, Need-of-the-Saxons, is in its second element an attribute of the Norse Odin (Othinn). The Sussex line is lost, but doubtless began also with Woden. Woden-Othinn in Scandinavia was Lord of Valhöll and god of war, poetry and magic. *Woden id est Furor*, says Adam of Bremen; and as the maddened and maddening war-spirit he was linked with the Berserks. He was especially the god of warrior-chiefs. The *Harbardslod* states, 'Woden owns all the gentry [*iarla*] that fall in fight, but Thor the thrall-kind.' His fertility aspects helped to invest the king with similar powers. The Scandinavian King Olaf Tretelgia was sacrificed by his people to ensure good crops; Woden's day, Wednesday, remained the lucky day for sowing or planting, though the Christians tried to link it with the devil and make it unlucky.[8]

There had thus developed a theocratic system in which church and state were largely merged, the one buttressing the other. The anointed king shared the priestly status on a high level, which in effect put him above any prelate and made him the head of the church in his realm, just as the pope had made the German emperor. The bishoprics did not make up a separate hierarchical organization so much as loose groupings like the estates of magnates, and were controlled by the king, though at times they needed to express the point of view relevant to their role in the church-state. The church, aware that it could not survive without royal support, looked on the state as expressing in a sinful world something of God's purpose in so far as it brought about an orderly system within which the rituals of salvation could be carried on. It also recognized that only the state could guarantee its immense worldly goods and ensure the destruction of heathen and heretic.

In England then the king tended to draw to himself with considerable strength the *comitatus*-bond; and though the retainer of a lesser lord might feel a stronger sense of loyalty towards that lord, on the whole the process of subordinating the lesser bonds to the larger was much more successful than on the continent where the development from simpler tribal forms had been more chequered through the entanglement with survivals of Roman landlordism, and where there were more direct memories of Roman unification. Despite all the influences coming in from Gaul and the church, the English began developing state forms more organically out of the tribal bases which they had introduced. For long the attitudes that Tacitus had described among the Germanic tribes carried on almost unchanged:

> It is a lifelong infamy and reproach to survive the chief and withdraw from battle. To defend him, to protect him, even to ascribe to his glory their own exploits, is the essence of their sworn allegiance. The chiefs fight for victory, the followers for their chief.[9]

The followers of Oswald of Northumbria in the seventh century and of Aethelbald of Mercia in the eighth went off with their lords into exile; not long after that Charlemagne asked the archbishop of Canterbury to intercede with Offa of Mercia to allow some exiles to return as their lord had died. Bishop Aldhelm of Sherborne tried to persuade the clergy of Wilfrid of Northumbria that it was their duty to share his exile; he pointed out that a layman who refused to go into exile with his lord would be a creature of scorn and ridicule.[10] Lillia, thegn of Edwin of Northumbria, in 625 saved his lord from a murderer by thrusting himself in the way of the poisoned dagger. Bishop Wilfrid's retainers in 666 swore to fight to the death, if necessary, against a much superior force of heathen South Saxons; King Egfrith in 685 fell at Nechtansmere, 'all his bodyguard having been killed'. The *Chronicle* under 755 (757) tells how Cynewulf of Wessex was murdered while visiting his mistress at Merton in her *bur* (bower, chamber):

> And then from the woman's cries the king's thegns became aware of the disturbance and whoever there was ready and quickest ran up; and the prince offered each of them money and life, and none of them would accept it, but in fighting all the while until they lay dead, except one Welsh hostage and he was badly wounded.

Next morning the other thegns heard the news and came up, and they too died to a man, except one who had been wounded several times. They refused all offers; and when the prince (the killer) said that he had some of their kinsmen with him, 'they replied that no kinsman was dearer to them than their lord, and they would never follow his killer'.[11] Not only warriors obeyed the ethic of loyalty. Under the same year we are told how a swineherd avenged his lord, earldorman Cumbra. In the *Battle of Maldon* the simple *ceorl* Dunnere is as ready to die for his lord as any thegn.

Alfred laid down that a man who plotted against his lord should forfeit life and property. Christ commanded that a lord should be loved as oneself. Alcuin in 801 had praised Torhtmund who avenged King Aethelred, and declared that to avenge one's lord in honest feud was not murder or sin. A writer states that any man who observes the proper fasts of the church need not fear hell – unless he is 'a traitor to his lord'.[12] Alfred's laws, while allowing a man to fight in defence of a wrongfully attacked kinsman without becoming liable to a feud, forbade his action if it meant fighting against his lord: 'that we do not permit'. By Edmund's reign everyone was required to swear fealty to the king 'as a man ought to be faithful to his lord'. Wulfstan wrote, 'It is the greatest of all treachery in the world that a man should betray his lord's soul, and a full great treachery it is also in the world that a man should betray his lord to death or drive him in his lifetime from the land; and both have happened in this country. Edward was betrayed and then killed, and Aethelred was driven out of his country.' The church also encouraged a man to do service to his dead lord by taking alms to Rome or making grants to a religious house. A passage in Cnut's laws, perhaps by Wulfstan, declares, 'For all that ever we do, through just loyalty to our lord, we do to our own great advantage; for truly God will be gracious to him who is duly faithful to his lord.'[13]

But we inevitably find outstanding acts of disloyalty as well as of devotion. Aethelbald of Mercia in 757 was murdered by his own bodyguard; next year the same fate befell Oswulf of Northumbria. In 796 Aethelred of Northumbria died through the plot of one of his nobles.

We see how strongly the church supported the ethic of fealty; the death of Jesus became the great instance of a lord's betrayal. And in the theocratic state the king became more than a priestly and anointed character; he was Christ's deputy and approximated to Christ himself:

At God's Judgement you will have to produce and lead forth
the flock of which you've been made the shepherd in this life,
and then give account how you held that which Christ before
bought with his own blood...

> Let no one dare to conspire to kill a king for he is the *christus*
> [anointed] of the Lord, and if anyone take part in such a crime,
> if he be a bishop or anyone of the priestly order, let him be
> expelled from it and cast out from the holy heritage, as Judas
> was ejected from the apostolic order; and everyone who has
> consented to such sacrilege shall perish in the eternal fetters of
> anathema, and, associated with Judas, be burnt in the eternal
> fires...[14]

So, while the premature unifications represented by Charlemagne
broke down on the continent, and were followed in the eleventh
century by endless conflicts of small states, with much local anarchy,
which we have discussed in connection with the rise of Normandy,
in England there was, despite setbacks and periods of confusion, a
steady movement towards a single state. The Danish invasions, we
saw, played an important part in the final stages, breaking down old
divisions and making possible a relatively complete unification as the
English made their retort under Wessex leadership. The regions that
had made up the more effective old kingdoms, together with Welsh
and Scottish princes, acknowledged the overlordship of Edgar (959–
75), the first English king crowned and anointed in a rite adapted
from the consecration of a bishop.[15] He ceded Lothian to Scotland
and ruled over the whole land from Wessex to the Tweed. It was
because of the high degree of unification now reached that the Danes
under Cnut were able to take over the whole area and rule it. England
was only one of the regions that Cnut had to consider; and looking at
the problems of control with the detached eye of a conqueror (as
William was able to do more completely later), he imposed a system
of three great earldoms which brought together big groups of shires.
These earldoms were not compact constitutional units, like Anjou,
nor were they like the great German fiefs of the tenth century; they
were too well integrated in a single royal system. In particular they
coordinated defence over big areas and collected the necessary
finance. The *jarl* or earl got a third of the profits from the shire
courts and a third of the customs rendered by the boroughs. He or
his deputy (a king's reeve, a shire-man, later the shire-reve or
sheriff) presided over the shire court, acting with the bishop.[16] Lesser
earldoms were made up out of the great units, usually to gratify
kinsmen of the three great earls. A Danish warrior married to an
Englishwoman was put over the unruly region of Northumberland;
Mercia and Wessex were under Englishmen, Mercia under Leofric,
Wessex under Godwin. The latter, we saw, owed much of his rise to
his marriage with Gytha, sister of a *jarl* who had married Cnut's
sister. Wessex, Alfred's original kingdom, which controlled the

routes to the continent and contained towns like London and Winchester, was by far the most important earldom. After the creation of the great Mercian kingdom in the eighth century, many lesser dynasties had had to make submission, take gifts from the king, and promise fealty. We see, for instance, Sigered, the last king of Essex, sinking from *rex to subregulus*, then to *dux*, earldorman. The typical ealdorman of the eighth and ninth centuries was, however, a member of the king's household, set over a shire or *regio* and removeable at his lord's will. The king wanted known and trusted men to lead the district's fyrd, enforce the decisions of its folkmoots, and impose terms on any of its nobles who let their household-men break the peace. Under Cnut the earls show a further stage in this development, foreshadowing the advent of the large provincial governments that are prominent under the Confessor.

The ease with which Cnut asserted his rule was then a sign of the general acceptance of an over-all kingship, even if the large numbers of Danes in the Danelaw helped him. What is as significant is the effect of such a situation on Cnut himself. King of England in 1016 at the age of twenty-two, he succeeded his brother in Denmark three years later, and in 1028 got Norway by bribery and war – thus gaining as dependencies Greenland, the Orkneys, the Shetlands, the Hebrides, and the Isle of Man. No system at this time could hold together such an empire and this had broken up by 1049. Apart from an increase of trade with the Baltic, England showed few signs of being affected; but the way in which the people had been drawn suddenly into a wider range of politics could not but bring about many changes, which ultimately facilitated the Norman conquest. Cnut himself developed from a war-chief with a piratic host into a ruler seriously pondering forms of government; he who had been a merely formal Christian became a keen supporter of the church. In 1018 he told an assembly at Oxford that he would enforce the English laws of his predecessors; in 1020 he announced that he would govern in accordance with the counsel of the bishops. His comprehensive law code was indeed based on English tradition; and his firm control ensured twenty years of peace, order and internal development, and in turn made possible Edward's secure reign.[17]

Now let us look at what class differentiations existed side by side with what we may call the exaltation of tribal kingship, aided by the church. In general the social divisions in England were similar to those we find elsewhere in western Europe in this epoch; but just as the differentiations in Scandinavia had taken on their own specific colourations, so the English ones had developed their own unique characteristics.

Lowest were the many slaves or *theows*. In all the stages of feudal society we find an attempt to distinguish the free and unfree. Looking back to a Roman law-maxim, a Carolingian cartulary could declare, 'There is none other than free and unfree [*servus*, serf]'; but the shadings between the two levels were always complicated. At that early phase we find the unfree in administrative posts, *ministrales*, and carrying on industrial work; but the mass of them were on the land. *Serf* came from *servus*, slave, while *slave* seems to be derived from Slav, since Slavonic areas were in early medieval times the main source of slaves, especially after the eastward expansion of the Germans had begun. Slaves were mere chattels, instruments for production on the land or in a workshop, provided by masters with food, clothes and shelter; they owned nothing. Serfs possessed the means of producing their own livelihood, even if they didn't legally own them: farm-buildings, tools, land and common rights, which together constituted the peasant holding. Some may have gone to a lord for grants, but many had held from time immemorial and fell under the lord's power only in difficult periods. The serf was thus distinct from the slave of ancient society or the wage worker of capitalism with whom the market system is the means of compelling him to work and of regulating wages and profits. Under feudalism the lord deals with the producer in an open way, taking products, money or services directly by means of his superior power, whether that power is expressed nakedly through his retainers or in a legal and political form through feudal courts. As Bloch has put it, the feudal system implied the existence of 'a subject peasantry'; it meant 'the rigorous economic subjection of a host of humble folk to a few powerful men'. The land was 'valued because it enabled a lord to provide himself with "men".' It followed that 'whatever the source of a noble's income, he always lived on the labour of other men'.[18]

The existence of this non-economic compulsion in a society where the main source of wealth comes from the land is what we have claimed is the distinguishing factor of feudalism: the one constant factor in many varying stages, each of which needs to be marked with a qualifying phrase. The early stages, when old tribal forms are breaking down, when the war-chief becomes king, when he finds his main support in companions or lesser lords, whose military value is rewarded by gifts of land (without necessarily any clearcut relation between tenures and services), we may call tribal feudalism. It contains many aspects of the old tribal society and also of the more mature feudalism where the fief, its burden, duties, and privileges are precisely defined. Other terms would be needed to characterize the phases from the period when the fief had developed to that of what have been described as the absolutist monarchies of the sixteenth and seventeenth centuries. For the moment it is enough to note that the England of Cnut and Edward represented the highest possible level of what we have called tribal feudalism. We see a complex society of varying levels, which has been developed under a rule that embodies the characteristics of the tribal kingship in an extended form, with a system of law based on local, popular courts and yet centred in the person of the king. On the other hand in Normandy we saw a society moving rapidly towards the feudalism of the explicit military tenure or fief.

In early feudal days there was no simple division between slave and serf. In the late Roman period and the first stages of the barbarian kingdoms, there were various forms of subjection and various ways of becoming subjected, which were reflected in the many terms for a servile class of peasants. Some serfs came from the *coloni* of the late Empire, who, though suffering legal disabilities, were not rated as slaves. They kept on sinking, however, through the burden of obligations imposed by the state and the estate-owners. In so far as the estate structure of the late Empire carried on into the successor states, the story of the *coloni* is fairly clear. They had not changed much in status when the polyptyques or surveys of the big Carolingian estates were made. But other peasants came from families that had been slaves proper in Roman times or who were enslaved during the wars. Now these were *servi cassati*, provided with holdings. Other serfs were originally free men who entered into some sort of dependence under a lord; such men turned to a lord or to the church for security of tenure. On the whole there was a tendency to depress and equalize the status of all peasants, though at any one moment there was much variety among the enserfed – as indeed also among the remaining free men. After the tenth century private jurisdictions grew stronger in the west. In a world of failing central controls it was easy for the landlord's economic power to become political and judicial; *pouvoir banal* became *pouvoir domanial*. By the twelfth century the lord's demesne, worked by forced labour, was, however, beginning to lose its importance; the *mansus*, the traditional peasant tenure, had been much subdivided; labour services were dying out and money rents losing their value. But private jurisdiction still brought in much profit, as did various land services reimposed as a subject's duty rather than as a tenant's rent, and as did the exploitation of seigneurial monopolies: oven, mill, winepress, and the like. Our investigation here is essentially into the period between the lapses of central control and the great changes in feudal relations in the twelfth century.[19]

In England, we have seen, there was never such a failure of kingly controls as on the continent. Also larger numbers of slaves persisted than in Gaul. There are many references to slaves in the law-codes; the *Domesday Book* gave some nine per cent of the population as slaves in 1086 and in the eastern counties the proportion rose as high as forty per cent. There were some 25,000 of them. Many of these slaves were part of demesne resources; their typical occupation was that of demesne ploughman or oxherd. Such is the ploughman in Aelfric's *Colloquy*:

'Ploughman, how do you work?'
'I go out at dawn to drive the oxen to the field, and yoke them to the plough. However hard the winter I dare not stay at home for fear of my lord. Every day I have to plough an acre or more. I have to fill the ox's bin with hay and give them water and carry the dung outside. Hard work it is because I am not free.'

But some slaves worked outside the demesne and may have been ignored by *Domesday* commissioners who were more interested in demesne than in tenant holdings; the *bordarii* may be *servi cassati*. Before 1066 men, women and children could be reduced to slavery as a punishment (e.g. for a false oath), or sold into slavery because of famine or poverty. Slaves had a low wergild of 40 pence. Far back in Pope Gregory's days English slaves were being sold in Rome; and there was long a flourishing trade of slaves from Ireland, who were carried to Bristol. This trade was still active in the eleventh century. Kent had three subdivisions of *theows*. In the thirteenth century the remaining demesne slaves were given holdings as part of their wages for the job.[20] The large-scale persistence of slavery in England was perhaps the result of its relative stability and a conservative attitude to demesne labour.

Above the slaves were the *ceorls* or churls, the relatively free peasants. *Ceorl* originally meant husband: man as correlative of wife. By extension it meant the head of a peasant household: its usual sense in the texts. It corresponds to *rusticus* and its best equivalent in modern English is *husbandman*.[21] The *Rectitudines Singularum Personarum* (probably dated to the generation before 1066) divided *ceorls* into three main groups: *geneatas* (radknights of *Domesday*), *kotsetlan* or cottagers, and *geburas*. As a class they were weakening, caught between the warriors and the *theows*; they tended to lose their economic freedom and with it all other freedoms. Any sort of trouble or mishap was liable to drive a man into dependency: illness, heavy taxes, Norse raids, land tax like the Danegeld. Kings rewarded servants or conferred favours by granting out food rents and other dues payable to themselves. Big landowners, especially churchmen, put tenants on their estates on service conditions. Dependent tenures appear in the Laws of Ine of Wessex (668–726), but must have existed much earlier. These laws deal with lords who grant lands to dependents and demand services as well as rent; dependents who have dared to leave their lords must return and pay compensation; men, even free men, incur penalties by working on Sunday without their lords' consent.[22] The *Dialogue of Salomon and Saturn* states, 'A wealthy *ceorl* may, according to his own inclination, easily choose a mild lord, perhaps a prince; the poor man has no such choice.'[23] The cohesion of the kin-groups, which once gave an individual much protection, had been breaking down, despite its tenacity in certain respects such as the carrying on of blood feuds. One reason was the fact that members settled far apart, so that kindreds ceased more and more to be compact groups; another was the idea that property was alienable, which the church did much to bring in and foster. The limiting of heirs to a certain kin-range grew stronger. By Cnut's time a man who had satisfactorily carried out the obligations on an estate could give it at death to whom he liked. Formal rules suggest that wife, children and close kin were expected to be the main heirs, but there was much freedom of disposal. After land had been legally sold or given away, the kin lost all claim to it and could not even exercise a right of preemption. These situations differ greatly from those of early Scandinavia.[26]

If the *ceorl* was free in comparison with the *theow*, he was not free in any complete way. Alfred in his version of Orosius equates *ceorl* with *libertinus* (freedman, who kept obligations to his patron). His laws show that some Wessex *ceorls* were rich enough to own slaves; these men may have been as free as a man could be in such a world, but there is nothing to suggest that they were typical. The treaty with the Danish King Guthrum equates the East Anglian *ceorls* with Danish freedmen, the half-free *liesengas*. In a will drawn up about 950 a woman directs that two men and a woman are to be set free; she leaves to her daughter the rest of the men 'except the freedmen', with the livestock. She or her predecessor, it follows, stocked the estate with husbandmen and oxen, both of which remained her property; those not freed might presumably be sold off or moved to some other estate by her daughter. The freedmen passed with the land and thus had security of tenure; but as they gained it by express stipulation they seem to have been very much at their mistress's disposal.[25]

We must never think that there was ever a simple struggle between nobles and peasantry. War-chiefs and *comitatus* were present from the start. Ine's laws show nobles who hold land; and they mention both tax-exempt demesne and land with tenant settlers and no exemptions – here already is the distinction between demesne and peasant land. Alfred's version of Augustine's *Soliloquies* assumes that a follower will hope to live only for a time on 'land loaned from his lord', until at last, 'through the lord's kindness, he may earn bookland and perpetual possession'.[26] One element of continuity was the village community, which passed through many phases but was always the basic unit of rural organization. Political life in the last resort rested on the village communities. Village meetings, of which we know little, were probably held at first to deal with problems such as allocating work and controlling refractory individuals, and later to assign police duties in a more regular way. Peasants at all stages of dependence and independence were liable to be found in the villages. The leading member of a family might hold a farm and a share in the village field; but around him would be landless kinsmen and farm labourers. From a rough legal viewpoint they were all of much the same status; but their social and economic roles were very different. A *ceorl*, though in some form of dependence on a lord, was still under the protection of common law. Custom regulated his obligations whether involving *geld* (money rent), *feorm* (rent in kind), or labour services. A lord's estate rarely coincided with a village; persons and lands might be commended to different lords. Peasants with full control of their land and owing only light services to lords were common as sokemen in the Danelaw; but generally peasant status was becoming lower.

Above the peasants were *gesiths* or companions, who had left the kindred to serve the king, accepting him as lord and entering under the shield of his peace, and becoming legally and economically dependent on him. Their role was mainly military and they were classified with a higher wergild than the ordinary *ceorl*: 1200 shillings to his 200. They rose in status by being given grants of land. Their oath had a higher value; their houses were more sacrosanct. Their name fades out during the ninth century; for some time it had been giving way to that of *thegn* – though in effect there was little difference between *gesith* and *thegn*. With both of them what had been an office became an hereditary status. Thegns did both military and administrative work; the magnates' households needed them as well as did the king's. There were not many of them in the eleventh century, but they held a lot of land – though the king could make or break them as his servants at will.[27] Peasants, we must recall, were both tenants of a lord and taxpayers of the king. A lord's motives in letting out his land might be mixed. Some tenants might be asked only to give an oath of loyalty as well as paying the taxes on the land; others to provide various rents and services. The entanglements grew more complex when the king alienated public rights to a landlord.

Probably at the outset estate and village, manor and vill, were all one, and expansion led to the formation of estates covering more than one settlement. In outlying parts lords may well have allowed a fair degree of territorial autonomy. As sections broke off as separate manors, estate structure could become even more complicated. Further differences in grouping could come about through a lord getting hold of nearby estates and rights. The whole picture would in time be made more involved and tortuous through sales and mortgages, leases and rewards, partitions or accretions through provision for women, inheritance and family arrangements (e.g. by co-heirs), forfeitures, illegal tactics, and pious gifts. Aelfhelm, in a will made 975–1016, left half his estate at Conington (Cambridgeshire), already lessened by four and a half hides he had granted to others, to his wife and daughter 'to divide between them', while he left his property at Troston (Suffolk), less a part already given away, to be shared among three brothers. Followers as well as relations had to have their gifts and rewards; such grants could lead to the division of an estate or could alter the structure of a manor. Thus a highly complex pattern of change, breakdown, and conglomeration appears, at work over a long time.[28]

Some suggestive points emerge from an analysis of the Charltons already mentioned: the *tuns* of *ceorls*, though *karl* may have taken over from *ceorl* in areas open to Danish occupation. Were the *ceorls* dependent? In *Domesday Book* many Charltons appear as satellites of other manors; in several cases they are not far from royal seats. So it has been deduced that they were appendages of royal manors, or of manors made up out of the royal domain for the endowment of favoured subjects. But far back the *cyninges tun* or *regia villa*, precursor of the royal manor, was a basic unit in the organization of justice and finance. Here the peasants from the surrounding country paid the food rents that kept the king, and often the profits of justice from the hundred courts were rendered here. These *tuns* seem usually to have had a prison, for Alfred enacts that a pledge-breaker is to be jailed for forty days at the *cyninges tun*, doing whatever penance the bishop ordains. (During the tenth century they attracted traders on account of their good order.) Sites like Axminster, Wantage and Mansfield were not only administrative centres of districts covering a hundred hides or more, but also heads of farming units (perhaps made up of several villages and hamlets). However, such systems began breaking up early with grants, rewards, and gifts to avid churches. So we meet names that speak of the grantee, e.g. Sibton the *tun* of Sibba. Yet the king needs a subordinate *tun* for its food rents and for the services of its *ceorls* in running the central manor. If the latter has a home farm, slaves will be used there, but the *ceorls* will be needed for harvests and the like. The *tun* takes the name of Charlton as the site of the king's *ceorls*, working for themselves but also for the king.[29]

There were three kinds of land that could be held: folkland, bookland, loanland. The first was owned outright by custom; it was held by individuals and normally it reverted only to kinsmen; as disputes about it came up in the folk courts, we know little of it. The second was also owned outright, by those who had managed to get a charter for it. The third was held on conditions and was in many ways like the continental benefice or fief. The Church with its desire to hold in perpetuity had brought in the charter or diploma, *boc* (book), which, couched in a florid Latin influenced by the Celts, conveyed land in terms of the vulgar law of the late Roman empire.[30] By the time of Edward the Confessor the charter had given way to the writ in the royal court. Land which the king granted could not be reclaimed, unless a thegn-owner neglected his duties such as fyrd-service or deserted in battle. The system was spreading from the church to the laity – though for the church it meant land capable of being held for ever, and for the layman it meant land that could be alienated or bequeathed. From the eighth century *boc*-land had been given to the thegns. But the charter was not itself the grant, which was made ceremonially, by symbolic gesture and word of mouth. As in Germanic custom law every gift needed a counter-gift; the formulas of Roman law no doubt obscured the fact that a return was expected: prayers and masses from the church, a price or services from the layman.[31] Disputes about it bypassed the folk courts and went straight to king and witan. As usual in the feudal world, even outright ownership was not absolute; the land was liable to be burdened with some service or other. And there was heriot, paid to the lord on a tenant's death by the heir in money, horses or arms, but remitted if a man fell in battle. For *boc*-land, however, the emphasis was not on services or dues, though it involved the burdens common to all land: maintenance of bridges and fortifications, and military duties. The charter or grant did not create the duties, which were linked with all landowning; but by the eleventh century the *Rectitudines* could consider that a thegn held his land in return for military services.

Leases, traced back to the late seventh century, multiplied in the period before the conquest. The church, wanting land for perpetuity, hated giving things away on the same terms; and anyway it could not give lands for which it was in effect a trustee. Yet it had to reward servants and thegns, and so it used loanland, which was a sort of benefice. Thus land could be lent to servants or leased for rent in money or kind, and life interests could be created in land for widows, younger children, and such dependents. Religious houses

granted leases to household retainers, *cnihts*, and thegns in return
for personal services or for taking over common burdens due to the
king – of which military service was the most important. In the
terms of Anglo-Norman lawyers the land was burdened with both
intrinsic and forinsec services. No doubt laymen also used leases, but
we lack evidence. The extant leases (of churchland) are mostly for
three lives, but could cover shorter times. Within the stated period
leaseland could be inherited or bequeathed; but failure to carry out
the entailed services could mean the loss of the land.

Land could change hands a lot, often begetting confusions and
lawsuits. In a charter dealing with Hurstbourne (Hampshire) we find
the lordship passing from the Wessex king to an ealdorman, then to a
church in Berkshire, then back to the king. It stayed in royal hands
half a century, though from 858 under promise of finally coming to
the Old Minster. In Alfred's reign the minster gained possession; but
with all the stress of war and tribute the clergy had to borrow money
from the king and repay him by handing back the usufruct. Ten
hides at Stoke were detached and entrusted to a thegn or royal reeve.
Alfred was now dead; Hurstbourne and Stoke were to be reunited and
at long last the minster would get permanent possession. But in the
bustle of a new reign the transfer took several months; perhaps the
witan was called in, as the matter is described as contentious, settled
not without trouble, *elucabratim*. The charter shows a wish to close
up every loophole.[32]

Land, we saw, was burdened with military obligations. Much
argument has gone on as to whether we can then equate such land
with the Norman military fief. The landed nobles were certainly
bound to answer the king's call and serve him in war, or else to lose
their land. The tenure had its military aspect, but this aspect was not
made the explicitly defined basis on which the grant was made. The
thegns had to fight, but their main function was administrative.
Thegnship was a status. A merchant who voyaged three times oversea, or a priest attending the king, might be promoted to it. If a
thegn broke with his lord or gave his land away, he still had his
military duties. Since England, an island, did not have to meet
enemies on horseback in large battles, specialization had gone less far
than in France. A thegn would be better armed than a *ceorl* in the
fyrd, but there was no such gap as between mounted knight and
footsoldier in Normandy. The thegn did not have to buy, rear, or
train destriers. Thus England with its high degree of tribal-national
integration did not find itself driven to explicit fief feudalism; but the
general concept of land-ownership involving military obligations was
as alive there as anywhere else.[33]

We see then that England had developed a relatively stable society, with broad class distinctions based ultimately on a man's relation to land. Inside the main divisions there was much differentiation; but the strong tribal basis, with power concentrated in the hands of the king, who was seen as the war-chief, prevented the *gesiths* or companions developing into barons such as we have seen in Normandy. The later earldoms indeed suggest great baronies and begin to take on some of their characteristics; but the king still has a supreme place for which we find no parallel in post-Carolingian Gaul. The stability of the kingship, however, cannot be properly understood without a consideration of the popular courts and the king's peace, which we shall look at later.

For the moment it is enough to note that there were two great binding forces in this society: forces which in some respects merged to strengthen one another, and in other respects were antagonistic. These were the bond of lordship, which we have considered, and the bond of kindred. In everyday village life the two bonds continually interlocked. A man in his home and in the fields was affected continually by both relationships; and it was the harmony of the two bonds that gave him many of his impulses, satisfactions and organizing energies. And yet, in the full historical process, the overriding needs of lordship were breaking down the broad and rich kindred systems. At first the commendation of person or land was a private matter, a private bond. But it greatly affected a man's place in the kindred, drawing him into a different sphere of controls. And the kings soon saw its use in their police administration. In such a society a man for whom no one was responsible was a suspicious and unreliable character. Was the kindred or the lord responsible for this or that man? The kindred had certain protective functions, especially in connection with acts of violence against him; but more and more the lord controlled his economic and social life. As the law codes developed, we see the weakening of the kin bond. Already in the early seventh century, in the laws of Wihtred of Kent, an accused *ceorl* had to clear himself, with the help not of his kinsmen, but of three oath-helpers of his own status. A century later the laws of Ine enjoined, in the case of a man charged with homicide, the inclusion of a man of high rank among those who testified; and for a *ceorl* such a witness could only be the lord to whom he was bound. Theft was a common crime. But the kindred, possibly scattered about, were not the most likely to know the facts; the accused had to get oaths sworn by neighbours whom he chose and who were then named for him by the court, provided that he did not thus suffer disparagement. An embryonic notion of trial by peers is present here. If the offence were against the king, a man was better placed if he could

call on neighbours chosen by royal officials. In general we may say
that territorial connections had begun to oust the kindred and that
fealty to a lord disrupted the kin bond. We saw how Alfred allowed
a man to fight for a wronged kinsman only if it did not mean fighting
his lord.

Not that in such a world the kin element could ever be quite
driven out or reduced to the family in its narrow sense. We have no
clear proof that there ever were corporate holdings of land by kindreds or if the latter ever existed as territorial units; but right into
the eleventh century the kindreds carried on as a powerful source of
social control. A law of Aethelstan mentions a kin group strong
enough to resist the central authority, but it may refer to a man
who gathered members of his kindred from far as well as near.[34] The
stress was on patrilineal descent and the kin thus involved; on the
spear side rather than on the spindle side. Surnames did not exist,
though additional names might be given to help identification, amid
the crowd of Aelfwines, Wulfrics, and the like. Children's names
were compounded from parents' names, but there is no trace of
reference to a named kin group.[35]

How far did reality live up to the ideal of loyalty, not in the high
exciting moments, but in everyday life? We see the steady intrusion
of economic bargaining in the forms of commendation and dependence. Except among household troops and the like the old element of
devoted adherence between lord and man could hardly have been
felt. In theory all free men were obliged to join the royal fyrd in an
emergency. Alfred called up sections at a time and so could extend
the length of campaigns, but in general a peasant soldiery could not
stay long away from the fields. Something of the old *comitatus*
relationship was carried on by the king's thegns. The number of such
retainers was much enlarged by Cnut with his house-carles or com-
panions-in-arms, Anglo-Danish courtiers well endowed with land.
But we must not think of all the thegns as being on their level or as
much involved with the king. No doubt free men on the whole felt a
definite loyalty towards the king in the sense of looking to him as the
ultimate source of what they most valued in life; and at certain
moments this emotion could be intensified. But it could also be
jeopardized by heavy exactions. Alfred had built a fleet of ships too
large, we are told, for his people to handle them; and later kings
maintained the right to seize any ship in times of need. But a regular
fleet was too expensive for the revenues of those days; Cnut reached
England with forty ships, then quickly reduced the number to sixteen.
When Harthacnut tried to bear the cost of forty-two ships, he caused
much discontent and two of his house-carles were murdered.

Still, the kings did their best to remain at the centre of the situation and keep a constant grip on men's loyalties; and partly through the workings of the local courts they were able to appear as the effective fountain-head of justice and security. The ideal position was expressed in the *Battle of Maldon* where the warriors are ready to die for their lord Byrhtnoth, but he sees himself in the role of 'guardian of the people and of the country, the home of Aethelred my prince – who'll defend this land to the last ditch'. Here is the perfect feudal situation: the retainers, nobles and even lesser *ceorls* all faithful to the lord, and the lord faithful to the king, his overlord, who in turn embodies an embryonic sense of the nation.

In that ideal situation the kindred systems did not intrude; they merely helped men to exist and work together in a cooperative brotherly sort of way. But in practice there could be clashes of kindreds, especially when the member of one was killed and his fellows felt impelled by the bond to avenge him on the killer, who in turn invoked the solidarity of his own group. And villagers in areas where kindred groups had at all strongly survived would talk over any grievances they had against the lord and would be encouraged to resist. Later we will look at two matters that show the power of the kindred in English society: the way in which the kings sought to keep peace by inducing kindreds to take wergild in compensation for a killed member rather than turn to the feud, and the way in which, as the kindred forms weakened, men sought to devise new forms of cooperation, guilds, on the same model. Here we can well consider the hide, which in this period was seen as a territorial unit, used for assessing taxes and rents, renders and services for king or lord, but which has a complex story behind it, a story that helps us to grasp the early English concept of family and kindred.

The hide can be traced back in documents to the seventh century; and the laws of Ine, the East Saxon king, have a rule defining the food render due from ten hides. The Northumbrian Bede several times refers to the hide and calls it the normal unit of land measurement used by the English. Kings and lords use both the manse and the hide in their systems; but it is most unlikely that they devised the forms or criteria of the measurements of land which they applied. To do so they would have needed methods of surveying and administration which plainly they lacked. The unit they used would certainly have been taken over from earlier stages in the evolution of their society. The Frankish *manse*, a unit equivalent to the hide, may have existed since the late Roman empire, when administrators may have taken it up in assessing taxes and services; but again they certainly did not create it. (By comparing the Anglo-Saxon evidence with that from Ireland in this period, where there is no question of Roman influences in such matters, we see that both Celtic and Germanic society had fairly similar systems.) The hide had three main aspects: it was the land of one family, the land of a normal freeman, the land worked by one plough.[36]

The key question is how a family was defined. Was it as wide as a kindred, or was it the limited family of man, wife, and children? In Germanic tongues the term for the home (Old English *ham*, Old High German *heim*, Gothic *haims*, village) is linked with the Old English *hæmed*, sexual intercourse. The home is the place where a man and his wife cohabit. So the Old English words for hide (*hīd*, *hīwisc*, *hiwīscipe*) seem definitely to refer to the limited family, its house and holding. As early as the late seventh century in Wessex, and perhaps earlier in Mercia and Northumbria, the emphasis on the term hide shifted from the home aspect to that of the land unit. A passage in Bede's *Historia Abbatum* shows that at a landholder's death the estate was divided among the sons, but the eldest son was given a preference. Ine's laws show that his prerogative was the 'first seat'. The inheriting sons each set up his own home.[37]

The normal freeman or *ceorl* belonged to the main body of freemen entitled to share fully in the life of the community. The hide was the unit of land he held, an area enabling him to enjoy his status. The noble held at least five hides.) Already in Ine's Wessex many peasants, legally free, were in fact tenants of manorial lords; they were probably often yardlanders, holding a quarter of a hide. There was thus a loosening of the link between wealth and status.) Where does the kindred come into this system, and how was it constituted? For any precise information on this point we must turn to wergild. In Ireland, the four-generation, agnatic lineage was the basic kin group for feuds as for other matters. The status of a lord required that the holders of a five-hide unit, namely a lineage, should be his vassals; lineage, lordship, status and land were bound up in a closely knit unity. We best make sense of the English situation by assuming that 'at an early stage in the history of the Germanic speaking peoples a corresponding system existed in their society. This would involve three essential elements: the status of the normal freeman, an appropriate holding of land and a kinship system which included the lineage as a normal form of kin-group' (Charles-Edwards).

It seems clear that the structure of Anglo-Saxon kinship was agnatic; but such a structure did not imply that men who were not members of the same agnatic kindred might not have close kin ties. In agnatic systems there is often a close link between a man and his mother's brother – perhaps a carry-over from matrilinear systems. In certain circumstances a man may then become attached to his maternal kindred as if it were the paternal one. Such a tie was possible in Ireland; it is also recognized in some Welsh lawbooks.

Tacitus tells us of his Germans:

> The sons of sisters are highly honoured by their uncles as by their own fathers. Some even go so far as to regard this tie of blood as peculiarly close and sacred, and, in taking hostages, insist on having them of this group; they think this gives them a firmer grip on men's hearts and a wider hold on the family. However, a man's heirs and successors are his own children, and there is no such thing as a will; where there are no children, the next to succeed are, first, brothers, and then uncles, first on the father's, then on the mother's side. The larger a man's kin and the greater the number of his relations by marriage, the stronger is his influence when old.[38]

The laws earlier than the Danish invasions do not define kindreds; the latter were so integral a part of society that their role and nature is assumed. We must look to Bede for information. Genealogies of kings in Kent and East Anglia are agnatic in form: the members of royal kindreds could trace their descent back in the male line to a particular ancestor. A man could become king in one of three ways. A member of the royal kindred who showed powers of leadership, especially in war, might be elected; the eldest son might succeed; the kingdom might be divided among two or more sons. Partible inheritance meant that if there were at least two or three sons in each generation, we should after a while get a cluster of farmsteads held by agnatic kinsmen. (This point does not apply to lords with scattered estates; hence the impermanence of their kindreds.) The clusters were at times called by the name of the kindred: for example, one type of early place name is formed on the same pattern as were the names of royal kindreds such as the Oiscingas or the Wuffingas. The suffix -ing was attached to a personal name, with the masculine plural -as added. Not that all -ingas names can be assumed to be originally the names of kindreds, but many of them probably were.[39]

Such groups, we noted, did not own land collectively, though the rule against alienating land outside the kindred shows there was still a feeling that a kindred had a territorial unity, into which non-members should not intrude. Ine's laws reveal neighbours (clusters of agnatic lineage?) cooperating in agricultural matters. There is strong evidence for the long life of kindreds; one late Northumbrian vendetta carried on for four generations.[40] The *Chronicle* says that Uhtred was killed by the advice of Eadric Streona; but the main agent seems to have been a noble, Thurbrand. Uhtred, it seems, came with forty companions to treat for peace with Cnut, but they were all killed by Cnut's soldiers through Thurbrand's guile. Thurbrand was then killed by Uhtred's son, earl of Northumbria, who in turn was killed by Waltheof, son of Earl Siward, whose mother was the earl's daughter. The *gegildan*, the group of associates who supported each other in feuds (and later in other ways) formed a corporate body and played a role analogous to that of the kindred. And indeed the kindred was used as a model for various kinds of social and political groups. A whole people might be called a kin, *maeg* or *cynn*; and thus the kindred in its final emotional extension foreshadowed the later nation.[41]

Despite then the silence of the laws on the kindreds (apart from wergild), it is clear that they played an essential part in holding English society together. We know a good deal about the forms of exploitation of the normal freemen by the lords; but in the concrete details of everyday life the ties of kindred must have operated in a myriad of pervasive ways that are largely lost to us.

We now turn to the system of kingly or centralized government which had been built up, and its relation to the popular local courts. The royal household showed a mixture of primitive elements and advanced methods. A great deal of the income was still food rent; but there was a certain amount of cash kept in a chest. The chest was at first put with other belongings in the wardrobe next to the king's chamber, to be looked after by his *bower-thegns* (chamberlains) and his *hraegel-thegns* (wardrobe attendants). But as the quantity of money increased and the king still moved round much of the time, by Cnut's reign it had to be stored in a single place where it could be watched over and be available for auditing; the coins were weighed or assayed as to their silver content. Lesser store points had also to be set up. The sheriffs of each shire farmed the various items of the royal revenue (profits of justice, customs of boroughs, *feorms* of royal estates) and paid in the stipulated amounts at Winchester, together with any extra sums that had come in. 'No other fisc in Europe had developed so far; and it was accepted and developed by the Normans. Its archives, like those of the *scriptorium*, have disappeared. Its records were superseded by, and started anew with, Domesday Book' (Barlow). We saw that in a smaller and more circumscribed way the Normans had begun to move towards a monetary system in their treasure; but the English system was far more complex and far-reaching. After the Conquest the Normans were able to build upon it, driven by their keen and ruthless quest for profits, and their capacity to see the potential in systems worked out by others.

There were also the usual officials of any court of the time. Thegns served as butlers, stewards (table-waiters), chamberlains (or stallers, the Danish term), with priests and clerks in the oratory. In the country the king and his thegns dominated each shire, reeves supervised his estates and the hundreds, port-reeves in the boroughs and sheriffs in the shires. His system was that of a magnate writ large, while the magnates used the system on a smaller scale. The clerks, apart from religion, acted as scribes, but there was no definite *scriptorium* or chancellor, though *Domesday* uses the latter term of one of Edward's clerks. We see clear signs of administrative continuity from Aethelstan on.[42] The diploma faded out at the conquest; but the writ or summary letter, setting out in English the grant of land or privileges, was taken over by the Normans and underlay most of the diplomatic forms used in medieval England. The use of the vernacular was remarkable for western Europe and carried on till 1070 when the Normans reverted to Latin, without significantly changing the form. The writ's virtue lay in its direct simple form as an order sent to the king's officer in the shire court where it was read to the assembly.[43] How clear and even curt it could be may be seen in the writ (1045–53) issued to the monastery of St Mary in Coventry: 'King Edward declares that he has granted to Abbot Leofwine judicial and financial rights over his lands and over his men as fully and as completely as ever Earl Leofric had.' A more detailed example is that issued to the twelve canons at Bromfield serving the minster of St Mary:

> King Edward sends greetings to archbishop Ealdred and bishop Begard and earl Harold and all my thegns in Herefordshire and in Shropshire. And I inform you that I have granted to St Mary and to my clerks at Bromfield who dwell in the minster in the service of Christ, that they be worthy of their sake and their soke (jurisdiction) over their lands, and to payments made as penalty for breach of the peace and for forcible entry into other people's houses and for committing ambush and to the right of doing justice on a thief taken within the estate in possession of stolen property, and that they be entitled to every fine within borough and without, to toll and to vouching-to-warranty on strand and in stream. And I will not allow anyone to take anything therefrom, neither bishop nor any other person, save whomsoever they may themselves desire. And I will not permit anyone to violate this on pain of losing my friendship.

Cnut had used a double image on his seal as king of two realms, a seal that enabled the writ to be sealed open. He seems to have drawn on the seal of the successors of the Emperor Otto III (983–1002); and Edward carried on the style. His seal, three inches wide, showed the king enthroned in majesty on both its sides, and was the first of its kind in Europe, providing the type for most 'great seals'.

We see then that a relatively advanced central system was built up expressive of the high degree of efficiency in the local courts and their interrelations with the crown. But the development was fairly recent; the administrative structure of shire and hundred was a product of the tenth century. The kingship had been extending and coordinating its rule ever since Alfred. The creation of the great earls as viceroys of wide tracts was Cnut's work. Structures at lower levels had been strengthened and given a cohesive force, while at the same time the unifying role of the kingship was intensified. The way in which the system had been built appears especially in the shires with their various origins and in the diversity shown by the hundreds or the wapentakes.

In all decisions of importance the king was associated with the *witangemot*.[44] The *wita* (plural *witan*) was a man whom he consulted, a councillor. But the group was not a constitutional body, with a list of secular and ecclesiastical magnates who had a right to attend. It was simply the group who happened to be present and whom the king consulted, traditionally composed of members of his household, earls, bishops, abbots and thegns with court offices or an influential role in the area where the meeting took place. A king or any lord was in custom expected to take counsel of leading vassals. The unlucky Aethelred II was called *Unraed*, Uncounselled. In a sense the witangemots were household occasions, held often at festival times when the great men were likely to attend court for social reasons, to keep in touch with the king and with one another. The linking up of these high court gatherings with festivals was older than Christianity and went back to the days of the sacral kingship, of which so many survivals remained. Under Edward we can make out twenty-six meetings of varying size in his twenty-four years as king; on the average thirty to forty persons seem to have been present. They discussed whatever was the most pressing business of the moment, political, judicial, diplomatic. Grants were now made, dooms issued, geld imposed, treaties or high appointments dealt with. The witan was not meant to represent different or conflicting opinions or interests that had to be resolved. The assumption of a tribal or feudal society was that custom held all the answers and reflected the needs of everyone. Men only wanted to clarify custom for new application; counsel was a form of aid, not a way of thwarting or correcting the king's judgment. In fact, opinions did differ at times and there could be a pull of opposing interests; but these were expected somehow to find their place in a unanimous agreement as to what constituted the customary solution. The witan too could play a part in disputed successions. There was no rigid scheme of succession by an eldest son. If the direct heir was a child, some other suitable member of the royal kindred could be chosen. A certain elective element survived from remote times in the notion that the ruler needed the approval of the people, expressed by acclamations. Councils of the same general type as the witan (descended from the gatherings of tribal elders) were characteristic of all the kingdoms with a tribal basis in western Europe; we saw that the Normans too had their ducal council. But the scope of the witan was unusually large because of the scope of the English kingship.

Law too was seen as the expression of immemorial custom which bound everyone including the king. It was long before men could feel that to change the law was not to break it. (The earlier laws consist of kingly dooms distinguished from customary law by being judgments on doubtful points or edicts for a better administrative enforcement.)[45] In fact new problems and solutions kept arising as society grew more complex, but generally these could be dealt with in a way that did not appear to harm the rule of custom. The collections of dooms that have come down, beginning about 600, are the earliest body of law in any Germanic tongue and have no continental parallel.

An important part was played by wergild, the price at which a man's life was assessed according to his social status. But the dooms became much more than a reassertion of the wergild principle as the kindreds weakened; they also contained the assertion of the over-riding power of the state, of the king's pervasive legal presence. Elsewhere kings were losing the power to issue laws as judicial power was fragmented; in England that power was never lost. Not that the fragmenting process was absent; if it had been, the key tensions through which feudalism operated and developed would have been lacking. At least from the seventh century the magnates had policing powers and the obligation to present men in their own courts, first their retainers, then their tenants. Thus forces were set into movement that kept on sapping the strength of the kin groups, which found their most obvious expression in bloodfeuds. A strong king in the tenth century could to some extent treat the lords as if they were officials carrying on the day to day work of administration; but at the same time the counter-movement was present, with kings granting away jurisdiction rights and their profits. Many hundred courts thus ceased to be directly under the crown. But the presiding lord took the profits, not by inherent right, but through a royal grant. The danger was that where there was little or no profit, there tended also to be a slackening of royal interest. A basic medieval

adage was that 'Justice is a Great Profit'. Justice without profit was
liable to lose its whole basis of existence; and the king had ceaselessly
to watch its workings. Asser stresses how Alfred was constantly
struggling to control his bishops, earldormen, thegns and reeves,
'who next to the king had all the power in the kingdom'. He continually praised or censured them, watching out for obstinacy, slackness or corruption; if need be, he threw them out of their offices.[46]

By the middle of the eleventh century a wealthy thegn held land
'with sake and with soke, with toll and with team, and with *infan-
genetheof*'. The first phrase, arising from a lord's jurisdictional
rights, had now become a vague general expression; its jingle form
shows its distant folk roots. The second phrase referred to the lord's
right to demand a sum out of the sale of goods or livestock on his
estate and to hold a court for dealing with disputes over ownership.
The third showed a more direct intrusion on the king's preserves;
it expressed the right to carry out summary justice on a thief caught
in the act. As in Normandy, graver crimes were reserved for the
ruler except where an express concession was made. By 1066 such
grants had been made to several magnates, bishops and monasteries.
But the exceptions did not affect the principle that all justice was
royal justice: a principle alive in England more than anywhere else
in Europe. A free man looked to the folk courts to enforce his rights
under the law.

The shire had several origins. Some shires began as administrative
units set up by the kings round the towns, e.g. Wilton administered
Wiltshire; Dorchester, Dorset. But other shires represented tribal
kingdoms absorbed into larger groupings: Kent, Essex, Sussex. Others
were sub-divisions of such kingdoms: East Anglia was cut into Norfolk and Suffolk. Mercia copied the Wessex system; and Alfred's heirs
created more shires in the east as they took over the Danelaw. Apart
from Rutland (created out of the dowerlands of Edward's queen) all
the shires had been established by the middle of the eleventh century,
reaching from south England to the Tees. The earlier shires thus had
a more organic element than some of the later ones, though the
Danelaw shires may have borne some relation to the various Danish
groupings there. Shires existed long before we hear of their courts,
but the latter no doubt descended from the folk moot, a tribal
assembly. The ultimate origin must have been the tribal gathering of
all free men in a particular grouping, however the social relationships changed. In Alfred's Wessex each shire had its head, the ealdorman, whom the king named; but the tendency was for the ealdorman
to deal with more and more shires till he evolved into Cnut's earl
or viceroy, with the shire-reeve or sheriff taking over his earlier

role in the court – though earl or bishop might preside there in special circumstances. The court, where decisions were final, met twice a year to deal with all sorts of disputes between free men. By Edward's day the function of declaring the law of the shire and of giving judgment had passed to the king's thegns.[47]

Here is the record of a Herefordshire case under Cnut:

> This writing is to declare that a shire-moot sat at Aegelmoth's Stone in the days of king Cnut. There sat bishop Aethelstan and Ranig the ealdorman and Eadwine the ealdorman's son and Leofwine Wulfstig's son and Thurkil the White, and Tofig Pruda came there on the king's errand, and there was Bryning the sheriff and Aegelweard of Frome and Leofwine of Frome and Godric of Stoke and all the thegns of Herefordshire.
>
> Then came Eadwine son of Eanwene to the moot and made claim against his mother for a piece of land...And they appointed three thegns from the moot to ride to the place where she was...and when they came to her she was vehemently angry with her son...and said...'Here sits Leofled my kinswoman, wife of Thurkil the White, to whom after my death I grant my land and my gold...and all I possess.' And she said to the thegns, 'Act like thegns and duly announce my errand to the moot before all the good men and make known to them to whom I have granted my land, and ask them to be witness to this.'
>
> And they did so. They rode to the moot and made known to all the good men what she laid on them. Then Thurkil the White stood up in the moot and asked all the thegns to give his wife clear the lands her kinswoman granted her, and they did so. And Thurkil rode to St Aethelbert's minister, by leave and witness of the whole people, and caused this to be recorded in a gospel book.

But the peasant was not likely to have affairs that needed to go beyond the hundred court. The hundred may once have been made up of a hundred hides, the land required to support a hundred *ceorls* with their families; as a military term it is known to Tacitus. It appears as an administrative unit under Edgar, when it may have been a recent creation. It was probably a division of the old *regio*, introduced into other areas as the Wessex kings expanded. (The *regio* was a governmental unit or district centring on a royal *tun* and administered by a royal reeve: perhaps rated at a hundred hides and legally described as *manung*, jurisdiction.)[48] The courts met in the open every four weeks under the king's reeve or his bailiff, and transacted every-day business. In this interlocking system, the king's officials or delegates could deal with disputes or crimes at the differing levels of shire and hundred, while petty matters were disposed of at yet a lower level. Thus the kings could build up a fiscal organization without parallel elsewhere.[49] And they were able in emergency to send an order to sheriffs for a sum of money, which was divided up among the hundreds and there assessed on groups of hides. Such tax demands were gelds, raised for example by Aethelred II several times. That king probably brought in Danegeld, levied to buy off the Danes. No attempt was made to impose a new and uniform rating everywhere; the local forms of assessment were taken over.[50] By Edward's time the system had grown unequal and complicated because of exemptions or reductions for the estates of favoured persons. The *Domesday* commissioners, baffled, merely recorded the geld assessment of an estate. Yet with all the imperfections, the application of such a tax at this time was a remarkable achievement.

The growth of the king's function of regulating the system, keeping order and centring it on himself, may be seen in the extensions of the notion of what constituted his peace, *grith* or *mund*. In a sense he became the embodiment of the kin groups he displaced, and so exacted payments or *wites* from the offender. His *mund* was the most generalized form of order of which the society at its various stages were capable; it was reflected in the *mund* of every free man's house. In the hierarchical system, in the scale of wergilds, the violation of *mund* grew more villainous the higher the status of the man concerned. With the king's increasing scope, his enlarged household and group of officials, his *mund* could more easily be violated. (By the time of Henry I it embraced the whole of the country where he happened to be.)[51] It thus became like a shield reaching out all over his subjects and finding expression through shire and hundred courts. Under Edward the king's sheriff could proclaim the king's peace as well as the king himself. His peace tended to take over areas where it was uncertain what individual or group was responsible for order : highways, big rivers, churches, monasteries; and in periods of special sanctity, when God's *mund* should be reigning: Christmas, Lent, Easter and Whitsun. (We see here a point of contact with the continental Truce of God, which was however never so closely linked with secular justice.) The king's *mund* was then not as yet omnipresent, but it tended to pervade social life and law. His *grith* could be given to a favoured person, who was then always under his protection and who could invoke it in the courts. (Again the logical conclusion was reached under Henry I when the king could claim jurisdiction over certain crimes wherever or against whomsoever they were committed.) Appeals could be made to the king. Throughout the medieval period unjust or over-rigid applications of law could only be dealt with through his mercy: a personal act rather than a decision derived from the legal system itself.[52]

As always in feudal society the contrary principle was at work. All authority had its *mund*, but an earl's was less than a king's, a thegn's less than that of an earl's, a *ceorl's* less than a thegn's. The *mund* was fragmented as well as made ever more cohesive. But the king's reserved rights to try major crimes and derelictions of duty that affected him had again the effect of spreading his peace over the whole country. Asser in his account of Alfred shows how hard a king had to struggle with what he calls the judges, *judices*. There were constant quarrels in the moots, among the thegns and free men, because of discontent and questioning of decisions by ealdor-men and reeves, and constant appeals to the king. We get a picture of a suitor asking for justice. 'And the king stood and washed his hands in the chamber at Wardour.' Then he investigated the case and decided that the accused, a biggish landowner and king's man, though thievish, must 'take the oath if he could', on an appointed day in the folk moot. Alfred, 'inquired in a wise way into the judg-ments given in his absence throughout almost the whole kingdom', probed the motives of those who had been unjust, and gave advice on studying Saxon books to those who erred through ignorance.

But if the idea of the king's peace and the systems for spreading it had to contest centrifugal forces, they also had to overcome yet deeper tribal resistances, those based on the kindred. We have glanced at this, but need to look closer. On the continent efforts had been made early to control the feuds of the kindreds; England too with its dooms tried to bring order into the system and gradually subordinate it to the king's law. In England there was a more pro-tracted struggle, for the whole process had to go on in a more organic way, feudal and tribal aspects interacting with one another in a series of shifting and extending tensions which did not exist so continuously elsewhere. In such a world a man had three points of dependence, three bonds of scurity: his relations to kindred, lord, and king. No one of the three was satisfactory by itself, so that a man had to try to make the best fusion of the three that was possible at his point in time and space.[53]

Under Alfred and as late as Aethelred and Cnut issues of kinship were still very important. Under Alfred a man without paternal kin was supported by the king and his associates: they were the ones to collect wergild if he were killed. Aethelstan took strong measures against men who were so rich, or who belonged to such a cohesive kindred, that they could not be punished. If necessary, they were moved, noble or commoner, with their goods, wives and children, to another part of the country. (We have seen that a certain territorial concentration was necessary for a kindred to exert much power.) If the moved men came back, they were to be treated like thieves caught in the act. The harbouring of thieves by powerful kindreds was specially condemned; reeves were to ride against such groups and to kill the thief and all who fought at his side. Edmund, who was himself murdered, tried to break the kindreds by enacting that a killer must bear the feud alone unless the kindred arranged composition. Anyone taking vengeance on a kinsman of the offender was to incur the hostility of the king and his men, and to forfeit all his property. Aethelred's code of 1014 stated that a kinless man was to clear himself of a bloodfeud with his associates or to undergo ordeal; Cnut's law ten years later was on the same lines. We find too that a monk must renounce the claims of kinship and his misdeeds must be atoned for by religious means.

There are three main texts dealing with wergild: that called *Wer*, the second code of Edmund, and the *Laws of Henry I* (a twelfth century compilation which used material from a source other than the *Wer*). *Wer*, in the tenth or early eleventh century, bases its calculations on the sum appropriate for a noble, the man with a wergild of 200 shillings; like other sources it distinguishes between the close kinsmen and the more remote kin. The former were entitled to a preliminary compensation, called the grasp-of-the neck (*healsfang*), to halt those most directly affected from starting off the vendetta. *Wer* and the *Laws* disagree as to who shared the *healsfang*. *Wer* says the children, brothers, and paternal uncles, the other source says the father, sons, and brothers. Only if these are lacking is 'he that is nearer from the father' (the paternal uncle) to get it. The second group is the limited family; the group in *Wer* is wider. The notion of the limited family is supported by the *Leis Willelme* (c. 1190–1135), which assigns the *healsfang* to the widow and children of the killed man. The differences here may be in part explained by a law of Aethelred which forbids marriage within a certain degree of kinship; *Wer* says that those who get *healsfang* are those 'within the knee'. Thus: 'Let it not happen that a Christian man should marry his own kin in the degree of six men: that is, within the fourth knee' – what is forbidden is marriage with a fourth cousin.

We see here again how the wide scope of marriage taboos was linked with the wide scope of kindred systems. Cnut's laws say that the penalty for incest is paid according to the degree of kinship, and that, if a man dies intestate, his property is to be divided among his wife, children, and close kinsmen, 'each in the proportion which belongs to him'. It is possible that this latter law merely meant that the kinsmen shared the moveable goods; but in any event we see two divergent rules in late Anglo-Saxon times: one restricting inheritance to the limited family of which the dead man was father, and one not thus restricting it. This divergence corresponds to that between *Wer* and the *Laws* on wergild.

The process of payment is set out in Edmund's code. Wise men start off the reconciliation; the killer uses an advocate to approach the dead man's kinsmen; only then does he himself approach them under safe conduct, and promises to pay wergild. He then finds a surety for the sum. The king's peace is thus established over the persons concerned; any violence that may follow involves a heavy fine to the king. Twenty-one days after *healsfang* is paid; twenty-one days after that the dead man's lord gets his compensation; twenty-one days later again comes the first instalment of wergild – the whole to be paid within a year of the death. We see here a distinction between the close kin and the more distant; but there is no precise delimitation or explanation. There must have been a well known rule, or there would have been endless quarrels on both sides. But apparently the rule was so well known that it was never spelt out.

In later times associates or friends tended to take over some of the functions of the kindred; but as these men would normally belong to the same lord as the kinless man, this is only an aspect of the dependency on that lord. The matter is complicated by the fact that *freond* or *frynd* may also mean kinsman, but we also see associates gaining importance as oath-helpers.[55] The kin were still claiming wergild in the early eleventh century; and though bishop Wulfstan complained that 'now too often a kinsman does not protect a kinsman any more than a stranger', he himself gives us an example of feud-obstinacy. Preaching at Gloucester on his usual text of peace, he found one of the listeners complaining that though he had killed a man by accident he could not buy pardon and peace at any price from the five brothers of the dead man. Wulfstan had to work a miracle before the brothers called off their feud. The concept of wergild was so familiar that the term came to be used for a fine, the aspect of blood-compensation forgotten. In the *Laws of Henry I* even a slave has a small wergild allotted.[56]

Historians have tended to underestimate the significance and importance of the kindreds. Because they impinged on the king's peace only in the bloodfeud, they have been treated as if they existed simply to deal with murders of their members. But the solidarity expressed in the feud could only come into existence and continue to exist from quite other causes. The feud was, so to speak, the outward expression of what arose internally from fraternal and co-

G

operative activities; its strength gives the measure of the inner bonds which it sought to protect and avenge.

Notions of commendation and wergild or ransom are embedded deeply in early medieval theology. It was held that Christ's death was a ransom-payment that ended the devil's rights over mankind. Anselm argued instead that God by his mercy united himself with mankind through Christ, who, sinless, gave God back much more than was due; so men were saved by identifying themselves with Christ. The Penitentials were based on the idea that a wronged person (God) had to be satisfied (paid) by some form of compensation as in secular law; so they categorized sins and allotted the appropriate penalty. Abelard began a revolution in religious thought by rejecting the concept of a ransom and arguing that the self-giving love of Christ must evoke a corresponding love.[57]

In considering the early medieval period we must never forget that the essential life of the church lay in the monasteries. In England, despite the triumph of the Roman over the Celtic church, and the attempts of men like Benedict Biscop and Wilfred of Ripon, the Bene-dictine rule had never been firmly established and the regulations in the monasteries, in so far as they functioned at all, were very diverse. Still, there was the dominant idea that one could live in a truly Christian way only under a system enjoying celibacy, rejection of private property, and communal living with work, meditation and prayer. Celtic monasticism had been a direct growth out of tribal systems, with the abbot as the main official and the bishop of minor importance. The abbot indeed was often the tribal chief or a close relation of his; and the monastery was thus an effort to recreate tribal fraternity on a new level, without any of the elements that had broken the earlier unity. Though English monasticism did not formally carry on the Celtic system, something of the fundamental idea survived in it. (We may compare the ways in which Celtic and feudal ideas merged in Breton knighthood. 'When a monastic recorder styles a man *Miles quidam Daniel Eudoni mattiern* (*mactiern*),' says Stenton, 'the French knight and the Celtic chief are brought into close association.') After the breakdown partly caused by the Norse invasions, it was some time before a new life could be breathed into the reconstituted church. There was no sign of the Cluniac spirit of reform. On the contrary: in 944 King Edmund gave the abbey of Bath to monks of St Bertin who had come as refugees from the discipline of Gerard of Brogne.[58]

However, the second half of the tenth century was on the whole a period of peace and stabilization; and there was a revival in the church, of Benedictine monasticism (The Black Monks), mainly in the south and the eastern midlands, under Eadwig (955–9) and Edgar (959–75). The climax came in 973 when Edgar was crowned at Bath; the ritual included not only the coronation, but also a solemn anointing and a form of coronation oath. The delay in the ceremony was not without its point; Edgar had now reached the age of thirty, the minimum canonical age for ordination to the priesthood. At the close of the rite mass was celebrated and the king was enthroned in company with the archbishops of Canterbury and York. In thus enhancing the priestly role of the king, the church was also celebrating its own revival, its triumphant part in the theocratic state.[59]

Dunstan had been the main agent in these changes. He had been a monk at Fleury on the Loire and knew well what was involved in the Cluniac reforms. Influences from Fleury had been active in England before him through Oda, archbishop of Canterbury, who died in 958 and had been a monk at Fleury, and who sent his nephew Oswald to the same monastery. But it was Dunstan who brought the new forces fully into play in England. Born about 909 near Glastonbury Abbey, he was educated there, and through powerful family connections in both church and state he soon rose in the world, joining the household of his uncle, archbishop of Canterbury, and winning the intimacy of the Wessex kings. About 936 he became a monk and some four years later was made abbot of Glastonbury by King Edmund; he worked there for some fifteen years, reforming its system, refusing to allow entry to married men, and insisting on the use of a common refectory and dormitory. King Edred made him his chief adviser, so that when the king died he was driven into exile by a jealous group of Wessex magnates. When Edgar succeeded to the throne, he returned. Edgar approved of his ideas and appointed him in turn to the sees of Worcester, London and Canterbury (960).

Aethelwold, after staying at Fleury, was in fact the man who did the most zealous work for monastic reform. Bishop of Winchester in 963, he set himself to rebuild monasticism in the south Danelaw; and among the houses which he reorganized were Peterborough, Thorney and Ely. A regular system of services was ensured by the *Regularis Concordia* which he drew up with aid from Cluny and Lorraine, and which was authorized by a royal council at Winchester. The strong monastic trend appeared in the arrangement that tended to bring cathedrals under the control and government of monks, as at Winchester and Worcester, and by about 1000, at Canterbury, Sherborne and elsewhere. At Worcester, however, Oswald did not abolish the secular clergy but set a community of monks beside them. The systems of cathedral organization thus remained varied and confused till after 1066, indeed till the end of the twelfth century. In some cathedrals, to which the secular clergy were attached, the latter were brought together in a community or chapter of canons under a dean.[60]

The main trend was thus to exalt the monks afresh at the expense of the secular clergy, though Dunstan seems to have been concerned with the church as a whole, convoking ecclesiastical councils of his province, trying to get decayed churches rebuilt, and discouraging (with little effect) the marriage of country priests. He, like Oswald (bishop of Worcester 961, archbishop of York 972), preached regularly; and Oswald, a careful administrator of church lands, also made frequent visitations throughout his dioceses. But though the development of what we may call the church-in-the-world was not wholly neglected, it is notable that all the leaders of reform were monks and that monks filled the sees, including the metropolitan ones, for many years. The rebuilding of schools and the revival of literature was also the work of the monks at Glastonbury, Winchester and Canterbury. Book decoration reached such a high level that it influenced continental *scriptoria*; the so called Winchester style was a local creation with its acanthus leaf scrolls as initial letters and its outline drawings. The artists developed fine animated patterns out of the old designs, figures with craned necks and fluttering drapes; the style, agitated, expressive, yet controlled, spoke of new energies trembling on the edge of liberation. At Worcester a splendid organ was installed about 980.[61] The peasant priest of the parish seemed an almost negligible part of the church, though the bishops had prestige as magnates. It was the monks who were the 'religious', the true followers of Christ.

After Edgar came an odd episode of anti-monastic reaction, with strong popular support. A monk writer, Oswald's biographer, admits that the monks were ejected with 'the counsel of the people and the noisy support of the vulgar'; in those days, 'if one of the ignoble vulgar caught sight of a man in our habit, he yelled out as if he'd glimpsed a wolf among sheep'. The outburst was made possible by the confused situation after Edgar's death, when Edward and Aethelred (then a child) disputed the succession, and conflicts broke out between the two most powerful men of the realm, Aelfhere of Mercia and Aethelwine of East Anglia. Aethelwine supported Dunstan, who had backed Edward, and Aelfhere expelled the monks from houses founded largely by Dunstan and his associates. But behind the political cleavages there were many social grievances over Edgar's policies. It seems sure that during the period of decay in the eighth century the properties of the monasteries had often been swallowed up by the royal fisc, as at Abingdon and Ely, or taken over by lay lords; the houses that survived, with the possible exception of St Augustine's, Canterbury, were occupied by clerks; and clerks did all they could to resist the reforms which entailed the return of the monks. When Edgar restored to Winchester the parts of the great Taunton estate that had fallen into his hands, he 'commanded every one of his thegns who had any land on the estate that they should hold it in conformity with the bishop's wish, or else give it up'. What the bishop wished, we have no idea. Even the intervention of Queen Aelfthryth merely gained for one of the thegns a life interest in the estate; after the death of the thegn and his wife, 'the land should go to Taunton, with produce and with men, just as it stood. And with great difficulty we two brought matters to this conclusion.' When monastic lands had come into the hands of lay lords, they seem to have been simply confiscated for the monks' benefit. Thus Edgar restored to Malmesbury two estates which had been 'unjustly' held by the 'contentious Adelnoth', and the *Gesta Pontificum* tells how the king ordered an inquiry into the former possessions of Chertsey to discover what lands had fallen into lay hands, so that they might be recovered. We find Edgar violently dispossessing magnates so as to return the land to the monks, and we can imagine how lesser holders were treated. Later pleas against the monastery of Ely declared that lands had passed to it by forceful dispossession of the holders. Many lawsuits occurred (as the records of Ely and Ramsey show) on the grounds that monasteries had persuaded pious layfolk to make gifts or grants of land and so had alienated the kinsmen of the grantors; and it seems clear that the Ely monks took advantage of the embarrassments of smaller landholders in their area.[62]

There was more than piety in Edgar's policy. The monasteries as landholders in close dependence on the crown made for cohesion in the body politic; by strengthening them Edgar was seeking to offset the growing power of the great ealdormen. (The chroniclers of the time even refer to the earldoms as *regna*, kingdoms.) We may compare with Edgar's policy that of the kings of Germany in the same century; they 'bound the churches of the realm to themselves by the immunity and thus acquired a new means of unifying the realm' (Barraclough). We see that England, though free from the endless petty anarchy of somewhere like Normandy, had its own problems of keeping a balance between the central power and the regions, and that in this matter its affinities were with the Germanic area.[63]

By 1066 there were forty monasteries and twelve nunneries. As the English church was rudimentary in its institutions, the monks had provided most of the bishops for over a century; they were the source of all religious and historical literature, and of most religious art; with their wide estates, jurisdictional immunities and treasures, they played an important part in economic and administrative life.

Self-contained and self-governed, they owed allegiance to no prelate outside their walls, to no community (apart from the post–1066 Cluniacs). They often housed a number of children, ranging from infants to adolescents, who had been brought in by parents who wanted them educated. Some, 'offered to God', became monks; indeed recruitment in the tenth and eleventh centuries was largely from such young folk.

If then the monks were the respected and dominant element in the church, what of the parish priest? The position here was complicated by the claims of the local lord.[64] On the basis of Mosaic law, tithes had been demanded since the fifth century when Ambrose and others identified bishop, priest and deacon with highpriest, priest and levite of the older dispensation. Gradually parishes grew up inside dioceses (modelled on the Roman administrative framework), and parish tithes were seen as the normal endowment of a parish church. Not that such a humble person as the priest could hope to get the whole of such a contribution. A papal letter of 494 (later called a decretal) divided the tithe into four parts, to be shared among bishop, ministering priest, the poor and the church fabric. This scheme was brought to England by St Augustine and applied to parochial as well as episcopal churches; then the bishops dropped out and a triadic system appeared. But the situation grew confused when the lay lords claimed a *dominium* over parish priests. The church tried to whittle the claim down and after long struggles a compromise left the patronage to the lord as a piece of property, but (in theory) denied his other rights over the church. Assertions of lay control, however, went on right to the end of the Middle Ages. The parish was usually part of the lord's domain. No doubt in some areas he set up the church in place of a pagan temple and held power over it as he had over the latter; the glebe was then a legacy from heathen days, to which Christian tithes were added.[65]

Till about 1000 the power of the local lord over the parish was hardly challenged; but it is not clear how far the lord took the tithes or controlled their use by others. There was thus a tendency to deprive tithes of religious significance, and by the eleventh century in England their payment was enforced by king's law. When lay lords granted tithes to monasteries, they were doubtless arrogating the right; they looked on the priests as their men and assumed they had the right to give away their fees when the offices fell vacant. We know more of the way that monks singly or corporately took over parish churches on the continent; but things must have been the same in England, where the boundaries of manor and parish tended to coincide.[66] But boundaries must at times have been unclear; Wulfstan in the eleventh century forbade one priest to lure away another's parishioner with his tithe and dues.

The rites most coveted by the priest were baptism, confession and burial; if he performed them he got a source of revenue and the local folk had the least trouble. Most lords drew revenue from their churches; the value that *Domesday* assigned to the larger churches was the rent taken by the feudal superior. To the commissioners a church was merely a bit of property, differing in no significant way from other estates or valuable buildings; all were subject to lords who expected to get a profit from them. But their economic and tenurial variety was considerable. The lord had the right to appoint the priest; the bishop had the right to investigate a candidate's suitability, but we know of no case where a lord's man was turned down. To interfere with rights of patronage was a serious matter in a world where all persons of property depended on them. At times a new lord tried to throw a priest out and install his own man; but this was against canon law. The king normally treated churches like any other dominical estate; they provided similar services and revenues. No doubt he also owned demesne manors with small churches. Most lords drew revenues from churches; clerical estate-owners enjoyed both transferred royal rights and revenues, and ecclesiastical ones. When an estate was booked to a church, *feorm* and other customs went to the beneficiary; so bishop or monastery drew *feorm* or its commutation from the churches thus owned. What was the benefice's value to the incumbent is not clear, nor who paid the amount to the bishop. Later it was the parson and the payment was known as a pension. If he himself served, he was the church's rector; if he was an absentee or not in priestly orders, he put in a vicar. Even in the thirteenth century there could be confusion between a rector burdened with a pension and a vicar farming the church for an owner.[67]

Monasteries were the worst and most callous exploiters. Churches were often made over to them as gifts, as well as some minsters in totality. A few grantors tried to safeguard the tenures of the priests; but on monastic estates priests and churches were liable to fade out. There seems to have been a clear policy of taking individual endowments into monasteries and of repressing lesser churches. The East Anglian houses, greedy for land, no doubt wanted to exploit their churches as capably as they did their agricultural holdings, but they found local customs hard to break or get around. In this region priests were more likely to be freemen or sokemen than villeins. Cathedral chapters, if monastic, behaved as badly as did the monasteries, unless the bishop, wanting to have churches available for his clerics, prevented them. The easiest way for a monastery to exploit a church was to rackrent it to a farmer (in practice not unlike a parson). Unless monks or canons themselves served a church, they had to put in a vicar and share the proceeds with him. That meant they usually took the tithes (or the greater tithes, those from corn) and left other payments and dues to the priest in charge as *altalage*.[68]

One argument, attacked by reformers, was that the church building could be considered apart from the altar. The abbot of Fleury wrote:

> There is another grave error by which the Altar is said to belong to the bishop and the Church to a certain other lord; since from the consecrated house and altar is made a certain thing called a church, as a man consists of body and soul. See, most just princes, whither avarice leads us, while charity grows cold.[69]

Important in the English system were the minsters. *Mynster* comes from *monasterium*; and many ancient parish churches certainly represented early monasteries which had disappeared. Such monasteries were no doubt missionary centres, as we know Breedon in Leicestershire was. But we must also recall that in the eighth century and later the term *monasterium* could be used of a church served by a group of clergy sharing a communal life. Thus the larger parish churches came to be called minsters. The earliest parishes seem to have been wide districts served by clergy from the bishop's *familia*, who were grouped round a central church. At one time there seems to have been one of these mother churches for each hundred or set of hundreds, which was in turn connected with a royal *tun* or vill. Well endowed, their parochial rights often reached out over a large area.[70] Many had now been alienated by the crown, especially to monasteries proper. At Elstead we see how a minster could be broken up to reward royal clients and give pickings for an earl. The early system had been confused or destroyed by the intrusion of many small churches set up by bishops, abbots, lesser nobles, even groups of freemen, for private estates or newly colonized areas. So we find the old minster parishes based on hundreds together with new church parishes based on manors or vills. But the first set was given fresh strength by the advent of rural deaneries in the twelfth century. Gifts made to minsters show the regard people kept for them; even in *Domesday* some minsters held all their rights intact. But generally they were archaic and decaying by 1066. Vainly they tried to assert a paramount right to baptism, and royal laws protected their claim to church-scot and tithe. On the continent, however, the filching of rights from old baptismal churches by lords had gone much further.[71]

In late times churches were classified as chief minsters, middling ones, smaller ones (with graveyards), and field churches or country chapels. Churches cited in *Domesday* vary greatly in wealth and prestige.[72] By 1066 manorial churches must have been the most numerous, mainly linked with estates of thegns (whether bookland or loanland). A thegn with lands assessed at five hides was expected to have his own church; laws of Aethelred assume that a vill can supply priest and reeve. In Kent the church was often associated with the slaves and so with the demesne; in openfield regions, with the villeins. In boroughs churches were affected by burghal customs. There were usually several, a man with fair-sized holdings there being expected to build one for his tenants. We find such churches pledged as loan security, sold, 'invaded' by the sheriff, or handled by speculators who buy and sell the valet.[73]

Occasionally protests were made. Aelfric denounced the sale of churches for money and attacked the lay domination of churches: 'Some men sell even a church for hire, as if it were worthless mills.' But no one could really question lordship; even the reform movement, gathering strength in the eleventh century, never came into collision with the trend towards stronger lordships. Usually a priest was a *ceorl*, a free man, and Wulfstan looked on him as mediator between manorial lord and servile tenants. He should be guardian of weights and measures; he should urge the *theows* to work for the lord and the lord to protect the *theows*. We do find a priest in a vill of Ely resisting a monk who wanted the peasants to work on a day when they normally went to make offerings to a saint (St Ives). If a priest was a celibate, he ranked with a thegn.[74]

The local priest had his importance as a dispenser of the sacraments; but he had little authority, partly because of his social status, partly because of his illiteracy and his appearing almost a secular character beside the monks. Still, in the cases where he was better equipped, a powerful weapon had been put in his hands, confession of sins. The early church had practised public confession; the private form seems to have been an Irish invention, brought to Europe by the Celtic missionaries in the later Merovingian and Carolingian periods. The priests of northern Europe came to be provided with penitentials and manuals for the examination of sins; and this monastic method of inquisition enabled the priest to question his people systematically and to get a deep grasp of their inner life. The detailed probing shook the confidence and self-reliance of penitents, gave a new urgency to their need to be united with the church, purged by penance, and afforded them a conviction, however temporary, of a new life.

Another important factor in breaking down old relationships and supports, was the substitution of the saint for the old local deity or spirit of the place. Thus men took a decisive step towards alienation from nature, which was generally regarded as evil, the haunt of evil spirits and tempters. The saint, mediating with the terrible God in his unapproachable power, attracted a strong and sustaining devotion. Men were thus put in a psychological condition in which they felt it right to attack nature, to attempt by all means to control a sphere which was seen as in its essence hostile and implacably opposed to them. This movement of alienation, appearing in its first embryonic forms in the early medieval era, was something which was in the long run necessary for bourgeois society. That society, with its basis in money power (as the keystone of the free market of an industrial system), immeasurably increased the alienation of man from his fellows and from himself; but this latter aspect was inseparably linked with the alienation from nature which was inherent in Christianity. Only when the triadic set of alienations had begun to operate decisively could the quantitative science be born that arrived with Galileo.

The power of the saint, we must add, was externalized in the relic, without which no church was considered a true church; and one of the great problems of the west, with its very few martyrs, was to beg, buy, or steal relics from the vastly richer east.

The bishoprics, as they had developed in both east and west, had come to represent what we may call the element of state power in the church: an element which both merged with secular state power and stood apart from it, ready to assert itself as the superior half of the partnership. In England two independent provinces had been set up in early years, with sees at Canterbury and York. Other dioceses were then formed, but in a somewhat haphazard way; the north had only one, the south had thirteen. The continental system of dioceses based on Roman administrative districts, with sees in urban centres, could not be applied. The layout had to conform to the boundaries of existing kingdoms, and so the diocesan areas changed with the political fortunes of the kings. This at least gave the church more elasticity in outlook and practice than in Gaul. The earliest foundations, made by kings or bishops with large endowments, were the minsters – called the Old Minsters by the eleventh century. We have already looked at these and at the growth of thegns' churches which produced a parish system. The resulting complexity was such that not only did a bishop often have trouble in controlling the lesser churches in his diocese, but some of them might even belong to another bishop. (Such peculiars lasted into the nineteenth century.) But by the eleventh century the rough basis of the medieval parish system was present. For the state of the local church much

depended on the bishop. If he travelled around, preaching, confirming, and making his presence felt, the local priest had to be careful;
if the bishop was lax, the priest tended to be lax as well.

The administrative system of the diocese, where it can be said
to have existed at all, was primitive. The bishop must always have
had a few priests and other clerks around him. They carried out
arrangements for him and helped him with such work as ordinations,
consecrations and confirmations. Also he needed clerks to look after
the charters which were so important in assuring the see's properties.
So there must have been some simple form of chancery and archive;
and when, shortly before 1066, trained royal clerks, like Leofric of
Exeter and Giso of Wells, gained bishoprics, more efficient systems
may have been built up. But in general the household and the chancery must have been simple and rough in character. Records of the
bishop's judicial work, carried on in the hundred courts, were kept
by the clerk of the court and the bishop was not concerned with
them.

The relations of the two metropolitan sees were never clearly
defined, though Canterbury in the more developed south could not
but have a more prominent role. However, it was only after the
Conquest that dissensions of a serious kind arose.[75] Connections with
the papacy could hardly be other than loose and occasional, and the
popes accepted this position. But relations were good. There was a
fortified area in Rome for Englishmen who formed a *schola* or section
of the militia there, as early as the eighth century; Alfred asked for it
to be freed from taxation and his request was granted. Later in his
reign, money described as the Alms of the King and the West Saxon
People was sent yearly to Rome; and following kings issued laws to
continue the payment, which was made in at least the latter part of
the Confessor's reign. This payment seems to be what was later called
Peter's Pence. Also, at least from early in the tenth century it was
customary for the archbishop of Canterbury to go to Rome for his
pallium; under Cnut we find the archbishop of York also making the
journey. Nicholas II wrote to the Confessor: 'To you and all your
royal successors we commit the advowson and protection of...all the
churches in the whole of England, so that with the counsel of the
bishops and abbots you may on our behalf establish just laws
everywhere.'

The first papal interference seems to have come in 1051 after
Robert of Jumièges had visited Rome. It was thus made on behalf
of the Normans. After that date churchmen began looking to Rome
for confirmations, and Rome began looking for the chance to make
them. Victor II, 1055–7, confirmed a privilege to Chertsey Abbey;
Ely asked him to confirm its *liber*. Nicholas II granted a privilege to

the bishop of Wells and heard an appeal from Worcester against encroaching York; in 1062 papal legates demanded the separation of York and Worcester, and made sure that Wulfstan, prior of Worcester, was installed in the see there. Edward built a monastery dedicated to St Peter. But all did not go smoothly, though the conflicts were still slight. Robert of Jumièges, for all his papal letters of reconstitution, failed to get back into England. Later Stigand had trouble with his pallium; he had had the bad luck to get it from Benedict X, soon afterwards declared a usurper, and he was closely linked with the party of Godwin.[76]

Now a glance at the economic advances that were being made, the development of towns, money, and new forms of union to meet the changing situation. The English had done much to clear wasteland and to transform the landscape. From the east coast they had worked along the river and attacked the forests and heavy clays of the Midlands. The Norsemen began the settlement of the northern dales. By 1066 a large proportion of the villages of today already existed, especially south of the Humber-Mersey line. Monasteries often helped to extend cultivation, for example in the wooded Severn valley and the fenlands round Ely. Nevertheless, the pre-1066 population has been estimated at only one and a half million, and half the kingdom waste-land. There were royal forests (not necessarily all woodland) and some thickly wooded regions, in Essex and on the Weald between the north and south downs, where the Mickle Wood was, which a ninth century chronicler described as 120 miles long and 30 miles broad; though reduced by this time, it was still big. In 1086 only southern Essex was heavily occupied; at least a third was part of the wild belt reaching into Surrey, Kent, and Hampshire. In Surrey only two settlements are named on the wealden clay.[77] In the Forest of Arden, however, despite the clays, the woods were subordinated to villages and manors. There could have been few areas where wild patches did not lie close at hand. Even in Norfolk, with a density of population greater than anywhere except Suffolk, and with no part apparently ever under forest law, *Domesday* shows enough woodland in the central area for swine to be numerous and demesne sheep farming little developed.[78]

Whatever the date of the introduction of the heavy plough, the system built up around it was well established by the tenth and eleventh centuries.[79] In *Domesday* the plough team is normally made up of eight oxen. Where a team of four is mentioned, it is set down as a half team, though one or two beasts more or less were not allowed to upset the standard reckoning. The threes and sixes gave the most bother. After harvest one field was left fallow next year; a second field by the first was ploughed and divided between spring and winter corn. This two field system seems normal throughout the twelfth century. After that a three field system was used, though both systems coexisted for a time. Many villages had open fields. After harvest the ground was used for common pastures, as distinct from the permanent closes found all over England. Beyond were the meadows, usually kept fenced and shared out yearly in agreed proportions among the farmers. Also there was wasteland where at any time cattle could be put and brushwood or timber gathered. Horses and pigs were turned out there; but as late as 1209 at Mardon (Hampshire) two foals belonging to the bishop of Winchester were eaten by wolves.[80] Arable and pastoral fields were both needed for a self-sufficient economy; and as the meadows didn't bring in much hay, rights of common pasturage were highly valued. Not that open fields were found everywhere. Kent had its closes and scattered fields, though co-aration was also carried on; much of the west from Devon to Lancashire did not come under the open field system, but had pastoral villages and isolated homesteads. The nature of the land played its part in determining the type of settlement, but there were also perhaps influences inherited from as far back as the Britons.[81]

The extension of cultivation and pasture helped to increase the population, and the increase in population in turn drove men to bring more land into use. In general, economic expansion had been going on from the eighth century, with effects that in time led to a decisive growth of trade and urban development and of the political systems and building programmes which emerged between the eleventh and thirteenth centuries. The earlier stages of this development are unclear; and it may be argued that the main factor was not so much a stepping up of productivity as the creation of a more efficient system by the lords for extracting the surplus from the producers. Probably both factors operated in complex interactions. Any increase in productivity was liable to stimulate the lords to demand more in rent and taxes, and the pressure from the lords helped to drive the peasants into producing more from the land. The systems of exploitation would in some ways inhibit the free activity of the village community; in other ways they would tend to bring about a more comprehensive organization. What we call the manorial system of exploitation grew up especially in areas where arable land could be effectively and widely tackled: France north of the Loire, Franconia, Lorraine, England south of the Humber. The Normans shared in this development.

One way in which the pressures of the lords and the initiatives of peasants came together usefully was in assarting, that is clearing forests and wastes. For instance, the work of clearing and dyking began in Flanders in the late ninth century. The workers who settled in the cleared areas formed associations which later got the name of Wateringues. Their method of drying out the polders of Holland and Flanders was applied to the gulf of St Omer, where new lands were gained from the sea; also on the Atlantic coast in Poitou and Saintonge. The Parisian region was cleared and became the centre of a kingdom from the end of the tenth century; the Capetians multiplied clearings on the Paris-Orleans route and we find places with the significant name Les Essarts: from *exarare*, to plough or dig up soil. As a result came the growth of villages and ultimately of towns, *bourgs*, *burhs*, communes. William the Conqueror carefully fostered the expansion of Caen; he founded two abbeys there and raised a castle of strong stone. Germany was expanding eastward, especially after the defeat of the Wends (a Slavonic people between the Elbe and the Oder) and the Magyars. Henry I, after beating the Wends, turned south and drove into Bohemia, where he forced the prince Wenceslas to surrender and then regain his land as a fief to the German crown. The Slavs were defeated in 933, though they were to keep on attacking the Germans for some time. By 955 the Hungarian danger had been disposed of by Henry's son. *Burhs* (small fortified towns) were built, and *marks* (defensive areas) set up beyond the Elbe. New dioceses were carved out of the conquered land for the ecclesiastical provinces of Mainz and Bremen. The eastern expansion of Germany had begun, carried on largely by the higher clergy and the margraves. Monasteries played a key-part, for example in Pomerania and Rugen.[82]

Assarting, reclamation of land, and colonization certainly had much to do with the economic expansion, as did such planning as the lay and monastic lords were capable of. But there must have been other elements, hard to isolate now, which played an essential part in producing the new quality of medieval society, something that cannot be paralleled in previous societies. The relations of the village community, and later the town and commune, to the exploiting ruling classes, were indeed of the utmost significance; but the peculiar quality of which we speak has deep roots in the tribal past and involves the steps taken by members of the tribal groups in their resistance to exploitation: their attempts to reassert cooperative methods and to keep the kindreds alive, their resolute taking advantage of all the interstices in the exploiting systems. Hence the way in which a large number of new technical devices and applications, new materials and uses appeared in the Dark Ages and were developed throughout the medieval periods. For instance: the easily heated house (as against the Mediterranean type), felting (which led in time to paper making), trousers and the use of furs for clothing, skis, soap for cleansing and butter for food (instead of oil), barrels and tubs, cloisonné jewellery, crops of rye, oats, spelt, hops, the fore-and-aft rig, the sport of falconry, the stirrup. Many of these had long existed, but they all now assumed a new importance. By the thirteenth century further devices or more effective applications had come in: crossbow, church bells, fiddle-bow, wheelbarrow, spinning wheel, functional button, cast iron, and finally fire-arms, gunpowder, clocks, paper, distilled liquors, roads paved with cubes of stone on a loose earthbed, instruments embodying reciprocal and rotary forms of motion – first in hand querns and rotary grindstone, later in all sorts of machinery.[83] Of much importance was the invention of the horse collar, with tandem harness and the horse shoes, which made the horse available for work. The ancient yoke harness strangled the horse if it pulled heavy weights. Here we may certainly give the credit to the nomads; the name for horse collar in Germanic and Slavonic tongues (English *hames*) is derived from central Asian sources.[84] A picture of a collar appears in the illuminated *Apocalypse* of Trèves done about 880; but in Swedish tombs of the middle and later years of the ninth century the frames of metal collars have been found; and near the end of the century Alfred, we saw, noted with surprise that in northern Norway the horse was used for work. This seems to be an instance of how receptive the independent Norsemen were to new ideas.[85]

To the new technological devices that appeared in the Dark Ages we must add the water-driven mill and the windmill. The watermill was worked out in late Hellenistic times, but it spread widely only after the Roman breakdown in the west; and by the eleventh century it was a common feature of the agricultural landscape.[86] How well it was developed through the Dark Ages can be exemplified by the watermill at Tamworth in Staffordshire, the capital of Mercia. Here much information has been provided by what is probably the earliest watermill in Europe to have been excavated. There survive from a first mill the levels of the leat by which water was led to the wheel, and timbers forming a framework of thin pegged planks. Parts of this first mill were reused in a second one, which was substantial, with massive oak baulks, planks, posts and pegs, showing a wide variety of carpentry techniques. Components included a three-sided millpool of timber baulks in which a head of water was built up and fed along a wheelrace and overflow channels. The wheelrace seems to have had a grid to stop debris from fouling the wheel, which is thought to have been of the vertical undershot type. Fragments of millstones (some of local gritstone, some of Rhineland lava) have been found, and a block of iron with a spindle socket set in a plank represents part of the machinery, perhaps the hopper. The superstructure seems to be of timber, with window leading in small lozenges for horn or glass panes. If the panes were glass, here would be one of the few instances of its use in an Anglo-Saxon context other than in monasteries as at Jarrow and Glastonbury.

The origins of the western windmill are lost. A document, apparently from about 1180 or even earlier, shows a windmill in Normandy. One existed in 1185 at Weedley (Yorkshire), rented at eight shillings a year. Before Henry II's death in 1189 one of his constables gave a windmill near Buckingham to the abbey of Oseney; and about the same time a witness of the third crusade tells how German soldiers constructed the first windmill in Syria, thus demonstrating that the idea was not imported from Islam. Diffusion must have been fast, for Pope Celestine III (1191–8) decreed that windmills should pay tithes.[87]

Despite the new collar and harness the use of horses on the land was erratic and slow to catch on. The earliest representation of this occurs on the Bayeux Tapestry (about 1077–82), where a horse draws a harrow while a mule is harnessed to a wheeled plough; the fields are no doubt those of Kent rather than Normandy. In 1095, at the Clermont council that launched the first crusade, Pope Urban II put under the protection of God's Peace 'Oxen and horses ploughing (arantes) and men who work ploughs and harrows, and the horses with which they harrow'. Material gathered from near Kiev reveals that the peasants there used horses for all possible tasks: a fact that perhaps helps us to understand the advanced level of Kievan culture at this time. But Domesday gives no hint of working horses, perhaps because the ox team was used as a standard assessment.[88] In the Liber Niger of Peterborough about 1225, we find a horse used for harrowing and a few years later in an account of the Friday market at Smithfield horses for ploughing are mentioned. Horses for harrowing turn up at Durham in 1183 and in the Inquest of the Templars, 1185.[89]

In short, the Dark Ages and the early medieval period saw the breakthrough which was in time to make possible the development of industrialism and which the ancient world with its slave economy had been unable to achieve. We see the operation of new free energies on the material inherited from the collapsed Roman world of the west – an operation which, though at certain points influenced by the Byzantine east, was essentially the work of the peasant and craftsman of the semi-tribal societies – men who, despite all the disorders and oppressions, were yet able to retain certain free and fraternal elements of the tribal organization, and to use their initiative and inventive powers at crucial points. The seventh century may be taken as the turning point after which, despite local setbacks, expansion goes strongly on, with a new momentum after 1000.

All communities from small hamlets to grandiose monastic households were more or less self-supporting if necessary. The old Roman roads had mostly fallen into decay through lack of repair; men had found the shortest routes from market to market. There was a fair amount of moving about, probably more than in later centuries. Free men had to attend folk courts; the royal court moved around. One of the main problems was to keep up the bridges over rivers, so the building of *burhs* and *brucgs* (bridges) was among the essential public burdens. The early *burhs* seem to have been mostly stockaded country houses, as we see from Ine's law that fixes the scale of penalties for breaking into them, starting from the king's and going down to that of the ordinary noble landowner. But by the eleventh century the boroughs were sites that had been fortified with ditch, bank and palisade during the Danish wars, or else reused old Roman sites. Mostly they had the administrative functions suitable for a fortress. Before 850 we don't know of even ten such sites that could be called *burhs*, fortresses or towns; within a century there is a record of over a hundred more. Before 850 there was the open port or trade town, the reused Roman site with good position and sheltering walls, the promontory *burh*, and the fortlet of the king's residence. The model for the new sort of *burh* was probably a town like Canterbury, which had streets, market, wall, and houseplots before 800. Throughout the period Iron Age sites were used. Alfred took the key step in seeking to build effective lines of defence against the Danes. Each fortress was kept in repair, and, when necessary, garrisoned by the men of the country around. Responsibility for the work was distributed among the villages which the fortress guarded, in accordance with the number of hides which each was considered to contain. It was assumed that four men were needed to hold each perch of wall or earthwork, and that each hide in the attached district should be able to supply one man. The system was completed before the reign of Alfred's son Edward. By the early tenth century no village in Sussex, Surrey or Wessex east of the Tamar was more than twenty miles from one of the *burhs*.[90]

Where did Alfred get his system from? As far as we know, the Danes built no fortifications in England before 868; but there were diplomatic connections between England and countries reaching from Ireland to the Mediterranean, and a lot was known of Scandinavia. However, comparison of the design and layout of towns in Scandinavia and the Danelaw suggests different lines of development, though the Norsemen may have provided various techniques such as timber lacing in the construction of banks, towers and gateways. There were certainly also many links with the Franks as we see in coinage and church architecture; Alfred's father married a daughter of Charles the Bald. There is only one clear example of a rectangular *burh*, Cricklade; but the bridge or double *burh* played a large part in the strategy of Alfred and Edward the Elder, sometimes straddling quite small streams, though the documentary evidence presents the double *burh* as meant to block the river on which it stood. Bridges and their fortifications played a big part in Frankish campaigns of the late ninth century; bridgeworks used by Charles the Bald ante-date the *burhs* of Alfred.[91]

By the eleventh century the distinction of port or market town and *burh* or defence position was blurred. A borough was generally the seat of a mint and market, and sometimes of shire and hundred courts. But there was no hard line cutting it off from the countryside. A royal reeve, here a port-reeve, headed its administration; it was assessed in the usual way in hides or carucates. Only London had its own government, with divisions into wards, each of which was presided over by an alderman owning a court; for more serious cases there was the husting court and a great folk moot three times a year. Land tenure inside a borough worked out in the same way as land tenure outside; the fenced tenements or buildings were usually held by payment of a rent (*landgable*) and by performance of services. Most boroughs were on royal demesne, but the king often granted away the tenements, customs, and jurisdiction. A borough could thus contain the same fragmented lordships and obligations as a village, with commendation and anything bringing in profits held by nobles or churchmen. The burgesses, *burhwaru*, were not all the inhabitants; they were those responsible for the customs. Many townsmen did work in the borough fields; but a growing population with a lessening field area suggests that more and more men lived on town activities. There was no borough court, but when other courts like the hundred met there, they may have taken on new coloura-tions; further there may have been some rough sort of communal organization not considered in the royal system. A town could have a recognizable corporate character; Edward arranged for a supply of ships from the ports of Dover, Sandwich, Romney, Hithe and Ford-wich, in return for which he allowed the ports to keep the profits of justice. In the wars of Alfred and his son we hear of the burgesses carrying on war work such as the defence of their area or local operations; in the following wars we hear of 'king's thegns at home in the *burhs*'. And the towns could develop guilds. By *Domesday* at least twenty of them had populations over 1,000; Norwich may have had over 3,000 *burhwaru*, Thetford almost 5,000, Lincoln and

Norwich 6-7,000, York about 9,000. For London and Winchester we can only guess. At least we can say that some genuine towns had emerged as a result of military and administrative organization together with the growth of trade.[92]

England was advanced in its monetary system, which was centrally controlled through the dies and thus brought in profit to the king. The one coin, the silver penny, was of a good weight, which was ensured by heavy penalties. A large amount of money was in circulation. In Edward's reign, till 1051, pennies of 18 gr (300 to the pound) were usual; then for a while the weight was raised to 27 gr, and in 1065 there were more reforms. Cnut called on English craftsmen to make dies for Scandinavia; his aim was to create a national coinage there also. Dies were cut in London, or, for a short period, at various sites under royal supervision; they were then sent to the boroughs. In *Domesday* we meet at Hereford seven moneyers, who, at a change in the coinage, paid 18 shillings for the dies, with a further 20 shillings within a month of their return. Most moneyers were directly under the king, but one of these seven belonged to the local bishop. From 973 the coinage was changed every six years, then under Edward every three years, with seventy mints operating. The old coinage was called in and melted down for the new issues. In general we may say that analysis of the number of dies and the probable number of coins struck from each of them suggests that money circulation was very much greater than our historical sources imply. It has been estimated that the coins are to be numbered in fives and tens of millions at a time when the population was less than a million. The moneyer (named on the reverse) seems to have been a man of substance, his profitable office hereditary. The strength of the administrative system is shown by the considerable issues from the forty-four mints during Harold's brief reign; the distribution of the finds (from the mints of York, Chester, Romney and Exeter) suggest that preparations for war helped to stimulate the local economies.[93]

The close trade links of England and Scandinavia at this time are shown by the efforts made in Denmark and Norway to imitate English coins, and by the introduction of English moneyers. The *Life* of *St Oswald* shows that soon after 1000 York was filled with the treasures of merchants, mostly Danish, who had come from every quarter. The Danes seem to have formed a colony there in the tenth century, like the Frisians in the eighth.[94] Edward granted Dover freedom from toll throughout England to help the diffusion of imported goods not produced in England, cattle, salt and iron implements.

Under Cnut and Edward no other town had so many moneyers striking coins as London, which was also the centre of a large rural area. We find in 1097 shires owing work to the town, and in the next century Londoners still held old hunting rights in Middlesex, Surrey, the Chilterns, and perhaps Kent as far as the Cray. William I found it necessary to forbid them to take stags, hinds and roe deer from Lanfranc's manor of Harrow. (These rights may go back to the days when Middle Saxons were a separate people with London as their centre.) The folk moot ranked with the shire court as a place where outlawry was proclaimed. The burden of suit fell on all men of London; everyone was assumed to be within the sound of St Paul's great bell that rang for a meeting. There were three sessions a year, at Christmas, Michaelmas and Midsummer, probably with the sheriff presiding. The Christmas meeting dealt with the keeping of the wards; the Midsummer one with fire precautions; the Michaelmas one with the question of who the sheriff would be, and with the hearing of his commands. Land-ownership was dealt with at the *husting*, a Norse term, which seems originally to have meant the meeting of a great man's dependents, but to have gained a wider reference by the eleventh century. It may have come in during the Norse occupation under Alfred; but London moneyers of the tenth century all have English names. More likely the husting emerged from the need of the citizens to deal with Norse traders. The earliest reference suggests a concern with the standard weight of silver; but later the court's business was much concerned with trading regulations. In the twelfth century it met every Monday in the Guildhall, with its suitors on four benches as in other old assemblies. It could deal with civil matters, pleas of debt, land disputes. A special summons was needed to enforce an answer in a suit. The court also controlled weights and measures, and dealt with cases involving foreign merchants. Aldermen, in charge of wards, also did the adjudicating in the husting.

London citizens might own the rights of jurisdiction over their own city properties. Such sokes obstructed the growth of a single court system. No inhabitant of a soke could be arrested in his house or penthouse; only in the middle of the road was he vulnerable. The soke-reeve had to be brought in to enable distraint in a soke; and temporary dwellers there owed customary payments only to the lord of the soke. Disputes between men of the same soke had to be settled privately. Thus, right into Norman London there survived small centres liable to erupt with violence and filled with a wergild atmosphere.[95] With the soke, again, was closely associated the defensible house, the *burh*. In the precincts of St Paul's was such a *burh*. The idea of a private stronghold was familiar to tenth century society. One text says that such a lair was necessary for a *ceorl* advancing to the status of thegn. Lothbury, for example, seems to have been the *burh* of a man whose name began Hloth. No doubt such a *burh* would merely have had a wall round the house and gives us some idea of what the houses of rich Londoners were like. A name like Bucklersbury (from Bucarelli, a name of Italian origin) reveals the merging of English and invasive elements. But generally English names are strong among London citizens, as in all the ancient boroughs. In lists of the early canons of St Pauls we find men with family connections in the city.[96]

An important proof of how deeply rooted in everyday life the kindreds were is afforded by the offshoots from them that we find both in boroughs and villages. These organizations, which used the model of the kindred for activities in new spheres of life, were the guilds. We meet guilds of *cnihts* in London, Winchester and Canterbury; a thegn's guild in Cambridge. These were clearly bodies with a long history during which many changes might have come about. No doubt at first the *cnihts* were servants put by a lord in charge of his town property. They thus provided a link between his upland estates and the borough markets. A class of burghal *cnihts* existed by the mid-tenth century, as is shown by an attestation to a charter of Aethelberht's reign referring to the Canterbury guild. Other associations may well also go back to the pre-Alfredian period. If such a group had grown up in London, it had had time to change its character by the eleventh century. The growth of trade could have developed a group of men who ministered for lords into independent merchants such as we find in the first list of the *cnihtena gild* of London. According to a survey under Henry I there were two *cnihts'* halls in Winchester, at one of which 'they drank their gild and held it freely under king Edward'. Other Winchester sources tell of a chapman's hall and later of a hall 'where the good men of Winchester drank their gild'. William Rufus and Henry I confirmed the London guild's land-holdings and privileges as it had enjoyed them under William I and Edward; and in 1125 the members, in return for religious benefits, gave all their land to the newly founded priory of the Holy Trinity, Aldgate. They included some of London's leading citizens. Their land took in the big tract outside the eastern city wall (afterwards called Portsoken Ward). The guild had now certainly become an association for religious purposes.[97]

We must not think of these *cnihts* as warriors. A document in English of 1093–1109 describes the Canterbury *cnihts* as of the Chapmen's Guild. The guild-principle could be used for organizing any group of a lord's servants, who might be settled on some outlying part of the estate for his convenience. Thurstan, magnate of eastern England, left to his knights 'the wood at Ongar, apart from the park and the stud I have there'. We surely see here a group of hunt servants

quartered in their master's park. Similar groups no doubt lay behind
placenames containing *cnihta tun*, e.g. Knighton. A lord might found
a guild or lend his name to it. Thus, Urki, founder of Abbotsbury
abbey, also founded a guild at this site, from which one of the few
surviving sets of Old English guild statutes has come down. (He was
certainly Norse; his wife Tola had a Danish name. Cnut gave him an
estate near Abbotsbury in 1024, and he attested the charter of an
estate in Dorset granted to Bovy in 1033; Edward called him *min
huskarl* in a writ and 'my faithful minister' in a charter of 1044.)[98]

But we must not look for the origin of the guilds in the wishes of
the lords. Men got together with the aim of gaining special benefits
from the church, and the king and the lords accepted the associations
for this reason. Besides Cambridge and Abbotsbury, Bedwyn (a royal
manor in Wiltshire), Exeter, Woodbury and several other villages or
hamlets near Exeter, had left their rules. The latter guilds were
post-conquest, but almost all the members had English names; and
we can safely see in them formations that go well back into the
English period. They differed in social status, object and character,
but all had some religious colouring. At Abbotsbury was a thegn's
guild, and the members at Bedwyn and Exeter seem to be men of
substance. But the fourteen guilds attached to St Peter's, Exeter,
were rural and humble; at times the chief member was the village
priest. All were burial societies and possibly confraternities for obits.
But their other aims give us clues as to the impulses driving men to
come together. At Cambridge the members wanted mutual assurance
against legal penalties and such troubles. At Exeter the group seems to
have been mainly concerned about prayers for the dead; they met
three times a year, not to feast, but to hear the priest sing two masses,
one for living friends, one for the dead, while they themselves recited
two psalters. Failure to attend brought the penalty of having to
provide further masses. (We may compare the *fratres kalendarii* of
twelfth century Exeter.) The village guilds were also associates for
obits.[99]

Usually a guild had a meeting place with benches. We find a
Guildhall at Abbotsbury. There was an entrance subscription, perhaps
a probationary period, and rules, with an oath and fines for infringements. Banquets and drinkings were usual. Benefits were worked out
to meet mishaps such as fire, damage to one's house, and above all
death. The guild might deal with the carriage of the dead man to
his burial place, generally the church to which it was attached, for a
special service – six masses or psalters (Exeter), five (Bedwyn), a
penny apiece at the body for the soul (Abbotsbury) and a burial
feast (Cambridge, Bedwyn). Some guilds had regular provisions for
services (Exeter, a ha'penny for their souls at each meeting), or made

payments to priest or church: at Bedwyn a young sheep or 2d on Rogation days to the priest; at Abbotsbury 1d or wax to St Peter's minister. At each death 2d a head went for almsgiving or food. Some guilds distributed alms; at Exeter they raised 5d a head when a member went on a pilgrimage to Rome.

We do not know of other village guilds, but may surmise that there were many. There were women beneficiaries in one Woodbury guild, perhaps the wives of members. We have short regulations for two of the Woodbury guilds, then a list of twelve other guilds, apparently with the same rules. Twelve guilds are from villages and hamlets southeast of Exeter, three from Woodbury (one called Alwin's guild), one from the near hamlet of Nutwell, two from Coly-ton, one each from Sidmouth, Whitestone, the near hamlet of Hals-ford, Exmouth, Clyst St George (Cliftwike) and Broadclyst (Cliftune); also a guild in the north-west of the diocese at Bideford, another at Lege (Leigh, perhaps East Budleigh) : two priests were members of it. The stated aim was to enter into confraternity with the canons of the cathedral church of Exeter: hence the lists of names. Members were to pay the canons 1d a year from each hearth (Easter, Wood-bury I, Martinmas, Woodbury II), and 1d at the death of each guild-brother as soul scot. In return the canons were 'to perform such services for them as they ought to perform'.[100]

The system is one of the many signs of the hold that the old minsters or mother churches had on the people. Encouraged by the clerics, the guilds represent villagers or townsfolk coming together for mutual help of various kinds and then diverging into more specialized groups, whether for the convenience of lords or of trade groups. In the later developments of craft and trade guilds the old basis is transformed, partly by internal forces of growth, but also by the impact of the Byzantine guilds, whether directly through traders or indirectly through the guild forms growing up in the industrial areas of north France and Flanders. Still, basically what we see are forms of association built up to fill the void left by the decline of the kindreds.

We can indeed prove this thesis by looking, say, at what happened in Holstein where the tenacious kindreds were not broken down till the sixteenth century. They then transformed themselves into guilds or mutual aid societies with *kluftbücher* setting out the duties that the members must perform. These guilds were still essentially based on kinship even if strangers were admitted. 'Long years ago our ancestors founded and established a *Vetterschaft* and Brotherhood among themselves, by virtue of which one *Klufts Vetter* must help and succour the other, like a brother, in all difficulties.' How well the guilds functioned is shown by the fact that till about 1760, it is claimed, no workhouses were needed, nor fire insurance societies.[101]

Looking back over the whole field, we see that England was continuing its own peculiar development right up to 1066, steadily expanding from the early tribal basis and building up an effective state system, with a corresponding culture, out of the unifying kingship. Nowhere else in the west was there anything at all comparable: a living vernacular literature and popular courts linked with the king's peace, the legal system of a centralized government. Germany alone had certain similar elements, but these could not cohere as in England because of the lack of clear geographical boundaries, the conflicting pulls in the eastward colonizing movement, and the imperial ambitions to dominate Italy.

Certain insular elements inevitably persisted in English culture, leaving the country to some extent out of the mainstream of European development; but there were many positive aspects in this situation. We see many forms of expression which could have come together to create an art and architecture belonging to the mainstream and yet highly original in style and content: Celtic, Norse, and Germanic ingredients, plus the traditional Latin culture of the church and its links with continental developments. We have only to consider the stone crosses of the north, the illuminated manuscripts with their many vital native aspects, the Norse decorative patterns and the architectural variations that were being made of the Romanesque style, to see how rich and complex were the possibilities in Anglo-Saxon art.

At the same time there were many backward aspects of the situation, especially the wide persistence of slavery. In many ways the royal organization covered too extensive and varied an area; to draw it together more tightly and effectively without disintegrating the local bases on which it reposed was no doubt too great a problem at this stage. Potentialities were not enough. The diverse artistic elements did not come together in a single stream where they could enrich one another; the output of vernacular literature slackened, despite the fine start given by Alfred and carried on to some extent in homiletic forms. Despite the existence of such a work as the noble fragment of the *Battle of Maldon*, poetry does not seem to have been developing enough to reflect the national life in anything like its fullness.

William of Malmesbury gives us a lively account of how the Anglo-Saxons appeared to the Normans.

In process of time the desire for letters and religion had decayed for several years before the arrival of the Normans. The clergy, content with a very slight degree of learning, could hardly stammer out the words of the sacraments; and a person who understood grammar was an object of wonder and astonishment. The monks mocked the rule of their order by fine vestments and the use of every kind of food. The nobles, given up to luxury and wantonness, did not go to church in the morning after the way of Christians, but merely heard matins and masses in a careless way from a hurried priest in their chambers, amid the blandishments of their wives. The commonalty, left unprotected, became a prey to the most powerful, who amassed fortunes by seizing on their property or by selling their persons into foreign countries, though it's an innate quality of this people to be more inclined to revelling than to the accumulation of wealth. There was one custom, repugnant to nature, which they adopted: the sale of their female servants after they'd made them pregnant and satisfied their lust upon them, in public prostitution or foreign slavery.

Drinking in particular was a universal habit, in which occupation they passed whole nights as well as days. They consumed their whole substance in mean and despicable houses, unlike the Normans and French who in noble and splendid mansions lived with frugality. The vices attendant on drunkenness, which enervate the human mind, followed. Hence it arose that, engaging William with more rashness and precipitate fury than military skill, they doomed themselves and their country to enslavement by one and that an easy victory...

In short, the English at that time wore short garments reaching to mid-knee, they had their hair cropped, the beards shaven, their arms laden with golden bracelets, their skin decorated with punctured designs. They were accustomed to eat till they grew surfeited, and to drink till they were sick. These latter qualities they imparted to their conquerors. As to the rest they adopted their manners.

He then retracts his contemptuous picture to some extent by adding that there were also many fine clerics and laymen 'of all ranks and conditions'. His account may well contain many true points, even if it is partisan and exaggerated as a total picture. The Norse attacks in the late tenth century, leading to Cnut's conquest, must have done much to check a coherent and well rooted development. Cnut no doubt did his best, and not without effect, to continue the work of unification; and to this task the church made its contribution. But the rapid changes of dynasty tended to disrupt the military organization and the link between the king and the local lords. There were new men in power at the court, and also in the regions; the house-carles, the king's retainers, were very important. The thegnage was held back from getting deeper roots and taking over more specific services, including military ones. The earls, great as was their power, were set over somewhat makeshift systems. We see a premature attempt to build up an overall kingly organization which was not in fact possible for hundreds of years, not indeed till the sixteenth century. That is why England was both archaic and highly advanced: it rested still on bases with many strong tribal elements and yet attempted a unification that the many fissiparous elements made unstable. Here, and not in the slackness and self-indulgence which William of Malmesbury blames, lay the reasons for the failure to build up any effective resistance to the Normans after a single battle, Hastings.

We now turn to that battle and its results, to the immediate and the long term effects of the union of the two systems, English and Norman, which in their different ways were the most remarkable of those developed in western Europe since the breakdown of the Roman empire there.

PART II

THE NORMAN CONQUEST

CHAPTER VIII

THE CONQUEST

In the earlier 1060s William had had little to fear from his neighbours. The threat of a Breton attack had been removed from his southern borders; Anjou was torn by war between Count Geoffrey's two nephews; France had a boy king with Baldwin of Flanders as regent. Further off, the Germanic Emperor Henry III was also a minor and the papacy had become wholly pro-Norman. Harold in England was facing a very different situation. In October 1065 the Northumbrians had revolted against their earl, his brother Tostig; and King Edward, out of affection for Tostig, seems to have wanted to fight. But Harold had no wish for civil war; and he was perhaps pleased at a chance to get rid of his firebrand brother. He may even have instigated the revolt or at least connived at it.[1] He probably saw that Edward would not last much longer and may well have decided already that his best policy was to work with Edwin of Mercia, who, with his brother Morcar, had joined the rebels. He accepted Morcar as the new earl of Northumbria. The *Life of Aedward* attributed the disasters of 1066 to the break between the two brothers Harold and Tostig: 'the kingdom's sacred oaks, two Hercules', who excelled all Englishmen when linked in peace. Both were serious, careful men who persevered with what they had begun, but Tostig vigorously, Harold prudently; 'the one in action aimed at success, the other also at happiness'. The English were to rue the 'vicious discord sprung from the strife of brothers'.[2] Certainly Tostig was to complicate Harold's problems and his actions may indeed have caused the latter's downfall and the end of the Anglo-Saxon kingdom.

The *Encomium Emmae* says that Edward lost his speech on 3 January, then at last regained it. The queen warmed his feet in her bosom. He prophesied woe to the land, frightening everyone but Stigand, who whispered to Harold that the old man had lost his wits. Dying on the 5th, he was buried next day, when, says Florence of Worcester, Harold the *subregulus* was elected king by the magnates and crowned with much ceremony by Ealdred, archbishop of York. William of Poitiers says that Stigand did the crowning. But the Normans wanted to suggest that the ceremony was irregular because it was the work of an archbishop with pallium from a dubious pope, while from what we know of Harold he was likely to have taken the more cautious way and turned to Ealdred. Now he quickly married Ealdgyrh, sister of Edwin and Morcar, and broke off the union, contracted *more Dannico*, with Edith Swannhelas, by whom he had had four or even six children. The administrative system went on working as well as ever, but Harold knew he must soon face severe threats.

William was watching closely and preparing to act. Accusing Harold of perjury, he appealed to Pope Alexander II, who he knew would support his cause. An extra point in his favour was that Harold was burdened by having Stigand as archbishop of Canterbury, even if he had avoided being crowned by him. No doubt his envoy, archdeacon of Lisieux, had many bargaining points; but the main question was decided by the pope's dependence on the Normans in Italy and his hope of getting England as well as Sicily as a papal fief by sending William a banner with his blessing. How far he exacted promises, and how far William accepted the role of a papal vassal, we do not know. Doubtless the pope was ready to take general assurances without demanding a definite oath; but we can be sure that the envoy did not contradict his assumption that England would become his fief. There is a certain sardonic humour in the fact that at the moment when William was staking his future on the denunciation of Harold as a perjured vassal, he was himself deceiving the pope in much the same way. Now, with papal backing, he ordered all the Norman monasteries to pray on his behalf and when he landed in

England he wore round his neck the relics on which Harold had sworn. The oath of fealty, we may note, was normally taken on relics; there was nothing unusual about Harold's oath. This is the form of such an oath:

> By the Lord, before whom these Relics are Holy, I will be loyal and true to..., and love all that he loves, and hate all that he hates, in accordance with God's rights and secular obligations; and never, willingly and intentionally, in word or deed, do anything that is hateful to him; on condition that he keep me as I shall deserve, and carry out all that was our agreement, when I subjected myself to him and chose his favour.[3]

The advisers of the young German emperor announced support for William; Baldwin of Flanders seems to have taken the same position, though he was ready enough to support Tostig as well. Lords, knights, and mercenaries, who saw a good chance of land and loot in England, flocked to William from all over the west, especially from north France and Brittany. He did his best to draw in ecclesiastical support: thus he told the abbey of Fécamp that when victorious he would restore to it the manor of Steyning, Sussex, a gift from Edward which Harold had seized. With Matilda he attended the dedication of the Trinité, Caen, in June, and about this time gave the queen charge of their eldest son, Robert (some fourteen years old), whom he declared his heir. The barons swore loyalty to the lad; and he decided to leave behind some of them, on whom he could rely, to control the situation: Roger of Montgomery and Hugh of Avranches, later earls of Shrewsbury and Chester. Each baron, it seems, contributed a member of his family as squadron commander. Thus, of eleven nobles that William of Poitiers mentions at Hastings, at least four represented their fathers. Robert of Beaumont, cited for gallantry on the right wing, was fighting his first battle and must have been quite young.

William's main problem was to gather an adequate fleet. No one in this period could maintain a regular fleet for long. A naval quota seems to have been imposed on groups of nobles, with Matilda setting an example by her gift of the flagship, the *Mora*. At all Norman ports ship building went on. The Tapestry shows men chopping down trees, shaping planks and constructing ships, which are then dragged down to the water. A cart follows, piled with armour and a wine cask; more men bring up hauberks, which are heavy enough to need two men to carry them. William had decided against diversionary strikes; he meant to risk everything on a single compact thrust. The transportation of large numbers of horses was a new problem;

the Vikings had relied on rounding up horses after a surprise landing. But the Byzantine navy was familiar with such matters; and the Normans had learned from them when attacking Sicily in 1060–1. William would have known all about their methods and may well have had advisers come from the south.

William of Poitiers makes it clear that his army could be divided roughly into barons, middling knights, and common knights. The term for the latter is *gregarii*, which is often met on the continent to distinguish the ordinary knight from the superior.[4]

William gave instructions to each section in turn. Because of the low status of so many knights or vavasours, we must not draw a sharp line between vavasour and mercenary. In early days the terms must often have been interchangeable. Later we find soldiers who had been mercenaries enfeoffed at Abingdon and Peterborough. As such men became linked with the land or unfitted for service, others of the same kind were used in the army. Indeed we often find mercenaries more loyal to a lord than those feudally linked with him. Thus, later at the siege of Bridgenorth they were the fighters most zealous in the cause of their rebel lord; they were disgusted when the other defenders submitted; they went off muttering that such behaviour left a stain on their character. William in all his main campaigns made extensive use of mercenaries; and his action as he lay outside London shows that he did not differentiate between them and the feudally summoned men. He asked the whole of his army if he should be crowned at once or wait for his wife. Haimo of Thouars, the army's spokesman, was upset and astounded; he must have had both the common knight and the hired soldier in mind when he answered that rarely or never was the army consulted on such questions (which would normally be discussed by a ruler's council).[5]

The question of Harold's perjury or disloyalty was crucial for the Norman case, and William did everything he could to stress it. His formal challenge of Harold to single combat was a feudally correct action in the circumstances, which no one expected to end in a duel. The Bayeux Tapestry is conceived throughout in the vein of the *chansons de geste*, where a vassal's betrayal of his lord is a central theme in those with feudal rather than crusading backgrounds. These *chansons* were already known in some form in the second half of the eleventh century, and there may even have been a jongleur at Hastings. We may discount the stories of Wace, but we have also the statements by Guy of Amiens and William of Malmesbury. The latter says that William

with serene countenance declared aloud that God would favour his side as the righteous one and called for his arms. Presently when through his attendants' haste he had put his hauberk on back to front, he corrected the mistake with a laugh. 'My dukedom will be turned into a kingdom.' Then he struck up the *Song of Roland* so that that man's warlike example might stimulate his soldiers, and called on God for aid. So the battle began on both sides.[6]

As the hauberk was of mail, such an accident could easily happen in a hurry. A minstrel Taillefer (*Incisor Ferri*) rode before the duke; later he was credited with singing of Charlemagne and of Roland and Oliver at Roncesvalles as he charged. The Tapestry says that William urged his men to fight *viriliter et sapienter*, bravely and wisely: terms that suggest the virtues of the epic hero, who is *sage et preu, sage et hardi*.[7] The two qualities are typified in the *Chanson de Roland* by the heroes Roland and Oliver. The traitor betrays both his feudal and his crusading duties; Ganelon is a faithless vassal who joins with the Saracens and betrays Roland, the epitome of loyalty. The barons might excuse him for the disaster he brings on the Frankish army if his motive had been personal revenge, but the charge of treason can have no pardon. The theme of betrayal pervades the Tapestry and gives its narrative a unifying force; the oath over relics is prominent in the *Chansons*. Betrothals are thus sworn; and the whole action of the *Covenant de Vivien* is based on an oath taken on a Gospel Book; in *Raoul de Cambrai* the emperor and the forty hostages promise Raoul his fief by an oath on relics. Gautier swears that Bernier is a traitor; on relics Guerri takes the oath to avenge Bernier. The theme of the Tapestry is that of *Roland*: 'A traitor causes both himself and others to perish.' The lesson of the main narrative on the Tapestry is underlined by the little fable-scenes that run along the borders; they have been carefully chosen to express the same moral from all sorts of angles. At times the tale is a simple one. A goat is allowed a short time to say mass by the wolf preparing to devour him, but at once he breaks his word and calls up the shepherd and his dogs. Other fables are more complex. A lion cheats his three companions and takes all the four quarters of the quarry, the first three by guile. The wolf is to be king while the lion is away; the lion makes him take an oath (in which relics are mentioned) not to eat flesh. The wolf swears, then by various tricks and a final outburst of violence he eats up all the lion's subjects. He, the vassal, cheats the true king. And so on. A further aspect of loyalty emerges in the *Chansons*, which, though not directly relevant to Harold's plight, is worth noting because it brings up the question of the feudal bond as opposed to the tribal bond of the kindred. The kin of Ganelon rally to

H

his cause and bring about the fight between Pinabel and Thierry; when Pinabel is killed, the Franks say that Ganelon and his kin sureties should all be hanged; and so they are, on a single tree. In *Girard de Viane*, the kinsmen of Ganelon, whom the queen has affronted, fight against her, so that again kinship comes before feudal loyalty. We may compare the way in which Ydelon objects when Charlemagne orders him as liegeman to avenge his emperor on Richard son of Aymon. Ogier goes even further in a similar situation. In other cases, to save the breaking of faith with a lord, kinsmen have recourse to stratagems, as Turpin does to save Ogier or as when kinsmen of Renaus urge Roland to strike only one blow at him *por sa foi aquiter*. In actual life the same sort of symbolic trick was used. In 1047 Ralph Tesson was one of the conspirators against William and had sworn to smite him at the first chance; but realizing that William was going to win, he galloped up and struck him lightly on the shoulder. He then felt he was free of his oath.[8]

The Normans stressed the story of Harold's perjury to cover up the weak case they had. William of Poitiers throws in: 'And if a claim by blood is demanded, let it be noted that the son of duke Robert touched king Edward in near kinship, for Robert's aunt, Emma, sister to Richard II and daughter of Richard I, was Edward's mother.'[9] But we may be sure that once William had asserted his claim, he passionately believed in it. The eastern crusades, soon to follow, exemplified the way in which these men so often found it hard to distinguish an exalted religious aim from the crudest material objective. The church itself set the way with its complex set of rationalizations and its confusion of worldly power and property with heavenly rewards, and men's minds shifted easily and excitedly from a base earthly motive to a spiritual or moral one, which was fervently accepted – even if a certain cynicism refused at times to be stifled and came out into the open in characters like Rufus.

To return to the war preparations. The largest foreign quota seems to have been the Bretons, who came from a rough area thick with poor knights. They formed the left wing at Hastings. Despite the many conflicts of Normandy and Brittany, there was much penetration by Bretons into Normandy, for instance in the Bayeux area, where in the eleventh and twelfth centuries the ruling class included many of them.[10] Troops were also recruited from Maine, Aquitaine, Flanders and France: these made up the right wing at Hastings.[11] Footsoldiers, among whom were many archers, a few crossbowmen (according to William of Poitiers) and engineers, came from unknown areas; and there was a large crowd of camp followers, squires, valets and purveyors. Many horses had to be collected; the Tapestry shows them in nearly every ship. The largest number in one ship is ten, though we cannot expect verismilitude in such details; the artist no doubt put in as many as he could. Wace, the Channel Islander commissioned a century later to write an epic on the Norman dukes, was told by his father that William gathered 696 ships and many small boats. Other writers, wanting a more impressive number, speak of one to three thousand. We can only be sure that the flotilla was huge by the standards of the day.

It began to assemble at the mouth of the Dive, and by 12 August was ready to sail. The speed of the mustering and the ability to hold such a large body of men and ships in good order for several weeks were proofs of the high reputation that William enjoyed, his organizing ability, and his ducal resources, which he must have long been building up for this moment. His magnates were abashed at the largeness of the project, but he maintained a steady confidence. The attack had to be made in 1066, otherwise Harold would consolidate his position, and the army gathered under papal blessing and banner would break up and the Norman barons would lose heart. William had hoped to sail in July and the delays taxed his energy and resolution. Poitiers says he caught an English spy and returned him unpunished, with a message for Harold. 'Tell him that if he does not see me within a year in the place he now strives to make secure against my coming, he may remain quiet for the rest of his days and need fear no harm from me.' Harold could not find out when and where to expect the blow. After gaining recognition at York he came back to London. Between February and May his people had been agitated by Halley's Comet, which had begun to streak the north-west sky.

William was following up his diplomatic contacts. Eustace of Boulogne was keen to share any English plunder, but as Edward's brother-in-law he was a possible claimant to the throne. So William demanded his son as hostage. Baldwin of Flanders as usual had an equivocal role; he was William's father-in-law, but a sister of his had married into the Godwin family. It has been suggested that he refused William aid as the French regent, but gave it as the count of Flanders. However, the only direct evidence is from Wace and William of Malmesbury. Wace says Baldwin was sent a blank piece of parchment on which to fill in what reward he wanted for his help, and that he deceived Harold as to the number of troops mustering under William; Malmesbury, that he helped 'with sagacious counsel, in which he was very strong, and by supplying troops'. But neither statement is worth much, though Baldwin certainly helped William with his benevolent neutrality.[12]

Moreover, William had to take into account what Tostig, the Danes, and the Norwegians were doing. Sweyn Estrithson of Denmark, Cnut's nephew, was persuaded to promise support, through fear of a Norwegian attack. But the stalwart Harald Hardrada was more dangerous. He had fought in Sicily, the east Mediterranean and Persia, had made a fortune while Varangian guard at Byzantium, married a Russian princess, and gouged out the eyes of a Byzantine emperor. The last of the wild, roving Norsemen, he had returned in 1047 and managed to withdraw Norway from Danish control and bring it under his rule. He had a claim to the English throne, based on a pact between Harthacnut and Magnus. Tostig meanwhile had been harboured by Baldwin, together with his wife Judith; the pair wintered at St Omer in sumptuous quarters. Tostig was in touch with Hardrada. Scandinavian sources tell of his visits in quest of aid, but may merely dramatize the arrival of envoys with letters. In early May he had made a trial attack, perhaps with covert aid from both Flanders and Normandy, ravaging the coasts of Sussex and Kent. At Sandwich he landed, seeking recruits (as his father had done some fourteen years earlier). An old comrade of northern campaigns, Copsi, joined him with seventeen ships from the Orkneys. Plundering along the eastern coast, he was beaten off by Edwin and the Lindsey fyrd; and barred by Morcar from Northumbria, he went north to Malcolm in Scotland, where he spent the summer, hoping for men from Norway. A pact was finalized, no doubt with the Orkneys men as intermediaries. Hardrada gathered a fleet (said to be three hundred ships) and sailed for the Tyne. Tostig was promised that his aid would earn him the restoration of his earldom. This time there must have been many Flemings with him.[13]

In September Tostig and Hardrada devastated the coast of Yorkshire and sailed into the Humber, then up the Ouse to Riccall. Some two miles south of York, at Gate Fulford, they routed at much cost a force under Edwin and Morcar on 20 September, Wednesday. York submitted and Hardrada moved to Stamford Bridge on the Derwent. Harold decided to risk leaving the south unprotected against William and to march north. He had had trouble in holding his levies together for three months while William was detained by the steady north winds. On 8 September he disbanded the fyrd, who were keen to get home for harvest, and went to London with his retainers. A part of his fleet followed him; the rest were dismissed. In September William moved his ships, or had them forced by a westerly gale, up the coast to St Valéry (in the county of Ponthieu); whether or not he intended the move, it cost him many ships. Drowned men were secretly buried; some soldiers deserted. The main wind was still contrary. The saint's body was taken from the church and carried round, while the army prayed for a change of wind.

Hardrada had set up headquarters at the old royal manor of Aldby, while hostages were brought in from all over Yorkshire. By 24 September Harold was at Tadcaster. Next day, Monday, he defeated Hardrada at Stamford Bridge. Norse accounts cast the battle into heroic formulas. Tostig, confronted with Harold, finds the call of kinship stronger than the recent act of homage he is supposed to have made to the Norse king; Hardrada, promised the traditional seven feet of earth, is contrasted with Harold, who is short though standing up well in his stirrups.[14] The Norsemen seem to have been caught off guard, and were without their *byrnies* (leather jerkins sewn with studs or metal rings) on account of the heat of the day. The saga says the English used cavalry and archers, while the invaders fought on foot with axes, swords and spears. The bridge was forced. Then, perhaps after an interval, the main attack was launched on Hardrada's shieldwall up a slight slope about three hundred yards above. The banner passed from Hardrada to Tostig, who was then also killed. Reinforcements from Riccall came too late. (The account reads rather like the battle of Hastings in reverse and may well have been modelled on that battle.) Harold, with his usual cool prudence, let Hardrada's son, Olaf, and the earl of Orkney go home with the survivors in twenty-four ships. One of the defeated, Godfred Crovan, an Icelander, later conquered the Isle of Man. Stories told how Harold was at a triumphant banquet in York when a messenger arrived with news that William had landed at Pevensey on Thursday, 28 September. The first of October would have been the very soonest the news could have reached York. Harold's losses had been heavy; the survivors must have been exhausted. But at least the north was now safe.

William had sailed at last, late on 27 September. The wind had changed. On the Tapestry the *Mora* and one other ship alone have no horses; he was no doubt unencumbered so that he could sail ahead in a fast ship. Indeed by midnight he found himself separated from his fleet, despite his masthead lantern. If Harold had had patrols out, William might have come to an abrupt end. But he kept his nerve, ate a high-spirited meal with spiced wines, and at last his fleet caught up with him. Early in the morning he landed on what is now a dried up basin, Pevensey Bay. (The Tapestry sets the banquet here on land; William is with his two half-brothers, and we see a woman and child escape from a burning house.) With his large and loaded fleet he could not try hit-and-run tactics, as Tostig had; he needed a secure beach-head. He must have had many sailors and guides who knew the coast well, and we may guess that he had first aimed for

Southampton Water – Tostig in May had raided the Isle of Wight and Edward had landed thereabouts in 1035–6. It was further away than Kent, but the Isle would have made a good base for attacks in various directions, across land to Winchester and on to the Thames. At the worst it could have been held through the winter, for fresh invasion attacks in early 1067. Driven to the north, William now decided to make for the Cinque Ports. He had lost so much time that he may have wanted to land nearer London and try a quick decisive action.

He began building fortifications at once, with a rampart dug inside the Roman fort; but the site was too exposed. The coastal area was backed up by the big Andred forest and contained many ports loyal to Harold's family. He could hardly have known as yet what a favourable moment had been thrust on him against his will, with Harold far away and his army weakened by its losses. The westerly gales had caused Harold at least as much trouble as they did the Normans, driving his ships up the Channel and round into the Thames. If William had had some desertions, Harold had had to release all his local defence bands. William decided to move a little eastward to Hastings; there, on what was a peninsula made by the swampy estuaries of the Brede and the Asten, he could set up a castle and lay waste the hinterland. For a fortnight, apart from the building and some reconnaissance, nothing much happened. The site was not much use for attacking from, but excellent if a retreat became necessary. Local labour was conscripted to help with the fortifications. Robert fitzWomarch (Wymarc) is said to have sent a message that William had no hope against Harold's forces and if he didn't give up the expedition, he would have to fight behind fortifications. William of Poitiers says Robert was 'a certain rich man, Norman by *natio*'; presumably he knew both Normandy and England. (He may have been a Breton who had settled down after service at Edward's court.)[15] 'In my opinion,' he declared, 'against Harold your troops are no more than contemptible dogs.' William sent back thanks for the counsel, but announced that he would stay on the defensive. 'I'm confident that even if I had only ten thousand men as good as the sixty thousand I've brought with me, through their courage and God's aid he and his army will be destroyed.' He certainly did not have even 10,000 men; possibly there were about 5-6,000 fighters on either side. But we are reduced to guesswork; 4,000 men was a portentous army in those days. Closed in by downs and forest and lacking clear news, William must have been uncertain what to do.

Meanwhile Harold, with his liking for speedy campaigns and forced marches, seems to have covered the 190 odd miles to London by 6 October. He stayed there some five days, waiting for what reinforcements he could hastily collect, and perhaps hoping Edwin and Morcar would arrive. According to Poitiers, he was infuriated by the devastations made by the Normans around their camp; he hoped to make a night attack or catch them by surprise, cutting off their bridgehead while sending a strong fleet to hem them in from the sea. About 11 October, with his brothers Gyrth and Leofwin, he led his men south over the weald, along a forest track. By the night of 13-14 October he had reached the Sussex downs. His men came out of the trees at Caldbed Hill on to higher ground which was linked by a lower neck to a cross-ridge running south-east. In the small hours of the 14th, William, warned by his scouts, moved north-west from his camp along the line of the present Hastings-Battle road. On Telham Hill, three quarters of a mile west of the highest point of the ridge, he saw the English gathering along the next ridge. The *Chronicle* suggests that Harold was taken by surprise. He 'gathered a great host and came to oppose' William 'at the grey appletree, and William came upon him unexpectedly before the army was set in order'. Again, Harold 'marched from the north and fought against him before his host came up'.[16]

Harold and his house-carles, his brothers and their retainers, had horses. Most of his men were tired and posted in some confusion. On the other hand, William and his men were in a very narrow bridge-head; only a slight reverse would have been disastrous. Perhaps it was at this moment that William challenged Harold to single combat; more likely, if the challenge was ever made, it was done months before by envoy. (Poitiers reports an exchange between William and Harold, in which each punctiliously set out his claims; and William offered to take his case to court to be judged by English or Norman law, or else to undergo a *duellum*, an ordeal by battle. More likely, each man briefly justified himself and defied the other.) When a Fécamp monk pressed for an answer, Harold is said to have replied, 'We march straight on.' Then, 'We march to victory.' The place recalled by the English as the Grey Appletree was called by the Normans Senlac, a corruption of *sand-lac*, sandy brook. (*Senlac*, *Sanguelac*, could be interpreted as Blood-lake.) William chose to attack. He addressed his men, reminding them that they had always won under his command and pointing out the desperate nature of their situation if they failed; he denigrated the English as soldiers and vaunted the justice of his cause. The Normans then marched out of their encampment. The English seem to have believed that they would not be assaulted in their superior position.

We are lucky to have three early accounts of the battle: in the prose of William of Poitiers, William's chaplain, in the verse of *Carmen de Hastingae Proelio* which seems certainly to be by bishop

Guy of Amiens (written by 1068 or at latest 1070), and in the designs of the Bayeux Tapestry. The weapons of both sides were much the same. Though in the battle only the English had axes, the Tapestry shows Guy of Ponthieu with an axe as he receives William's embassy. One English archer is depicted, but he is no different from the four Norman ones; perhaps we are to infer that there were four times as many Norman archers as English. The latter were certainly not ignorant of archery. Bows appear in the *Battle of Maldon*, though it is not clear which side uses them. A century after the Conquest, William fitzStephen found archery practice a part of London holiday pastimes; and under Henry I accidents from careless archery practice were common enough to call for special legal notice.[17] But possibly because of losses in the north Harold was now short of archers. The battle accounts show the Normans as superior in them as well as in cavalry. Against William's army were Harold's shire levies, a close phalanx, a shieldwall up to ten or twelve ranks deep, with house-carles making up the front line. The latter would have dismounted as horses were used for attack, not defence. Each side had its standard, the Normans the papal banner charged with cross and roundels, Harold the dragon of Wessex and his own sign of the Fighting Man. The Tapestry shows a model dragon on a pole over him as he dies. Heraldry had not yet been born, though emblems of various kinds had long been used. Asser's *Alfred* tells of a dragon woven by the daughters of Ragnar Lothbroc on a banner called *Reafan* (Raven), which was captured from his sons in 878. Some knights on the Tapestry have shields painted with dragons; some shields are plain, others have markings that may be cognizances or merely constructional forms. Wace says that the Normans had devices on lance flags and shields so as to tell one another in the mellay. But in general these were not personal or family emblems like the later heraldic ones.

Harold had been with William on his Breton campaign and must have known something of his methods. Most likely, he had decided to meet any cavalry attack with the phalanx. On the right ground light cavalry could hardly hope to breach a solid line; and when the enemy weakened, the defenders could move into attack. William, however, had his archers ready to harass the phalanx. His forces were divided into three groups, Bretons on the left, a mixed Franco-Flemish contingent under Robert of Beaumont on the right, and Normans in the centre. With horsemen and archers he had a freedom of movement denied to the compacted English. He set his archers in front, probably backed by light-armed footmen with slings and spears; then came the heavier footmen, with mounted knights at their rear. He deployed his men without response from the English.

The trumpets sounded and the battle began about 9 a.m. William's formation suggests that he envisaged three tactical phases: shooting by the archers, assault by the heavy infantry, and attack by the cavalry, penetrating any breaches in the enemy line. The archers stuck their quivers in the ground and shot uphill; their arrows would have been easy to catch on shields unless they passed high overhead. The paucity of English archers would have one disadvantage for the Normans; there would have been few enemy arrows for them to pick up and use for return volleys. Next the infantry advanced up the hill and were met with a shower of missiles that is described as unprecedented. The Normans failed to break the English line and suffered from the axes of the house-carles. The Bretons, who had the easiest slope to climb, would have been the first to meet the English resistance. Unsupported for the moment on their right, they fell confusedly back, forcing their cavalry with them, into the marshy depths of the valley where heavy casualties were suffered. The English are said to have chased after them down the slopes.

The Norman contingent, unprotected on its left, also fell back, and the Franco-Flemish one further along followed their example. Even the baggage guard was affected, and there was danger of a Norman rout. William at once galloped down into the tumult. The tale got around that he had been killed. Pushing back his helmet, he shouted that he was still alive, and, with the aid of bishop Odo and Eustace of Boulogne he rallied the fugitives and after a while was able to launch some of his own cavalry, which then charged downhill and attacked the Englishmen who had broken ranks in pursuit of the Bretons. He thus struck them between the hillock and the marsh. Most of them were killed, though some succeeded in getting back to their line or climbed on to the hillock. Probably after these events there was an exhausted pause. Both sides needed to reform.

Harold has been blamed for not taking advantage of the period of Norman disorder and launching an attack. His failure to do anything of the sort is so remarkable, so out of character, that it has been plausibly suggested that he did in fact launch a counter-attack, that he made it too soon, and that, through William's prompt and resolute action, it was met and beaten. The episode in question was treated at length by the Tapestry, and during it Harold's two brothers, Gyrth and Loefwin, were killed. We can well imagine that they would have led a counter-attack, but would not have been carried away by some of the fyrd breaking ranks; and unless they did lead such an attack, it is hard to see how the Normans were in such straits.

It was now that William decided on the third phase of the operations: the heavy cavalry attack up the ridge. There could be no question of a thundering impact such was possible on level ground or

downhill. The English again let loose a hail of missiles and many of
the Normans were cut down by the battleaxes of house-carles. The
struggle seems to have gone on some time, till at last the Normans fell
back. Again either the fyrd broke line or there was an attempt at an
English counter-attack. But William was ready. He had cavalry in
reserve which were sent to fall on the English. Two similar incidents
are said to have occurred on the Franco-Flemish front, with similar
results. Now the English had suffered so many losses that they had
to draw in their flanks and gather round the standard.

In most of the accounts of the battle including those of the *Carmen*
and of Poitiers the Normans are said to have made feigned retreats in
order to get the English to break their line and the Englishmen stupid-
ly went on breaking it. But we cannot credit that the Normans would
have acted so rashly on such ground. The fact that this tactic turns up
repeatedly in the accounts of battles of the period makes the story
more suspect, not less. The Normans are said to have used it at Arques
in 1053 and against the imperial troops at Larissa in 1082; the crusaders in Syria in 1099 found that the Moslems were said to make
common use of it. We can safely assume that it was the sort of tale
that winners were liable to tell after the event in order to explain
away any failures on their part in the battle.

What William seems finally to have done was to throw all his
forces into the attack on the weakened English. The archers had presumably drawn fresh supplies of arrows from the munition waggons
like the one shown on the Tapestry. They shot high so that the arrows
would come down on to the closely packed English. Such knights as
still had horses charged; those who had lost their horses joined the
infantry. A strange battle, commented Poitiers, where one side was in
ceaseless movement, the other rooted to the ground. The Tapestry
brings out the high trajectory of the arrows. By the end of the day
the English were worn out, and their shieldwall breached; the house-
carles died round their lord, and at last, 'towards the twilight hour',
Harold was killed. The Tapestry shows an Englishman with three
arrows in his shield as he plucks a fourth from his eye; dropping his
axe, another dies under the sword of a mounted Norman. Baudri of
Borgeuil, at the end of the century, says that Harold was shot through
the eye, but he may have been misinterpreting the Tapestry. Most
experts now think the man with an arrow in his eye is a house-carle;
Harold is the man being struck down. Guy of Amiens says the killers
were Eustace of Boulogne, a son of Guy of Ponthieu, Walter Giffard,
and Hugh of Montford.[18] Just where he fell, nobody knew. His mutilated body was later found among the huddled corpses. (The high
altar of Battle Abbey was erected on this spot.) At his death the
English gave way and fled, with the Normans in pursuit. Where

broken ground helped them, they turned and rallied. Eustace was hard pressed and called on William to sound the retreat; he was answered by a blow between the shoulders that brought blood gushing from nose and mouth, and he had to be borne off. William once more held his men steady, but the pursuit had cost him some of his best men. Despite the victory, the Normans seem to have been too exhausted and uncertain to rejoice; the next day, for all they knew, might have brought a fresh army on them and they would have been done for. But when the bodies of Harold and his brothers were found, they began to believe in their triumph.

The sequence of events and the events themselves are substantially the same in the Tapestry, in William of Poitiers' account, and in the poem on the battle, though with many minor variants. The poem mentions the duke's long and vexatious delay at St Valéry, but Poitiers adds that there were shipwrecks and desertions. The poem says that the fleet, sailing at night, had torches on every ship; Poitiers says the duke only had a fire lit at mast-top to signal the resumption of the voyage after the pause; the Tapestry shows the lantern signal on the ducal vessel. The poem says a comet shone in the sky; Poitiers that it appeared after Harold's coronation. The poem says that an Englishman who watched the Normans landing rode off to tell Harold; Poitiers describes it as the visit of a Norman settled in England. Early in the battle the poem speaks of a simulated flight of the Norman army; Poitiers speaks of a genuine flight, though later of a simulated one. The poem says that Gyrth, Harold's brother, dismounted the duke but was at once killed by him; the Tapestry just says that Gyrth was killed. The poem says that fitzHelloc killed the duke's horse, then the duke killed him in revenge; Poitiers, merely that the duke was dismounted thrice and each time took his revenge. The poem says that Count Eustace gave his horse to the duke and took one from a knight of his, then the pair ravaged the English camp, and the duke gathered Hugues de Ponthieu and Gilard to launch the assault on Harold; Poitiers draws up a list of honour, which mentions Eustace and Gautier Giffard, together with others whom the poem ignores. And so on. We get the impression that each of the three sources is independent and was based on direct experience or contemporary accounts. The battle was in no sense a simple victory of expert and trained knights against antiquated footsoldiers. William owed a great deal to his superiority in archers. Without a large body of horsemen he could not have kept on making attacks uphill against the English line, but the nature of the ground prevented a shock onslaught. The outcome of the battle was largely determined by the haphazard way in which the English had been got together at London. Harold could have had few of his northern army with him, and such as were there must have been very tired. William of Malmesbury says that after Stamford Bridge:

> Harold, elated by his successful enterprise, allowed no part of the spoil to his soldiers. So many of them, as the chance came, stole off and deserted the king as he was proceeding to the battle of Hastings. For with the exception of his stipendiary and mercenary soldiers, he had very few of the poeple with him: on which account, circumvented by a stratagem of William's, he was routed...

Harold may well have had no time to arrange what to do with the spoils from Stamford Bridge; there may have been much discontent at a second forced march; men may have fallen back through exhaustion. The few days at London could not have brought in large levies. Malmesbury stresses the small size of Harold's army at Hastings:

> Those persons seem to me to err who swell up the numbers of the English and underrate their courage; who, while meaning to extol the Normans, load them with ignominy. A mighty commendation indeed: that a very warlike nation should conquer a set of people who were obstructed by their own multitude and fearful through cowardice. On the contrary they were few in number and brave in the extreme; and sacrificing all concern for their bodies, poured out their spirit for their country.[19]

William's steadfastness certainly must have helped a great deal; but we must not think there was tactical control except of the simplest kind. The Tapestry gives us no hint of any uniformity in Norman equipment, or regularity of formation. What we see are knights riding at the English in a succession of columns with two or three abreast. There is one scene with an Englishman being ridden down. Most Normans throw spears; only two or three have their lances under their arms. The artist stresses this point by making the throwing spears thin and the couched lances thicker. What is shown is nothing like shock cavalry tactics. One interesting detail is that spears and lances used by both English and Normans have a cross-piece near the top to prevent deep penetration. Poitiers speaks of the terrific clamour on both sides. There would have been no possibility of orders except of a very local kind. On the other hand, the English system of defence by means of axes and javelins could not have been very effective, yet it seems to have repelled the Normans for many hours. And it may be that if Harold have been able to disengage his forces without disorder, he could have gone to collect fresh troops and then met the weakened Normans again, but he seems to have been too tenacious for such tactics.

In *Heimskringla* the English horsemen at Stamford Bridge ride against the Norse footmen with spears, but fail till the latter break formation; in the mellay Harald Hardrada is killed by an arrow through his windpipe.[20] This account was written a century after Hastings and seems to be based on that battle; but it is not inherently impossible. Certainly the English leaders and their retainers would normally have been mounted. The *Chronicle* of 1055, dealing with the Welsh marches, says that the English went off 'because they were on horses', which becomes in Florence of Worcester the statement that the English were bidden to fight on horseback against their custom. But even if correct, the *Chronicle* is telling of warfare on steep broken ground, thick with trees, and no doubt the fyrd normally did not use horses. Still in 1063 the English seem to be mounted under Tostig against the Welsh on the coastal strip of north Wales; and in 1054 Siward defeated Macbeth of Scotland despite his Norman allies. Florence states that Siward led 'a mounted army'. The existence of horses in 1016 is implied, when Edmund Ironside, says the *Chronicle*, pursued the Danes in Kent 'with their horses to Sheppey', killing those he could overtake. An Anglo-Saxon drawing shows two horsemen riding side by side, one throwing a spear, the other holding a two edged axe; there are no hounds and the nearer horseman has a shield on his bridle arm. The way that the men ride, two abreast, with missiles, suggests strongly the charging knights of the Tapestry. We may take the drawing to represent thegns or house-carles in action. Under William in Brittany Harold played his part in a mounted force; and at Gerberoy in 1080 Englishmen fought on horseback for William.[21]

What was unusual for a battle in England was the large number of horsemen in the Norman army. In the sense that this mass of knights represented the serried might of feudal France opposed to a phalanx of the traditional English kind, there was an historical significance in the contrast between the armies; but what was crucial for Harold was rather the hurried and restricted way in which he had got together his forces, and the rash way he rushed into battle in his eagerness to deal with the Normans as he had dealt with the Norsemen. We may discount the charge that Edwin and Morcar deliberately left him to fight alone. They had lost heavily at Fulford, and Harold's hurry gave them no chance to join him with fresh forces. Perhaps his death was more disastrous than his defeat. His accession had broken the line of kings with their Woden genealogies; the Aetheling was young and unknown; Edwin and Morcar lacked the prestige to aspire to the crown. There was nobody round whom resistance could gather. Only a great figure, capable of arousing a strong sense of the English tradition and with a legitimate claim to the throne, could have unified and roused the national forces. And there was no such figure. Only local resistance was possible and this had no hope of success. So the fact that Harold had broken the line of legitimate descent, and intruded as an outsider on the royal kindred, was of enormous help to William, once he was dead.

A vain attempt was made to find a substitute. Ealdred of York turned to the one person who might have aroused English loyalties: Edgar Aetheling, now about fifteen. He was helped by Stigand, Edwin and Morcar and the Londoners, with varying degrees of resolution. But when he had to make the final decision – whether or not to crown the lad – his heart failed him. The family of Godwin had so long been the real centre of power in England that since their disappearance no one had the courage or resolution to attempt a new start. And William, whether out of caution or good sense, did not advance on London at once and so gave time for the vacillations of Ealdred and the earls to increase. He himself could not yet believe his own good luck: that with one battle he had crushed all opposition. Steadily devastating the land he moved along the south coast. A sally of men from Romney was ferociously beaten back. He went on to Dover, then turned inland for London, where he arrived by the end of October. He was now delayed by dysentry. Queen Edith surrendered Winchester. He advanced to the south end of London Bridge, but lacked the strength to take the city. So he laid waste Southwark and marched west, once more destroying everything in a swathe through Surrey, north Hampshire and Berkshire. Then he turned to cross the Thames at Wallingford. He was ringing London with a black band of death. Twenty years later in the *Domesday Book* his course could be traced in the clumps of manors which slumped in value after 1066. We can see that the usual distance his army travelled was twenty-five miles a day.

Stigand lost his nerve and submitted, being told that William would recognize him as his spiritual father. The other English magnates were cowed. William was met at Berkhamstead by Ealdred, Edgar, the earls and bishops, Wulfstan of Worcester and Walter of Hereford, with representatives of the Londoners. He promised to rule as Edward's legal successor and marched on London, still systematically laying waste the land. Admitted to London, he repeated his promise at his coronation on Christmas Day in Westminster Abbey. How unsure the Normans still felt was shown by their reaction when he was presented to the people for acclamation, with the question put in both English and French. The responses were misunderstood by the men-at-arms on guard, who at once set the near houses on fire. While the houses burned, the ceremony went on. William had had doubts whether he should be crowned without his wife present, fearing that later objections to the king-worthiness of his sons might arise. But he knew the magnates and Londoners wanted to get as good a bargain as possible by pushing him quickly on to the throne, now they had no choice; his own lords also must have been keen to see him crowned. He was in an ambiguous position, which was inherited by his sons. All his actions were based on the claim that he was the lawful king of England, chosen by Edward and continuing his line after disposing of a perjured usurper; yet he was the conqueror of a foreign country which he had to rule by ruthless military power.

Both his roles, that of king by right and that of king by might, carried on throughout his reign. In the first of his declarations he said 'He wished above all things God to be revered throughout his realm, the faith of Christ to be preserved inviolate, and peace and security to be kept between English and Normans.' He granted all men the laws of King Edward; he confirmed London's customs and ordered the ports and certain roads to be opened to traders. He also ordered his troops to behave well: they were to refrain from outrages liable to provoke revolts among those justly subjected to them; they were not to shame their homeland's good name amid strangers; they were not to visit brothels or drink too much in taverns, as drunkenness begot brawls and brawls begot murder. He appointed judges to deal with offenders, Normans, Bretons, or others. In all this he was sincere enough; he wanted no unnecessary trouble and still felt insecure. He had the Norman determination to wring every penny of profit out of a situation, together with a realization of the limits which must not be transgressed if he wished to maintain the basis on which the pennies could be extorted. The Normans, quite lacking in original ideas, were highly adaptable and able to take over the systems of others and make them work better or more profitably. Where there was no system on which to build, as for long in Apulia, they were at a loss and reverted to simple freebooting; but where, as in Sicily and in England in different ways, there were effective systems of government and exaction of taxes, they did their best to make no unnecessary alterations.

William's call for good order among his troops was thus meant to be taken seriously; but the nature of the situation ensured that vast oppression and harrying of the English would go on – accepted by William as long as the administrative structure, on which his profits depended, was still able to function. Many noblewomen had to find refuge in nunneries or be raped, and we can but dimly imagine how the commonfolk suffered.

> To the natives it appeared that 'devils had come through the land with fire and sword and havoc of war', 'that under the scourges of the chastising God many thousands of the people are thrown down and the kingdom is ravaged by fire and plundering', and what can we expect but a miserable end in slaughter unless the infinite and inestimable mercy of the Lord ...should give us pardon.' The same, or another, contemporary wrote, 'How many thousands of the human race have fallen on evil days! The sons of kings and earls and nobles...are fettered with manacles and chains...How many have lost their limbs by the sword or disease or have been deprived of their eyes, so that when released from prison the common light of the world is a prison for them!' The last of William's statutes reads, 'I forbid that any man be executed or hanged for any offence, but let his eyes be gouged out and his testicles cut off' (Barlow).[22]

One great advantage of Hastings for William was that he was able to declare a considerable portion of England forfeit to the crown: all the wide lands of the house of Godwin (in the southern and south-west shires, Herefordshire, the south-east shires, and East Anglia) and of any other landowner who had opposed or fought him. He could also claim that no Frenchman was given anything unjustly taken from an Englishman; in such a situation there was little need for 'injustice'. And soon further revolts made more and more land forfeit. William, protesting his good intentions, could hardly feel secure or beloved.

He at once began building a castle by the river in the south-east corner of London. This was later in his reign replaced by the White Tower, ninety feet high, which is still the centre of The Tower of London. Poitiers admits that it was needed to scare the citizens.[23] Perhaps Baynard's Castle in the south-west of the city was also built for the same reason at about this time. William made his first allocations of lordship: Odo was given Kent, with the royal steward William fitzOsbern probably in the Isle of Wight. Count Brian, second son of Eudo of Porhoët, count of Penthièvre in Brittany, may have been promised the south-west peninsula; the Anglo-Breton Ralf de Gael, son of Ralf the staller, servant of Edward, was given East Anglia (perhaps only Norfolk). More troops were brought over from France and installed in castles and strongholds. William himself moved about west of London. Several English magnates were summoned to Barking to give him allegiance. William no doubt went as far as Winchester, to get the treasury and for strategic reasons. Odo was based on Dover Castle to control the south; William fitzOsbern was to watch the north from Winchester; Edwin was left over Mercia; Copsi was put over Northumbria. There was still a Scandinavian threat. Edgar, Morcar, Stigand and others were kept at court under surveillance and taken along when William crossed the Channel.

He must have completed many dispositions in January, for in February he was back in his duchy. He had laid a heavy geld on England and already some of the war loot had reached Normandy; he himself brought more, appearing at Rouen in magnificent vestments to match his new kingly title. As there had been no time to gather taxes, what he brought must have consisted of 'gifts', many no doubt extorted from the church. Poitiers is eloquent about the wonderful treasures, embroideries and ornaments which the monasteries 'bestowed' upon their new king. At Pevensey he had paid off his mercenaries. Splendid gifts had to go to the papacy for its important aid; in return for his banner he sent Harold's flag embroidered in gold with an armed man. Gold and jewelled crosses, golden vases, bullion and embroidered palls were distributed, we are told, to churches in France, Aquitaine, Burgundy and Auvergn; the Norman churches must have been given even more valuable plunder. At Fécamp, during Easter, visitors admired the gaudy glitter, but they seem to have been most attracted by the long-haired English nobles who looked lovelier than girls. For the first time, William, inured to hardship and careless of display, found the time and the means for luxuries.

How much his heart was in Normandy and not in England is shown by the fact that at this crucial period he stayed on for nine months, and only returned to England when trouble broke out. Not that the duchy needed him: everything was quiet, as could be expected with so many turbulent nobles killed or busy grabbing wealth in England; there was no external threat. He must have thought his measures would keep England cowed and tranquil. While the country provided him with a title, profitable revenues and with lands to grant his adherents, he had no further interest in it. But he misjudged the situation; and his attitude helped to precipitate further warfare and decisively deepen the gap between conquerors and conquered. Orderic tells us that the Normans behaved as badly as might be. The castellans oppressed rich and poor with unjust exactions and added insults to the injuries. The commanders acted brutally and had no interest in hearing or judging the complaints of the tormented people. Soldiers raped and looted with impunity, protected by their superiors. If any English were fools enough to object, they were punished. The lack of any English rival for the throne meant that the opposition had no focal point. In desperation the men of Kent called on Eustace of Boulogne, whom they would have known to some extent under Edward, to intervene and save them from Odo; they must have heard that the count, apparently considering that he had been insufficiently rewarded, had quarrelled with William. He made an attempt on Dover, but was driven out of the town by the castle garrison. William was compelled to return on 6 December 1067 with reinforcements, bringing Robert of Montgomery. He was able to use his authority to quieten things. Before Whitsun 1068 Matilda, pregnant with the future Henry I, came over to be crowned queen at Winchester by Ealdred; she stayed till her son was born, then went home.

England, angry and discontented, but lacking a leader, was inevitably breaking up into areas of revolt: the south-west, the Welsh borderlands, the north. In other parts some English prelates were working hard to damp down the wraths: Bishop Aethelmaer (Stigand's brother) in East Anglia; Aethelwig, abbot of Evesham, and Wulfstan bishop of Worcester, in west Mercia. On the borders Eadric the Wild (a Welshman?), a Worcestershire thegn, was helped by Welsh princes to attack Richard fitzScrob and other Normans who had settled earlier in Herefordshire. Northumbria, which always had a strong feeling of independence, had no effective ruler and was growing rebellious, looking for some scion from the family of earlier native earls and ready to ask for aid from Scotland or Denmark. The Scottish king had thoughts of carrying his realm down to the Humber; the Danish king had his claim to England. With such aliens as the Normans and their allies swarming over England, Danes and Scots seemed like brothers to the English. Copsi, whom William had appointed to the north, was murdered in March 1067 or 1068; there was only the archbishop Ealdred of York, who lived mostly in the south, to support Norman rule.

William proceeded to attack his opponents, who had no castles in which to take shelter, but only walled towns or boroughs. The fighting went on from 1068 to 1071. English nobles turned on William in the dissident areas, but the opposition remained localized: no unifying leadership emerged. At the height of the troubles William had several armies in the field, his own and those of kinsmen and trusted comrades such as William fitzOsbern or Brian of Brittany. The commanders had their retainers, but most of the soldiers were hired. As a result, with the arduous conditions and prolonged campaigning, the composition of any contingent kept changing, and much expenditure and skill in management were required. Heavy taxes and much plunder were needed to meet the costs. There was the further problem of garrisoning the castles William was building as the necessary basis for a stable repression of the people. He proved astute in calling up native levies on the old system and in using them with effect in the south.

He turned first to the south-west where Exeter had defied him and was seeking to build a league of boroughs. On his arrival the rich citizens wanted to surrender, but the people disavowed them and shut the gates. The siege lasted eighteen days, during which he had a hostage blinded before the defenders and set to work undermining the walls. The city gave in. William saw that savage reprisals would make things worse; he demanded only the right to build a castle on the highest point inside the walls, which his men garrisoned. Then he made a circuit of Cornwall and was back in Winchester by Easter. Harold's illegitimate sons, who had been exercising some of the family influence in the region, sailed off to Norse Ireland (as their father had once done) and for some summers kept up raids on the south-west. But they merely annoyed and injured the people there, to William's benefit. When they attacked Bristol, the citizens drove them off. In Somerset they met a local force under Ednoth (staller under Harold). Ednoth was killed, but the invaders were expelled. Harold's son attacked again next year and failed. This sort of fighting had the effect of dividing the English. In the north Oswulf, who had challenged Copsi, himself died, and his cousin Gospatrick bought the earldom from William. But by the summer both Mercia and Northumbria were in revolt. Edwin and Morcar went off to the Welsh; but when Henry of Beaumont was put over a castle built in Warwick, they gave in and were pardoned. Edgar Aetheling, with his mother and two sisters, left for Scotland, where Malcolm Canmore reigned. (He married one of the sisters, Margaret, in 1069–70. A very influential woman, she was later canonized; three of her sons became successive kings of Scotland, and her daughter Edith married Henry I in 1100.) William built a castle at Nottingham, which he entrusted to William Peverel, then he took York, where another castle was raised. Aethelwine, bishop of Durham, persuaded Malcolm not to intervene. The county of Durham, now or soon after, was put under the Flemish count of Comines.

On his way south William built castles at Lincoln, Huntingdon and Cambridge. We can gauge the morale of the Normans in England at this time by Orderic's tale that their wives in Normandy, afraid to venture into England, clamoured for the men's return. William replied by granting the discontented soldiers rich fiefs, with promises of more when England was subjugated. But there were some grave defections, including, it seems, Hugh of Grandmesnil, a Hastings fighter, who had been put over the Winchester area. William got together more mercenaries, with increased promises of reward. Early in 1069 Roger de Comines marched on Durham. He ignored warnings, was enclosed in the town, and burned in Aethelwine's house. A York castellan was also killed. Edgar moved in from Scotland, with rebels flocking to join him. Welcomed at York, he attacked the castles. But before Easter William drove him out, executed many, gave the city up to loot, and put William fitzOsbern over it. Gospatrick resumed the earldom. In the summer Harold's sons were beaten off from north Devon by Brian of Brittany. Small revolts went on all over the west. Men from Dorset and Somerset assailed Robert of Mortain's castle at Montacute, but were put down by Geoffrey bishop of Coutances. On the Welsh borders there were uprisings. Men from Chester were helped by the Welsh in an attack on Shrewsbury, where the burgesses joined them together with men from Shropshire and Eadric the Wild. Exeter was attacked by rebels from Devon and Cornwall, but this time the citizens resisted. William had returned to Winchester by Easter; fitzOsbern and Brian, sent to quieten down the situation, found Shrewsbury burned out and deserted, but they routed the besiegers of Exeter. We may note that Orderic rated the value of the castle for defence highly and considered that the English suffered much from lacking them: 'For the fortifications called castles by the Normans were scarcely known to English provinces; and so the English, in spite of their courage and love of fighting, could put up only a weak resistance to their enemies.'

Now at last came the Danish challenge, from Sweyn Estrithson, son of Cnut's sister, cousin of Harold and Queen Edith, claiming that Edward had left him the throne. He got together a large force, not much smaller than that of William in 1066, comprising volunteers from Poland, Frisia, Saxony and Leuticia (probably Lausitz). His brother Osbern (expelled from England in 1049) and two of his sons commanded the fleet, said to number 300 (or 240) ships. They ravaged the coast from Kent northwards, till they anchored off the Humber. Yorkshire again rose. Edgar arrived to join the fleet, with Gospatrick and other nobles. The army of Danes and English took York with its castles on 20 September, and killed or captured the garrison. The city was again on fire. Ealdred died during the struggle. William had a dangerous situation to face, as the south-west was in revolt again and Eadric the Wild struck from Wales into Staffordshire and Cheshire.

But the northern combination did not hold together. If it had the story of the Normans in England might have had a different ending; for a strong stand would have badly weakened William and stimulated further risings, with the Scots joining in. Edgar retreated back into Scotland, and Osbern withdrew to the Isle of Asholme in Lindsey. When William arrived, the Danes, thinking more of their loot than their cause, moved off to their ships. William left the counts of Mortain and Eu to watch them, and marched west to deal with Staffordshire while the south-west rebels were held up at Exeter. Again the bishop of Coutances dealt with them. He took the risk of removing most of his troops from the south-east and reduced Somerset and Dorset. William was returning to the east coast when he heard that the Danes were moving north again. So he turned north himself. Once more he tried the tactic of devastation. Instead of making a direct attack, he hovered round in a semi-circle, laying waste, burning, murdering, looting. The Danes went back to their ships and were bribed to sail away. William then felt it safe to enter York where amid terrible slaughter he celebrated Christmas, ordering his full coronation regalia to be sent up. He decided to smash the north once and for all. In January 1070 he rode onwards to the Tees, destroying everything as he went. Two of the chief English leaders, Waltheof and Gospatrick submitted. He pushed on to Hexham on the Tyne, then returned to York. Despite the sharp winter weather he crossed the Pennines, while mercenaries from Brittany, Anjou and Maine mutinied and left him. Still, he reached Chester with enough men to build a castle and lay waste Mercia. All the while he tried to hearten his men with promises of the great rewards they would get in land and money if they stayed with him. At Salisbury, before Easter, he paid off his soldiers, who included Englishmen, but bade the mutineers be kept under arms for forty days more in punishment.

The destruction in the north was ghastly. On his march to York everyone, man or boy, had been slaughtered. After that he broke his forces up into small bands with orders to destroy everyone and everything of use to man. Fugitives were hunted down. Houses, crops, cattle and implements were all burned. Between York and Durham a whole generation was eliminated; in 1086 York was still largely deserted. Though the devastation was less complete in Staffordshire, Derbyshire and Cheshire, it was severe enough to ensure that no one there would think of resistance for a long time. Simeon of Durham, writing some fifty years later, recalled the days of cannibalism, of highways littered with rotting corpses, of starvation and pestilence following in the wake of the butchery. Even Norman chroniclers had to admit that there had been 'an act which levelled both the bad and the good in a common ruin'. (And yet, to see the devastation in perspective, we must recall how cruel the men of the north themselves could be. In 1065 the Northumbrians who had risen against Tostig wrought much havoc round Northampton while waiting for the king's answer to their demands: 'They killed people and

burned houses and corn and took all the cattle they could get...and
captured many hundreds of people and took them north with them,
so that the shire and other neighbouring shires were the worse for it
for many years.') To meet the heavy demands on his finances,
William is said in February to have plundered all the monasteries; in
such a situation rents and taxes must have been hard to collect.

The worst was now over. William had been able, through the lack
of a unified opposition, to apply the methods he had learned in
Normandy for tackling pockets of resistance, even though in England
the whole thing was on a larger scale. His castle system had proved
its worth; and barons or sheriffs must have dealt with many smaller
spots of trouble. To leaders he was often mild. Waltheof was pardoned and married Judith, William's niece; Eadric too was pardoned.
In spring 1070 King Sweyn at last joined his fleet in the Humber and
sailed down to raid East Anglia. At Easter William had deposed
Stigand and bishop Aethelmaer, perhaps no longer trusting any Englishmen; these prelates seem to have been the biggest landowners in
the region. The people rose and welcomed the Danes. Sweyn sent
Osbern with an army to Ely. Hereward the Exile plundered Peterborough Abbey to stop its treasures falling to a Norman abbot, and
took them to Ely. But the Danes had now decided that William was
too strong to attack directly; they merely wanted loot and bribes.
William offered to let Sweyn sail home unchallenged with the Peterborough treasure. Sweyn accepted but autumn gales dispersed his
ships and much of his loot sank. Hereward stayed in Ely.

Edwin and Morcar chose this unpropitious moment to leave
William's court. Perhaps they feared disclosures about their implication in the uprisings. But both their careers were full of vacillations;
and now instead of making for Scotland, Morcar turned to Ely and
Edwin was killed by one of his own men. Aethelwine of Durham had
also gone to Ely; and there in the Fens the last English stand was made.
William invested the resisters by sea and land, and at last drove them
out. The leaders were imprisoned, the lesser men mutilated and turned
free. Hereward escaped.

William could now turn his attention to strengthening his north
and west frontiers. While he was at Ely, the Scots had been laying
waste Lothian. In 1072 he attacked Scotland by sea and land, with
Eadric the Wild in his army. Crossing the Forth, he marched into the
valley of the Tay, while his fleet followed up the estuary. In these
combined operations he must again have been drawing on the
experiences of the Normans in Sicily. Malcolm at Abernathy accepted
him as overlord and gave his eldest son Duncan as hostage; Edgar
went off to Flanders. On the Welsh borders William set up three
earldoms with extraordinary franchises to match the problems they

had to meet. Hugh of Avranches, earl of Chester in 1071, built an outpost at Ruddlan under his cousin; Robert of Montgomery was earl of Shrewsbury with an outpost at Montgomery. The earls were able to contain the princes of Gwynedd and Powys; the commander of Ruddlan was so powerful that in 1086 he paid £40 'for North Wales', appearing thus in the same role as the native Rhys ap Tewdwr for the south. The third border earldom, that of Hereford, functioned well till the second earl's disgrace in 1075. Later barons continued with the task of beating Rhys (1093) and strengthening Norman control of the south from the lordships of Brecon and Glamorgan.

William's later difficulties came more from discontent among his own followers than from the defeated English. In 1075 three of his earls revolted, having come together at the wedding feast of Ralf of East Anglia and Emma, sister of Roger of Hereford. Waltheof, who had been made earl of Northumbria, was drawn in. The *Chronicle* bursts into one of its few verse passages. 'There that Bride-ale led many to bale.' And, 'All the Bretons who attended that bridal at Norwich were ruined: some of them were blinded, some of them were exiled, some were brought to shame. So all traitors to the king were laid low.' The grievances are not clear, though Roger resented the king sending sheriffs to hold pleas on his lands. A number of discontents had been gathering; inevitably when large-scale plundering was going on and gifts and grants of conquered land being made, many men felt they had got too small a share. Orderic says that in 1075 rebels complained that William had not properly honoured those who made his conquest possible; he had ungratefully defrauded those who gave their blood to his cause; he had granted infertile and war-wasted lands to wounded veterans, and then, when they had restocked them, he sometimes gave them away again. Elsewhere, naming some of the leading beneficiaries, he observes that William had created tribunes and centurions out of the meanest Norman soldiers. What happened at Norwich was, however, more than a drunken protest, for Cnut, the Danish king's brother, appeared off the Northumbrian coast with two hundred ships. But whatever happened, no English support was gained. Too many areas had been depopulated; and the English were not likely to support barons against the central authority, in which their sole hope of any sort of justice now lay. The regents quickly put the revolt down. Ralf got away to Brittany and Roger to Denmark, later returning to be imprisoned and lose his fief. Lanfranc advised Waltheof to throw himself on the mercy of the king, his wife's uncle; and William at first seemed to take the matter lightly. Then in May 1076 he executed Waltheof, last of the great English earls, at Winchester. Now England had without exception a Norman ruling class.

The 1075 revolt was said to have led to a 'purge' of England from Breton influences; not only did Ralf cease to be earl of Norfolk, but Brian also made way in Cornwall for Robert of Mortain. The Flemings, who had taken over much land in the north, with Gerbod becoming the first earl of Chester in about 1070, also suffered something of an eclipse, since Flanders had become hostile to England from 1067 onwards. Gerbod, after fighting in the battle of Cassel, disappeared from the English scene, his place being filled by Hugh, son of the vicomte Richard of Avranches. Thus the Normans became ever more dominant on the baronial level and much of the union of the invading army was lost. William was doubtless not displeased.

Northumbria was still a problem. William tried the device of a marcher bishopric under Walcher of Durham. But in 1080 Walcher had to deal with a feud involving his own household; his Norman adviser was entangled in the killing of a descendant of the earls. Walcher offered to clear himself by oath and rode to Gateshead where the crowd chased him into the church, set fire to it, and killed him and his party as they emerged. William built a new castle at Newcastle on Tyne, fostered a strong Breton group in the Honour of Richmond, and did his best to build up the Mowbray interest in the north. No simple administrative solution could be found for the region.

William was still primarily duke of Normandy. He was in his duchy from February to December 1067, in early 1072, again in early 1073, from April to December 1075, from spring 1076 to summer or autumn 1080 (four years), in summer and autumn 1082, at Easter 1083, in summer 1084, and from summer 1086 till his death on 9 September 1087. He was continually caught up in petty feudal conflicts until at the age of fifty-nine he was fatally injured when fighting the Capetians in the Vexin. In 1069 Maine had shaken off Norman domination, while Fulk le Rechin was getting control of Anjou, and was liable to take advantage of the confused state of Maine to intrude there. Baldwin VI had died in 1070, and his widow was striving to defend her children against his uncle, Robert le Frison. Doubtless through William, she married Osbern of Hereford, who joined her and was killed at Cassel in February 1071. William lost an old friend, and Flanders also went to an enemy. Philip of France, no longer a minor, was friendly to Fulk of Anjou and in 1072 he married Robert's half-sister. Moreover, he was keen to humble a vassal who had now become a monarch. Normandy was encircled by enemies. While William was in Scotland, Fulk seized Le Mans. William got back to Normandy as soon as possible; Fulk was away and William soon reduced the whole of Maine, transporting Englishmen over the Channel to fight for him. The *Chronicle* says:

> William led English and French levies oversea and conquered the province of Maine, and the English laid it completely waste. They destroyed the vineyards, burnt down the towns, and completely devastated the countryside, and brought it into subjection to the king. Then they returned home.

There seems to be a note of pride there. English levies are mentioned before the French ones. But we can hardly sympathize with the English pleasure at finding that, acting under William's orders, they could be as destructive to other people as the Normans had been to them.

Under 1074 the *Chronicle* tells us that Edgar returned from Flanders to Scotland and was received by Malcolm with much ceremony. 'At the same festival, Philip, king of France, sent a letter to him, bidding him come to him, and he would give him the castle of Montreuil so that he could do daily mischief upon his enemies' – by sea raids. He seems to have meant to accept the offer; but when he sailed off with great treasure, he met severe storms. His ships were wrecked and he gained shore with difficulty. Malcolm advised him to make his peace with William. 'And the king revoked the sentence of outlawry against him and all his men,' and he stayed at William's court. Philip may have had a finger in the 1075 revolt, and he would have been pleased when Rolf escaped to his border castle at Dol in Brittany. By September 1076 William had invested the castle, but Philip brought up a relief army and drove him off. Such a repulse provoked another Angevin attack on Maine, while the French penetrated the Vexin. The year 1077 ended with patched-up truces and with Philip's power reaching to the Epte. Family discords erupted to worsen William's troubles. His son Robert Curthose, short, stocky and dashing, without a trace of his father's shrewdness, demanded control of Normandy and Maine. When refused, he tried to seize Rouen, then fled with many nobles to Flanders and on to Germany; envoys from Philip and other enemies of William offered him support. The rebels gathered in Gerberoy.

> Robert fought against his father and wounded him in the hand; and his horse was killed under him; and he who brought up another for him – that was Toki, son of Wigod – was immediately killed by a bolt from a crossbow, and many there were killed or taken prisoner; and Robert returned to Flanders (*Chronicle*).[25]

Toki was an Englishman. In spring 1080 William made peace with Robert, but his defeat had roused his many wary enemies. Malcolm began depredations again in 1079, and in May 1080 came Walcher's murder. But a Norman expeditionary force imposed new terms on Malcolm; William was kept in Maine because of fresh attacks by Bretons and Angevins. Somehow battle was averted and a pact was signed. But, back at last in England, William had trouble with a man who had been his staunch supporter, his half-brother Odo. He arrested Odo: why, we do not know. Odo may have been trying to lure knights off to Italy in a bid for the papacy. (Rome was in confusion. In June 1080 Robert Guiscard had knelt before Gregory in homage for lands granted by previous popes; he did not yet know that the emperor Henry IV had deposed Gregory at a council of Lombard and German bishops, who had elected Gilbert of Ravenna as Clement III.) Odo spent the rest of William's reign in prison. Robert ran off in July 1083 to become again a pawn in King Philip's plots and plans. Queen Matilda died in November; and William, ageing and obese, heard that another Danish invasion was being prepared by Cnut.

Using the proceeds of a heavy geld, he took a big mercenary force across the Channel, a force said to have been the largest army yet seen in England. He met some expenses by quartering troops on vassals. The men were drawn from all the western lands north of the Alps; Florence says there were many thousands of archers and footmen from all parts of France. The statement that he quartered them on vassals, 'each in proportion to the produce of his estate', suggests a more complete control of the system of services than we would expect; it indeed suggests both the new kind of feudal duties and the old English type of responsibility based on the number of hides held. Probably it was because of the problems raised by such a measure that the *Domesday* survey was projected. The *Chronicle* moves straight on from the matter of quartering to tell of an assembly held at Christmas at Gloucester where there took place 'important deliberations and exhaustive discussions about the land, and how it was peopled, and with what sort of men'. So the decision to make the survey was taken. Orderic stresses its link with the question of manpower, though his description of the work itself is incorrect: 'He made a survey of the military strength of the kingdom of England, and he discovered 60,000 soldiers, whom he ordered to be made ready whenever need demanded.' Orderic, who had lived his first ten years in England close to Earl Roger of Montgomery's household, was sent as an oblate to St Évroult in Normandy in September 1085. It seems unlikely that he would have got the motives of the survey altogether wrong. From his account it follows that if the hidage of an estate were established, so were the attached services.

The decision to make the survey was indeed an astonishing one and shows what an advanced administrative system was enjoyed by England. Also it shows with what strength William had asserted and established his controls. At Lammastide, 1 August 1086, 'all the people occupying land who were of any account' were summoned to Salisbury. 'All the people' here must mean all the tenants-in-chief and their main sub-tenants (sometimes called honorial barons and capable of themselves developing into tenants-in-chief). In theory the king needed no fresh oaths of fealty; and William was not trying to cut across the feudal tangle of loyalties by a direct appeal to the lesser lords. Rather, in a moment of great stress, he was striving to grasp something of the totality of the system he had created by his various disparate measures, and was anxious to produce an appearance of solidarity and to draw the whole network closer to himself. Fear of a big Danish attack, the problems of supplying and quartering the huge mercenary army he had gathered at Lanfranc's advice, interest in how the English settlement had worked out and what forces were at his disposal, the wish to assemble the notables to do him homage afresh: all these factors were interlinked.

Cnut was murdered and the Danish threat vanished. Edgar, restless, was allowed to leave for Italy. The year 1087 was a disastrous one, with a terrible outburst of disease, followed by great storms and a bad famine. The largest and best part of London was burned down. The *Chronicle* bursts into a denunciation of Norman rule:

…no righteousness was to be found in this land in any man's heart, except among the monks where they lived virtuously. The king and the leading men were fond, yes too fond, of avarice. They coveted gold and silver, and did not care how sinfully it was obtained as long as it came to them. The king granted his land on the hardest terms and at the highest possible price. If another buyer came and offered more than the first had given, the king would let it go to the man who offered him more. If a third came and offered him still more, the king would make it over to the man who offered him most of all. He did not care at all how wrongfully the reeves got possession of it from wretched men, nor how many illegal acts they did; but the louder the talk of law and justice, the greater the injustices committed. Unjust tolls were levied and many other unlawful acts were committed which are distressing to relate.

How long the memories of 1087 and William's behaviour persisted is shown by a passage in Henry of Huntingdon (born about 1180–90), which is also interesting in that it puts the events in England in the wider perspective of Norman expansion:

> For it is the nature [of the Normans] that when they've so cast down their enemies as to add no more to their burdens, then they proceed to oppress each other, reducing their own folk with their lands to poverty and devastation. This appears more and more plainly in Normandy, England, Apulia, Calabria, Sicily and Antioch, lands of great fertility which God has subjected to the Normans. In England, therefore, unjust taxes abounded in those days, and abominable customs. All the great folk were so blinded with greed for gold and silver that the poet's words were true of them: 'All must needs get and get, while none asks how his gains are gotten.'
>
> The more talk there was of right, the more acts of unrighteousness; those who were called Justiciaries were the fountainhead of all injustice. Sheriffs and reeves, whose duty was to dispense law and justice, were more savage than the thieves and robbers, and more barbarous than the most barbarous of all. The king himself had farmed out his lands as dearly as he could; he would transfer them to another who offered more, and again to another, ever making light of his own covenant, and greedy of greater gain. So in this year 1087 God sent plagues of sickness and famine upon England, so that he who escaped the fever died of hunger. He sent also tempests and thunder, by which many men were killed, nor did he spare either oxen or sheep.[26]

Henry had been brought up in the *familia* of Robert Bloet, an important prelate who was bishop of London 1093–1123; he was later employed by Alexander of Blois, who succeeded Bloet in the see of Lincoln. He had an independent mind, which is shown in his treatment of the great men of the time; in his *Letter to Walter* he says, 'I'll relate nothing not told before save what is within my own knowledge: the only evidence that can be held authentic.'

William returned to Normandy. He hoped to take advantage of a county in the Vexin passing by marriage to an ally. Philip's troops from Mantes advanced into Normandy. William took revenge by treating Mantes as viciously as he had treated York. But as he was entering through the wreckage of fire and rubble, he felt a sharp pain, perhaps a rupture caused by his horse jolting. He had to retire to Rouen, where he grew worse. He was borne to the priory of St Gervais overlooking the city, and the magnates hastened to his deathbed. For several days he lingered. We may discount the edifying speeches and penitences put into his mouth, though, as with so many men of his time, the approach of death may have stirred a sense of guilt for his greed and violence, which had been stoutly resisted through a vigorous lifetime. He inveighed against Robert, still in exile, and wanted Odo excluded from the general amnesty he was to order. (His bitterness against Odo suggests a greater disloyalty on the latter's part than any known facts warrant.) The barons begged him to be lenient and at last, against his better judgment, he agreed that Odo should be freed and Robert made duke of Normandy, for which he prophesied a sad future. England was to go to his second son, William Rufus, while Henry was to get some £5,000.[27]

CHAPTER IX

WILLIAM RUFUS TO HENRY II

As soon as William died, early on 9 September 1087, all respect for
him vanished. His corpse rapidly stank. The nobles hurried off,
leaving the cell and its body to be despoiled by servants.[1] But an
imposing funeral service was organized. As the procession entered
Caen, part of the town caught fire. In the abbey of St Etienne,
Henry attended the service, which was interrupted by a man claiming
that the burial plot had been stolen from him. Orderic says that the
rite had to be rushed, so great was the stink now coming from the
coffin into which the fat body had been crammed. Morcar and
Harold's young brother Wulfnoth were freed, but Rufus at once
clapped them back in prison. The barons hastened to take advantage
of the relaxation of harsh ducal controls; frontier fiefs fell away.
Orderic says, 'The Norman barons expelled all the royal custodians
from their castles and again plundered their rich country with their
own soldiers. And so the wealth they'd taken by force from the

English and other peoples they deservedly lost through robbery and pillage.' In many ways Normandy reverted to the condition it had been in before William brought it under his controls. In England the need for a common front against the defeated population ensured that there would be no anarchy. Further, the survival of the old English administration kept intact forms of order which had never existed in Normandy. After the first excesses of the foreigners had ended and William's devastations had made more large-scale revolts impossible, the lack of any alternative candidate for the throne slowly made the English accept him as the only possible source of order, security and law. Hence the way in which they began to rally to the king's defence. Above all, the old fyrd obligation was carried right into the Norman epoch and formed a basis on which English loyalties could slowly gather afresh round the kingship. The gathering took a long time before it was completed, but the process had already begun under William.

The Norman kings continued to use both the great fyrd and the select fyrd. The great fyrd was linked with the Anglo-Saxon custom of general allegiance to the crown and the subsequent obligation for all free men to defend the realm when in danger. (It corresponded to the continental *arrière ban*, which was to be called only when an invasion took place, and the continental custom for the burghal militia to serve within half a day's march of their town.) The Anglo-Saxon system is to be more found in the *Dooms of Edmund*, and the duties are set out even more definitely in the *Ten Articles of William the Conqueror*, which declare that all freemen must pledge loyalty to King William within and without England, preserve his lands and honour, and defend him against enemies. The obligation was made yet more definite in a revision of the *Ten Articles* dated to the reign of John.[2] The fyrd was different from the *arrière-ban* because of the whole administrative system in England with its folk moots, which tended to draw men under the king's peace; so in war there was generally a far higher degree of allegiance to the crown. The fyrd thus provided an important means whereby that allegiance was slowly attached to the new monarchy at new levels of national development.

All this does not mean that the English soon accepted William or his successors in any whole-hearted way. What militated more than anything else against a quick assimilation of the conquerors, as was the case to a certain extent under Cnut, was the cleavage in language and culture. For several generations the Normans could not but be isolated from most of English life, and sharply marked off as a conquering race, who regarded with varying degrees of contempt the defeated race they exploited. In any feudal society there could not but be a continuous tension between lords and peasants, whatever social differentiations existed within these two basic classes. But when the lords were seen daily as alien intruders the tensions could not but grow deeper and clearer. However it was not until the thirteenth and fourteenth centuries that these tensions reached an explosive level. By that time the process of assimilation was far advanced; but elements from the past, however diffused and hard to analyse, must have continued to affect people. The peasant revolts from the fourteenth to the sixteenth century, with their climax in 1549, differed from the Jaqueries of France because of these elements, though they were in turn based on the specific forms of English development rooted in the situation we have been discussing.

William Rufus quickly took advantage of the bequest of England. He had himself crowned by Lanfranc, put down a revolt in favour of his elder brother Robert, duke of Normandy, and set out to rule as closely as he could in his father's way. Looking at the treasure at Winchester, he was dazzled at the wealth that the avaricious William had heaped up. 'It was impossible for anyone to describe how much was accumulated there in gold and silver and vessels and costly robes and jewels and many other precious things that are hard to recount' (*Chronicle*).[3] He carried out his father's testament. For William's soul, he gave ten gold marks to each of the larger minsters, six to each of the smaller, 60 shillings each to the ordinary churches and £100 to each shire for distribution to the poor. He commissioned Otto, a German goldsmith in England, to make a silver gilt gem-studded superstructure for the tomb (perhaps recalling Einhard's account of Charlemagne's). The epitaph in gold on the monument was composed by Thomas archbishop of York.

William's empire seemed to be breaking up. Something of a crisis in feudal tenures was involved, strikingly expressed by the fact that the ruler's eldest son inherited a duchy while a younger son gained a kingdom. No effort had been made to build up a system by which a single ruler could rule over both England and Normandy. Estates in Normandy were held by hereditary right; in England the nobles had gained land by right of conquest, by acquisition, and such land was not governed by the rules of inheritance. It could be used, for instance, to provide for younger sons. There were nobles who held land in both England and Normandy, or who were members of a family where the elder son had been given the Norman patrimony while the younger took the acquired land in England. With one brother ruling the Norman duchy and another the English kingdom, and both continually at loggerheads, there was all sorts of divisive pressures at work on the barons; and the threat of depriving a baron of his land in one region, or of actually dispossessing him, merely

meant that he became a rebel turning to duke or king as the circumstances led him. Orderic puts into the mouth of Odo of Bayeux a
speech that sums the situation up: 'How can we give proper service
to two mutually hostile and distant lords? If we serve duke Robert
of Normandy properly, we shall offend his brother William, and he
will deprive us of our revenues and honours in England. On the other
hand if we obey king William, duke Robert will deprive us of our
patrimonies in Normandy.' Duke and king were compelled to intervene in title and succession – as was particularly easy where land was
acquired rather than inherited. This sort of situation, greatly worsen-
ed in 1087, was to carry on for a long time, with divisions and
conflicts sharpening as the strains between Normandy and England
intensified.

But for the moment we must return to William Rufus and the
problems he faced as the result of divided Norman allegiances or
interests. Normandy was anarchic; Maine and various border fiefs
had fallen away or were rebellious. In such a situation William and
Robert could not remain quietly content with the areas they had
received, and Henry threatened to cause trouble. A long struggle over
Normandy began. Rufus and then Henry, using English resources,
were to take it from Robert; finally, after 1144, it was to be ruled by
Angevin counts and in 1204 lost by John to the French king. All the
while it caused unbalance and distraction for the rulers of England.
For long William I's attitude prevailed: England was a necessary
source of title, prestige, wealth and land for the kings, but they saw
themselves as Normans, continental potentates, and strained every
nerve to maintain their foothold in Europe, in their ancestral duchy
and the regions it dominated. They were French princes who luckily
happened to have England to exploit. Yet all the time forces were at
work anglicizing the Normans in England while they in turn greatly
affected the English.

Meanwhile Rufus's gifts to the church impoverished his treasury;
and he made an amiable error of judgment in restoring his uncle
Odo to the earldom of Kent. Odo was smarting from his years of
confinement, and at once began intriguing against Rufus, who by
1088 found that his chief lords were turning to Robert and awaiting
his arrival. They wanted a single ruler over England and Normandy,
and they must have felt that the eldest son who had inherited Normandy was somehow more their overlord than Rufus, even though
their English estates had been acquired or won and had thus been
directly enfeoffed to them by William I by right of his conquest of
the land and gaining of the English title. Some vassals, however,
were loyal: Hugh of Avranches earl of Chester, William of Warenne,
Robert fitzHamon. The minor barons, especially in the midlands,

waited to see what happened and who was likely to win. The church, except perhaps the bishop of Durham, stood by the king; and Rufus won over the lesser landholders, who included Englishmen, by promising to restore 'Edward's Laws' and to give relief from geld and the forest laws. He decided to deal first with the region where Odo was strong and forces from Normandy might land; he took Tonbridge and moved on towards Rochester. Odo got away to Pevensey, but Robert did not join him. The forces he sent by sea were driven off. Odo had to surrender, promising to persuade Rochester to yield. But when he arrived there, the garrison rescued him. Rufus was enraged. He called up more levies, under the Norse penalty of dishonour: being held *nithing*. The barons had begun to find out what a strong character he was. Rochester surrendered. The defenders, granted their lives, came out to the jeering of trumpets. It was significant that the English levies shouted for the hanging of the traitors. Rufus could now deal with the west, which the Mowbrays and William of Eu had been devastating while Roger de Lacy had attacked Worcester where the aged English bishop Wulfstan had stirred the citizens to resist. By autumn Rufus had only one important rebel to crush, the bishop of Durham, a churchman who refused to accept a lay court's judgment affecting his bishopric.[4]

Rufus seems to have been a sceptic in religious matters, so that it was all the easier for him to raise revenues by pillaging monasteries; but his actions in this repect were not much different from those of many magnates, a Mortain or a Meulan. What created antagonisms towards him was his effort to extend the royal authority and the way he thus annoyed his tenants-in-chief; he interfered increasingly in local affairs through itinerant justices and the shire councils. His minister Ranulf Flambard was hated for his part in these measures; when released after his imprisonment by Henry I, he feared that the people would stone him to death. His origin was said to be lowly; but so was that of many ministers raised by Henry I 'from the dust'. Lords, resenting royal intrusions, resented them doubly when the agent was in their eyes of base birth. Ranulf seems to have come from the backstairs of the royal household, one of the many men of fairly menial status, clerks, crossbowmen and engineers, whom medieval kings, considering them capable, turned into bishops, seneschals and justiciars. There was already a permanent board of officials who had more complicated duties than those who had run the old treasury; they had the duty of ensuring that all revenues due to the king did indeed reach the treasury and of judicially determining what was due to him. The abacus, the technical device of the treasury, was known to members of Rufus's curia; Robert of Hereford, who heard pleas in his court, was skilled in the new methods, as was Walcher, prior of Malvern. Both these men had come under the influence of Arab ideas. (Gerbert, who became Pope Sylvester II in 999, knew the abacus and used the Hindu-Arabian signs for numbers. An early account of the abacus in England describes the form used by Gerbert; it was written by a monk of Ramsey in about 1111.)[5]

Relations between Rufus, Robert and Henry continued to be complicated. Rufus instigated a revolt at Rouen in 1090, which Robert suppressed with the help of Henry and Robert of Bellême. A burgher leader of the English party, Conan, was thrown by Henry himself off the city tower. But because he intrigued with both his brothers Henry was in the end distrusted by both. Rufus expressly disinherited him, though he was heir presumptive to both England and Normandy. Yet at times all three combined, as in August 1091 when they dropped plans to restore order in Normandy in order to cross the Channel and deal with troubles in Wales and Scotland. Rufus had no title to Normandy, but could not keep out of its politics. Late in 1093 Robert, tired of waiting for help from him, denounced the treaty they had made. Rufus was on good terms with the Flemish count, who had been angered at the French king's repudiation of his step-daughter. He now raised money with help from the barons and called the feudal host to Hastings in February 1094. Archbishop Anselm consecrated Battle Abbey on the old battle site, and Rufus complained about the meagreness of his aid, receiving retorts from Anselm about the vices of the court and the scandal of vacant abbeys. On 19 March Rufus went off. At a conference the twenty-four guarantors of the treaty with Robert found him at fault. There was an inconsequential war in which Robert, helped by his French overlord, did better than Rufus, who then called for 20,000 English footsoldiers; which seems an impossibly large number. But when the fyrd gathered at Hastings, Flambard took from each man the 10 shillings provided by his district for maintenance; and with the money Rufus hired mercenaries. In the autumn he won Henry, now lord of Domfront, to his side; and in October Henry, with the earl of Chester, went to England, where Rufus joined them late in December. There were rumours of plots, discontent in the church, a dangerous situation in Wales, and yet another Scottish invasion. Rufus was arguing once more with Anselm, who wanted to go to Rome for his pallium, when a baronial revolt broke out. Rufus's harsh controls had stirred anger in Robert of Mowbray, earl of Northumbria, who had plundered two Norwegian merchant ships taking refuge in a northern port and who then ignored the order of restitution and the summonses to attend the Easter and Whitsun courts of 1095 to stand trial. He conspired with the marcher lords of Wales and Scotland, who also resented interference, the earl of Shrewsbury and his brother Philip, Roger de Lacy, and William

of Eu (a kinsman of Rufus). They hoped to kill Rufus and crown
his cousin Stephen of Aumale (son of William's sister by her third
husband, who had been disinherited as count of Champagne but was
lord of Holderness in England). After the Whitsun court Anselm was
put in charge of Kent to block any invasion from France while Rufus
went north, captured Newcastle, then, after two months' siege,
Tynemouth, and finally invested the stronghold of Bamburgh. He
turned next to Wales. Mowbray was caught by a trick and his wife
yielded Bamburgh to save her husband from being blinded. Rufus now
saw the full scope of the conspiracy, jailed Mowbray, and decided
to appoint no northern earl. Some plotters bought their peace; the
earl of Shrewsbury was said to have paid £3,000. The remaining
malcontents were brought up before the large gathering of barons
at the Christmas court. William of Eu, worsted in ordeal by battle,
was mutilated; his steward was hanged; others were mutilated or
disinherited. Rufus was secure enough now to scare the barons from
making further combinations against him.[6]

His last years were taken up by Normandy. From November 1097
to April 1099 he was there fighting. He triumphed; but in June,
hunting at Clarendon, he learned that a vassal of Anjou, his enemy,
was investing the castle of Le Mans. He hurried to France, relieved
the castle, and was back hunting in England by Michaelmas. Robert
had mortgaged Normandy to him for 10,000 marks so that he might
go off crusading with several neighbouring rulers; in September 1099
he was returning from Jerusalem. But we shall never know if Rufus,
who was negotiating a similar business venture with the duke of
Aquitaine, would have restored the duchy. In August 1100 he was
shot while hunting in the New Forest.

He had been a strong king, but without his father's all-enveloping
sense of martial purpose. He confirmed the royal power in England
and managed to end the anarchy in Normandy. A bold, mocking,
merry character, he has come down in history as a villainous debau-
chee because he had no respect for the church and its property. But
he handed on his legacy intact to his younger brother, who was
astute at building effectively on the base created by William and
strengthened by Rufus. Henry had been waiting for the chance to
assert himself. The day after Rufus's death he took decisive action
in grabbing the royal treasury from its reluctant custodian. He won
over most of the court officials and was supported by some leading
families, such as the Clares and the Beaumonts. By 5 August he was
crowned at Winchester by the best available bishop, Maurice of
London; Anselm was in exile and Henry did not want to wait till
the archbishop of York arrived. He quickly rewarded his adherents
and put Flambard into the Tower. Henry issued a coronation charter,

which was confirmed by the next two kings and influenced John's *Magna Carta* greatly. In content, however, it did not differ much from the proclamations of William and Rufus. It promised that the church should be 'free' and not robbed by the king when appointments were vacant (as Rufus had done), and it rejected the 'unjust oppressions' of Rufus, swearing to maintain peace and re-establish the good old laws (those of Edward as amended by William).[7]

William of Malmesbury stressed his continence, his moderation with food and drink, his dislike of warlike solutions, but adds, 'We have learned from those who were well informed that he was led by female blandishments, not for the gratification of incontinency, but for the sake of issue.' He was of middling stature, with black hair scanty near the forehead, 'his eyes mildly bright, his chest brawny, his body fleshy; he was facetious in proper season, nor did multiplicity of business make him less pleasant when mixing in society'. Henry of Huntingdon states that he was pre-eminent for great sagacity, foresight, eloquence, success in war, and wealth; but 'others take a different view', seeing him as greedy, 'since, though his wealth was great, imitating his progenitors, he impoverished the people by taxes and exactions, entangling them in the toils of informers', as cruel, since 'he plucked out the eyes of his kinsman the earl of Mortain in captivity, though the horrid deed was unknown till death revealed the king's secrets', and as wanton, 'perpetually enslaved by female seductions'.[8] Suger of St Denis tells us that he was so scared of his chamberlains conspiring that he frequently changed his bed and increased his guards, and had a shield and sword set ready near him at night.

He married Eadgyth, daughter of Malcolm of Scotland and Margaret (the Aetheling's sister), in an effort to conciliate the English, strengthen his dynastic claims, and broaden the basis of his rule. Anselm had to carry out investigations to disprove the rumour that the girl had taken nun's vows; but the charge was revived later by Stephen so as to bastardize Henry's children, Matilda, who married the German emperor, and William, who was drowned in 1120. Having begotten this pair, Henry returned to his mistresses and Eadgyth turned to religious matters.

By the end of a year he had received an oath of allegiance from his subjects; at Christmas 1100 the French king's heir visited him at Westminster. But Robert was back in Normandy, relieved that Rufus' death had saved him from meeting a huge debt. He took over all the duchy except the castles with Henry's garrisons. He had strengthened his position by marrying a woman whose father was grandson of Tancred of Hauteville and nephew of both Robert Guiscard and Roger of Sicily. He soon found out which barons were disaffected and

began building up his partisans in England. In February 1101 Flambard escaped from the Tower and joined him. (He had got the guards
drunk and gone off with his aged mother and a boatful of
valuables.)[9] By July Robert had his fleet mustered at the mouth of
the Bresle. Henry did his best to prepare. He renewed the traditional
money fief to the Flemish count, and this time we know what it
entailed: aid to Henry against all men apart from the count's French
overlord; the provision of mercenaries on specified occasions – 1000
knights if England were invaded or had a serious revolt; each year
the same number for Normandy and half as many for Maine, if
Henry asked for them. If the count had to fight under his liege lord
against Henry, he would take as small a contingent as possible, ten
knights, leaving the others with their paymaster. (The treaty was
renewed in 1103 and 1110.) Henry sent ships against Robert, but
they deserted. Robert, outflanking the army at Pevensey, landed on
20 July at Portsmouth. But Henry had raised so large a force that
when the two armies met at Alton, (Hampshire), Robert was daunted
and a settlement was arranged without bloodshed. Henry kept
England but paid Robert a yearly pension of £3,000; Robert took all
Normandy but Henry's castle at Domfort. Each ruler was to pardon
his faithless vassals and make the other his heir. Henry did not keep
his word about the pardons. He shrewdly used legal pretexts to punish
one rebel after another. By Easter 1102 he felt he could deal with the
strongest one, Robert of Bellême. When the latter failed to appear in
the royal court, Henry marched against him, reduced his strongholds,
and advanced on Shrewsbury. Robert surrendered. He and his
brother lost their English honours, and Henry even confiscated the
lands of the Norman monastery of Almenèches, where the abbess
was Robert's sister. (Bellême was a 'man intolerable for the barbarity
of his manners and inexorable to the faults of others', full of craft and
dissimulation, so that when those who knew him saw him affable and
mild, they were terrified. 'On account of some trifling fault of the
father, he blinded his godchild, who was his hostage, tearing out the
little wretch's eyes with his accursed nails.')

As Robert of Normandy proved incapable of controlling the duchy,
Henry set out cautiously and astutely to supplant him, gaining
supporters, sending in agents, harbouring exiles, and using all his
diplomatic skill to isolate the duke. In the end a pitched battle (a
rare thing in those days) was fought in September 1106 at Tinchebrai
with decisive victory for Henry. Edgar the Aetheling was among the
prisoners and was at once pardoned. Henry proceeded to subordinate
Brittany and beat back the French, thus enlarging his territory. A
second French war was provoked by his nephew Theobald of Blois,
who ambushed and seized a friend of King Louis. Henry defeated

Louis at Brémule, and though Louis again invaded Normandy, Henry did well from the peace negotiated by Pope Calixtus II at the council of Rheims (October 1119). His influence reached from Flanders to Anjou, and he controlled Boulogne, Brittany, Bellême and Maine. His nephew ruled Blois and Chartres.

But the drowning of his one legitimate son on 25 November 1120 in the wreck off Harfleur did much to break down his system. His rivals were stirred up afresh: Fulk of Anjou, back from the east, demanded the return of Maine and began a revolt in 1123; other revolts stirred in Normandy itself. Despite his military and diplomatic measures, which even drew the emperor Henry V into invading France and marching on Rheims, his scheme was defeated by the rallying of the people to Louis. His second marriage was childless. He resorted to getting the barons and bishops to accept Matilda as his heir. But there was a portent of trouble when his nephew Stephen of Blois successfully challenged his (Henry's) bastard Robert of Gloucester for precedence in taking the oath. The French king re- torted by calling on his barons to support William Clito's claim to Normandy, by marrying William to his wife's half-sister, and by en- feoffing him with the Vexin and its castles. But Baldwin IV was murdered on 2 March 1127 as he prayed in a church at Bruges, and several claimants for Flanders appeared. William Clito belonged to the senior line; and when Louis VI marched into Flanders, the barons and most towns accepted William as count. But he became unpopular through his opposition to the interests of the merchant class, and had to fight various rivals including Stephen of Blois. Louis intervened and Henry then invaded France. William Clito died of a wound near the end of July 1128. Thierry of Alsace, grandson of Robert le Frison, became the strongest claimant and was recognized as count; Henry could now scheme for an alliance of Flanders, Normandy and Anjou. To settle his uneasy relations with Anjou, he proposed to marry Matilda to the heir there, Geoffrey Plantagenet. But Matilda, a wilful woman of twenty-six, disliked marrying a lad ten years younger; the English barons had not been consulted; the Norman barons abhorred the idea of an Angevin overlord; the French king feared the alliance, especially when Thierry of Flanders married William Clito's divorced wife, Sybil of Anjou. Geoffrey soon threw out his over- bearing wife Matilda; Henry tried once more to arrange for her to be his heir, then decided to send her back to Geoffrey, who had asked for her return. On 5 March 1133 she bore a son, later Henry II of England; next year she bore a second son. When Geoffrey demanded the homage of the Norman barons and was refused, he made war on Normandy. In the midst of this confused situation Henry died on

1 December in the forest of Lyons, having eaten too many lampreys after a hard day's hunting.

He left a number of difficult problems for his successor. By marrying Matilda to the count of Anjou he had greatly provoked the French king; for the combination of Normandy, Anjou, Maine and Touraine was something that French rulers had long dreaded. At the same time he increased the distrust of Anjou and Blois for one another, since Theobald and Stephen of Blois were both first cousins of Matilda. Stephen had on his side the advantage that his wife was grand-daughter of Margaret, sister of Edgar the Aetheling. So he combined in his ancestry both the Norman and the English royal lines. But Henry had done his best to ensure that Matilda would be accepted as his heir. She had to face the great obstacle that she was a woman, and it was unprecedented for a woman thus to succeed her father. At first the position was indeed unclear: whether her claim was to be vested in herself or to pass through her to her husband – though he might resign in favour of his son. For the barons to ignore her claim after an act of homage was to commit perjury, the very sin imputed to Harold by William I. Stephen's only good way round her claim then was by means of papal approval; and this approval Stephen got. The barons in Normandy wanted to recognize Duke Theobald IV of Blois and Champagne, but it was Stephen, the younger brother and the greatest landowner in England, who crossed the Channel quickly with a few resolute knights. Pushing aside the garrisons of Dover and Canterbury, he entered London. The Norman trading interest there seems to have supported him, and he had a powerful friend in his brother, Henry of Blois, bishop of Worcester, through whom he gained the castle and treasure at Winchester and a quick coronation from the primate. Theobald archbishop of Canterbury, made no resistance.

Henry I had built up royal power in quite a different way from that of William and Rufus. Though he was involved in wars from 1109 until his death in 1135, the main characteristics of his reign were the extension and strengthening of the administrative, fiscal, and legal systems. Though in part he was driven by the need to finance his continental schemes and ventures, the bent of his mind was towards such tasks. He and his officers, who were often drawn from professional classes of low birth, did their best to extend the centralized rule of law. But their motive was profit, and in fact there was much legal and financial oppression. Thus, Henry created great areas of 'forest' subject to special laws, and increased his revenue from the host of fines inflicted for special offences. In effect he drove the system to its limits and ensured trouble for his successor. In his

Charter of Liberties he insisted on concessions to the under-tenants, which the magnates were not to take advantage of:

> To the knights who do service with hauberks for their lands, I concede their demesne ploughs exempt of all taxes and all works by my grant, so that, relieved of a great burden, they may furnish themselves so well with horses and arms that they may be properly equipped and prepared for my service and for the defence of the kingdom.[10]

Such provisions gave him the loyalty of the poor knights, which could be used against the magnates. Florence of Worcester tells us how in 1101 the 'common knights' of his bishops stayed loyal to him against the rebellious magnates. In a discussion after Bellême's revolt in 1102, the latter declared it would be dangerous to draw up a peace which left Henry in too strong a position. At news of this 'three thousand rustic knights', *pagensium milites*, protested and warned the king of the lords' measures. Henry in fact continued Rufus's policy, but without its boisterous note and its irreligious side and with a consistent drive of greed. The *Peterborough Chronicle* complained in 1124 that 'the man who had any goods was deprived of them by harsh gelds and harsh lawcourts'. The same accusations were made against other kings trying to carry out a centralizing policy: Philip Augustus in France, Henry the Lion in Germany; but that does not disprove charges of brutality and injustice. Eadmer gives an account of the merciless methods used by Henry's agents in collecting the monies needed to pay for his wars:

> They showed no regard for piety or pity; but as persons coming from England assured us, extortion, frightful and cruel, beat down like a raging storm upon all. Then you might see, so they reported, those who in fact had nothing to give, driven out from their cottages or the doors of their houses torn away and carried off, and themselves left open to be plundered of everything. Or their paltry bits of furniture would be taken and they reduced to abject poverty, or at any rate ground down and tormented with some form of wretchedness or another. But against those who seemed to have everything, certain new and carefully thought-out forms of confiscation were applied and in this way, as they dared not institute a suit in their own defence against the king of the land, their possessions were taken and they themselves plunged into serious hardship.

He adds that many similar practices were used by both Rufus and William; he is perhaps exaggerating, as an aggrieved ecclesiastic, but there must have been much violent and overbearing behaviour by the tax collectors.

Under Stephen the inner conflicts of the Anglo-Norman state, partly masked and held down in the phases of conquest and consolidation, began to emerge and threatened to destroy it; his reign therefore deserves a closer attention than those of Rufus or Henry I. The government was still at root a personal matter: the system imposed by a strong king to maintain his position as overlord of the barons, master of the armed forces, and controller of the main revenues of the kingdom. There was little government machinery to carry on by itself, so the failure of the direct male line after Henry I was liable to beget a crisis in the situation of England and Normandy.

The crisis duly came, speeded and intensified by Stephen's character and attitudes. He lacked the drive for supremacy that in different ways had dominated William and his two sons. He saw himself as a feudal noble with a primacy over the others, but essentially acting on a contractual basis; he did not assert his position as overlord to whom the tenants-in-chief had to pay homage. Hence his stress on the elective principle in the kingship: a stress also necessitated by the fact that he had stepped over his elder brother in grasping the crown. The nobles thus came to look on their relation to him as feudal in the simple sense: something that they could terminate if he went beyond what they regarded as the limits of his role. He took the same attitude to the church as to the barons; when it declared that he had broken his contract, he merely sent an envoy to plead his case. Matilda on the other hand stood firm on the hereditary principle, as if the kingdom was a bit of property that her father had the right to bequeath as he wished. She had no hope of making an effective claim unless she had a party of English nobles supporting her; and as Stephen's methods went on increasing discontent and disorder, such a party did in fact form. From 1137 her half-brother the earl of Gloucester was working on her behalf.

Stephen was a good soldier, chivalric, and far more likeable than Rufus or Henry, Matilda or her son. His disadvantage was not weakness, but the attitudes we have outlined. At the outset he had much on his side. The church, we saw, rallied to him, largely because of his powerful brother Henry of Blois, bishop of Winchester; and the high officials acquiesced, glad to see the interregnum ended. But very soon his policy of concessions was encouraging the discontented or greedy nobles and stimulating them to press for more. He increased the number of earls and found himself dependent on Flemish mercenaries; his resources began to fail him and he debased the coinage. By 1136 his weakening grip on the magnates was reflected in such events as the seizure of Norwich castle by the earl of Norfolk and the pillaging of Exeter castle by a local lord on the grounds that there was talk of the king's death. Next year he visited Normandy and irritated or stirred up the barons there as he had done in England. A threat to northern England was bought off; he gave Cumberland to Henry, son of king David of Scotland. Such an act could only lead to further demands. When Henry asked to be earl of Northumbria also, Stephen demurred. The Scots harried the border shires in early 1138 and in the summer made an invasion; the aged archbishop of York had to take the lead in organizing resistance. The Scots were beaten at the Battle of the Standard. Yet next year Stephen, hoping to gain Prince Henry's help against rebellious barons, handed over Northumbria after all.

To make things worse, he upset the administration by becoming suspicious of the powerful family of Le Poer. Roger of Salisbury, justiciar under Henry I, had carried on with the office, with his son as chancellor and two nephews as treasurer and bishop of Ely, and bishop of Lincoln. Stephen now bade them surrender their castles, the last thing they wanted to do in such an uncertain situation. When they resisted they were imprisoned. But, defending themselves behind their ecclesiastical privileges, they drew the church into conflict with Stephen. They had him cited at a council held in Winchester and used the threat of excommunication. He had thrown away their support; when war came, the bishop of Ely held Ely castle for the rebels.

The ecclesiastical exponents of reform in England were now stimulated to take full advantage of the king's difficulties. To conciliate them, he granted a charter setting out the church's privileges and in effect abdicating from any royal control of the church: 'Justice and power over ecclesiastical persons and all the clergy and their goods and the distribution of ecclesiastical property were to be in the hands of the bishops.' Laymen too were to come under the church's jurisdiction in actions dealing with the sacrament of marriage and the probate of wills. The church was brought near the point of being accepted as a self-contained corporation, free from royal controls. Nothing like this had happened before in the medieval world. For the first time the church had the full right to appoint all bishops and abbots; church councils could be held without the supervision of royal representatives; and prelates seem no longer to have been obliged to pay homage to the king – an oath of fealty sufficed. All this meant was that the pope was able to take over all the rights which the king had given up. He welcomed English bishops at Rome, and the legates whom he freely appointed controlled the church in England, not the king.

In practice this situation also meant that the papacy was able to intrude in the political sphere and ensure that its directives were carried out there. The very existence of the kingship as an independent organization was threatened. Thus, in 1148 Stephen exiled archbishop Theobald, who had been abbot of Bec, for attending a papal council contrary to royal orders; but he had to retract at the threat of interdiction. He dearly wanted to have his own son Eustace crowned during his own lifetime; but the pope forbade him and Theobald slipped out of England so that he could not be compelled to take part in any proceedings. A new type of churchman was coming up, not at all like the lowborn servants (such as the Le Poers) who were rewarded for services by being given bishoprics. Stephen's own brother, Henry of Blois, who had helped him so much in gaining the throne, now turned on him, perhaps offended at Theobald being made archbishop. As papal legate, he was able to wield a great measure of power in his own person; he called the council at Winchester which so embarrassed Stephen. We may add that he had built six castles for himself and had no intention of surrendering them.

Matilda correctly decided that now was the time to make her attack and precipitate civil war. In 1141 the earl of Chester, enraged that Cumberland could not be got back from the Scottish prince, revolted with his half-brother the Earl of Lincoln. The earl of Gloucester joined them. Stephen was defeated at Lincoln, and captured and imprisoned at Bristol. The breakdown of the state strengthened further the independence of the church, whose councils were the only deliberative assembly left in action. Also, the church could dominate the situation by holding a balance between the two battling factions. Two months after Lincoln, Henry of Blois took advantage of his brother's disaster. He called a council at Winchester and declared that Stephen, by breaking his compact with the church, had forfeited allegiance. In effect, then, the church deposed Stephen; and Matilda was elected as ruler in his place – a wholly unprecedented event. The implication was that a king elect was not king until he was crowned and, as coronation depended on the church, the latter had the right of veto, which in turn involved the right of election.

Matilda was no wiser than Stephen, but she had, beside the unpleasant arrogances of her character, much obstinacy. When she invaded England Stephen could have soon disposed of her; but, accepting the counsel of a papal legate, he courteously let her out of the trap into which she had fallen and gave her safe-conduct to join her half-brother Gloucester. Civil war in England was accompanied by anarchy in Normandy. After much confused fighting and shifts of fortune, the objectionable Matilda was thrown out of London and Henry of Blois once more changed sides. The earl of Gloucester was captured and exchanged for Stephen. At a legatine council at Westminster in December 1141, Henry denounced Matilda on the same grounds as he had denounced Stephen, called for her excommunication, and urged support of Stephen. He had however sapped his own authority by such rapid volte-faces, and in 1143 the new pope did not renew his position as legate. Stephen as usual made the most possible mistakes; his appointment to the see of York brought denunciations from archbishop Theobald and St Bernard of Clairvaux, and it was annulled by the pope in 1147. But the Angevin party was also in a bad way. Gloucester died in 1147 and next year Matilda left England. (Stephen we may note had made one of his useless chivalric gestures when her son Henry, about fourteen years old, had attempted to enter England in 1144 with slight resources. He sent the boy money to pay his knights off so that he might return home with honour untarnished.) Success in the war had varied largely according to the amount of money available for paying mercenaries.[11]

Geoffrey de Mandeville was an outstanding example of the way in which an unscrupulous magnate could extend his lands during the disorders. A Essex magnate, he first supported Stephen and gained the earldom of his shire; in 1141 he left Stephen and Matilda rewarded him by making him sheriff and justiciar of Essex and constable of the Tower of London. Late the same year he transferred his allegiance back to Stephen; he was then made local justiciar of Essex, London, Middlesex and Hertfordshire, with precedence over the sheriffs there and full control of London. So he proceeded to intrigue again with Matilda, seeking a yet higher offer for his support. Stephen arrested him in 1142, but was unable to keep hold of such a slippery and powerful baron. However Geoffrey happened to die in 1144. On a grand scale he reflected the sort of tergiversation and treachery that was typical of the period.

Even more ominous as symptoms of the declining royal power were the treaties that some leading barons made with one another, as if private war and private combination were now in order. The earls of Chester and Leicester made such a treaty, as did the earls of Gloucester and Hereford in the uneasy months immediately after Henry II's coronation, when they renewed an 'alliance of love' by which their fathers had bound themselves to maintain each other's interests 'during the present war between the Empress and king Stephen'. The treaty of Chester and Leicester, despite some formal references to the 'liege lord' (the king), reflected the attempts of some of the barons to create a system of balances which would save them from being engulfed in the growing anarchy. But, as well as recognizing the right of a great baron to make war at his pleasure, the document brings out clearly the military aspects of the private castles in central England; and one clause implies that a tenant who feels aggrieved by his lord may well refuse to stand to right in his court and withdraw his fealty altogether from him. The bishop of Lincoln is cited as security for the agreement:

> on his Christianity, so that if anyone departs from this agreement and refuses to make amends within fifteen days after he has been requested to do so, without ill will, then the bishop of Lincoln and the bishop of Chester shall do justice upon him for broken faith. And the bishop of Lincoln and the bishop of Chester shall each give up the two pledges whom they have received as security for the observance of these agreements, to him namely who shall keep these aforesaid agreements.[12]

It has been suggested that the church in the person of the bishops arbitrated or intervened; but the terms of the charter are wholly feudal, with no sign of a church mediator from outside. What is of interest is the way in which the church gains from the disorders, appearing as the sole stable body able to stand above the conflicts.

Meanwhile Angevin power had been increasing. In the early summer of 1144 Geoffrey Plantagenet took the title of duke of Normandy, and in 1149, when his overlord King Louis VII returned from his crusade, he gave up the Vexin to him and was rewarded by recognition of his conquest. He had done much to restore the governmental system of exchequer and chancery to order (as his son was later to do in England), and the methods of the Norman chancery were imported into Anjou. He used the sworn inquest extensively to recover ducal revenue and demesne; and the privilege of using this ducal machinery was sold to lords who had suffered losses during the years of anarchy. (Henry was to introduce this practice in England.) The Norman church had been posing a threat to the state as had the church in England; here the reasons lay in the general growth of papal centralized organization, with the fading out of such local forms of expression as the provisional council. The Norman church was thus being drawn into the French system, with political effects leading in the same direction.

Later in 1149 Geoffrey resigned the duchy to his eldest son Henry Fitzempress, who made an unsuccessful attempt to get hold of his maternal inheritance. Until 1151 he was occupied with sporadic warfare with Louis, who had allied himself with his brother-in-law Eustace of Boulogne and had various grievances against the Angevins.

But in August that year peace was made and Henry paid homage to Louis. At once he began preparations for invading England. His father died on 7 September, leaving him all his fiefs and advising him to keep the various customs distinct and intact. There might have been a provision in the will that the younger brother Geoffrey should get Anjou and Maine if Henry won England.

It was natural enough for Normans in England to feel for some time that Normandy was their homeland and that the conquests in north and south redounded essentially to its glory. It was still the custom for a great lord often to leave his Norman estate to his eldest son, his English estate to a younger son. Thus in 1107 the count of Meulan got from Henry I a charter authorizing the division of his large inheritance in England and Normandy between his twin sons Waleran and Robert. Robert the younger twin was to get the English lands apart from those at Sturminster. If Robert died or proved incapable of ruling, the English inheritance was to go to Waleran, and similarly if Waleran died or proved incapable, the Norman part was to go to Robert. If land in either country was lost, what was left was to be divided among the brothers. (We also see here how the kings could control the devolution of even the greatest fiefs of England or Normandy). With Geoffrey as duke of Normandy, there seems to have been a resurgence of Norman patriotism. An anonymous poem, cited by Henry of Huntingdon, declares that Rouen, Rothomagus, is a noble, ancient, fair and mighty city, adorned by imperial favour – the empress Maud having taken up residence there in 1147. It is like Rome, not only in its good report, but even as a name: take out the middle of *Rothoma* and you get *Roma*. Normans had chosen Rouen as their capital, and it had reduced to tribute Brittany and England, Scotland and Wales, and now reposed under the rule of Duke Geoffrey, whose very name spells Joy: Gaufregus, *gaudia fert dux*. Another son of Rouen is Roger, 'ruler of Italy and Sicily, Africa, Greece, and Syria; even Persia trembles, even the bright skies of Ethiopia and the dark gloom of Germany seek protection. Rouen alone is worthy of the empire of the world.' And indeed Rouen was soon to send forth Geoffrey's son to gain England.

In March 1152 Louis VII was foolish enough to divorce his wife Eleanor duchess of Aquitaine; and in May Henry hastily married her. He was nineteen and she was eleven years older; but she was a great political prize. He outwitted the others, including his brother Theobald, who were after her, and gathered afresh an invasion army. Louis belatedly repented his action, and with Theobald of Blois, Geoffrey Plantagenet, and Eustace of Boulogne, he attacked Henry. But by the end of August the latter had scattered his enemies and in January 1153 he invaded England. Stephen was weary of fighting and depressed by the loss of his wife and his son Eustace. He agreed that his other son William should be barred from the English throne and be satisfied with the fiefs his father had held before becoming king. Stephen was to rule until his death, treating Henry as an adopted son and acting on his advice. The church added its threats of anathema to deter any breaking of the agreement. There seems also to have been an understanding that all castles built since Henry I's death should be razed, foreign soldiers (especially Flemings) sent away, and the rights of the crown regained.

On 25 October 1154 Stephen died in Kent and was buried beside his wife and son at the Cluniac monastery he had founded some six years before at Faversham. On 8 December Henry landed on the Hampshire coast and was accepted as king. With him began the Angevin line of kings, though perhaps they ought more properly to be called the Norman-Angevins.

He set about restoring a centralized government and repairing the damage of Stephen's reign. There had been much ravaging and destruction in the civil war, and much building of unlicensed castles. Normal life could not but have been deranged by campaigns in which both sides used bands of mercenaries, the resumption of private feuds, the banditry liable to irrupt on unsuspecting areas, the conflagrations and lootings that struck many towns, and the disturbances in regions long inured to quiet developments: East Anglia, the Thames valley, Berkshire and Wiltshire. There had been local dearths and pestilences, economic growth had been checked, legal and fiscal systems built up since 1066 disrupted. Yet it is a tribute to the general toughness of the underlying structures in English society that no lasting breakdowns occurred. The governmental system was never totally paralysed: writs went out, in many areas sheriffs and justices continued to administer justice. Henry II, despite the difficulties he had to overcome, was able to continue with Henry I's centralizing work on a new level. But England could never be quite the same again. The civil and ecclesiastical clashes were the precursors of Magna Carta and Thomas Becket's challenge to the secular state. The struggle to re-establish royal power in a world that had suffered so many disruptions and separatist trends could not result in the recreation of the situation that had prevailed before the disorders. Either things had to grow more chaotic or the centralization had to be more complete and effective. Under Henry II the second alternative was realized.

We cannot here examine his reign in detail, but we must look at the main lines of his reconstruction. England was now, under the first Norman king without rivals, to become one of the leading

European powers, with territory stretching from the Solway Firth
to the Pyrenees. It was by the extension of royal justice that Henry
set about building his central controls; for in this way he could best
get rid of anarchy, strengthen his hold on the country through one
deep-rooted and comprehensive system of government, and at the
same time gain ever greater profits. In 1166 he brought about a new
feudal assessment, asking all his tenants-in-chief, lay and ecclesiastical, for the details of their owed services and their enfeoffed knights;
there was a great outcry from the church, which he overrode. All
knights were to pay him homage as liege lord, though they paid their
incidents to their direct lord as usual. Thus the Anglo-Saxon concept
of fealty was given a primacy over the Norman idea of feudal homage
At the Assize of Arms in 1181, which regulated the military equipment to be used by nobles and all free men, Henry forbade the export
of ships and timber for ships, and reconstituted the fyrd. The Cinque
Ports, in return for various privileges, contracted to provide ships
in time of war.

In 1170 he made a survey of the administration called the Inquest
of Sheriffs; he removed the local justiciars, first appointed by Rufus,
who he felt had gained too much power, and developed the system
of itinerant justices. The eyres or circuits existed before 1166, but
we know little of them then; by 1170 an almost complete circuit
system was operating. Henry made an increased use of writs, and
sworn juries became an essential part of the judicial machinery. He
transferred the work of punishing criminals to royal courts, while
keeping the old English method of communal prosecution. The
criminal jury emerged from the obscure levels of the local courts, into
the full light of royal records. Free men (though not villeins) were
enabled to use the king's prerogative; if they wished they could
establish their title to land by means of a sworn inquest. Some central
tribunal continuously at work was now necessary; so Henry set the
curia regis at the disposal of ordinary men.

These changes struck hard at many of the barons' powers. Their
courts were ignored. The assize of *mort d'ancestor* was in effect aimed
at them, since it was they who would most likely try to keep an
heir out of his property. The Grand Assize sapped their rights to
administer justice as it laid down that no freeholder need defend
his title to property unless called on to do so by royal writ; and if he
wished, he could have the case transferred from the lord's court to
the king's, where he could buy the privilege of trial by jury instead
of having to undergo trial by battle.

If such developments weakened the power of the aristocracy
by producing an administration which no longer depended on

feudalism for its support, they were certainly favourable to the middle classes. They lifted the free tenants out of their feudal surroundings and gained their support; they brought about a permanent liaison between royal justice and the justice of the local courts. The magnificent result of these vast and unremitting labours was the foundation of a rule of law, a royal law, and not a customary or feudal law, a law which commanded respect all over the country and obedience in places where the king had no direct authority (Sayles).[18]

All that is true of the new tendencies, but the actions of Henry II and their results were not so clear-cut or so final. He, like many kings to follow, was king in a feudal world. Still, the system he worked out had indeed lifted the whole internal struggle of feudalism to a new level, in which many new possibilities had been opened up.

CHAPTER X

MORE ON THE NORMANS
IN THE SOUTH

We left Roger de Hauteville engaged in the conquest of Sicily, but still far from complete success. After defeating the moslems at Cerami, he was safely established in the hill-city of Troina; but he had an uncertain hold on Messina and could not extend his control south and west. He was, however, able to take advantage of quarrels among the emirs, who came together only in their dislike of the Arabs despatched from Africa to fight in the cause of their overlord. In 1068 Roger moved towards Palermo, winning a victory at Miselmeri near that city. But it was three years before he was able to break the resistance. In 1071 Robert Guiscard, helped by Roger in the siege of Bari, set sail with him with a fleet of fifty-eight ships manned by Greeks, Calabrians and Apulians. They declared themselves friendly to the Moslems of Catania, were admitted, and at once took the port over. Through the sweltering summer Roger led the main body of their forces via Troina across the island, while Robert went round the north coast by sea. At Palermo they began a siege by sea and land, as at Bari. The defenders were weakened by hunger; and on 7 January 1072 the Normans began their assault. Roger attacked the citadel on a hilltop. The Normans forced their way in, while Robert, moving round to the coast, entered the lower city, climbed the hill, and assailed the citadel from the rear. The Moslems held out a few days, but they were doomed. On 10 January the Normans were in secure possession of the great city, a trading and cultural centre of the Byzantine-Arabic world, surrounded by parks and fountained gardens, with some quarter of a million inhabitants. The butcher's guild alone had some seven thousand members.

A century earlier it had been described as containing three hundred mosques, countless markets, exchanges, streets of craftsmen, and one of the first paper mills in Europe. (A deed sealed by Roger in 1102 is the oldest known European document on paper.) When the Normans camped in the district of palaces and orange groves owned by the big merchants, 'even the knights', says Amatus, 'were royally provided for in what was truly an earthly paradise'. After Byzantion, Palermo was now by far the most populous and magnificent city in Christian hands; and the Christian hands were those of the Normans. Robert Guiscard did not behave at all like the crusaders who, twenty-seven years later, massacred all Moslems on taking Jerusalem and burned the Jews alive in the chief synagogue. He demanded only allegiance and a yearly tribute, and permitted the continuance of Islamic religion and law. Apart from Palermo, half Messina, and half the mountainous region of the north-east where he had shared in the conquest, he appointed Roger as tenant-in-chief over the island. Roger then set himself to subjugate it completely. He had more trouble now with the Greeks than with the Moslems. They found the knights more brutal than their previous masters, and disliked their use of the despised Latin liturgy. But, though Latin priests and monks thronged in, Roger did not try to suppress the Greek church; rather, he helped the Greeks in its material reconstruction. All he asked was that they should cut themselves off from Byzantine patriarch and emperor. The Latin hierarchy was to be dominant, but the Greeks were treated mildly and even at times exempted from the local bishop's jurisdiction.

After the fall of Bari in 1071 the Normans in south Italy set themselves to consolidate their position. Not that their troubles had ceased. The Lombard duchy of Naples was still hostile to Richard of Capua; and the Greeks still held enough cities to keep Count Roger at Mileto watchful. Though Robert held Bari, Brindisi and Otranto, he had yet to assert his authority over the coastal towns to the north. Full control of Apulia was slowly achieved in the years 1072–85.

Further, the Normans were no longer in easy accord with the papacy; Hildebrand became pope as Gregory VII in 1073. Though the papacy had gained much from the aid of the Normans after 1059, their too successful expansion posed a threat, especially after Robert gained Amalfi and was looming up over the papal patrimony. Gregory therefore tried to set the Normans at one another's throats. In 1072 he made an alliance with Richard of Capua and launched the first of his three excommunications of Robert Guiscard. His feelings are clearly revealed in a letter of 22 January 1075 to Hugh, abbot of Cluny: 'There are no longer princes who set God's honour above their own selfish ends...and those among whom I live, Romans, Lombards, and Normans, are, as I've often told them, worse than Jews or Pagans.' He tried to build up an army; but the Pisans in it were outraged at finding among the ranks the pirate Gisulf of Salerno. The army broke up. The pope was dragged from the crypt where he was saying mass and imprisoned. Further, the emperor Henry IV was on the point of descending into Italy to depose him. The great investiture conflict had emerged fully into the open.

Henry IV decided to take the Guiscard as ally, but the latter had his own ideas. He came to an agreement with Richard of Capua, and Gregory excommunicated Henry: the first time such an action had been taken by the head of the church since Theodosius seven centuries before. All the ruler's subjects were in religious law exempted from allegiance. In October 1076 Robert, with Capua's support, attacked Gisulf in Salerno with a sea and land blockade. The citizens suffered badly, and on the last day of 1076 they opened the gates to the Normans. The citadel fell in May 1077 and Gisulf went off to Rome. The last stronghold of Lombard power was in Norman hands. Furthermore, Salerno was an important mercantile centre. In 1078 Richard of Capua died and Robert was beyond question the strongest ruler in the south. Gregory gave in. In June 1080 he came to an agreement with Robert at Ceprano. The thrice excommunicated Norman was confirmed in his conquests of Amalfi, Salerno, and the march of Fermo. He had no secular overlord, though he repeated the oath of fealty to the papacy which he had taken in 1059.

The conflict of German emperor and pope, which had come to its first head with the vindication of the imperial control of the see of Milan in 1046, now became fiercer and more far-reaching in its effects. Though Henry was backed by his own bishops, he had to deal with opposition at home: discontented Saxons and Thuringians who took up the papal cause for their own ends. Gregory's sentence was more effective than he could have hoped; the German princes gave Henry a year in which to seek absolution. He had to cross the wintry Alps and wait three days at the fortress of Canossa as a penitent. Things were patched up between emperor and pope, but a second ban came in 1080. The pope's release of Henry's subjects from their allegiance and the encouragement given them to set up a rival king had played a crucial part in strengthening the divisions in Germany. After the formal deposition of 1080 there continued to exist an opposition, half dynastic, half clerical, till the religious half of the friction was alleviated by the Compromise of Worms in 1122, under which the emperor kept his control over elections in Germany, and received the right to invest by the sceptre, though he gave up the investiture by staff and ring. At the same time, however, he surrendered his hard fought claim to intervene directly in the elections of Italian bishops. The Italian bishoprics were in fact growing less important because of the rise of the communes and the acceptance by the bishops of Lombardy of the reforming decrees of the papacy. So, out of this first long phase of the investiture dispute the papacy emerged centralized and strengthened, with a clear policy, while the empire, though still powerful, was bleeding from an internal wound. As we have seen, the Normans played a crucial part in ensuring this outcome, at moments when the papacy was in dire difficulties.

The Guiscard's ambitions now turned eastwards. The Byzantine empire had suffered a severe blow at Manzikert in 1071 at the hands of the Seljuk Turks. In 1074 Robert sent his daughter Helena to be betrothed to the son of the emperor Michael VII. He seems to have been scheming for a chance to grasp the eastern throne for himself. When Michael was deposed and killed, the contract for marriage with Helena was repudiated. Robert produced a bogus monk as the dead emperor and began refitting his fleet. Ever since his investment by the pope with the Calabrian duchy, Robert had been assuming the role of the eastern *basileus* or emperor, copying his insignia on seals and wearing imperial robes of state on formal occasions. At Crepano Pope Gregory had virtually recognized the bogus Michael as the true emperor; and now he sent his support, with a papal banner, to Robert for his invasion of the eastern empire. The fact that the Christian defenders of the east were hard pressed by the Turks made this a good moment to stab them in the back.

On May 1081 Robert with his huge, barrel-chested son Bohemund sailed from Otranto, crossed the Adriatic, captured Corfu, and moved on to assault Durazzo. The investment began, but in October the Byzantine army came up. The imperial bodyguard largely consisted of Anglo-Saxon exiles who had been waiting fifteen years to get their own back on the Normans. They made a fierce attack with two-handed axes. The Apulian knights could not break their line; but Sichelgaita, Robert's warlike wife, rode up to rally her side while Bohemund's left wing wheeled in support. Crossbowmen shot down the Varangians. The last English took refuge in a chapel of the arch-angel Michael, which the Normans set on fire, burning the men inside. The Byzantines were defeated, and the Normans moved on east to Kastaria. But once again the vassals in Apulia and Calabria rose against their overlord, this time stirred up by Byzantine agents, and Henry IV was at the gates of Rome.

We may pause to glance at the Anglo-Saxons who after 1066 had joined the Norsemen and Russians in the Varangian Guard at Byzan-tion. The Guard was given charge of the palace by Alexis Comnenos after he had suppressed the ancient corps of Excubitores. Alexis did his best to recruit western mercenaries, the chiefs of whom took a feudal oath to him, according to the customs of their own lands. Count Robert of Flanders in 1087, returning from a pilgrimage to Jerusalem, promised to send five hundred knights, who took part in an expedition against the Pechenegs. A chrysobull of 1088 for Patmos distinguishes the Englishmen from the Varangians; but a tale told by a Canterbury monk who went as pilgrim to Palestine shows that towards 1090 the Anglo-Saxons belonged to the Varangian Guard. Alexis put some of them in the town that he founded to keep a watch on the Turkish emir of Nicomedia.

Learning of the troubles in south Italy, the Guiscard left Bohemund in command, swearing by the soul of his father Tancred not to shave or wash till he returned. He found that Henry had gone off ravaging the lands of the papal ally, Matilda of Tuscany; so he turned to Apu-lia. Bohemund was beginning to threaten Byzantion itself, but in 1083 he was beaten at Larissa, and slowly all the Norman gains in the Balkans were lost. In Italy Henry, after a long siege of Rome, entered the city on 21 March 1084. Robert, having dealt with his Apulian rebels, moved north. Henry retreated, and when Robert reached Rome with a big body of Calabrian and Saracen mercenaries, he met little opposition. Forcing his way in through the Flaminian Gate, he hewed a passage through the burning streets to the Castello Sant' Angelo where the pope was in refuge. Three days later some disturb-ances among the citizens provided the pretext for setting fire to the city again, and it was given up to rape, arson, murder, looting and destruction. Many of the leading citizens who survived were sent as slaves to Calabria. The devastation was enormous. No barbarian attack over the centuries had done anything like the damage. Churches and temples crashed down, the Capitol and the Palatine were burned out, hardly a building was left between the Colosseum and the Lateran. Many people were burned alive, others were cut down as they ran about. The Normans had not only wrecked Rome, but had brought in Saracens to help in doing it.

Pope Gregory did not care. He had beaten Henry and nothing else mattered. But now he was so detested by the people that he could not remain in Rome; he was doomed to go off with the Normans whom he had once so loudly denounced. In May 1085 he died at Salerno and was buried in the new cathedral, which was built, according to the inscription, by 'Duke Robert Greatest of Conquerors with His Own Money'. To the end he was perfectly convinced of his own righteousness. 'Therefore I die in exile.'

In autumn 1084 Robert was back in Greece; but, as we saw, the tide had turned. This time the Normans had taken on an enemy too powerful for them, with far too many resources still despite set-backs and depletions. By the end of the year they held only a coastal strip. Robert tried to bring reinforcements across; but bad weather and the Venetians beat him, though at the close of his second defeat he rallied and drove his fleet into one more attack that capsized many of the heavier Venetian galleys. Anna Comnena tells of the mutilation he inflicted on his 2,500 prisoners. He took Corfu, but an epidemic, probably typhoid, broke out among his men and finally he himself was affected. On 17 July 1085 he died with Sichelgaita at his side.

His tomb at Venosa called him with something like truth the Terror of the World. Various incidents of his Byzantine expedition got into the *Chanson de Roland*, as did incidents from the career of William the Conqueror; Charlemagne was described as having 'con-quered Pouille [Apulia] and the whole of Calabrie' as well as having 'crossed over the bitter sea to England'.[1] William and Robert had shared many qualities, but Robert operated in a wider field. In Apulia and Calabria he had to deal with territory broken up into many feudal units and comprising several advanced mercantile cities: something as unlike England as could be found in that age. But, though he tried imitating the Byzantines, he could not devise an administrative system to hold his conquests together. William, his admirer, died two years later; and with their two deaths the old Norman world disappeared. Something more sophisticated had to emerge.

We noted that elements drawn from both William and Robert went into the *Chanson de Roland*, in which the concept of the holy war was maturing. To enter into the minds of the period we must understand how they could celebrate the violent and ruthless Robert as being under the special shield of the Virgin Mary, as being the Most Christian Duke guided by God and assured of his victory by the direct intervention of Jesus Christ. Amatus calls him and Richard of

Capua (the Wolf of the Abruzzi) the Lord's Anointed. A series of tales about visions and miracles supported these assertions. Robert, says Malaterra, preached a sort of sermon to his men before the invasion of Sicily in 1061, bidding them seek remission of their sins before setting out on so holy an exploit. Roger, at Cerami in 1063, called on his men not to be daunted by the hosts facing them, since they were the sturdy soldiers of Christ's army; and St George appeared on a white horse, with a shining banner, to lead the Normans to victory. Robert told his troops before Palermo that Christ was their leader, and the first Norman on the wall made the sign of the cross. Amatus tells us that, when Palermo was taken, the Normans cleansed the church of St Mary, which had been turned into a mosque, and celebrated mass there. During the ceremony angels descended from aloft and the whole church was filled with music and light. William of Poitiers stresses with strong conviction the view that William's conquest of England was above all a Christian mission.[2] Eadmer thought that the victory at Hastings was 'without doubt entirely due to a miracle of God'.

To see in such actions and statements mere hypocritical sham would be as wrong as to take the expressions of piety at their face-value, nor can we rightly see in them a confessed mixture of hypocrisy and piety. We must realize how strong a magical element entered into the attitudes. Men did not feel drawn to compare the tales of miracles with such facts as that Robert had devastated Rome with the help of large numbers of Saracens. Since William won at Hastings, he must have had God on his side; and the protestations of men like Robert and Roger about their pure Christian mission had behind them a feeling that they were thus binding God and Christ to their cause. God ought to support his own cause; and the vehemence with which the fighters convinced themselves of the truth of their claim was felt as a force binding them to God and God to them; the emotion was the proof of the claim, which found its external vindication in success.

We cannot follow in detail the further story of the Normans in the south; but a few words are needed about the way in which Roger developed his state in Sicily, and about the Normans in the crusades.

Robert was so taken up in his last ten years with the affairs of the papacy and his invasion of Greece that the struggle in Sicily was left more and more in Roger's hands. Roger, however, still depended on his brother for reinforcements from Italy. At first he was concerned to strengthen the hold he already had, and probably built several more castles. In 1075 he came to an agreement with the sultan of Mehdia, under which the Moslem troops from Africa, particularly valiant fighters, were withdrawn. But he had a ten year war with the emir of Syracuse, with moments of drastically changing fortunes; the emir in 1084 even ravaged Calabria and carried off the nuns of Reggio for his harem. But Roger built a new fleet, besieged Syracuse for some months and, at last, captured it. This was the decisive victory. In 1090 Roger took Malta and Gozo, and next year had made himself the secure lord of Sicily. By the time of his death, in 1101, he was dominating the whole political situation in south Italy. His position had thus already foreshadowed the emergence of a single Norman state in the south, with its capital at Palermo.

Roger, who died aged seventy, had been the youngest de Haute-ville; and three rulers – Philip of France, Conrad son of Henry IV, king of Italy, and Colman of Hungary – had sought to ally themselves with him in marriage. The dependence of the papacy on the Normans had not ceased. The pope Urban II, a Frenchman elected outside Italy, got into Rome through the Normans, in opposition to Clement III; he seems indeed to have had to spend nearly a year in the South under the aegis of the two sons of Robert Guiscard, the rival half-brothers Roger Borsa and Bohemund; not till the pair were reconciled could he go to Rome under Norman escort. Later in 1091 the supporters of Henry IV's pope threw Urban out of Rome and again he had to seek Norman aid. Henry, having just beaten the forces of Matilda of Tuscany near Padua, was at the most succesful point of his career; but the Normans yet again won control of the situation and in 1093 Urban was back in Rome. Two years later Roger's daughter Constance married Conrad, Henry's rebellious son. Urban was becoming a powerful figure, with influence all over western Europe, and through him the first crusade was launched. We see that throughout the eleventh century the Normans in Italy played a decisive role in the relations of the papacy and the German empire, and thus in determining many of the main lines on which the medieval world was to evolve. If they had not played this role it is hard to see how the crusades could have come about as they did. The Easter synod of 1059, made possible by their support, was of key importance in the development of the whole reform movement. Part of that development was the creation of a coherent body of canon law in place of the vast compilations gathering conciliar acts and papal decrees (some of them forged, though uncritically accepted at this period).

The English monk Eadmer gives us a picture of Roger of Sicily in 1097–8 when the exiled Anselm came to see him as he laid siege to rebellious Capua.

Having heard the fame of Anselm, he sent messengers and asked him to come to him, wishing to see him and talk with him and be instructed by him in all that might conduce to his salvation. So the Father set out to go to him. But when we were yet a great way off, the duke himself, supported by a large company of soldiers, met him and ran to kiss him and thank him for coming. After that we spent many days at the siege living in tents some distance from the coming and going and the turmoil and din of the camp.

Pope Urban arrived, and he and Anselm were together 'in such a way that they seemed to form one household'. William Rufus wrote letters and sent presents to turn Roger and the others against Anselm.

The duke himself, to whom these messages were particularly directed, so far from paying any attention to them, tried by repeated requests to induce Anselm to do him the favour of staying on with him and accepting as a gift the best of his lands both in manors and in his cities, whether fortified or open.[3]

In 1096 a high watermark of Norman unity was reached, in the union of Roger of Sicily, Roger of Apulia, and Bohemund of Taranto, against Amalfi. In the same year there came the first crusaders from the north, and Roger, as Duke of Apulia, received and entertained Robert, duke of Normandy, William's son, treating him as his natural lord – as if the Normans everywhere recognized the duke of Normandy as their overlord.

Roger's third wife, Adelaide, a Ligurian, bore him two sons: Simon, who died in 1105, and Roger, who at the age of ten became ruler of Sicily under his mother's regency. Roger I had still loved his mainland castle of Mileto; Roger II was brought up as a Sicilian, a man of the Mediterranean inheriting three great cultures. His mint, controlled by Greeks, was mainly staffed by Moslems; and about this time the Italian term for mint, *zecca*, was taken from the Arabic. In Palermo the governor, a Christian, was called *emir*, *ammiratus*: whence our *admiral*. In 1127 Roger II united the states of Apulia and Sicily, and outlawed all rights of feud. In 1130 he took the title of King of Sicily. He kept a harem in Moslem style, exercised the authority of a papal legate, and thus had more complete control of his church than had any other western ruler; he issued orders in Latin, Greek, and Arabic to officials variously called justiciars, constables, logothetes, catapans and emirs. No western kingdom of the twelfth century had so strong or so complex a constitution, a mixture of feudal customs and Roman-Byzantine-Moslem laws, and with the king's will and the justice of his courts providing the basis of unification. Roger II's policy aimed at developing the sea power which his Norman pre-

decessors in the south had lacked, and at promoting trade and industry; he conquered the north African ports below Sicily and
made his island the strongest sea power in Italy, so that in the end his
rivals, Genoa, Pisa and Venice, had to combine to regain, later in the
century, the mastery of the Italian seas.

The glamorous perspective in which the south was viewed from
England may be gauged from an Anglo-Norman romance, *Ipomedon*,
by Hue de Rotelande, a light-hearted poet who seems to belong to the
same line of Norman-Welsh clerks as Walter Map and Girald; he has
the same flippant and witty note; probably born at Rhuddlan, he
lived at Credenhall near Hereford. *Ipomedon* has a reference to the
siege of Rouen in 1174; it was inspired by the wedding of our Henry
II's Joan in 1176 to William II of Sicily – the betrothal had been
made in 1164. Most of the poem's action occurs in Apulia, Calabria
and Sicily. The heir to the Apulian kingdom falls in love with the
duchess of Calabria when he hears her described; and after many
adventures and mishaps he finds and marries her.[4]

In Apulia and Calabria the Normans, as soon as they were able to
settle down, used the system of the military fief that was being
developed in Normandy. Certainly Robert Guiscard and Roger I
systematically endowed their supporters with the lands they won.
But the situations of Apulia and Sicily were different. In Apulia the
conquests were made first by small bands, often under Lombards
or Greeks, and any form of central authority developed slowly,
whereas in Sicily, as in England, a big area was gained in one concerted effort. We find a large number of small fiefs, and a few large
lordships with an autonomy that was only gradually modified. Among
the latter group were the many comital families, who provided
a long lasting source of rivalries and turbulence. The setting up of
central control in the feudalized system was also delayed by the
existence of great monasteries like Monte Cassino and La Cava, with
vast estates. These houses resisted the burden of military services,
though the Normans exacted feudal dues and counsel.[5] But fully
feudal forms were steadily built up; a charter by Bohemund for St
Nicholas of Bari, ascribed to 1090, is wholly feudal in character.

Inevitably, especially in early days, the Normans were much
affected by the customs of the regions where they settled. The comital
dynasties often took over Lombard jurisdictions; Richard of Capua
in 1065 granted an estate to be held 'according to the legal customs
of the Lombards'. Other lords took up Byzantine forms and terms.
Some counts in Apulia appointed catapans to act as their deputies in
administration, while Bohemund created his dukes. And Roger I in
1094 granted to the bishop of Messina lands that were to be defined

'according to the earler divisions of the Saracens', while he continued to use Byzantine *strategoi* in Calabria and later introduced them into Messina.[6] In Sicily Roger was able to introduce a centralized system far more quickly than had been possible on the mainland. By 1077 Robert Guiscard seems to have created some very big fiefs in the north of the island, but at his death Roger broke them up into small fiefs and handed them out among his knights; and when he died, Sicily was divided into small fiefs in the north, and some big ones he had created in central and south-east Sicily. Of these latter many were held by the church. We hear of two *comtés*, but these were made for close relations.[7]

In south Italy the Normans used Byzantine methods of assessing and collecting taxes; a charter in 1087 shows that at Bari the administration carried on the fiscal registers known as *Quaterniones*. In Sicily Roger carried on the centralized financial bureau of the diwan.[8] The Moslem system however was reorganized, and we find members of the bureau making visitations, so as to ensure local control. As in England the sheriffs were to be called to yearly account – while in the earlier part of the twelfth century the use of the local units or *iklim* has been compared with the use made of the hundreds under Henry I of England. The Moslems had kept detailed records or registers, which the Normans took over; a Greek charter to the refounded bishopric of Catania in 1095 adds to the list of granted estates a *platea* of the dependent peasants. The *plateae* were rolls (in Greek, or sometimes in Arabic) made up out of the diwan's records; and it has been conjectured that Roger used such lists to make a survey of his economic and military resources on the same sort of lines as *Domesday* in England. In any event there are analogies between the way in which a Norman aristocracy was set up in England and in Sicily, and in which advances were made towards a centralized administration.[9] The scope of the system developed under Roger may be gauged by the fact that before the end of the century the emir of Palermo had expanded his jurisdiction so as to become emir over all the dominions in Sicily and Calabria, subject to his lord.[10]

Bohemund was an outstanding leader in the first crusade. On his return for new forces in 1105, he visited France and married the king's daughter. Eadmer tells us how Anselm was at Rouen when Bohemund arrived with a cardinal, Bruno, who had with him a Master of the Knights, Ilgyrus. The latter,

being on terms of friendship with Anselm, entertained him with a great deal of agreeable talk about the wars he had been through, of cities captured, of the situation of the places and

not a few other pieces of information which he had picked up
on the Jerusalem campaign. He also disclosed to him the fact
that he was in possession of many relics of saints and the way in
which he had come by them. Among these, and indeed above all
those he possessed, he prided himself especially on some hairs
of Mary, the blessed Mother of God, of which he said that some
had been given him by the Patriarch of Antioch when he held
there the post of Master of the Knights under Bohemund...These
hairs had been torn out by that Lady herself when, standing
beside the cross of her Son, a sword pierced through her soul.

Two of the hairs were taken to Bec; two were reserved by Anselm and
reverently guarded by Eadmer as the Keeper of his Chapel. As for
Bohemund, intoxicated by the sense of power that the new army gave
him, he treacherously turned from his crusading task to march on
Byzantion, the main bulwark against the infidels. But the Venetians
helped the emperor, and he failed. Humiliated, he returned to Apulia
and died in 1111.

 During these years a fleet of English Varangians was cruising in the
Mediterranean under the Byzantine emperor's orders. Edgar the
Aetheling took command, and we find him again entangled with the
Normans. In 1097 Guynemer of Boulogne captured the port of Lat-
takieh. In March 1098 Edgar drove him out and occupied the place
in the emperor's name. But he could leave only a few men as garrison;
so the crusaders were asked to help with the defence. Robert of
Normandy turned up and the port was handed over to him in trust
for the emperor. But his only idea of government was to extort as
much money as possible from the people, and he was soon driven
out.[11]

 All the crusading chiefs were seeking for kingdoms, their personal
ambitions as usual fused with their religious fervour. Bohemund ruled
the principality of Antioch. We may assume that his court was made
up of leading Norman families as in south Italy, for we find such
families present under his successor. When he was imprisoned in
1100, the court might have appointed a regent, but it chose his
nephew Tancred, who would have been his nominee. Feudal institutions had been imposed on the area, probably from the outset.[12]
Following the Norman method of making use of existing governmental systems, Bohemund used Byzantine methods of administration – the empire had held Antioch until some twelve years before
the Normans conquered it – while the peasants carried on with
Moslem customs under the immediate jurisdiction of cadis of their
own faith and race.[13] So Frankish knights worked with officials
trained in the Byzantine tradition; and though the crusaders usually

persecuted Jews both before and after the establishment of the new Latin states, the Jewish community of Antioch, well known for its skill in glass making, seems to have been relatively undisturbed.

Tancred later became prince of Galilee. And other leaders of northern France played important roles in the east. Thus there were Flemish people at Jerusalem itself, where after Baldwin II tenure became hereditary and a highly logical application of feudal principles was worked out.

We see that the Normans, when faced with governmental problems, tended to consider seriously what they could use and adapt from the customs of the conquered land, and avoid any unnecessary breaks and confusions. They showed little, if any, originality in devising new forms; but it might be argued that in all the areas they controlled – Normandy, England, Italy, Sicily and Antioch – they had irrupted into regions with old traditions and well rooted administrative methods, and that they therefore needed the intelligence to absorb and apply what was best in those regions rather than to work out unnecessary novelties. There was one area, however, in which they did innovate, or at least sharpen and systematize trends in Frankish feudalism: they developed the fief with definitely defined military services or obligations. And we find them carrying this development with them into England, the South and Antioch. The system of liege homage, whereby a man might hold land from several lords but owed a special and complete allegiance to the chief of these lords, was developed by them and carried wherever they went. There were slight variations in application of these ideas and methods – for instance the exaction of what were called feudal incidents by the lord from the vassal seems to have been regularized in England earlier than in south Italy or Antioch – but in general the principles of Norman feudalism were the same everywhere. They did not try to transfer administrative methods found and expanded in one area, into other areas they had conquered.

In the early part of the twelfth century the Normans had developed the most strongly organized kingdoms of Europe, and they ruled the most effective of the crusading states. Two powerful empires, that of Henry II of England and that of Roger II, had been built up. They included some important ports, London, Palermo and Bari – the last named a point where many contacts between east and west were made. Under Roger I Mileto also became a centre for merchants and travellers, from the north beyond the Alps, the Italian ports of the west coast, the Byzantine world and the Moslem south. Under Roger II of Sicily there developed a magnificent culture with many inflowing and partly fused ingredients, which found expression in such buildings as the cathedral of Monreale. To examine this flowering is beyond our scope, but we may note that in January 1186 Henry, son of the emperor Frederick I, married Constance, heiress to the Sicilian crown, and the island entered into a new phase under the Hohenstaufens. In England the effects of the Norman conquest were in the end far more stable and more far reaching in their consequences.

CHAPTER XI

TENURES, FIEFS, AND MILITARY ORGANIZATION

We now turn to a more detailed examination of what happened in England. Here we can see how a Norman takeover and transformation of a native system worked out. First we must note the almost total dispossession of the native ruling class in favour of an alien group. At Edward's death there seem to have been between four and five thousand Englishmen holding estates of the king that the Normans were to call manors. When the *Domesday Book* (1086) was compiled, there were some 1400 to 1500 tenants-in-chief holding direct from the king, with some 170 or 180 of them getting a yearly income of £100; and there were about 8,000 sub-tenants. Only two of the tenants-in-chief were English; a mere eight per cent of the land was left in English hands. The total population was somewhere between one and two million, having been much reduced by warfare, deaths, ravages and disease since 1066. The thegns were still to be found in most parts of the country, but with diminishing status. Many sank

K

down to peasant level; the more adventurous wandered off to Scotland, Ireland, Denmark or Byzantion. Goscelin, a monk of St Bertin, tells of a *vir honorificus*, who, though a layman, seems to have been brought up in St Augustine's Abbey at Canterbury; after Hastings he went with other *optimates* to Byzantion, where he became a duke. He must have entered the Varangian guard. Marrying a rich noblewoman, Eudoxia, he built a basilica by his house, and dedicated it to St Nicholas and his old patron St Augustine; the English exiles used to gather there.[1] A few Normans got estates by marrying English heiresses; and a few Englishmen bought back their lands at high rents. Others survived at a low level as sub-tenants of the new lords. At the end of the county surveys in *Domesday* we meet groups of thegns reduced to holding tiny pieces of land. Thus, the lands of Merleswein, a great thegn under Edward and William (in his first years), were taken over by Ralph Paynel, ancestor of the Luttrells of Dunster, lords in Lincolnshire, Yorkshire, Devonshire, Somersetshire and Gloucestershire.

The two Englishmen who were big landowners in 1086 are worth a glance. They were not great men surviving from Edward's day, but unscrupulous characters who had risen on the backs of their fallen fellows. Thorkill of Arden had a big fief in Warwickshire, mostly made up of the lands of dispossessed Englishmen, valued at over £120; it was assessed at over 135 hides for geld and as able to support nearly 220 ploughs. The value had increased by almost a third since 1066. Thorkill held seventy-one manors, of which only four are known to have been his father's. He seems to have risen through his zeal as sheriff. But even so his heirs failed to carry on at his level: most of his estates went to Roger of Beaumont, to swell the earldom of Warwick, while his heirs became modest military tenants of the Warwick fief. The other rich Englishman was Coleswain who seems to have made his fortune by building schemes in Lincoln. He held forty-four manors, eleven pieces of sokeland, and seven berewicks, none of which had been his in 1066. He inherited four tofts in Lincoln and got from the king a stretch of wasteland outside the city, on which he built thirty-six new houses; he also built and owned two churches. But his family too, failed to keep up.[2] A few Englishmen, however, like Eadnoth, father of Harding and grandfather of Robert fitzHarding, did beget families that finally rose in the world. Smallholders remained common, especially north of the Humber; in the south the thegnage was driven down in status or its members were replaced by aliens.

By 1070 only two English earls were still in office, Waltheof and Gospatrick; and Ralf de Gael had a Breton father and English mother. But neither of these lasted long. Nor did the English bishops. In spring

1070 a papal legate came with orders to depose Stigand and the bishops he had consecrated; but William wanted much more. Most of the bishops had unimpeachable orders, and among Stigand's men was a Norman monk, Remigius, who had been made bishop of Dorchester. So at two councils, besides Stigand, his brother Aethelmar of Elmham and Aethelric of Selsey (transferred to Chichester in 1075) were deposed, while Leofwine of Lichfield, a married man, resigned; Ealdred of York died before action was taken against him. William appointed his own clerks to the vacancies. Only three English bishops remained. One was old and died in 1075; the other two had been keen supporters of William and so were tolerated, as also was the abbot of Evesham. No Englishman now became bishop for several generations. As the abbots died, Normans took over. By William's death only some small houses had English heads. The lands of the sees and abbeys thus passed into the control of foreign churchmen.

There were certainly many usurpations of land. We hear of them only when a Norman is wronged by another Norman. Thus in Cambridgeshire *Domesday* gives us clues to such seizures. Twice we are told that Aubrey de Ver's predecessor (according to the testimony of the Hundred Jury) had grabbed certain land despite the king's arrangements. Earl Ralf lost holdings in Whaddon through his revolt; now Richard fitzGilbert had it, though the Hundred declared that his predecessors had never held it. Ely claimed much land that was in lay hands; perhaps it had been taken by aliens after the revolt of 1070 in which Ely tenants took part. Clearly many lords, backed by the sheriff, took estates without the king's licence and in defiance of the principle of heredity. 'Aubrey de Ver is convicted in *Domesday* of having acquired illegally a holding in Abingdon which in 1066 had been held by a sokeman of the king, and which three years before the Inquest Picot the sheriff had proved was not properly Aubrey's and had recovered' (Finn).[3]

One factor, however, that tended to preserve continuity was the desire of the aliens not to lose any profits they could get from old customs or contracts. *Domesday* shows that in general English tenures could be described in Norman terms. The new pattern did not mean so much a displacement of the previous one as its complication and tightening up. Processes of change, already at work, were speeded up. *Domesday* shows how carefully the Normans found out and recorded the customs of the boroughs and shires, and the hidage of estates. The picture is complicated by the fact that tenants-in-chief could be sub-tenants in some of their holdings. Sub-tenancies enabled a tenant-in-chief to gain bases in parts of the country where he held no land as tenant-in-chief. Thus, the count of Eu, who had been given the greatest of Sussex castles, Hastings – to be guarded by the sixty knights of his rape – gained a foothold in Kent through a manor held by knight service which was granted to him by the archbishop of Canterbury. And at times the system gave a magnate the chance to gain land conveniently near his own main holdings.[4]

Only some forty names of lords who came over in 1066 are definitely known. Some invaders were killed; others for one reason or another decided that they preferred Normandy, Anjou or Brittany, for instance Aubrey de Coucy and Gherbod the Fleming. Perhaps they found the terms of settlement too onerous; William may have tried to impose unusually strict systems on his vassals. Humphrey of Tilleuil, who had visited England under Edward and was for a while put over Hastings castle, heard that his wife was being unchaste and hurried back to Normandy. His brother-in-law, Hugh of Grandmesnil, also returned to see what his wife had been up to, but decided on England after all and became a great landowner there. Many important families of the twelfth century derived from troop commanders of 1066. A large number of lords felt that their roots were in Normandy, but moved to and fro; when they had more than one son, as we saw, they often asked William to allow the elder to inherit the Norman estate, and the younger to settle in England. William himself followed that course in 1087.

The small group of advisers who helped William to deal with such matters as land grants was mostly related to the ducal house and came from the Rouen district; among them were Odo and possibly William fitzOsbern. About half the land in England was held in lay tenure; about a quarter of the landed wealth was granted to ten men, mostly relatives of the king, who himself held about a fifth.[5] The great magnates made up a group which usually felt a strong sense of solidarity, though conflicts could arise. They were in a sense governors, the core of the king's council, though he kept up the witangemot as a Great Council at Christmas, Easter and Whitsun. With such a shrewd and ever watchful taskmaster, these barons knew that they could not relax without falling away from the centre of power and events. The second generation had less the sense of being an alien group in a country that hated them or accepted them only out of impotence; the close links between them began to weaken. For the men who wanted something to replace the fierce jostling and private wars of Normandy, there were the marcher earldoms with their difficult and changing frontier situations. The holder there was generally the largest landowner in the shire, at times almost the only tenant-in-chief. (Throughout the Middle Ages the marches of north and east produced many challenges to the crown, which, however, had no choice but to allow dangerous concentrations of power there.) However, William granted the lands of one or more English lords to the new beneficiaries; marcher lords often held estates scattered about the realm, like most barons. In many cases, especially with important men, rough bargains may have been struck before the expedition of 1066. But the amount of land forfeited by English resisters may well have exceeded estimates of what would be available. The result would have been increased demands, expectations and intrigues, which William and his advisers would have had to tackle decisively.

In return for the extensive lands held by his barons William demanded considerable services. No longer, as at home, could most of his great lords meet their dues to the ducal host by drawing on their household knights. The king was in theory the owner of all land; he could echo, with effect, the boast attributed to his ancestor Robert the Magnificent that he held from God alone. Under the late Saxon kings the royal estates had been slowly but steadily shrinking; now William was able to expand them again dramatically – though the shrinking process was to reappear through royal grants in the coming decades. And since this creation of the royal demesne took place in a situation where land tenures and military services were being closely linked, the demesne took on a new significance. William granted out bits of the demesne as in effect he had granted out the rest of the land – even if there was no specific act of giving involved for the mass of lesser landholders and peasants of varying status.[6] William fixed the services due when he made the grant of an honour. From now on rights and obligations were not to be built up in a confused way over generations; the ruler could settle everything from the outset. Not that there was any master plan; much must have been improvised. But William and his advisers must have given a lot of thought to the allocations made gradually from 1066 on. There must have been some correlation between the size and value of the lands and the services exacted, but there was no definite ratio. The whole thing happened too fast and there was too little knowledge of just what was being granted even if William did realize the virtue of uniform services. What happened was a result of the tension between the feudal concepts hammered out under William in Normandy and the actual situation in England: a tension resolved, in so far as it was resolved, by the practical necessity to keep the English down and get the maximum profits from them.

The barons were to a great extent left to meet the contracted services in their own way. They could maintain a large number of knights in their households, supplying them with food, equipment, and so on; or they could do in their sphere what the king did in his –

keep a demesne of their own and allot parcels of the rest of the estate
to knights, who thus in turn became enfeoffed. Most barons, especially in danger areas, preferred to have a troop of knights answering
their call; sometimes these knights held land or dwellings close by
and were available for such duties as escort. At times a churchman
felt the same preference, for instance at Glastonbury and Abingdon.
Or he could hire mercenaries. Walcher of Durham had knights in
his household and their presence helped to bring about the troubles
of 1080. Wulfstan at Worcester gathered a retinue whose yearly
wages were a heavy burden on the bishopric; he used to dine with
them as he thought it wrong to eat in private while they grumbled.
In the revolt of 1088 these knights did much to beat a rebel force.
But when Wulfstan died in 1095 many had been enfeoffed. Henry
of Huntingdon as a boy (about 1100) admired the pomp of the bishop
of Lincoln's retinue.[7]

As the magnates could settle differences at the royal curia and feel
that they played a part in the destinies of the realm, so at the lower
levels the courts made the sub-tenants feel that they had an important
relationship with the lords. Thus Haimo Daipfer, who held an estate
of St Augustine's, promised to 'give counsel, aid and succour to the
church, to the abbot and his successors, concerning all pleas of the
shire or in the king's court, against all barons, except those whose
vassals he will have become by the giving of hands'. The feudal relation thus gave the lord bonds of personal and political influence,
and often put him in active relation with men of yet higher rank. Not
that disputes could not break out at all levels. Thus, later bishops of
Worcester claimed that they owed the king fifty and not sixty
knights. Early enfeoffment charters are rare; we must conclude that
the early fiefs were granted mostly by word of mouth before
witnesses, with no written record.[8]

How far was there continuity between Anglo-Saxon customs and
Norman feudalism? The question cannot be answered in a few
words, but it is clear that the two worlds had many similar elements,
even if the Normans also made great changes. Anglo-Saxon commendation anticipated Norman homage; Anglo-Norman writers sometimes regarded the two terms as having the same meaning. For more
than a century before 1066 the lesser thegns had been insecure in
status, so they were more and more ready to give up their independence in return for a lord's protection. The process by which the
new relationship was brought about is often cited by *Domesday* as
commendatio: a ceremony of homage binding a man to be true to a
lord and kept alive year by year by payments recognizing the lord's
role. The lord was to support his man in pleas and use his influence

on his behalf at court or in the shires. The man might or not pledge himself to render service to the lord, obtain the lord's licence before alienating his land, or subject himself and his land to the lord's jurisdiction. A man might commend himself to more than one lord and could withdraw his allegiance – 'go with his land to whatsoever he would' (*Domesday*). Not only thegns commended themselves; we find the custom also among the Anglo-Danish peasantry of East Anglia and the eastern midlands.

There were many instances where Anglo-Saxon custom merged without friction into Norman feudal practices. Legists linked Norman feudal reliefs with English heriot; and the point is significant, even though reliefs may have been paid in pre-1066 Normandy. Among both English and Normans the failure to perform military obligations entailed forfeiture of land; and the five hides of the fyrd soldiers corresponded approximately to the hidage of the average knight's fee. Further, in the leases of English ecclesiastical estates we find services specified. We have some seventy leases granted by St Oswald as bishop of Worcester to men whose status is not sure, but who were certainly mostly above peasant level. In a long memorandum to King Edgar, Oswald shows that he looked on his tenants primarily as mounted retainers, bound 'to fulfil the law of riding as riding men should'. They had to ride on errands, lend him horses when he needed them, make fences when he wanted to hunt, help him to meet the king's demand for service, pay church-scot and other customary dues, apparently find lime for the church fabric and bridges, and be generally obedient to his commands – a phrase which may cover various services or agricultural work. (Hard manual work would have been done by their slaves, servants, or dependent peasants.) Oswald seems to have taken as his model the services due from *geneatas* as set out in the *Rectitudines*; and the *geneat*, whatever his condition in the tenth century, was originally a lord's companion.

We do not know how prevalent were such loan lands as those of Oswald's tenants; but the land grants have close resemblances to Norman enfeoffments and they come near to having feudal incidents connected with them. Thus, by the Confessor's time the grantor of loanland claimed the right to marry the heiress to the man he named. On the other hand the services exacted were vague and miscellaneous, unlike the specific military services of the fief; and loanland was generally given for three generations; it was not hereditary.

The English concept of kingship, implicit in the organization of the fyrd as the king's force, involved the view that the king owned the primary allegiance of all subjects, as above any particular commendation or obligation. This position emerged among the Normans as the reservation of allegiance to the ruler as above any particular homage.

The first document in which it directly appears is one of 1087–96 in which the bishop of Bayeux pays homage in the time of Duke Robert Curthose; here we meet an express reservation of ducal rights. But the vassal is a vicomte, whose allegiance to the duke would be a function of his office. The general obligation to join the *arrière-ban* held, however, an implication of the duke's paramount authority, though not in as clear a form as fyrd duty implied the English king's supremacy. A passage in William's *Ten Articles* carries the old fyrd duty forward into the new situation by ordering that all free men should swear loyalty to the king both in and out of England, upholding his lands and honour with all loyalty, and defending them against his enemies. The 1086 assembly at Salisbury put into practice the theory of the fealty of all important landlords, tenants-in-chief or sub-tenants to the king. At times lesser men defied the call of their immediate lord and clove to the king, as in the 1101 revolt. The Salisbury ceremony was repeated at the coronations of Rufus and Henry I. It is clear then that, whatever embryonic elements of such paramount authority existed in ducal Normandy, the big advance in England of the idea and its application owed much to Anglo-Saxon tradition. The idea still needed considerable working out but a turn of great importance had been decisively made. The 1086 oath not only brought the loyalty of sub-tenants more directly into connection with the king; we may argue that it also implicitly promised those sub-tenants security of tenure. We find the under-tenants of rebellious lords converted into tenants-in-chief of the crown and the estates of loyal under-tenants excepted from the grant of a rebel's land to a new tenant-in-chief.

We may claim then that practically all the elements of the Norman system were present in pre-1066 English society; but that the fief did not exist in the clear-cut and specific form in which it was imposed by the Normans. On the other hand the broadly based fiscal and administrative system enabled the Anglo-Norman state itself to emerge, giving to the fief a new meaning and decisively expanding its social and economic effects.[9]

The speed at which military tenures developed in England varied with the regions and the characters of the lords. Some barons made their fiefs microcosms of the king's realm. They too had their lords, knights and sergeants, they could enfeoff their men; and in each barony or honour the feudal law had to be worked out. But William kept to himself two rights. There were to be no private wars (save on the Welsh borders) and no baronial troops were to fight save in the royal army. Also the king could interfere with the barons, since a baron's vassal might appeal to him against denial of justice or wrongful action. The barons certainly considered the Salisbury oath of 1086 a high-handed intrusion on their sphere. Further William was ready, when he felt it necessary, to ignore a magnate and deal directly with an important rear-vassal. His interference might have had as an object the supplementing of one of his officials' income or the support of a nepotic enfeoffment. A writ of William's orders that the *dapifer* Eudo be given an estate (Easton) to be held as fief of the abbot of Peterborough; the abbot refused to comply, but *Domesday* shows Eudo in possession. It also mentions several enfeoffments made at the king's command, especially on ecclesiastical lands. Occasionally the intrusion was merciful. A knight, caught in an attack by pirates as he sailed home, had had his hands cut off; he was a professional knight of Abingdon Abbey, who had not yet got any land, and the abbot did not want to enfeoff a useless man. The knight somehow got his case before the king, who, 'feeling pity, commanded the abbot to provide for the man enough land of the king to support him while he lived'. In the marcher-earldoms independence from the king reached its limit. The knights had no obligation to serve on the king's expeditions except when he joined with their lord in operations against a near enemy.[10]

Roger of Montgomery, a tenant-in-chief who left his name to a county, had a capable financial system; he seems to have appointed his own sheriffs in Shropshire and the Rape of Arundel. We may assume that a baron began by enfeoffing his own kinsmen, his trusted officials, or his leading warriors, constables, marshals and seneschals. Each sub-tenant would be given land to maintain, say, four or five knights, and was responsible for calling up that number. Sub-tenants might when necessary, for instance in the baron's absence, lead the feudal levy or a part of it. The knights, we saw, might be men of modest or even poor means. No doubt at first they gathered round the head, *caput*, of an honour; but some of them, perhaps after a period of service (the rules of which were then familiar but are lost to us), were settled in more various ways or were endowed with a revenue corresponding to that from whole villages. There was certainly no standard knight's fee, perhaps not even at the end of the Anglo-Norman era. Sub-infeudation developed more in some areas than others; even when we allow for the devastations, it was rare in northern Danelaw. Many honours in Lincolnshire were much under-enfeoffed, perhaps as a result of less manorialized conditions, or perhaps because the lord wanted to have fighters ready in case of Danish attacks.

We find some knights holding about five hides, men who were probably of the later gentry type (at least in embryo). Others had a hide or two and were on much the same level as well-to-do peasants.

Even a single district can provide contradictions. In general we may say there were two main types holding fiefs: the substantial sub-tenant and the professional knight. But as the twelfth century went on, the minimum needed to maintain and furnish a knight increased, so that soon the small professional, and then the superior kind, found difficulty in carrying out the knightly role.[11]

Efforts have been made to argue that the inheritability of fiefs was far from established in the period immediately following 1066. In support of this position it has been pointed out that life tenures certainly survived for a time and can indeed be cited up to the reign of Henry I; but the grants in question come from ecclesiastics such as the bishop of Hereford or the abbots of Westminster and of Abing-don. All we can safely argue is that the church took a conservative view and wanted to stick to the old *laen* grants, which gave it much more control of its lands than grants with an hereditary basis; this ecclesiastical attitude is illustrated by *Domesday*.[12] It is more than unlikely that the marked development of hereditary fiefs in Normandy would have been reversed in England. What constituted the main difference between the situations in the two areas was the fact that for some time the fiefs in England had all been granted out of conquered territory and so had not been inherited. The royal rights to the land were much more direct than in cases where a family had held a fief for generations. William I was able, it seems, to readjust the initial acquisitions of his Normans in England without much difficulty or friction; exchanges were made and compensation was provided when a new tenant-in-chief was accommodated on land already held, as we see in the Sussex baronies. Under Henry I it was still possible for Ranulf le Meschin to exchange one acquisition, the lordship of Carlisle, for another, the earldom of Chester. The king was also liable to intervene in disputes concerning twins, claims through an heiress, collateral title – cases for which there was no clearly established procedure.

Till 1087 the whole structure of inheritance involved dependence on a single feudal lord; but then, as we saw, title and succession could come into conflict with the calls of political allegiance. Hence the increased rebellions among the great families, and the use of *disseisin* or disinheritance as a penalty by the crown. The uncertainties thus produced explain why even in later times an heir wanted if possible to get a new charter confirming or restoring his father's land to him. From the third quarter of the twelfth century such charters have come down in considerable numbers. Men of high rank, experienced in the law, like Richard de Lacy, who had been joint justiciar of England, thought it prudent to get a confirming charter. Gerard de Limesi granted him the manor of Chigwell for a knight's service and confirmed it by charter, getting three marks in recognition of the lordship as well as a gold ring from Richard's son, who became his *affidatus*.

The wardship of heirs did not belong to the family, as generally in western-France; in Anglo-Norman custom it belonged to the feudal lord. In 1100 Henry I promised in his charter of liberties to accept the system of family wardship, but seigneurial wardship continued to be the rule. Indeed no other system would have worked after the separation of Normandy and England. Questions of uncertain or indirect succession thus played an important part in what has been called the tenurial crisis of the early twelfth century. The more distant and dubious the claim, the more crucial became the overlord's consent and the more likely that he would take political aspects into his decision on the settlement. Also, he would be better placed for exacting a high cash return for his assent. The heir would need to pay a substantial *finis terrae* and offer a high price for the good will or arbitration of the king on his side. Titles to castles were even less secure than titles to land, and claims to property in offices varied greatly in strength, e.g. foresterships-in-fee showed hereditary office at its most precarious. The nobles were keen to hold local office by the time of Stephen; and here the issue of hereditary title would have been one of principle between crown and vassals. If that were so, with Henry II came a heavy setback for hereditary claims. 'The sheriffs were investigated, many were removed, and the office ceased to be hereditary. Another local office to which heritable title had been claimed, the county justiciarship, was abolished. Title to local office became more precarious as title to land grew more secure. By 1215 it was beyond revival' (Holt).

We see that these tenure problems, which were very much intensified by 1087, had their positive as well as their disturbing and upsetting effects. After the confusions of Stephen's reign the hand of the crown was much strengthened. The inner conflict of Norman feudalism was deepened; certain aspects tended to disappear and there was an overall movement towards greater unification within the governing system, and towards more effective interaction of its parts. The Angevins seem to have grasped some of the difficulties which the Norman system had created for itself, and less drastic means were devised for dealing with rebellion; payment of ransom and demolition of castles tended to replace confiscation and disinheritance. Security of tenure and succession went together with the strengthening and elaboration of the royal system of law. The feudal contradictions were not eliminated, but they were lifted on to a new level.[13]

Perhaps it was also partly a sense of insecurity, a wish to make the most out of any given situation while it lasted, that had made lords enfeoff far more knights than they needed for service to overlord or king. Abbot Turold of Peterborough 'evilly gave lands to his relatives and to the knights who came with him', says the *Chronicle of Hugh Candidus*. An archbishop of York explained that he had an over-large number of knights because his predecessors 'had enfeoffed many more than they owed the king, not on account of the obligation of service that they owed, but because they wanted to provide for their kinsmen and those who served them'. A panegyrist says of an abbot of Ely that he enfeoffed knights only through compulsion, 'not by intention or rather partiality for riches, not by exerting himself for relatives'. In a late case we see how men could grow confused about the service they owed. The bishop of Winchester owed the service of twenty knights and had seventy enfeoffed; one of them, Nigel of Broc, in 1201 put himself before the grand assize so that a jury could decide whether he owed the service of one knight for the fee held at Braishfield or whether his obligation was 'to rise for the bishop in the king's court and make room for him so that he can speak with the Lord King'. By 1135, of sixty-five lay honours that have been analysed, seventeen (which had five or more fees) were over-feoffed, forty were under-feoffed, eight were enfeoffed exactly to the extent of the quota. But by 1166, seven of the under-enfeoffed ones had a surplus. As for ecclesiastical honours with five or more fees, in 1135, eighteen were over-enfeoffed, three under-enfeoffed, one was exact. Some baronies were very heavily over-enfeoffed. After 1166 *(Cartae Baronum)* the crown seems to have tried to raise the quota on over-enfeoffed honours, at least for scutage purposes, to a figure corresponding to the actual situation, and the tenants-in-chief strongly objected.[14]

Some of the reasons stimulating lords to over-enfeoffing are given in the protests cited above. We may add that one value of sub-infeudation was that it spread the problems of management, supervision, and collecting of revenues. Throughout our period an educated administrative class was lacking. Hence the recourse to farming out responsibilities. Instead of having to organize things himself, the baron or his officer had only to deal with a single man and get in an agreed sum. As money transactions increased, the pressure to find ways of raising cash through the existing systems also increased. Sub-infeudation in general had a dual effect. On the one hand it provided a stable and definite framework, both social and economic. The majority of fees on the honours were created under William or Rufus; the resulting pattern in its main lines carried on for decades, even centuries; the royal quotas themselves remained relatively stable till the drastic reductions of the thirteenth century.

On the other hand sub-infeudation had aspects that sapped the whole system. It was not a once-for-all process; it went on and on, complicating questions of loyalty and lessening the services demanded; above all by helping to replace personal services with commutation, it speeded up the increasing use of money in transactions originally controlled by feudal relationships.

The effect of money in breaking down the institution of knighthood was of great importance; and we must therefore stress the distinction between the enfeoffed knight, bound essentially by feudal ties, and the mercenary knight, whose relationship with his master was primarily financial, even though feudal attitudes entered into it. When we hear of a ceremony of initiation, the subject is a member of the highest level of knights, the son of a king, an earl, or a great baron. The most elaborate account is perhaps that of the knighting of Geoffrey of Anjou by Henry I at Rouen in 1129. Occasionally we find a lesser person going through the ritual. Walter de la Haule was taken into custody for giving his sister to William de Bodiham and making him a knight 'while he was not yet of age'. In 1220 Henry of Tracy claimed the manor of Barnstaple which 'King John surrendered to him as his inheritance on making him a knight'. The lesser person was no doubt simply dubbed a knight by the baron giving him a fief.[15]

Mercenaries consisted roughly of household retainers, some of whom were hired on a permanent basis; of professional fighters hired individually or in bands for a specific purpose; and in Normandy also of armies of neighbouring regions such as Maine or Anjou, which in certain circumstances might be hired by Norman kings under command of their own rulers or lords. One of these lords might be the vassal of the king, but his aid normally needed subsidies. By the second half of the eleventh century mercenaries played an important role in warfare; by the later twelfth, and yet more in the thirteenth, they dominated, not only as the roving bands who were dreaded as reckless and ruthless looters, but as the paid soldiers of the armies. Even the enfeoffed knights had to be paid; wage-service came overwhelmingly to take the place of tenure service.

Only now and then household knights show up in the records. When Rufus in 1095 marched into Northumbria to put down Earl Robert, 'he captured many prisoners in a fortress, including almost all the best men of the earl's retinue'. A charter of 1094–1100 shows a lord making a grant to a continental church while at his house in England in presence of many knights of the *familia* (household). A knight from the *familia* of Hugh de Lacy founded a house of Augustinian canons in the wild Black Mountains about 1108.[16] In the early years of the Conquest king and barons liked to be surrounded with ready and trusty fighters; as they grew more secure, they often enfeoffed such men. The king had the biggest retinue of knights, but even the church lords needed them. Here we meet another clear link between the systems under the Confessor and those under William.[17]

The diversity of status and the miscellaneous nature of the functions of knights needs to be stressed; we must not think of them as at all a homogeneous class. We find a considerable and striking variety of status if we approach the class from the military, tenurial, social, economic, or legal angles. Important sub-tenants of the abbey at Bury St Edmunds had 'to ride in the saint's service', but their main duty was to find knights for him. In *Domesday* these knights appear after a list of bakers, ale-brewers, tailors, washerwomen, shoemakers, ropemakers, cooks, porters, agents 'who daily all wait on the abbot and the brothers'. Also, 'there are 14 reeves over the land, who have their houses in the said town, and under them 22 bordars'.[18] The magnates or superior knights gave the professionals as little land as they could. Alexander de Alno recalled in 1166, 'My father gave his brother Hugh de Alno a small amount of land from his demesne so that if it became necessary he could do one knight's service for the whole of my father's land. And that grant was made to him and his heirs in king William's time.' (Note the claim to hereditary right.) From *Domesday* we learn that a knight normally held about one and a half hides, just a trifle more than most well-off peasants. Very few had more than three and a half hides. So the feudal middle-men did very well out of the arrangements.[19] Probably one to two hides would just have supported a knight in the eleventh century: he needed weapons, one or two horses, and the means to maintain them. Besides war-service such a knight did lesser duties such as aid and escort of his lord. Thus, Gilbert count of Brionne often sent Herluin, founder of Bec, on missions to other courts, and when Herluin refused to take Duke Robert a message that he considered morally wrong, he lost his fief. As at Ely, household knights would get food from the cellarer as well as being paid; the Ely abbot supplied many of his men with arms.

The rise of the paid soldier could not have come about without a wide economic expansion, the growth of towns and trade, and the money economy that tended to break down economic localism. In earlier times, when money was short, services could be substantially paid for by grants of land, the lord retaining various rights to exploit it and its tillers; but this method of payment, once it involved hereditary rights, was based on a commodity steadily becoming less available, though events like the vast dispossessions after 1066 could give it a new life. The more that money was used and needed to sustain a rising standard of living for the lords, lay or ecclesiastic, the more the fief-system must disintegrate. Instead of the fyrd or *arrière-ban* of the feudal host, the king could use soldiers who were at his disposal as long as he was able to pay them. Through the relative wealth of England in the first half of the eleventh century, paid soldiers had come to the fore, producing an élite force.[21]

The *stipendiarii*, the men hired for a particular campaign, had their English parallel in the *lithsmen*, *butsecarls*, and related groups in the pay of kings. These men were trained in Viking tradition to fight on foot and to man ships; the post-1066 *stipendiarii* fought as heavy or light cavalry, as archers or ordinary footmen. The kings taxed the people heavily through Danegeld, and used scutage and many other dues to pay the men, who were also called *solidarii*, men who served for a shilling. (The term *milites stipendarii* is first found in a Pipe Roll of 1162. The men were then paid 8d a day; under John the general rate had risen to 2s. These were high rates for the time. Our word for soldier is from *solidarius*, server-for-pay. The noun *sold*, common down to the sixteenth century, meant pay; *solidus* was Latin for shilling. A shilling per day was the normal pay for a knight at the end of the twelfth century.) Apart from their place in retinues, knights came to be officers in command of a considerable body of men-at-arms, who were mounted or foot sergeants and who got 4d or 6d a day if on horse, 2d or 3d if on foot.[22]

Rufus preferred mercenaries and seems to have used up much of his inheritance treasure on them; his fame for generosity brought him soldiers from all over Europe. To meet the wages he used the heavy taxes administered by Flambard and plundered church monies. Henry I was more careful, but he too used many mercenaries, especially Bretons. In his later wars he was almost wholly dependent on them. Apart from the problems of long campaigns, he trusted mercenaries far more than men who had sworn him feudal loyalty. When Robert of Bellême revolted in 1102, he put his stronghold of Bridgenorth under three captains with eighty mercenary knights. Henry I threatened to hang all prisoners if the castle did not surrender in three days; the captains and the burghers of the surrounding town agreed, but the hired knights refused. The burghers shut the knights in part of the castle and opened the gates. Henry ordered that the knights should go free with their equipment as men who had kept faith with their lord; and as they went out, they loudly complained of the way they had been deceived by captains and burghers. Orderic says that they did so in order that their withdrawal should not discredit other mercenaries. We can see what a high degree of solidarity was felt by such men and how much they valued their reputation for loyalty.[23]

In the letter that Henry wrote to Anselm after Tinchebrai he referred to his battle 'on a named and fixed day' with Robert and 'all the forces of knights and infantry which by begging or buying he was able to collect'. The close connection between his forces and his fiscal system is brought out by the fact that in 1123–4, when his knights 'complained of the coins they got in wages', he ordered the mutilation of all English moneyers who had debased the system.[24] Thus, by the late twelfth century mercenaries were ousting the knight of military tenure; obligations of host service and castle guard were mostly commuted for money payments; the money fief was playing an increasingly significant role in recruitment; most of the men serving in Angevin armies were paid regular wages. By the time of *Magna Carta* the Anglo-Norman type of feudalism was in rapid decline; the feudal levy had ceased to act as an effective fighting force, and there is no sign of it having been summoned in this period.[25]

The way in which the motive of the mercenary as the typical character in twelfth century society was coming up in men's minds is shown by Orderic's description of monks who gained promotion by currying favour with lay authorities as *stipendiarii non monachi*; and Lawrence of Durham remarks in the preface to a poem that the poet too needs incentives, and cites the farmer driven on by hopes of harvest, the pedlar by hopes of gain, the soldier by thoughts of pay.

Another example of the increasing efforts to extract profit, preferably in cash form, from the system of feudal relations is to be found in the extension of 'incidents'. These, we saw, had a pre-1066 history, but it was at this time that they were systematically worked out. A man on taking up a fief paid a relief to his lord; when he died, his heir made homage and paid a relief, if of legal age. The lord took guardianship of an heir under age and arranged the marriages of heiresses. The tenant made aids of free gifts on various occasions: after the lord's eldest son was knighted or one of his daughters married, or if he himself had to be ransomed. Henry I in his coronation charter promised to make the succession relief just and lawful. What did that mean? The compilation *Leis Willelme* (probably 1095 –1135) linked the relief with the English heriot, and expatiated on Cnut's law of heriots, which deals with horses, arms and armour. But it adds that if the vassal lacks the horse and arms his father had, he may acquit himself by paying 100s; for a man holding his land by a yearly rent the relief is to be a year's rent. A baron, however, had a chance to bargain. The *Dialogue of the Exchequer* says, 'He is not to satisfy the king according to a settled sum, but as he may be able to arrange with the king.' A relief was often £200, even for an estate of fifteen fees or a mere three. The general understanding was that a baron's relief should be reasonable; *Magna Carta* laid down that the relief for a whole barony should be £100.[26]

The rights of wardship and marriage were the most irksome. The lord got all an estate's profits during an heir's minority. Boys were minors till twenty-one, girls till the nubile age of fourteen. The lord also controlled the marriages of wards, male or female, and of all widows. A villein paid a merchet of a few shillings for leave for his girl to wed – merchet being regarded as the supreme test of servile status. Yet when a baron's widow paid a hundred or a thousand pounds for leave to remarry, the payment was taken as mark of her high rank. Henry I promised reforms, but his concessions were ignored. Widows and orphans were still sold for large sums. What the ladies feared was not so much the hole made in their estates as the disparagement – to be forced to marry below their rank, perhaps by being given by the king to some official who had risen from a lower status. They at times paid large sums to remain free; disobedience to the king's commands involved severe punishment. At times the bidding for a ward was brisk. The itinerant justices collected information so that the king could charge as large a sum as possible and also be sure the estates in question were farmed as profitably as possible. They inquired, for example, as to the age of a widow, the number of her children and the value of her dowry. (We find shameless neglect, profiteering and theft on the part of the crown agents farming estates in wardship.) By the late twelfth century payments were often taken in small instalments, with much inefficiency or carelessness on the part of the officials. To offset this, often very precise details as to payment were laid down.[27]

Scutage, the payment made in place of a knightly military service, became more and more common, and it gives us information as to the current value of a knight. In the twelfth century we find it levied sometimes in the early years at 13s 4d, sometimes at £1, only once at more than that amount.[28] A serving knight around 1086 had an income of 32s to £2, which enabled him to keep going, but not to rise in the world. *Domesday* has hardly any cases of a knight holding a whole manor (the unit of tenure). Where once or twice there is an exception, the knight stands third, not second, in the tenurial scale. Generally he holds a small unit (akin to an important manorial appurtenance, for example 'There, four slaves, a church and three knights') or something like the berewick, an outlying piece of land within the manor's system but geographically distinct.[29] Some knights held bits of demesne manors; such knights come up in the questions put to tenants-in-chief in 1166, as again in the Assize of Arms of 1181. These men seem to be in and about the tenant-in-chief's household.

Many *Domesday* knights hold villein land. Once the professional knights, both French and English, are called *milites probati*, proven knights, and we find peasants 'dwelling under them'. So they seem more tied to the soil than others who merely get rents. In early years the small land fief might be linked with a rent payment, as knights could not be expected to attend much to agriculture; and this sort of assigned grant may be termed a type of money fief.[30] The knight with revenues from villein-holdings (perhaps merely the non-homefarm sector) was getting rent charges and was moving just slightly away from complete dependence. Knights had to be ready for service 'beyond or within the kingdom, wherever and whenever the abbot wants to have his own knight' (a Bury charter of enfeoffment). It has been argued that elsewhere, but not in England, the *fief-rente* was much used for ensuring a supply of castle guard, a duty much suited for lesser knights. However, *Domesday* shows knights gathered in the largest numbers in Sussex, Kent and Herefordshire, counties of strategic importance.[31]

Equipment must have been a worrying matter for the small knight. Under Stephen the knight tended to have a low status and was often linked with crossbowmen. Common rustic knights fought beside mercenaries or hired knights; and the upper knights were distinguished as 'belted military men', paired with bishops, 'finely equipt', or 'highly equipt'. Yet, about 1150, the knight's equipment was simple compared with what it was a century later. A writer of the 1210s speaking of the 1150s, remarked, 'The world was not then so proud as in our days. A king's son would ride with his cape bundled up, without any more equipage; now there is hardly a squire who doesn't want a baggage-horse.'[32]

The early years of Henry II's reign saw a crucial change in knightly status, making the cleavage between the higher and the lower levels more acute. Late twelfth century feodaries say, 'Five hides make the knight's fee.' The century had seen an extension of cultivation, plus an increase in hereditary tenures, which weakened the lord's juridical control.[33] Knights with nothing but rent from a small piece of land suffered badly. Military service ceased to be their prime function and became an imposed burden. Not that there was any lessening of the need for fighters. The wars about the inheritance in Anjou and Aquitaine demanded more men than ever, and also more equipment and supplies; transport costs were high and campaigns were long. The small knight was incapable of fighting in such wars. Indeed many of them were by now liable only for a fraction of their former services. A fragmentation of twelfth-century tenures had gone on, which has been explained as being the result of a lack of male heirs and of devolution upon heiresses, and the effect of sales, farmings-out and family commitments, but which was generally produced by the whole trend of feudalism we have been tracing. The small knight's economic basis was insufficient to keep him equipped and active in a world of rising prices and increasingly expensive weapons. The vavasour knight insisted that his land, even if it stayed undivided, was inadequate for the provision of a full knight.

Fractional fees existed quite early, perhaps deliberately introduced; thus at Canterbury in 1090 and at Rochester several knights got together to provide one ready for service. The knight seems to be feeling already a pull between his role as soldier and that as land-holder anxious to hold his own in the developing agricultural situation. Pressure for fragmentation may have come from below. Also, at the lowest levels of organization, the effects of Anglo-Saxon practices persisted. On some ecclesiastical estates (Ramsey, Malmesbury), responsibility for military service may not have been complicated and 'distorted through so many stages of personal and tenurial ties usually consequent on the Conquest and redistribution from above' (Harvey)[34]. In the twelfth century, in the records of the upper and middle sections of society, we seldom meet tenants with an integral knight's fee; we find even a 'fifth part of the third part of a fee of one knight'. Large fractions of fees (half, third, quarter) might have been worked out by holders who were all on a single well organised estate; but with small, broken-up and scattered sites, the reckoning could have been only in terms of money. At a date that must be in Henry I's reign, a man and his heirs were to hold land in Warwickshire 'by a third part of the service by the yearly payment of 20's'.[35] By 1100 we saw Henry I was driven to lend aid to the small knight. The *Dialogue of the Exchequer* (by the late 1170s) deals at length with the knight in debt:

[The belted knight] When the other chattels are sold, a horse will be left to him, and it must be a trained horse, lest he who is entitled by his rank to ride, should be compelled to go on foot.

[The active knight] The whole of his personal armour, along with the horses necessary shall be exempt from distraint so that when need arises he can be employed on business for the king and realm, fully equipt with arms and horses…always supposing he is to serve not at his own cost but the crown's.

[Royal intervention] If the tenant-in-chief, who is responsible to the king, fails to pay scutage, not only his chattels but those of his knights and villeins are indiscriminately sold. For the principle on which scutage is raised mainly affects the knights, since it is only due to the king from knights and by reason of their service. Yet I myself, though not yet hoary-headed, have seen not only the lord's chattels lawfully sold for his personal debts, but also those of his knights and villeins. But the king's ordinance has restricted this practice to scutage alone...that if the knights have paid to their lord the scutage due from their fees, and can produce pledges to prove it, the law forbids the sale of their chattels for the lord's debts.[36]

We see here one of the results of the knights' tenure consisting of villeinland. By 1181 the Assize of Arms was worried at the amount of armour come into the hands of Jews. Scutage and a recognition of the knights' plight tended to disrupt the whole balance of lord and vassal in their interlinked obligations, on which feudal society depended. Near the end of the twelfth century an alternative method was devised, by which the tenant-in-chief could pay a fine, a sum fixed arbitrarily by the king, which relieved him of his entire burden of military service; its acceptance by the king authorized him to go on collecting scutage at the current rate from his sub-tenants. As usual magnates tried to use the situation to gain as much as possible for themselves, getting the money from tenants for both scutage and fine. They made a good profit especially if they were over-enfeoffed with knights, for then they collected scutage from them all. Thus, at Bury St Edmunds the abbey had fifty-two knights but owed service for only forty; so, as Jocelin of Brakelond explains: 'so often as 20s are charged upon the fee, there will remain £12 to the abbot; if more or less is assessed, more or less will remain as a balance to him'. If a baron could recover his fine from tenants, he was in the pleasant position of being relieved at no cost to himself from many onerous duties. We find the fines on the rolls described as for 'not crossing in the army of Normandy' or for 'having peace when he does not cross', or for 'leave to stay in England'; later they are merely said to be instead of his 'passage'. Later we hear of fines *pro servitio*, and the principle is then applied to service in Wales and Scotland. But whether or not the barons found the fines acceptable, the fines were primarily a device of the king to raise revenue.[37] The royal officials did not fail to note that profits were made from scutage on over-enefoffed estates. Henry I kept a close watch on such honours and asked for extra scutage: a policy carried on by Stephen and reasserted by Henry II with only partial success. As for the way in which tenants-in-chief passed scutage down to mesne-tenants, who passed it on at times to rear-vassals and even to peasants, there was much argument as to who should get the profit from surplus fees.

Scutage, payment in place of military service, was then closely linked with the existence of knights' fees, though in a broad sense it had a long history, going back to late Roman days. We must not identify it with fines for failure to carry out war duties such as the English *fyrdwite*. True commutation appeared with the expansion of a monetary economy. It is found in Germany and France in the eleventh century, in France particularly linked with the wish of the people of the communes to avoid war service; it was prominent in Normandy by 1172. It was fundamental to French feudalism by the thirteenth century; in England, relatively prosperous, it appeared earlier. Under the Confessor men were already paying wardpenny to escape commonward duty; towns could at times commute war-service by paying the crown for replacement at the rate of 20s a soldier; and castle work and even castle guard were at times commuted under Rufus and Henry I. *Domesday* states that several towns owing fyrd duty according to the five hide system of recruitment compounded their service at times for a fixed payment. However, in the late English period, Danegeld was the main military impost, looked on as a tax to be used chiefly for paying mercenaries. A Danegeld (usually 2s a hide) was imposed by the Normans until Stephen's reign, and briefly tried by Henry II; but by then it lacked its primarily military aspect and was assessed by hides and carucates rather than by knights' fees or by revenues or chattels. After 1162 the term went out, though it carried on in effect in hidages and carucates of the Angevin kings. Under the Normans many methods were used for meeting the costs of war. The *Dialogue* says that in the early period the wages of mercenaries were met by the profits from royal justice, payments for privileges, revenues from town communities; and it implies that when Henry I commuted food rents from his demesne, there too was a source of military funds.[38]

By 1100, when Henry I granted exemptions including scutage to the monastery of Lewes, his casual tone indicates that the tax was already well known. After that references to it multiply; and as we saw, the services due from many fragmented knights' fees must have been commuted for money. Scutage is mainly mentioned in church records, as ecclesiastics were particularly interested in bypassing war services and they kept many more records concerning property than did laymen. But it was as important for laymen, and by the early twelfth century, or even earlier, it was effectively displacing knight service as the basic war obligation of Norman feudalism.[39] Yet, although knight service almost disappeared, the idea of it was so deeply imbedded in feudal society that the obligation survived formally until the reign of Charles II.

The twelfth century saw a fluctuation of the wages of knights, scutage rates, and the length of war service. The interconnections are hard to show with any precision, but clearly a general crisis of feudal tenures underlay the various developments. Later scutage assessments in France can at times be related to replacement costs. Philip II had a schedule of commutation rates for barons, bannerets, knights, and squires or sergeants. Signs of a similar system can be found in thirteenth century Normandy. In England during the century after 1066 it seems that scutage rates were usually linked with the daily wages of knights multiplied by the customary length of service. But while scutage had the advantage of supplying more revenue to meet war costs, it had its disadvantage in the lack of any clear equation between the services lost and the services for which scutage money had become available. The Angevins could not recover the full cost of replacement; Richard and John tried hard to get their vassals to attend them in person on overseas expeditions. (After 1204, with Normandy lost, English barons no longer owed continental service for Norman estates.) No doubt it was the crown's difficulties in such matters that had led to the creation in the later twelfth century of the fine on barons, which we have discussed. By the late thirteenth century scutage had lost its original meaning and was just one more way of raising revenue. Tenure for military service had been thoroughly undermined.[40]

But we cannot understand this development by considering it only in relation to war revenues. The rising price of equipment, for instance, was linked with the whole rise in prices in the twelfth century.[41] Between 1050 and 1150 rents and prices seem to have more or less doubled. Then, after a while, they went up still faster. The wages of knights had to rise as well. Early evidence shows the knight getting 4d a day; in 1173 payment to castle guard rose from 8d to 1s a day; under John 2s a day had to be paid to a knight, and later 3s or 4s.[42]

A glance at agricultural prices will give us some idea of what was happening. Between 1172 and 1176 came a sharp rise in the price of cereals; the years 1178–1204 saw a slower but still steady increase, affecting the cost of provisioning households. For livestock the years 1163–83 seem fairly stable, with an ox costing 3s, sheep 4d, a cow or a bull at times 2s 8d, or even 2s, but usually 3s, and a sow or a boar bringing in 1s, though at times only 8d. With the 1180s came a rise to 4s or 5s for plough beasts, with sheep at 6d each. In 1196 the itinerant justices were told in September to see to the stocking of royal manors at set prices:

> The price of an ox shall be 4s, and of a cow the same, and of a farm horse the same, and of a fine-wooled sheep 10d, and of a coarse-wooled sheep 6d, and of a sow 12d and of a boar 12d.[43]

The restocking of 107 manors is recorded. Except for cows bought at Black Boughton for 3s, the prices paid were those laid down. Only at Sulby (Northamptonshire) were sheep with fine wool introduced. But the prices were actually set high. On a group of fifteen estates, mainly in the south-west, 3s was the rate for horses, oxen, cows and bulls; and this seems to have been the current rate for most of the country.[44] The agricultural situation was putting up the price of traction animals, including horses. By the second decade of the thirteenth century the cost of grain had doubled, and the price of livestock since 1180 had doubled or more. (Needless to say, in a medieval economy there must have been many minor variations in prices in different parts of the country; statistics are limited. But the figures cited above may be taken as showing the general pattern of price movement.)

In such a situation equipment inevitably kept on getting more costly and complicated; the common or rustic knight, *gregarius* or *rusticus*, found it ever harder to maintain his social position. The last decade of Henry II's reign saw the armour for man and his mount growing stronger and more elaborate; the knight needed a complete mailcoat and a heavier helmet. Later in the thirteenth century came plate armour.[45] The knight kept needing a stronger horse. A *Domesday* horse cost £1; a century later the heavier horse must have cost at least five times that sum; another century and it cost from £40 to £80. These prices included a certain amount of inflation, but behind them was great economic expansion, reflected in the advance of town life, crafts and trade, and in changing agricultural methods.[46] Here it will be sufficient to cite the growth of population as an example of what was happening. The growth had been going on ever since the eighth century, it seems; but the eleventh and twelfth centuries saw the maturing and converging of a number of factors that allowed the trends of the previous period to gather a new momentum. England in 1086 is estimated roughly to have had 1,100,000 people; by 1348 the number had risen to some 3,757,500; by 1377 it fell back to some 2,224,000, and by 1438 to 2,100,000. Servile status held back population. Of two villages dependent on the Benedictine priory of Spalding (Lincolnshire) in the thirteenth century, one was mostly made up of free peasants able to divide or bequeath property at will, and they married early and increased in numbers, while the other, with folk of servile status, who were unable to divide the land, saw late marriages and a dwindling population.

A break up of the demesne was going on in England and on the continent in the twelfth century. The evidence comes mainly from ecclesiastical estates: their surveys show such land as being leased out, with tenants exerting pressure to free themselves from labour services in favour of money rent. The one surviving Pipe Roll of

Henry I's reign reveals how increasingly important money had become in the administration; we find country farms rendered in money and not in kind, and so on. Not that we can ignore the demand for money and its effects even in earlier years: military tenures themselves had from the outset aimed at getting in a certain amount of money, from the tenant-in-chief down to the rustic knight. And the money bond and the feudal bond were liable to merge; the mercenaries at Bridgenorth in 1102 saw Robert of Bellême as *princeps* as well as paymaster. But generally cash transactions tended to dissolve what we have called fief feudalism, the tenures with military service.

As demesne land was reduced or leased out, less labour services were needed, so the tenants had a favourable situation for changing the form of their obligations. Not that a large amount of labour rent was not still being called for; and the customary tenants or villeins owing the services were not called servile. Rather they were distinguished from the few *servi* or *ancillae* who were cited. And they were not yet usually burdened with dues such as merchet, heriot, toll, or arbitrary tallage, whereas on the continent such dues were being asked of free as well as servile dependents. The tenants were helped in their demands for money rents by the wish of the lords for easily realized revenues, and also by the vulnerability of the ecclesiastics. A change came under the Angevins, however, a sort of counter-attack by estate lords, who sought to tie customary or villein tenants down to hereditary labour services: and the courts, concerned only about the rights of free tenants, were ready to leave customary tenants to the jurisdiction of the manor courts. The lords, seeking ready cash, did their best to exploit their private courts fiscally. In such a situation the knights had to rise higher in the social scale or rapidly sink.[47]

The better-off knight was changing from a warrior to a man of social importance in his locality, concerned with assize work and tax assessment. The change matured by mid-twelfth century, but rising prices faced these gentry knights with the same problems as the small professional knights; many fell into debt. (Distraint of knighthood seems to go back to John.) The crown tried to keep up their numbers by stipulating in 1181 that laymen with land or chattels to the value of sixteen marks should hold the equipment of a knight, and that those with ten marks should own a hauberk. But many men with military tenures had turned wholeheartedly to developing their land and taking advantage of an expanding market; so the Assize produced complaints that 'unskilled rustics, accustomed to furrows and ditches', were being against their will 'vaunted with knightly arms'.[48] The gentry knights who survived became occupied with the administration; they bore the main weight of judicial matters. They became more and more involved with the Grand Assize, which was extending its amount of business in often long and tedious procedures with continual postponements of cases. Four knights as a committee elected twelve others to serve on the jury; as their numbers dwindled, the same men had to keep on serving. They were at times even called on for juries at the petty assizes where ordinary freemen were competent to serve. And they had many side duties. If a litigant pleaded confinement to bed through sickness, four knights visited him and testified as to his condition. They inspected lands in dispute, perambulated bounds, made assignment of dower and marriage portions, made land valuations in a settlement by a final concord, or audited accounts of an estate in wardship. Transfers of cases could take up much time and be expensive.

In criminal cases they acted as coroners with manifold duties. From the late twelfth century they were given policing duties. A sheriff might commit a prisoner to their custody; they inspected the scene of a crime or a victim's wounds, which they measured. In trial by battle they kept the ring, acted as seconds, and made records of the fight. Such work had its hazards. They could be fined for wrong pleading or making a bad record of a case before a higher court; if convicted of giving a wrong verdict as jurors or taking a false oath in an assize, they could lose their chattels or spend at least a year in jail. Further, their powers were limited. Some knights astutely followed a band of robbers by noting their horses' hoofmarks (one horse was unshod on the hind feet); but when they came up, they had to wait for the king's sergeant, who arrived too late. However, they liked the sense of importance that their duties gave him. Richard Revel, a Somersetshire knight, told the court of his *gentilitas*, and how he, his father, and his brothers were *naturales homines et gentiles de patria*.[49]

We know of Revel because of a case going back to 1166 when the abbot of Muchelney enfeoffed him to carry out half the service of a single knight, with a woman for the other half. In 1206 in a Scottish campaign the two tenants failed to provide the service; the abbot was fined a hundred marks and he took proceedings against the defaulting pair; Revel pleaded that he had been ill (he died three years later); the woman (not the same as the one of 1166) had to make good the abbot's loss and was fined half a mark.

Many factors came together to turn the knight into a noble figure, so that by the early thirteenth century men of noble birth were pleased to define themselves as knight, *miles*, in documents. Only the rich could afford the arms. Further the Crusades and the advent of the military religious orders, the growth of an idealizing courtly literature, all helped to raise the knightly status and hand it over to the wellborn. 'Richard de Lucy was well aware of the higher status of those called knights in the later twelfth century, and was contemptuous of those who were not. "It was not the custom in the old days," he said, "for every petty knight (*militulum*) you care to name to have a seal." By the thirteenth century the word knight did not denote a military function; it had become a title with attendant civil duties' (Harvey).[50]

Two texts from the later twelfth century will show how the chivalric ideal was still proclaimed, and how strongly men felt the failure of the military knight to live up to these ideals. The first passage is from the *Policraticus* of John of Salisbury; the second from a letter of Peter of Blois to John the archdeacon:

(1) But what is the function of orderly knighthood? To protect the church, to fight against treachery, to reverence the priesthood, to fend off injustice from the poor, to make peace in your own province, to shed your blood for your brethren, and, if needs must, to lay down your life.

(2) I cannot bear the vaunting and vainglory of the knights your nephews...The Order of Knighthood, in these days of ours, is mere disorder. For he whose mouths are defiled with the foulest words, whose oaths are most detestable, who least fears God, who vilifies God's ministers, who does not fear the church: that man nowadays is reputed bravest and most renowned of the knightly bans...The knights of old were used to bind themselves by an oath to maintain the state, never to flee in battle, and to set the commonweal before their own life. No, even nowadays aspirants receive their swords from the altar so that they may profess themselves sons of the church, acknowledging that they've received their weapons for the honour of the priesthood, the defence of the poor, the avenging of wrongs and the freedom of their country. Yet in practice they do the contrary...

These men, who should have used their strength against the enemies of the cross of Christ, contend in wassail and drunkenness. They stagnate in sluggardy and rot in riotous living. Dragging through their degenerate lives in uncleanness, they dishonour the name and order of knighthood...If these knights of ours are sometimes constrained to take the field, then their sumpter-beasts are laden, not with steel but with wine, not with spears but with cheeses, not with swords but with wineskins, not with javelins but with spits. You'd think they were on their way to a feast, not to fight. They bear shields bright with beaten gold, as who should hope for prey rather than for hard fighting; and in truth these same shields (if I may say so) come back intact in their virginity. Still, they embroider their saddles and blazon their shields with scenes of battle and tourney, delighting in a certain imagination of those wars which in very deed they dare not mingle in or behold.[51]

There was no period when the chivalric ideal was lived up to; but when men so clearly felt the hopeless gap between the ideal and the practice, the system in question must have been badly in decay.

One aspect of the decay of knighthood was the advent of the tournament, a mixture of play-fantasy and hard-headed money making. Devised in France, it appeared in England under Stephen when, in the general disorder, knights were spurred on by boredom and excitement to fight among themselves. Thus, in 1139, the company which Stephen had left to invest Ludlow castle grew 'so arrogantly active that they couldn't keep off fighting for a moment', and arranged a tournament, which drew in a small host of knights. The knights at such gatherings galloped about wildly for days in open fields with no rules; but already we find jousts, with lists, before the *Mêlée*. Richard I legalized tournaments to raise money and help in training. But the areas where tournaments flourished were France, Flanders, Burgundy and Champagne. Good money could be made by a champion. William the Marshall and his comrade Roger de Gaugi spent two years from 1177 fighting and captured 102 knights within ten months. Henry II whose son Geoffrey was killed thus in France, forbade tournaments; but Edward I, another son and a keen fighter, approved rules which were made statutory in 1294.

The popes objected in vain. In 1179 Alexander III declared that men killed in tournament must be forbidden Christian burial. Celestine III forbade tournaments on the grounds that young men could get better training for war by fighting infidels on crusades. The development of elaborate formal devices on helmet and shield was linked with jousting. Gradually the sport grew less violent, and blunted spears were used. The joust entered into romances as a chivalric activity linked with the devoted love of a lady. The earlier aspects appear in Geoffrey of Monmouth's *Historia* where Arthur jousts with Frollo and in a three-days tournament at his court the knights 'contrive cavalry games in mimicry of war'. The full fantasy appears in the thirteenth century *Fulk fitzWarin* where 'all valiant knights who wished to tourney *pur amurs*' were exhorted to turn up and gain as prize a lady's hand and love. In general the tournament belonged to the period when the knighthood was decaying and the past being glamourized.[52]

This decay can be illustrated from records of the numbers of

knights in action in the thirteenth century. In 1230, when Henry III
made his main effort in Poitou, he had only some 400 knights with
him; and in 1242 he had about the same number. Again in 1265 some
400 knights seem the limit for any campaign. Under Edward I the
cavalry consisted at most of one to two thousand lances, and two
thirds of these were troopers: *servientes*, sergeants. In the first Welsh
war there were only 228 knights and barons with 294 troopers.
In November 1295, when there was fear of invasion, a coastguard
in Essex was organized, made up of all the knights in the county;
they number 101, of whom 11 were *impotens* (old or ill) and 66 held
land in Essex but did not live there; only 24, fit to fight, were left.
When under Edward II knights of the shire were sent to Parliament,
half of them turned out not to be knights at all. Earlier, under John,
cases in the shire courts at times had to be adjourned as too few
knights were present and they could not agree. Though these figures
do not give the numbers of men constituting the knightly class, they
are significant of what was happening to that class.[53]

As the original class of knights thus decayed or changed in
character, the idealization of the knightly role matured, largely the
work of the princely courts. There numbers of young people, *juvenes*
both lay and cleric, were gathered in the ruler's entourage; and this
group 'was the focal point of rivalry and emulation. The concept of
the prize to be gained in military or oratorical competition is
fundamental here; and the types of perfection whose characteristics
were determined by this emulation were natural points of reference
which had to be accepted by all' (Duby). In these competitions not
only was the ideal of each type developed and defined, but also the
theme of contrasts or rivalries between the two, perfect knight and
perfect clerk, was worked out. Each ideal was thus strengthened
and clarified; and by the late twelfth century a major theme in the
games played in the lady's quarters was which man, clerk or knight,
was the better one to love.

Already in the eleventh century courts the concept of holiness was
taking in elements of heroism, and heroism claiming some elements
of holiness. One ideal affected the other. After 1100 the old type of
monastic ideal was losing its central force; the *avantgarde* cleric had
to show intellectual expertise as well as skill in prayer. Abelard is the
supreme example, seeing himself as a knight of the spirit, his quests in
philosophy like conquests of a new land; he opposed his masters in
the same challenging way that young knights opposed the established
seniores who stood in the way of their reputation; he was a great, if
necessarily tragic, lover. The knights themselves now tended to become *litterati*. The ideas, ideals, and images thus developed in the
courts were diffused into all levels of the upper classes, and reached

out into the wider world beyond, finally influencing medieval society as a whole. They merged in an extended expression in the final stages of the Arthurian material.

So far we have been looking at Anglo-Norman society mainly from the angle of military tenures and of the knight's changing social status. Now we must consider the way in which the army functioned, and the role of the castle. No force in the Middle Ages was actually called the feudal army, *exercitus feudale*; the term used was simply *exercitus* or some such general word. Often an army was named after some particular campaign for which it was raised, e.g. the army of Poitou or of Ireland. There was no standing army: the only forces summoned for a particular occasion and made up of the soldiers available at the time. In general, however, what we may call the feudal army consisted of the tenants-in-chief with all the knights in their quotas, household or enfeoffed, but vacancies were filled with mercenaries in varying numbers. Besides knights there were men holding sergeantry tenures: footsoldiers, archers, light horsemen and the like. Inferior to knights, sergeants do not seem to have been included in the quota system, though sergeantry was a tenure of the same general kind as the other fees. They did not fight in a separate host, but went alongside the knights and were responsible for auxiliary services. In later times a mounted sergeant was valued as half a knight. As for the masses of unfree status, they seem to have lacked any military standing.

Knightly duties lay mainly in the host or in castle guard, though a third duty might be added, *chevalchia* or equitation. Only the heads of feudal hierarchies could summon the host, but lesser lords might call a body of men together for some specific local purpose; *chevalchia* seems roughly to cover this right and obligation. It was less commonly used in England where there were no private wars; but in the absence of a royal summons a lord might call his vassals up for peaceful activities such as escort. The king, too, might ask *chevalchia* of his vassals for some minor expedition or perhaps for a formal tour of the countryside.

The king called up the host by means of a writ to the sheriffs, to the tenants-in-chief. The knights were expected to be properly trained and equipped. The commanders might be earls, sheriffs, bishops, abbots, leading barons, members of the king's *familia*, foreign princes or mercenary chiefs. Knights tended to fight under their own lords; the units, varying in size, were combined under a man chosen for military skill as well as social rank. The later twelfth century saw units called *constabulariae* of five hundred men; but we must not antedate such forms. Constable was a term used in the Middle Ages for anyone in a position to command men: from the village constable of thirteenth century peace ordinances to the Constable of England, one of the highest royal household officers, from a ship's captain to commanders of castle garrisons – this last an early use.

Service had been for forty days in Normandy and two months in England; William seems naturally to have preferred the longer term. A record of 1130 speaks of two months in wartime and forty days in time of peace, 'as the knights of barons ought reasonably to do'.[54] Perhaps the forty days were used for training. Henry of Huntingdon, dealing with the Battle of the Standard of 1138, contrasted the inexperienced Scottish warriors with the Anglo-Norman knights whose skill was born of many exercises in times of peace. It seems that under Stephen the wartime period also was reduced to forty days, which approximated to the standard duty of the shire infantry in the later twelfth and thirteenth centuries. But in prolonged campaigns disputes could arise. Perhaps the kings avoided too precise a statement of lengths of service; there may have been a duty, explicit or implicit, to continue fighting in an emergency. Later we find long campaigns but also, it seems, reductions of quotas. But such quotas might be used even when there was no threat of long service; a third was called up in 1157 and 1191. Bargains between individual barons and royal officials show the proportion of the full service that might be accepted; a full quota seems unusual, and never summoned for service overseas.

The idea of a geographical limitation to service was found in every feudal state; hence the tendency to fall back on mercenaries for all long, difficult, or distant campaigns. England also had the problem of transport over the sea. The Norman kings seem often to have used the select fyrd for expeditions across the Channel – though on the continent the feudal host of Normandy could be used.[55]

Little is known of the sergeants in Anglo-Norman times. They covered almost every possible service from holding the king's head when he crossed the Channel (apparently to help in sea-sickness) to finding him three arrows at a hunt on Dartmoor. Henry II enfeoffed his servant Boscher with a manor in Warwickshire that had a mill and appurtenances with £5 a year; Boscher had to keep a white hound with red ears and deliver it to the king at the end of the year, then he got another puppy to rear. Under Henry I a larderer, as well as doing larder service, had to keep prisoners caught for offences in the nearby forest of Galtres, guard the king's corn measures, and make distraints at York for debts due to the king, then selling the chattels he took. He was also said to be Alderman of the Minstrels. He got 4d for every distraint as well as 5d a day, and in addition:

on Saturday for every window of bakers selling bread a loaf or
a halfpenny; of every alewife a gallon of beer or a halfpenny;
for every butcher's window a pennorth of meat or a penny;
of every cartload of fish at the bridge over the Foss 4d
worth of fish, for which they paid 4d at the price paid at the
water's edge; similarly of every horse-load of fish 1d worth of
fish, for which they paid.[56]

One difficulty is that while every military sergeant may have been
a *serviens*, certainly every *serviens* was not a military sergeant; and
the translation of *serviens* in all documents as sergeant has brought
about an inflated notion of the influence of sergeant tenures in medieval armies. There is in fact no precise term for sergeant, as distinct
from sergeantry tenure. The earliest known such tenure appears in a
charter of about 1082 from Maine, in which, in return for the fee of
Mont-Greffier, a pantler is to serve for a month in England or
Normandy with one horse, provide the Paschal candle, and be the
champion of the granting chapter at Le Mans; the charter was given
by order of William I. Mounted sergeants appear again in a charter
of Henry I (or II) granting Wilton (Herefordshire) to Hugh de
Longchamps for the service of two light horsemen in the Welsh
wars. Indeed sergeant tenures are often associated with garrison
work in the Welsh marches or in castles such as Porchester; and the
information as to the military roles of sergeants in the Pipe Rolls
(especially of 1173–4) probably also reflects earlier practices. But by
the thirteenth century sergeantry tenures covered all free tenants not
holding by knight-service, frankalmoign or socage. Perhaps they were
an invention of royal officials of the later twelfth century, who
wanted a category into which to put a large assortment of older
services. The precedents seem continental; yet some sergeantry
tenures show a link with Anglo-Saxon days; a sergeantry tenant at
times led the popular militia or great fyrd of a district. Cornage, a
tenure of Anglo-Saxon origin, which involved service in the vanguard
of a royal military expedition (into Scotland and Cornwall) and in the
rearguard on its return, persisted into the thirteenth century and is
later identified with sergeantry tenure.[57] Indeed sergeants were
obliged to serve only on war expeditions led by the king.

But then was the king's presence not necessary for all feudal
expeditions? No doubt he was expected to be there, but he did not
always attend. The feudal army in England was a royal one. In the
thirteenth century, however, by the time of Edward I, the king's
presence was required as one of the many limitations and specifica-
tions breaking down the simple system of military origins.

In battle the commanders knew how to make use of the combinations of foot and horse, and of reserves. Generally the infantry formed a defensive wall, from which the knights could charge; if the latter failed, they could withdraw behind the infantry and regroup. This method was employed by the Guiscard in Italy and by the crusaders in the east. The rise of the mounted soldier did not mean that footmen became unimportant, and these footmen had many of the qualities of the infantrymen who won such victories in the fourteenth and fifteenth centuries; in infantry tactics, as in so many other things, England was much ahead of the continent. So far from thinking that the Englishmen at Hastings used out-moded tactics, the Normans seem to have been much impressed. At Tinchebrai, the first major conflict after Hastings, an eyewitness, a priest of Fécamp, says that ninety-six per cent of the royal army fought on foot, including the king Henry I. Henry looked on the footmen as effective enough not only to brigade them with horsemen in each of the two leading divisions, but to take his place among them 'so that they might fight with more constancy'. His brother Robert on the other side opened the battle with a cavalry charge, which failed. The men of Brittany and Maine, posted out on a flank, then decided the issue with a mounted attack. In a smaller engagement in Brémule in 1119 Henry dismounted most of the knights under his own command; and it was this group on foot who defeated the loose cavalry attack on the French. At Bourg Theroulde in 1124, the force that stood loyal to him won a victory in the same way. The important Battle of the Standard in 1138, in which the English defeated the Scots, saw the whole of the former force, partly made up of shire levies of the fyrd and partly knights, fight on foot in a single close formation. Three years later, Stephen at Lincoln drew up part of his army on foot, and fought on foot in their ranks himself. (Dismounted knights were also used elsewhere, e.g. by the Flemish at Cambrai.)

Not that the mailed horseman ceased to be the most powerful type of warrior; at Lewes and Evesham in the thirteenth century it was cavalry that won the day. But the value of trained footmen as a solid defensive force was recognized, and measures were taken to organize them in units under capable command. In the late twelfth century we find records of constabulariae of footmen, often under the command of knights; and we see that one important use made of the lessening number of fighting knights was to put them over fair-sized bodies of men-at-arms. A century later the organization of foot units had much advanced; the men in charge of groups comparable to modern platoon, company and battalion were paid in accordance with their rank. These vintenars, centenars and millenars carried on through the rest of the medieval period.[58]

We may now ask afresh what part did the English fyrd and English ideas about obligation play in the development of Anglo-Norman feudalism. The question does not admit of a simple answer, yet without doubt the interplay of English and Norman elements was profound, complex and enduring. We have noted how the English army was both archaic and advanced; at Hastings its footmen had many of the characteristics of the infantry of the fourteenth century, in which we see a strong defensive formation with good weapons, able to meet cavalry charges and to afford adequate logistic support, and which heartened the men and gave them confidence and solidarity. The analogy holds despite changes in weapons. The later footmen had pikes, and longbows. By their time the cavalry too had had time to grow and change. William saw and made use of the qualities of the English soldiery, just as Edward I, conquering Wales, learned to know and use the Welsh archers. The final reason why the English could anticipate these later developments was that they had a degree of social unity, evolved organically out of tribal bases despite divisive forces, which in some ways corresponded to the growing national cohesion of the later Middle Ages. That cohesion was linked with the economic forces which led to the building of communes and towns, and brought interrelationships among men to a far higher level than in the eleventh century; but the element of continuity was there.

In English practice the free man had been as much involved in keeping the peace as in fighting wars; and this tradition that it was the duty of all able-bodied men to carry out police duty at local level was carried on in the Norman period.[59] Furthermore, despite differences, there was continuity of the idea of having retainers. The French term *chivaler* was not taken over; instead the English word *cniht* became in time *knight*.

We have noted how, when any united resistance had become clearly impossible, the English often rallied to the Norman king against malcontent nobles. They were in part recognizing that nothing was to be gained by anarchy, which made the lords more free to make exactions from them, but they were also in part carrying on their traditional loyalty to the king. The *land folc* supported the king against the earls in 1072, and many examples of this sort of thing could be cited from the following years. In 1088 Rufus twice called on the English, and the second time he raised a huge force, containing more English than French. (Some English, however, did join the rebels.) The first summons, directed to both French and English, may have been meant to gather the feudal host and the select fyrd (a section of the great fyrd, drawn from the inhabitants of every five hides); the second was an appeal to all freemen. By the time of Henry I the term English is perhaps ambiguous, meaning both the native English and the generation of Anglo-Normans since 1066. Henry seems to have felt, at least at certain moments, that he could trust the English more than his Norman nobles; but like Rufus he relied mainly on mercenaries. However, some English levies no doubt served in such armies as those of 1114 or 1121. Freemen of Yorkshire fought at the Battle of the Standard where the sheriff Walter Espec seems to have commanded them, the units being parish levies led by their priests. How far this was typical of the great fyrd, we do not know, but parochial units appeared in the *arrière-ban* of the continent as early as 1038 – there, however, villeins played a large part while at Northallerton there would have been only freemen.[60]

Anyway, in some form or another the fyrd carried on through the Anglo-Norman period and beyond. We meet sokemen serving *cum militibus*, with the knights; the reference cannot be to fyrd service in general and seems to touch on men of a status high enough to have obligations beyond those of the normal freemen, yet not holding knight's fees. Generally we may say that knight service tenures were linked with the territorial fyrd structure without much affecting it. In East Anglia fief tenants took over roles that had belonged to groups of freemen and sokemen; but what happened was merely that the earlier tenants dropped down to the next level in the tenurial scale.[61] The existence of two systems, to some extent superimposed, must have been a great burden on resources. Drastic hidage reductions altered the pattern of the five-hide groupings on which calling-up had been based; and the process which drove the knights up into the gentry or nobles or down to the free peasants, completed the dislocations. At the same time the mass of middling free tenants was moving towards villeinage. Reorganization was necessary, with the stress changed from hidal recruitment to customary service in war and a dropping of the other big hidal obligation, Danegeld.

What we see is a slow penetration of Norman conceptions about tenure by certain deep English attitudes. All moot-worthy men had had the responsibility of attending the shire and hundred courts; gradually the liability was attached to particular tenures. We see sokemen, through their fyrd duties, becoming men who held land by military sergeantry tenures; the levying of taxes shifted from an assessment in terms of hides or carucates to one in terms of yearly rent or income. A more exact way of measuring land values grew up.

In Henry II's Assize of Arms of 1181 England's military force was divided into four categories. The first corresponds to the feudal host. The second and third seem to represent the select fyrd cut into two levels (that of the freeman with chattels and rents of sixteen marks and that of the freemen with ten marks). The fourth brings us to the broad level of free commoners, the general fyrd. All groups are to swear fealty to the king. Their arms are specified: mailcoat, helmet, shield and lance for the first; the same for the second; hauberk, iron cap and lance for the third; gambeson, iron cap and lance for the fourth. A similar assize was arranged for Henry's continental domains; but only in England do we find an emphasis on the military obligations of all free men and a denial of arms to the unfree.

The Assize of Arms, when examined, shows underneath a strong likeness to the Old English select fyrd, with recruitment-system based on hide and carucate. The national army was serving for wages by the end of Edward I's reign; wages were the accepted basis during the fourteenth century. But in any event the duty of keeping arms and bearing them in the royal service went on being based on the value of lands or chattels. So the idea of a national territorial system based on land-value had a long and varied history. 'The Conqueror himself had been quick to appreciate its potential value, but even he could not have foreseen its crucial contribution to the stability of the Norman monarchy, much less its central role in the great tradition of territorial infantry service that extended from Edington, Maldon, and Stamford Bridge, to Crecy, Poitiers, and Agincourt, and far beyond' (Hollister).

The castle was as characteristic a Norman contribution as the fief. The few castles in England in 1066 were the work of Norman favourites of the Confessor. English society knew nothing like the private fortress with a distinctive structure. The *burhs* were larger and quite different in nature. The castles that the conquering Normans raised were built of earth and timber, and could be set up quickly, without skilled labour. Their weakness lay in the timberwork set in the earth, as it was vulnerable to fire. On the Bayeux Tapestry we see the Normans using fire weapons at Dinan against the timber. These early castles were of the motte and bailey type, and were based on elements that were later to be developed in stronger and more complex ways: mound, tower, ditch and palisade. At times a natural knoll was used, to save time and work in throwing up earth. The largest mounds have tops more than a hundred feet in diameter; three could carry halls and have been called residential mottes. The smaller ones, quickly constructed, could be as little as twenty feet across. Documents give few details except that timber was generally used. In the *Vita Johannis episcopi Tervanesis* by Walter, archdeacon of Térouanne, we find an account of a motte at Merckeghem (France, Nord):

They make a mound of earth as high as they can, and encircle it with a ditch as broad and deep as possible. They surround the upper edge of the mound, not with a wall, but with a palisade of squared timbers firmly fixed together and with such turrets set around it as are fitting. Within, they build their house, a citadel that commands the whole. The gate can only be reached by crossing a bridge, which springs from the outer edge of the ditch, and, gradually rising, is supported by double or even triple piers trussed together, at suitable intervals; thus ascending as it crosses the ditch, it reaches the mound-top level with the gate's threshold.

When the visiting bishop was going out over the bridge, the weight of the gathered people and the devil's agency made it collapse; all fell at least thirty-five feet, but the bishop's saintliness ensured that no one was hurt. The description of the flying bridge tallies with the structures spanning the ditches of mottes on the Bayeux Tapestry, which also shows a motte being constructed at Hastings. Excavations at Abinger showed the palisade, represented by an outer circle of deep post-holes and an inner circle of more widely spaced and shallower ones. The outer uprights were taller than those inside; the cross-bracing between the two series provided the basis for an inner parapet. A gap in the south-west indicated the gate, which was deliberately not right in line with the bridge foundation in the ditch. The central tower, twelve feet square, was represented by very deep post holes; it was built as a lookout tower, a vantage-point. Mortices or slots in the sides of the north and west corner-posts (preserved in the sand) showed that the vertical members were slotted for timbering that lay below the surface and stabilized the structure; no doubt the same slotting system was used above ground. Horizontal planks were slipped edgeways down continuous slots in the facing of each pair of corner-posts, forming a complete wall, edge to edge.

This motte must have been one of the adulterine constructions under Stephen, soon broken down; we have no documentary reference to it. The nearby manorhouse lasted at least until the late thirteenth century. But the structure revealed is of the early type and enables us to understand the Tapestry drawings. Here, however, the bridge was not a flying one. The lower parts of the tower framework were probably left open; there was shelter from arrows unless they were shot up almost vertically. (That technique, used at Hastings, was doubtless evolved to solve the problem of shooting into a motte.) On the Tapestry a soldier at the foot of Dinan castle passes his arm behind the lefthand corner-post and it reappears on the outside of the tower; it seems the tower was a sort of box on stilts. A capital from

Westminster Hall shows just such a stilted and embattled building (1090–1100). The massive stilts are of wood, for a shielded soldier attacks one with an axe. Also, the carving shows the enclosed upper part divided into rectangles, each with a central boss and raised rim round the sides; the Tapestry gives a conventionalized version of these units. The Dol castle has rectangles treated as a chequer pattern of dark and light, and shows rims and bosses. The units cannot be hides stretched on wooden frames on account of the bosses (really raised rings with a central hole); they must be protective plates of some kind – not shields, though the idea of using them may have come from the practice of hanging shields on castle walls and the sides of ships. The holes may represent the means by which they are fastened on, or perforations in the walls. They do not seem to be loop-holes for archers; but they may have been used for thrusting out lances to defeat attempts to scale the tower.

The motte tower may go back to such works as the Romans timber watchposts on the frontiers; stilted towers of this sort appear on Trajan's Column. From Charlemagne's time there was a rash of private fortifications, which in 864 Charles the Bald ordered to be demolished. A stilted watch tower may have stood in the middle of the Viking fortresses such as that at Trelleborg, where also, in a larger scheme, we meet the palisaded ringwork of earth. Indeed a motte at east Jutland helps us further to grasp the method of construction. Large vertical posts had been put through the centre of the mound from the top to the original ground level, where they rested on a bed of sill or stone rubble to prevent lateral movement; and part of a large slotted timber was found. The main uprights were reared first, then the earth thrown up to enclose them. Indeed we can perhaps make out four kinds of motte: (1) where the superstructure rests on the mound (Abinger, Hoverberg near Cologne), (2) where the substructure rests at original ground level and is quite buried in the mound (made in wood in Denmark, perhaps at Burgh castle, Suffolk; made in stone perhaps at Totnes, with superstructure of wood), (3) where the substructure rests at the original level, but is buried only on its outside, the interior being kept as a cellar (made in wood at South Mimms; in stone at Farnham, Ascot Doilly, perhaps Wareham – Farnham had two storeys underground), (4) with a freestanding tower to which a mound was later added (Aldingbourne, Sussex, with fine ashlar facing the tower-base; Lydford, where the material of the mound covers tower windows).

The sequence is hard to determine. It has been suggested (by Bloch) that the wooden tower was primary, the motte arising as a protective mound at the base. But from the Tapestry it seems that the first two types were prevalent in the eleventh century; the third type seems to be transitional; and with stone superstructures we come to normal keeps. The Abinger type would then be the last phase of the motte, not the first. But by 1050 the first phases may have been left far behind and the Tapestry types may not represent the primitive form.[63] In the fully developed motte a palisaded bailey was added at the side.

William's reign was a great time of castle building, often done hastily, since the Normans did not feel safe without their castles. Some five or six hundred existed by 1100. The Laud *Chronicle* stresses the oppressive burden this laid on the poor; the Winchester *Chronicle* says that in 1067 when William left Odo and fitzOsbern in charge, castles were built far and wide, causing great hardship among the common folk, who must have been impressed for the digging, timber-cutting, and building. To the burden of such heavy labour were added at times when the central control slackened, all sorts of ravages. We read of Matilda and her friends under Stephen:

> She built castles over the country wherever she might to best advantage; some to hold back the king's men more effectively, others for the defence of her own people – one at Woodstock, king Henry's place of most private retirement, another at the village of Radcot, surrounded by water and marsh, a third at the city of Cirencester, next to the holy church of the religious like another Dagon before the Ark of the Lord, a fourth in the village of Bampton, on the tower of the church there, which had been built in ancient days of wonderful design by the amazing skill of ingenious labour; and she allowed her helpers to build other castles in different parts of England, from which there arose grievous oppression to the people, a general devastation of the realm, and the seeds of disorder on every hand.

The *Chronicle* of 1137 speaks even more strongly, 'And they filled the land full of castles. They cruelly oppressed men of the land with castleworks; and when the castles were made they filled them with devils and evil men. And they said openly that Christ slept, and his saints.' Without the castles we cannot imagine the full development of the baronial system and the fiefs. Back in the tenth century the raising of castles in regions like Poitou had already started off the movement in this direction; and castles had the same effect wherever they appeared.

Timber was used for a long time, especially where extended defences were needed. The new borough of Montgomery, founded in 1223, was merely palisaded; in 1278 a stone wall was built, but what timber was still sound was taken to the castle to enclose one of the baileys. In the midst of the Welsh war of 1282–3 timber was used to protect the refounded borough of Rhuddlan, and it was not superseded till the fourteenth century. But stone was used early where it was easily available: for example, at Richmond, probably while Alan of Brittany held the honour, 1071–89. Parts of the enclosing wall of Peveril in the Peak district also seem to be early, as do the fortifications at Ludlow in the Welsh marches, begun 1085–95 – a curtain wall flanked by four, small, rectangular towers and cut by a rectangular gatehouse, later incorporated in a late twelfth-century keep. London tower was probably completed before the death of its chief architect, Gundulf bishop of Rochester (1077–1108); it served as a model for strong keeps, and only Colchester was larger. The latter, also of the late eleventh century, was reared on the base of the great Roman temple. Both it and the White Tower of London had an unusually large space for the chapel, while the other floors were divided into two unequal rooms. Rochester and Dover castles of the twelfth century were comparable structures. Most rectangular tower keeps were set inside a bailey; the outer defences were not of stone till the thirteenth century.

The motte mounds were not suitable for bearing heavy weights; but in the twelfth century the palisades were often replaced by roughly circular or polygonal walls following the crest of the mound; they are usually called shell keeps. Inside was a simple tower, doubtless for long often made of timber; where there was enough space inside, a hall and ancillary compartments were sometimes added. Occasionally the shell was built from the base of the mound. At Orford in Suffolk the polygonal tower was flanked by three projecting square turrets so that the defenders could command the whole face (1166–73); at Conisborough in the 1180s we find a round tower, perhaps the earliest in England of stone, with six wedge-shaped turrets around it, serving as both buttresses and fenders. Thus we see the transition from the solid dignity of the rectangular keep to circular keeps or tower houses, always with great concern to maintain a flanking cover of continuous wallfaces, which were characteristic of the thirteenth century. By the early thirteenth century it was found possible to build round towers on the tops of mottes where the earth had settled firmly down, as on the southern Welsh marches. In the late twelfth century a new seige engine, the trebuchet, working on the tip-cat principle, had come in, with higher trajectory and heavier missiles. The area of defence had to be widened and obstacles to attacking forces added; much labour and higher costs were involved. Wards and baileys were enclosed by thick stone curtains strengthened at all salient points with projecting towers. The round or half-round towers had no doubt been suggested by Byzantine constructions seen in the east by crusaders.[64]

There was no direct correlation between the Anglo-Saxon obligation to do fortress work and the forced labour put into the mottes, though many mottes were inside towns. We may assume the Normans drove the peasants to do the building without concern for legalities. But after a while the old system may well have been invoked; in Anglo-Norman charters there was a tendency to link castle work and bridge work. The inferior fiefs rendering castle guard in late Carolingian times, which were continued in Germany and Normandy, were perhaps reflected in England in sergeantry tenures with no service but castle ward. But host service seems in general to have involved castle guard, though we meet instances where this obligation is linked with exemptions or strong reductions in host service. Often it was demanded only in wartime. Like other war services it came to be widely commuted.[65] For a big royal castle, groups and fees had to provide rotating garrisons, with control of the military aspects under a sheriff. A baronial castelry was more cohesive as a feudal unit, and the castle was often the administrative seat of a barony. An analysis of the sites, which were mainly in towns or at crossings of rivers or roads, shows that the aim was not safety in an inaccessible position; the considerations were strategic, whether for war or for the imposition of authority over a valuable area. In Normandy, where by 1172 the ducal demesne was no longer administered by vicomtes and prévôts, it was regrouped in bailiwicks, each centred and dependent on a castle.

The military strategy involved in the distribution of castles in England need not have been worked out in a system covering the whole country. Even on the Welsh marches the system may have been devised by barons not the king. William knew most of his magnates well, and, especially at the outset, he may have felt that the more castles there were, the more assured was his domination. On the Scottish border fortifications were fairly thin, no doubt reflecting the relatively scanty Norman immigration into the far north.[66] But more than a hundred castles guarded the approaches to London in a belt reaching out from twenty-five miles to fifty miles. William may have encouraged his lords to build here, but they may also have been attracted by the area. Invasion was always a possibility, but William's main need was to overawe the English. Henry II, wanting to consolidate his hold on Normandy, built castles along its geographically indecisive frontiers.

The essential characteristic of the feudal castle was its expression of power; and though this power was meant to frighten off enemies and impede them if they invaded, it was also meant to warn the people, to let them know who were their masters. The administrative system was naturally linked with the fortress which nakedly announced where power lay.[67] The medieval castle was to go through many more phases until the central government, in Tudor times, was strong enough to abolish livery and maintenance, and to end the need or right of nobles to fortify their residences. The duke of Buckingham, Edward Stafford, who refused to accept this situation, lost his head in 1521 and left his arrogant castle unfinished at Thornbury. Fortifications then became wholly a royal prerogative; Henry VIII, for example, built a chain of artillery forts along the southern and south-eastern coast. But the castles, even if an archaic survival, still had a lessened military role to play in the Civil War of the seventeenth century, as was fitting enough in a conflict that ended with the defeat of the feudal state in its last stage.

There is one more aspect of the castle, not primarily military or administrative, which must be noticed. In the eleventh and twelfth centuries there emerged a definite court culture, with common attitudes, juridical rules, manners and morality, which had its effects, not only on royal or baronial families, but also on the household knights and soldiers of fortune who were the servitors of such groups. This development was strongest in north-western France and was linked with the forces that matured fief feudalism; it involved a sense of lineage and of *nobilitas*, of a house or family with a genealogy based on strictly agnatic rules, patrilineal descent, primogeniture, and so on. It had first appeared among the princes and comital families of the tenth century, but by 1100 it had spread to the castellan families and it was absorbed by the knights – or rather by the superior section of them which we have discussed. This court culture was essentially linked with the castle; and as it spread socially, its exponents came to be persons who owned small castles or some kind of moated and defended manorhouse. Largely through the ladies in their quarters it was merged with other currents and had important literary effects, some of which will come up later in our inquiry.[68]

CHAPTER XII

STATE AND CHURCH

William took over English institutions, with their main basis in the courts of shire and hundred. He strengthened the office of sheriff, feeling that it had affinities with that of the Norman vicomte and could be made to act yet more directly for the crown. When Latin replaced English in official documents, the sheriff was given the Norman name, but no Norman vicomte was ever turned into an English sheriff. Already under the Confessor the sheriff had been growing in importance as his superior colleagues, bishop and earl, left more and more work in his hands. Now only a few strategic earldoms survived and bishops no longer sat in shire courts; the advent of church courts deprived the sheriff of influence in church pleas, but gave him more autonomy in his secular role. Also, that role was given further scope by the extension of feudal dues and by the forest laws, while, like a vicomte, he took over the duty of keeping the king's castles as well as commanding shire levies. But his biggest advance was on the judicial side. Royal writs laid down his powers more specifically, bidding him send on a case to the royal court or to assume that court's role. (Visits from royal judges, whenever they began, were very important only in the twelfth century.) Sheriffs were often appointed from among barons of the second degree, and *Domesday* shows that they were often changed. They paid a special premium to the king for the privilege of farming out the shire. As with other officials, the right of farming out tempted the sheriffs to extortion or increasing the farm with the king's permission.

The best known peculator was Picot of Cambridgeshire. The Ely chronicler complains, not only of the wrongs he inflicted on the abbey, but also of the bitter hostility to St Aethelthryth and her properties manifested by one of his *ministri*, Gervase, to whom 'he had committed the business of the whole shire'. Picot imposed a new carrying service on the men of Cambridge, seized their common pasture, pulled down their houses to make room for three mills, compelled them to lend their plough teams nine times a year instead of three. At the Ely monks' protest he sneered that he knew nothing of their saint. 'Do you hear this, O Lord, and stay silent?' cried a monk, profuse with epithets. Picot was a ravenous lion, a filthy hog, and many other beasts, with such an insatiable belly that he would share nothing, not even with God and the angels. We are told that the saint appeared to Gervase and beat him to death: 'which reveals how marvellous is God in his saints'.[1]

But though at times a sheriff might have to disgorge illgotten gains, William prized efficiency above scrupolosity and humanity. The neighbouring magnates, churchmen or lay, however, kept a jealous eye on the sheriffs. In 1075 Roger earl of Hereford revolted when William sent sheriffs to hear pleas in his earldom. Sometimes the sheriff took over management of royal estates, for which there was no regular system. The office grew in stature till there was little likeness to the *gerefa* of the eleventh-century *Rectitudines* or to the seneschal or steward of thirteenth-century bishop and baron. By 1071 local administration was wholly in Norman hands.

Under Henry I more and more expedients were devised to increase the yield from the counties. Some old shrieval families held their ground, but new men were brought in and methods were changed. The king sold the shires for sums higher than the traditional farm of royal manors; or he put in custodians who paid over, not the fixed farm, but the actual profits. Groups of counties were granted to members of the court. In 1129–30 eleven shires were jointly held by Aubrey de Vere, who had been made master chamberlain in 1133, and Richard Basset, one of the king's justiciars. But Henry outreached himself in trying to work out direct control

of the royal demesne; and many of the new men were acting as the
previous sheriffs had done, and were making the shrievalty hereditary. Still, Henry II carried on much the same shrieval system as
Henry I; the office never grew into a fief and continued to be an
appointment made by the king at his will and totally accountable
to him. The use of itinerant justices reduced the scope of shrieval
powers, but the sheriff was now firmly established as an important
servant of the king with much influence in local matters.[2]

In Cnut's reign we find grants of hundreds to laymen; eight and
a half were assigned to Emma as her dower. The Confessor granted
hundreds in various shires to religious houses; *Domesday* shows both
laymen and clergy holding shires. By 1086 there seem to be at least
130 private hundreds. In some the crown gave up almost all its
rights, though it never quite dropped control; and as the hundred
was a police unit concerned with the taking of thieves, the sheriff
never lost all his rights of supervision. Throughout the medieval
period the police and military systems of the realm reposed on the
hundredal organization. So, as the king's justice tightened its hold on
crime and the pleas of the crown became once more the crown's
affair, the lords of hundreds found themselves turned into the king's
justiciars (as Edward I's lawyers called them). When a lord was lord
of both hundred and honour, the courts of the two might be held on
the same day, but they did not merge – though some confusion
occurred when the lord held all the territory of an hundred. The
hundred courts kept their own identity and survived the honorial
courts.[3]

William carried on the English fiscal system. Unlike Edward's quiet
reign, his was full of wars, so he had to find means of expanding the
revenue; his reign was one of crushing taxation. In 1083 what seems
to have been the usual charge of 2s a hide for the geld was raised to
a crippling 6s. The sheriffs had the main task of getting in the
revenue, but more specialized financial officials appear under Henry
I. The treasury was still at Winchester, with accounting done by
split sticks, tallies, on which the sums were recorded by notches.
Revenue was under the control of a Norman master chamberlain –
though England had its separate official until 1087 when Tinchebrai
reunited it with Normandy. At some date in the Norman era finance
came under two chamberlains of the treasury. In Henry I's reign
appeared a new head, the treasurer, who became one of the great
state officers, while the master chamberlain carried on as head of
the royal bedchamber.

The Latin term *scaccarium*, first found in 1110, gave its name
during the century to the Exchequer. Meaning a chessboard, it

referred to the chequered cloth over the table where the counters were set. Calculation was now done by the abacus, a frame with bells strung on wire, brought in from Laon or Lotharingia. (Arithmetical calculations on the Arabian system were coming into use in the twelfth century; but a gadget like the abacus, which made the processes of addition and subtraction visible, was better suited to illiterate laymen.) William's need of money made his agents sharp and forceful in collecting revenues; their efficiency was reflected in their thoroughness and their record-keeping. Feudal incidents were increased. Their profitability to the crown now and for centuries to come was shown by the way they went on being exacted long after military fiefs became obsolete. Henry VIII set up a new court to exploit them systematically; and after the Cromwellian revolution, in 1660, the Restoration was linked with an act confessing that 'the Courts of Wards and Liveries and Tenures by Knight-Service either of the King or others...and the consequents upon the same have been much more burdensome, grievous and prejudicial to the Kingdom than they have been beneficial to the King'. Thus only under Charles II was there a formal renunciation of feudal dues; in France they continued till the Great Revolution.[4] William was much taken up with adding to revenue through taxes and dues of all kinds, but neither he nor his sons issued any law codes like those of the English kings. Their chief innovations were the forest laws, the creation of separate church courts, and the regulation against murder aimed at protecting Normans from attack. The English kings had owned their own chases; but these were now much extended. The royal forests were not wholly woodland; they were reserves set aside for the king under special regulations. Certainly he hunted there, but he also used the system to raise money. The Hampshire reserve was widened to make up the New Forest, with much depopulation on the outskirts; some 2,000 people are said to have been driven out and 20,000 acres added to an already sparsely populated area of 75,000 acres. These forests were usually open to certain agricultural uses; the king got revenue from pannage, a rent for pasturing swine and other beasts, and from fines for purprestures, which worked out as land rents.

William brought in a forest law of Frankish origin to protect his hunting and applied it, in addition to existing laws, across vast tracts. By Henry I's time all Essex was forest, and few counties lacked wide preserves. Penalties for taking deer or boar grew steadily harsher, and special officials enforced the laws. The nobles disliked the royal forests which limited their own; the church was annoyed at the disregard of its privileges; the people hated the harassments and penalties, the obstructions of agriculture and the closing off of a food supply. But the kings mercilessly defended their forests at all costs as sources of food, sport and revenue. In many districts lords put peasants to work on deer hedges, building temporary hunting lodges or making drives. We meet a Wealden obligation to erect a *sumerhus* (probably under William).[5] Blinding and castration were the common fate of those convicted of destroying game, but the Angevins preferred fines. The limits of expansion seem to have come under Henry III, when nearly a third of the realm became a royal game preserve, with only Norfolk, Suffolk, and Kent unaffected. Under Henry III itinerant justices held pleas of the forest every three years, and in the next century every five years, so an accused man might spend years in jail before being tried.

In the development of the whole governmental system a key part was played by the court, *curia*, which in the Norman period was generally a small group of servants dealing with judicial, financial and administrative matters. Men of this sort usually attested the writs of William II and Henry I. But at any time the group could take in the greatest magnates, who enjoyed the social side of the court. They had their own ideas on how things should be run, and when they were present there were likely to be arguments and discussions of the sort that would inevitably have to be carried on before any general rules of feudal law could be formulated and put into action. Many of these magnates would have known the king and his chief ministers well; some may have been reared at the curia, as often happened with the heirs of noble families because of the royal right of wardship. (An epitaph in Lincoln Cathedral refers to William de Aincurt as of royal stock and as brought up at William II's court.) At the early stage there would have been no sharp and formal line drawn between the *curia regis* where the king met and entertained his barons, and the Curia Regis from which the later departments of state were derived. The court in the eleventh and twelfth centuries was the judicial centre of the realm, the place from which writs went forth, the seat where ultimate judgments were given, and equally the place where king and barons met to feast, talk, and discuss events and problems. The group of magnates with the king did not constitute a formal court of law, but out of their meetings must have come many decisions which had important effects on all branches of the administration. It was one of the duties of the barons to give the king counsel when he asked for it.

For the most part only short and formal statements of royal acts and commands have come down from this curia regis. They scarcely ever cite any guiding principle or rule. Most come from religious houses and thus do not tell us much that we would like to know of the relations of king and barons. But we can be sure that the king often discussed with the barons such matters as the disposal of escheated fiefs, the settlement of conflicting claims to estates, and the marriage of heiresses; the decisions thus taken in the end determined the lines on which feudal practice was to develop.

Great Courts were normally held at the three great church festivals. The king sat enthroned in majesty with crown and regalia; the *laudes*, hymning his praise, were chanted; the archbishop celebrated a votive mass; and to the glorification of the anointed king was added the feasting of the magnates. There was nothing much to distinguish such a Great Council from the witanagemot, except perhaps that William held his meetings more regularly, as befitted his difficult and complex situation. In such a gathering there could be no voting. In a society which considered itself ruled by custom what was sought was a consensus, and all men had the duty to work together.

Coleman, who wrote in English the *Life of Wulfstan*, describes such a court held by the River Parret in Somerset (at North or South Petherton, both royal manors), 1070–1. A case had been brought by Wulfstan, the old bishop of Worcester, who claimed from Thomas, the Norman archbishop of York, the return of twelve villages. These had been kept by the previous archbishop, Ealdred, when promoted to York from Worcester. Odo of Bayeux and all the barons stood by Thomas; only Lanfranc supported Wulfstan. The parties took their stand and the hearing began. After the plaintiff had set out his case, Thomas withdrew with his advisers to compose an answer. Wulfstan went to sleep. His councillors woke him on Thomas's return, but he merely recited psalms while Thomas eloquently pleaded his case. He was then sent out to compose his reply, but he recited the office of *Nones*. When his men complained that there were more pressing matters to deal with, he declared that he left the justice of his cause to God and the saints who had preceded him in his see. Back in court, he was asked by William what counsel he had got; he answered, 'My counsel rests with you.' The king, moved by Lanfranc, gave judgment for Wulfstan.[6]

Slowly in the thirteenth and fourteenth centuries the Great Council, from one of its aspects, evolved into Parliament; but this evolution was not the result of a legislative act or of any conscious process of distinguishing one meeting from another; we cannot put our finger on just when and how Parliament appeared. Certainly in the earlier phases Parliament did not need the presence of the Three Estates, of the representatives of shires or boroughs; its development as a distinctive form of the Council was largely brought about by the discontent and insurgency of the barons in the thirteenth century. However that may be, 'already in 1258 a parliament has an authority, a status, superior to that of other afforced sessions of the Council, and it would appear to be a corollary, for which there is much evidence, that in parliament specially solemn acts may be expected to be performed, a higher justice administered' (Richardson and Sayles).[7]

William's household was based on that of the French kings, with steward, butler, chamberlain, constable and chancellor. The first four officials were laymen dealing with the king's food, drink, bedroom and sport. But Edward's court no doubt had had the same officials, who then held the general title of staller or placeman. As the court and its duties grew in complexity, the work of the main officers multiplied. The steward dealt with pantry, larder and kitchen as well as dining hall; the butler with winecellar and chapel; the chamberlain with laundry, bath and beds; the constable with stables, kennels and mews. As the head officials got more helpers, their positions in time became honorary. William generally did not allow magnates, apart from William fitzOsbern, to hold any of these court dignities; though Hugh of Ivry was butler. The earliest account of the household is the *Constitutio Domus Regis*, drawn up on Henry I's death in 1135 as a guide to his successor, which deals with all servants from steward to scullion. The liveries (pay and allowances) are set out. The underlying pattern is that of a medieval house divided into hall, chamber, chapel and yard. The chancellor controlled the priests and clerks of the chapel, who performed religious services and acted as secretariat. The hall (main living and dining room) was under the steward (sewer, *dapifer*) who controlled the dispensers of bread (pantry) and meat (larder), and the butler who looked after the cellar. The chamberlain supervised the chamber (private and sleeping quarters). A new servant, the treasurer, might also be found in the chamber as well as at Winchester, since the king kept some of his money under his bed. The constables in the yard, with the marshall's aid, dealt with stables, kennels, mews and policed the whole court.

> The chancellor shall have 5s a day and one lord's simnel [a loaf of best quality] and two salt simnels and one sextary [4 gallons] of dessert wine and one sextary of ordinary wine and one large wax candle and 40 candle ends.

All that was in addition to the two main meals he took in the common hall. The duties sound crude and even menial, but they led to high preferments. Most of the king's clerks gained lands, bishoprics or churches.[8]

The court travelled with the king on horses or in carts, as he was seldom still; the government of the land was carried on in castle, hunting lodge or the like, in England or Normandy. The sudden appearance of the court could be a disaster for a township. However, the financial side of government needed something more settled than this roving court. Flambard was Rufus's agent in England, and under Henry I the appointment of a permanent deputy was more carefully considered. He was to be called the chief or capital justiciar, or the Justiciar of All England; once *procurator* in a Latin document. The first holder was Roger, a Norman from Caen, who was later bishop of Salisbury, while in Normandy the bishop of Lisieux held a corresponding post. Much of the governmental system was able to carry on by its own momentum, but twice a year, at Easter and Michaelmas, the court sat round the exchequer board at Winchester to audit the accounts of sheriffs and other officers directly rendering monies, and to deal with disputes arising from them. King or justiciar presided at this special meeting of the curia, and most great household officers were present: the barons of the exchequer. Michaelmas saw the final audit. Later the meetings were held at Westminster. A statement of each account was enrolled on two sheep membranes stitched together, end to top; when the membranes were rolled up, the effect was cylindrical, as of a pipe. This pipe was the Great Roll of the Exchequer. That of the thirty-first year of Henry I is the oldest extant. In his reign the exchequer took definite shape, and was again reorganized after Stephen's. We may contrast the state of things in the German empire where there was a great lack of professional administrators; no archives were kept before Henry VI (1190-7) and no register of the chancellory till the early fourteenth century.

Writs and charters were in Latin under the second chancellor, Osmund. For his first four years William had had to carry on with Edward's clerks. Chancery clerks attending the king continued to be clerks of the chapel, and we also find clerks of the scriptorium attending justices in eyre. The scope of writs was quickly widened. William found in them a convenient way of making his will known without delay all over England. What had been a title deed became a way of sending out all sorts of commands. The writs were authenticated by the Great Seal held by the chancellor, whose authority grew with the scope of the matters treated. He remained a royal chaplain who left the administration on being rewarded with a bishopric; he had no special judicial duties. The full importance of the later office was foreshadowed, however, when in 1133 the chancellor, given the see of Durham, kept the Seal.[9]

Sealing was a classical device and by the sixth century the popes had sealed letters with a two-faced leaden *bulla*: the pope's name and number on one side, the head of St Peter and St Paul on the other. Merovingian and Carolingian kings impressed a wax seal on charters; but this meant that the parchment was cut to give the wax a grip and the seal could be easily removed. At last in the eleventh century Edward's writing office devised the pendant, a wax seal like a coin attached to a parchment strip cut at the document's foot; the king was shown on both sides seated in majesty; a position used by the emperor Otto III and his successors, but on single-faced seals. The idea of the double face, as we saw, probably came from Cnut, the head of a dual monarchy. This new kind of *bulla* was soon taken over, via the French court, by every European chancery, royal, baronial or episcopal. (The apex of seal-using was in the thirteenth century; in the fifteenth century we find jurors signing their names to inquisitions; the Tudors introduced the personal signature or sign manual into affairs of state.) William seems to have had no pre-1066 seal of his own; he took over Edward's, though on the seal's obverse he put a horseman. However, there are perhaps some signs of an occasional use of a seal under him and Richard II in Normandy.

The name and office of justiciar suggests the exchange of administrative ideas between Norman England and Sicily. In Sicily we met itinerant justices, who on account of the settled conditions tended to become justices for a particular district. Nothing similar can be found in Italy, France or Germany at the time. 'In England and Normandy, on the other hand, Henry I had established a system of judicial and fiscal visitations, which could hardly have failed to be brought to the notice of Roger II, and the relations of the two kingdoms under Henry II were such as to keep the Sicilian rulers well informed of the development of the Anglo-Norman institution' (Haskins).[10] Thomas Brown was an official both of Roger II of Sicily and of our Henry II; the *Dialogue of the Exchequer* describes him as serving Roger *in regis secretis*, in the *Diwan* or *Doanna de secretis*. Other Englishmen, Robert of Selby, Richard Palmer and Walter Offamil, were employed in the Sicilian chancery.

Feudal society saw endless disputes over land at all levels. When tenants-in-chief were concerned, the dispute called for a decision by the king, who was for them both *dominus* and *rex*. Such trials were instituted by royal writ and the judge presided as the king's deputy, with tenants-in-chief attending. Geoffrey bishop of Coutances was often appointed to hear such pleas; he and others of the period who received such appointments were not professional lawyers. Indeed we do not get men to whom that term could be applied and who may be called justiciars with entire correctness until a century after Henry I's reign. The hearings were held at the full meetings of the

shire courts where local men, including Englishmen, could pro-
nounce on the custom of the country. Thus native tradition and
feudal law were able to some extent to merge. There was not always
time to examine the many witnesses closely. So the method was used
of a sworn verdict being given by a group of men whom the court
appointed. We cannot find a definite precedent in Normandy,
though the Franks were familiar with the idea of a collective verdict,
as also were the most populated parts of the Danelaw. The origins
of the jury are lost in obscurity. but the wide use of it certainly
goes back to William; *Domesday Book* was compiled from the verdicts of juries all over England. It was returned in terms of shires,
and then the information was rendered hundred by hundred according to a list of landholders headed by the king.[11]

Domesday needs a further glance. This remarkable work is the
best testimony to the extent to which the Norman curia and its
officials had been able to grasp the nature of the English system and
to begin integrating it with their own. At Christmas 1085, as we saw,
under the threat of Danish invasion, William wore his crown at
Gloucester and the decision was taken to carry out a nationwide
survey: to record how much land was held by the king and how
much by the barons on whose knight service he depended; to discover all taxable values; to sort out questions of ownership by setting
down the positions and conditions in Edward's day, and thus finding
out just what changes had occurred. The survey was at times called
a *descriptio*, a tax assessment; but there were other aspects, feudal
and judicial, as well as fiscal. The *Chronicle* says that William
wanted to learn about his conquered land: 'how it was occupied
and with what sort of people'.[12] England was divided into seven
circuits, to be visited by royal commissioners. Only the most northern shires were to be ignored. Despite the scattering of many estates,
the information was returned in terms of the shires. The survey
was partly a book of fees, a record of the way in which England had
been parcelled out in fiefs; and it revealed how thoroughly England
had in fact become a Norman dominion. But it was not concerned
with the personal duties of vassals to lords. Indeed the extent to
which the duties of the king's barons were a controversial subject
in the twelfth century makes it clear that no detailed conditions
were imposed when William made the grants. The customs involved
were so well known at the time that they were assumed and never
put on paper; they may also have been very varied.[13]

The survey disregards many of the finer distinctions of old English
social status, and lumps the mass of cultivators, save in some eastern
counties, into two groups, *villani*, villagers with a landed stake in the

village fields, and *bordarii* or *cotarii*, cottagers, village labourers and craftsmen. We must not here read into *villani* the later colourations of the servile villein. The term is used for some groups of petty thegns holding a small estate as joint heirs, and for larger numbers of sokemen. Certainly a levelling effect became apparent immediately after the Normans took over the land; but this was the result of their general way of ordering the situation, their imposition of fief systems, and the attitudes inevitable in an alien ruling class towards a subject people. One notable effect of the levelling trend, with its ultimate heavy depression of peasant status to a servile level, was a quick elimination of the class of slaves. This was solely an economic process; no one ever set out the desirability of ending slavery. There was simply nothing for the Norman lords to gain by retaining a slave-class as well as a peasant class which they wanted to subject to as many rents in kind, labour, or money as possible. They had no use for slaves whom it would be their responsibility to maintain while putting them out to work. From the 1190s the records of the *curia regis* show the lords waging a successful fight against customary or villein tenants on the question of freedom: that is, on whether the tenants had an hereditary obligation to perform labour services.

The name given to the survey, *Domesday Book*, shows how dreadful the glare of its inquiries appeared to the men of the times. (In earlier days Leontius of Neapolis had compared the ruthless Roman fiscal system with the inexorable terrors of a last judgment; and the text of the medieval *Dies Irae* abounds in metaphors from the technical vocabulary of tax exaction.) The report enabled William to settle once and for all many of the thorny disputes about land that had kept arising throughout his settlement with its many usurpations, encroachments and high-handed transfers; the churches were always liable to have land or other valuables stolen in times of confusion, and must have become involved in many complicated lawsuits.[14]

One detail of *Domesday* terminology is worth noting, for it shows how the Norman clerks, faced with the problem of ordering the new system of fiefs and land grants, were forced to generalize and make precise definitions to replace vague terms. They called the seigneurie a *manoir, manerium, manor*. The root is the Latin *manere*, to remain, to dwell, and the term had been given a special reference to a well built house, often with defences: something less than a proper castle, but more than a peasant's home. All the Norman texts which use the word before 1066 preserve this meaning. But in *Domesday manerium* takes on a technical meaning; it refers to the seigneurie, the tenure, with the demesne, the fields, the wastes and the forests in the territory under the lord's rule. A piece of land depends on the manor; the lord's court is the manorial court.

There is here something of a new concept. Previously the Normans had spoken of the *seigneurie* of such and such a thing; the word did not include the land itself or the attached rights. In the Frankish epoch the old Latin term *villa* was used to refer to landed property. But by the eleventh century *villa* had come to refer to an agglomeration of houses – to a village as well as to a township. The diminutive *village* came later. A Norman lord before 1066, referring to his estate, would speak of 'my land, ma terre', just as speaking of his vassal, his serf or his tenant, he would say 'my man, mon homme'. The term *manerium* or manor thus has the flavour, in its English applications, of an official creation, a deliberate use of an old term with a quite new significance. The clerks used the term *manerium* because the manor house was the seat of power which endowed the attached territory with its feudal values and meanings. The English had used the term *hall* for the residence of the chief, the lord; and indeed in *Domesday* we find *hall* and *manor* used as interchangeable terms, e.g. of Ingelric, where on one page he puts men under the dependence of his *hall*, and on the next joins them to his *manor*. But naturally the foreign word served better for technical usage, as it had fewer local associations. In the processes of thought probably leading to its adoption we see how the Normans were led to generalize, simplify, and interrelate their feudal ideas and practices: when confronted with a strange country, they had to ask themselves just what had happened there, and how best they could find categories for the effective organization of the system of land-holdings that had resulted from the Conquest.[15]

As we go on, we find fines grew more and more customary, so that the greatest possible profits could be got out of justice. Further, when a man for some reason, often quite innocently, found himself embroiled with the authorities, he was adjudged *in misericordiam;* he was at the king's mercy and was amerced. By the twelfth century we get the impression from the eyre rolls that nobody, however law-abiding, could hope to escape amercements at some stage. (Eyres were the itineraries of the king's justices, and the rolls were the records of the proceedings before the justices, made by the clerks as a simple record and as a memorandum of fines imposed.) We understand why the coming of the justices under Henry II stirred such a general dread. In 1180 Leicester paid the large sum of eighty marks 'that they may be quit of murder fines and common pleas' on the visit of the judges; and later, in 1202, Lincoln, where there were eleven charges of murder, thirteen of robbery, and four of breaking peace, paid a hundred marks that they might not be interfered with in the pleadings, plus £100 compounded for licenses to settle matters out of court and for their misdemeanours. The idea of amercement may well have owed something to the Old English system of *bot* and *wite*, by which crimes were atoned for by money payments to both wronged person and the crown, according to a finely graded tariff. But if there was a link, the Norman application threw out any notion of compensation, and in an arbitrary way used the system wholly for the benefit of the king. The only cases in which fines were now linked with compensation for damages were cases of disseisin (wrongful dispossession of real property) and infringement of rights, for example by obstructing watercourses or tampering with landmarks. (Landed property was the sacred thing.) Amercements were not even imposed as penalties for crimes; they were tariffs for the profit of the state. Only minor misdemeanours such as selling wine or cloth contrary to regulation were punished by money fines. Over £25 was got in by the justices in 1200 from a group of Lincolnshire men 'for putting a woman unjustly on the tumbrel', and more than twice that amount next year for catching a fat fish, a whale or porpoise (royal prerogatives). Common law (the law of the royal courts common to the whole realm, not regional or sectional like the law of custom or the law of the honorial courts) was growing faster than the machinery of justice and policing. The burden of detecting crime rested almost wholly on the unpaid and unaided labours of the community of peasants and townsmen.

The changes made by Henry II in the legal system in the end led to our commonlaw procedure; but in these early stages the law was a crafty business, which 'certainly favoured the criminal' (A. L. Poole). 'Perhaps the rough justice meted out in Henry I's day was better suited to the times...The new procedure was little more than an expensive game of forfeits when the minimum stake was half a mark, 6s 8d. It was also a compulsory game at which heads I lose, tails you win.' You were sure to leave court poorer, whether you had attended as plaintiff, pledge, or juryman.[16] Hence the twentieth clause of Magna Carta, which tried to protect freemen, merchants, and even villeins from amercements.

Trial by battle was brought into the legal procedure, with mutilation in place of the death penalty. An Englishman, accused of theft or murder, could still clear himself by compurgation, the corroborative testimony of a sufficient number of witnesses, or by the more familiar forms of ordeal by water or fire. If there was a duel, it might have to be fought by witnesses as well. (Ordeals were condemned by the pope in 1205; but trial by battle and compurgation went on till the end of the Middle Ages, and neither was abolished till the early nineteenth century.) One of the parties might get off

by claiming that he was maimed or over sixty. Here is a record of
1202:

> Ralph the blacksmith appealed Ralph son of Jordan that he
> infringed the peace of the lord king and basely assaulted Agnes
> his wife and robbed her of 5s and 3 rings and 2 silver brooches,
> and he gave her a wound in the head, and besides that he broke
> the window of her house, and this he offers to prove against him
> in the consideration of the court as of his sight and hearing. And
> Ralph defends the whole. And it is considered that there be a
> duel between them, because the jurors bear witness that he
> raised the hue and cry and that he exhibited a little wound.
> They came armed on Tuesday after the octave of the feast of
> the apostles Peter and Paul at Lincoln. Afterwards they came
> and put themselves in mercy.[17]

That was a common ending to such ordeals. There was no fight. But
a late account says that if the disputants did engage, they must go on
battling 'with their hands, fists, nails, teeth, feet, and legs', and
Bracton considered the front teeth a valuable asset in the scrimmage.

Generally in ordeals (according to Glanville) the freeman had to
carry the hot iron, the unfree went through the ordeal by water.
The nobles seem seldom to have been required to face either ordeal.
In the Pipe Roll of 1168 we read: 'for the cost of one knight hanged
and for the ordeal of one man who failed and was hanged, 8s'. Water
was in fact the common ordeal. Both the Assizes of Clarendon and
Northampton prescribe it for all cases; and from the Pipe Rolls it
appears that only Hampshire disagreed. There in 1176 *iudicio ignis*
was substituted for *iudicio aquae* in the lists of all who failed to
pass the tests. Usually only women offenders had to carry the iron.

The church had shown itself more amenable to the Conqueror than
the lay lords; only the bishop of Durham had joined in the revolts.
The bishops might well have expected to be accepted as upholders
of the invasion which the papacy had blessed; and even the abbots
though less conforming, could not be accused of stirring up trouble.
But they failed to reckon with the fact that William, intent on creating a secular power structure based on the fief, could hardly leave
the church alone and treat it as something separate. He looked on
the church entirely as an aspect of the state; he had to consider the
bishops as instruments of government and bring them into the same
system as the secular tenants-in-chief. Besides, the Normans could not
but look on the English church in general as rather slumbrous and

old-fashioned. While admiring its treasures, they despised the vernacular of most of its ministers; and they found many churches at
important sites unimpressive. The Norman church had for some years
been committed to the cause of reform through houses like Bec, and
there was much to reform in England, where the marriage of the
clergy was perhaps even more tolerated and accepted than on the
continent. Above all, the Norman churchmen and their friends were
hungry for English bishoprics, abbeys, treasures and lands.

Not that William did much before 1070. He did not want to complicate the situation and his spoliations were limited to what he
urgently needed to reward the churches which had supported him,
and to meet his war costs. He even flattered Stigand, who thought he
had got himself accepted. A warrior-priest like Ealdred of York was
at home with the Normans; but in any event he soon died. By 1070
William no longer felt it necessary to court the English churchmen.
Shrewdly he once more drew in the papacy to strengthen his stand,
while giving Rome the illusion that it was entering the situation as a
prelude to claiming England as a papal fief. Ermenfrid, bishop of
Sitten, was sent with two cardinal priests as papal legate; he had
some knowledge of Norman affairs, having operated against Mauger
in 1054–5; and he may have visited England in 1062 with Ealdred
to carry out some agreed reforms. William could rely on him.

The legates arrived in 1070 and called the bishops, and the abbots
in their dioceses, to a council at Westminster on 7 April. Their aim
seems to have been merely to depose Stigand and the bishops he had
consecrated. But that didn't suit William. The first of his own new
men had been consecrated by Stigand, and he wanted to get rid of
Englishmen whose orders no one could challenge. Stigand was
accused of intrusion, of getting his pallium from a false pope, and of
pluralism; four other bishops, mostly with no definite charges against
them, were deposed. Only seven of Edward's bishops were spared,
and of these four or five were foreign-born. Lanfranc became archbishop of Canterbury; he nominated a monk from Bec for Rochester,
and then when this bishop died, he put in another monk from Bec.
William in all made sixteen appointments, to twelve sees; he promoted no Englishman. Already in 1066 he had made one of his chaplains a bishop in Normandy. Such appointments were an English
tradition, which he carried on. His men were mainly Norman,
though two were Lotharingian and one from Maine (probably of
Norman origin). At least a third of his sees were held by monks, and
an even larger proportion of monks appeared under his sons. He
chose his bishops and invested them with ring and staff himself,
making them his vassals. (We do not know the form used by
Edward.) Reformers declared that the investiture was with tem-

poralities only; and later Henry I had to give up using ring and staff, though he kept control of appointments. But William did not sell his sees, and in this respect was in line with the reform movement. In general he made no attempts to meddle with English customs though he formulated them more precisely. He wanted an obedient church and had no interest in putting his magnates into sees. Efficiency was his test, together with readiness to cooperate; other qualities were incidental. Walkelin of Winchester was pious, Herfast of Elmham loose-living, Thomas of York (favoured by Odo) a musician and a scholar.

Before he brought Lanfranc into the see of Canterbury, he had taken a decisive step aimed at integrating the church into his feudal order. He drew the whole network of bishoprics and abbeys into the tenurial system, imposing on all bishops and most abbots the obligations of knight service and feudal incidents. The church thus had secular as well as ecclesiastical status in a far more systematic way than before 1066, and was joined with the crown in an economic and legal dependence. At the same time, precisely because the church was now being definitely organized and was losing the loose uncoordinated structure it had before 1066, the possibilities for it to assert its independence were increased.

William had forged his power in a fairly small duchy, where he might have had trouble with individual churchmen but where the church itself could not have hoped to resist him; Lanfranc, both lawyer and theologian, had grown up in an Italy that did not yet know the reform movement, and, despite his loyalty to the papacy, his whole outlook was based on the idea of harmony between pope and theocratic ruler. Like the compilers of the pre-Gregorian canonical collections, he looked on the regional metropolitan as the indisputable centre of authority for the English church.[18] He and the king, aided by papal legates, set about creating a new order and regularity in the hierarchy. Unconcerned with English tradition, they had four sees moved, with the sanction of canon law, from backward villages to townships with a promise of growth. The bishops of Dorchester, Ramsbury, Elmham and Selsey became the bishops of Lincoln, Salisbury, Thetford (later Norwich) and Chichester. In two other cases the movement of the see did not extinguish the ancient cathedral; Bath was added to Wells in the title, and Coventry to Lichfield. There were then fifteen dioceses, and this number remained until 1540, except that Henry I added the two small sees of Ely and Carlisle, the latter in a region that William I had not effectively controlled.

There was also a scheme for developing the whole of the British Isles into a single ecclesiastical area, which would reflect the secular unification by the crown. A great difficulty here was the position of metropolitan York, and Lanfranc ran into trouble when he tried to assert the primacy of Canterbury. Thomas of York in the end was forced to accept the royal position; but his see's ancient claims to equality were so strong that Lanfranc did not profit much from his victory. As part of the wider scheme, however, York was encouraged to claim rights over southern Scotland. Wales was permanently drawn into the English system; and monks educated in England were consecrated for some Irish sees. One of them, archbishop of Dublin, even took an oath of obedience to Lanfranc. But the scheme envisaged political controls which were not established in Scotland and Ireland, and it was soon to run counter to the new canon law which wanted stronger papal assertions everywhere and did not like metropolitans with huge provinces.[19]

In 1070 William allowed the reformers to start the struggle against laxities in the church. Reforming activity in Normandy also led to the councils of 1072, 1074 and 1080: two of them at Rouen, one at Lillebonne. In England the fifteen canons attributed to the 1070 council condemned simony and the holding of two bishoprics at the same time, and bade clerics live chastely or give up their offices. In 1076 Lanfranc interpreted this injunction to mean that married village priests and deacons could keep their wives, but none in the future was to have wife or concubine. He called councils yearly, though with some intervals, and attempted a number of reforms. Not much attention was paid to lay morals except to prohibit marriage within seven degrees and to insist that the ceremony should have a priest's blessing. Procedures strengthening the position of bishops were drawn up, and laymen were obliged to accept the jurisdiction of the bishop's court, which, with the synods, was to enforce canon law. Penalties were excommunication and constraint by the sheriff.

William did not foresee any challenge to the secular power, and no sign of such a challenge was to come for many years; but the basis had been laid for an ecclesiastical independence that he did not dream of. He aimed at increasing the theocratic aspect of the kingship, not at undermining it. The separation of church courts and secular courts had worked well in Normandy, where the system was reaffirmed at Lillebonne in 1080; and William may well have felt that by clarifying what was ecclesiastical and what was secular in legal matters, he was making royal control easier — especially in England with its network of old folk law. Lanfranc, and maybe others, had introduced a book of canon law, which was used to deal with issues as they came up; but it was old-fashioned and did not raise any uncomfortable questions. William in his own way felt himself a faithful defender of canon law. 'I have ordained that the episcopal laws shall be amended, because before my time these were not properly administered in England according to the precepts of the holy canons.' But he certainly looked on the new church courts as being as much a part of his governing system as the shire courts.

The lesser offices in a diocese were now something like enfeoff-ments, territorial archdeaconries which were subdivided into rural deaneries. With their enhanced powers the bishops needed arch-deacons and officials to govern and carry out their jurisdictions. In a writ of 1072-6 they were confirmed in their sole control of ordeals, and about the same time came their separate courts, in which lay officials were ordered to give them as much help as before. Moreover, they got the profits of justice from cases that came up before them. William would have considered a church court as much a part of his governing structure as an honorial court granted to a baron; the bishop was his vassal and he himself through unction was a representative of God. In the *Tractores* written by an un-named Norman about 1100 the power of the king is exalted; by unction he is sacramentally transformed; he is *christus Domini*; he has been turned into a *sanctus*; and his office is in some way a re-flection of God's own authority. Somewhat later the mosaic in Martorana church at Palermo shows Roger II getting his kingdom direct from the hands of Christ himself. Such ideas of Christ-centred kingship were weakening in the later eleventh century; but con-quering Norman rulers like William held fast to them. We noted earlier how he was hailed by specific royal *laudes*; in these litanies the Virgin Mary, St Michael and St Raphael were invoked on his behalf; and he was thus recognized as one of the few divinely ap-pointed rulers of western Christendom.[20]

Though the situation had not yet been reached when an open conflict between church and state in England could break out, there were moments of strain, showing the lines on which dispute was sure to emerge sooner or later. After Hastings a papal legate in Normandy drew up an elaborate code of penances for every man killed in the battle, with a severity that varied according to the status and motives of the killer; there were also penances for wound-ings and killings before or after the battle. We cannot believe that these injunctions were ever seriously applied; but they bring out the way in which Rome considered itself to have been in ultimate con-trol of the operations. In the years 1079-81 Pope Gregory (Hilde-brand), seeing that William was meeting setbacks on the continent, tried to exert pressure. Exultant at having humiliated the German emperor, he felt that he could at last deal with William. He de-manded Lanfranc's appearance at Rome; he put the province of

Rouen with Sens under the primacy of Lyon; he asked for the payment of the interrupted Peter's Pence; and he finally brought up the need for William to admit himself a papal vassal. He was basing his case on the new canon law and hoped to have Peter's Pence interpreted as an old form of vassalage. William made a plain reply:

> To Gregory, the most excellent shepherd of the holy church, William by the grace of God the glorious king of the English and duke of the Normans sends friendly greetings. Hubert the legate you sent me, most religious father, has urged me to do fealty to you and your successors and give better thought to the money which my predecessors used to send to the church of Rome. The latter I accept; the other I refuse. It was never my purpose, and it is not now, to do fealty. I neither promised to do it, nor do I find that my predecessors ever did it to your predecessors. The money has been collected negligently during the three years I have been in France; but now by divine mercy I have returned to my kingdom, I am sending you through Hubert what has been collected, and the balance will be forwarded at a convenient opportunity through the envoys of our vassal, archbishop Lanfranc. Pray for us and the state of our realm, for we have always loved your predecessors and it is our sincere desire to love you above all others and to hearken to you most obediently.[21]

He emphasizes his point by describing Lanfranc as his vassal. He resisted the threat to depose the latter and defeated the pope on the Rouen issue despite the withholding of papal authorization of his nominee for the see; and through his opposition the papal decree against lay investiture, which had precipitated the crisis of 1074 in the German empire, did not reach England till the end of the century. By 1081 Gregory had to give way: his legates were told to restore the Norman bishops who had been suspended after William prevented them from attending a council. Gregory summed up, making the best of a bad job:

> The king of England, though in certain respects he is not as scrupulous about religion as we could wish, still shows himself to be more acceptable than other kings in this: that he neither wastes nor sells the churches of God, that he causes peace and justice to prevail among his subjects, that when he was asked by certain enemies of the cross of Christ to enter into a plot against the apostolic see he refused his consent and that he bound priests by oath to dismiss their wives and laymen to give

up the tithes they were withholding. So it is not unfitting that his power should be dealt with more leniently and that out of respect for his upright conduct the shortcomings of his subjects and his favourites should be borne with indulgence.

Eadmer set out what he saw as William's innovations. They were all concerned with centralizing church authority in his own hands and preventing the pope from gaining any direct relation with the English church. No pope was to be recognized in England without royal authority; all papal letters must pass through the king's hands; the primate could issue synodal decrees only after the king approved them, and he could not issue any in the king's absence; no baron or servant of the king could be excommunicated or proceeded against by a bishop, even when publicly defamed for incest, adultery or any other capital crime, unless the king ordered it; no papal legate could enter England without the king's invitation; bishops could enter or leave his dominions only with his assent; no appeals were to be made by the church courts to the papal curia without his permission. For the moment there was no great churchman in England who wanted to challenge such rules, and the papacy could not attack them until it had settled the investiture conflict with the emperor.

The situation changed under Rufus, not because his ideas were different from William's but because his methods were harsher and more arbitrary. He squeezed the church for money to pay his mercenaries and he made profits out of ecclesiastical estates by delaying the appointment of new prelates. Eadmer describes the situation as the church saw it:

[After Lanfranc's death] soon, not to mention other wrongs he committed, he laid hands upon the very Mother of the whole of England, Scotland, and Ireland, and of the adjacent isles, that is, upon the Church of Canterbury; and all that rightfully belonged to her within and without he by his agents ordered to be listed and, having estimated what was needed for the bare subsistence of the monks who served God there, all the rest he ordered to be taken into his own hands or let out at rent. In this way he put the Church of Christ up for sale, granting the right of lordship over it in preference to all others to whoever to the church's detriment outbid his rival in the price he offered. With miserable regularity the price was yearly renewed. For the king would not allow any bargain to be made for a term certain, but he who promised more ousted him who offered less, unless perhaps the former bidder, littering his first bargain be set aside, increased his bid up to the offer of his rival.

Moreover, you might see daily all the most odious of men, without any respect for the religion of God's servants, engaged in exacting the king's moneys, making their way through the precincts of the monastery with grim and threatening looks, giving orders on all sides, uttering threats, displaying to the utmost their dominance and power. What scandals, disputes, and disorders arose...[22]

Archbishop Anselm, though not very different in his attitudes from Lanfranc, could not but protest. Rufus replied, 'Are not the abbeys mine? You do as you like with your manors and shall I not do as I like with my abbeys?' Thus the beginnings of a deep conflict with the papacy appeared, though neither side was ready for some time to push things to a full clash.

Henry I carried on much the same policy as Rufus and William, but with the more controlled methods of the latter. A compromise was arrived at between king and pope after Anselm had been exiled a second time. 'The pope,' says Eadmer, 'while standing fast on the sentence promulgated on that matter [investitures], had allowed homages, which pope Urban had prohibited equally with investitures, and had by that concession brought the king to agree with him on the investiture question.' Stephen, we saw, through his insecure position, was driven to make unprecedented concessions to the church. Henry II hoped to turn back the tide by working with Becket as William had done with Lanfranc, but misjudged both the man and the times. Becket, on fleeing to France, widened his protest; the original argument over the powers of church courts turned into a claim to the full freedom of the English church to obey papal laws. On Becket's murder the claim was half won: Henry allowed appeals to Rome and new extra-territorial jurisdiction was instituted in England.

But in fact a much wider series of conflicts had been opened up than the direct one between crown and church: conflicts that were to have repercussions in all spheres of medieval life. First we must note that the Hildebrandine reforms, aimed at strengthening the papacy and extending its organizational controls, were not at all identical with the aims of the monastic or Cluniac movement, which were to exalt the monastic ideal and find grandiose means of expressing it. In some respects the Cluniacs preferred the theocratic system to the Hildebrandine stress on the supremacy of the pope. And indeed a wide resistance was stimulated throughout the church, which had effects in the secular world and on political theory. The lesser clergy objected, and the bishops argued that Gregory had usurped powers of legislation and powers of determining doctrine, which belonged only to general councils; he had thus lapsed into heresy and was no true pope. Then the cardinals, who had gained a strong position through the reform movement, which gave them the right to nominate the pope, wanted to extend their powers to include the right to judge all bishops. The lesser cardinal clergy were not consulted by Gregory on the investiture issue; they reacted by proclaiming that supreme power was vested, not in the pope alone, but in the pope together with the college of cardinals. Finally came the protesters who noted that, in calling on the populace to abandon corrupt priests, Gregory was in effect stimulating secular forces. The German bishops in an edict of deposition directed against him declared, 'Through you all administration of ecclesiastical affairs has been handed over to the madness of the people.' Bishops had lost their powers; discord had been 'stirred up through terrible factions' and 'spread with raging madness through all the churches of Italy, Germany, Gaul, and Spain'. (It was a long time, however, before the full results of the appeals to the people became apparent – though the new ferment did in time lead to the ideas of men like Marsillio of Padua and William of Ockham : that complete sovereignty in both state and church lay with the commons.) The position of the schismatic cardinals had further ramifications; for Gregory's attempt to turn Augustine's mystical concept of the Congregation of the Faithful into the basis for a power system led to the general relating of the various church levels to feudal hierarchies, with each group, from pope and cardinals down to the lesser clergy and the laity, possessing its own rights and dues that could not be infringed.[23]

Though 1066 brought in some sort of a diocesan secretariat and the church court, it was some time before there was much advance on the rough and ready system previously existing; the bishop and his household clerks did most of the work. By mid-twelfth century, secretariat and archives were better organized; but administration was still not much regularized and a great deal depended on the personal and direct activity of a bishop or his clerks, who were often able and cultivated men, later to become bishops or curialists themselves. At Canterbury the *familia* had an unusual character, since the monastic chapter carried out some of the duties of the see's regular officials; but from York and Chichester we see the same close association of bishop and clerks in an unformalized way. The decisive change came after the Lateran Council. Wider and more clear-cut duties emerged, with the application of the new developments in canon law; professional lawyers and secretaries appeared, bringing an end to the old kind of freelance literary man, half scholar, half ecclesiastic, such as Peter of Blois and John of Salisbury.

The new set of officials varied from diocese to diocese, and from time to time; there was not a full crystallization till the fourteenth century. Though the officials were still called the bishop's clerks, they could act as his council and executive, and they had clearly defined spheres of action.[24]

Occasionally we catch a glimpse of a bishop in his daily life. Wulfstan worked a miracle while at one of his episcopal manors, where he was consuming food rents on the spot. In one of his vills he had a cell or humble dwelling where he retired to study or contemplate, but he built no halls in his vills. Instead he restored village churches. We see that it was usual for a bishop to spend much time on his manors; what was unusual here was Wulfstan's asceticism. In the next generation we meet very different churchmen. Roger of Salisbury built so lavishly that William of Malmesbury doubted if his successors could maintain the edifices. Lanfranc built many houses in his vills, and Anselm seems to have lodged in one of them while deliberating whether to accept his see. Some monastic leases laid down that the grantee was to provide lodging and hospitality when an abbot was in the neighbourhood; such systems went back to Anglo-Saxon days.[25]

The monasteries of the Black Monks continued to be self-governing. They lay mainly in Sussex, the Fens and the Severn valley, with some nine hundred monks in all. In *Domesday* their revenues amounted to almost a sixth of the kingdom's (£11,066). Incomes varied however, from Ely with £768 to Horton in Somerset with £12. Of the nine nunneries, Wilton and Shaftesbury were the richest; they at this time expanded through the influx of ladies in distress. Nuns and monks came from the ruling class of landowners, and abbots were men of the highest rank. The monasteries were centres of wealth and political influence as well as nurseries of future leading churchmen. The last thing that monks or nuns normally did was any manual work. Far back, St Maur, who had been Benedict's pupil, remarked that since monasteries had become well endowed, monks no longer needed to work like labourers. The original idea of withdrawing – throwing off the entire network of subjections to power and money, property and possessive emotions – was thus not merely perverted: it was turned upside down, since the monks became parasites dependent on endowments and estates. Reformers kept on over the centuries trying to revive the old rule of manual labour, but their effects were always short-lived. Apart from a talented few who were devoted to illuminating manuscripts and similar work, it had become exceptional well before 1300 for a monk to work at a craft, let alone in the fields. Later, accounts rolls show that they could not even shave themselves; they had long since given up any idea of working in a kitchen or mowing the cloister garth. They kept accumulating private property, apart from the corporate property of the monastery, though just before and after 1200 popes decreed that a monk found at his death to have owned things should be buried in a dunghill in token of his damnation. To escape the interdiction of meat, monks built a chamber halfway between refectory and infirmary, where they ate meat and still claimed that it was banished from the refectory; such a room was often called a misericord.

The Normans disliked the independence and laxity of the English houses, and wanted to bring the abbeys and their estates into the feudal structure. The houses founded in Normandy under William were certainly not outside ducal control. Now the sometimes unruly English houses were subdued under Norman abbots. Many Normans were selected for the office, from such houses as Fécamp, Jumièges, Mont St Michel and Caen; Bec wielded great influence through Lanfranc; but no attempt was made, as under Edgar, to develop uniformity of observances. The rebuilding of monasteries, which often involved destruction of hallowed edifices linked with revered saints, must have deepened the gulf between Norman abbot and English monks. A side effect was to drive out the most devout, who then made new foundations. Monks from Evesham and Winchester moved north in 1074; they or their recruits refounded or created Jarrow, Wearmouth, Tynemouth, Whitby and Melrose. Houses were relatively sparse in the north, and it was at Fountains that the new White Monks, the Cistercians, made their first English foundation in 1132.[26]

There was little legislation about monks. Lanfranc's constitutions for Christ Church, Canterbury, were not meant for general use but were copied. They drew on the customs of several continental houses, modifying them to suit English conditions, but they differed little from the *Regularis Concordia* of a century earlier. Monks still kept the highest prestige in the church. It had long been held that only a very few persons would be saved, and that that few would doubtless be monks. Anselm said that heaven would more likely be inhabited by monks than by secular priests or laymen. The idea of a middle state between heaven and hell, Purgatory, seems to have been first elaborated in the writings of Gregory the Great. It was useful to the church, as it alleviated the pessimistic view that handed heaven over to a handful of monks and ascetics; it brought the mass of mankind into the scheme, in a chastened but not wholly hopeless position, in which they would surely be ready and eager to pay

M

for masses and prayers on behalf of the dead, and to give land and property to the church. St Hugh of Flavigny set out the graded hierarchy of blessed and sinful when he said that at the Last Judgment hermits and monks would come immediately after the apostles and saints, followed by the bishops, priests, and laity.[27]

The growing prestige and administrative importance of the bishops was reflected in a premature effort, recorded by Eadmer, on the part of the bishops who had been clerks, to break the links between cathedral and priory; the Normans with their drive for clear-cut definitions seem to have disliked the system of some of the reformed minsters, where the clergy were not distinctly monks or secular priests.

> Urged by the same desire, engaging in a like attempt, with one consent and accord, the bishops who were not bound to the monastic order began to exert themselves to root out the monks at any rate from the primate's see of Canterbury, thinking that if this were done, they'd have very little trouble in turning out others elsewhere...The king and other princes of the realm had been won over to this view, but Lanfranc opposed it.

At the cathedrals the bishops set up individual houses and prebends for the canons, and in time installed the system of dean, treasurer, precentor and chancellor.[27]

Monasteries, with their often scattered estates, had stewards who went round to collect produce and rents. The office rose in importance and often became hereditary; for its holders, who had little direct control over them when they worked in distant districts, were able to extend their own profits. The Cluniac houses developed a system of deans who administered properties, sometimes with stewards, sometimes without; and at times small groups of monks were sent to perform the rites on an estate church and live on part of the income. A good example of the monastic dean is provided by the activities of Osbert of Lewes priory, resident in Norfolk about 1170. Inefficiency and a weakening of controls resulted, with a breakdown of Cluniac economy in the twelfth century. The Cistercian movement thus did not merely represent a refurbishing of pieties; it also revealed the need for a more workable system of monastic economies, with increased centralization and (where sheep were brought in) a ruthless depopulation of an abbey's lands. But though the Cistercians were keen on good estate management and on sheep-farming, the monks did not do the manual work. Thus, Walter Daniel tells of Ailred of Rievaulx (1147–67) that he doubled all things in it: 'monks, *conversi*, laymen, farms, lands, and every kind of equipment', so that when he died there were '140 monks and 500 *conversi* and laymen'.[28]

For a century and a half after 1066 the invasion of England by monks from the continent went on. We have noted some of the orders in our narrative, but we need now to consider them in more detail. First came the monks from Normandy. Some were picked men, sent to govern existing houses; others were colonizers for new foundations such as Chester (Bec) and Battle (Marmoutier), or were put in to strengthen existing communities or their daughter houses, Canterbury, Rochester and Colchester. Yet others went into the small priories or cells, of which by 1200 there were at least two hundred. Lesser lords established them in a castle or near a hall, or where owners of churches felt that monks would be more edifying than a married peasant priest. But often their religious duties were few or non-existent, and their main task was to channel wealth out of England. Hence their common name, Alien Priories, and the way they later fell victims to the rising national emotions of the Hundred Years War.

Lanfranc, Father of Monks, was always ready with counsel. Foremost of the new orders were the Cluniacs. William of Warenne founded a house at Lewes, and they branched out into a number of houses directly or indirectly connected with the Burgundian mother house. Most of them were small and remained outside the general life of the land, free from feudal dependence on the king. However at Lewes, Thetford, and Much Wenlock they carried on the rich liturgical traditions of their order. After the monks came the Austin or Black Canons, based on the brief Rule of St Augustine and bringing the customs of some important church of Flanders or north France. They too were taken up by the landowners, but they concentrated on their liturgical offices in their semi-monastic groups with little concern for apostolic work. The Cistercians, the White Monks, were very different, with an austere programme of following the Rule of St Benedict *ad apicem litterae*, to the last letter. They began in Yorkshire, but spread over England and then Wales, as they were ready to tackle wastelands and remote districts. They aimed at clearing woodland, draining marshes, and introducing crops of flocks into wild places; they recruited cottars and small freeholders as lay brethren; and they thus acted as a powerful economic force in a period when concerted and informed efforts to advance productivity on the land were badly lacking. After them came the White Canons or Premonstratensians, who developed from apostolic preachers into a semi-monastic order with a Cistercian type of drive, gathering their flocks in Yorkshire and Lincolnshire.

Then there were the men of the order of Grandmont, with constitutions as complicated and harsh as those of the Old English houses had been loose; and the order of the Chartreuse which at this time was made up of two different communities: the hermit monks in small houses round a large cloister, and the lay brethren in a group of buildings half a mile or so distant. The first two Carthusian foundations were in Somerset, and they only slowly expanded. Then came the two orders born of the crusades, the Templars and Hospitallers. The Templars were a military order, and by attempting to fuse warfare and monastic discipline they were doing their best to make a single way of life out of the two most hopelessly opposed ideals of the medieval world, and to provide a religious profession for knights and men-at-arms. The originators of the order were two knights, a Burgundian and Godeffroi from St Omer; with six others they took a vow of chastity, obedience and poverty, and guarded the pilgrim ways to Jerusalem. They drew in excommunicated men (after absolution by the bishop) and thus hoped to discipline what St Bernard called the unruly rabble of 'rogues and impious men, robbers and committers of sacrilege, murderers, perjurers, and adulterers', who rushed east in search of loot and rapine. This work was to gain them the privilege of immunity from excommunication by bishop or parish priest; it was also liable to stir the suspicions of the papacy. But the order gained the enthusiastic support of St Bernard of Claivaux, and was sanctioned at the council of Troyes in 1128. Very soon it was richly endowed. Henry I gave it lands in Normandy; Stephen gave it the manors of Cressing and Witham in Essex, his wife that of Cowley near Oxford. Templars were exempted, as defenders of the church, from tithes – finally even from the action of general censures and decrees of the papacy, unless specifically mentioned. Soon they were so arrogant that they rejected all episcopal jurisdiction and formed a separate ecclesiastical organization under the pope as supreme bishop. Within twenty-five years of their foundation they were in open feud with bishops and priests, and the popes had to issue decree after decree to protect the order from violence and spoliation. (In the early fourteenth century Philip IV of France did manage to suppress them in order to grab some of their wealth.) So little then did the attempt to harmonize warfare and a meek monastic spirit succeed.

The Hospitallers were formed to help, receive, and heal pilgrims. They too became rich rapidly. Both they and the Templars set up centres for recruitment and for the exploitation of their estates and collection of revenues. But apart from the London Temple and the priory of St John at Clerkenwell the preceptories and commanderies strewn about England were small and had little significance on the religious side. Far more socially important were the quasi-religious bodies, the groups of sisters or brethren (or both) who staffed the hospitals that sprang up in the twelfth century, and who often followed some rule. Before 1066 there seems to have been nothing resembling a hospital, except perhaps in a few monasteries set in towns. The urban growth of the twelfth century, the considerable expansion of trade and of travel, the threat of new diseases, or what were thought to be new diseases, such as leprosy, created an urgent need for such institutions, which acted often as hospice, clinic, and almshouse. The experiences gained by crusaders and pilgrims in the east helped both to spread the idea and to provide forms of organization. However crude the methods, the very existence of such institutions was a great step forward.

By the end of the century the energies which had been released in and through the new orders were growing stale. More than six hundred houses of monks and canons were flourishing; they had taken over a considerable proportion of the land and potential wealth of England. The stage was set for new orders, which would be better suited to deal with a society that was developing more and more centres of urban population. These new orders were the Friars, Preachers and Minor – later called the Dominicans, the Black Friars, and the Franciscans, the Grey Friars. Now the monks were to yield to the friars the direction and development of theological thought, and so of the emerging universities.[29]

One more point, small in itself but with important repercussions: the monks, as part of their superior collective organization, had led the way in cleanliness. Anglo-Norman kings had a bath at least three times a year, before the great courts; at other times the ewerer, *aquarius*, who prepared the bath, was paid 4d for his extra duty. John, who bathed twice in 1212, and had a bath at Pentecost, only paid 4*d* for the two baths; but he took twelve between January and November 1209, and eleven in the next six months. Hot water was carried in jugs to a tub. The ewerer also dried the king's clothes when they got wet; but we find no reference to their being washed until under John we meet Florence the laundress, who, like other humble household servants, received 18*d* for shoes. The monastic tradition was against washing; Gregory the Great, following St Benedict, thought baths should seldom be indulged in by the healthy and especially not by the young. But monks were expected to wash their hands before and after meals; and many houses supplied soap and warm water three or four times a year for a bath. The head was shaved every third week and feet washed on Saturdays. In the twelfth century the priory of Christchurch had a good water supply, with settling tanks to purify, a vent to control pressure, pipes connected with the main rooms, and running water to flush the latrines (which normally were mere cesspits). Each cell at the London Charterhouse had its own water tapped from near springs at Islington. By the thirteenth century many towns had learned the lesson and had relatively efficient water supplies.[30]

A few points about the rich developments in culture during these years may be made here. Monastic libraries were much extended. Lanfranc and Anselm were learned men. They looked back mainly to early medieval ideas, but could not help being affected by the new currents, as we see for example in the *Similitudines* in which the monk Alexander wrote down an account of Anselm's conversation. Henry of Blois exemplified quite a different kind of churchman, with a wide and restless range of interests which reflect the opening up of new horizons in the twelfth century. A capable politician and a prince of the church, he was not limited to feudal ambitions as, say, Odo of Bayeux had been. In some respects he was more concerned with art than with canon law – though when he became papal legate, he used his powers to fight his own brother. He suggests the ecclesiastical prince of the Renaissance rather than the monastic magnate of the eleventh century. While intriguing in Rome in the years 1149–50, he bought ancient statues and brought them back to Winchester. None survives, but an inventory of his gifts to the cathedral show how widely he collected works of art: gospel books, crosses, frontals, carpets, embroidered tapestries, reliquaries, a font of carved Tournai marble and copper plaques, products of English, French, Flemish, Roman and Moslem styles.

There was also a strain in religious expression which broke through the more formal theology of the past and stressed a sense of emotional immediacy in worship, the total identification of the self with Christ which illuminated the deep patterns of human growth, involvement and change. Such attitudes largely threw off the old urge to self-abasement before beings of supernal power. Abelard typified this aspect of the century, which was also to be found in England. Thus, it seems sure that the most outstanding utterance of Cistercian piety, the long and ardent hymn of meditation on the name of Jesus, *Dulcis Jesu memoria*, was composed in England. 'This piece, which sums up in a few lines what Cîteaux meant for countless nameless people, has an English as well as a Cistercian context, and belongs to a strain of piety discernible in England from the school of Anselm to Richard Rolle' (Southern).[31]

The land was not yet divided up into parishes normally comprising the territory of a single village, or pair of villages, each served by a parish priest. The process had been going on for centuries, but was still far from complete. Sometimes churchmen as well as laymen built a church, and some of the evidence derives from disputes about the rights of the mother church. The local church was still rated low in importance next to the cathedral or abbey; and in view of the high estimation of monks, it was common for two parts of the tithe to be transferred to an abbey, one part being left for the incumbent; and besides abbeys, by *xenodochia*, the sick and the pilgrim might make claims on the grounds that contributions were primarily owed to the clerical militia. 'The church may hold what it possessed in common with the poor; how much more with those poor [the monks] who have left their own possessions and bearing Christ's cross not by compulsion, are following the Poor Christ.'[32] Monks thus became professional alms-takers. The early Cistercians, however, reacted against this attitude and attacked the Cluniacs and Benedictines for claiming parts of tithes. About 1160 the abbot of Darley and Lichfield in the Coventry diocese was recognized as a dean over all the churches of the abbey in Derbyshire; he was empowered to hold a decanal council of their secular clergy to stop anyone demanding more than the customary dues. In England the council of Westminster in 1102 declared: 'That monks do not accept churches without the bishop's consent nor rob the revenues of those which are given them so that the priests who serve them lack that which they need for themselves and their churches.' In 1122 the Lateran council forbade monks to take the office of parish priest; they should have their churches served by vicars. Pope Alexander III in 1179 forbade the archbishop and chapter of York to detract from the due income of the clergy serving their churches, and ordered all monks of the Canterbury diocese to present fit priests to their churches; he also wrote to the bishop of Norwich that no vicar was to appoint a substitute to perform the duties of his benefice. Honorius III declared that vicars should be forced to reside on their benefice and become priests, under penalty of losing the profits. We see that secular clerks were non-resident rectors as well as monks. John of Salisbury in the twelfth century declared:

Those who live, not to say luxuriate (as the people reckon) on the altar, don't want to be burdened with the priesthood or to serve the altar, but have introduced parsonages, the burdens of which belong by law to one man and the emoluments to another. And though the apostle says, 'He who works not neither shall he eat' (*II Thess.* 2), yet he who deserves less gets more, and enters on burdensome and outside labours.

In a decretal letter of 1199 to the archbishop of Canterbury, Innocent III protested against the usage by which the laity gave two thirds or the whole of tithes to other institutions, not to their own parish church; he required the archbishop to annul all pensions recently imposed on parish churches of his province, contrary to the canons. Canon 32 of the Lateran council of 1215 was the magna carta of the parish priest:

> A vicious custom that must be extirpated has grown up in certain parts, where patrons of parish churches, and certain other persons claiming the profits for themselves leave to the priests deputed to the service of them, such a scanty portion that from it they cannot be suitably sustained. For as we have learned for certain, there are some regions where the parish priests have for their sustenation only the fourth of a fourth, to wit, the sixteenth part of the tithes; whence it comes that in those regions scarce any parish priest can be found who is even moderately well-educated. Since therefore the altar should live of the altar: we have ordained that by a certain custom of the bishop or patron, not withstanding any other, a sufficient portion be assigned for the priest.[35]

This canon was often ignored, misinterpreted or misapplied, yet stood as the basis of the vicarage system. The perpetual vicar, instituted by the bishop and removable only by force of judicial procedure, with a separate endowment of his own, was the typical vicar of the system; even to resign a benefice without special permission was difficult. The bishops, if friendly, now had a strong weapon with which to defend the parish church against usurpations and attempt to raise it from the lowly status to which it had so long been submitted.

The abuse most generally attacked in twelfth-century councils was the inadequate service given by untrained clerks whom the monks hired. There were often grants of tithes that did not amount to the whole proceeds of a church, but which were confirmed by bishops to the monasteries as yearly pensions, e.g. of half, one, two, three or four marks, four shillings, a pound of wax or of pepper. When there was a vacancy, there was liable to be a dispute as to who got the revenues, the bishop or the monks; the monks of Evesham transcribed in the cartulary a bull to the archbishop of Canterbury, which stated that churches belonging to monastic houses were never vacant and that till parson or vicar was instituted the monks got all the fruits. The monks thus had a temptation to leave churches vacant; and churches granted to cathedral chapters were used as prebends for the canons. We can find few genuine examples of vicarages in the twelfth century; the system seems to have grown in the early thirteenth century and then rapidly expanded. In 1204 the bishop of Ely sent Innocent III, a good lawyer, a number of queries about the relations of monks and bishops. The preponderance of English examples among the decretal letters of Alexander III and Lucius III shows that canon law as a whole had only recently been absorbed in England and regarded as universally valid. The monks greatly resented the extension of the vicarage system. Matthew Paris, speaking for the abbey of St Albans, called the bishop of Lincoln the 'persecutor of the monks and the hammer of the canons and the religious', because of his zeal for the vicars. The *Liber Antiquus*, compiled about the same time, records nearly three hundred cases of vicarage ordinations in churches of monasteries and of absentee rectors; and that was not all. Thus, in October 1220 Hugh of Lincoln visited Dunstable priory and ordained vicars in five of its churches. In 1222 the Council of Oxford took up the cause of the parish priests and laid down rules by which the bishops might carry on the struggle; but even so there was still a hard fight ahead.

Norman lords detached peasants from demesne work and its obligations, and set them to collect tithes; such men were granted lands and churches, even foreign abbeys and alien priories. Walter de Lacy, who died in 1081, gave or bequeathed to St Peter's church in Hereford, which he had founded, two thirds of the tithe and a *villanus* in each of ten villages. The man granted with a tithe was at times called a *hospes*; and it has been suggested that the name derived from his function of acting as host and entertaining monks as they travelled round to collect rents. One deed of 1177–87 seems to support the idea; but there is no proof that even here, at Harlton, the *hospes* was originally given for such a purpose. The Longueville monks, who held the grant, had begun to lease out their tithes, so they no longer needed a peasant tithe-collector. In Normandy a *hospes* in a town might be a man obliged to provide his lord with lodgings, among other duties; but the term was simply used for tenant. In Normandy and elsewhere on the continent it meant a settler: *hospites* were men brought in from outside, generally in groups, and given lodging, especially on newly cleared land or land waiting to be cleared. In Normandy they had all sorts of odd duties, such as catching fish.[34]

In England tithe grants were often made without any mention of peasants, and no doubt there was often no such transfer; but at the same time there were probably many more tithe-collecting villeins than we can trace. The peasant put in a role of authority had risen in the world and grown independent of the village community. The

lord or abbey to which he was responsible might be far off; and he
would have to go over the demesne arable at harvest time, undeterred
by bailiff or farmer, to see that one sheaf in ten was taken out and
(where the usual system operated) to ensure that the parish priest got
only a third of the seized sheafs. He might have had to deal with
tithes of livestock as well. Such an agent would hardly have been
popular with his fellows, and he would have had chances of enriching himself. In the records we find these peasant agents owning two
virgates or perhaps one and a half (land for one ox); the rustics
granted to Hurley were to have eight acres each, but others have
only five and there are bordars with only two.

Domesday shows Suffolk and Huntingdonshire well supplied with
churches, but we cannot check if other areas were on the same foot-
ing. We would expect the 'free men' and sokemen of Lincolnshire
and East Anglia to judge communal needs and control resources for
building churches in villages, while in more manorialized areas the
thegn, lord of several vills, might build a church only on his chief
site of residence. But Huntingdonshire had very few *liberi homines*
or sokemen in 1086, and we do not find here the subdivisions of rights
in village churches we would expect if men had clubbed together
to build them. Certainly it is odd to find an unusual number
of churches in areas that had suffered from heathen attacks – more
than in the counties south of the Thames and west of Watling Street.
We can only assume that *Domesday* scribes used differing principles
for various parts. In Cornwall they seem interested only in collegiate
churches; but clearly there must have been churches at the seven
places named after Celtic saints, the twenty-four starting with *lan*,
the one that starts with *eglos*, and the one that ends with *circa*.[35]

Domesday is confusing also about the priests. Sixty churches in
Surrey are mentioned with no reference to priests; now and then we
meet a priest serving two villages or a church with two priests; a
manor may be cited with two priests but no church. In such cases we
may be dealing with the remnant of a collegiate minster, or one of
the priests may be the landowner who did no duty in the church.
Once in Leicestershire parson and curate seem to appear. Tithes are
rarely mentioned; only for Suffolk (and to a lesser extent for Norfolk)
do we learn much about the parson's glebe, which tends to fall into
the general pattern of peasant holdings. These churchlands are
similar to the holdings of the villeins, but a fair amount are humbler,
akin to those of bordars or cottars. One, however, at Long Melford
was an estate comparable to a small manor. Elsewhere village
churches seem rather better endowed, though there are many variations and a tendency for the churchland to approximate to some
regular agrarian unit. We have no way of estimating what dues came

in from plough alms, burial fees, and the like. At times even a resident incumbent might have to pay rent for his glebe to a lord or a monastery. Churches were often linked with mills as a source of manorial profit; we find property in a church divided like that of a mill in the same manor. Though a parson occasionally had a glebe approximating to a small manor, in general the priest was reckoned as a member of the peasant community; often, but for dues, he would have been on the lower levels. A rare example of independence appears at Abbots Bromley, Staffordshire, where Aisculf the priest gave up his holding of inland and joined with four other peasant tenants to make up the whole manor, apart from woodland, to farm, on a twenty years' lease, with a rent of 100s.[36]

The priests were almost all of English stock, though no doubt in time there were Norman priests. William of Malmesbury called the Anglo-Saxon clergy illiterate or semi-illiterate; and the same was true of the cleric *rustici* throughout the Norman period. They were given to tippling. But there were also men like Brichtric of Haselbury, Somersetshire, who, according to John of Ford's *Life of Wulfric*, was a simple pietist who painfully felt how dumb he was before the French-speaking bishop and archdeacon. He married Godia whom we meet sewing a linen alb for the anchorite Wulfric; their son Osbern, who succeeded him, was probably not married as he generally slept in the church.

It was perhaps an expression of the slow rise in the status of the ministering priest that in the twelfth century there came in the custom of giving the laity only the bread in communion, while the priest alone drank the wine from the chalice. The practice widened the gap between layman and priest, though in theory the consecration made the bread and wine each into the flesh and blood of Christ, so that one was concomitant with the other. However, the change may rather have reflected the way in which the church as a whole was separating itself from the secular world and asserting its superiority.

England had a tradition of monastic preaching at least as far back as Bede, and such oratory flourished under Cluniac and Cistercian revivals. Joscelyn depicts abbot Samson in the twelfth century setting up his pulpit in the abbey of St Edmund's and addressing the layfolk 'in the Norfolk tongue'. But he also remarks, 'How can a man who is unlettered deliver a sermon in chapter or to the people on feast days?' Bishops, seen as the successors of the apostles, were considered to possess the sole power to grant the right to preach – and that only in their own dioceses. There are many objections to anyone except the learned clergy preaching. Even by 1281 there was extreme

doubt about the capacity of a village priest to preach or teach, as we
see from the synodal decree of archbishop Peckham:

> The ignorance of the priests casteth the people into the ditch
> of error; and the folly or unlearnedness of the clergy, who are
> bidden to teach the faithful concerning the catholic faith, doth
> sometimes tend rather to error than to sound doctrine.

Still each priest over a flock should 'personally or by deputy'
expound four times a year on one or more solemn days

> in the vulgar tongue, without any fantastic texture of subtlety,
> the 14 articles of the faith, the 10 commandments, the 2
> evangelical precepts of charity, the 7 works of mercy, the 7
> deadly sins with their progeny, the 7 chief virtues, and the 7
> sacraments of grace.[37]

English nunneries had been few and mainly aristocratic; and though
a few were added after 1066, there was no real change until the
foundation of a new order, a wholly English creation though the
rule was Benedictine. The founder, Gilbert of Sempringham, deserves
a few words. He gives us a glimpse of the more humane sort of men
in this brutal world: men who sought to find some way out of the
impasse without a total surrender to monastic or eremetic seclusion.
He was the son of a small Norman knight (who in *Domesday* held land
in some half dozen Lincolnshire villages) and an Englishwoman of
lower rank. As a boy he had some deformity: perhaps the reason
why he was given a clerkly education. He progressed slowly at home,
then went to France where he won 'the name and degree of a master'. Back home, he taught country children, boys and girls. We are
told that he 'checked them from freedom of jesting and roaming,
compelled them according to the statutes of monasteries to be silent
in church, to sleep all at the same time (as if in a dormitory), and
talk and read only in appointed places'. His father at last provided
him with the livings of Sempringham and West Torrington to be
held in plurality. The young rector was not yet in priestly orders,
and had a chaplain with him at Sempringham. Perhaps he put a
chaplain or vicar into the other church. Lodging in the village, he
was attracted by his host's daughter; so he fled and lived with his
chaplain, perhaps at first taking only enough from the villagers to live
on, giving all he could spare to the poor and turning the parsonage
into an almshouse. Ordained priest, he was offered an archdeaconry,
but returned to Sempringham, where he set up a nunnery for seven
village girls by the church. He thus started off an order, the only

English one, to which his name was attached. When he died in 1189, the order had thirteen houses, of which four were of regular canons, and the rest primarily nunneries. We hear that if any Sempringham people went into another church, they were recognized by their devout manner. When a parishioner failed to pay tithes, Gilbert had all his corn taken from the barn while the man counted out the correct number of the sheaves; these sheaves were then burned on the village green, since what was stolen from God was unfit for human use. There were many tales of cures through an old stocking he wore, the cup he drank from and the bread he blessed. His prayers brought about opportune weather changes or halted a fire in London before it reached his lodgings.[38]

Gilbert, who was an excellent organizer, had added lay sisters to the nuns; later lay brothers were added on the Cistercian system, as were the Cistercian Uses for the exploitation of the nuns' property, and finally an institute of canons with the rule of Augustine. In the end he reluctantly joined the order himself as its Master; his elaborate constitutions were aimed at preventing any scandals in the double establishment of nuns and canons, where the two families dwelt each round its own cloister and a wall divided the choir between the sexes. The houses were mainly in Lincolnshire, with extensions into the north-east midlands and south Yorkshire, and a few scattered elsewhere.

There was another double order, that of Fontevrault, which was more aristocratic, with its main house at Amesbury, but it had much less appeal. During the twelfth century the Cistercians and Premonstratensians, against their original intentions, were forced to allow communities of women to use their customs, under chaplains of their order. Also Augustinian canonesses appeared and settled in many houses, multiplying throughout the thirteenth century. We see then that women had intruded far more into religious life than before 1066, though they had a subordinate position to that of the monks and did not play the active roles that came in from the fifteenth century – teaching, nursing and doing works of charity. Also, in the absence of strict enclosure, they enjoyed a certain amount of freedom.

Revulsion from the corruptions and cruelties of the world more often led to withdrawal than to educational work such as that of Gilbert. A striking example was the Wulfric of Haselbury, whom we mentioned above. He was a man of middling station, who must have had some education, since later he copied out books. Ordained before he reached the canonical age, he was priest of a Wiltshire village, Deverill, where he spent most of his time with hawk and hound. He was converted by meeting a beggar who guessed correctly the amount of money (two silver pennies and a half penny) in his purse and who blessed Wulfric for giving him alms and foretold his future. Invited to be parish priest at his native place, Compton Martin, he suffered at having to dine in the lord's hall, so went to Haselbury, a village belonging to the same lord near the southern borders of Somersetshire, and spent the rest of his life there as an anchorite in a cell by the church. Giving himself up to extreme mortification, he was famed throughout England for his prophetic and miraculous powers. Henry I and Stephen visited him, and St Bernard asked for his prayers. One day he emerged from his cell into the midst of the congregation and narrated how his sleep had been broken by a sexually exciting dream (which could be considered as inflicted on him by the devil). Once he cursed a mouse for nibbling his clothes; the mouse fell dead and 'by its death gave glory to God and peace to the saint'. But Wulfric felt remorse, sent for the priest, and confessed. The priest said that he wished Wulfric could curse all the mice of the district.[39]

Anchorites passed all their life in cells, with the sanction of the local bishop. Hermits, however, were solitaries who might stay in an enclosure or roam about, like Peter the Hermit preaching the crusades or Richard Rolle of Hampole (about 1349); they were generally males, at times hard workers, building or maintaining roads and bridges, cultivating wasteland, helping lost travellers, collecting alms for good causes, preaching and holding services in their little chapels. Recluses were often females, as we find by a study of the names. They communicated with the world only through a small window. 'Recluses dwell under the eaves of a church,' says the *Ancren Riwle*, 'so as to understand that they ought to be of a life so holy that all holy church may lean and rest upon them, and for this reason is an ancre called an ancre, and anchored under a church, as an anchor under a ship to hold the ship.' *Ancre* is in fact from the Greek *anachorein*, to withdraw. Before 1066 England had recluses and hermits; thus in 890 abbot Hartmuot was immured in four walls, with a small opening, for good, and we have a *Regula Solitariorum* by the presbyter Grimlaic, probably of the late ninth century. But the period with most recluses was about 1225–1400. Two later works on the theme were *De Vita Eremetica* by Ailred, abbot of Rievaulx (mid-twelfth century) compiled at his sister's request; and the *Ancren Riwle*, written in Middle English, apparently about 1200–25, for three sisters who in the 'bloom of life' took to solitude. But there was no authoritative book of rules. Probably the arrangements depended on the discretion of the bishop's deputy at the examination or enclosure of the postulant, the control exercised by chaplain, confessor or parish priest, and the recluse's character. Grimlaic says that youth was no obstacle. Stress was laid on the stillness of life. Ailred forbade beggars. 'Let not the poor clamour' around the cell. 'The orphan wail, the widow lament...When they know they'll get nothing they'll soon be off, tired out.' The *Riwle* says that any morsel which can be spared should be sent out secretly to the poor. But though the recluses were expected to work hard to escape the lures of lust – making their own dresses, praying and reading, especially praying – the commonest charge against them was that they gossiped. Kindred spirits visited them and they even seem to have carried on the entertainment of guests outside. Later we find them with child. At Pontefract an anchoress went out for a yearly pilgrimage. Grimlac thought it permissable for her to address a gathering from her window, outside or in the church.

Some recluses lived in a church, at times over the porch, or in a cell built up against the outer wall; some dwelt in the churchyard; others in or near busy thoroughfares of towns, or scattered in the countryside, by highways and near bridges. The cell might be a single room or have several compartments with a garden. The *Riwle* mentions as a transgression: 'I went to [the] play in the church-yard.' Most recluses were of the upper or wealthy classes, and were helpless unless someone looked after them. There had to be at least one servant to attend and cook for them. The sisters of the *Riwle* had two maidens and an occasional kitchen boy. Julian of Norwich had two servants of her own. It is hard to see how they had any soli-tude at all; indeed the *Riwle* goes so far as to say, 'Who has more facility to commit wickedness than the false ancre?' They could take fees or gifts from persons consulting them. At times anchorages were supported by endowments; and later came bequests to recluses. The Exeter ceremony treated the postulant as dying (to the world) with the office of extreme unction and a suggestion that the cell was heaven; the antiphon, 'May angels escort you to paradise', was sung as the woman went to her cell.[40]

At least to some extent the recluses of the Anglo-Norman period seem to have been withdrawing from an alien world that repelled them. Thus Christina of Markyate, born near the end of the eleventh century and dying about 1150, had to repel an attempt at seduction by Flambard when bishop of Durham; his mistress was her maternal aunt. Like most of these recluses she was of Anglo-Saxon descent; her father was one of the submerged native landowners, who combined a moderate landed wealth with commercial interests and town properties. She and her friends were patronized by powerful men and felt the hostility of their own kindred; we can understand how a sense of guilt and revulsion took the form of becoming an anchoress.[41]

We may then summarize by saying that the Norman period saw both a closer integration of the church into the state and the creation of powers in the church which were certain to lead to deepened conflicts between the two – especially when we realize that at the same time the papacy was rapidly developing its own catholic organization and its demands for independence from state controls. The growth of the parish system meant that in due time the priest, not the monk, would become the typical representative of religious self-dedication. This growth was linked with the increase in state organization as well as with the detachment of the bishop from the monastic system, since the monasteries were no longer the recruiting ground for the episcopacy or the centres of erudition. The advent of the friars left the old kinds of monasteries more and more out of the main picture, since it was they who played the main role in the universities and in missionary work among the new urban populations. The friars may thus be said to represent the transition from the monk to the priest as the key representative of the church, and to foreshadow the day when the role of the Christian would be seen to lie in his capacity to function in the world – with the Protestant conscience and direct relation to God as the final concomitant of such a role, disrupting the catholic church and its all-pervading claims. The Cistercians also represented something of a halfway house from the old monasticism to the new concept of religion in the world; they dropped alike the primitive monastic concept of a group of men living simply by their own work, and the parasitic concept of a group living on its granted or bequeathed estates; they introduced the idea of a group increasing its assets and income by economic development and exploitation. The increase of recluses we may take as a minor by-product of the dislocations we have been analysing, a by-product in which, despite the apparently greater immolation of the self, there was in fact a new wilful and self-assertive element, very different from the spirit that in the early eighth century drove Guthlac, of royal lineage, into the fens, where he saw devils in all sorts of animal forms and one night devils talking like Britons – 'at a time when the Britons, the troublesome enemy of the Saxon race, were invading and harrying the English'.[42]

CHAPTER XIII

COUNTRY, TOWN, TRADE

We have already looked at the countryside, but mainly from the angle of tenures. *Domesday* worked on the assumption that the land was divided up into estates of a manorial kind. The inquisition was meant to be made hundred by hundred, with each village finding a priest, a reeve or six villeins to provide the evidence. The name of the place was given as that of the manor, which was held by a lord. The manor was normally made up of two main sections. There was the lord's demesne: the homefarm, often small in size and generally composed of a number of strips scattered about the manor. The primary duty of the tenants was to cultivate the demesne. Administration was centred in the manor house, with steward and bailiffs directing the staff and cooperating with the reeve who represented the tenants; arrangements and regulations as to agricultural duties were made at the manorial court, which also saw that they were performed. Secondly, there were the dependent holdings of peasants with ploughs of their own. The peasants comprised *liberi homines* (free men) and sokemen, villeins, cottars, and *servi* or slaves. The first group was less closely linked with the demesne and owned property that needed to be separately considered.

The sokemen were small landowners who acknowledged a lord's *soc* (the term is Danish); in return for his protection they paid him dues which had come to be identified with rents in kind or money, or light labour services. But the lord was not lord of their land; they paid any taxes on it direct to the king. *Domesday* has some references to the obligations of sokemen and *liberi homines*, escort, guarding and carrying services owed (or once owed) to king or sheriff, and it mentions small payments due if these services were not required. Now and then the men are said to render money payments; but the reasons are obscure, since even when the sums are clearly related to the area at which the land was assessed, the figures vary a great deal. But serfdom was the essential basis of the manorial system; the manor was the means found most effective for managing an estate through compulsory labour service. It was the agricultural unit, largely self-sufficient, which brought together the exacting lord and the peasant producers in a way that enabled the lord to obtain both services and surplus. Villein was a term brought in by the Normans; *Domesday* seems to use it for the dependent peasants who had a share in the field system, while using cottar for those who lacked such a share and provided an indispensable reserve labour force for agricultural and other needs.[1]

Domesday also aimed at recording woods, meadows, pasturages, mills and fisheries. But the neat pattern did not fit. The Norman concept of the manor was, as we saw, the result of a remarkable effort of abstraction. *Domesday* itself gives much evidence of the artificial nature of the construct. *Liberi homines* have been 'added' to this or that manor in King William's time. A demesne team is at times shown to be an intruder by the fact that without it the peasants' teams exactly equal in number both the carucates at which the land is assessed and the estimated 'teamlands'. Further, there are many examples of fair-sized manors formed by the combination of small properties, which in fact must have differed little from the holdings of substantial sokemen and were probably called manors only because of the thegnly rank of their holders.[2] Apart from *Domesday* we have to rely for evidence about the countryside mainly on manorial records, which by their nature deal only with manors and which come only from part of the midlands and southern districts — in addition they largely derive from the conservative and rather static estates of ecclesiastics.

In areas with no demesne ploughs there was usually no arable cul-

tivated as the homefarm, but the lord might keep mills or dairy
farms in his control. Berkshire shows a score of small estates where
all cited ploughs belonged to the demesne. The diversity is very large.
Derbyshire villages at times were populated by sokemen; in other
places there were only villeins; in one place only bordars. Mostly
these villages contained both villeins and bordars; at times the numbers were equal, but once the bordars were in a majority. At one
site we meet five *cenarii* (rent-paying tenants), two sokemen, four
villeins and five bordars; slaves were rare.

Northumbria cannot be said to have been manorialized; we find
there villages where the people have a personal, not a tenurial tie,
with the lords, paying rents often in kind or money, and where no
strict line was drawn between free and unfree. The south-west and
the counties bordering Wales also showed a strong resistance to
manorializing trends, partly because of Celtic traditions and methods,
and partly because of the strength there of pastoralism. In eastern
England, south Yorkshire, Lincolnshire and Norfolk the manor by no
means dominated the situation; and whatever *Domesday* might
assert, Kent claimed that villein tenure was unknown inside its borders. When we look in detail at the countryside, we find lordless
villages made up of freeholders; manors with no demesne or courts,
no villeins or villein tenures, no labour services. Even in more or less
standard manors, the lord might have surrendered part of the demesne land, rents and services to another lord; and at times freeholders or even villeins held land in nearby manors and so had more
than one lord.

The village, which had been the fundamental unit of rural organization before 1066, still maintained its character. The manor was a
unit of property or of seigneurial jurisdiction, while the village was
a territorial unit, which might be inside a single manor's boundaries,
but which might also be divided among several owners – it was also a
unit of royal administration. When personal taxation was brought
in, the collectors dealt with the villages. Even in the thirteenth century, when the manor was at its height, out of some 650 villages it
has been calculated that more than half did not coincide with manors
in their bounds.

We may assume that the need to discuss their affairs and to make
the necessary arrangements and adaptations for daily life led to village moots, of which the hall moots mentioned in the twelfth
century were the descendants. Anyhow the vills remained important
in the country's governmental system because of the police duties
laid on them. Everyone had to find other persons who would appear
in court if he was charged with misconduct or debts; thus members
of a family became *borh* or surety for one another, a master for his

servants, a lord for his tenants. Also in late Anglo-Saxon times in most areas of the country every male (unless excused because of high social rank or large property) had to be enrolled in a tithing, a group of ten under a tithingman. If a member was accused of any wrongdoing, the others in the tithing had to produce him for trial or pay a fine to compensate the wronged person. In some places the tithing became identified with a territorial unit of the vill, and in matters connected with producing and punishing wrongdoers the vill became a subdivision of the hundred. The lords, who had often been granted the fines imposed in the hundred courts, did not want to be in the position of guarantors of the fine to be paid to themselves, so they wanted to escape being held responsible for their tenants' acts. They pressed their tenants to seek *borh* among their neighbours. Along these lines the customs of *borh* and tithing came together to produce what the Normans called *frankpledge*: the system under which the medieval peasants were set in tithings without the right to choose their own pledges. The commonfolk were thus bound together in a communal way that had no analogy on the upper levels of society.[3]

In *Domesday* slaves employed in the manorial *curiae* seem to be in a numerical relation to the demesne plough teams, though slaves were certainly not used only as ploughmen. In 1086 a class of workers, *bovarii*, appeared, whom twelfth-century surveys show to have largely taken the place of demesne slaves. They had the same function, but their status was now rather that of serfs. Other farm services and minor manorial offices were met out of the same sort of service holdings or base sergeantries. The strong tendency to link all services with land and to model them on military tenures played its part in this development, and was reinforced by the wish of the lords to escape all responsibility for looking after their workers, as they had to do with slaves. The apparent drop in *servi* between 1066 and 1086 was in part a mere matter of terminology; many *servi* had become bordars; others, unfree ploughmen, are often linked in pairs with one demesne plough, and appear, as noted above, as *bovarii*. But the change in terms is an aspect of fundamental social changes and the tendency to drive all dependent peasants down towards serfdom.[4]

We saw how the thegnly class was either wiped out or declined in status. Free farmers were generally forced by the addition of labour services to money rents into becoming tenants bound to a lord; or they fell in status because their land was granted to the lord. We find a castastrophic fall in the number of sokemen in Cambridge-shire: from over 700 to 213. And the same tendency is to be traced in other counties; we can perhaps see it behind the descriptions in

Domesday of the inhabitants of sokelands as consisting wholly
of villeins and bordars. By the time of Henry II the villeins, not yet
deprived of their personal as distinct from their economic freedom,
found that they were on the unfree side of the sharp line being drawn
between free and unfree.

The dissolution of slavery by the Normans was thus entirely the
result of economic developments. There is no sign of any argument
that slavery was humanly undesirable. Servile status was recognized
and defended by canon law, where we find bishops severely condemned for freeing church serfs. There was a difference here between
east and west; Theodore of Tarsis, becoming archbishop of Canterbury, had noted: 'Greek monks keep no slaves; Roman monks possess
them.' Churchmen were no more ready than laymen to free bondmen except on attractive financial terms. Anselm made an explicit
defence of hereditary servitude, seeing it as a reflection of the
principle that unbaptized babies were damned. St Thomas Aquinas
defended servitude as economically expedient. However, as slavery
became economically unacceptable, criticisms began, not of slavery
in itself, but of the slave trade. The 1102 council condemned the sale
of men into slavery. William of Malmesbury, looking back, says of
Godwin's mother: 'She was in the habit of buying up companies of
slaves in England and sending them off to Denmark; and especially
girls whose beauty and age make them more valuable, so that she
might accumulate money by this horrible traffic.' The reason why
men could not attack the principle of slavery itself was that they
found it hard to distinguish it from the principle of subjection and
servitude which lay at the heart of feudalism. Monks were in servitude to God, to what was considered the moral law; by their conscious and rejoicing acceptance of such a status they transformed
what was a matter of naked force to the slave or serf. Pope Gregory
the Great declared, 'No society could exist in any other way than if it
was maintained by such a great differentiated order'; and Anselm
of Laon in the twelfth century argued that

> servitude is ordained of God, either because of the sins of those
> who become serfs, or as a trial, in order that those thus
> humbled may become better. It would seem pride for anyone
> to wish to change that condition which has been given to him
> for good reason by the divine ordinance.[5]

William de Fougères held that labourers were created by God to
toil for the support of other men and to eat what their lords rejected.
Not till the days of Lollardism, the first embryonic stage of
protestantism, do we find a leading schoolman, Wycliff, making an

outright attack on hereditary bondage. 'It is their lust of dominion' that persuades the magnates 'it is just and natural to hold whole tribes of serfs in bondage to them and theirs, by the law of the state, as it is natural for fire to burn.'[6]

Peasant farms tended to concentrate on subsistence and to resemble one another, though for boonwork the men might get a meal of herrings or cheese now and then, or materials for clothes and tools not locally available. The usual diet consisted of foods produced within the village bounds: beer, bread, meat, eggs and cheese. The village organization is obscure. Later Anglo-Saxon laws mention a village reeve who worked with priest and tithingmen to enforce secular or ecclesiastical obligations; and *Domesday* still thus links reeve and priest. Such a reeve was never classed with serfs and at times he was shown to be superior to bordars and cottars. Saxon *gerefa* and Latin *praepositus* were used for many kinds of officials, but we may safely assume that a local community had its reeve. What is not so clear is whether they were manorial officials. Some certainly were; others seem to have been village headmen. But the distinction may have been wavering; official and headman alike would have had to deal with customary positions. Their way of performing their duties and of interpreting them would often have depended on circumstances, on the varying pressures of lord and peasants. The *Rectitudines* refer to beadle, hayward, and woodward. Beadles turn up occasionally in *Domesday*, perhaps as assistants of the reeve. These were a sort of petty constable, calling on people to fulfil their obligations, and were probably rare in 1086.

The economy of peasant holdings tended to be much more limited than that of the demesne, where the lord or his *firmarius* (farmer-out) could indulge in specialization and then exact carrying services from the tenants so that the product would reach the necessary markets. *Firmarii* were a highly varied set of men. Those of royal estates were often sheriffs, but some of them do not seem to have held that office. Perhaps, at least in some cases, while sheriff they had let out a manor to themselves to farm, and then had gone on holding it after vacating the shrievalty. In much of south England *firmarii* are found in *Domesday* renting big and valuable manors. Sometimes a great baron held land at farm. Thus Robert d'Oilly farmed a ten-hide estate, clearly because it was only six miles from the head of his own honour. And lords who were not tenants-in-chief might be *firmarii* on a large scale. But we also find ordinary leaseholders as farmers of a manor, as well as reeves and monks. (Two pre-1066 examples of monks in the office are given by the chronicler of Ramsey Abbey.) The passage in the *Anglo-Saxon Chronicle* in which William is accused of letting land to the highest bidder shows the way in which the royal estates were farmed out. (Here again we meet a pre-1066 practice; for a grant made by the bishop of Winchester to a kinsman in 902 of Ebbesbourne for a rent of 45s contains the clause: 'that no one be permitted by offering a higher rent to turn him out'.) It seems that Englishmen who were able to come into the market were forced to pay excessive rents if they wanted to gain or hold on to land.[7]

One of the landlords who early turned to careful estate management was Ernulf of Hesdin, lord of Chipping Norton and tenant-in-chief in ten counties. *Domesday* shows some of his estates stationary or even making a small loss, but those in six counties had made much headway since 1066 (or the date when he took over). In twenty-five sites on his fee, values had gone up and the total net gain exceeded £90 yearly value. Similar advances were made on some manors he held from Odo of Bayeux. William of Malmesbury says that he was 'wonderful in his skill in agriculture' – though he mentions him only in connection with the healing powers of St Aldhelm's tomb. Though Ernulf was outstanding, there were other barons concerned with agricultural efficiency or lucky in having capable officers – though again there were large numbers interested only in what they could extort from their tenants. Abbeys were beginning in some cases to realize that profits could be made by good management, resumption of demesne lands, investment in improvements, and attempts to increase yields. They hoped to use the money in lavish building, extending their own numbers, and raising their standard of living. Houses that thus made efforts to increase agricultural gains were those at Abingdon, Battle, Hereford, Lincoln, Durham and Winchester. But it was not till the Cistercians that a really thorough effort was to be seen. At the outset the increase in efficiency was probably more in methods of collection than in management proper. The abbot of Rochester arranged for himself or his successor to take a long ride into Suffolk yearly rather than lay on the monks or the poor folk of a vill the task of transporting grain.[8]

In the Norman period leases were generally for the lessee's life or for the lives of him and his wife. Until Stephen's death the leasing of estates for a specified rent was so common that it seems certain that a large proportion of estates or manors in 1086 were held by a life lease or for a term of years. Stock and land leases (under which the landlord provided much of the stock) went back to Anglo-Saxon days. But the relation of lessees and manorial tenants is not clear, though no doubt a lessee obtained the right to demand such customary services as were needed for cultivating the demesne. There was recognition of the likelihood of a farmer-out abusing his position.

In the later twelfth century clauses in leases insisted that he should treat the men on a manor reasonably and that he should not oppress them. The big landowners were certainly often mere receivers of rent, though, as we saw, some of them took a hand in running things.

In considering the role and status of the peasants we need to note the variations between nucleated villages and scattered hamlets, and in the amount of near forest. Apart from the use of forest for pasturing swine, it made peasant expansion possible. At times the denes in the Weald, which were some distance from their manors, grew into fair-sized settlements through assarting. In such places peasants were likely to grow more independent.[9] An important area of reclamation in the twelfth and thirteenth centuries was the fenland; more than a hundred square miles were saved from fen and sea. A great deal of the reclaiming work in Lincolnshire was done before 1200, most of it in the second half of the twelfth century. The next century was one of bad weather and incessant rain, which may have affected the movement, though it did not halt it, since work went on in the wapentake of Elloe until 1241 on the fen side and 1286 on the sea side.[10] We need to glance at this development since it shows us the free peasants of the period at their best, and it is likely that there was a considerable Danish strain among them.

Between 800 and the close of the eleventh century the east coast was emerging from the North Sea, but in the twelfth century a marine transgression began, worsening from 1236 onwards. Archaeological evidence supports this thesis. By the time of the Danish conquest the area round Breydon Water was used for settlement; by 1086 there were many free peasants with wide sheep pastures in the estuarine area. These Anglo-Danish settlers no doubt began the digging of turf, which was sold up to 1340. But the great flood of 1287 started off a process of deterioration that in the end brought the sea some thirteen feet higher than it had been in the late thirteenth century.[11]

An account by the prior of Crowland shows what sort of men these fen peasants were:

> So when according to the usual custom the abbot of Crowland placed his fen in defence, as used to be done every year about Rogationtide, and had publicly announced the fact on Spalding bridge, so that the men of Holland and others might keep back their livestock from the entrance to the fen, that the hay might be at liberty to grow, they were unwilling to do this, but incited each other to enter more than before. So the abbot's ser-

vants, who were appointed by custom to do this work, upon his order just as they had been in the habit of doing in other years, impounded the beasts. But the men of Holland, who are our neighbours in the northern side, strongly desired to have the common of the marsh of Crowland. For since their own marshes have dried up [each village has its own], they have converted them into good and fertile ploughland. Whence it is that they lack common pasture more than most people; indeed they have very little.[12]

These men were a disorderly crew ready to rush in and take advantage of the weakness of others, while the abbot was ready to use forged charters to grab land. We may note that there is no hint of a soke and its constituent townships; the abbey wanted to enclose and the fenmen objected, the abbot set himself up as supreme lord of the fen. Later the prior of Spalding got permission to build a great wall round the *curia* against the violent raids of the men of Deeping, who used to attack the town of Spalding across the fens and carry off the cattle of the men of Holland when they thought they could get away with it.

There was a fen reeve whose office was ancient and who seems to have been an officer of the sokes of Horncastle and Scrivelsby. We get a glimpse of how independently and unmanorially the fenmen acted in an account of sokemen from three sokes dividing Wildmore from West Fen in about 1140–53. 'These men set down the Stones and Marks as follows...' Many fen regulations were communal in origin and operation, but the lords were liable to intrude. In the great fens of the northern marches in this region they hatched an agreement among themselves in connection with demesne farming.

The size of townships in these fenlands had increased much by 1086, in part through the reclamations; but the reclamations themselves had been the result of the pressure of population on the small amount of arable available in the eleventh century. In *Domesday* the townships are among the largest in England, and a striking feature is the weakness of the lordships. Considerable proportions of tenants lived on unmanorialized land, with no demesne farm and no heavy work weeks.[13] Sokemen are found living on sokeland in manors with a homefarm, but many such manors were very small in 1086 and some were made up wholly of sokeland. Throughout we see communal activity and initiative in the methods of reclamation and fen management, and much land continued without a manorial lord, as did Kirton and Skirbeck wapentakes.

Ecclesiastical manors tried hardest to impose feudal systems of work and rent. The priory of Spalding treated its bondmen harshly and had made its sokemen unfree. On lay manors in the thirteenth century the labour services of villeins varied, but were mostly moderate or even light. There was a proliferation of small holdings among both bond-sokemen (molemen) and freemen, with whom we must place at least some of the *liberi tenentes* of the inquisitions. This came about mainly through the custom of dividing the heritages of sokemen and freemen among the father's descendants, both male and female. In some villages, a freeman carried on a craft or engaged in trade; but the majority were sokemen and molemen. The customs of partible socage, of inheriting an estate while the father still lived, and of free and frequent sales, were advantageous to the younger generation, who could marry early, beget big families, and feel little need to emigrate. Where these free customs were weaker, we find larger holdings and smaller families (with less branches), and the population growing much more slowly.[14]

The fenmen were skilled drainage engineers from an early date, able to build big sluices to control the rivers as early as Stephen's reign and probably well before that. We can still walk on their fen banks and sea banks. They had a system of local government that took effective charge of the drainage works, as we see when the system comes into our view in the verdicts of sewers (under Henry VIII onwards). By 1160 the dyke reeve is well attested. Alan of Craon carried out one of the first examples of water-engineering in medieval England; he helped the port of Boston by encouraging a river to change its main course from Bicker Haven to the present Haven. The date, 1142, is perhaps the earliest for the construction of a great sluice in England. Agricultural technique was reflected in the movement of reclamation. In the siltland openfield husbandry gave way to enclosed tofts and crifts; there is also evidence in places of two-course and three-course husbandry. These men were capable of flexibility of outlook in their response to challenges. They liked to grow flax and hemp, with wheat on the drier siltland where monastic estates lay. At all times pastoral farming was important for them. 'Mutual aid for the good of all (in spite of transgressions),' says Hallam, 'was the ideal of a neighbourhood where lordship was at a discount and togetherness the ideal. The results of these sentiments were admirable. The Fenland communities formed the most successful culture in medieval rural England. Together they tamed the fen and marsh for posterity, but they also gave us something for which we must always be their debtors – the finest parish churches in England. These and their great banks are their monuments and the labour of their hands is our reward.'[15]

Not much change in technique came about for generations, but the amount of stock and number of cultivated acres went on growing. The staple crop was corn, with peas and beans as an extra. A few commercial crops were grown: flax for linen, woad and saffron for dyes. But these did not loom large. Bartholomew Angelicus in the thirteenth century remarked: 'Many medly beans with bread-corn' and he cites the many stages needed for treating flax.

When the hop begins to wax, then the flax is drawn up and gathered all whole, and is then lined, and afterward made to knots and little bundles, and so laid in water, and lies there long time. And then it is taken out of the water and laid abroad till it be dried, and twined and wend in the sun, and then bound in pretty niches and bundles. And afterward knocked, beaten, and brayed, and carfled, rodded, and gnodded, ribbed and heckled, and at the last spun. Then the thread is sod and bleached, and bucked, and oft laid to drying, wetted and washed, and sprinkled with water until it be white, after divers working and travail.[16]

There was still no way of producing enough fodder to feed large herds through the winter, so animals were slaughtered when winter came and then salted. There is little evidence of any change in the nature of the crops since the Carolingian period. In the early centuries on some well organized estates perhaps a third of the arable soil may have been sown with spring crops, but mostly winter-sown bread grains predominated. However, as time went on, spring grains were no doubt more generally sown: barley, oats, according to circumstances. Where oats were sown in large quantities, it was not to provide fodder for horses, but to make the best use of the particular soil and climate. In England beans and peas were certainly not grown in significant amounts before the fourteenth century. We cannot make any strong distinction between two and three-field systems. The basis of rotation was throughout the *cultura* or furlong rather than the field. Spring crops were not necessarily the cause of reduction of fallow from a half to a third of the ploughed area. Many villages were able to put only half the arable under crop while they grew on that half a high proportion of spring crops, mostly barley and oats, that had a long history in the north.

Alexander Neckham in his *De naturis rerum* of the late twelfth century describes the two main farm machines, the plough and the cart; and in *De utensilibus* he tells how the prudent villein has wicker baskets and panniers, cheese moulds, sieve and bolter cloth for sifting meal and straining beer, spades, mattocks, a threshing sledge, a seed-bag for sowing, a wheelbarrow, a mouse-trap, a gin-snare for wolves, fire-hardened stakes, an axe for rooting up thorns and the like, butchers-broom to make and repair his yard-hedges, a small knife for grafting, a hoe and hook for weeding, nets and snares for hares and deer, and a gaff for fishing. Many herbs and vegetables were grown in cottage gardens. Neckham tells us expansively what should be planted in a noble's garden – fruits, vegetables, herbs. The few flowers named all have their uses: rose, lily, viola, heliotrope, peony, daffodil, purple iris, yellow gladiolus. Herbs include lettuce, parsley, mint, sage. There are beds of onions, leeks, garlic, pumpkins, shallots, cucumber, with beet under pottage vegetables. Fruits include medlars, quinces, warden-trees (a pear), peaches, pears of St Riole, pomegranates, almonds and figs. For the truly keen growers: lemons, oranges, dates. (Apple or pear seem not to be considered a noble fruit. Pears are harmful unless taken with wine; and all soft fruit, including apples, should be eaten on an empty stomach, never after dinner.)[17]

Sheep were found everywhere in England from Anglo-Saxon days, but we find them especially in the marshlands of Essex, East Anglia and the fens. A record of 1160 mentions that Crowland Abbey had over two thousand sheep besides lambs at Monklode, with nearly as many at Langcroft. But there were also large-scale sheep farms in areas like the Breckland and on into the upland regions of Cambridgeshire, in other parts of Norfolk and Suffolk, in the west, in Dorset, and on parts of the Mendips. In areas with an exceptional amount of meadow, cows competed with ewes and goats in providing milk and cheese. Much cheese seems to have been produced in the Berkshire meadowlands. But it is rare to meet *vaccaria* in *Domesday*, and cows are seldom distinguished from other *animalia ociosa*. We meet a few sites specializing in horse-breeding, for instance William granted Westminster Abbey the tithe of a stud of two hundred horses somewhere in Surrey (probably in the hundred of Kingstone, where *Domesday* mentions the king's forest mares). The abbey at Burton-on-Trent had a *haraz* or stud farm with seventy horses, including foals, under abbot Nigel, 1094–1114. The untamed mares at Brendon and the wild mares at Lynton seem to have been Exmoor ponies.[18]

But there is no sign of the breeding of work horses. It was long before the possibility of the horse's traction power was realized. When the population began to increase considerably in the thirteenth century, men were not stimulated to make a more extensive use of horses and to provide more fodder for them. Rather, they took the easy way out by reducing fallow and using more ground for crops, with unfortunate results in the long term. The area of meadow and pasture was reduced, so that more cereals could be

grown; as a result there was even less feed available for animals, so
that their manure and traction power was lessened instead of increased. Peasant holdings became understocked and demesne flocks
suffered from shortage of pasture. This setback occurred despite what
seems to have been an increased use of horses in the later twelfth
century, at least in seven contiguous counties in eastern England:
Norfolk, Huntingdonshire, Suffolk, Essex, Cambridgeshire, Bedfordshire, and Buckinghamshire. Horses that seem to have been used
in mixed teams or alone have been noted in twenty-three places
there. But apart from some Yorkshire cases, the only other data suggesting a use of plough horses elsewhere

> are some *instauramentum* figures in the *Liber Henrici de Soliaco*
> which may perhaps indicate that by 1189 they had begun to be
> combined with oxen on some of the Glastonbury manors, and
> two payments recorded in the Pipe Roll of 1166 – one for 10
> horses and 6 oxen at Chelesherst (a lost village in Kent) and
> the other for 22 oxen and 2 horses that were provided for Wash-
> field and Tiverton in Devon (Lenard).

In Bedfordshire in the later thirteenth century the horse called the
affer or *stort* was indeed the draught beast of the poor man, while
the lords preferred the ox.

Salt was much needed, especially for salting meat or fish for winter
consumption. Saltpans appear in *Domesday* in every seaboard
county from Lincolnshire to Cornwall. The single village of Caister
in Norfolk had forty-five – though some such entries are composite,
covering several settlements. In some places the saltpans were an important part of the economy, for example in Lyme in Dorset with
twenty-seven saltworkers, ten *villani*, six bordars, and an unstated
number of fishermen. The coastal saltpans seem to be let for rent to
the workers. The works at the brine springs in Cheshire and
Worcestershire were almost industrial settlements. Before 1066 at
several sites such as Droitwich and Nantwich the king had taken two
thirds of the income and the earl a third. After the Conquest there
was a decline, even at Droitwich. But there were other works on
rural manors, sometimes the manor owning only one or a part of one.
In such cases the products were no doubt in the main used
locally; but when there was a group of saltpans attached to
a moderate-sized manor, the profits could be high. Saltpans needed
fuel and thus affected the economy of near villages. *Domesday*
shows that there was much traffic to the Cheshire wiches; tolls were
paid for carts drawn by two or four oxen, for horse loads or for men
carrying salt on their backs – with higher rates for those coming

from another hundred or shire. Here the transport system was fairly humble; but when weighty objects were involved, large teams were used. For timber needed at Abingdon six waggons came all the way from Wales, each with twelve oxen; for the great bell cast in London for Durham, a team of twenty-two oxen was used. The timber carts took six or seven weeks on the round trip. In 1121 Henry I cleared and deepened Fossdyke, the canal linking Lincoln and Torksey; thus boats could go from the Wash to the Humber by inland waterways.

Fisheries were important in the fenlands, some river valleys, and parts of the coast. *Domesday* has many references to fisheries and renders of fish. A fishery there seems to be a fixed device of some kind such as a weir. Generally *piscariae* seem to be let for a rent of fish or money. In Shropshire we find five rented by *villani*; but at times one or more were reserved for supplying the lord's hall. Apart from repairs now and then, they needed little care for the taking of eels or salmon. We meet village mills paying a rent of a thousand eels (apparently caught in eel traps), and occasionally a man called a *piscator*. Sea-fishers appear mainly in Suffolk and the eastern section of the south coast. Among freshwater fisheries, those of the eastern fens were outstanding. Only rarely was a fishery large enough to affect a village's character, though there were exceptions in the west. At Etone (Eaton Hall) on the Dee above Chester a fishery rendered a thousand salmon.[19]

Watermills were to be found almost everywhere, though in no exact ratio to population or plough teams, and varying in value and capacity. Where we find a number close together we may be sure that the manorial mills ground more than the manor's corn. The lords tried hard to keep a monopoly. When Cecily de Rumilly (1131–40) gave the Silsden mill to a priory, she denounced the use of handmills and threatened severe penalties for anyone evading the suit owed to her mill by sending a horseload of corn elsewhere. At times mills are described as serving the hall, but as a rule they were let at a fixed rent; payments were mostly in money but at times they seem to have been made in kind. Clusters sometimes appear in towns, for example Louth and Thetford. In construction they might be of the simple vertical axle variety or of the more complex geared kind (described by Vitruvius). The millwright who built or repaired the mill was not uncommon among villagers; and together with the blacksmith he accustomed them to new metallurgical and mechanical technology. In the eleventh century water-power was applied to other industrial processes. Trip-hammer devices were used in the forges and in watermills for fulling cloth.[20] Water-power was also used for forges, perhaps in England by 1086, certainly at Caraden in Catalonia in 1104 and Soroï, in Sweden in 1197. *Domesday* tells us little of the mill occupants; as *custos* we meet a Frenchman, a reeve and a sokeman. But twelfth-century surveys suggest that the miller was a peasant who also had an agricultural holding. Fractional ownerships (down to an eighth) occur, especially in Lincolnshire and Norfolk; perhaps a group of men, rather than the village community, got together to set up a mill in some such cases.

We meet a few references to mines, for example *plumbariae* at five sites in Derbyshire; and another place makes a render of lead. Lead was no doubt also worked in the Mendips and Shropshire, where production was going on in the later twelfth century. *Domesday* also mentions Cornwall; and silver-bearing leads seem to have been worked on Alston Moor near Carlisle under Henry I. References to iron-works or workers and to renders of iron imply more than smithies, and are widely spread, from Devon to Sussex and north to Cheshire or Lincolnshire. We find an association of iron-workers with ironstone outcrops and with woodlands. At Hessle, West Riding, the population consisted of six iron-workers and three bordars with a single plough.[21]

Trade had been hampered to some extent by the Conquest. The Scandinavian links were dislocated; after 1071 Flanders was hostile and by 1074 relations with France were difficult. For a while economic development was held up, with a falling back from the expanded money system devised for the payment of mercenaries. Norman feudalism in some ways increased the particularism of the old English system to the extent that it cut the land into sharply defined manors; but at the same time, by strengthening the central grip of the government and increasing the demand for money rents, it set into action contrary movements, which made for economic advance. All the while there was a certain influx of foreign traders and craftsmen, who at times set up a community inside or outside an old borough, or settled by a new centre, often a castle. For a while the effects were slight. The Norman kings seem to have left things much as they found them in the towns, making few administrative changes and granting no new privileges. But the boroughs continued to grow slowly, until they began expanding in the middle of the twelfth century.

The origin of the English boroughs is uncertain. They were certainly not simply a development of Alfred's fortified *burhs*, and their courts seem to be not municipal institutions, but merely the hundred courts that sat within the walls and extended their jurisdiction over the districts around. Clearly the growth of trade played a key part in creating a borough, which had civic consciousness of a new kind. The inhabitants were mostly free men, and before 1066 the term burgess applied to those of its folk who held property by a burgage tenure, under which their tenements (houses, shops or booths) paid a fixed money rent, were inheritable, and could be freely mortgaged or sold. There were none of the agricultural or other services attached to other tenures; and this fact played a great part in developing the peculiar social character of the boroughs. Guilds had appeared, which, whatever their original nature, were coming to include the leading merchants and to act as trade organizations; the new burgess way of life, with its strong trading characteristics, was already before 1066 building up its special set of rules later called borough customs. Moreover, burgesses may have begun to develop their own courts for dealing with the regulation of business affairs. In a few places the Norman castle was accompanied by a Norman borough, especially on the Welsh marches; such a borough was granted the free customs of the small *bourgs* known in Normandy. The earl of Hereford was castellan of Breteuil, so he conferred that *bourg's* customs on Hereford.[22]

What later brought about a uniform movement towards self-governing status was the sale of privileges to the boroughs by the kings. Henry I granted to the peasants of the royal borough of Cambridge a charter giving them a monopoly of river trade in the area. About 1120 at Leicester the citizens, tradition declared, gained one of their chief liberties in an odd way:

The jurors say on their oath that in the days of earl Robert, two cousins, to wit Nicholas son of Aco and Geoffrey son of Nicholas, waged trial of battle for a certain plot of land which each claimed for his own. And they fought from sunrise even to noon and longer; and as they thus fought, one of them drove the other to the verge of a little ditch. And as they stood there on the verge and would have fallen in, his cousin said to him, 'take heed of the ditch behind you or you'll fall into it.' At that there arose so great a shouting and tumult from those who sat or stood around, that the lord earl heard their clamour even in his castle and asked then what it might be. And men answered him that two cousins were fighting for a plot of land and one had driven the other to the ditch and warned him that he stood on the brink and would have fallen in. So the burgesses, moved with pity, made a covenant with the lord earl that they should give him threepence yearly for each house that had a gable in the High Street, on condition of his granting them [the right of judging their own pleas by a jury of twenty-four citizens]: which right the lord earl granted them.[23]

In 1130 London and Lincoln asked for the privilege of paying dues to the crown direct, without any control by shire officers; Lincoln offered two hundred silver marks and four gold ones 'that they might hold their city of the king in chief'; the Londoners offered a hundred silver marks 'that they might have a sheriff of their own choice'. The Lincolners chose their own reeves to collect dues and take them to Westminster; the Londoners were given control not only of the dues from their own city, but of those from the county of Middlesex where it lay, and gained the right to choose the justiciar who tried pleas of the crown in London.

London was the pace-setter in urban and trading developments, and deserves some examination. It lay on a tidal river that ran far back into the country. The Confessor's city had stretched a mile on the north bank, east of the Fleet, and run half a mile inland. It was sheltered by the patched Roman walls, though already there was some settlement around them. A wooden bridge, under which ships could go, ran across to the suburb of Southwark. The site covered the valley of the Wallbrook, with low hills to east and west. Here was the one organized body of Englishmen with whom William had to reckon. The citizens could even interfere with effect in civil war, as in the summer of 1145 when Stephen captured the strategically important castle of Faringdon, Berkshire, with the aid of 'a terrible and numerous army of Londoners', in Henry of Huntingdon's words. The link between civil and military administration lay in the wards, which formed the basis for organizing defence or for keeping the watch. Probably already under Henry I there were twenty-four wards, each with its ward moot (corresponding in function to the court of a rural hundred). The profits of justice were the king's, though in the Norman period more and more properties passed to the lords of sokes. The respect the Normans felt for the citizens was shown by William's efforts to conciliate them by confirming their old rights. His fear of them was reflected in the early building of castles. At once after his coronation he went to Barking, 'while certain strongholds,' says William of Poitiers, 'were made in the town against the fickleness of the vast and fierce populace.' Baynard's Castle preserved the name of Ralf Baignard, a tenant-in-chief of eastern England. (The last baron of the family in England lost his inheritance in 1140.) The lord of this castle probably held a position of official authority in the city from the outset. In the west was another castle, later called Montfichet, which played a part in the revolt of 1173–4.[42]

The urban immunity of the sokes under the Normans reached a level here that had no parallel in other towns. This fact derived

N

from the city's commercial importance. Magnates and lords wanted houses in or near the city to ensure access to its market. Like other towns London had houses appurtenant to country estates; in *Domesday* the king himself had thirteen burgesses there belonging to Bermondsey. Monasteries acquired properties in London, and in the eleventh century some of them gained royal writs conferring jurisdictional powers. By the earlier half of the next century, Londoners, knowing what was going on on the continent, began to aspire to the status of a commune. After the battle of Lincoln, William of Malmesbury says, at the council of London citizens were sent 'by the Commune, as they call it, of London', to ask for Stephen's freedom, and 'all the barons who had already been received into their commune very earnestly begged this of the lord legate of the archbishop and clergy'.[25] Indeed London was known abroad as a commune. The archbishop of Rouen thanked the illustrious senators, honoured citizens, and the whole commune of London for fidelity to the king, and asked them to do right in a dispute between Algar the priest and Reading Abbey.[26] By 1191 the commune, from which the later mayoralty grew, was established. This development had come about through steady pressure, not through violent struggles such as often accompanied the creation of a commune on the continent. For all its varieties of tenure and jurisdiction the city had built up its own effective unity.

A commune was a sworn association of burgesses or citizens who sought to exclude all control by a lord, rule their own town as a sovereign body, and maintain a force able to defend its walls. Norman kings would not tolerate such a development in England, where in any event London was the only place big and strong enough to aspire to such freedom. The London burgesses, however, took advantage of Stephen's difficulties to assume quietly the title; but Henry II crushed the movement such as it was, raising the annual rent to the crown (reduced by Henry I) and imposing on the citizens frequent aids and gifts. Attempts made in his reign by Gloucester and York to form communes were sternly repressed. In 1196 the poorer citizens of London revolted against the city fathers, but were put down by the king's justiciar. Henry II was thus strongly opposed to burghal rights, and at the end of his reign only five English boroughs, apart from London, were directly responsible to the crown for their dues, and none of them could feel safe about retaining the right. But the financial problems of Richard I and John enabled many towns to gain charters, and the tide became irreversible.

Norman laws recognized no distinction of status among the citizens and thus helped the growth of civic unity. There were *principes* or elder citizens, but their position derived solely from the personal authority of wealth and influence. Henry I in his charter gave every citizen the wergild of 100s, the sum allotted to the pre-1066 *ceorl*, the early Norman *villanus*. (Not that this wergild implies that the citizens had servile status; what it implies is the relatively free status of the early twelfth-century *villein*.) William had addressed writs to the *burh*-thegns of London, but no later custumals or writs recognize such a patriciate of birth in the city. We may note further that the influx of foreign traders would have helped to break down any English system of ranks.

London was much more purely urban than the semi-agricultural boroughs of the south and midlands. Londoners were aware of the dangers proceeding from their way of life, and they used them to support claims to exemption from taking part in inquests under oath:

> Further, there are many folk in the city and they are housed close together and are more crowded early and late than other people are, and notably more so than those of the upland, who hold their county court and ought to swear concerning such matters. For if any one in the city should swear against his neighbour, whether concerning an inquest of an assize, or concerning that in which he has offended, great mischief might arise from it. For when the citizens are thus crowded together, whether at their drinking or elsewhere, they might kill one another and the city would never enjoy steady tranquillity. And for this reason, and by reason of the franchise, and for many reasons, it was established that they should not swear.[27]

Not that we must imagine as yet much huddling together. An average street frontage seems to have been about thirty to forty feet, though such properties were already being divided into smaller *mansurae*: under William big houses had already sprung up along the road from London to Westminster. Acts of violence, however, did occur. In 1130 there was a riot with thirteen persons mentioned, English and foreign, 'an assault on the ships and houses of London'.

So far we have seen the Danes on the land or in villages, though they were ready enough to gather in towns when they had the chance. Recent excavations have shown us Danish York. The core of the settlement seems to have been densely built with long narrow timber-framed houses. The main impression is of a somewhat damp and dirty town with thriving industries. There were furnaces here, tan-pits there; functional and luxury goods were being produced in quantity; commodities were arriving from several parts of Yorkshire and probably from beyond; and merchants' houses stood in close proximity to industrial premises. More important still, the Danish re-

mains prove conclusively that the present streetplan and the general
pattern of the arrangement of messuages were already in existence
before the Norman conquest (Radley). At the Conquest the town held
some 30,000 adults and was ready to take on the role of military
capital of northern England through a reorganization of the town
that involved the destruction and levelling of the Danish industrial
area to make way for William's new castle. The main industry seems
to have been leather: many remains of shoes, laces, belts, garments,
bags, sheaths and gloves have been found. The tan-pits were big
enough to stack cattle hides in without folding them, and shallow
enough to make emptying easy. The earliest freemen's rolls (1272–
8) show that the leather trades continued their importance in the
city.

The growth of new towns in England was slow. Under William I
Windsor and Ludlow were built; then we jump to Portsmouth under
Richard I, and Liverpool under John. The tradition of royal action in
such matters perhaps goes back (if we may take the grid plans of
streets as evidence) to Saxon Oxford, Wallingford, and Wareham.
But it was not till the first half of the thirteenth century that the
economic forces maturing during the twelfth found expression in a
considerable number of new towns, for instance six that were the
works of bishops of Winchester in Hampshire, Wiltshire and the Isle
of Wight: three in open country, a mile or more from previous
settlements, and three separated by rivers from existing villages.
These towns then antedated the plantation of towns begun by
Edward I, which was based on his experiences in Gascony. Towns
planted by landlords included Newton Abbot in about 1200, and
Chipping Sodbury in 1227; we may note also the move from Old
Sarum to Salisbury.[28]
   We may glance at this process since it shows the working out of
the economic and social forces liberated in the twelfth century. We
see, for example, how the population was increasing. The new towns
could be filled while the old ones extended their shop and house
space. (The period is that of the colonization of the empty spaces
from the Baltic to the Danube, and the multiplication of houses in
old settled parts like south Germany and Gascony.) In the hinterland
of Winchester the new forces produced Yarmouth and Newport
(I.O.W.), Portsmouth, Poole, Lymington, Beaulieu and Haslemere, as
well as abortive efforts at Newton in Purbeck and near Chichester;
and old trading centres were strengthened. We know little of the
effects of the new towns on the rural hinterland, of the ways in
which they were planned and built, or the motives behind their
founding – though the desire for profit certainly played a big part.

Documents merely refer to a market house, stalls, oven, weir, canal, fulling mill, churches, boulting house and well, not to mention a fourteen fathom rope and an iron bucket. The liberty of action enjoyed by the burgess in comparison with the villein is shown by the entries on the bishops' account rolls for *manerium* and *burgus*. The *burgus*-roll is short, often holding some half a dozen entries (rents, arrears, market and fair tolls, profits of justice); but a single manor might cover four to six feet of closely written parchment, dealing with rents collected, demesne services commuted, produce gathered, and goods transported to market or taken to the stock of farm equipment, farm animals and grain. Here the profits of justice included many payments from manorial villeins, including fines paid on the inheritance of land, fines paid for the marriage of a villein woman, heriots paid on deaths, and yearly recognitions for permission to remain away from the manor as long as the bishop would allow. The four short *burgus*-entries reveal the progress made by the towns: the taking up of burgage plots, the success of markets, the bustle of legal activity, the large amounts of folk drawn in by the yearly fairs. The next stage of the lord's withdrawal from a direct share in rents and revenues came when fixed yearly payments were made in lieu of them; the lord turned into a mere money-collector.

From at least the end of the eleventh century onwards the royal grant of a license to hold a fair seems to have implied also a license to hold a court of summary jurisdiction for offences committed at the fair itself. These courts got the name of Piepowder (*piepoudreux*, dustyfeet) as the suitors appeared informally in their travel-stained condition. A jury of merchants found the judgment or declared the law; so suitors and doomsmen were of the same class. England is the only country with records of such courts.[29]

London was the centre of far-flung trading connections. It lay at the end of a route from Byzantium, which the men of lower Lorraine controlled. Along that route came goldwork, precious stones, cloth from Byzantium and Regensburg, pepper, cummin, wax, fine linen and mailcoats from Mainz, and wine. The king, through his chamberlain, had the right of pre-emption over such goods; then the Londoners might buy what they liked, then the men of Oxford, then those of Winchester, then anyone else. Danish and Norwegian traders could live in the city a year, dealing in timber, sailcloth, marten skins, and the like; they probably still connected London with the east via Russia.[30] William fitzStephen associated the Norwegians with the Russians (the Swedish colony at Novgorod). At Bruggen, the old Hanseatic wharf in Bergen, continental wares predominated before 1200, then English pottery was in the ascendant till about 1400, after which it gave out. In 1186 the Norwegian king Sverri in a speech declared that the Germans brought in so much wine that it was no dearer than ale. In a second speech he said :

> We desire to thank the Englishmen who have come here bring-
> ing wheat and honey, flour and cloth. We also desire to thank
> those who have brought here linen or flax, wax or cauldrons.
> We desire next to make mention of those who have come here
> from the Orkneys, Shetland, the Faroes or Iceland; all those
> who've brought here such things as make this land the richer,
> which we can't do without. But there are the Germans who've
> come here in large numbers with large ships, intending to carry
> away butter and dried fish, of which the exportation much im-
> poverishes the land; and they bring wine instead, which people
> strive to purchase, both by men, townsmen, and the merchants.[31]

The compilers of customs at London may have ignored the Flemish through trade jealousy, as we know of them under the Confessor and they are seen established in the city by royal authority in a char-ter of Henry II to the men of St Omer, which allows the latter to lodge where they wished, and to sell their goods without view of justiciar or sheriff and without paying dues for setting them out; also to visit fairs and markets anywhere in England.[32]

There was a large number of goldsmiths at work. Craft associa-tions were being formed in the Norman period. We meet the guild of weavers in 1130, represented by an Englishman, Robert son of Leustan; and in the 1150s the weavers got a charter to confirm the liberties enjoyed under Henry I and to forbid any non-members to weave in London, Southwark or other places belonging to London, except in so far as had been the custom under Henry I. In 1156 the bakers appear with a debt of one gold mark. By 1180 at least nineteen guilds were fined for being formed without warrant; they included pepperers, goldsmiths, butchers, cloth-dressers. How long they had existed we do not know.[33]

The importance of trade is shown by the political use of embargoes. William of Malmesbury says that Henry I's relations with Murchertach, high king of Ireland, were normally good, but they deteriorated at one point. Soon, however, the high king 'was brought to reason by the embargo declared on shipping and trade. For what would Ireland be worth if goods were not shipped from it to England?' The Pipe Roll of 1130 shows that the Gloucester burgesses considered Henry I's influence in Ireland strong enough to justify their offer of thirty marks for the recovery of money stolen there. William of Malmesbury, dealing with regional specialization in agriculture and trade, described the fertile orchards of the vale of Gloucester and the volume of shipping handled by Bristol; he stressed the pastoral economy of Cheshire and its dependence on trade with Ireland. In 1127 the claimant to the English throne was invested with the county of Flanders (already importing much wool from England); an embargo drove the citizens of Bruges to rise against him. (The connection with Flanders was further shown by Henry's settlement of Flemings in Pembrokeshire shortly after the Tinchebrai campaign; these were presumably mercenaries whom he now used as a counter-balance to the Welsh.)

Edward I's abolition of the right of wreck has been taken to mark an important point in the growth of trade, which was then able to override old feudal privileges. But if we look back we find Henry I declaring that the right of wreck must end and that any goods from a wrecked ship should go to the survivors.

A trader about whom we happen to know a good deal was Godric of Finchale, born of poor peasants in Lincolnshire in the late eleventh century. At first he walked the beaches in quest of wreckage, and at last was able to set up as a pedlar, travelling the land with a little pack of wares. He gathered a small sum, enough to enable him to join a band of town traders whom he had encountered. He went with them from market to market, fair to fair, town to town. Now a professional merchant, he soon got the money for chartering a ship with a group of others and for engaging in coastal trade along the shores of England, Scotland, Denmark and Flanders. The group did well by taking to foreign lands wares that they knew were scarce or unusual there, and by selling them at a high price, getting other wares in exchange and carrying these to places where they were in demand. After some years of buying cheap and selling dear, Godric was suddenly stricken with a bad conscience and the need to renounce the world; he gave his goods to the poor and became a monk.[34]

We know of him because he became a saint after settling in a hermitage on the banks of the Wear near Durham. Many others grew wealthy in the same way without qualms. Godric was a speculator and his contemporary biographer remarks that he preferred using his greater intelligence, *sagacior animus*, to toiling at agriculture. Such a man was called by Gratian the *mercator* 'who is turned out of the temple of God'. Godric was typical of the wandering trader of the times, a shrewd fellow who came from the country to the towns, which he made his base; but except in the winter he was mostly abroad. The impotence of a single trader in such a world, and the insecurity of the roads, encouraged such men to join in associations, guilds, hanses, *caritates*. The group took wares in convoy from town to town, bought and sold in common, and divided profits in proportion to their respective investments in the expedition. Their trade was wholesale; retail was left to the rural pedlars. They exported and imported wine, grain, wool and cloth. The statutes of the Flemish hanse in London expressly excluded retail dealers and craftsmen from the company.

The merchant associations of the eleventh and twelfth centuries had nothing exclusively local about them. Burgesses of different towns worked side by side; the effect was of regional rather than urban groupings, which were still far from the exclusive, protectionist groupings of the fourteenth century. Trading regulations were not hampered by restrictive clauses and public authorities exercised no supervision. The men were left to carry on as long as they paid the fiscal dues levied by the territorial princes or lords with jurisdiction at the passage of bridges, along roads and rivers, or at markets. The only restrictions were economic: the various merchant associations, meeting at a market for buying and selling, opposed one another in strong competition. Each excluded members of other groups from any share in its affairs, though without any legal title to do so. Down to the end of the twelfth century the number of towns with a strong mercantile basis was relatively small; only places with favourable geographical sites drew large numbers of merchants, and these places exerted much influence on secondary regions where the merchants, too few to act on their own, affiliated themselves to the hanse or guild of the main town. Merchants of Dixmude, Oudenbourg, Ardenbourg, and so on, sought admission to the hanse of Bruges. Town activities were more concerned with trade than with craft or industry; commodities like wine, grain and cloth were often produced in the country.

Travel over long distances was slow; but the speed at which news got about varied. The usual time for travelling from Rome to Canterbury was seven weeks, but urgent news could arrive in four. The story of Frederick Barbarossa's death in Asia Minor took four months to reach Germany, but that of Richard I's captivity in Austria reached England in as many weeks. Men travelled at an average speed of twenty miles a day, or possibly thirty, though if necessary they could speed up to fifty. There was considerable movement among pilgrims, merchants, churchmen going to synods and scholars to universities, crusaders, mercenaries, pedlars, and peasants seeking for land.[35] Ideas and cultural influences could thus be exchanged far more than one might think. The French *chansons de geste* were connected with the ambulatory public of the pilgrim centres and fairs, and show a close link between monks and jongleurs. The

annals of a group of Anglo-Norman houses were based on annals
that had come from the Rhine via Burgundy, and went back to the
Easter tables of Bede; the annals of Margam on the Welsh border
described King John's condemnation by the court of Philip
Augustus; Bury in 1181–2 had a six months' visit from the Norwegian
archbishop Eystein; the monks of Mont St Michel in Normandy were
in close touch with those of Mont Sant'angelo on the east coast of
Italy. Matthew Paris had detailed information about the Tartars; and
the miracles of St Nicholas, of much importance in the history of
ritual drama, came from the east via St Nicholas in Bari as far as Bec
and Hildesheim – not only to churches with this patron saint, but to
others along the road, like St Salvatore in Lucca (as we see from the
portal).[36] Rulers took part in the exchanges. Manuel Comnenos sent
Ptolemy's *Almagest* to the king of Sicily; King Roger drew to Palermo
men of learning from all lands. Peter of Blois was the friend of the
rulers of both England and Sicily. The pilgrim routes also helped the
diffusion northwards of Byzantine influences and the church-type of
the Holy Sepulchre; Cluniac art spread into Burgundy, then into
England, Galicia, Apulia and Palestine, but especially along the great
road to St James at Compostella.[37]

At sea were the hazards of bad weather and piracy. Goscelin tells
us of a man bringing Caen stone for Canterbury under William who
ran into a storm. Even during his lifetime St Wulfstan rivalled St
Nicholas as the saviour to whom sailors of the Bristol–Ireland passage appealed. Eustace the Monk was a famous pirate whom we shall
later consider. We hear of sailors driven on to Lundy Island, which
was held by the pirate William de Mareis, son of Geoffrey de
Marisco, and used as a base for attacks on passing ships. Till the end of
the eleventh century the line between trade and piracy, raids and
war proper, was not clearly drawn. Gruffyd ap Cynan was a Welshman with Norse blood; in about 1087 he sailed to the Orkneys to
gather a fleet of pirates for a descent on Wales to restore him to his
kingdom. The fleet entered the Severn estuary and ravaged the
church of St Gwynllyw, which looked out over the marshy flat near
the mouth of the Usk. Other churches were raided: St David's in
1080 and 1091. The second time the raiders came from the Isle of
Man, 'pagans from the isles'. This seems to have been the last pagan
assault on a church in Wales.[38]

The urbanizing and mercantile trends were inevitably linked with
an expansion of the cash nexus, which undermined a great many
medieval preconceptions and feudal institutions. An important
aspect of the medieval world was precisely the way it functioned
to a considerable extent without the intrusions of money, despite

the continual drive to transmute service relations into money contracts. There was thus what we may call a pervading concreteness in
human relations, which was in ceaseless conflict with the abstracting
powers of money. Men normally made whole things, and made them
with their hands; they carried through the whole of a process of
work. Fragmentation of labour was little developed. Profits and rents
were essentially extorted by sheer force; but at least this meant that
there was nothing difficult to understand in what happened. In such
a world the abstracting force of money, involving a mechanism
that seemed to be outside human control, appeared as something hostile, uncanny, and insidious; its operation seemed to be based on
cheats and tricks; profits could only result from some underhand
theft. Hence a trader was liable to have something of the alien aura
of the usurer or Jew, a man who made money unnaturally, by
'breeding'.

The scriptural condemnation of *Deuteronomy* (xxiii 20–1) was
taken by Jerome and medieval writers to apply to all Christians. It
was argued by Peter Comester that the Jew was forbidden to engage
in usury with his brother, but was allowed by God to lend to
Christians to save them from temptation. Anyone indulging in usury,
said the Lateran council of 1179, was unworthy of Christian
burial. When Aristotle's influence increased, his idea that money
should not breed strengthened the prevailing view. To buy cheap
and sell dear was a sin equal to usury. William of Rennes declared:

> though business can scarcely be conducted without sin,
> merchants may receive a moderate profit to maintain them-
> selves and families. As they work for all and perform a sort of
> common business by transporting merchandise back and forth
> between fairs, they should not be held to pay their own wages.
> From the merchandise itself they can accept a moderate profit
> which is regulated by the judgment of a good man, since the
> amount of profit permitted cannot be exactly determined in
> shillings, pounds, and pence.[39]

The church's doctrine of the just price collided with the Roman law
of sale (revived by the school of Bologna) that prices should be the
result of free bargaining between seller and buyer, as long as there
was no fraud. But lawyers took up a qualification in the code of
Justinian – that the price agreed on for land should not be less than
half of the just value – and applied it to all sales. Thus a compromise
was found with the notion of the just price, which was interpreted
simply as the current market price or as the decision of a judge or
competent valuer. Everyone considered it fair and right to ask

interest from an enemy, from infidels, heretics or Saracens, though
not from Jews. And a way was found round the condemnation of
selling dear and buying cheap; the canonist Rufinus said that all was
well if the transaction was based on necessity rather than profit. The
labour spent in transportation or improvement must be allowed for;
profits were fair if not inordinate. Aquinas concluded that a
trader's profit should bring adequate repayment for services he had
rendered, gain him a livelihood, and give him a surplus to be used
in works of charity and grace; and if a debtor out of gratitude
wanted to make a gift freely to his creditor, the law wasn't broken.
Slowly qualifications of this sort corroded all the church's positions
about the just price and about usury. The upper classes naturally felt
that the only respectable money was that earned without labour
and simply extorted by armed power; their attitudes thus merged
with the people's fear of money as a strange alien compulsive force.
'It is difficult among buyers and sellers not to fall into sin,' said the
canonist Histiensis. There was a confused linking of usury and
heresy; Flemish merchants were much suspected, perhaps because of
their connections with the Albigensian south, perhaps because
money itself had a set of unholy connotations, especially where
profits or increases (breeding) were concerned. But gradually the
world was made safe for the early capitalist ethic of thrift and profit-
making.

The Jews played an important part in the growth of money transactions. By their nature they were a group both related to Christianity and cast out from the Christian community. In France they
had long been forced to restrict themselves to money matters; in
return the kings had protected them and until the ninth century
had indeed left them free to own their own land and carry on ordinary trade. In the early medieval world they thus had a close connection with royal finances; and being compelled to limit their
talents to a single field, they did much to advance its systematiza-
tion. William of Malmesbury says that they were brought to England
by William I; and this statement is supported by a petition of 1275
in which the Jews of England speak of their establishment 'since the
conquest of the land'.[40] William may well have meant to use them
as financial agents who would collect dues in cash rather than in
land and produce. They continued to have a peculiarly close link
with the king, and were considered his legal chattels. Thus their
wealth was not technically theirs at all; at their deaths the king
could, and at times did, take over the whole estate, not the third
which was the usual tax. When the biggest financier of the thirteenth century, Aaron of Lincoln, died in 1186 his estate became

an escheat to the crown and a special branch of the exchequer was set up to deal with it; fifteen years later the king had still not got settlement of all his debts. Two other rich Jews were the brothers Jurnet and Benedict of Norwich. Jurnet was said to have married a Christian heiress and converted her to Judaism, so that she lost her lands and was fined six thousand marks – all the Jewish communities in England being jointly responsible for the debt. The tale has been disproved; but it was a fact that a consortium of the two brothers and some London Jews was forced to buy the king's pardon for some offence (probably financial) in 1177 for the same sum. And a similar fine had to be met by Jurnet in 1184; the Pipe Rolls show that his bonds were transferred to the English Jewry as a community – apparently the usual way of realizing a debtor's assets. But he remained a man of substance; he bought a house in Norwich in 1189, and in 1190 he accounted for a fine of £170 imposed on him at Windsor.[41]

Jews thus formed a cooperative banking system that spread over the whole realm, and they advanced large sums to the exchequer to meet sudden calls. Repayments were generally made through drafts on sheriffs to be met out of the taxation of the shires. When a property tax was levied in 1188 to finance the third crusade, the Jews were told to contribute a fourth of their property and were expected to provide £60,000 as against £70,000 to come from a levy of a tenth on all the other citizens of the land.[42] They could sue debtors in English royal courts. Henry I gave them a charter of protection and allowed them to travel freely, to be exempt from toll, and to hold land taken in pledge as a security. Their heydey was under Henry III, with his extension of the fiscal system, when they were given the right of internal jurisdiction according to Talmudic law. Their numbers were swollen by the expulsions from France in 1182. The kings, as we saw, were ready to squeeze them, but did not want to see them broken or wiped out. If a Jew got hold of most of a Christian's estate, the king could confiscate the property on his death; and at times the crown took over a Jew's debts, scaring the noble and ecclesiastical debtors since it was likely to show less mercy. Attacks on Jews were liable to destroy their archives and thus threatened the crown as residuary legatee of Jewish debts. So Archbishop Walter set up archives in the chief towns where bonds between Jew and gentile could be safely kept under the supervision of the so called Exchequer of the Jews.[43]

The Jews were thus the obvious 'inner enemy': they were held by the church to be responsible for the execution of Jesus and at the same time had been compelled to embody the alienating force of money. The crusades piously stimulated their massacre and oppression. On Easter Eve of 1144 the corpse of a young apprentice was found in woods near Norwich and a rumour spread that local Jews had crucified him on the second day of the Passover in imitation of Christ. The sheriff tried to protect the Jews, but the bishop opposed him and encouraged the agitation. At Richard I's coronation, Sunday 3 September 1189, there was a murderous riot against London Jews, with fresh outbursts in Lent, probably stimulated by the approaching crusades. The Jewish leader, seeing that the situation was hopeless, set fire to a funeral pyre in the castle tower where the refugees had fled. The church did its best to make things hard for the Jews. The Lateran council of 1179 forbade Christians to live in Jewish communities and Jews to employ Christians; that of 1215 ordered Jews to wear a piece of yellow or crimson cloth to mark them out – on the grounds that otherwise a Christian might copulate with a Jewess or a Jew with a Christian female. Excited by the story of a deacon converted to Judaism and marrying a Jewess (for which he was burned), the church council of Oxford promulgated a series of anti-Jewish laws, which grew harsher throughout the thirteenth century.

The odd sardonic nature of William Rufus comes out in the tales of his relations with Jews. Once he staged a debate between Gilbert Crispin, abbot of Westminster, and a learned Jew from Mainz. William of Malmesbury says:

> At Rouen they tried to prevail through gifts on some converted Jews to return to Judaism; at another time at London they entered into controversy with our bishops, because the king in jest, as I suppose, had said that if they mastered the Christians in open argument he'd become one of their sect.[44]

Eadmer tells how a Jewish lad at Rouen had a vision in which St Stephen bade him be baptized. He obeyed, but his father rushed to Rufus and begged him to compel his son to return to his ancestral faith. He had heard that recently the king 'in return for a money payment had restored a number of persons in the same situation to Judaism'. At first Rufus took no notice of the pleas; then the Jew promised to give him sixty silver marks. Rufus called the lad in and ordered him to abandon his conversion. 'My lord king, I think you must be joking,' cried the lad. The king shouted back, 'Joking with you, you son of the dungheap, you'd better go back and obey my command, and that quickly, or by the holy face of Lucca I'll have your eyes torn out!' The lad refused and was at last driven away. William then asked for his sixty marks. The Jew demurred on the grounds that William had failed on his side of the bargain, but after some argument agreed to pay half the sum.

The Jews did not have a monopoly of money-lending despite the prohibitions of usury. There was for example William Cade, with his headquarters at St Omer, who flourished in mid-twelfth century and was long remembered on the continent as a man of vast wealth with agents 'through all the *climata* of the world'. Under John the exchequer was still struggling to collect all the debts under his bonds that had fallen into Henry II's hands at his death. The latter king paid him for supplying gold for crown and regalia by a precept on the sheriff of Berkshire. Payments over ten years amounted to about £5,600.[45]

Already in the eleventh century, as part of the general economic and social advance, the basis of many technological ideas and applications was being laid, and this was to bear important fruit in the following centuries. The later developments are well known; what is more obscure is the way in which during the Dark Ages and the early medieval period peasants and craftsmen, because of their relative freedom and their initiative and readiness to experiment with labour processes, were able to take the first crucial steps in new directions. Foremost among the new devices were the treadle loom and the fulling mill. In the late tenth and in the eleventh century evidence starts coming up to show that water-power was being used for other processes than the grinding of corn. There are fulling mills in Italy, using the cam; and water-driven trip-hammers began to work in the forges of Germany. At Grenoble was a fulling mill, and about 1085, one for treating hemp. St Wandrille near Rouen was getting in tithes by 1080 from a fulling mill; and at least by 1086 two mills in England were paying rent for blooms of iron, showing that water-power was used at forges.[46] By the thirteenth century mechanical fulling of cloth, supplanting the method by hand or foot, was decisive in shifting the centre of textiles from the south-east to the north-west where water-power was easier to get at. More and more, all over Europe, we meet mills for tanning or laundering, for sawing or crushing anything from olives to ore, for reducing pigments for paint or pulp for paper, for producing mash for beer, for operating the bellows of blast furnaces, fore-hammers, or grindstones for polishing weapons and armour. Those developments lay well ahead, but the basis for them was laid back in the tenth and eleventh centuries, and earlier.[47]

Though we cannot enter here into the growth of the universities, in part out of the old cathedral and monastic schools, nor into the great advances in many fields of thought in the twelfth and thirteenth centuries, we may note the part played by Englishmen in the early phases of learning from Arab culture and of preparing for the birth of a new scientific approach. The godless reign of Rufus had seen the stirring of scientific interests and attitudes. Early in the twelfth century Adelard of Bath went abroad in search of Arabic learning; later in the century Daniel of Morley did the same. Both men returned to England. Adelard translated Euclid's *Geometry* and introduced the works of Khwarizmi to the west in fragmentary form; Robert of Chester, in about 1144, translated the same mathematician's *On the Restoration of Opposition of Numbers*, called *Al Gebra* (*The Book*) by Arab scholars; hence our term Algebra. Michael the Scot (who died in 1224) was described by the pope while still alive as 'burning from boyhood with the love of science'. He introduced Avicenna and Averroes to the west.

An element of the English situation which did much to inspire such men to start their quests was the strong interest in the calendar and technical chronology, which had existed in monastic circles since Bede's time. We see this interest in Byrhtferth's *Manual* early in the eleventh century and in the works composed by Abbo of Fleury for the Ramsey monks. It was still alive in the later part of the century, especially in the group around Wulfstan at Worcester. Wulfstan's friend, the Lorrainer Robert of Hereford, introduced the chronicle of Marianus Scotus (an Irish monk living at Mainz) into England, and Wulfstan had a copy made. This led to the connecting up of the English history in that large work to bring about the chronicle that goes under the name of Florence of Worcester. These studies, which led to much interest in mathematics and astronomy, were linked with the Easter Tables worked out at Worcester. A second Lorrainer, Walcher, prior of Malvern, seems to have been the centre of another scientific group in the west country; he was one of the few men to whom William of Malmesbury admitted a debt. He seems to have been the first man in England to use the Arabian astrolabe; and he acted as interpreter or *amenuensis* to a converted Jew from Spain, Petrus Alphonsi, who arrived some time after 1106 and was Henry I's physician. Petrus clearly did much dissemination of information and helped to set curious minds off on further quests. A twelfth-century book from Worcester contains works by Petrus, Robert of Hereford, Walcher, and Adelard. If we consider a few of Adelard's comments, we see what a vast gap lies between his thought and that of men like Lanfranc and Anselm. Nature, he says,

is not confused and without system, and so far as human reason has progressed, it should be given a hearing. Only when it fails utterly, should there be a recourse to God.

Those now called authorities reach that position first by the exercise of their reason...So, if you want to hear anything more from me, give and take reason.[48]

CHAPTER XIV

PORTENTS AND PROPHECIES

We have dealt so far mainly with the social, economic and political aspects of the changes going on in the medieval world between the tenth and the thirteenth centuries. Now we shall look at some of the expressions of the inner strain born from the many conflicts and contradictions which resulted from those changes. Tenth-century folk had felt increasing fears of the end of the world, which seemed likely to come with the year 1000. For some time there had been warnings that the 'world was growing old' and that certain signs foretold the end. A donation of Arnaud count of Carcassone et de Cominges to the abbey of Lezat in 944 remarked, 'world end is approaching'. In 948 the deeds of the foundation of the priory of Saint-Germain de Muret echoed familiar phrases, 'the end of the world approaching and ruins multiplying'. In 909 the council of Trosly had invited bishops to be ready to give an account of their acts, as the day of Judgment was near. About 940 Abbo of Fleury, while a youth

in Paris, heard a preacher announce that the world would end in
1000; he also heard later (about 975) in Lorraine that the world
would end when the day of the Annunciation coincided with Good
Friday, as would happen in 992. He wrote a book attempting to
discredit these fears. In England the main authority on the end of the
world was Bede, who based his account on Tyconius, a commentator
of the African church in the fourth century (when violent social
struggles had been going on among Christians). Bede took over from
Augustine (through Isidore of Seville) the scheme of six ages. The
sixth reached from Christ's incarnation to the end of time; the
seventh would be the eternal Sabbath of the new Jerusalem. Bede
was cautious about giving an exact date for the end of the world.[1]

When the year 1000 was at hand, there seemed to be many portents.[2] Gerbert the learned pope was said to be a diabolical magician,
a sort of anti-Christ; famine and pestilence were widespread; there
were signs in the sky, meteors; and the church of St Michael the Arch-
angel, 'built on a promontory of the Ocean, and which had always
been a special object of veneration in the whole world', was soon
after burned. The abbess of Jouarre and the abbot of Rebais organized a big procession. Many people went on pilgrimages or haunted
monasteries. Relics were found and displayed. Wulfstan in his
homilies of the early eleventh century saw 'many signs of world-
end'. There was complete breakdown of all social bonds, he said. The
relations of thrall and thegn were reversed; a thrall often bound the
thegn his master and forced him into thralldom; one Dane in battle
often put to flight ten or more English; women were outraged; the
bonds of kinship were broken; brother would not protect brother,
father his child or child his father. When Jerusalem fell in 1009–10
many people again saw it as an unmistakable sign of the end.

Famines had preluded the year 1000 and they continued. Glaber of
Cluny tells of the years after 1032–4:

Famine extended its ravages to such an extent that one feared
that almost the whole human race would disappear. Climatic
conditions were so unfavourable that the weather was never
suited for sowing, and through the floods there was no way of
harvesting...Ceaseless rains had so drenched the earth that for
three years a man couldn't dig small furrows capable of receiving the seed...If by chance one could find food for sale, the
seller could exact as excessive a price as he liked. However
when men had eaten wild animals and birds, under the impetus
of hunger they collected dead carcasses and things too horrible
to speak of...Raging hunger made men devour human flesh...
Some persons travelling from one place to another to flee the

famine and finding hospitality on the road had their throats cut in the night and served to nourish those who welcomed them.

A recluse by a church in the wood of Chatenay buried the remains of his victims; forty-eight skulls of men, women and children he had eaten were dug up.[3] After 1033 (taken as a thousand years after the Cruxifixion) there was a brief period of peace and plenty; hence the councils ushering in the Peace of God.

In such a world dreams and prophecies were taken very seriously. Many that have come down deal with the royal family. Of Edward the Confessor William of Malmesbury says: 'He was famed both for his miracles and for the spirit of prophesy.' His future reign had been shown in vision under Cnut to the bishop of Wilton, who was brooding on the extinction of the English royal line, when he saw 'Peter consecrating as king Edward, at that time an exile in Normandy; his chaste life too was pointed out, and the exact length of his reign, twenty-four years'. To the inquiry as to what would happen after him came the reply, 'The kingdom of the English belongs to God; after you he'll provide a king according to his pleasure.' At an Easter banquet at Westminster, as Edward sat crowned amid a crowd of nobles all greedily eating after the fast of Lent, he grew abstracted and burst into laughter. Harold, a bishop, and an abbot later helped him to unrobe and asked why he had 'burst into a vulgar laugh while all others were silent'. He said that he had seen something wonderful. After much entreaty he explained.

> The Seven Sleepers in Mount Coelius had now lain for 200 years on their right side, but that, at the very moment of his laughter, they turned upon their left; they would go on lying like that for 74 years, which would be a dreadul omen to wretched mortals. For everything would come to pass in these 74 years which the Lord had foretold to his disciples about the end of the world. Nation would rise against nation, and kingdom against kingdom; earthquakes would be in various places; pestilence and famine, terrors from heaven and great signs; changes in kingdoms; wars of the Gentiles against the Christians and also victories of the Christians over the Pagans. Telling all this to his wondering audience, he descanted on the passion of these sleepers and the make of their bodies – things quite unnoticed in history...

So the listeners sent a knight, a priest and a monk to Byzantion; the emperor there sent them on to the bishop of Ephesus, who showed them the relics of the Seven. The Greeks had a tradition that they lay on their right sides, but they were now on their left. What Edward had foreseen came to pass: irruptions of infidels in the east, rapid changes on the imperial and papal thrones, troubles brought on Rome by the Germans, the death of Henry of France, and a comet. William I was said to have his own astrologer, who was in one of the ships lost during the crossing of 1066; later at Ely he was said to have used a witch. Margaret of Scotland foretold certain things, says Turgot her biographer of his last visit to her: her own death and 'the elevation of sons and daughters of hers to the summit of earthly dignity'. Some years later, about 1106, he considered it astonishing that she was proved right by her son Edgar being king of the Scots and her girl Maud (Matilda) queen of England.[4]

The death of Rufus begot a number of omen tales, which are of interest in bringing out how any strange event, or one which took place at a moment of great change or conflict, was liable to be seen as revealing some deep plot of fate or of spirit powers. FitzHamon, a friend, was visited by a monk who had had bad dreams the night before: he saw Rufus enter a church and tear a crucifix to pieces. 'The image at length struck the king with a foot in such a way that he fell backward; from his mouth, as he lay prostrate, issued so copious a flame that the volume of smoke touched the very stars.' FitzHamon, alarmed, told the king, who, with much laughter, exclaimed, 'He is a monk and dreams for money like a monk; give him a hundred shillings.' Here we see Rufus as the devil despoiling the church. But in the version of the *Brut* he himself dreams 'that he was [let] blood, and bled a great quantity of blood, and a stream of blood leapt on high toward heaven more than a hundred [fathom]; and the clearness of the day was turned all to darkness'. He is also said to have had visions in which bishop Gundolf, who had warned him to amend his ways, appeared as a herald of approaching doom. We learn that he couldn't sleep the night before his death, ordered lights to be brought into the chamber, and made his chamberlain talk with him. The dream of spouting blood presents Rufus as the cosmic victim, the fellow or the opposite of Christ. In another dream, he went alone into a forest chapel, where the walls were hung with purple tapestries of Greek work, embroidered with ancient legends; suddenly the trappings all vanished, walls and altar were bare; and on the altar he saw a naked man, whose body he tried to eat. The man said, 'Henceforth you shall eat of me no more.' In another version the body on the altar is that of a stag. Here the rejection of Rufus by Christ whose flesh and blood is consumed in the rite of communion is repeated by the world of nature, by the animal on whom predatory human beings live and who was the special prey of kings.[5]

There were also tales about the foreknowledge of his death and the impossible speed at which news of it spread. Within a few hours it was known in Italy and in more than one place in England. In Belgium, Hugh abbot of Cluny was warned of the death the night before. On the day of his death Peter de Melvis in Devon met a rough common man with a blood dart, who said, 'With this dart your king was killed today.' The same day the earl of Cornwall, walking in the woods, encountered a big black hairy goat carrying the king's figure. When questioned, the goat replied that it was the devil taking Rufus off to judgment. Anselm heard the news in Italy through a splendid young man who told the clerk on guard at the door that all dissension between king and archbishop was now at an end. A monk of the same order as Orderic had a vision early in the morning after his death. Chanting in church, he saw through his closed eyes a person holding a paper on which was written: King William is dead. Opening his eyes, he saw no one.

Some of these tales clearly reflected the hatred felt by ecclesiastics who wanted to make his death a portentous warning. But perhaps the manner of his death in the forest stirred fantasies among the English that the king had indeed been a sacrificial victim and that his death would somehow shake the power of the aliens. To see him as a victim of the old religion, a seven-yearly sacrifice of the king or some leader, is going too far, however, though the day of his death, we may note, was 2 August, the Morrow of Lammas (1 August), and Lammas was one of the four great festivals of the old creed in Britain.[6]

Rufus was a strange man, probably reckless in blasphemy rather than a heretic or a pagan with worked out ideas. We saw how he liked to set Jews and Christians arguing. To a monk who denied that his house had any money to give the king, one of his ministers said, 'Have you not chests full of the bones of dead men but set about with gold and silver?' Rufus himself declared that neither St Peter nor any other saint had influence with God, and that he'd ask none of them for help. When fifty deer-stealers cleared themselves by ordeal, he remarked that God didn't know the deeds of men or else he weighed them in an unfair balance. He was angry if anyone added the proviso of God's will to some work he undertook or was ordered to do. The monks insisted that Ranulf, his chief adviser, was the son of a pagan or witch. He had an odd oath, 'By the face of Lucca!' which we find him using furiously when arguing with the bishops.

Dreams seem to have entered much into daily life and its problems. Peter, prior of the Holy Trinity, London, 1197–1221, wrote a huge compilation of revelations from the other world; he also held

strong millenary beliefs. He tells us about a man John of the village
of Orpington, who recounted events connected with his father
Jordan and his grandfather Ailsi. Ailsi lived in Cornwall, intent on
pleasing God and St Stephen, so he clung to the canons at Launceston
(Llanstephen), from whom he held his land. The saint 'familiarly
revealed to him many hidden matters and prophecies, and graci-
ously cherished him in all his anxious cares, and often healed his
infirmities'. He used to appear as a man of venerable aspect. Ailsi
acted as treasurer for the canons when they were building a tower
for their church; he attended 'not only to the work itself, but also
to the workmen and servants'. The saint would come to him
in visions and 'show him how he wished all things to be done,
diligently teaching him which of the workmen were faithful and
should be kept, which were faithless and should be sent away'. Three
of his miracles are recorded. Once Ailsi was diseased in the eye.
Leaving his work, on his way home he lamented, 'O blessed Stephen,
for long I've toiled in your service, yet now it seems in vain. If I'd
served the earl of Moreton, who's now Lord of Cornwall, as faith-
fully as I've served you, he'd have enriched me with many gifts. But
you, to whom I've committed myself and my whole soul and all
my property now give me over to torture.' He reached home as he
was thus inveighing; but that night the saint visited him with gentle
rebukes and cured his eye by touching it.

Ailsi often talked with the saint 'as a man speaks with a
friend'. Afterwards he described the meetings to his friends, so that
he was called the Holy. His children, 'who were also justified in their
kinship to him', he used to call the Half-Saints. He had four sons
'over and beyond the daughters he begot'. The two eldest, Bernard
and Nicholas, 'through their learning and their virtues earned the
familiarity and affection' of Henry I, 'and were esteemed first
among the foremost of the court'. They gave the saint's church a blue
banner embroidered with gold, in the middle of which was shown
the Lamb, with the stoning of Stephen below and the symbols of
the four evangelists in the corners; they also gave a carpet and a
silver-studded ivory casket full of relics (the casket had been their
writing case and still held their great silver inkstand).

The third son, Jordan of Trecarl, a layman like Ailsi, was the
heir. 'To his servants and serfs he was almost a companion. He was
learned in secular law and customs beyond all his brothers.' Many
persons asked for his help, 'but he would take no cause for gain
unless he knew it to be just'. The fourth son, Paganus, was not baptized till he was twelve and died soon after. God 'sent to Ailsi in a
vision of the night his son Paganus' to tell him about the pains and
rewards of the afterworld, 'to lead him down to the place of hell-

pains and up to the mansions of the blest'. Peter the prior recounts the dream in much detail, 'until at last both child and vision melted away together, and the father awoke to find himself in his own house, much troubled by reason of the dream'. (The fourth son's name, Paganus, and his late baptism, are strange in this pious setting.)

To understand the pressures which made men grasp at wild intuitions of unknown forces ceaselessly playing upon them, we must look at the vast changes taking place over the whole of western Europe. England was involved in these changes, though with her own particular situation, and her own way of refracting the general ideas and images of clash, conflict, change, hopeless suffering and desperate hope. The expansive movement in western Europe from the eighth century onwards, which brought about increases in population and a fuller use of economic resources, also had its oppressive and dislocating aspects.

The Viking migrations were the last great movement inwards of barbarians (that is, of peoples outside the Roman and the Christian enclave), but they were followed by the crusades, which, despite their religious aspects, reflected the same desire of warrior groups for loot and land. And at home, in the regions where agriculture and industry were most successful, there were many painful changes going on, uprooting people, destroying them, and combining them in new forms of association. There was over-population (in terms of the capacity of the regions to employ and feed people) from the eleventh to the thirteenth centuries, especially in the area between the Somme and the Rhine, with its concentration of people in the parts that the counts of Flanders were seeking to control. Already in the eleventh century the lowlands and the Rhine valley could not support their populations under the existing agricultural systems, though the situation was slightly alleviated by efforts to reclaim land from sea or marsh and to cut down woodlands. The Germans were moving back eastwards into areas where the Slavs had settled. The same centuries saw the growth of the great cloth industry in what is now Belgium and north-east France. The Rhine valley was closely linked with this development through its merchants, who by the thirteenth century dominated the markets of north Europe. Through them Flemish cloth found its way to new markets in central and south Germany and in the Levant. Cologne was a point where many routes met, with fine textile and copper industries. Impoverished or landless peasants were drawn in. Some settled to the industries and crafts, some got lesser jobs, towing boats, hauling merchandise and so on, while others gave up the land and its way of life without being able to satisfy their new needs. Beggars crowded the markets and roamed

in gangs from town to town. Landless men swelled the bands of mercenaries. But campaigns were short and the soldiers were continually
in desperate straits. The name Brabaçons came to mean marauding
bands of soldiers from Brabant and around it. In Flemish towns, with
populations of 20–50,000, the wretched went down as they could
not have done in the villages; kin groups could not persist or guild-
substitutes take form, except in the settled crafts. So we get a mass of
journeymen, unskilled workers, peasants with no land or tiny plots,
beggars, vagabonds, and workless men on the edge of disaster. Such
folk provided a miserable and restless herd (unlike anything in Viking
days), which was one of the great unsettling elements of the period.

The crusades were launched in 1096 and 1146. We saw how Pope
Urban II made his appeal in Clermont at a council concerned with
the Truce of God. While he offered remission from temporal
penalties for the taking of the Cross, and total remission of sins for
death in battle, he also contrasted the impoverished condition of
many nobles with the prosperity they would enjoy after conquering
new fiefs in southern lands. A vast enthusiasm swept the assembly;
they cried, 'It is God's will!' The agitation was carried on by
preachers, prophets and hermits.

The decade 1085–95 had been harder than usual in north-east
France and west Germany, with floods, droughts and famines; since
1083 there had been plague. Whole families moved with children
and chattels piled on the carts, the horde of paupers swollen by all
sorts of crooks and adventurers. Men felt that if they could only
reach Jerusalem and capture it, they would enter a blessed life. The
mass movement which had shown itself in such pilgrimages as those
of 1033 and 1064 had become a militant, desperate eruption. The
feeling that safety lay in destroying the enemies of the faith led to
the first massacres of Jews in Europe; the first crusade led to the
attack on Jews in Speyer by crusaders in May 1096. But this involved
little murdering compared to the later large-scale destruction at
Worms and Mainz, with sacking of synagogues, looting of houses,
and murdering of all who refused to be baptized. Children were
killed or taken off for baptism. Preparations for the second crusade
provoked the people of Normandy and Picardy to kill more Jews.
On the Rhine an ex-monk called on the populace to slaughter the
Jews as a fitting send-off for the crusade.

In 1198 a prophet, Fulk of Neuilly, called on the poor to start their
own crusade; they perished on the coast of Spain. Soon after came
the children's crusade; almost all the children were drowned, starved,
or sold into slavery. Prophetic movements at home demanded a total
change of the world, the day of doom, the last judgment, a
redeemed earth, paradise. The check to outward expansion, with its

hope of land and liberation, turned aspirations inward, where they were given a deep imprint of collective hope.

Tauchelm in the Lowlands in the late eleventh century denounced the churches as brothels and holy orders as hopelessly degraded. He called for the withholding of tithes. His area was one that had seen communal uprisings for years. Starting in 1074, town after town in the Rhine valley, Utrecht, Brabant, Flanders, and north France, struggled to get as free as possible from feudal overlords, lay or ecclesiastical: the merchants wanted to escape from the dues and levies. Tauchelm formed his followers into a devoted community, the one true church; he said he possessed the holy spirit as much as Christ and that he too was God; he ruled as a messianic king. St Norbert was brought in against him, a great noble who had taken the way of poverty.

About the same time a monk called Henry was entangled in the struggles of the folk of Le Mans with their bishop. He preached against the clergy and held a bonfire of vanities. Later, in Italy and Provençe, he more fully developed a creed of apostolic life and simplicity, saying that love of one's neighbour was the essence of religion and that the authority of the church must be wholly rejected. Out of Brittany in the 1140s came Eudes of the Star, organizing his own church and calling himself the son of God. (The winter of 1144 was terrible, followed by two years of dearth.) He made his lair in a forest and raided and destroyed churches and monasteries. In 1148 he was captured by a band that the archbishop of Rouen sent against him, under a portentous comet. At a synod presided over by Pope Eugenius he was condemned and handed over to the archbishop, who starved him to death in a tower. His chief followers were burned at the stake.

These outbreaks were part of a larger movement. Eudes may have been in touch with the Apostolic Brethren centred in the diocese of Chalons and found in most of the northern provinces of France. Their main tenets were that baptism was of no avail before the age of thirty, when Christ was baptized; that there was no resurrection of the body; that all property, meat and wine must be abjured. In the case of Arnold of Brescia, pupil of Abelard, apocalyptic views became directly political; he was inspired by the idea of Republican Rome to denounce the temporal powers of the papacy. After the defeat of his republic of Rome, one sect of Arnoldists called themselves the Poor Men. Other dissidents were the Pasagni or Circumcized in Italy, who preached the law of Moses and the Ebionite notion of Jesus. In France the Caputiati, with an image of the Virgin on their hats, sought a return to primal equality and freedom. The Apostolici, mostly poor workers, had their two main leaders burned. But the main centre of anti-papal heresies was Provençe, where in the early twelfth century Pierre de Bruys denounced the worship of images and veneration of the cross; Christ should be execrated rather than venerated; only a man's own faith could save him. He too was burned alive. Peter Waldo, a rich Lyon merchant, gave up his property to his wife and the poor, and went preaching in the streets. At the same time Catharism was appearing from the east, with its asceticism and its belief that the world was given up wholly to evil. In the early thirteenth century the papacy unloosed a bloody crusade against southern France and wiped out its brilliant civilization, in which the troubadors had founded modern literature with their subtle and complex poetry. The Franciscan friars, with their return to apostolic poverty, showed the effect of the heretical movements inside the monastic tradition; they did, however, become part of the church, though the section called Spirituals, who could not accept property even in a disguised form, was finally denounced by the papacy. Linked with the outlook of the Spirituals was the influential work of Joachim of Fiore, who found the Cistercian rule too easy and became a hermit in Calabria. The notes and introduction to his *Everlasting Gospel* announced the failure of Christianity and the birth of a new religion.[7]

During these years the English church seems to have been undisturbed by the deeper currents of inquiry and dissent. Yet these currents were strong in Flanders and north-east France, with which England has so many links. Catharism had appeared in the Rhineland and in Flanders by the mid-twelfth century. In 1157 Archbishop Samson of Rheims attacked a group described as *publicani* (clearly Paulicians); a group of heretics was burned at Cologne in 1163; in England a church council ordered the dissidents to be branded on the chin; in Burgundy the heretics were put to the ordeal in 1167 and then burned. Wandering weavers spread ideas, so that weaver and heretic became almost synonymous terms. But these ideas did not flourish in England to the extent of much disturbing the church. Perhaps the reason for this lay in the political situation. The mass of the English people, toiling in various degrees of subjection under alien lords and unable to find any effective basis on which to organize and struggle, may well have been in a condition of emotional and moral exhaustion and bewilderment, groping in darkness for the lost centres of their personal and social being, gathering new energies for resistance and renewal, but powerless as yet to find outlets for expression. The enemy and his nature were clear, and so there was not the recoil into deep fantasy hopes of a millenary kind. The distinctive aspects of the English situation were: that the ruling class was alien in a sense unknown in other feudalized regions of western Europe; that it had imposed a strong government also without parallel; and that, despite this alien rule, the folk courts and many other aspects of traditional Anglo-Saxon organization continued to function – the result being a maximum of tension between the popular and ruling levels. We must add that the urbanizing trends (with their basis in mercantile and craft activities) had not yet advanced in England to anything like the extent they had in Flanders and southern France.

On a broad view the idea of a golden age – an earthly paradise, a saturnian earth of brotherhood and equality, a pastoral condition freed from all the conflicts of property and power which bedevil a class society – is derived from the memory of tribal society in its earlier phases – a memory which greatly simplifies and glamourizes the facts. Projected into the future, the image appears as the resolution of all existing contradictions and conflicts; but, since there is no actual basis for such a resolution, the advent of the desired society of harmony and justice can only be conceived as brought about magically, by some divine intervention; and since productive powers are still at a low level, the achievement of plenty can also only be magically conceived. Hence the imagery of spontaneous production for human needs by nature in the utopias, whether secular or religious. In the tradition carried on by Christianity there were many ingredients, Persian, Greek (especially Stoic), Egyptian, and so on; but the reaction of people at any historical moment was entangled in turn with their specific relation to the tribal past and its surviving forms of association (such as the kindreds).

Still, if the situation in England was such that it held back the growth of large dissident movements, millenary-utopian or directly political, we can perhaps find an oblique connection with the Provençal developments in the cult of St Gilles, which had been particularly favoured by the counts of Toulouse; they fostered the town of St Gilles and Raymond IV said that he would prefer to have Count of St Gilles as his title. There is a charming legend about a white hind that gave the saint milk and was chased by a royal hunter; the latter's arrow hit the hermit by mistake. But what gave Gilles his special appeal was an anti-clerical note: the belief that he could forgive sins without the sinner having to confess them to a priest. To support the belief in this power a tale was invented about Charlemagne being unable to tell him some grave sin, which Gilles then read in an angel-borne scroll; he handed the scroll to the king and gave him absolution. As we saw, private confession was a comparatively recent custom, which vastly increased the church's hold on people, so that the legend of St Gilles and the practices it encouraged were opposed to this development and represented embryonic protestant views of the direct relation between Christian and God – even though here a saint still meditates.[8] The papal crusade destroyed the culture of Provençe and Toulouse, and did much damage to the town of St Gilles; but the cult spread much in north France and England. In France the saint's name was given to clowns of popular farces and to their waistcoats *(gilets)*; the saint was the patron of the poor, especially cripples (called in England Hopping or Hobbling Giles) and outcasts such as lepers or beggars.

In England he was in particular the saint of country workers, and some hundred churches were dedicated to him, mostly in small places. He had almost twice as many churches as even the popular martyr (killed by the king, the State) St Thomas of Canterbury. He was only beaten later by St George, but that was not until the eighteenth and nineteenth centuries. One of his earliest churches here was built under Rufus when Hugolina founded a monastery of six Augustinian canons near Cambridge castle with a church dedicated to St Giles; in 1112 the canons moved across the river to Barnwell, where they raised a church to Giles and Andrew. Under Rufus also came the first of the hospitals dedicated to him, outside Cripplegate, London. The founder was Alfune, friend of Rahere, the converted jester, who, after a vision of St Bartholomew, built a church for that saint at Smithfield on a site used for dumping rubbish and hanging criminals. Alfune was the first warden of Rahere's hospital. Soon after, Matilda, wife of Henry I, in 1117 founded a hospital of St Giles for lepers in fields outside London: St Giles in the Fields. Guillaume de Berneville (Barnwell Priory) wrote a *Life of St Giles* in Anglo-Norman verse, which was one of the sources of Lydgate's *Life* of the saint in Middle English. 'O gracious Giles, of poor folk chief patron.'[9]

St Giles, then, with his belief in forgiveness of sins without sacramental confession (against the church's doctrine), his links with folk drama and his championship of the poor and the outcast, preserved many signs of his origins in heretical southern France.

Looking back at the eccentricities of Rufus, we cannot rule out the possibility that he had been influenced by the heretical freethinking of Toulouse and Provençe. William IX of Aquitaine was friendly with him, came to his aid in his campaigns in France, and eventually pledged his duchy to him. This duke, who was also William VII of Poitou, was the first known troubador; his *Song of Nothing* is a witty and paradoxical expression of unorthodox ideas, foreshadowing the dialectic of chastity-copulation, dearth-plenty, of the whole troubador ethic and aesthetic. That there was much exchange of ideas between certain elements of Anglo-Norman culture and the south, is shown by the career of Bletheris or Bleddri whom we find cited by the second continuator of the *Conte del Graal* as narrating the adventures of Gawain and a dwarf knight, a poet 'who was born and reared in Wales...and who told it [the story] to the count of Poitiers, who loved the story and held it more than any other firmly in memory'. The story seems quite in the vein of many tales told by Girald of Wales; and other references, including one which says Blihis (Bliheris) insisted that the secrets of the Grail must not be revealed, authenticate the activities of the Welsh poet in France. The count of Poitou whom he knew must be our William (who ruled from about 1086 to 1127), not his son William VIII. The earliest known reference to Tristram as a famous lover came in the 1150s from two troubadors, Cercamon and Bernard de Ventador, both closely connected with the court of Poitou.[10]

In England, as elsewhere in these years, one of the main sources of strain in people was the persisting and not always consciously perceived conflict between the church and ingrained pagan attitudes. One result was a pervasive sense of insecurity. People felt surrounded by hostile and unsettling forces which they could not identify. The sacraments of the church gave a certain relief, but could only palliate their fears. Indeed in many ways the church increased the strain by opposing magical ideas of its own to the pagan ones, for example asserting that everywhere the air was thick with swarming demons who sought entry into human beings. Such beliefs easily merged with the old attitudes set out for instance in the Anglo-Saxon *Leechbooks*, that men were surrounded by dwarfs who could make themselves invisible, by elves who shot tiny shafts at their victims and caused diseases, by little wormlike things that wriggled under men's skin, and by elf breath that was wafted on the air to spread illness. There were nine specific venoms, Onflying Things, 'the Loathed Things that run through the land'. Sudden pains were the result of spears shot into a man by wicked women (witches) in league with the elves. Pagan and Christian imagery merged in magical formulas: 'A drink for a fiend-sick man: when a devil possesses a man or affects him from within with disease, a drink is to be drunk out of a church-bell...' Hell was the Mouth of the devouring Whale; and there were numerous paintings in the churches depicting the hell mouth.

William of Newburgh tells us of a man named Ketell, who lived in the village of Farnham, Yorkshire, and who had the gift of seeing devils if they were present. Once he entered a *domus potationis* and saw a little devil sitting on each man's drinking-cup. When prayers

were said 'as the custom is', the devils flew away and only came back
when the rustics resumed their seats and their drinking. (Whether
the *domus* of drinking was in a village or a market town we don't
know; Aethelred II had laid down penalties for a breach of the peace
in an ale-house, but we don't know if the law referred to villages as
well as towns. The ale-house must have been an important gathering
place of the folk, but we know little of it.) From the tenth-century
Blicking homilies to the later sermons of Friars and other ecclesiastics, the moment when the preacher comes warmly and passionately
to life is when he reaches the theme of death, burial, judgment, and
hell-pains – events that are seen as taking place in a vast panorama
of swarming devils.

> Gazing into the unknown abyss, helpless upon his deathbed, the
> devils whirling above him, or lurking under the furniture,
> friends and acquaintances waiting at his side, the stoutest
> medieval sinner becomes a trembling savage again. There in the
> awful air, in every nook and cranny we behold primeval mon-
> sters of the past, implacable spirits returned to haunt the
> enfeebled race (Owst).

The image of the individual death was linked with that of Judgment
Day, the Day of Doom. 'Alwey when I thenke on the last Day, for
drede my bodie quaketh.' Here was the personal anxiety reflecting
the general social crisis.

Yet, while stimulating certain elements of paganism, the church
had to fight obvious survivals of pagan cults. Much of the conflict
could not but be subterranean, ambiguous, and confused; but it
continually irrupted into the open. Under Aethelred we read, 'If
anyone is guilty of offering obstruction or open opposition anywhere
to the law of Christ or of the king, he shall pay wergild or *wite* or
lahslit, according to the nature of the offence.' Thus ecclesiastical
offences became secular crimes as well. The principle seems to have
been observed; for in the *Law of the Northumbrian Priests* secular
penalties are listed that are not given in any extant royal codes.
Offences include the oppression and sale of churches, heathenism and
witchcraft. Under Cnut we meet an increased concern with heathen
practices. (At the end of the ninth century the Mercian kingdom
had been overrun by heathen Danes; one of the greatest Mercian
kings, Penda, was a heathen. Sweyn son of Harald Bluetooth, was
baptized as a child, but as a man he waged a religious war against
his father; as late as the end of the thirteenth century a Norwegian
king was called Priest-hater.) Edgar is said to have attacked, at
Dunstan's request, the unlawfully married, false coiners, faith-

breakers, sorcerers (*veneficii compistores*), whoremongers, traitors, kinsmen-slayers, women who killed husbands 'by adulterous deceits', and those whose life was odious to God. His laws specified the unseemly marriage of widows, heathen practices, and witchcraft; he appealed to every Christian 'zealously to accustom his children to Christianity'.

Especially in the north and the Danelaw, Christianity must often have been not even a veneer; everywhere the old faiths were very much alive, directly and indirectly. Church-reformers were particularly interested in black magic and murder. Under the stress of the invasions there must have been a more active reversion to pagan ideas and practices, with a deepened sense that dark forces were at work. About 1020 Bishop Aethelric of Dorchester brought an action against Thorkell the Tall, Jomsviking of East Anglia, and his second wife Edith, after a witch confessed to being accessory to the murder of Thorkell's son by the stepmother. The earl ignored three summons, so the bishop bided his time till he could draw Cnut in. The king, told of the earl's contumacy, summoned him to court. Thorkell and Edith attended and were accused by the bishop. The judgment was that the earl with eleven compurgators and Edith with as many female ones should clear themselves by oath at a site appointed by Aethelric. The latter chose the meadow where he said the murdered child was buried, and bade the abbey of Ramsey bring out its best relics for the oath ordeal. Before a great crowd of clerks and laymen, Thorkell swore his own innocence, and then, to save Edith, swore on his beard that she too was innocent. His beard came away in his hand. Edith denied the charge. The bishop ordered the secret tomb to be opened. Then she broke down and confessed. Thorkell was found guilty of perjury and Edith of homicide. Penances were laid on them; and Thorkell gave Aethelric a piece of land for flouting his jurisdiction, which land he transferred to Ramsey. In 1021 Thorkell was outlawed, but we do not know if there was any connection with the trial. The story has come down to us only because the chronicler of Ramsey abbey wanted to explain the gift of land. There must have been many lesser cases of witchcraft that we know nothing of, but in any event it was only some three centuries later that the western church felt itself capable of trying to extirpate witchcraft.[11]

William of Malmesbury tells of a Berkeley witch, 'I heard it from a man of such character that I'd blush to disbelieve him, and he swore he had seen it all.' The witch was skilled in augury and devoted to gluttony and lewdery, 'as she wasn't old, though fast declining in life'. One day as she ate, her jackdaw, a great favourite, chattered more loudly than usual; she dropped her knife, paled and groaned. 'This day my plough has finished its last furrow; today I'll hear and suffer some dreadful disaster.' At that moment a messenger arrived: 'I bring news from the village of the death of your son and the whole family by a sudden accident.' She took to bed. The disorder approached her vitals, so she wrote to her surviving children, a monk and a nun. 'I've constantly administered to my wretched circumstances by demoniacal arts. I've been the sink of every vice, the teacher of every allurement. Yet, practising these arts, I soothed my hapless soul with the hope of your piety.' Now, near her end, she begged them 'by your mother's breasts', that if they couldn't revoke the sentence passed on her soul, they might perhaps save her body.

> Sew up my corpse in a stagskin, lay it on its back in a stone coffin, fasten the lid down with lead and iron, set on it a stone bound round with three chains of enormous weight, let psalms be sung for fifty nights and masses said for fifty days, to allay the ferocious attacks of my adversaries. If I lie three nights secure, on the fourth day bury your mother in the ground, though I fear the earth so often burdened with my crimes will refuse to receive and cherish me in her bosom.

They obeyed. On the first two nights, when a choir of priests was singing psalms, the devil burst the huge bolt on the churchdoor and broke two outer chains; the middle one stayed fast. Next night about cockcrow the monastery seemed to overturn; a yet more huge and terrible devil smashed the gates as the priests stood with hair on end. He called on the woman to rise. She replied that she was chained. 'You shall be loosed and to your cost.' Breaking the chain, he bashed the coffin lid in with his foot, took her hand, and dragged her out. At the doors appeared a black horse with iron hooks bristling all over its back. She was set on it and the whole group vanished, though her cries were heard for four miles around.[12]

William of Newburgh tells how a man, riding home from North Barton in the East Riding, heard sounds of merriment coming from Willy Howe (an early round barrow).

> He saw a door open in the side of the mound, and riding close to it, he looked in and saw a great feast. One of the cupbearers approached and offered him a drink. He took the cup, threw out the contents, and galloped off. The fairy banqueters gave chase but he managed to outdistance them and reached home safely with his prize. The cup is said to have been given to Henry I.

But despite all these superstitions there were also mockers such as William Rufus. Girald of Wales said, 'Many hide secretly their unbelief among us today.' One priest remarked to another, who criticised him for his indecorous way of celebrating mass. 'Can you out of this bread make flesh? Out of this wine make blood? Could you imagine that God the creator of all took flesh of a woman and wished to suffer? Do you think a virgin can conceive and remain a virgin? Do you think our bodies, reduced to dust, will rise? All that we do is hypocrisy.' Such ideas were in part stirred by the arguments going on about the Real Presence in the elements of communion. Lanfranc set out the plain magical belief in transubstantiation:

> We believe that the earthly substances which are divinely consecrated at the Lord's Table through the priestly mystery, are by ineffable incomprehensible wondrous operation of the heavenly power, converted into the essence of the Lord's Body, while the appearances and certain other qualities of the same realities remain behind, in order that men should be spared the shock of perceiving raw and bloody things, and that believers should receive the fuller rewards of faith.

This position was accepted at the Lateran council of 1215. But Berengar of Tours had declared that the elements cannot be 'the very body and blood of our Lord', and 'cannot be handled by the hands of the priest or broken or crushed by the teeth of the faithful with the senses'.

Perhaps because of the complexity of the struggle between ancient pagan ways and the imposed Christian creed in England, we find that it was a source of fantastic literature. Geoffrey of Monmouth was the greatest figure in the invention of fantasy-history and the embellishment of old traditions; but his writings were part of a wide trend. William of Malmesbury and others loved a tale full of marvels. William gave the first full series of tales about the magical powers of Gerbert, Pope Silvester II, the encyclopedist humanist who was an important precursor of the cultural outburst of the twelfth century, who in the legend sold his soul to the devil after seducing the daughter of his Moslem host in Spain and stealing a book that 'held everything that is to be known', and who had a human head cast that answered all questions. John of Salisbury was the first writer to mention the stories of Virgil the Magician, which became very popular. Probably through Petrus Alphonsi many eastern legends reached Britain and were there disseminated in Latin form. England contributed the fullest accounts of journeys to the other world;

Henry of Saltrey, Adam of Eynsham, the Yorkshire Orm, and Thurkill with his vision first told by Ralph of Coggeshall, all carried on a tradition going back to Bede. Under Henry I, with the queen as patron, Benedeit made an Anglo-Norman version of *St Brendan's Voyage* which, after many wonderful and colourful romantic scenes, ended in paradise. We may mention also the English illuminated manuscripts of the twelfth century, dealing with Bestiaries, Herbals, Lapidaries, the Marvels of the East, and later the Apocalypse; the menagerie kept by Henry I and the abbreviation of Pliny's *Natural History* made for Henry II.[18]

Though attempts to put the Virgin Mary at the heart of the scheme of redemption had got under way in the eleventh century, with men like Fulbert at Chartres and Anselm at Bec prominent in the movement, no signs of the impact of their thought can be noted in Anglo-Saxon England. Yet the church there pioneered in observing the feast of the Conception of the Virgin; and in the twelfth century England seems to have been the key source of Mary legends, which spread abroad with vast popularity. They widened the vein of fantasy in tales of miraculous cures, and stimulated devotional practices that had begun in the late eleventh century. The practices arose in the monasteries, and there also no doubt the stories, especially at Canterbury, Bury, Malmesbury, and Evesham; but they were aimed at drawing the laity in. Anselm, nephew of the archbishop, abbot at Bury in 1120, seems to have been the first to think of collecting the tales. He started off with several from foreign sources, but on arriving in England he encountered the wealth of recent inventions. In his final collection (about 1125) were some forty tales. Dominic, prior of Evesham, made his own collection at about the same time; and soon afterwards William of Malmesbury in his old age gathered some fifty-five stories, adding a devout preface. Then Master Alberic, canon of St Paul's, arranged the tales from Anselm, Dominic, and William; and his work became widely known. It was translated into French verse by another Londoner, a cleric Algar; and after that the tales appeared in all sorts of arrangements and versions in the vernacular of all European countries.[14]

Though in medieval society the class divisions were deep, the way in which people were thrown together in this world governed by direct personal relationships ensured that there was much cultural interplay between the different levels. For long the centres of cultural creation were located in the higher literate groups, especially the more active and responsive churchmen. Already in Merovingian times we find a deliberate use of popular elements, which we can call folklore, to bring home a message to wider circles; the climax of

o

this development appeared in the sermons of the Friars, which sought to reach the hearts of the townfolk, shake and terrify them, and exhort them to live better lives. But the same sort of drawing on popular levels for images and themes can be found throughout medieval literature from the twelfth century on. The traffic was indeed two-way. Ideas and values from the courtly level, such as the models of perfect knight and perfect clerk which we discussed, reached downwards, while elements from folklore, from folk custom and song, played an important part in courtly culture. We may note as instances the mayday dances and songs, with the theme of conflict between young lover and jealous old man, which is one key ingredient in the troubador ethic, and the pastoral imagery, with its interest in shepherds and rustic entertainments, which emerges in the fifteenth century. The resulting patterns of interaction of courtly and popular culture were highly complex.

England, like other lands of the Christian west, revealed in its culture an intense contradiction between the prevailing sexual morality and the symbolism of the church. Churchmen, sworn to celibacy and expressing the utmost horror of the sexual act, conceived the relation of Christ to the church or to its devout members as one of married copulation. Glaber writes: 'Each bishop, as the bridegroom of his own see, shows the likeness of the Saviour.' Pope Paschal objected to kings making church appointments because 'it is not right that a Mother should be so delivered into slavery by her son as to be given a husband whom she has not chosen'. Such imagery was universal and was consciously worked out. Hincmar in the ninth century stated that 'marriage lacks the symbolism of Christ and the Church if it is not treated as marriage, that is, if there is no intercourse of sexes'. Peter Lombard said that in a marriage based only on consent, the union of Christ and his Church was symbolized, since it was a union forged by charity, but in a consummated marriage the union of the members of Christ's body was signified, both being complementary aspects of a single sacramental union. We may note too the stress on the church as the mother. The woman, rejected from a system where a male Trinity ruled and expressed the universe, reappeared as mediator; the faithful were reborn in her womb. As the deep cleavages of early feudal society were partly veiled and modified by the beginnings of a burgess class, the cult of the Virgin Mary gained a new momentum.[15]

Out of the same general development came new attitudes to love and women in secular literature. In many ways the Conquest, with its intensification of the concept of private property, and its emphasis on war and law, brought about a fall in the moral and social position of women among the upper classes. An estate had to be kept intact; daughters and younger sons could rely only on the father's generosity. A woman could still inherit land and in theory alienate it; but she was not supposed to appear in court or make a will without her husband's leave. The reformed church stood out strongly for womanly submission to the male. Even a woman freed by widowhood from male guardianship could, if an heiress, be forced by the king into a new marriage; or he might instead take money from her. The first glimmer of women's rights appeared when Magna Carta laid down that a widow could remain single if she promised not to marry without the lord's consent. Yet, when the chance came, women showed themselves as capable of wielding power as men, even of fighting as brutally (as we saw with Robert Guiscard's wife). A baron's wife was left with only a third of her husband's land by law; but a villein's widow could hold all the land as long as the customary service was done; her place in the home was secure as long as she stayed unwed. A labouring woman in general, as in almost any society, was freed to some extent by her need to mix with people and do her job.

The extension of church controls also helped to darken the whole idea of womanhood, strengthening the denunciation of sexual activity as evil and of woman (Eve) as the agent of man's fall. Peter Lombard accepted the maxim: passionate love of one's wife is a form of adultery. Even when the scholastics played chop-logic with the theme (as when Aquinas said that the evil lay, not in the carnal desire and pleasure, but in the suspension of intellectual activity), the essential horror was there. Yet, as a result of the same general forces that issued in the cult of the Virgin Mary, we find the advent and growth of the idea and practice of Courtly Love, finding its first great expression in the troubadors. They almost inverted Peter Lombard's maxim and said: 'Then let adultery be our passionate love'. The whole complex dialectic of their poetry, as it developed through the twelfth century, was a retort to the ecclesiastical notion of Woman. They used paradoxes of loss and absence to define the psychological and social situation in which they adored Woman as the ultimate source of joy and satisfaction, of life itself, but in which they felt cut off from that source, an unbridgeable gap between actual and potential. The troubador ethic and aesthetic had little direct effect on twelfth-century England; but it did have effects on the position of women, with which it was both directly and symbolically concerned. We may therefore glance at the cultural role of upper class women at this time.

The literature of the first half of the century was the work of clerks, whether regular, secular, or merely literate. But patrons played an active role. We must visualize the nobility as living most of the year in castle or manor, in a rather isolated way. They looked in at the patronal feasts of religious houses which they or their fathers had founded. A chaplain lived with them or was borrowed from the nearest monastery, combining religious work with work as secretary, librarian, and tutor. Every morning the family attended chapel; and if there was no fighting, the day might be taken up with hunting or games of backgammon or chess in bad weather. Orderic gives us a good glimpse of the high-spirited sort of horseplay that the men indulged in. 'Once Rufus and his brother Henry played with *tesserae* [dice] as is the custom of soldiers' on the solar in a house in the castle of L'Aigle. Hearing an uproar below, they poured down water on their brother Robert and his men (apparently outside the house). Robert rushed into the dining room to retaliate. Rufus and Henry seem to have been in a first floor hall; Robert dashed up an external staircase and found them at their game in the hall (such as we see at Christchurch or Boothby Pagnell). Tales would be told when the tables were taken away or the nobility retired to the room called the solar, where Rufus and Henry were playing. Though children had to be superintended as they came from the nursery, and husbands or guests required food and entertainment, the ladies were often left alone for long periods and wanted distraction. They discussed things with the chaplain. Books were needed. They were borrowed from neighbours and supplemented with story-telling, family traditions, local legends, lives of patron saints, romances or songs gathered from wayfaring minstrels. Thus the ladies could become the centre for tales and poems from all sorts of quarters, where the creation of new works was stimulated and various influences converged. Though men did most of the travelling, wives too moved about, to pilgrim shrines, to friends in England or across the Channel, where the family might also have estates. Soon the universities were to be in full swing and town life was to grow richer; but the lords' country houses survived in one form or another as important social and cultural centres until the eighteenth century.[16]

A graceful tribute to the way the lady's chamber became a centre for the culture of the feudal world appears in the poem that Baudri of Bourgueil wrote for Countess Adela, daughter of William I: a detailed vision of her vast and magnificent bedroom. The poet had no doubt never seen the room; he described it as it should be. On the walls of the alcove are tapestries depicting the battle of Hastings; on the other walls the story of man's creation and fall is shown, with Old Testament history up to the Kings; then comes Greek mythology and the story of Rome's foundation, with the names of a hundred kings. The ceiling is painted to represent the heavens, with zodiac, planets, sun and moon; on the floor is a *mappa mundi*, with the sea and its monsters, its fishes, the rivers and the continents, together with all the marvels of nature. Lastly comes the bed, adorned with statues representing Philosophy and the Seven Arts. As an example of the way in which the lady in her chamber could help in the development of poetry, we may take Benedeit and his poem on the *Voyage of St Brendan*, perhaps the oldest work written in octosyllabic rhyming couplets, which, we noted earlier, was dedicated to Maud, great-niece of the Confessor and wife of Henry I. This poem, derived probably from an Irish *imram*, seems to have been written first in Latin, then translated into Anglo-Norman for the queen, her ladies and maidens. It is full of vivid marvels: a deserted city of great splendour, an Easter feast on the back of a sleeping whale, a paradise of birds with its choir of fallen angels, a frozen sea, a magic, intoxicating spring, fights between sea-monsters, griffins and dragons, the smithy of hell, the volcano of Hecla (where Judas is imprisoned), and at last paradise itself.[17]

As a final example of the way in which even small matters could be moralized upon and made into portents, we may take the question of the long hair of the knights, which is also interesting in that it shows the first important borrowing by the Normans from the conquered English in the social sphere. Wulfstan of Worcester had attacked the morals of the English on the eve of 1066, paying particular attention to the men's long hair. This long hair he took as a proof that they would be unable to defend the land against invaders. He urged Harold when in Northumbria in 1066 to reform such corrupting customs, which had grown up in an age of peace and easy affluence. His biographer Coleman held that his prophecy was confirmed. 'For such was the feebleness of the wretched people that after the first battle they never attempted to rise up for liberty behind a common shield.'

In fact the Vikings may have worn their hair long. A stele shows a Frankish warrior of the late seventh century combing his hair: this seems to represent a survival of the forces of life; while a double-headed serpent surrounding his head represents the forces of darkness that take the dead into their realm.[18] The Normans, who had cropped their hair, adopted the English fashion of long hair, apparently charmed by the comeliness of the young English nobles. Eadmer tells us:

Now at this time it was the fashion for nearly all the young men of the court to grow their hair long like girls; then, with tresses well combed, glancing about them and winking in ungodly fashion, they would daily walk abroad with delicate steps and mincing gait.

Anselm preached against the fashion at the start of Lent and many had haircuts. The moralists regarded the long hair as a certain sign of homosexuality. Eadmer goes on to tell how Anselm rebuked Rufus:

> This most shameful crime of sodomy, not to speak of illicit marriages between persons of kindred blood, and other wicked dealings in things abominable, that crime, I say, of sodomy, but lately spread abroad in this land, has already borne fruit all too abundantly and has with its abomination defiled many.

Unless king and church quickly suppressed it, the whole land would become 'little better than Sodom itself'.

Rufus seems certainly to have been homosexual, and in a semi-military caste like that of the Norman nobles sodomy was no doubt a common practice. Later Eadmer returns to the theme, citing a letter sent by 'a man of no mean standing' to Anselm at Bec. He remarks of the laity:

> They, but most of all the princes, take to themselves wives almost always of their own family; they plight troth secretly; girls plighted contrary, as they well know, to the law of the church they keep and maintain for themselves. What of Sodomites, whom you yourself in the great council excommunicated until they should repent and make confession; or of those affecting long hair, whom just afterwards at the Easter celebration you, robed in your episcopal stole, publicly expelled from the doors of the holy church?

Near the end of his *Historia* Eadmer again takes up the subject, the men with long hair who 'now so abound and so boastingly pride themselves on the shameful girlish length of their locks that anyone who is not long-haired is branded with some opprobrious name, called country-bumpkin or priest'. In his summary of the transactions of the 1102 council, the last and far the longest section deals with the curse on those who commit sodomy or abet it, whether churchman or layman. The council also enacted that men should cut their hair enough to show part of the ear and the eyes.

William of Malmesbury describes the court under Rufus:

All military discipline being relaxed, the courtiers preyed on the property of the country people and consumed their substance, taking the very meat from the mouths of these wretched creatures. Then was there flowing hair and extravagant dress, and then was invented the fashion of shoes with curved points, then the model for young men was to rival women in delicacy of person, to mince their gait, to walk with loose gesture, and half naked. Enervated and effeminate, they unwillingly remained what nature had made them; the assailers of others' chastity, prodigal of their own. Troops of pathics and droves of whores followed the court.

Orderic tells us of Robert, Rufus's brother, that he was 'desperately abandoned to indolence and effeminacy'; at his court in Normandy 'the Venus of Sodom stalked boldly in the midst of such scenes, with her wanton enticements', while at Rufus's court 'the effeminate predominated everywhere and revelled without restraint'. Henry of Huntingdon saw the wreck of the White Ship as a punishment for sodomy:

In the passage the king's two sons, William and Richard, and his daughter and niece, with the earl of Chester and many nobles, were shipwrecked, as well as the king's butlers, stewards, and bakers, all or most of whom were said to have been tainted with the sin of sodomy. Behold the terrible vengeance of God. Sudden death swallowed them up unshriven, though there was no wind and the sea was calm.

William of Nangis says that on the ship, 'The lascivious and showy young men' were all, or most of them, 'tainted with the sin of sodomy', and Gervase agrees. Finally, William of Malmesbury adds an anecdote of an event of the late 1120s.

A circumstance occurred in England which may seem surprising to our long-haired gallants, who, forgetting what they were born, transform themselves into the fashion of females by the length of their locks. A certain English knight, who prided himself on the luxuriance of his tresses, was stung by conscience about it and seemed to feel in a dream as if someone strangled him with his ringlets. Waking in a fright, he at once cut off all his superfluous hair. The example spread through England; and as recent punishment is apt to affect the mind, almost all military men allowed their hair to be cropt in a proper manner, without reluctance. But this decency was not of long continuance. Scarcely had a year elapsed before all who thought themselves courtly had fallen back into their former vice. They vied with women in length of locks, and wherever they were defective they put on false tresses.[19]

At the Council of Nablus in 1120 under Baldwin II of Jerusalem the penalty of burning was decreed for sodomy; a contemporary says that the practice caused earthquakes, Saracenic attacks, and all sorts of disasters. The main denouncer of sodomy was Peter Damian in his *Liber Gomorrhianus* in which he says that it was prevalent among the clergy; he wanted all found guilty to be degraded from the order; but Pope Leo IX, to whom the book was dedicated, thought this too harsh. The English lawyer Fleta, in about 1290, wanted the penalty of burning alive; his contemporary Bracton also wanted the guilty to be burned like sorcerers and heretics.

CHAPTER XV

RESISTANCES
AND RECONCILIATIONS

It is hard to estimate just what the English suffered, how they reacted, what they felt and suppressed, as they watched the arrogant
Norman knights. Before we go on to deal with some of the evidence
which, directly or indirectly, shows us some of those hidden emotions, we had better take a few more examples of the way the
Normans behaved – a better documented matter. Thus Orderic
describes Hugh of Avranches, earl of Chester, the sort of ruthless
bully whom the English had to watch in stricken impotence and
dumb rage. The picture is a curious mixture, a bitter indictment that
cannot help revealing a fascinated admiration.

> This man with the help of many cruel barons shed much Welsh
> blood. He was not so much lavish as prodigal. His retinue was
> more like an army than a household; and in giving or receiving
> he kept no account. Each day he devastated his own land and

preferred falconers and huntsmen to the cultivators of the soil and ministers of heaven. He was so much a slave to the gluttony of his belly that, weighed down by fat, he could scarcely move. From harlots he had many children of both sexes, who almost all came to a miserable end.

He loved the world and all its pomps, which he regarded as the chief part of human happiness. For he was an active soldier, an extravagant giver, and found great pleasure in gaming and debauchery, and in jesters, horses, and hounds and other such vanities. An enormous household, which echoed with the clamour of a crowd of youths, both noble and common, was always in attendance. Some good men, clerks as well as knights, also lived with him and rejoiced to share in his labours and wealth.

He especially praises Gerold, a clerk from Avranches, in his chapel.[1]

Eadmer gives us a terrible picture of the behaviour of Rufus's court, a picture, we must recall, which deals with the situation after some decades of Norman rule. Even allowing for his ecclesiastical prejudice against the king, we cannot discount the general truth of what he says.

A great number of those attending his court had made a practice of plundering and destroying everything; and there being no discipline to restrain them, they laid waste all the territory through which the king passed. Not content with that, they adopted another malicious practice. Very many of them, intoxicated with their own wickedness, when they could not consume all the provisions that they found in the houses they invaded, made the owners of the goods take them to market and sell for their benefit; or else they set fire to them and burned them up; or if it were drink, they washed their horses' feet with it and then poured the rest of it on the ground or without fail found some other way of wasting it. What cruelties they inflicted on the fathers of families, what indecencies on their wives and daughters, it is shocking to think of. So, when it was known that the king was coming, all the inhabitants would flee from their homes, anxious to do the best they could for themselves and their families by taking refuge in woods or other places where they hoped to be able to protect themselves.

The royal court, we must recall, was continually on the move. The truth of the accusations of rape is supported by the story that Queen

Matilda told Anselm when he was investigating the charge that she had been made a nun as a girl.

> I did wear the veil, I don't deny it. When I was quite a young girl and went in fear of my aunt Christina, whom you knew quite well, she – to save me from the lust of the Normans which was rampant and at that time ready to assault any woman's honour – used to put a little black hood on my head, and when I threw it off, she would often make me smart with a good slapping and a most horrible scolding, as well as treating me as being in disgrace.

During the civil wars under Stephen there was a return, at least in many areas, to conditions in which the knights and retainers did as they pleased. A later lawsuit has preserved for us the career of one of the lawless soldiers, Warin of Walcote. He desired Isabel the daughter of Robert of Shuckburgh, but was refused. After Robert's son was killed in the wars, Warin carried the girl away with a host of men and held her for a long time.

> At length, after the death of king Stephen, when the peace of king Henry was proclaimed, Warin fell into poverty because he could not rob as he used to do; but he could not refrain from robbery and he went everywhere and robbed as he used. And king Henry, having heard complaints about him, ordered that he should be taken. At length, when he was sought out and ambushed, he came and hid himself at Grandborough in a certain reedy place, and there he was taken and led before the king at Northampton, and king Henry that he might set an example to others to keep his peace, by the counsel of his barons ordered him to be put in the pillory and there he was put and there he died.

Isabel, returning home, was married again and bore a son.[2] But even before Stephen we encounter much lawlessness. We may recall for instance the hanging of forty-four thieves in 1124 at Huncot in Leicestershire. It is a pity that the *Chronicle* does not specify what crimes the men were accused of. Were they mere criminals, or poverty-stricken peasants driven to theft, or members of a group taking revenge on their masters? Did they represent a moment of unrest, or was it merely that the thief-apprehenders were particularly active in late 1124 in that area?

Discontent at peasant level is hard to prove; but we have evidence of flight from estates. A precept of Rufus bids the sheriffs compel the return of fugitives from the lands of Ramsey Abbey; and more than a generation later Stephen issued similar orders. The second precept covered the chattels of the men as well as their persons. Under Henry I the same sort of trouble occurred on the lands of Abingdon Abbey; in three documents (issued from Woodstock, Wallingford and Westminster) the king ordered sheriffs and others to see that the fugitives were recovered with all their *pecunia* (probably livestock).[3] William of Poitiers, despite his attempts to idealize the situation, admitted how unreconciled the English were when he complained that neither kindness nor severity was sufficient to make the people prefer a quiet life to turbulent rebellion. In the great peasants' revolt of 1381 the people often appealed to the ancient charters of Saxon kings, which they believed had guaranteed the liberties denied them by the Norman lords. The men at St Albans appealed to a lost charter of Offa, those of Bury to one of Cnut.[4] Perhaps the *murdrum* fine instituted by William most clearly reflected the Norman fear of the English in the early days: this made a sharp distinction between Englishman and Frenchman, and sought to scare the English from killing Normans caught on their own. By it a hundred had to prove that the victim of a murderous attack was English or else lay themselves open to a corporate fine. Henry I in a dream aptly saw peasants threatening him with scythe and pitchfork.

What Richard fitzNeale, bishop of London and Treasurer, who died in 1198, has to say in his *Dialogue* of the *murdrum* brings out its significance clearly.

The Master: Murdrum is, properly, the secret death of a man whose killer is unknown; for the word *murdrum* means secret or hidden. Now in the earlier state of the realm after the Conquest, those English who were left were used to lie in wait for the dreaded and hated Normans, and secretly to kill them here and there in woods or secluded places. as the chance came up. So the kings and their ministers for some years inflicted the most exquisite tortures on the English, yet without full effect, till at length they imagined the following device. Wherever a Norman was found thus killed, if the killer didn't show himself or even betray himself by flight, then the whole of the district called the Hundred was fined on behalf of the royal treasury, some in £36 sterling and some in £44, according to the diversity of districts and the frequency of murders: which (as we hear) was decreed in order that this general penalty might secure the safety of wayfarers and all men might be spurred on to punish the crime or to hand over to justice that man who had brought so enormous a loss upon the whole neighbourhood. You must know that they who sit at the Exchequer are free from the payment of these fines.

The Disciple: Should not the secret death of an Englishman, as of a Norman, be imputed as *murdrum*?

The Master: Not at the first institution of this law, as you have heard; but now that English and Normans have lived so long together and have intermarried, the nations have become so intermingled (I speak of freemen only) that we can scarcely distinguish in these days between Englishmen and Normans, except of course those serfs bound to the land whom we call villeins and who cannot leave their condition without permission of their masters. So in these days, almost every secret manslaughter is punished as *murdrum* except those of whom (as I have said) it is certain that they are of servile condition.

The law however was not repealed till 1339.

Ailnoth of Canterbury speaks of the great hopes of the English in East Anglia in 1085 that the Danes would invade. An effective invasion might well have led to a large-scale uprising. Cnut remained highly popular in the area; his rowing song, 'Mury sung the muneches binnen Ely', is one of the oldest snatches of popular song in the Norman period. In 1108 Henry I married his daughter to the German emperor, taxing every hide in England 3s for the cost; but what the people really remembered was the marriage of Cnut's daughter some hundred years before to the emperor Henry. 'The splendour of the nuptial pageant was very striking,' wrote William of Malmesbury, 'and even in our times frequently sung in ballads about the streets.' Much later Matthew Paris declared, 'To this day men in their songs in taverns and at gatherings strive vainly to recapture the pomp of that wedding feast,' and from what follows it is clear that he is not just repeating William.

Orderic tells us that in 1132 a plot was discovered. All the Normans in England were to be killed on the same day and the kingdom was to be handed over to the Scots. No doubt there was more fear than fact in the story, but the fear was none the less significant. The *Gesta Stephani*, at their fragmentary end, tell how Walter de Pincheny took Christchurch castle by surprise, ravaged the neighbourhood, and secured the lordship of a large district.

But though he ought to have given up his old ways of cruelty and violence, lest through his sins he should fall once more into his enemies' hands, he continued to be fierce and tyrannical, to plunder mercilessly the church's possessions, to worry his neighbours with quarrels, and ceaselessly to extort money and offerings from all around, torturing some and killing off others from mere love of cruelty. But God the just judge at last repaid these grievous wrongs by a righteous judgment. For the inhabitants of the place, with some of the countryfolk, were no longer able to bear his barbarity. They formed a conspiracy with the soldiers on the lordship to which they belonged.

Walter was assassinated. Such plots were possible in disordered times; the failure of central controls that gave Walter his head also made it possible for the people to strike back at the ravagers.

An example of the conflict in the monastic world is the fight at Glastonbury in 1083 when the Norman abbot Thurstan tried to install the Dijon type of rites and chants in place of the Gregorian chant of which the monks claimed to be the inheritors. The *Chronicle* tells us:

Its origin was the abbot's folly in abusing his monks about many matters. The monks made an amicable complaint to him about it and asked him to rule them justly and have regard for them and in return they would be faithful and obedient to him. The abbot however would have none of it, but treated them badly, threatening them with worse. One day the abbot went into the chapter and spoke against the monks and threatened to maltreat them. He sent for laymen, who entered the chapter fully armed against the monks. Not knowing what they should do, the monks were terrified of them and fled in all directions. Some ran into the church and locked the doors against them, but the pursuers went after them into the monastic church, determined to drag them out since they were afraid to leave.

More, a pitiful thing took place there that day when the Frenchmen broke into the choir and began pelting the monks in the direction of the altar where they were. Some of the men-at-arms climbed up to the gallery and shot arrows down into the sanctuary, so that many arrows stuck in the cross standing above the altar. The wretched monks lay about round the altar and some crept underneath, crying aloud to God, desperately imploring his mercy when none was forthcoming from men. What more can we find to say except to add that they showered arrows and their companions broke down the doors to force an entrance and struck down and killed some of the monks, wounding many there, so that their blood ran down from the altar on to the steps and from the steps on to the floor. Three of the monks were done to death and eighteen wounded.[5]

The knights used to subdue the monks seem to have been members of the abbot's *familia*. The gallery was probably a timber construction at the end of the nave such as once existed at Deerhurst, or else a chamber above the side aisle.

In the works of Goscelin we can luckily find what the literate Englishman thought of the conquerors. Of St Bertin, who lived for twenty years under the protection of Bishop Herman. About 1080 he wrote from Peterborough, where he had taken refuge, to an old pupil and friend now at Angers:

> How many thousands of the human race have fallen on evil days. The sons of kings and dukes and nobles and the proud ones of the land are fettered with manacles and irons, are in prison and in jail. How many have lost their limbs by sword or disease, have been deprived of their eyes, so that when released from prison the common light of the world is a prison for them. They are the living dead for whom the sun, mankind's greatest pleasure, now has set. Blessed are those who are consoled by eternal hope; and afflicted are the unbelieving, for, deprived of all their goods and also cut off from heaven, their punishment has now begun.

We may suspect that William preferred mutilation to hanging because the blinded or crippled man remained as a spectacle of warning for the others. Goscelin goes on to lament the end of asceticism in the church under the Normans.

> They would do far better to learn through education how to preserve humility, which is the guardian of all virtues, and to stamp out the barbarous pride and bragging of the undisciplined. We shall soon see the unlearned deriding and despising the learned and counting illiteracy secular wisdom or holiness of life. No wonder they neglect what they do not know, and prefer what they do know, that the blind despise those who can see, and ignorant men take pride in the cult of humility.

He saw the Conquest as the imposition of rule by ignorant, arrogant and prejudiced barbarians, who sought to crush English scholarship and civilization. (Later he became reconciled.)[6]

The Normans retorted in kind. At St Albans, Paul called his venerated predecessors uneducated simpletons; the abbot of Abingdon dismissed such saints as Edmund and Aethelwold as rustics; Lanfranc overrode his chapter and omitted many English saints from the calendar. Writing to Abbot Paul, who was Anselm's nephew, he declared that the barbarians would fail to understand him, but his labours would not be in vain. 'What you cannot say to them, you can show by your life.' We see the veiled hostility in the jokes made at Bishop Wulfstan, who had to be tolerated as useful to the Conqueror. Wulfstan dressed modestly, and Geoffrey of Coutances, also a bishop, asked why he did not wear sable, beaver and wolf, as he could and should, but wore lamb skin instead. Wulfstan replied that it was right for men of secular wisdom like Geoffrey to use the skins of crafty animals, but he himself was content with lamb skin. Geoffrey persisted, suggesting he should at least wear cat skin, and Wulfstan answered, 'Believe me, we chant more often of the Lamb of God than of his Cat.'

The resistance in the spirits of the English to the Norman conquest appeared in tales told about the English kings. A strong peasant element intrudes in these versions. Athelstan is given a peasant pedigree; Alfred wandered among the common folk in the guises that brought him close to everyday life. The story of the burnt cakes first turns up in Henry of Huntingdon; in Layamon's *Brut* he has become England's Darling; and he is regarded as a Solomon, a repository of all wisdom. His *Proverbs* were collected; in the English *The Owl and the Nightingale* a host of sage comments are attributed to him. And as we shall see the band of the resister-outlaw Hereward came to be made up of peasants in the tales.

William of Malmesbury in his tale of Athelstan's birth says that his source was 'old ballads popular through the times that followed, rather than books expressly written for posterity's information'. The lovely daughter of a shepherd saw in a vision the moon shining from her womb 'and all England illuminated by the light'. She told her friends next day; and the tale reached the woman who had nursed the kings' sons and who then adopted her as daughter. Edward, Alfred's son, passed through the village and stopped at his nurse's house, where he fell in love with the girl. He spent one night with her, and she bore Athelstan.' Even a character like Godwin had a folk tale attached to him, in which he too was a peasant in origin. He takes the role of the lowborn hero who is to act a saviour part. Map tells how King Aethelred, when hunting, strayed and at night sought shelter from the cold in a cowherd's house. He was hospitably entertained, especially by the son Godwin, whom he took into his service. Godwin rose to be earl of Gloucester. (There were no such earls at the time, but the story-tellers gave the setting of their own times.) However, at this point a counter-tradition, that of the tales told by the Normans, breaks in; the popular hero becomes a villain. He rapes the nuns of Berkeley and cheats the archbishop of Canterbury of his Bosham lands. The existence of an English epic is further shown by passages from the *Knytlinga Saga* and from Randulph Niger, which correspond with the first parts of Map's story.

Some of the English even began looking to Arthur. At least one Londoner of the twelfth century attributed to his days the city's folk moot. And lesser heroes were not forgotten. Thus the account of Byrhtnoth in the *Book of Ely* seems to be from a later and longer poem than the extant *Battle of Maldon*. Veneration quickly began to gather round the tomb of Waltheof, last of the English earls, whom William executed at Winchester. Anselm sent an archdeacon to tell the abbess and nuns of Romsey to drop all 'superstitious veneration of a dead man whom they considered a saint'. (There was as yet no fixed method of canonization; the main principle was that there should be no veneration without episcopal authorization. But sanctification often happened fast; at Winchester Bishop Aethelwold's body was performing miracles and was translated to the choir twelve years after his death.)[8]

Edward the Confessor was said to have made a death-bed prophecy that anticipated events of the early twelfth century. After two speechless days, the tale said, he spoke out. Two monks whom he had known in his youth in Normandy had appeared and told him that after his death England would pass for a year and a day 'into the hand of the enemy and devils will wander over the land'. The cause was that the heads of England, the dukes, bishops and abbots, were the ministers not of God but of the devil. The monks said that the English could not repent and thus save themselves. 'When would the calamities end?' asked Edward.

> When a green tree shall be cut down the middle, and the part cut off, being carried the space of three acres from the trunk, shall, without any help, become again united to its stem, bud out with flowers, and stretch forth its fruit as before, from the sap again uniting; then may an end of such evils be at last expected.

This prophecy was obviously invented after Henry I's marriage with Matilda, which brought together the English and Norman lines; the three acres represent the reigns of Harold, William and Rufus. Henry and Matilda had three children: a son who died in infancy; Maud born February 1102; William born before August 1103. The prophecy was doubtless connected with this third birth. We are now entering the territory of Geoffrey of Monmouth; but we must leave him till we have considered the tales about Harold and Hereward.

The legend of the dead hero who cannot die, who will return in time to free his people, found its most powerful form in the tales of Arthur; but a rationalized version appeared in connection with Harold Godwinson. The folk could not believe that he was dead. Tales of his survival occur in three Norse texts; in all three he ends as a hermit. The most interesting is the Icelandic tale of Heming Aslaksson. The full account deals with the conflict between Heming and King Harald Hardrada. Heming started as a 'fool', who however beat the king in a series of athletic tests or ordeals but was almost murdered by being forced over a cliff. (One test involved a William Tell feat of shooting a nut on a brother's head.) He went off to England, Rome, and back to England where he became athletic instructor to Harold, accompanied him on the visit to Normandy, and fought for him at Stamford Bridge and Hastings. At the end we are told that Harold was found by a cottar and his wife; they put him in a waggon and took him home, where they hid him from the Normans. When he was recovered he sent for Heming and asked him to get a hermitage built in Canterbury, where he could watch King William in church. When he died, William found out about him, pardoned Heming, and offered to make him a powerful baron; but Heming asked only for the same hermitage.

Norse tradition, despite Stamford Bridge, remained friendly to the Confessor, Godwin and his sons; but it did not invent the theme of Harold's survival, which we find also in Gervase of Tilbury. The *Vita Haroldi* insists he was rescued from the battlefield, conveyed to Winchester, and there nursed back to health by a Saracen woman. Two years later, he went abroad, failed to win help in regaining his kingdom, and travelled east as a pilgrim. Returning, he lived as a recluse in a cave near Dover. At last, while wandering disguised on the Welsh marches, he reached a hermitage and stayed there till his death. His brother Gyrth is reported to have turned up at Henry II's court at Woodstock, 'by then indeed very old'. The link with Chester represents a strong tradition. Florence of Worcester says that after Hastings the queen was sent by her brothers there; and Girald tells a story of a disguised emperor (apparently Henry V) ending his days in a hermitage near the city.[9]

The theme of defeat, exile and return of a dispossessed hero appears in the stories of *Haveloc* and *Horn*. There are strong Viking elements here. Haveloc was connected with Grimsby. He had been deprived of his rights by a treacherous regent in Denmark, the princess Goldeburh of her rights in England. Haveloc fled to England with the fisherman Grim, earned his living as a kitchen-boy, and was forced to marry Goldeburh by the regent who meant to degrade her. As a man Haveloc went back to Denmark, gathered those faithful to his line, defeated the regent and gained the throne. Then he returned to England with his wife, rallied her adherents and won her throne as well. Grimsby was where he landed; the place was called after the fisherman who saved his life and was made an earl. The town seal of Grimsby, said to be not later than Edward I, showed the figures of Haveloc, Grim and Goldeburh. A local legend seems to have been conflated with material from Norse sagas.[10]

But it is in the historical character of Hereward that the theme of the exile was given full relevance to the hopes and fears of the defeated English; we may note that elements from his story as well as others from *King Horn* survive in the ballads of Robin Hood. The exile was the outlaw, the total outsider in Anglo-Saxon or Norman societies. A decision of the king or his courts put him outside the protection of law; he lost his birthright, privileges at law for which the king was only the guardian. A price was put on his head as on a wolf's, so he was said to have a Wolf's Head. *Civiliter mortuus*, he could be killed with impunity. (Gradually the full harshness was modified; by the thirteenth century he forfeited chattels and rights, but did not lose all claim to inheritance, nor was his killer free from a charge of homicide.) His only hope was to elude authority and sue for pardon from the men who had condemned him. In making him an outlaw the system admitted its weakness, its inability to bring him to justice; and if he had enough support, he could withdraw to a remote place and defy the law. Hereward went to Flanders as an exile. He was shipwrecked near St Omer where Count Manasses welcomed him; he took part in a war against the count of Guines and was captured by the count's nephew; he wooed and wed Torfrida; he joined in two expeditions with Duke Robert to Scaldemariland. The material is legendary, but possibly with factual elements. The future Robert I did lead an expedition against Zealand (probably in 1067); Manasses seems to have been count of St Pol at about this time; the shipwreck faintly suggests the Harold story. But we meet sheer folklore in the tale of the fight with a bear with human intelligence; its father, carrying off a princess, begot on her Bearn of Norway, a man with a bear's strength, and the bear with a man's mind. Hereward also killed the Giant of Cornwall, saving a king's daughter; the jealousy of the king's knights made him flee to Ireland; and he had his wonder mare Swallow. Such tales are valuable in showing how popular he was as an heroic figure.[11]

The *Gesta* says he returned from Flanders in 1068; he wanted to see if any kinsmen had survived the Conquest. Leaving Torfrida and his two nephews, he went with a single servant to his ancestral home at Bourne. (The tales link him with Bourne; *Domesday* shows him holding land of the abbey of Crowland; and Hugh Candidus says he held from the abbey of Peterborough. He or another Hereward had Warwickshire lands in 1086.) Without revealing himself he entered the house of Osred who had been his father's knight, and was offered hospitality. He found the household mourning. Only the day before, the Norman lord and his men had come to the village to demand the whole family estate. Hereward's younger brother killed the man who laid rough hands on Hereward's wife; he was surrounded and cut down, and his severed head was set over the door of the house. As Hereward was going to bed, he heard noise and singing. Cloaked, he went with his servant to see. The Normans were celebrating. He took down his brother's head and wrapped it in a cloak. Inside he found his enemies lying drunken in the arms of the village women whom they had forced along; a dancer entertained them with songs insulting the English and with mimes of their coarse manners. One girl protested, 'If our lord's other son Hereward was here, he'd change your tune before tomorrow morning.' The Norman lord jeered, 'That particular rogue isn't likely to show his face just now this side of the Alps.' The jester took up his words. Hereward, leaping from the shadows, cut him down with one blow. Some of the drunken Normans he killed while at the door his servant dealt with those who tried to dodge out. None escaped. In the morning fourteen heads grinned down from over the door in place of the brother's. Other Normans in the district fled.

There is nothing impossible in the tale. About twenty years earlier, in Italy, a large number of peasants, monks and townsfolk had resorted to guerrilla warfare against the Norman marauders. Amatus tells how a young baron Rodolf came with his band one day to the monastery of Monte Casino, and went in to pray. They left their swords outside, as was the custom. At once the servants seized the weapons and horses, closed the doors, and rang the bells. The country folk, thinking the monastery was being attacked, rushed to the rescue and burst in. Soon the Normans, armed only with daggers, gave in, asking to have their lives spared out of respect for God's house. But by the time the monks arrived, Rodolf was a prisoner and his fifteen men lay dead on the floor.[12]

Countryfolk now came hurrying to join Hereward, who chose a small body of retainers, mainly men of his own kin. They drove out any Frenchmen who dared to linger in the lands of his inheritance. He seems to have gone as far afield as Peterborough; for he was said to have been knighted there in the Saxon manner by the last English abbot, Brand. Frederick, brother of the earl of Warenne, swore to hunt him down; but when he met Hereward late one evening, he was killed. So Earl William himself became Hereward's bitter foe. Hereward meanwhile decided to fetch wife and nephews from

Flanders, and disbanded his men, promising to return in a year and give them a sign. (Warenne also had links with Flanders; he had married Gundrada, sister of Gerbod the Fleming and was given control of Surrey while Gerbod gained Chester.) Hereward duly returned and as a sign set fire to three villas on Brunneswald above his Bourne manor, where no Norman had dared to set foot. He gathered the bravest of his men, many of whom were old rebels: Leofric the Mower who with his scythe drove off the score of Normans who tried to take him as he harvested alone; Leofric the Crafty who had often escaped captivity by his guile; Wulric the Black, who once darkened his face with charcoal, slipped among the Normans by night, and killed ten of them; Wulric Hraga who rescued four brothers from execution and killed the guards; Leofric the Deacon; Utlamhe (the Outlaw); Hereward's cook; Winter; Hurchill; Grugan; and the two nephews, Siward the White and Siward the Red.

The monks of Ely, who were averse to having a French abbot, were helping another rebel band. With them, says the *Gesta*, were Earl Morcar, Count Tosti, and the abbot. Later tales added Earl Edwin, Stigand, Frithric (an exile from St Albans), and even Edgar Aetheling. Hereward, summoned, joined them the safest way, by water; but Warenne tried to cut him off where the channel was narrow, at Herberche. Hereward got there first and the earl found him on the far side. Hereward shot and knocked him down with an arrow that glanced on his armour; then in the familiar fens he and his men slipped through to the isle of Ely, a site that was impregnable as long as the garrison could live on what they caught or grew. The best line of attack was through Aldreth village to the south-west, but even there a bridge had to be built over the marshes. Gaimar says that the king called up his host, French and English, shipmen, sergeants and freebooters, against Ely this year, 1171; and if this is correct, William then summoned his feudal host for the first time in England. His first attack failed; the bridge sank under the weight of armed men, those in front slithered into the bog and many died. The writer of the *Gesta*, some forty or fifty years later, recalled seeing their skeletons in rusty armour hauled up by fishermen. Only one Norman, Deda, keen for the rewards promised the first entrant, reached the isle. Hereward treated him with courtesy and after a while sent him back. He gave William a full account of the garrison's way of life. Desperate men, they were ready for any hardship, as servitude was the alternative. Well defended, the isle could stand four sieges. The rebels were ever prepared to meet an attack, and the monks would join in with arms. They all dined together, monks and soldiers, with weapons hung ready on the walls; at the high table dined the abbot, the three earls, and the two outlaw leaders,

Hereward and Thurkill. Each day was busy. Strong defences had been raised. The isle was fertile and everyone joined in tilling the soil; the garrison could almost live on the proceeds of hunting alone; the waters were thick with fishes, the woods with wild creatures and herons; waterfowl were trapped (no doubt in the traditional way, by netting). Deda had seen a thousand birds taken at the same time from a single marsh. The many fenmen in Ely knew how to live off the fens. There was no point in surrounding the place year after year, and the outlaws would not be able to drive investors off; the best thing was to offer terms.

William came near to agreeing; but Warenne and Ivo Taillebois wanted to fight on till the end. Ivo had a new plan. He knew a witch with spells strong enough to put the garrison's courage to sleep and fill them with fear; and he won William over. Everything was done with the utmost secrecy so that the Englishmen might not be warned and concoct some magic of their own; but rumours of the preparations reached Ely. Hereward volunteered to go into the Norman camp as a spy and find out what was going on. He set off on Swallow, ungainly looking but the fastest of horses; her ugliness helped his peasant disguise. Meeting a potter, he borrowed his pots. Then, reaching the camp before nightfall, he found lodging in an old woman's cottage, where Ivo's witch was also. Dozing off, he heard the two old women discuss their plans – in French, which they thought a rustic couldn't follow. Then he watched them go to a spring, where they asked questions of the unseen guardian; but he failed to catch the answers.

In the morning he cried his wares in the camp. Servants from the king's kitchen came; but a soldier noticed that the potter was like Hereward. The crowd argued as to whether a warrior could really be so short and stocky. They asked the potter if he had ever seen Hereward. 'Indeed I have, and I've good cause to remember it. He stole my cow and four sheep, all I had apart from my pots and this old horse – and me with two sons to rear.' The cooks invited him to their quarters, where they got on with the king's dinner. Wanting more tales, they plied him with drink, and they too drank. One of them suggested a joke that involved shaving the potter's beard and crown with a kitchen knife. Hereward laid out the joker with one blow and was immediately surrounded by angry cooks with knives and forks; but as they led him off he broke loose, grabbed a sword, and dashed down the steps into a lower court. (William seems to have been lodging in some sort of mansion.) He leaped on his horse, pursued by a passing group of young knights, whom he soon shook off in the marshes. One knight, who did catch him up, was soon forced to yield and was sent back with news of who the troublesome potter had been. (The episode looks back to the tales of Alfred entering the Danish camp, but even more strongly forward to those of Robin Hood and his stratagems; it provides the basis of one of the earliest surviving ballads; it was also told of Eustace the Monk.)

Hereward and his men got rid of the witch. As she cast spells from a wooden siege tower, they fired the dry sedge. The wind fanned the flames and the Normans retreated, while the tower burned. The *Chronicle* gives a more sober account of William's progress: 'He ordered out naval and land levies, and surrounded the district, building a causeway as he advanced deeper into the fens, while the naval force remained to seaward.' (The *scyp fyrd* was hardly likely to have been the product of service owed by a select fyrd; more likely it was made up of sea-mercenaries, as is suggested by Florence's use of the term *butsecarl*.)

Another story tells how Hereward, disguised this time as a fen fisherman, joined the labourers on William's pontoons. Then one night he burned them all. However the monks began to lose heart; they heard that the king's vassals were sharing their estates outside the isle. Afraid for their property they entered into secret parleys and agreed to yield up the isle if allowed to keep their lands. With their guidance William's men began the march to Ely. Hereward was away on a raiding party, says the *Gesta*. He turned back, hoping to burn the place down before the Normans got in. A monk met him and his band with faggots on their shoulders; he argued that William was already too near. Hereward, at last persuaded, made for his boats on one of the big marshes and took refuge in the heart of the fens. Gaimar says that with five men he eluded William's guards under the net of a fisherman who had sold his catch to the soldiers. He returned to Brunneswald and made raids near and far, sometimes from his home base, sometimes from the deep forests of Northamptonshire near Peterborough. He used all sorts of tricks and devices to fool the enemy. Once his band reversed their horses' shoes to deceive pursuers. Once Abbot Turold and Ivo almost hemmed them in, but they broke through. Turold in turn was captured, then freed for a ransom of £30,000. He failed to keep his word and pay the money, so Hereward fell on Peterborough, burned the town, and took the monastery's treasures. But a midnight vision of St Peter brandishing a huge key made him return the spoils. In return, lost in the woods at night, he and his men were guided by a great white hound, while unearthly lights, like will-o'-the-wisps, played about their lance points. At dawn they saw that what they had thought a hound was a white wolf, which disappeared into the forest.

He continued his struggle, raiding, fighting and encountering William's champions, and was even joined by some French. One tradition has it that he took part in the revolt of Norman earls in 1072. But he had fallen in love with a beautiful Englishwoman, Alfthrida, who undertook to make his peace with William. They were betrothed and Torfrida went to a nunnery. But, lacking her counsel, he never did so well afterwards. Alfthrida got his lands restored, but he had too many enemies. Through intrigues of Ivo and Warenne he was imprisoned. Rescued by his old companions, he was again admitted to the king's peace. Finally he settled at Bourne and ended his life quietly, says the *Gesta*. Gaimar says his enemies never forgave him. Though he was always guarded, one day a sentinel slept and they surprised him at table. In a great fight he was at last struck down, but with his last blow he killed his killer. Gaimar adds that had there been four such men in England, William would not have won. 'Under his command assembled all those who were outlaws.'

All we can be sure of is that Hereward did exist, that he fought at Ely, and that he became the emblem of resistance to the Normans. His story includes elements from ancient folktales and from the sagas; it moved towards romance (as in Gaimar) and begot much imagery of popular resistance to all forms of oppression. Storytellers tried to raise the hero's status by emphasizing the romantic aspects. One version called him grandson of Leofric, earl of Mercia under Edward; another called him nephew of Ralph the Staller. But the pull of the outlaw theme was stronger and Hereward became the symbol of popular resistance. There are distortions of history in the tales, as when Gaimar and the *Gesta* both put the sack of Peterborough after the siege of Ely; and some of the persons said to be on the isle could not have been there, for example Edwin or Stigand, who was in jail at Winchester. The story divides clearly into several main stages. The first deals with the wonderful adventures of a young exile; then in the fight against William the chivalric elements fade out (though revived in some of the tales of his last years). The setting now is the wild fens; the themes are the tricks, guises, and ambushes of desperate men in waste places; the surrounding characters are cooks, potters, peasants and fishermen. The *Book of Ely* says that songs about him were still sung in taverns by the peasantry; and it refers to a *Life* by Prior Richard, who seems to have been working in the third quarter of the twelfth century. Gaimar gives no hint as to his sources. The Latin *Gesta* claims to use part of a book about Hereward in Anglo-Saxon by Leofric the Deacon, who was one of his contemporaries. It declares that many accounts were still to be found flourishing in the fens; but its author could not verify the story he had heard of some great book stowed away in a monastery. However, he had talked with men who could recall Hereward and even with some of his contemporaries; out of this material he made up his account.

Hereward's fame lasted long. In the thirteenth century men still went to see the ruins of a wooden structure in the fens called Hereward's Castle. Ingulph declares, 'His deeds are still sung to this day on the king's highway.' Ingulph was a fourteenth-century fraud; but this touch was clearly meant to give versimilitude and would not have been added if Hereward were unknown. He worked in Crowland, not far from the scene of Hereward's exploits.

A tradition that there were pockets of resistance was still alive in the thirteenth century, as we see from the *Flowers of History*. The author, while describing the peace that William had established by the end of his reign, insists:

> Those of the English who were of gentle birth were driven from their lands; they could not dig; they were ashamed to beg. So with their kindred they took refuge in the woods, living by what they could hunt, and only falling back on raids when all else failed them...
>
> In their lairs in the woods and waste places...they laid a thousand secret ambushes and traps for the Normans.[18]

We find traces of resisters other than Hereward. Twice his *Gesta* refers to Brumannus who captured a Norman abbot and ducked him in the sea in a sack. Evidently the story was very well known. And we can see that legends gathered round Eadric the Wild. *Silvaticus*, his epithet, Wildman or Forestman, perhaps means no more than *silvestris* used of the Wild Welsh; Giraud de Barri was called *Giraldus Cambrensis* alias *Silvestris;* and the Scottish Highlander is *silvester et montanus*. But it also suggests the outlaw whose home is the woods. Eadric led a revolt in the marshes of Wales in 1067–9. The chronicles of Wygmore Abbey have tales of his fight with the Norman lord Ralph de Mortemer; and Walter Map shows that there were many folk-tales about him. Wandering one night in the forest, we are told, he came on a remote house within which a band of lovely girls were at play; he went in and before morning one of them was his bride. They left the forest and lived together a few years; then one day he asked her if she didn't wish to visit her sisters, and at once she vanished. He could never find the forest house again.

The theme of the exile-outlaw also entered the upper levels of culture. Two historical figures under John were made the heroes of romances, in which magical and chivalric elements conflicted or merged with the motifs of revolt. These were Fulk fitzWarin and Eustace the Monk. In its prose texts *Fulk* has two quotations from the *Prophecies of Merlin*. It opens with references to the months of

April and May when a man's fancy should turn to memories of his ancestors' deeds. Giving a fanciful account of William I's pacification of the Welsh marches, it moves on to describe its hero's family; its main part consists of the story of the struggles of the third Fulk against John, his exile and wanderings in France under an assumed name, his turn to piracy, his return in the guise of a merchant, his further adventures, then his home-coming and pardon. The author was probably a monk of the New Abbey, a Benedictine house founded by Fulk II. Chronology and details are confused, perhaps deliberately; one sees here illustrated the background of innumerable forged charters. The romance has many elements that anticipate Robin Hood. 'In all the time he was a banished man neither Fulk nor any of his did damage to anyone, save the king and his knights.' He fights for the right, and 'was a good purveyor and a liberal, and he caused the royal highway to be turned by his hall at his manor of Alleston, so that no traveller should pass without food or other honour, or good of his'.

Eustace is a more dubious character, an outlawed knight, a renegade monk, a tremendous magician. As a sea captain he was a real person who became the terror of the Channel. The chroniclers call him the Archpirate, the Apostate, a man who 'from a black monk became a demoniac'. After his death the legends grew till under Edward II William of Hemingford took him to have been Monachus, a tyrant of Spain, who, hearing that England was ruled by a child (Henry II), aspired to conquer the land. He was in fact killed in a battle off Sandwich in 1217. His history contains many elements that were important later in the ballads of Robin Hood; and in general the tone is much more popular than that of *Fulk*. Like Fulk, the Monk is in the right; he combats a tyrannous count who has taken his land; but he is not the complete rebel like Hereward (in the core of his story) or like Robin. The popular elements in the Hereward saga had meanwhile disappeared from the upper levels of culture, or been absorbed into tales of other outlaws. Matthew Paris recalled his name and the siege of Ely, but little more.[14]

With the story of the Confessor's prophecy of the Great Tree we noted that we were trespassing on the field of Geoffrey of Monmouth, whose *Prophecies of Merlin* seem to have been completed and known in 1134, a couple of years later to be incorporated as Book VII in his *Historia Brittanorum*. Thus the Prophecies certainly seem to have been the originating core of the *Historia*. For us the interest of the Prophecies does not lie merely in the important way in which they brought Celtic traditions into the mainstream of medieval literature, but also in the fact that, by doing so, they revealed the need of the Normans to find a living relationship between their culture and the English past. By making Brut the Trojan the ancient invader of England, bringing a superior culture, the Norman conquest was justified and put in a new perspective. Trojans, Britons, Romans, English and Normans all had their place in this perspective as the creators of the complex reality of English life, its governmental forms, its institutions.

The Arthurian material was to take many forms with a variety of meanings, finally issuing in the great medieval epic-romance. In this on the one hand the Grail theme fused the monastic and the chivalric motifs in terms of a mystery quest, as the Templars never succeeded in doing in actual life; on the other hand the story of Arthur and his Round Table became the supreme expression both of the dream of a harmonious society of interlocked and dedicated hierarchies and of the disastrous awakening to the facts of pervasive treachery. The Celtic hope for a redeeming leader, who would restore freedom and unity to his people, was linked with the real conflicts and ways of life of the twelfth century (such as courtly love), lending the story its comprehensive range of meanings, its hidden force. That the Arthurian theme was thus able to win so central a place in the medieval world was in the last resort due to the skill and insight that Geoffrey showed in bringing together his materials and relating them to the deepest problems of his age, of Anglo-Norman culture in its quest for roots.

Most of the records we have of his earlier life as a churchman link him, not with Llandaff as in later Welsh tradition, but with the region of Oxford in the diocese of Lincoln; he is here found as witness in seven charters (1129-51) and is concerned with houses of Oseney, Godstow, and Thame, and with the canonical house of St George in Oxford castle. Among his fellow witnesses are Walter archdeacon of Oxford and Ralph of Monmouth; he himself may have taught at Oxford. He was also known as Geoffrey Arthur, as early as 1129. He seems then to be of Breton rather than Welsh blood, reared in a Norman environment on the Welsh marches; linked politically with Robert of Gloucester, ecclesiastically with Oxford and Lincoln.[15] He tells us that he made a start with his *Historia* when the prevalence of rumours about Merlin led Alexander bishop of Lincoln and others to ask him to make a Latin version of the prophet's British utterances. His Merlin he concocted of various figures including the prophet Lailoken who had encountered St Kentigern (Glasgow's Mungo) just outside the city. The prophecies were long compositions in symbolic language, with imagery from the animal world. The Kingdom of Arthur is foretold, with six inheritors (the *Historia* gives only five); then we find some events drawn from the later struggles of the

Saxons, the coming of the Normans, the slaying of Rufus, the dominion of Henry (the Lion of Justice), and the wreck of the White Ship. Here historical allusions stop. A reference to Henry's death seems to be an interpolation. Some vague comments can be made to fit later events. Thus, a king is to overthrow the Walls of Hibernia: which suggests Henry II in Ireland. But an expedition had long been contemplated. We can dimly make out references to the Celtic peoples and the expulsion of aliens. The animal images thicken: a goat of the Castle of Venus, a Lioness of Stafford, and so on. Many geographical names are English. The work ends with an astrological version of chaos or world-end. Stilbon of Arcadia will change his shield, the helmet of Mars will call to Venus, the Virgin will mount on the back of the Archer and darken her maiden honour, the Moon's chariot will disturb the Zodiac, and so on.[16]

We see how strongly men's minds had turned to prophecies, recent and ancient, in their efforts to understand history, its pattern and its working out. Orderic in the Twelfth Book of his *Historia* tells of the death of Duke Robert of Normandy on 10 February 1134, then calls attention to the fulfilment of much of the prophecy of Ambrosius Merlin to Vortigern, from which he cites some points that 'seem relevant to our time'. He does not name Geoffrey, but relates the struggle of the red and white Dragons, with the variation that the red one becomes Saxon, the white one British. Then he deals with the Norman domination and the final expulsion of the invaders, in much the same language as Geoffrey's *Historia*, but without the addition on the death of Henry I. He was writing before that event of 1 December 1135; for he comments that much of the prophecy was destined to bring joy or grief to those yet unborn, but that parts would be comprehensible to those who knew histories of Hengist and others; he mentions several English and British princes down to the days of Henry and Griffith, 'who yet await the doubtful lot of forthcoming events divinely ordained for them by the ineffable decree'. He was writing between the deaths of Duke Robert and King Henry.[17]

The prophecies, which are so concerned with Arthur the great liberator who will return, and which foresee the expulsion of the Normans, could only derive from a deep popular agitation, even though many of the sources are Breton or Welsh. In 1113 some canons of Laon visited England with relics on a fund-raising tour. In Danavexeria (? Devon) they were told that they trod the very land of Arthur and were shown his chair and oven; at Bodmin a dispute broke out between one of their company and a man with a withered arm who had come to be healed. 'Just as the Bretons are wont to wrangle with the French on behalf of king Arthur,' says the narrator Hermann, the cripple insisted that Arthur still lived. A brawl broke out, a crowd gathered with weapons, and bloodshed was narrowly averted. Alanus de Insulis in the twelfth century said that the belief in Arthur's return was so deeply and widely held in Brittany that to deny it might cost a man his life. (The tale of the canons of Laon and their Bodmin troubles exists also in an Icelandic version.) The legend spread to Sicily, for Gervase of Tilbury, the first to tell of Arthur sleeping in the otherworld of a Hollow Hill, says that recently a groom of the bishop of Catania, following a strayed horse into the recesses of Aetna, came on a fair plain full of all manner of delights and Arthur lying on a bed, with wounds that broke out afresh each year. Arthur sent back gifts to the bishop which many saw and marvelled at. (Gervase had been in Sicily as a follower of its king William about 1190.) Geoffrey's *Historia* was translated into Anglo-Norman verse by Wace, who refers to Wassail and Drinkhail, but knew no English, a language which he compared with the barks of dogs. Layamon translated it into English verse about 1205.[18] The most remarkable illustrations of the Arthurian legend are found, not in France, but in manuscripts from Naples, Bologna, and Milan.

Geoffrey claimed that he based his work on old books. In 1129 at Oxford he came to know Walter of the collegiate church of St George and borrowed from him, he says, a history in the British tongue which he translated into Latin. Holding back the *Prophecies*, he did not issue the *Historia* till after the death of Henry I, whom it was meant to glorify. But it had a great success in both England and Normandy, and as early as 1139 Henry of Huntingdon saw a copy at Bec. Before that, between Henry's death in 1135 and the remarriage of Adeliza of Louvain in 1139, a copy was held by the northern baron Walter Espec (whom we met at the Battle of the Standard). It was borrowed by Ralph fitzGilbert, a man of importance in Lincoln-shire, who married Constance, a Hampshire heiress with some educa-tion. The poet Gaimar says that she gave him a silver penny for the *Life of Henry I*, written by David for Adeliza; she kept it and read it in her chamber. It seems then that she could herself read; and as Gaimar compares the work with his own, it must have been in French. (It is doubtful if Adeliza could read Latin, though her predecessor did.) Constance got Geoffrey's *Historia* from her husband and gave it to Gaimar to work on. He began his *Estorie des Engleis* in Hampshire and completed it in Lincolnshire. With the presumed exception of David's lost work, it was the oldest chronicle in French; the first of its kind, it was called a *Brut* after Brutus the Trojan, the legendary founder of the kingdom of Britain. Gaimar added a sequel bringing the country's story down to the present; he thus set the pattern for popular history for some three centuries. According to his epilogue, he used not only Walter Espec's book (Geoffrey's) but also 'the good book of Oxeford' which had belonged to Walter the archdeacon; in fact he was using this good book before he got hold of Espec's book. He evidently thought that Walter had two books, one in Latin which he used, and one in Welsh, translated by Geoffrey.[19]

He drew much on the *Anglo-Saxon Chronicle*; so he seems to have been capable of working with English books. (He seems to have used two copies of the *Chronicle*, probably because he moved about.) His name is perhaps Norman. We see that the Normans were now taking a strong interest in the past of their conquered land, the Norman-Welsh in the British and Anglo-Normans in the English past. Gaimar tells of St Edmund of East Anglia, his martyrdom and the finding of his severed head by a wolf, of King Edgar's wooing of Aelfthryth and his marriage. He was also familiar with Danish traditions (probably met in Lincolnshire). He used the tale of Haveloc but had some trouble fitting him into the list of English kings. He has four short passages dealing with Danish kings, apparently local legends which he modified in terms of contemporary feudalism; he may also have had direct access to Celtic traditions. Lives of Irish and Scottish saints, some now lost, were being read in English: an interest stimulated by Henry I's marriage and his later links with Scotland.

Gaimar was thus one of the many twelfth-century writers who, while stirring interest in the English past, did much to depress English writing through their translations into Latin or French: later writers were not concerned about going back to the originals. No one wrote in local dialects any works that aspired to be of lasting value. Works like Gaimar's further show the transition from the epic to the romance, which we find fully developed in, say, *Tristam* by Thomas about the time of Henry II. Like Wace, Thomas may have been patronized by Queen Eleanor; her daughters would have been the agents introducing his poem to Spain, Germany and Sicily; her grandson Henry III would have introduced it to his ally Haakon IV of Norway. Wace the Jerseyman was living at Caen; he finished his *Brut* in 1155 and presented it (according to Layamon) to the queen. It became fashionable and supplanted Gaimar's work.

The work of Gaimar is of interest as showing again the importance of the lady's chamber in the development of poetry, and in the convergence of elements from many quarters to build an Anglo-Norman culture which retained English (or Celtic) elements and looked forward to the day when English and French traditions would merge. We see the same sort of attempt at harmonization of English and Norman view points, in a simpler and more direct way, in the work of William of Malmesbury. No Norman had recorded the life of an

English bishop who died after Oswald and before Wulfstan. William wrote in the prologue of his *Deeds of English Pontiffs*;

> What task could be more agreeable than to tell of the favours conferred on us by our ancestors, so that you may come to know the deeds of those from whom you received both the rudiments of your faith and the encouragement of right living. I thought it was very slack and shameful not to know at least the names of the leaders of our province, when in other respects our knowledge extends to the lands of India and whatever lies beyond hidden by the boundless ocean. And so, for these reasons, I have dragged my pen, both here and elsewhere, through the most obscure histories, although the sources for this work are not as plentiful as for the *Deeds of the Kings*. For there, when I had made an abstract of the chronicles which I had before me, I was advised, just as by a torch shining from a high watchtower, in which direction I could freely bend my steps. But here, deprived of almost all comfort, I grope within the thick dark clouds of ignorance, making my own path, with no lantern of history to lead the way.

Behind such statements many deep cohesive forces were at work, socially and politically. We saw how some Englishmen rallied early to the royal cause. These groups would have come from the middling and lower sections of free landowners, who, when it became clear that no effective basis remained for a revival of the English monarchy, were ready to support a foreign king in preference to his foreign barons. By the time of Henry I the possibility of rallying yet wider sections of the English to the king was stronger, as he was aware. Hence his marriage with Matilda who had inherited the claims of the English royal house. The Norman lords mocked at him and his wife as Godric and Godgifu, but the union was an important step forwards. Ailred of Rievaulx complained that Stephen's intrusion had once more broken the ties of the crown with the old English royal family.

Orderic (probably following William of Poitiers) gives a rosy picture of the situation after 1070:

> The English and French lived peaceably together in the boroughs and towns, and intermarried. You would see some places and markets full of French traders and goods, and everywhere you would notice that the English, who, when they used to wear their native dress, were considered uncouth by the French, were now affecting foreign fashions.

The account of the influx of French traders and wares may well contain much truth, but the picture of ensuing harmony is certainly overdone; Orderic himself often gives us a much more realistic account of the conflicts between the two peoples. And in the passage cited above about *murdrum*, fitzNeale is certainly exaggerating when he insists on the complete uniting of English and Normans above serf level by the mid-twelfth century. The significance of these statements lies rather in the recognition that the two people should and must become one. The men whom Henry I 'raised from the dust to do him service' were almost all aliens; only under Stephen a slow change began. By the early thirteenth century, probably soon after the loss of Normandy, a poet like Chardri, writing in French, could in his *Petit Plet* set English women and knights above French ones. He is a poet with a note of ironical gaiety, and this work of his is the only medieval one in which youth vanquishes old age in argument. But who are his 'English'? Anglo-Saxons, Normans who have inter-married with the natives, Normans who see themselves as belonging to England rather than to the continent?

Events that decisively stimulated the growth of English-Norman unity were the loss of Normandy under John and the outbreak of the Hundred Years War. The nobles then had to consider themselves landlords in England without a network of feudal connections on the mainland. The fall in the status of the peasants that occurred was part of a development in all the west and would have happened whether there had been a Norman conquest or not. The fact that the landlords were intrusive aliens complicated the social issues, but throughout the thirteenth and fourteenth centuries the conflict of alien landlords with indigenous peasants became more and more the plain antagonism of peasant and landlord. The great revolt of 1381 expressed not only a maturing of the inner conflicts of feudal society but also something like the re-emergence of the English people as a united and conscious force. We find too in Lollardism the advent of an English form of heresy. (Heresy is too simple a term to use of Lollardism without qualification, but the movement reflected burgess elements in the situation which, linked with the general upheaval and the growth of the textile industry, led in due time to protestant and puritan positions.)[20] The delayed development of certain aspects of social cohesion – aspects concerned with the relation of the free peasants and craftsmen, the burgesses, to the governmental structure and the forms of exploitation used by the ruling class – meant that when this cohesion did begin to appear, it was extremely strong, and led on in time to the Tudor State and the English Revolution.

The crucial factor preventing a quick absorption of the Normans was the difference in language. Probably a few men at Edward's court spoke French, but only a few. England had been unique in developing a vernacular as well as a Latin literature, even in church culture. By 1000 a matured and rich prose style had been formed, and soon after came the official English used by the government. Under the Normans the displacement of the native tongue in many spheres was not rapid; men still pleaded in it in the shire courts under Henry I; official documents sometimes used it, e.g. the confirmation of the privileges of Londoners by Henry. William is said to have tried to learn English, but after 1071 he had little motive for doing so. A certain amount of inter-marriage seems to have gone on at the level of the smaller landholders, but not enough to have much effect for a long time. Latin officially displaced English, then French crept into the official sphere and became the language of the lawcourts, then (in the thirteenth century) of the first universities and of early parliamentary procedure. However, English gradually reasserted itself. Henry III issued a trilingual proclamation as early as 1258; but it took the Hundred Years War to drive French out and to end the Alien Priories. We see a growing effort by the court to find English roots in such matters as the move to canonize Edward the Confessor and the advent of a Norman king named Edward. In the mid-thirteenth century the barons reiterated that castles must not be entrusted to aliens and that heiresses were not to be married with disparagement: 'that is, to men not of the nation of the realm of England'. In 1362 at the opening of Parliament the chancellor first read his speech in English, and soon afterwards English displaced French in the lawcourts, though records were still kept in Latin, as in most medieval departments of state. The lawyers resisted, and a mangled French persisted till its formal abolition in 1731 – though Cromwell had long past condemned it.

The names of ordinary folk show a slow taking-over of Norman names. The old English peasants had names like Ragge or Bugge, while the west Saxon royal family liked names that began with *aéthel-* (noble) or *ead-* (rich) and ended with such words as *-weard* (guardian) or *-mund* (protection). Norsemen brought in names like Sweyn and Harold – Hereward was the Old English equivalent. (So we see that King Harold and the outlaw Hereward had in fact the same name.) The Normans carried on the names they had been used to in the duchy: William, Richard, Hugh, Robert, Roger, Geoffrey, Fulk, Walter, Rao (Ralf or Radulf), and Maud (Matilda in Latin), Alice, Agnes, Catherine, Margaret, Joan, Mary, Elizabeth, Ann. At first the result was to increase the stock of names; but soon a few Norman names began driving out the English ones. William and Robert became favourites; John in the thirteenth century, Thomas after Thomas

P

Becket's murder. Edward we noted was the one royal name taken over from the English. By the later thirteenth century most Old English names had faded out. Surnames gradually came in. The Normans had added the name of castle or estate; and in time ordinary folk used a calling, a locality or the father's name plus *son*, while nicknames or diminutives increased the variety.[21]

For long the Conquest dealt a deadly blow to vernacular literature, both prose and verse, though the English still had their songs and (we may strongly suspect) their minstrels who kept alive much of the old themes and techniques. Anglo-French writing had its lively aspects, but could not fill the gap. The chroniclers wrote in Latin, even when they owed a debt to Old English sources and origins, like William of Malmesbury, for all his interest in, and understanding of, the English past. Yet he:

> breathes nationality, and in excellent Latin. His very grasp of English history – so far in advance of anything seen for centuries – marks a step forward in national consciousness, and a very slight study of the *Gesta Pontificum* reveals an historical interest rooted in English soil. The same is true of his lesser contemporaries, such as Serlo, whose poem on the Battle of the Standard is entirely English in spirit. The stubborn and illiterate warrior-class, whose history and privileges alike began in 1066, held out rather longer (Galbraith).[22]

William speaks of the folk of Canterbury as 'more than other Englishmen breathing still an awareness of ancient *nobilitas*', and Serlo calls English the *patria*. Robert of Gloucester complained near the end of the thirteenth century that there was no land 'that did not hold to its own speech but England alone'. The latter half of the fourteenth century saw English returning to the chronicles and being revived in other literary forms. Ranulf Higden, monk of Chester, noticed the change in attitudes; since 1066 children had not been taught in their own language, gentlemen had learned French from their cradle, countryfolk who wanted to gain advancement had had to learn French. Ranulf disliked this 'corruption of the mother tongue'. John of Trevisa traced the return of English to the Black Death (1348–9), so that by 1385 'in all the grammar-schools of England children are giving up French and are construing and learning in English'. Even the gentry were changing their ways; by the end of the century the court could listen to Chaucer.

But meanwhile big changes had taken place in the English language, many losses but also great gains. Regional differences increased and Norman usages affected spelling, grammar and punctuation after English became again the official language. The new standard English of the fifteenth century was mainly based on the dialect of the east midlands, the most economically advanced area. The great burst of poetry, using modified forms of the old alliterative verse, came from the west midlands and the north-west: *Sir Gawayne and the Grene Knight, Wynnere and Wastoure, The Parlement of the Thre Ages, The Avyntyrs of Arthure at the Tarn Wadling*, and so on. (No doubt we have lost much; *Gawayne* has come down in a single manuscript.) The alliterative revival reached its climax in *Piers Plowman*, just as Chaucer was revealing the full potentialities of the new Norman-enriched English. The basic Germanic structure remained, but in more supple and elastic forms, wider in scope, and with a much extended vocabulary. In various indirect ways both the Latin and the Anglo-Norman culture of the centuries after 1066 had played their part in greatly increasing the potentialities of the language; the outburst of the fourteenth century was not simply an underground stream re-emerging into the light. We saw how writers like William of Malmesbury were strengthening the old traditions as well as departing from them, and how works like Geoffrey of Monmouth's *Historia* did much to fuse Norman present with English (and British) past, in anticipation of a new synthesis. In England as elsewhere the Latin-minded clerics gave an alphabet to the local dialects. After 1066 English fell behind French and Latin as a literary medium; but in the end the works produced in those tongues reacted on the vernacular, which in any event had not been standing still. The very existence of Norman French (as to a lesser extent the earlier existence of Danish) helped to strengthen men's consciousness of being English. By the thirteenth century we have evidence for literary activities in English, which presupposed a reading public. There is for example the fine setting at Reading of the lyric on the *Cuckoo*; and an English version of the romance *Floriz and Blanchflur* was produced. There were also poems such as *The Fox and the Wolf* and the satirical *The Owl and the Nightingale*. By the late fourteenth century the vernacular had become a matter for patriotism, partly through the wars with the French, partly through the conflict (and half-union) with the alien language at home. A summons to Parliament in 1295 declared that the French king proposed to abolish the English language from the earth if his power corresponded to his detestable aims, 'which God avert'. By the fifteenth century English was fully re-established. Henry V sent despatches from France to the city of London in English. England was strongly felt to be separate from Europe, with its own clear and vital identity. *The Libelle of Englishe Policie* in 1436 declared, 'Kepe then the See, that is the wall of England.' The poet anticipated the Tudor sentiment summed up in the speech in Shakespeare's *Richard II* (ii, 1, 45).[23]

Langland, Chaucer, the 1381 revolt, and Wyclif, were different aspects of the rapid emergence of a great new synthesis, English solidarities developing among the masses of the people. Their diversity and contradictions reveal the dynamic breadth and richness of the nationhood thus emerging from the many interrelated elements.

CHAPTER XVI

A WIDER PERSPECTIVE

Argument still goes on as to the exact definition of the term feudalism, though no doubt most medievalists would basically accept Hollister's definition of it as signifying 'an institution based on the holding of a fief, usually a unit of land, in return for a stipulated honourable service, normally military, with a relationship of homage and fealty existing between the grantee and the grantor'. Yet once such a definition is accepted, interminable argument goes on as to how one defines Anglo-Saxon society. Sayles comments: 'To deny the descriptive term of "feudal" to the changes which had produced the Anglo-Saxon social structure on the ground that it did not fully resemble the social structure in Normandy is begging the question; it could equally well be argued that Norman society was never feudalized because it did not reach the still more developed form of feudal society in the Latin kingdom of Jerusalem. Feudalism is an unsatisfactory word: however, if what went on in England before

1066 was not feudal, even though it was no more than tentative in military and political aspects, the word to describe it will have to be invented.' The term was unknown to the medieval world itself, and one is tempted to fall back on the witticism that feudalism was introduced into England in the seventeenth century by Sir Henry Spelman. To think that a whole new kind of social order can suddenly appear with the advent or completion of some particular institution is frivolous in the extreme – as if one were to pinpoint the day of opening of the first steam-driven textile mill and announce that capitalism was then born. The inadequacy of a definition of feudalism in terms of Norman fief systems alone is brought out by the fact that from the very beginnings of the Norman systems the seeds of something quite different were present: the *fief-rente* with its substitution of money payment for military service. 'Ironically, the Conqueror's system of military tenures, seemingly a consummate expression of the feudal idea,' says Hollister, 'was in fact compromised from the beginning by factors that would ultimately destroy it: a money economy, a strong monarchy with a long tradition of direct and general allegiance, a military situation that favoured the use of mercenaries, and a political situation in which Norman feudal vassals were often less dependable to the monarchy than native Englishmen.'[1] The factors of direct allegiance and native reliability were particularly English factors, which help us to understand the main points in which our developments differed from those on the continent.

There are certain common factors that operated in western Europe in the centuries following the breakdown of Roman authority and law – factors which remain as what we may call the bedrock structure of society, despite continuous changes and modifications in their forms of expression, until the definite intrusion of the first modes of capitalist production. These common factors include at their core the ownership of the land and the enjoyment of its profits by a ruling class which holds its own by sheer force. Even if its officials and agents play useful parts in different phases by helping to organize agricultural and other work, the position of the ruling class is based on armed might and not on an economic role. Such a system inevitably has a class of warriors or retainers in close relation to the lords, and since land is one of the most valuable gifts at the disposal of the lords, some of the land will be held by warriors or companions, so that in effect there will be a relation between war service and such holdings even if it is not at all legally precise. Further there will be some sort of homage relation between such landholders and their lords. From the outset then, after the breakdown of the Roman state, the tribal successors of that state reveal all the ingredients that we find in Norman feudalism, though in a more fluid form, without sharply defined conditions – though custom would in its own way have laid down clearly enough for the men of the time just what they expected to do in return for gifts or privileges.

We should naturally expect that as society advances, with more play of money forces, economic expansion, and the growth of literacy and governmental organization, the relations between lord and retainers or companions could tend to be defined in more precise legal terms, with more definite obligations on both sides. This tendency appears everywhere in western Europe in early medieval times, but, for a number of reasons (which we have analysed), it was in Normandy, and then in Norman-conquered England, that the tenurial obligations of the military class were most precisely defined. There can be no doubt then that the Norman fief represents a particular development of a general trend, and that to isolate it as a special and separate type of social order to be labelled feudalism is myopic in the extreme. The key aspect of feudalism is the ownership of the land by a ruling class that maintains its hold by force; all the other aspects flow from this central point. Whether the dues or rents from the land are paid in products, labour services, or money, may be highly important for determining the particular phase of the system, but does not affect that central point.

There is one more aspect of feudalism to be noted. In a feudal society there will certainly be a strong tribal element, at least in its early phases. The tribal groups may be settling down and developing the first stages of urban society, like the early Sumerians; they may be conquered by members of a society with more advanced techniques, like the Amerindians under the Spaniards; or they may irrupt on a world with a higher culture, which they help to disrupt, like the Germanic peoples who overran the Roman west. But though the circumstances may vary, the first phases of a feudal society will have a strong tribal imprint; and what we see is the steady breakdown of the original elements of tribal brotherhood and equality in a situation where the lords and their warriors constitute a superior class set over the class of peasants. Not that we must visualize a simple antagonism. As we have seen, what actually happens is a complex mixture of force and assent, ruthless exploitation and tangled loyalties. The way in which the old tribal elements of cooperation and the new feudal elements of compulsion merge and conflict is what constitutes the actual living energy and coloration of any particular situation. [2]

One problem raised by this kind of formulation is the wide range of societies to which it refers. Indeed it covers all societies beyond the tribal level (that is, in which classes have developed) and which

have not created a slave economy or become capitalist or socialist.
The result is a rather unmanageable conglomeration of societies
which includes ancient Sumeria, Egypt, China and India, as well as
western Europe in its post-Roman phases. European feudalism, for
one thing, was unique in issuing in bourgeois or capitalist society:
something that no other feudal society showed any real signs of
doing. Faced with this problem, one might be tempted to give up.
But categorizing the stages of historical development is useful –
indeed necessary if one is not to succumb to pragmatism and the
mere description of societies and their stages. The only proviso is
that we must keep watching that the categories are not pushed too
far or allowed to become rigid, so that the facts are fitted into them
rather than their being reconstituted to meet the facts. All general
theories need to be continually overhauled and tested in the light of
new facts or hypotheses.

I myself therefore incline to the use of the term feudalism for
the European west alone. Feudalism would then be seen as a particular form of what we might call serf society; and we could put it in
a larger category that also included, say, Sumerian serf society. In
turn we might subdivide feudalism itself. Fief feudalism would serve
as a term to define the phase developed in an intensified form by the
Normans; the earlier phases in England, where we find king and
warriors set against the free peasantry we might call tribal feudalism;
the final phase, emerging in England with the Tudors, we might call
the absolute monarchy.[3]

At almost every new start made in past history – apart from the turn
to bourgeois society – there has been an influx of peoples at various
tribal stages to the more advanced areas. In general, whatever divisions, social or economic, have grown up during the phases of tribal
development, there has survived a strong element of what we may
call primitive democracy: that is, notions of the equality of all able-
bodied clansmen, which are carried on as notions of the equal rights
of all arms-bearing men – together with various forms of assembly
through which the clansmen can express their opinions, discuss
matters that concern them, and play a part in the making of all
important decisions. The classic case of the carry-over of such tribal
notions into settled life, with a continual revaluation and reapplica-
tion of their forms of expression to suit the changed conditions, is
that of the ancient Greeks, above all in the city-state of Athens.
Such a development was made possible by the rejection of the kingship and of the organized priesthoods which had dominated the serf
societies of the Near East and Egypt, and had limited the extent of
their social development. The Romans too, in a different way,

showed the carry-over of tribal ideas and forms into the complex political situation of the city-state, despite the division of the citizens into patricians and plebeians. Hence the republican forms of government, voting, and assembly, which survived the many strains until the fall of the Republic. In both Greece and Rome class conflict, which implies some degree of freedom of action in the conflicting classes, was able to continue without either chaos or arrest of the system. The crucial point then in the development from tribalism into fully settled or civilized life is the way in which the tribal forms are broken down, transformed, or readapted, with the advent of urban life and of the state. An analysis which attempted to show the distinctive qualities of each emerging civilization would need to grapple with this question and to show the different ways in which the transition from tribal bases was carried out.

The influx of Germanic tribal groups into the breaking down West of the Roman empire introduced a new life, or at least the possibility of a new life, however much the situation was complicated by the degree of social differentiation and the emergence or strengthening of war-lords among the tribes, and by the extent to which the tribal societies assimilated elements from the Roman provinces they invaded and settled in. (Various social and economic elements had also been absorbed for long before the invasions.) In Anglo-Saxon England there was the cleanest break with the Roman past and therefore also the fullest development of the forms and attitudes of the tribal systems of the invaders. And this point is valid even if we make allowance for more contacts with and influences from the Romano-Celts than has usually been accepted, and for more connection with Gaul and other parts of the continent than is usually taken into account, especially after the conversion of the various Anglo-Saxon groups. Hence the strong folk element in Anglo-Saxon society, which we must not ignore or undervalue because it has been sentimentalized and seen by nineteenth-century scholars in terms of an idealized Victorian democracy. There was a richness of folk culture in English society not to be found elsewhere in western Europe. Whatever similar elements persisted in Germany lacked the English cohesive and unifying quality. The folk basis of English life implied all sorts of binding elements as well as elements of sturdy independence.

Despite all the pressures of Norman feudalism, the hundredal and the honorial courts never fused, and never showed the least signs of fusing or linking together. The hundredal system had embodied the determination of Edmund, Athelstan, and Edgar, to enforce peace through the king's justice. The Normans, by making the sheriff the chief military and police officer of the crown in the shire, and by associating the hundred with police measures like *murdrum* and frankpledge, prepared the way for the Angevin policy that worked the communal traditions of shire and hundred into the new bureaucracy. The juries of Henry II and the tax-assessing knights of Henry III not only paved the way for the shire representatives of Edward I, but also assured to the Anglo-Saxon system of shire and hundred 'a permanence that is unique in European history, and thus blended Teutonic and Roman elements into that characteristic hardy hybrid which we call the English constitution' (Cam).[4]

We may now try to summarize and extend some of the main findings that have emerged from our analyses. England, however different in many respects from the rest of western Europe in the eleventh century, was ultimately a part of the same general development. If we can imagine Harold as having won at Hastings, we can be sure he would have taken many steps that strengthened the links between England and the continent, especially Flanders and northern France. Just how he would have done it, we cannot tell; though he would certainly not have initiated anything like the sudden leap into fief feudalism which the Conquest brought about. But 'ifs' are usually not fruitful in the discussion of history. The Conquest did take place; and that involved a sharp collision of English and Norman forms, and the ultimate development of a synthesis out of them. On the one hand there was England, the one state in the West with a high level of unifying law, a close link between the kingship and popular courts, a kingship with a tradition of issuing law codes, and a relative absence of internal war; and on the other hand there was a highly militarized system, linking land tenures with specific services, with a powerful drive for centralization. The result might have been chaos, a country breaking down between unrelieved tensions; but the Normans, however ruthless and violent they might have been, always had a strong sense of the possible, allied to a capable organizing faculty.

We have noted the mixture of archaic and advanced elements in pre-1066 England. The society was archaic because it rested ultimately on a large-scale reaffirmation of tribal kingship; it was advanced because this aspect anticipated the more integrated relationship of the state system and the people which came about in England in the sixteenth century. Many changes had to occur before the Tudor state could be reached. There had to be a big expansion of mercantile and productive capacities, a considerable growth of towns and their burgess class, and an extension of kingly power as the result of a long class struggle in which king, lords, burgesses and peasants all played their parts. What gave an element of inertia to the old English kingdom was the high degree to which it was ruled

by consensus, customary law and tribal survivals in the courts and in
the relations of man with man, even of peasant with lord. But there
was slow, steady organic growth, despite all the warfare between
the early kingdoms and the many exploitations. This was something
unparalleled on the continent, except to some extent in Salian
Germany. But for a mixture of political, economic and geographical
reasons (at some of which we have glanced), Germany could not
attain the comprehensive solidarity that was emerging in England,
stage by stage, especially after Alfred. The intensification of feudal
tenures and services came about in Germany only in the anarchic
half-century after the investiture controversy; and what then
developed was not at all like the state emerging in England under
Henry III. The centrifugal forces were too strong.[5] Similar centrifugal forces in England, active both in the old English particularism
under the unifying kingship and in Anglo-Norman feudalism with
its baronial divisions, were controlled and redirected by the fusion
of Norman centralism linked with the fief settlements, with the
tough tribal cohesiveness of the Anglo-Saxon court system and
administration.

Thus England was saved from the over-simple fief feudalism of
Normandy itself and of other comital states like Anjou or Maine,
and from the cumbrous breakdown of effective centralization which
happened in Germany. A vital union of English and Norman elements came about: a maximum of central organization was merged
with extended local forms in the tenures and in the courts, shire,
hundred and honorial: that is, a maximum of centralization
in terms of the concrete possibilities of the epoch, where the limits
of governmental organization were determined by the level of the
social and economic nexus, the supply of literate and trained officials,
and so on. Perhaps something analogous had occurred in the creation of the Merovingian kingdom in Gaul, the first important
attempt to build a wide-reaching state on the Roman ruins. That
was brought about by the Salian Franks, who seem to have remained
quietly in Betuwe and north Taxandria, then to have started moving in the mid fifth century. As a result of their conquest, some
30,000 Franks were settled over the whole area between the Somme
and the Loire; all the tribal fighters thus constituted something of
a ruling class to hold the region together. But this development –
and that of the Carolingian state that followed – occurred at a much
lower level, economic, political and cultural, than that of the
eleventh century, and so had different though noteworthy effects.
France in the medieval era shared with England a strong centralizing trend, but without the rich set of cohesive factors.[6]

We must then see the post-1066 process as involving above all the imposition of the Norman fief system on the old English agricultural and land-holding basis, in which there were similar elements but in a looser form: and thus also the imposition of the sharp Norman concepts of property relationships on the very much broader field of old English law. This imposition was not achieved once and for all by a single set of actions, but was the result of a continuous tension, conflict, and synthesis of the two elements. The tension, we must stress, was continuous and prolonged; it took centuries in its working out. Indeed it was never worked out in the sense of reaching a complete synthesis. Rather it went on through a complex and hard-fought series of conflicts and integrations, each of which in turn transformed the ground on which the tension operated. One key tension was that between certain ruling class systems of ownership and exploitation and a comprehensive system of folk forms, which both stimulated the sense of immemorial local and personal liberties, and strengthened the royal struggles for unification. To say this is not to introduce later ideas of democracy and its opposite into the feudal situation – though we may validly claim that those later ideas would never have evolved without the earlier conflicts, compromises, unions and disunions. The folk in the England of the eleventh century were real enough, though harder to describe precisely than the lords who controlled the state system and its various expressions. They had their traditions, customs, ideas and methods, which were appropriate to their needs in their specific historical situation, and through which they expressed themselves; they had their notions and emotions of solidarity and freedom, as also many divisive activities and ideas, which limited their solidarities. The problem is to realize both the cohesive and the divisive aspects, and not to distort them by anachronistic perspectives, nor to lose sight of them or dissolve them in too abstract and remote an analysis of the society, and of the factors and forces both rending that society and holding it together. We may indeed say:

In the field of institutions continuity is the essential theme of English history. The monarchy, the shire courts, the hundreds with their courts, the towns, the geld system of assessment and collection were all products of Anglo-Saxon experience and skill. The principal means and instruments of royal administration, the royal chapel, the solemn charter, and the sealed writ were familiar in late Anglo-Saxon days. The very coinage and system of weights and measures were convenient and fostered by the Norman conquerors. Only in their feudal attributes do the Normans appear as conspicuous innovators. Elsewhere it is as constructive builders on solid Anglo-Saxon achievements that their principal virtues find expression (Loyn).[7]

And yet that gives too static an impression of what happened. The Norman system of fief feudalism was indeed all that the aliens introduced; but in the circumstances the impact was violent, pervasive, dynamic. The old institutions were set in a new framework, but this meant more than a mere new setting. It meant the slow but unceasing recreation of the old forms in terms of new needs and new relationships.

The kingdom of Jerusalem may be taken as an example of almost the exact opposite of the Norman procedure in England. There fief feudalism was imposed grandiosely on a society, or at least a region, which was in many ways richer and more complex than that of its conquerors; but though a clever dovetailing of the various components of the kingdom was worked out, there was hardly any significant cross-fertilization. In Sicily the advent of Norman power had much happier results, and a much more complicated system, drawing on Greek and Moslem experience, was evolved; but there was really nothing comparable to the total interpenetration of two systems, sharing certain important elements and yet powerfully opposed, which we find in England. Perhaps we can roughly suggest the difference between Norman Sicily and England if we compare the powerful and original structural unity of Durham cathedral, its sheer organic force, with the diverse elements, Norman, Byzantine and Moslem, brought most impressively together at Monreale, but never fused into a significant sort of new structure.

We may now ask afresh the question: what was it that held men together during the Anglo-Norman era – held them together as members of a group and provided for each of them an inner unifying element, a sense of spiritual security? If we consider the peasants and smaller landholders in the light of laws and charters, we see them mainly as economic or social groups; in the charters, if they figure as individuals, we learn little more than their names and status. At best we see them as men who must have shared emotions of satisfaction and comradeship as they worked and talked together in a village community, or of frustration and stifled revolt as they suffered the same exploitations or oppressions under the local lord.

Certainly the aspect of work was crucial; but we still have only a thin and too general impression; we are far from the fully concrete situation. We have seen how, as early tribal bonds tended to break down, the relation of man and lord emerged as a powerful force. But it operated most strongly at the upper levels of society, where a vassal could feel intensely his fealty to a lord and the lord in return could exercise much generosity and goodwill. The feudal bond at lower levels was entangled with the bonds of kinship, sometimes harmoniously, sometimes in fierce conflict. For the ordinary man his place in society was defined by this unstable merging of fealty ties and kindred bonds, with a hopeful turning to the king and his justice as an ultimate reconciler and unifier.

The kindreds certainly played an extremely important part in the life of the common man, filling the gap between his role as a worker in a system with many cooperative elements and his connection with king or lord through the courts.[8] We know about their nature and activities almost wholly from the law codes, so that they come into view mainly in connection with killings and bloodfeuds. This limitation inevitably gives us a perverted as well as a restricted notion of them; we have only a few general statements that enable us to guess how a man's place in a kindred filled out his life and gave him a sense of identity. Tribal concepts of the group were breaking down; the nationhood of the absolutist state and of bourgeois society was not yet born. It is thus hard for us to grasp just how medieval man saw himself in the world; the idea of nationhood has been so important since the sixteenth century that it is only by an extreme imaginative effort that we can think ourselves into the position of men who lacked it. In the eleventh and twelfth century class position was more basic than any embryonic national bond. A Norman baron felt warm affinities with a baron of Anjou or France, which he did not feel in the least with his own peasants – though the lack of mobility and communication among the lower classes prevented the English peasant from feeling any solidarity with Norman peasants in much the same conditions as himself. The peasant therefore tended to react only to local issues; but his sympathies too were essentially for members of his own class.

Revolts occurred in the thirteenth century, as when the Dunstable tenants fought the monks in 1229. By the fourteenth century the peasantry had learned many lessons about organization and communication with other groups in England. In 1336 the people of Darnall and Over rose against the Cistercians of Vale Royal on whose manors they dwelt. The abbot locked them up 'as though they were villeins and forced them to serve in all villein services'. Refusing to submit, they were again jailed. At last they gave in 'and confessed that they were villeins, they and their sons after them'. The abbey chronicle shows how they had learned common action and had used pilgrim routes to communicate with other parts of the country. They had:

called together all their neighbours of their own condition, and
plotted by night to get their liberty by rebelling against the
aforesaid abbot. And they sent some of their number on behalf
of them all on a pilgrimage to St Thomas of Hereford; and these
men, contrary to their oath, came to the king in the northern
parts and for many days were begging his favour, which they
did not deserve to find; and afterwards they came to unforeseen
adventures, for they robbed certain people of their goods and
were all to their great chagrin carried off to Nottingham jail,
being wholly stript of all their own goods that they had with
them. Afterwards, before the justices of the lord the king in
that place, they were condemned to be hanged.

Before the great revolt of 1381 the peasants were getting together
in 'conventicles'. Countryfolk, even when most scattered, had
systems of union. In ordinances of the tenth century it seems assumed
that men belonged to a village (villa or *tunscipe*); *Domesday* divided
the country into counties, hundreds (wapentakes), and vills; and in
the later Middle Ages the hamlet seems always to have existed within
the boundaries of a vill. Further, however isolated the houses, men
were drawn together by the rule that every male over twelve had
to be in a tithing for police purposes, if he were to enjoy the rights
of a free man. All men were joined also in ecclesiastical obligations
to a parish church. The police-group, the *parochia*, and the vill might
not coincide; but the village system tended to invade and control
others: village churches tended to take the place of the old collegiate
minsters, and in later years the tithing in some districts appeared in
territorial form, identified with the vill or a subdivision of it.

In one sense medieval man, with varying degrees of comprehen-
sion and sophistication, saw himself as a member of the universe
(reflected in God's church and concretized in the actual edifice of
worship); but except in so far as it bound him to the church, this
cosmic sense did not much pervade his social consciousness. If he
spoke of his *patria*, he would no doubt be referring to Normandy or
Mercia, even Pisa or Florence, rather than to France, England,
Germany or Italy. Primary groupings were provincial or regional,
effective only when small enough for the prince, duke or count to
know the area and its folk through personal contact and to control
all immediate vassals, even though groupings were being consolidated
in language as well as in geography by the time of the crusades.
William of Malmesbury remarks, 'The Englishman gave up his forest
hunt, the Scot [or Irish] his familiarity with fleas, the Dane his ceaseless boozing, the Norwegian his raw fish.' By the thirteenth century

a feudal sense of belonging to the larger entities foreshadowed the full sense of nationhood of the sixteenth century.

The term *natio* or nation was the sole word in medieval Latin to describe Slavs, English, Saxons or Florentines. In the fourteenth century it moved towards its modern sense; in the sixteenth century came the term 'national', in the seventeenth 'nationality' and 'nationally'; in the eighteenth 'nationalize', in the nineteenth 'nationalism' and 'nationalization'.[9]

A small concentrated unit such as the town was necessary for the rebirth of a strong sense of group solidarity after the break up of the territorially based kindreds. As we saw, substitute kindred forms appeared in the organization of associates and of guildsmen; but though these were very important in providing models, they could not suffice to create a bond to embrace all the townsmen. To the extent that a strong kindred element was present in the groups founding or decisively enlarging a town, the process of achieving a new civic sense of unity would be helped; but in any event the deep conviction that some sort of kin bond was necessary for a secure and satisfying life would have led to an infusion of kindred emotions into the new situation. In Holland and north France we can see with special clarity how tenacious kin groups played a key part in providing the new town spirit. It seems certain that often the immigrants who provided the nuclei of towns did not enter as individuals but as kin groups; and we can probably see the *conjurati* and *congildones*, against whom so many enactments of capitularies are aimed, as kin groups who had entered into various agreements. Such bodies were certainly formed to a considerable extent with kindred help and on kindred models. The strength of the great merchant families was clearly based on kin solidarity, and led in time to measures being taken to limit the number of close kinsmen who might serve as urban or rural officials or councillors.[10]

All this does not mean that we may claim that the kindreds were the sole bases of the new urban consciousness or of the town guilds. For one thing, as trade increased, there were strong influences from Byzantion, where guilds had developed out of the ancient corporations. From the twelfth century, we find in the western towns the same controls of trade and industry as in Byzantion: a strict surveillance of the members of guilds, the constant inspection of workshops, measures against middlemen and hoarding, restriction on the freedom of sales in the market, limitations of exports to what is not needed for consumption by the town's inmates. But in the west there was a concern with equality not to be found in Byzantion; the civic spirit had new elements and potentialities. However, the link was certainly there. Analogous measures were taken by the heads of the imperial government and the urban principates of the west; Byzantine corporations were under the prefect as the urban trades in Lombard towns in the patrician epoch were put under senior members appointed by the town magistrates; we can pair off the obligation of Byzantine silk-makers to get the prefect's seal on their bales with the sealing of cloth in the towns of Flanders and Brabant, to ensure quality as well as control export. (We must recall that 1147 saw the transfer of silk industries from Thebes and Corinth to Sicily.)[11]

The extent to which guild forms helped to create the sense of London's being the seat of a large body of citizens with a corporate existence can be guessed from the peace guild of late Anglo-Saxon days, which we noticed earlier. 'This is the decree which the bishops and reeves belonging to London, *eorl* and *ceorl*, have published and established with pledges in our peace-guild, in addition to the laws given at Grately, Exeter, and Thundersfield.' The guild was concerned with putting down thieves and keeping the peace of the district; but besides its policing duties it had both secular and religious obligations to its members, an elaborate organization, and a common purse. Its officials met once a month, generally when the butts were being filled, and had their meals together. 'And they shall feed themselves as they themselves think fitting.' This body perhaps gave its name to the Guildhall. The degree of political consciousness developed by the Londoners is shown by their claim in 1135 to have the right of choosing the king. They were known collectively as barons and were thus styled by the clerks who wrote the writs of Rufus and Henry I. Their city was *refugium et propugnaculum regni*, and it could be maintained that its liberties were necessary for the well-being of the whole kingdom. Civic consciousness was being tinged with a rudimentary national consciousness.

Taking a broader view, we may claim that the feudal bond and the kindred bond, with their mixture of unity and conflict, entered into the other forms of association, those of work and locality, and were powerfully affected by the growth of the king's law as a nationally unifying factor. The towns with their new concentrations of population, and new unions and exploitations, provided focal points for gathering and diffusing a new communal sense and new communal forms of organization, while at the same time they created new lines of class differentiation. Here we are still inside the feudal process; but in the countryside, with the steady breakdown of feudal relations, the lack of guild forms made possible the activities of the small entrepreneurs who laid the basis of capitalist wage relations in agriculture and craft industries – though their methods of exploitation also penetrated the towns, despite the many resistances there. Throughout this development the common man could not but have felt the hopeful pull of the varying unions as well as suffering the oppression of many divisive factors. Gradually the remnants of the extended kindred fell away and gave place to the restricted family as the normal unit; the feudal bond of man and lord was replaced by that of employer and wage-hand. What remained of the feudal period was the loyalty to the king and the acceptance of his law and administration as a unifying factor. The kingly system gradually became the expression of nationhood and men felt something of a sense of unity with all other members of the nation; the king was the symbol and effective expression of this unity. We must not idealize this new concept of unity, which in daily life was torn and denied by all kinds of oppressions, divisions, and exploitations; but it had its reality nevertheless, both in the new complexity of concrete inter-connections among men and in a general sense of human unity or brotherhood which it stimulated as well as distorted or limited. Men now existed in a tension between this new nationhood with its concept of unity, and their own particular loyalties in work, family, and linked associations; between this new corporate body with its multiple expressions in institutions and culture, and the various divisive factors ceaselessly acting upon them. A new stability had been reached, which overcame many of the conflicts and contradictions of feudalism, but which in turn created conflicts and contradictions on a new level, inside the new whole.

But these remarks need to be supplemented with an inquiry as to why European developments led to the medieval borough or commune, and to capitalist modes of production, and why such developments did not occur elsewhere. Why for example did the Byzantine or Moslem towns not evolve in similar ways? To answer such questions at all fully would need a new book, but we can glance here at some of the general points that would have to be discussed. The Byzantine world has never been properly analysed to bring out its similarities with and differences from the western states of the post-Roman era. Roughly we can say that that world for long stood out as far the most advanced section of Europe because of the extent to which it was able to retain elements from the ancient world, its governmental forms and its type of city, while modifying them to suit the new situation that was emerging. Feudalism therefore took a highly complex form, using and adapting ancient forms while giving them a new content. For long there was strong conflict between the lords of the big estates and the men who stood for the interests of the great mercantile cities with their extensive craft activities. This conflict is to be seen in the battles of the Green and Blue Factions grouped round the chariot teams in the great games. But the emperors maintained control, and with it they preserved a certain balance, though, as great landowners themselves, they inclined for the most part – or at crucial moments – to support of the feudalizing forces. Through the Theme system in its administration the state both facilitated the growth of feudalism (in the broad sense given to that term earlier in this chapter) and prevented the developing of full baronial power as in the West. The seventh century saw a decisive turn with the onslaught of Islam and the movement inwards of the Slavs throughout the Balkans and much of Greece. There is no need for us to follow the changes in detail, but we may note how under the Comnenes military service was largely determined by the system of the *pronoia*, under which the big landlords had to supply heavily armed cavalry in return for their grants, while the smaller landholders and the monasteries had to supply footmen. But such recruits needed to be supplemented by paid mercenaries. The defeat of Alexis by the Normans at Dyrrachium in 1082 was due to the lack of training of the *pronoia*-recruits. To raise new forces the emperor had to raid churches' treasures.[12]

This period saw the triumph of the military nobility; it also saw the weakening of Byzantion's world position. The persistence of ancient forms in state and city, which had given the empire its strength and superiority, was holding up development; the west was gathering the forces that were to bring it up to the Byzantine level – an achievement villainously expressed in the treacherous sacking of Byzantion in 1204 by the men of the fourth crusade. Above all, despite internal struggles, the Byzantine town could not compete with the communes of the west as a centre liberating new social and economic forces.

The conflict and merging of Arab and Byzantine elements created for a while new peripheral societies which generated powerful energies. These societies, however, lacked the capacity for development beyond a certain point; they perpetuated many of the Byzantine weaknesses in an intensified form. In Islam from the outset the rulers had a readymade stereotype of theoratic authority. The tribal assembly did not generate forms such as we see in ancient Athens and Rome, or in Anglo-Saxon England with its folk courts. No steady and effective class conflict could come about: that is, conflict within a system which provides a framework of continuity, so that the conflict can drive society ahead into new forms without breaking it up.

We may compare east and west again in the matter of military tenures. In the east we find the Ottoman *timariot* or the Moghul

jagirdar holding an allotment of land (temporarily, at least in principle) or rather getting land revenue in return for services; but we do
not find the growth of an aristocracy with anything like an
independent basis, even when a regime was far in decay. In the
west the kings had continually to face a body of lords settled firmly
on the land, with rights of renunciation of fealty, the *diffidatio* of
Anglo-Norman England or the *desonaturalizacion* of the Aragon
nobles, *ricoshombres de natura*.[13]Throughout, the kings had to consider and somehow control powerful barons. In such a situation, if
anarchy was to be avoided, there was a need for counter-weights on
the royal side, including a strong administrative and coercive
apparatus. The ceaseless tension between king and lords – who both
needed one another, but could never find a point of stable balance
in their relations – had a vital effect on every aspect of the situation,
allowing all sorts of interstices, deadlocks, or contradictory interests,
to develop, through which the burghers or peasants could in
different ways at different times assert themselves. A simple and solid
alliance of king and lords to hold down the lower classes would
have been liable to produce stagnation; and something of such an
alliance, though not in any massively articulated form, did exist in
late Anglo-Saxon England. At least that element existed to the
extent of producing what we have called the archaic aspect of the
society; the great value of the Norman intrusion was that it shattered the consensus for all time and sharply and pervasively
stimulated class conflict, thus freeing the potentialities of the English
situation in a way that could hardly have been done from within.

The existence then of continual conflict between king and barons,
who each needed the other, stopped them from simply making an
alliance against the commoners except at moments of extreme
crisis, and made possible the deep rooting of the idea that the king's
law was an essential mediator and dispute-settler at all levels, however imperfectly the idea may have been put into practice at any
given moment. There was security of landed property to an extent
quite absent from Asiatic systems, including that of the Moslems, and
justice was more fully embodied in definite laws. These laws might
be harsh and weighted against the peasantry in many respects; but
they were far less arbitrary in their application than anything in
the legal systems of the east. Only a comparatively small area of life
was covered by Islamic canon law, *Shari'a*, and this provided no
protection against arbitrary action from above. Hence the growth
of a large body of lawyers in the medieval west. Their activities
might often stir popular indignation; but without them the state
and its legal systems could not have evolved as they did – nor in time
could the revolts from below have achieved their clarity of goal.

The fact that the west had its inheritance of Roman Law could not by itself have brought about this development; but at almost every phase it helped to consolidate the emerging forms. If we turn to China we find that throughout its history there was nothing like the series of mediating and conflicting factors which make up medieval Europe.

Many further factors might be mentioned that made for a vital complexity, diversity, density, and at the same time brokenness of structure, in western societies: a continual balance and imbalance of forces that made possible effective pressures from below. Even geography helped. The way in which the sea spread around and into the area was useful for trade and for the definition of regional frontiers. The area could be split into a large number of sizeable regions, which could be effectively organized without (apart from such an area as Norway) being too cut off from one another. The ancient world had in general been able to bring about such coexisting regions only in the form of city-states. Now larger units, variously interacting, could be organized – units that in turn could expand and become strong centres of development, Old Castile in Castile, the district round Paris in France, London and the home counties in England. The stronger areas could then in turn draw in outlying territories such as Brittany, Wales, Granada, Navarre and Ireland, not by large-scale conquest but by prolonged warfare and penetration – though the movement outwards did not always succeed, as when Spain tried to take in Portugal, or England and Scotland. There was much destruction and suffering, but also much enriching integration, in which trade played its part. The movements, piratic, trading and colonizing, of the Scandinavians and Normans produced the last largescale upheavals and new integrations in this European pattern we are sketching out.

There was one more factor of great importance in begetting this fruitful balance-imbalance: the Christian Church, which had characteristics unlike those of any other ecclesiastical organization, ancient, Buddhist or Islamic. Here was a highly centralized and disciplined corporation, fiercely and ruthlessly destroying all competitors, pagan or heretical, and yet confronting secular states with which it might come variously to terms but could not subdue. It held its own traditional and steadily expanded set of ideas, and possessed a very strong cohesive inner force, produced by its rigid systems and its unchallenged appeal to supernal sanctions, which in particular played on the sense of guilt of a violent, deeply divided and oppressive world, and on the fear of death afflicting the inhabitants of such a world. Growing up inside the bureaucratic structures of the Roman imperial state, it had taken over many forms and methods of that harshly authoritarian system, with which it had once struggled. It had thus learned to maintain comparatively sophisticated forms of organization even in the worst periods of the Roman breakdown. The emerging tribal states learned much from it, using its clerics for their administration as they grew more stable; but the church played an even more important part in the creation of Europe when in the eleventh century it began to break its compact with the theocratic state and to assert its claims to a superiority which, though based on theological dogmas, asserted its rights to all sorts of independencies and dominances that impinged on the secular state. The conflicts of church and state from the eleventh century onward can thus be seen as the conflicts of a pair of superimposed states, both of which claimed to be uppermost in a great many important matters. The tensions inherent in such a situation might weaken at moments, but were ready to reappear at any challenge on either side, and provided a permanent aspect of the medieval world.

There is the further point that the church itself was divided into 'religious' and seculars, monks and priests. One section, at least in theory, totally repudiated the world (money, marriage, family, forms of social grouping), while the other sought to carry on in the world, with its upper levels aping all the pomps and grandeurs of the secular rulers and nobility. There was a deep contradiction here, which did much to stimulate critical and heretical thought. As we have seen, the relations of the religious and the seculars underwent many changes over the years, especially after about 1100; but the contradiction they represented persisted throughout the medieval epoch.

The existence of two systems of law, secular and canon, also had the effect of keeping before men the possibilities of choice and the need for discussion and inquiry. This effect operated increasingly from the eleventh century onwards, as the church widened the area of its claims. The study of secular law became important in the universities. We saw how Gregory (Hildebrand) stirred up much more than he had bargained for. In considering Roman law, men thought much on ancient Rome itself and its empire; and this trail led to such views as those set down in Dante's *Monarchia*: that the empire (the secular order, with the Holy Roman Emperor as its supreme ruler) was the instrument for the realization of the ends of the human race as a whole, of *humana civilitas*. By means of the empire 'the blessedness of this life' can be attained, a blessedness 'which is figured by the terrestrial paradise'. Such concepts were as far as possible removed from what Pope Gregory himself thought of the secular state and his thesis that all political authority had a 'sinful origin'.

In his Letter to the Bishop of Metz, 1081, he declared,

> Who does not know that kings and leaders are sprung from men
> who were ignorant of God, who by pride, robbery, perfidy,
> murder, in a word, by almost every crime at the prompting
> of the devil, who is the prince of this world – have striven with
> blind cupidity and intolerable presumption to dominate over
> their equals, that is, over mankind?

We can understand why the German bishops protested that his doctrines were stirring up the common folk.[14]

The church also, by claiming the right to assert its overriding
power against all the many states of the west, provided the idea of
an ultimate European unity. If asked for some term to cover the
common civilization of the west, men would have used some such
term as *Respublica Christiana* or *Christianitas;* yet an early Spanish
chronicler could describe the victory at Poitiers over the Saracens
in 732 as the work of *Europeenses.* In due time men began to recognize the imperial state behind the Rome of the martyrs and to apply
ideas from the ancient world to the present.

We must also consider the nature of the city in the west, where a
mixture of elements from the ancient world merged with elements
from the tribal present to produce with many variations a body
politic that had remote affinities with that of the old city-state,
though developing inside a different social whole. Nothing at
all similar could be found in the east. Not that there was any lack
of eastern cities. European travellers were for long astounded at the
many huge and thriving cities of the east; and Moslem civilization
was always urban rather than rural, since it inherited the strong
urban tradition of the east Mediterranean. But the Moslem city was
politically inert, enclosed as part of a burdensome bureaucratic establishment without any inner drive to self-government. Over it stood
not bishop or baron but a theocratic kingship. When we turn to
the early communes of Italy and Flanders we step into another world.

Not that things were made easy for the burghers of the west. On
the contrary. The early growth of strong feudal controls, from Spain
to Scotland, ensured that they did not get anything like complete
independence, while the nature of the towns and their inhabitants,
and their relation to the whole situation in which they grew up, ensured that they would not remain inert cells in a larger system. They
slowly but steadily found a secure basis on which to struggle for the
rights and privileges they most needed. In eastern (non-Byzantine)
Europe towns tended to be garrisoned centres for a colony planted

by the king; they were often alien in speech and character to the surrounding population and for long could not fruitfully interact with that population. The belt in which urban communities were able to develop their own political life ran from north Italy up to west Germany, the Low Countries, and along the Baltic. In Italy the town brought the nobility under its control and became the dominant political entity; but this very success broke down the growth of larger political systems in which the town might have played its part and in time led to an impasse; the towns became specialized feudal enclaves unable to stir or support the political struggle driving feudalism towards the final working out of its contradictions. In Germany the town separated itself from the near principalities, with something of the same effect in the long run. The Hanseatic League, the Lombard League, and the *Hermandad* or Brotherhood of Basque ports, could not evolve into true federations; the links remained comparatively external, without moving towards larger political or economic integrations. The Italian cities turned into petty principalities, partly through absorbing aristocratic elements which had at first been disturbed by them. The result was a set of unstable units, interacting only at certain levels, and unable to move into anything like a national system. Venice and Genoa remained republics and, like Athens of the fifth century B.C., they devoted their energies to building little empires – mostly outside Italy, as Athens had build an Aegean system. The decisive development occurred only in the Lowlands and in England – the two areas that were to produce bourgeois revolutions long before the rest of Europe.

In England the towns did not gain such independence as the Italian communes or the Hanseatic ports; the struggle for self-assertion went on as an integral part of the movement towards nationhood in which the burghers were increasingly important from the fifteenth to the seventeenth century. The Low Countries were cut off from the general development of the Holy Roman Empire by the river system that gave them access to the sea and stimulated economic activities, and by close links with England and north France, so that the towns were neither completely independent and separate, nor simply dominated by feudal lordships. Urban and feudal forces could conflict and merge, finally consolidating into a sort of proto-nationhood under the Burgundian overlordship of the fifteenth century and then maturing in the long struggle against Spanish domination. In England the same sort of development went on, but in a less sharp and particularist way, in forms that made for stable nationhood far beyond what the Netherlands could attain in the seventeenth century.[15]

Thus, because of the complexity of the situation and its multiple potentialities, the later Middle Ages saw a welter of varying trends, interactions, and intermediate forms, with all sorts of counter-attacks from the more backward-looking nobilities, who wanted to take advantage of greater profits while clinging to or reintroducing forms of serfdom to preserve their controls. The Italian city despot was a miniature precursor of the absolute monarch, while England and Holland drove on to create the first bourgeois nations.

We must beware of seeing any single line of movement from serfdom to capitalist wage systems. There is however one key factor that runs through all the centuries of feudalism, from the days when the barbarian states emerged coherently on the Roman ruins to the breakthrough of the bourgeoisie in Holland and England, and this is the struggle for feudal rent. The big growth of international trade, the industrialization of Flanders, Brabant, Liège, Lombardy and Tuscany, with the appearance of large commercial centres like Venice, Genoa, Bruges, Paris and London, all came after feudal de-velopments of agriculture and were ultimately dependent on them. They were products of the feudal process and by themselves could not have transformed it. The increase in production for the market extended and deepened the existing stratifications among the peasant producers. The rich peasants became richer, and the poor, poorer. But they became a different kind of rich and a different kind of poor, especially after the thirteenth century. Now the better-off peasant was concerned rather with sending his surplus to market than with consuming it; and he kept his eye open for more land and began to employ more wage-labour – drawing on landless men rather than smallholders. Such peasants resisted the extraction of their surplus-rent by the lords, and in this resistance they had the alliance of the poorer sections of their class, who were fighting against being driven down to a bare subsistence level. The struggle for rent sharpens and in the fourteenth century reaches the stage of general revolt (Hilton).[16]

The expansion of money and its circulation and uses, though a key aspect of later medieval developments, did not itself disrupt feudalism or create a different sort of society. Though at some periods feudalism operated at a level close to that of a natural (non-monetary) economy, with local sufficiency dominating the situa-tion, the development of markets, trade, and the circulation of money were not decisive in bringing about a fundamental change. That is, such things would not alone change a feudal economy into a bourgeois one – any more than they could by themselves change the slave economies of Greece and Rome into forms of capitalism;

or more relevantly, than they could change the Byzantine world, where they operated strongly, into such forms. The Norman lords were always concerned with *profit*, and in a sense it did not matter if it came in the shape of productive lands, tolls and taxes, or money rents and commutations. There was indeed a continuous movement towards money evaluations, despite setbacks, for money by its fluidity enabled the lords to enjoy a wider range of satisfactions and luxuries. But the ancient world and medieval Byzantion proved clearly enough that such a movement did not spontaneously generate capitalist modes or relations.

Because of the growth of trade in the twelfth century, men with money invested in land, especially that of the towns where they lived. Hence the urban patriciate, *viri hereditarii, divites, majores*, who held this land profited further from the rise in ground rents. Now they were no longer wandering traders. They lived in stone houses, with towers or battlements rising above the thatched roofs of their tenants' wooden dwellings. They took control of municipal administration, and some by fortunate marriages became part of the lesser nobility and modelled their way of life on that of the knights. As towns grew richer, more peasants were drawn in and their industrial character increased, with secondary localities developing around. Some towns were based on local trade, others became big exporters.[17] Instruments of credit, such as the Lettre de Foire, were used. Traffic in money expanded. The customs of fairs, especially in Champagne, gave rise to a sort of commercial law. By the mid-thirteenth century gold coinage (dropped since Merovingian days) was resumed. Much struggling went on between the merchant patriciate and the craft guilds. Municipal statutes fixed wages and regulated conditions of work as well as limiting the independence of the merchants. The church pressed in with its theory of the just price, forbidding usury, the lending of money at interest, sales on credit, and monopolies. But in fact monopolies were strong in the thirteenth century, with Flemish towns controlling the trade in fine cloth and merchant companies of Lombardy, Provence and Tuscany dominating banking. Lombard money-lenders financed Edward III in his wars against France. We even find men like Jehan Boinebroke (1280–1310) at Douai reducing workers (mainly women) to serfdom by advancing money and wool which they could not repay.[18]

By the thirteenth century a complex situation had developed on the land. Various kinds of labour were used on the demesne. Some work was done as rent by customary tenants with full holdings; some as piece-work by temporarily hired men; some by paid *famuli* working part or full time, who got in return, not land, but money or food; some by *famuli* who got part of their wages through service holdings (which were small and provided only the minimum subsistence needs of the worker and his family). Even *famuli* with base sergeantry holdings had to have their wages supplemented with money, liveries of corn, and the right to an acre's crop from the demesne, or the use of the lord's plough team on Saturdays. Service holdings in general were losing their function; most surveys show the tenants of such holdings paying rent, which was used for various kinds of paid labour. The wage labour used by the richer village peasants was beginning to approximate to capitalist wage labour, that is, it was determined primarily by economic compulsion; but on the demesne the lords were ready to use any form of pressure, including the legal status of their dependents as servile persons. We find, in the early fourteenth century, on the manor of the Yorkshire abbey of Selby, the lord using sons of his serfs (ploughmen, carters, a shepherd) as *famuli curiae* at half the wages paid to an extraneus.[19]

As rents fell, incomes had to be made up by intensified fiscal exploitation, warfare, and plunder, though these methods were often frustrated by policies of currency inflation. The most capable producers for the market, men not seeking luxury or display and thus not needing to keep servants and non-productive dependents, were the wealthy peasants and members of the lesser nobility who had given up trying to live in the wasteful style of the upper members of their class. These groups though as yet far from dominant carried out forms of exploitation that anticipated capitalist farming. What encouraged increases of production and improved methods was no longer feudal rent, which could still be an obstructive burden for the middle peasant, but the stimulus of the market, which grew ever more important in the fifteenth century, helping to develop production and to introduce new elements into the economy. The groups with political dominance kept on trying to maintain their power by various devices, of which the absolute monarchy was the last large-scale example; but they were carrying on a failing struggle to use their links with the state to preserve the essentials of the feudal system.[20]

The peasant revolts, whether in the form of the 1381 revolt or those of the fifteenth and sixteenth centuries, could not by themselves break up feudal society, however symptomatic they were of its crises. (In the Hussite wars the smaller gentry felt alienated from the lay and clerical magnates, but were an irresolute force. There were indeed revolts of both knights and peasants, but they did not coincide in point of time or in viewpoint, despite the common enemy. Anyhow, Luther was there to ensure that they did not merge.)[21] These later revolts took place, we may note, in eastern Europe where state power was relatively weak, as also were urban developments. The biggest challenge came in Bohemia with its considerable economic advance; but because of the lack of any true bourgeois challenge, the rebels, even when victorious, made no attempt to take over state power. The Taborites tended to a sort of religious anarchism and primitive democracy of a peasant type, as did the Anabaptists with their voluntary church membership. However shaken or worried, the feudal ruling class could always re-gather its forces and set about re-consolidating the state. The big landowners had the most to lose and were afraid of accepting any drastic reforms, as we see in Spain of the late fifteenth century. The new absolute monarchies were led by new rulers, Isabella in Castile and Henry VII in England, but they had to build on old foundations. The utmost they could do was to attempt to rationalize the feudal order; but they could only do this because of the high degree of social and economic integration that had been going on within feudal society. For the same reason the feudal state in the advanced areas could even resume its control of the church and submit it to considerable regulation from above, imposing a discreet and restricted version of the Reformation. One interesting point is that in this milder version of the theocratic state the king resumes some of his shorn divinity, in the form of a 'divine right'.

The expanding state system was able to lengthen its life and gain temporary stability by drawing in the smaller gentry, offering them jobs in the official spheres or the standing army. The appropriating classes were thus linked by multiple bonds of interest to the administration. The result of all this was (a) a far stronger structure where wealth was essentially dependent on land rent (as in eighteenth-century Poland) or was extracted by taxes (as in Islam) or (b) a governmental system which, on reaching the limits of its contradictions, provided a firm basis for the next level of development, that of the bourgoisie. The expression of the final stage of feudal integration, the stage before the bourgeois revolution, was the emergence of the national state. Strictly we cannot speak of such a state at earlier periods. We have tribal groupings or federations, feudal combinations and concentrations, city-states, empires, and so on, but only at the end of feudalism does the national state proper appear.

A complicated struggle had gone on during the transition from labour services to money rents, with the breakdown of serfdom in the fourteenth century, and the first effective intrusion of genuine capitalist relationships in sixteenth-century England. In that century the vast majority of peasants paid money rents; the well-off freehold farmers no longer paid feudal dues and had reached the status of independent free producers, who employed poorer neighbours in both agriculture and industry, though still on a small scale. The genesis of capitalism is to be sought here, in the petty producers, not in the *haute bourgeoise* who had accommodated themselves to feudal relations in banking or mercantile pursuits. 'To buy land is one of the objects for which merchants are accustomed to labour,' said Guicciardini in the fifteenth century. The yeoman farmers bought the labour-power of their poorer neighbours, the cottars, and not only kept on expanding the scale of their productive operations but also started off the country cloth industry, while entrepreneurs of the same kind appeared in the town crafts. Merchant capital on the other hand was often allied with feudal reaction or absolutism; the chartered merchants and monopolists belonged to the royalist party in the seventeenth century. Modern capitalism (observed Pirenne) did not come from medieval 'capitalists', that is, men of capital, but rather from their destruction. The basic contradiction in this phase lay between the rising small and middle bourgeoisie and the 'merchant or usurer capitalists' with their roots in feudal economy.[22]

Much more might be said on these points, but we have briefly considered the ways in which European feudalism differed from previous serf economies or the contemporary ones of the east, and how it alone led to a bourgeois society and industrialism. The antecedents of that later development lay in the distinctive nature of European feudalism with its rich and complex texture, social and economic, its entangled pattern of conflicts and contradictions inside a strong evolving structure. The pattern was too varied and vital, too full of conflicts, for any simple system of feudal exactions to settle down over society as in the east; the feudal structure was too firm to allow the variety to fall away into localism, into patches of particular or separated out interests seriously impeding the general social evolution.

In that evolution England had an important part to play – a part which can be understood only if we realize what happened in the Norman conquest, and how the juxtaposition and ultimate fusion of the Anglo-Saxon and the Norman contributions worked out. Conversely, the Conquest itself and its more immediate effects can only be understood if they are seen in the wider context of the whole trend of feudalism, and of the forms and forces in it which finally issued in a new kind of society.

BIBLIOGRAPHY

BIBLIOGRAPHY

For some abbreviations, see Notes. Also Med. (Medieval); Eng. (England or English); RKOR (*Register d. Kaiserurkunden d. äström. Reiches* 1924-32, F. Dolger.)

Adam, R. J., *A Conquest of England*, 1965. Adams, G. B., (1) *Councils and Courts in AS England*, 1962; (2) *Councils and Courts in Anglo-Norman England*, 1926. Adler, M., *Jews of Med. England*, 1939. Aelfric, *Colloquies*, ed. G. M. Garmonsway. Ailred, *Regula*, PL xxxii, 1451-8. Alcock, L., *Antiq. J.*, 1966. Alexander of Telese, *Rogerii Regis Siciliae Rerum Gestarum*, lib. iv (RCSS ii). Alexander, S., *St Giles's Fair 1830-1914*, 1970. Almgren, B., *The Vikings*, 1966. Amatus, *Ystoire de li Normant*, ed. V. de Bartholomaeus, 1935. Ancren Riwle (Camden Soc. lxii, 1953) ed. J. Morton. Anderson, J., *Orkneyinga Saga*, 1873. Anderson, M. D., (1) *A Saint at Stake*, 1964; (2) *The Med. Carver*, 1935. Anderson, O. S., *The English Hundred-Names*, 1934. Andréadès, A. M., (1) in Baynes, 51-70; (2) *Annali d. R. Scuola Normale Sup. di Pisa, Lett.* etc. (ser. 2) iv, 1935, 139-48. Anna Comnena, see Sewter. Anselm, *Opera* ed. F. S. Schmidt, 1950. Arbman, H., *The Vikings*, 1961. Archer, T. A., EHR ii, 1867, 103ff. Armitage, E. S., (1) *Early Norman Castles of the British Isles*, 1912; (2) EHR, xix, 209-45,

417–55; (3) *ib*. xx, 1905, 711–8. Arnold, T., ed. *Symeonis Monachi Opera Omnia* (RS lxxv, 1, 1882). Ashdown, M., in Clemoes, 122–36. Aston, T. H., TRHS 5th s., viii, 1958. Attenborough, F. L., *The Laws of the Earliest English Kings*, 1922. Ault, W. D., (1) *T. Am. Philos. Soc.*, n.s. lv pt 7, 2965; (2) *Sp.* xlv, 1970, 197–215.

Bagley, J. J., *Historical Interpretations*, 1965. Baker, T., *The Normans*, 1966. Baldwin, J. W., *T. Amer. Philos. Soc.* (Just Price), 1959. Ballard, A., (1) *The Domesday Inquest*, 1906; (2) EHR, 1915, 646–58. Barlow, F., (1) *The Feudal Kingdom of England*, 1961; (2) *The English Church 1000–66*, 1963; (3) transl. *The Life of King Edward the Confessor*, 1962; (4) *William I and the Norman Conquest*, 1965; (5) *Edward the Confessor*, 1966. Barraclough, G., (1) *The Origins of Modern Germany*, (2nd ed.) 1947; (2) *History*, 1954, (AS Writ); (3) ed. *Germany and Western Europe in the Middle Ages*, 1970; (4) *Medieval Germany*, 1938. Barrow, G. W. S., (1) *Feudal Britain*, 1956; (2) *Northern History*, iv, 1969; (3) BIHR xxix, 1956, 1–29. Bateson, M., (1) EHR, 1900, 73–8, 302–18, 496–523, 754–7; (2) *ib.*, 1901, 82–110, 389–99; (3) *Records of the Borough of Leicester*, 1899. Baynes, N., with H. St L. Moss, *Byzantium*, 1961. Bazeley, W. TRHS, 1921 (Eng. Forest 13th c.). Bean, J. M. W., (1) *The Decline of Eng. Feudalism*, 1968; (2) EcHR, 2nd s. xv, 1962–3. Beard, C. A., *The Office of Justice of the Peace in England in its Origin and Development*, 1904. Beaurepaire, Fr. de, AN x, 1960, 307–12. Becher, P. A., *Der gepaarte Achtselber in der franz. Dichtung*, 1934. Becker, P. A., *Zeits f. fr. Spr.* lxiii. Bédier, J., *Les Légendes épiques*, 4 vols., 1914–21. Beeler, J. H., (1) *Sp.* xxxi 1956, 581–601; (2) *Warfare in Eng. 1066–1089*, 1961. Bell, A., (1) *Mod. Lang. Rev.* xxv, 1930, 56f; (2) PMLA lxv. 1950, 601–40; (3) *Le Lai d'Haveloc*, 1925. Bell, C. H., *Sister's Son in Med. German Epic*, (Univ. Calif. Pub. in Mov. Phila. x, 1920–5). Benedict of St More, *Chroniques des Ducs de Normandie*, ed. F. Michel, 1834–44. Bennett, M. K., *Econ. Hist.* iii, 1953, no 10, 12–29. Beresford, N., MA iii, 1959, 187–215. Bertrand, S., (1) AN, 1960, x, 193–206; (2) in F. M. Stenton (2). Besnier, R., *Rev. hist. du Droit*, xxvii, 1959, 183–212. Bettenson, H., *Docs. of the Christian Church*, 1946. Beveridge, W., *Econ. J. (Econ. Hist. Suppl.)*, May 1927. Bezzola, R. R. *Romania* lxv, 1940. Birch, W. de Gray, *Cartularium Saxonicum*, 3 vols. 1885–93. Birette, C., BSAN xlii, 1934, 146–200. Blair, P. H., *An Intro. to AS England*, 1956. Bliss, W. H., *Calendar of Entries in Papal Registers*, 1893 on. Bloch, H., *Dumbarton Oaks Papers*, iii, 177–86. Bloch, M., (1) *Mélanges historiques*, i, 1965; (2) *Rois et serfs*, 1920; (3) *Seigneurie française et manoir anglais*, 1960; (4) *La société féodale: la formation des liens de dépendance*, 1939; (5) *Ann. d'hist. écon. et soc.*, vii, 1935, 538–63; (6) *Soc. féod.: les classes et le gouvernment*, 1949; (7) *Feudal Society*, 1961; (8) *Les caractères originaux de l'hist. rurale fr.*, 1955; (9) *Rev. hist. du Droit*, 1928, 46–91; (10) *Le Rois thaumaturges*, 1924 (1961). Blumenkranz. B., (1) ed. *Disputatio Iudei et Christiani*, 1956; (2) *Juifs et chrétiens dans le monde occidental*, 1960. Boase, T. S. R., *Eng. Art 1100–1206*, 1953. Boehmer, H., *Texte u. Forsch. z. eng. Kultur* (Festgabe F. Liebermann), 1921, 301–53. Bolin, S., *Scand. Econ. Hist. Rev.*, i, 1953, 5–29. Bonnaud, Delamere, M. J. *Bull. philos. et hist. du Congrès des travaux hist. et sc.*, 1955–6, 143ff. Bonnerm, G., *St Bede in the Tradition of Western Apocalyptic Commentary*, 1966. Bony, J., JWCI, xii, 1949, 1–15. Borges, J. L., *Nouv. Rev. fr.*, June 1955. Bosl, K., in Barraclough (2). Bosquet, A., *La Normandie romanesque*, 1845. Boüard, M. de, (1) *Guillaume le Conquérant*, 1958; (2) BIHR, xxvii, 1955, 1–14; (3) AN, i, 1951; (4) AN, ix, 1959, 169–89; (5) *Le Hague-Dickie, Cah. archéol*, viii, 1956, 117–45; (6) *Rev. hist. du droit*, xxxi, 1953, 327f. Boulay, F. R. H. du, (1) *The Lordship of*

Canterbury, 1966; (2) EHR, lxxvii, 1962, 504–11. Boussard, J., (1) *Biblioth. de l'éc. de Chartres*, cvi, 1946, 189–224; (2) *Le Moyen Age*, 1952, 253–79; (3) *Rec. à M. Clovis Brunel*, 1955, i, 193–208; (4) *Les mercenaires aux XIII, S.*, 1947; (5) AN, viii, 423–440; (6) *La seigneurie de Belléme*, 1951, (Mél L. Halphen). Boutaric, E., *Institutions milit. de la France avant les armées permanentes*, 1863. Boutruche, R., *Seigneurie et féodalité*, i, 1959. Bratanic, B. *Laos*, ii, 1952, 56–8. Brawn, H., *The English Castle*, 2nd ed. 1943. Bréhier, L., *Les Institutions de l'emp. byz.*, 1949. Breslau, H., *Die Werke Wipos*, 3rd ed. 1919. Bridrey, E., *Bull. Soc. Antiq. Norm.*, xvliii, 1946–7. Brittain, F., *Saint Giles*, 1928. Brogger, A. W., (1) *Ancient Emigrants*, 1929; (2) with Shetelig, *The Viking Ships*, 1953. Bronsted, J., *The Vikings*, 1965. Brooke, C., (1) *12th c. Renaissance*, 1969; (3) *Bull. Rylands Lib.*, 1, 1967; (4) *From Alfred to Henry III*, 1961; (5) *Camb. Hist. J.*, xii 1956, 1–21. Brooke, G. C., *English Coins from the 7th c. to the Present Day*, 3rd ed. 1950. Brooke, Z. N., (1) *Cam. Hist. J.*, ii, 213ff; (2) *Eng. Church and the Papacy from the Conquest to the Reign of John*, 1931. *Med. Castles*, 1954; (3) *Arch. J.* for 1969 (1970), 130–48; (4) *The Normans and the N. Conquest*, 1969. Bruce-Mitford, R.L.S., (1) ed. *Recent Arch. Excavs. in Britain*, 1956; (2) in Harden, 173–90. Brunet, P., AN, v, 1955, 12of. Bucher, (1) PP xlv, Nov. 1969, 3–18; (2) *Ann. della Fond. Ital. per la storia ammin. F.*, *Comparative Studies in Soc. and Hist.*, iii, 1960–1, 89–105. Bullough, D. A., 1949. Campbell, J. K., *Honour, Family, and Patronage*, 1964. Candidus, Hugh, Brooks, N., MA, viii, 1964, 74–90. Brown, Baldwin, *The Arts in Early Eng.*, AS Architecture, 1925. Brown, R.A., (1) EHR, lxxiv, 1959, 249–80; (2) *Eng.* ii, 1965, 647–59; (3) EHR, lxxxv, 190; (4) *Sp.* xlv 1970. Burchard, *Decretum*, xix, ed. J. T. McNeill and Garner. Burne, A. F., *The Battlefields of Eng.*, 1951. Butler, L. A. S., (1) *Arch. J.* cxxi (for 1964), 111–53; (2) *Procs. Camb. Ant. Soc.*, I, 1957, 89–100.

Cacheux, P. L., *Mélanges (Soc. de l'hist. de Normandie)*, xi, 1927, 203–17. Cahen, C., *Le régime féodale de l'Italie normande*, 1940. Cam, H. M., (1) *Liberties and Communities in Med. Eng.*, 1944; (2) *Studies in Manorial History*, ed. with M. Coate etc., 1938; (3) *The Hundred and the H. Rolls*, 1930. Campbell, A., (1) EHR, lvii, 1942, 85–97; (2) *Encomium Emmae* (Camden Soc.), see Mellows. Canton, N. F., *Church, Kingship and Lay Investiture in Eng.*, 1958. Capgrave, J., *Life of St Gilbert* (EETS 1940). Carabie, R., *La Prop. fonc. dans le très Anc. Droit Normand*, 1939 (*Bibl. Hist. Droit Norm.*, n.s. v). Carstan, F. L., EcHR, xi, 1941, 61–76. Carus-Wilson, E. M., (1) ed. *Essays in Econ. Hist.*, 1962; (2) EcHR, xi, 1941, 39–60; (3) MA, xiii, 1969, 148–66; (4) *Med. Merchant Ventures*, 2nd ed. 1967, esp. ch. iv; (5) EcHR, xiv, 1944, 43f. Cauvet, *Mém. Soc. des Antiq. de Normandie*, xx, (*droit du patronage ecclés. rel. aux paroisses des campagnes*). Cauzons, T. de, *Hist. de l'Inquisition en France*, 2 vols. 1909–12. Chadwick, H. M., (1) *The Nationalities of Europe and the Growth of National Ideologies*, 1945; (2) *Origin of Eng. Nation*, 1907; (3) *Studies on AS Institutions*, 1905. Chadwick, N. K., (1) *The Beginnings of Russian History*, 1946; (2) *Studies in Early British History*, 1954. Chalandon, F., *Domination normande en Italie*, 1907. Chambers, E. K., (1) *Arthur of Britain*, 1927; (2) *Med. Stage*, 1925. Chambers, R. W., (1) *England before the N. Conquest*, 1926; (2) *Beowulf*, 1932; (3) *Man's Unconquerable Mind*, 1939; (4) *On the Continuity of Eng. Prose*, 1932; (5) with Daunt, *London English*, 1931. Chaney, W. A., *Cult of Kingship in AS Eng.*, 1970. Chantepie de la Saussaye, P. D., *Religion of the Teutons*, trans. B. J. Bos, 1902. Chanteux, H., *Trav. de la Sem. de Droit norm. de Guernsey*, 1938. Charles, B. G., *Old Norse Relations with Wales*, 1934. Charles-Edwards, T. M., (1) pp, 1972, lvi, 3–33;

(2) Bull. Board Celtic St., 1970–2, xxiv. 107–11. Chefneux, H., *Romania*, lx, 1934, 1–35, 153–94. Cheney, C. R., *Studies in Med. Hist.*, cxi, 1966. Chenu, M. D., *Nature, Man and Society in the 12th c.*, trans. J. Taylor, L. K. Little, 1968. Chew, H. M., (1) *The Eng. Ecclesiastical Tenants-in-Chief and Knight-Service*; (2) EHR, xxxvii, 1922, 321–6; (3) *Ib.* xxxviii, 1923, 19–41. Chrimes, S. B., *Intro. to the Administrative Hist. of Med. Eng.*, 1952. Chibnall, M., (1) AN, 1958, 103–18; (2) ed. Ordericus Vit., 1969. Child, F. J., ed. *English and Scottish Ballads*, 1882–94. Clagett, M., etc., *Twelfth Century Europe*, 1961. Clapham, A. W., (1) EHR, xxv, 287–93; (2) *Eng. Romanesque Architecture before the Conquest*, 1930; (3) *E.R.A. after the Conquest*. Clark, J. M., *The Abbey of St Gall*, 1926. Clay, C. T., *Early Yorkshire Charters*. Clay, R. M., *The Hermits and Anchorites of Eng.*, 1914. Clemoes, P., (1) with K. Hughes, ed. *England before the Conquest*, 1972; (2) ed. *The Anglo-Saxons*. 1959. Cockayne, O., *Saxon Leechdoms*, (RS) 1864–6. Cole, H., *Docs. illustrative of Eng. Hist. in 13th and 14th cs.*, 1844. Collingwood, *Yorks. Arch. J.*, xxiii, 1915. Colvin, H. M., (1) in *Studies . . . to R. Graham*, ed. V. Reiffer & A. Taylor, 1950, 15–38; (2) in *Med. Kentish Society*, (Kent Records xviii 1964). Conant, K. J., *Cluny*, 1968. Constable, G., *Letters of Peter the Venerable*, 2 vols., 1967. Cooper, C. H, *Annals of Cambridge*, 1842–1908. Copley, G., *Conquest of Wessex*, 1954. Corbett, W. J., CMH, v, 1926, 581–520. Corrain, D. O., *Ireland before the Normans*. Coulanges, F. de *La monachisme fran.*, 1888. Coulborn, R., ed. *Feudalism in History*, 1956. Coulson. N. J., *A Hist. of Islamic Law*, 1914. Coulton, G. G., (1) *Med. Studies: Priests and People before Reformation*, 1907; (2) *Med. Village*, 1926; (3) *Five Centuries of Religion*, ii, 1927; (4) *Social Life in Britain from the Conquest to the Reformation*, 1919; (5) *Med. Garner*, 1910; (6) *Med. Scene*, 1930; (7) *The Meaning of Med. Money*, 1934; (8) *Med. Panorama*, 1938; (9) *Camb. Hist. J.*, v, (1), 1935; (10) *Inquisition and Liberty*, 1938. Cowdrey, H. E. J., *The Cluniac and the Gregorian Reforms*, 1970. Coxe, H. O., ed. Roger of Wendover, 1841. Cramer, A. C., *Amer. Hist. Rev.*, xlv, 1940, 327–37. Crawford, O. G. S., in *Custom is King*, 1936, 181ff. Crawford, S. J., in *Speculum Religions*, (to C. G. Montefiore), 1929. Crombie, A. C., *Augustine to Galileo*, 1961. Cromme, H. A., (1) *The Reign of Stephen*, 1970; (2) with Moody and Quin, *Essays in Brit. and Irish Hist. in hon. J. E. Todd*; (3) *History*, xxiv, 1939, 251–9. Cross, J. E., *Vetenskaps-Societens i Lund Arsbok*, 1956. Cross, S. H., *Sp.* vi, 1931, 296–9. Crossley, F. H., *The Eng. Abbey*, revised B. Little, 1962. Crossley-Holland, K., and B. Mitchell, *The Battle of Maldon*, 1967. Curschmann, F. *Hungersnote im Mittelalter*, 1900. Curwen, E. C., (1) *Plough and Pasture*, 1946; (2) *Antiquity*, xii, 1938, 135. Cusa, *I Diplomi Greci e Arabi di Sicilia*, 1868. Cutts, F. L., (1) *Parish Priests and the People in the Middle Ages*, 1914; (2) *Dict. of Church of Eng.*, 1895.

Daniel, W., *Vita Ailredi*, 1950. Darby, H. C., (1) ed. *Domesday Geography of Eng.*, 1952 on; (2) *Hist. Geog. of Eng. before A. D. 1800*, 1936; (3) *Geog. J.*, lxxxv, 1935, 439–43; (4) with R. W. Finn, *The DB Geog. of SW Eng.*, 1967. Darlington, R. R., (1) EHR, li, 1936; (2) *Anglo-Norman Historians*, 1947. Darwin, F. D. S. *The Eng. Med. Recluse*, n.d. Daumas. H. ed., *Host. gén des techniques*, 1962. Dauphin, Dom., *Le bien-heureux Richard, abbé de S. Vanne de Verdun*, 1946. David, C. W., *Robert Curthose*; 1920. Davidson, H. R., Ellis, *Pagan Scandinavia*, 1967. Davis, H. W. C., (1) EHR, xx, 1905; (2) *Regesta Regum*, i, 1913; (3) EHR, xxiv, 1909, 729f. Davis, R. H. C. (1) *Eng. under the Angevins and Normans*; (2) TRHS 5th s., v, 1955, 23–39; (3) EHR, lxxvii, 1962, 209–32; (4) ed. *The Kalendar of Abbot Samson* (Camden Soc.), 1954. Davison, B. K., *Arch. J.*, cxxiv, 1967, 202–11. Deansley, M., (1) *The Med. Church*,

1969; (2) Pre-Conquest Church in Eng., 1961. Deck, S., AN, 1956, 245–54. Deforneaux, O., Les Français en Espagne aux xie et xiie siècles, 1949. Delaborde, H. F., Mélanges . . . à C. Bemont, 1913, 173–9. Delbruch, H., Gesch. d. Kriegskunst etc., 7 vols. 1900–36. Delisle, L., (1) Le clergé normand au xiiie s. (Bull. de l'Ec. des Chartes viii); (2) Litt. latine et Hist. de M.A., 1890; (3) Études sur les conditions de la classe agric. et l'état d'agric. en Normandie au moyen âge, 1851; (4) reprint, 1903; (5) Mém Soc. des Antiq. de N., iv, 1852, xv-xviii; (6) J. Brit. Arch. Assn, vi, 1851. Delpech, H. La tactique du xiiie s., 2 vols., 1886. Demus, O., The Mosaics of Norman Sicily, 1949, (1950). Denholm-Young, H., (1) History, xxix, 1944; (2) in R. W. Hunt, 240–68. Dhont, J. (1) Annales écon., soc., Civil., xii, 1957; (2) Études sur la naissance des principautés territoriales en France, 1948. Dialogus de Scaccario, ed. C. Johnson, 1950. Dickinson, J. C., The Origin of the Austin Canons and their Intro. into Eng., 1950. Didier, N., Le droit des fiefs dans la coutume de Hainault au moyen âge, 1945. Digby, G. W., in F. M. Stenton (2) 37–55. Dimock, J. F., ed. Metrical Life of St Hugh, 1860. Dobb, M., (1) Studies in the Development of Capitalism, 1963; (2) in Transition; (3) Our History, xxix, winter-spring, 1963. Dodsell, C. R., (1) ed., Theophilus de diversis artibus, 1961; (2) Burlington Mag. cviii. Nov. 1966, 549–56. Dodwell, B., EHR, lxiii, 1948, 289–306. Doehaerd, R., (1) Le tonlieu d'Arras, 1945; (2) L'expansion écon. belge en moyen âge, 1946. Dolley, R. H. M., (1) ed. with D. M. Metcalf, A.S. Coins, 1961, 136–68; (2) Num. Chron., 1961, 151–61. Döllinger, J. J., Beiträge zur Sektensgesch, 1890. Douglas, D. C., (1) The Norman Conquest and British Historians, 1946; (2) with G. W. Greenaway, Eng. Hist. Docs. 1042–1189, 1953; (3) William the Conqueror, 1964; (4) Procs. Brit. Acad., xxxiii, 1947, 101–30; (5) EcHR, ix, 1939, 128–43; (6) The Social Structure of Med. E. Anglia, 1927; (7) EHR, xliv, 1929, 618–25; (8) EHR, 1953, 526–45; (9) EHR, lvii, 1942, 417–36; (10) Feudal Docs. from the Abbey of Bury St Edmunds, 1932; (11) EHR, xlii, 1927, 245ff; (12) Oxford Studies in Soc. and Legal Hist., ix, 1927; (13) EHR, lxi, 1946, 129–56; (14) Camb. Hist. J., xiii, 1957; (15) The Norman Achievement, 1972; (16) The Domesday Monachorum of Christ Church, Canterbury, 1944; (17) French Studies, xiv, 1960, 99–116. Drew, K. F., Medievalia et Humanistica, xv, 1963, 5–14. Drögereit, R., Mitteil. d. Inst. f. Osterreich. Gesch., lxx, 1962. Dubled, H., Le Moyen Âge, 1951. Duby, G., (1) Rev. hist., ccxxvi, 1961; (2) Le Moyen Âge, xlii, 1946; (3) La société aux xie et xiie s. dans la région mâconnaise, 1953; (4) Economie rurale et la vie des compagnes dans l'occident méd, 2 vols., 1962; (5) Rural Econ. and Country Life in Med. West, trans. C. Postan, 1968; (6) pp xxxix, 1968, 3–10; (7) Annales, E.S.C., xix, 1964 (les jeunes). Dudo of St Quentin, Re moribus et actis primorum Normanniae Ducum, ed. J. Lair, 1865. Dunning, C. G., in Harden, 218–33. Dupont, E., Recherches hist. et topog. sur les compagnes de Guillaume le Conquerant, 1907.

Edwards, E., ed Liber de monast. de Hyda, (RS) 1866. Ekblom, R., in A Philol. Misc. presented to E. Ekwall, 1942, 115–44. Ekwall, E., Scandinavians and Celts in the NW of Eng., 1918. Ellis, A. J., Y Cymmrodor, v, 1882, 173–208. Ellis, H., Intro. to DB, 1833. Ellis, H. A., Antiq., Sept. 1942, 216–36. Erdmann, C., Die Entsehung des Kreuzzugsgedanken, 1935. Espinas, G., Les origines du capitalisme, 1933. Evans, A. C., Antiq, xlv, (178), 1971, 89–96. Evans, J., Monastic Life at Cluny, 1937.

Fagarlie, J. M., Late Roman and Byzantine Solidi found in Sweden and Denmark. Fahnestock, E., A Study of the Source . . . of the Old French Lai d' Havelof

1915. Faral, E., (1) in *La technique litt. des chansons de geste*, Actes du Colloque de Liège, Sept. 1957, 1959; (2) *La Légende arthurienne*, 1929. Farmer, D. L., (1) EcHR 2nd s., xxii, 1969, 1–16; (2) Ib., ix, 1956–7, 24–43. Farmer, H., *Analecta Bolland.*, lxxv, 1957, 72–82. Farmworth, W. O., *Uncle and Nephew in Old Fr. Chansones de Geste (Columbia St. Romance Philo. au Lit.*, 1913). Farrer, W. D., (1) *Honours and Knights' Fees*, 3 vols., 1923–5; (2) *Early Yorks. Charters*, iii, 1914–6. Faulkner, P. A., *Arch. J.*, cxv (for 1958), 1960, 150–83. Fauroux, M., *Rec. des actes des ducs de Normandie*, 1961. Fawtier, R., *Europe occidental 1270–1328*, 1940. Fehr, B., *Archiv f. Stud. d. neu. Spr. u. Lit.*, cxxx, 1913, 381. Fest, S., *The Hungarian Origin of St Margaret of Scotland*, 1940. Finberg, H. P. R., (1) *Lucerna*, 1964; (2) *The Early Charters of Wessex*, 1964; (3) *The Early Charters of the W. Midlands*, 1961; (4) *Tavistock Abbey*, 1951; (5) EHR, lxvi, 1941, 67–71; (6) ed. *Gloucestershire Studies*, 1957. Finn, R. A. W., (1) *Intro. to DB*, 1963; (2) *The Domesday Inquest*, 1961; (3) *Procs. Camb. Antiq. Soc.*, liii, 1960, 29–38. Fisher, D. J. V., *Camb. Hist. J.*, 1952, x, 254–70. Fisher, E. A., (1) *AS Towers*, 1969; (2) *The Greater AS Churches*, 1963. FitzStephen, W., (1) *Descriptio* (London) in J. Stow *Survey*, 1603; (2) with S(1). Fixot, M., *Les fortifications de terre et les origines féodales dans le Cinglais*, 1968. Flack, J., *Les origines de l'ancienne France*, 1886–1917. Fliche, A., (1) *L'Europe Occidental 888–1125*, 1930; (2) *La règne de Philippe Ier*, 1912. Flita, *Commentarii Juries Anglicani*, ed. H. G. Richardson and G. O. Sayles (Seldon Soc.), 1955. Flodoard, *Annales* ed. D. Lauer, 1905. Florence of Worcester, see B. Thorpe. Focillon, H., *L'an mille*, 1952. Folz, R., *The Concept of Empire in W. Europe*, trans. S. A. Ogilvie, 1969. Foreville, R., (1) *Le Moyen Age*, 1953; (2) ed. *Guillaume de Poitiers' Hist. de G. le Conq.*, 1952; (3) *Le Livre de S. Gilbert de Sempringham*, 1943. Fosbroke, T. D., *Brit. Monachism*, 1843. Foster, C. W. and T. Longley, *Lincolnshire Domesday and the Lindsay Survey*, 1924. Fournier, P., (1) *Mél G. Glotz*, ii, 1932, 367–76; (2) *Rev. d'hist et de litt. relig.*, vi–ix, 1901–4. Fowler, J. T., ed. *Coucher Book of Selby*, 1891. Fox, C., *Antiq.*, iii, 1929, 135ff. Frappier, J., *Les chansons de geste du cycle de Guillaume d'Orange*, 1955. Fredericq P., *Corpus doc. Inquisitionis haereticae pravitatis Neerlandicae*, 5 vols., 1889–1906. Freeman, E. A., (1) *The History of Norman Conquest*, 5 vols., 1867–76; (2) EHR, iii, 1888. French, W. H., in *Essays on King Horn*, (Cornell Stud. in Eng.), 1940. Fuaino, M., *Archivo Storico Pugliese*, ii, 1–2, 1949.

Gad, F., *Hist. of Greenland*, trans. E. Dupont, 1970. Galbraith, V. H., (1) TRHS, 1941; (2) EHR, xliv, 1929, 353–72; (3) EHR, 1954, 289–302; (4) *Studies in the Public Records*, 1948 (1949); (5) in R. W. Hunt, 283–95; (6) EHR, lvii, 1942, 161–77; (7) *The Literacy of the Med. Kings*, 1935. Gaimar, G., *Lestorie des Engles* (RS), ed. T. D. Hardy and C. T. Martin, 2 vols., 1876. Ganshof, F. L., (1) *Qu'est-ce que la féodalité*, 1947; (2) *Feudalism*, trans. P. Grierson, 1952; (3) *Byzantion*, iv, 1928, 659; (4) *Ann. Soc. d'arch. de Bruxelles*, 1942–3; (5) *Nederlandsche Historiebladen*, i, 1938; (6) *Settimane di St. d. Centro Ital. di St. sull' altro Med.*, i, 1954 46ff; (7) *Mém. de l'Acad. roy. de Belge (cl. des lettres)*, 2nd s. xx, 1926; (8) as (6), 1955; (9) *Rev. du Nord*, xxx, 1948, 97ff; (10) *The Carolingians and the Frankish Monarchy*. Garmonsway, G. N., *Peterborough Chronicle*, 1954. Garner, H. M., *Med. Handbooks of Penance*, 1938. Garufi, C. A., *Censimento e Catasto*. Gautier, L., *Le Chevalerie*, 1891. Gautries, J. Adigard des, (1) *Les noms de personnes scand. en Normandie 911 1066*, 1954; (2) AN, 1954 and 1959 (names). Gay, J., *l'Italie méridionale et l'empire byz.*, 1904. Gaydon, A. T., ed. *The Taxation of 1297*, (Beds. Hist. Rec. Soc., xxxix). Gaythorn-Hardy, G. M., *The Norse Discoverers of America*,

1921. Geanakoplos, D. S., *Byz. East and Latin West*, 1966. Geidel, H., *Alfred d. Grosse also Geograph.*, 1904. Gem, R. D. H., *Arch. J.*, cxxvii, 1970, 196–201. Genestal, R., (1) *La tenure en bourgage*, 1900; (2) *Nouv. rev. hist. de droit*, 1904, 766ff. Genicot, L., (1) *Ann. écon., soc., civ.*, xvii, 1962 (*noblesse*); (2) *Biblioth. de l'éc de chartes*, cvi, 1946, 189–224. George, R. H., *Rev. belge de philol. et d'hist.*, v, 1926, 81–97. Gervase of Canterbury, Chron. ed Stubbs, RS, 1877. *Gesta Herewardi*, RS, see Gaimar. *Gesta Stephani*, (1) ed. K. R. Potter, 1955; (2) R. Howlett, RS, 1866. Gibbs, M., *Feudal Order*, 1949. Gierke, O., *Political Theory of the Middle Ages*, trans. F. W. Maitland, 1900. Gilbert, E. C., *Arch. J.*, cxxvii, 1970, 202–10. Gilchrist, J., *The Church and Econ. Activity in the Middle Ages*, 1969. Giles, J. A., (1) trans. Will. of Malmesbury, 1847; (2) ed. *Gesta Willelmi Ducis Norm.*, 1845. Gille, B., (1) *Techniques et Civilisations*, iii, 1954, 4–9; (2) *ib.*, ii, 1951. Giraldus Cambrensis, *Anglia Sacra*, H. Wharton. ii. Gjesset, K., *Hist. of Iceland*, 1923. Gleason, S. E., *An ecclesiastical Barony in the Middle Ages*, 1936. Glob, P. V., (1) *Danish Prehist. Mons.*, 1971; (2) *The Bog People*, 1971. Glover, R., EHR, lxvii, 1952, 1–18. Gluckman, M., PP, 8, Nov. 1955, 1–14. Godfrey, C. J., *The Church in AS England*, 1962. Goebel, J., *Felony and Misdemeanour*, 1937. Goff, J. le, (1) *La Civil. de l'occid. méd.*, 1964; (2) *Annales, E.S.C.*, xxii, 1967. Gomme, G. L., *Folklore as Hist. Science*, 1908. Gordon, E. V., *The Battle of Maldon*, 1937. Graham, R., (1) *J. Brit. Arch. Assn.*, 3rd s. iv, 1939; (2) *St Gilbert of Sempringham and the Gilbertines*, 1901; (3) *Eng. Eccles. Studies*, 1929. Grand, R., (1) *L'agriculture au moyen âge*, 1950; (2) *Rev. hist. de droit*, 1942, 149–72. Gras, N. S. B., (1) *Hist. of Agric.*, 1925; (2) with E. C. Gray, *Econ. and Soc. Hist. of an English Village*; (3) *Evolution of Eng. Corn Market*, 1906. Graus, F., with others, *E. and W. Europe in the Middle Ages*. Gray, H. L., (1) EHR, cxvi, 1914, 625–56; (2) *Eng. Field Systems*, 1915. Green, V. H. H., *Med. Civil. in W. Europe*, 1971. Grendon, F., *J. of Amer. FL*, xxii. 1909, 105–275. Greenwell, N., *Boldon Buke*, 1852. Grégoire, H., *Byzantion*, xiv, 1939, with R. de Keyser. Grierson, P., (1) EHR, lxxvi, 1961, 311–5; (2) TRHS, xxiii, 1941, 71–112; (3) EHR, li, 1936, 90–7; (4) *Les annales de Saint-Pierre de Gand*, 1937. Grivot, D., with G. Zarneck, *Gislebertus, Sculptor of Autun*, 1961. Gross, C., (1) *Select Cases on the Law Merchant* (Selden Soc.), 1908; (2) *The Sources and Lit. of Eng. Hist. to 1485*, 2nd ed. 1915. Grundmann, H., *Deut. Archiv f. Gesch. d. Mitt.*, v, 1942, 419–92. Guicciardini, P., *Opera* (V. de Caprariis), 1953. Guilhiermoz, *Essai sur l'origine de la noblesse en France*, 1902. Guillaume de Poitiers, see Foreville. Guiraud, J., *Hist. de l'Inquisition au moyen âge*, 2 vols., 1935–8. Guitries, A. de, *Les Noms de personnes scand. en Normandie de 911 à 1066*, (Mon. Germ. xi 1954), 265–70.

Hagen, A., *Norway*, 1967. Hall, D., *Eng. Med. Pilgrimages*, 1965. Hall, H., (1) *Pipe Roll of Bishopric of Worcester*, 1903 (2) *Red Book of the Exchequer*, 1896. Hall, J., PMLA, xviii, 1903, 1–83. Hallam, H. E., (1) *Settlement and Society*, 1965; (2) EHR, xiv, 1961, 71–81. Halphen, L., (1) with Poupardin, *Chroniques des Comtes d'Anjou au xie s.*, 1946. Hamilton, J. R. C., in Bruce-Mitford, (1). Hammond, N., ILN, Arch. no 2364, 1971. Hampe, K., *Le haut moyen âge*, 1943. Harden, D. B., ed. *Dark Age Britain*, 1956. Hardy, G. M. G., *The Norse Discoverers of America*, 1921, Hardy. T. D., (1) *Descriptive Cat. of Materials rel. to Hist. of G.B. and Ireland*, 1862–71. (2) *Rotuli de . . . Misis*, 1844. Harmer, F. E., in Clemoes, 89–103. Harrison, F., *Medieval Man*, 1947. Hartmann, L. H., *The Early Med. State*, 1965. Hartridge, R. A. R., *A Hist. of Vicarages in the Middle Ages*, 1930. Harvey, A., *The Castles and Walled Towns of Eng.*, 1911. Harvey, J., (1) *Sussex Arch Coll.*, xcviii, 1959, 21–34; (2) *Antiq. J.*, xlviii,

1968, 87–99. Harvey, S., PP no 49, Nov. 1970, 3–43. Harvey, T. E., *St Ailred of Rievaulx*, 1932. Haskins, C. H., (1) *Studies in Med. Culture*, 1929; (2) *Renaissance of the 12th c.* 1927; (3) in *Essays in Med. Hist. pres. to T. F. Tout*, 1925; (4) *Rise of Universities*, 1957; (5) *Normans in Europ. Hist.*, 1916; (6) EHR, July and Oct, 1911; (7) *Norman Institutions*, 1918; (8) EHR, xxvii; (9) *Studies in the Hist of Med. Science*, 1927. Hassall, J. M., with D. Hill, *Arch. J.*, cxxvii, 1970, 188–95. Hatem, A., *Les poèmes épiques des Croisades*, 1932. Hauck, K., *Seculum*, vi, 1955, 189f. Haudricourt, A. G., (1) *Ann. d'hist. écon. et soc.*, viii, 1936, 515–22; (2) with M. Delamarre, *L'homme et la charrue à travers le monde*, 1955. Havet J. *Oeuvres*, 1896, ii, 117–81. Hay, D. *The Emergence of Europe*, 1957. Hearne, T., *Adami de Domerham Hist. de Glaston.*, 1727. Heer, F., *The Med. World*, 1962 Hefele-Leclercq, *Hist. des Conciles*, 1907 on. Hemmeon, *Burgage Tenure in Med. England*, 1914. Hencken, H., *Procs. R. Irish Acad.*, liii, sect. C, no 1, 1–247. Henderson, E. F., *Select Hist. Docs. of the Middle Ages*, 1892. Henderson, G., (1) *Early Medieval*, 1972; (2) JWCI, 1962, 172ff; (3) *J. Br. Arch. Assn.*, xxxi, 1968, 38ff. Hennig, R., *Byz. Zeits.*, xxxiii, 1933, 295–312. Henry of Huntingdon, *Hist. Anglorum*, ed. T. Arnold, RS, 1897. Henshall, A., *Arch. J.*, cxxi, for 1964, 154–62. Herteig, A. E., MA, iii, 177–86. Hill, D., MA, xiii, 1969, 84–92. Hill, J. W. F., *Med. Lincoln*, 1948. Hilton, R H., (1) *Decline of Serfdom in Med. Eng.*, 1969; (2) *Econ. Development of one Leicestershire Estate in 14th and 15 c.*, 1947; (3) *A Med. Society: the West Midlands at the end of the 13th c.*, 1966; (4) EHR, lvi, 1941; (5) PP no 31, 1965; (6) in Carus-Wilson, (2); (7) *Univ. Birmingham Hist. J.*, iv, 1952; (8) EcHR, 2nd s., ii, 1949–50; (9) in *Transition*; (10) EHR, Oct. 1954, 623–5; (10) PP xiv, 1963, 95–100. Hocking, W. J., *Num. Chron*, 4th s., ix, 1909, 68f. Hodgen, M. T., *Antiquity*, xiii, 1939, 261–79. Hodgkin, R. H., *Hist. of AS*, 1952. Höfler, O., in *Sacral Kingship*, 664–701. Hollings, M., EHR, lxiii, 1948. Hollister, C. W., (1) *AS Military Institutions*, 1962; (2) *Military Organization of Norman Eng.*, 1965; (3) EHR, lxxv, 1960; (4) EcHR, xvi, 1963, with Holt; (5) *Am. Hist. Rev.*, lxvi, 1961, 641–63; (6) *J. of Brit. Stud.*, ii (2), 1963, 1–26; (7), *Spec.*, xxxvi, 1961, 61–74. Holmes, G. A., *The Estates of the Higher Nobility in the 14th c.*, 1957. Holmes, M. R., MA, i, 178–82. Holmes, W. T., *Spec.*, 1955, xxx, 77–81. Holt, J. C., (1) EcHR, xiv, 1961, 334–6; (2) *ib.* xvi, 1963, 114–8; (3) PP, lvii, 1972, 3–52. Homans, G. C., (1) *Eng. Villages of the 13th c.*, 1940; (2) *Ann. d'hist. écon. et soc.*, viii, 1936, 438–48. Hope, W. H. St J. *Archaeologia*, lviii, pt. 1, 293–312. Hope-Taylor, B., (1) in Bruce Mitford (1) 223–50; (2) *Arch. J.*, cvii, 1950, 15–43. Hoskins, W. G., *The Med. Landscape*, 1955. Hoyt, R. S., (1) *The Royal Demesne in Eng. Constit. Hist.*, 1950; (2) in *Early Med. Misc.* (Pipe Rolls S.), 1962 for 1960; (3) ed. *Life and Thought in the Early Middle Ages*, 1967. Hübener, G., *Eng. Studien*, lx, 1925, 37–57. Hughes, A., *Dialogus de Scaccario*, 1902. Hugill, R., *Borderland Castles and Peles*, 1939. Huizinga, J., *Meded. d. kon. Akad. v. Wetensch. afd Lett. deel 84*, ser. B. (2) 1927, 2–11, (86–95). Hunt, N., *Cluny under St Hugh* 1967. Hunt, R. W., ed. *Studies in Med. Hist. pres. to F. M. Powicke*, 1969 Hurnard, N. D., EHR, lvi, 1941. Hussey, J. M., *Church and Learning in the Byz Emp.*, 1937.

Imbart de la Tour, P., (1) *Les paroisses rurales du ive au xie s.*, 1900; (2) *Questions d'hist. soc. et relig.*, 1907.

Jackson, E. D. G., and F. G. M. Fletcher, *J. of Arch. Assn.*, xxv, 1962. Jacobs, J. J. and L. Wolf, *Bibliotheca Anglo-Judaica*, 1888. Jamison, E., (1) *Procs. Brit. Acad.*, xxiv, 1938; (2) *Brit. School of Rome*, vi, 1913. Janko, S., *Wörter u.*

Sachen, i, 1909. Janssen, A. L., AN, xi, (3), 1961, 179–95. Jansson, S. B. F., *The Runes of Sweden*, 1962. Jenkinson H., (1) in *Essays . . . to R. L. Poole*, 190–210; (2) EHR, xxx, 1913, 209ff, with M. T. Stead. John, E., (1) *Land Tenure in Early Eng.*, 1960; (2) *Bull. J. Rylands Lib.*, xli, 1958, 59–63; *ib.*, 1959, 82ff. John of Ford, *Wulfric of Haselbury*, ed. M. Bell, 1933. Johnson, C., (1) EHR, xlix, 1937; (2) ed. *Dialogus de Scaccario*, 1902. Joliffe, J. E. A., (1) *Constit. Hist. of Med. England*, 1937; (2) EHR, xli, 1–42; (3) *Angevin Kingship*, 1955; (4) *Schweizer Beiträge z. allgemein Gesch.* x, 1952. Jones, G., *A Hist. of the Vikings*, 1968. Joranson, E., *Spec.* xxiii, July, 1948, 353–96. Jordan, E. *Le Moyen Age*, 1922–3, 33–4. Joscelin de Brakelond, *Chronica* (Camden Soc. xiii).

Kantorowicz, E. H., *King's Two Bodies*, 1957. Katzenellenborgen, A., in Hoyt (3) 66–84. Keen, M. H., (1) *The Outlaws of Med. Legend*, 1961; (2) *A Hist. of Med. Europe*, 1967 (1968). Kemble, J. M., *Codex Diplom. aevi Saxonici*, 1839 etc. Kemp, E. W., *Canonization and Authority in the Western Church*, 1948. Kendrick, T. D., *A Hist. of the Vikings*, 1930. Keyser, C. E., *A List of Norman Tympana and Lintels*, 1927. Kiernan, V. G., PP, no 31, July 1965, 20–38. Kil. V., *Archiv f. nord. Filologi*, lxxv. Kimball, E. G., *Sergeanry Tenure in Med. Eng.*, 1936. Kinard, J. P., *Study of Wulfric's Homilies*, 1897. Kirbis, W., *Gött. geogr. Abh.*, x, 1952, 45–7. Kivikovski, E., *Finland*, 1967. Kjellman, H., *La deuxième coll. Anglo-Normane des Miracles de la Ste Vierge*, 1922. Klindt-Jensen, O., (1) *The World of the Vikings*, 1969; (2) *Denmark before the Vikings*, 1957; (3) with D. Wilson, *Viking Art*, 1966. Knowles, D., (1) *The Historian and Character*, 1963; (2) *The Monastic Order in Eng.*, 2nd ed. 1963; (3) with Obolensky, *The Middle Ages*, 1969; (4) *The Religious Orders*, 3 vols., 1948–59; (5) in A. L. Poole (1); (6) with Brooke and London, ed. *The Heads of Religious Houses: Eng. and Wales*, 940–1216, 1972. Koch, A. C. F., *Tijdschrift v. Rechtsgechiednis*, 1953, 420–58. Kohn, H., *The Idea of Nationalism*, 1945. Kölbing, E., *Ipomedon, in drei eng. Bearbeitungen*, 1889. Kosminsky, E. A., (1) EcHR, iii, 1931, 16–44; (2) in *Studii in Onore di A. Sapori*; (3) *Studies in the Agrarian Hist. of Eng. in the 13th c.*, 1956. Koyré, A., *L'idée de Dieu dans la philosophie de S. Anselme*, 1923. Krappe, A. H., (1) *Mitt. d. Schles. Gesell. f. Volkskunde*, xxxiv,, 1934; (2) *Spec.* xx, 1945, 408–11. Kroeschell, Z. F. *Savigny-Stiftung*, Abh., lxxvii, 1960, 1–25.

Laborde, E. D. *Byrhtnoth and Maldon*, 1936. Lagarde, G. *de La naissance de l'esprit laique au déclin du moyen âge*, i, 1934. Lagouëlle, H., *Essai sur la conception féodale de la propriété foncière*, 1902. Lair, J., *Matériaux pour l'édition de Guillaume de Jumièges*, 1910. Lamb, H. H., *The Changing Climate*, 1966. Lammens, E., *Islam, Beliefs and Institutions*, 1929. Lammert, F., *Klio*, xxxi, 1938, 389–411. La Monte, J. L., *Feudal Monarchs in the Latin Kingdom of Jerusalem*, 1932. Lamouche, *Hist. de la Turquie*, 1953. Lancaster, L. *Brit. J. of Sociology*, ix, 1958, 230–50, 259–77. Lanfranc, *Opera*, ed. J. A. Giles, 1844. Laporte, J., *Inventio et Miracula S. Vulfranni*, 1938, (Mél. S.H.N., 1938, 7–87). Larson, L. M., (1) *Canute the Great*, 1912; (2) *The King's Household in Eng. before the N.C.*, 1904. Latham, L. C., *The Manor*, 1931. Latouche, R., (1) *Le Moyen Âge*, 1937, 44–64; (2) *Les origines de l'écon. occid.*, 1956; (3) *Textes d'hist. méd.*, 1951. Lea, H. C., *Hist. of Inquisition*, 1887. Leblond, B., *L'accession des Normands de Neustrie à la culture occid.*, 1966. Le Bras, G., (1) *Pénitentiels* (in *Dict. Theol. Cath.*); (2) *Cahiers de Civil. méd.*, 1968. Leclercq, J., *Jean de Paris*, 1942. Lees, B. A., *Records of the Templars in Eng. in 12th c.*, 1935. Lefèvre, G., *Les variations de Guillaume de C. et les questions des universaux*, 1898. Legg, L. G. W., *Eng. Coronation Records*, 1901. Legge, M.D.;

(1) *Anglo-Norman Lit. and its Background*, 1963; (2) in *Stil und Formprobleme in d. Lit.*, 1959; (3) *Anglo-Norman in the Cloisters*, 1950. Legras, H., *Le bourgage de Caen*, 1911. Lejeurwe, R., and J. Stiennon, *The Legend of Roland in the Middle Ages*. Lemarignier, J. F., (1) *Rev. du moyen âge latin*, iv, 1948, 191–6; (2) *Études sur les privilèges d'exemption et de jurisdiction ecclés. des abbaies normandes*, 1937; (3) AN, 1958, 191–6; (4) *Recherches sur l'hommage en marche et les frontières féodales*, 1945; (5) *Sett. di Stud. del Centro Ital. di Stud. sull' Alto Med.*, iv, 1957, 365–7. Lemmon, C. H., (1) *The Field of Hastings*, 2nd ed., 1960; (2) in *The Norman Conquest*, 77–122. Lennard, R., (1) *Rural Eng. 1086–1135*, 1959; (2) EHR, 1954, 580–96; (3) EcHR, xiv, 1944–5, 51–63; (4) *ib.*, 217–33; (5) EHR, 1960, lxxv, 193–207; (6) EcHR, xvii, 1947, 150; (7) *ib.*, iii, 1951, 342f. Le Patourel, J., (1) EHR, lix, 1944, 129 58; (2) AN, xi, 1961, no 3, 171–7. Le Prévost, ed. *Ordericus Vit.*, HE, 1852. Lesne, E., (1) *Hist. de la propriété ecclés. en France*, ii, 1922; (2) *Les écoles de la fin du viiie s. à la fin du xiie s.*, 1940 (vol. v. of first title) Lestocquoy, J., (I) EHR, xvii, 1947; (2) *Rev. belge de Philol. etc.*, 1944; (3) *Les dynasties bourgeoises d' Arras (Mém. Comm. des mons. hist de Pas-de-Calais)*, v, fasc. 1, 1945. Levett, A. E., in Cam (2). Levison, W., *Eng. and the Continent in the 8th c.*, 1946. Lewis, A. R., *The Northern Seas*, 1958. Lewis, C. S., *The Allegory of Love*, 1936. Leyser, K., pp, 1968, xli, 32–6. *Liber Eliensis*, ed. D. J. Stewart. Liebermann, F., (1) *Die Gesetze der Angelsachsen*, 1898 16; (2) EHR, xxviii, Liebeschutz , H., *Med. Humanism in the Life and Writings of John of Salisbury*, 1950. Liestol, K., in *Maal og Minne*, 1933. Lindsay, Jack, (1) *Byzantium into Europe*, 1952; (2) *Medieval Latin Poets*, 1934; (3) *Short History of Culture*, 1962; (4) *Cleopatra*, 1970; (5) *Origins of Astrology*, 1970; (6) *Norseman*, iii, no 6, 1945 (Beowulf); (7) *Coll. Latomus* cxiv 20–30. Lindsay. P. with R. Groves, *The Peasants' Revolt*, n.d. Lloyd, R., *The Golden Middle Ages*, 1939. Lobel, M. D. (1) *Oxoniensia*, iii, 1938, 83ff; (2) ed. *Historic Towns*, i, 1969. Lokeren, van. *Chartes de St-Pierre, London and the Vikings*, Lond. Mus. Cat. i, 1927. Loomis, R. S., (1) *Wales and the Arthurian Legend*, 1956; (2) *The Grail*, 1963. Lopez, R. S., (1) *Spec.*, xx, 1945, 1–42; (2) *ib.*, xxviii, 1953, 1–43; (3) *Byzantion*, xviii, 1948, 139–62; (4) in Hoyt, (3) 30–50. Lot, F., (1) *Les derniers Carolingiens*, 1891; (2) *Les invasions germaniques*, 1935; (3) *L'art militaire et les armées au moyen âge*, i, 1946; (4) with Fawtier, *Hist. des institutions fr.*, 1957–62; (5) *Naissance de la France*; (6) *Études critiques sur l'Abbaye de St Wandrille*, 1913; (7) *Nouvelles recherches sur l'impôt etc.*, Bibl. Ec. Hautes Études, 1955, cciv. Loth, J. *Hist. de l'abbaye roy. de Jumièges*, 1882 5. Lottin, O., *Recherches de théologie anc. et méd.*, xiii, 1946. Loyd, L. C., (1) *Origin of some Anglo-Norman Families*, 1951; (2) ed. with Clay and Douglas, *Sir C. Hatton's Book of Seals*. Loyn, H. R., (1) *AS Eng. and the Norman Conquest*, 1963; (2) *History*, xlii, 1957; (3) *The Norman Conquest*, 1965; (4) EHR, lxx, 1955, 533–40. Luard, H. R., *Lives of Edward the Conf.*, RS. Lyon, B. D., (1) *From Fief to Indenture*, 1957; (2) EHR, lxvi, 1951, 161–93. Lyon, C. S. S., *Num. Circular*, lxxxiii, 1965, 180f.

Macdonald, A. J., (1) *Lanfranc*, 1925; (2) *Berengar and the Reform of the Sacramental Doctrine*, 1930. McFarlane, K. B., *Bull. of Hist. Research*, xx, 1945. McIlwain, C. H., *Constitutionalism and the Changing World*, 94–8, 1939. Maeri, C. M., *L'organisation de l'écon. urbaine dans Byzance*, 1928. Magoun, F. P., (1) *Eng. Stud.*, xxxv, 1954, 203f; (2) *Spec.*, xxviii, 1953, 220; (3) *Mod. Lang. Rev.*, xlvi, 1951, 249f; (4) *Anglia*, lvii, 361–76. Maissoneunve, H., *Études sur les origines de l'Inquisition*, 2nd ed., 1960. Maitland, F. W., (1) *Domesday Book and Beyond*, 1960; (2) *Coll. Papers*, 1911. Malaterra, G., *Historia Sicula*

(MPL cxlix) and (RIS v). Malone, K., (1) MLR, xxv, 78–81; (2) Spec., v, 1930, 159–67; (3) ib., viii, 1933, 67–68. Manitius, M., Gesch. d. lat. Lit. d. Mitt., ii, 1923. Mann, J., (1) An Outline of Arms and Armies in Eng., 1960; (2) in F. M. Stenton (2). Marcus, G. J., EHR, lxxi, 1956, 56–61. Maréchal, J. R., AN, ix, 1959, 257–72. Martin, J. P., Normannia, Oct.-Dec. 1933. Marx, J. ed. Gesta Norm. Ducum, Guill. de Jumièges, 1914. Mason, J. F. A., EHR, 1934, 283–9. Mathieu, M., Guillaume de Pouille, 1961. Matthew, D. J., The Norman Conquest, 1966. Megaw, I, in Cromme (2). Mellows, C. and W. T., (1) Chron. of Hugh Candidus; (2) Peterborough Local Admin, i, 1939. Menager, L. R., (1) Cahiers de Civil. Méd., ii, 1959; (2) Q. u. F. aus ital. Arch., xxxiii, 1959; (3) Rev. d'hist. ecclés., lii-iv, 1958–9. Messent, J. W., The Round Towers to Eng. Parish Churches, 1958. Metcalf, D. M., (1) EcHR, xviii, 3, 1965, 475–82; (2) with Dolley, AS Coins, 1967. Meyer, P., ed. L'Estoire de Guillaume le Maréchal, 1901. Michaud, E., Guillaume de Champeaux et les écoles de Paris, 1867. Mickwitz, G., Ann. d'hist. écon. et soc., viii, 1936, 21–9. Miller, E. G., Eng. Illuminated MSS from 10th to 13th c., 1926. Miller, F. Abbey and Bishopric of Ely, 1951. Moore, N., The Church of St Bartholomew the Great, 1892. Moore, W. J., The Saxon Pilgrims to Rome and the Schola Saxonum, 1967. Mor, C. G., Rev. hist. de droit fr. et étr., sér. 4, xxxvi, 1958. Morey, A. with Brooke, Gilbert Foliot and his Letters, 1965. Morris, W. A., (1) EHR, xxxiii, 152–6; (2) ib., xxxvi, 1921; (3) Med. Eng. Sheriff, 1927; Morrison, K. F., (1) in Hoyt (3), 143 59; (2) The Two Kingdoms: Ecclesiology in Carolingian Political Thought, 1964. Morton, C. with H. Muntz, The Carmen de Hastingoe Proclio, 1972. Müller-Wille, M., Mittel. Burghügel im Nörd. Rheinland, 1966. Munro, D. C., Amer. Hist. Rev., xl, 1906, 231–42. Murray, M. A., (1) God of the Witches, 1962; (2) Witch Cult in W. Europe, 1921; (3) The Divine King in Eng., 1954. Musset, L., (1) Mél. de linguistique...F. Mossé in memoriam, 1959, 330–9 (2) AN, vii, 1957, 345ff; (3) AN, ix, 1959, 285–99; (4) AN, iv, 1954, 31–8; (5) Mél. du treizième centenaire de Fécamp, i, 67–79; (6) Bull. Soc. des Antiq. de N. lii, 1952–4, 117–41; (7) ib. 142–53; (8) AN, xii, 1962; (9) Bull. S.A.N., xlix, 1942–5, 7–97; (10) Les peuples scand. au moyen âge, 1951; (11) Rev. hist. de droit 4 sér., xxix, 1951; (12) Rev de moyen âge Latin, (4), 1954, 237–66. (13) Rev. hist. de droit 4 sér., xlvii, 1969. Napier, A., Anglia, xi. 1889. Naumann, H., Wirtschaft u. Kultur: Festschrift A. Dopsch, 1938, 1–12. Needham, J., (1) Arts and Sciences in China, no 2, 1964; (2) Clerks and Craftsmen in China and the West, 1970; (3) Science and Civil. in China. Neilson, N., Customary Rents, 1910. Nevinson, J. L., in F. M. Stenton (2). Nicolaisen, W. H. F., Scottish Studies, iv, 1960, 49–70 Nissen, W., Die Diataxis des Michael Attaliates, 1894. Nithard Hist. des fils de louis le Pieux, ed. P. Lauer, 1926. Noonan, J. T., The Scholastic Analysis of Usury, 1957. Norlund, P., Viking Settlers in Greenland, 1936. Norman Conquest (Battle and District Hist. Soc.), 1966. Norwich, John Julius, (1) Normans in the South, 1967; (2) Normans in Sicily.

Oakley, T. P., Eng. Penitential Discipline and AS Law in their Joint Influence, 1923. Odegaard, C. E., Vassi et Fideles in the Carolingian Empire, 1945. Oleson, J. T., (1) in Hoyt (3), 122–42; (2) The Witangemot in Reign of Edward the Conf., 1955. Olivier-Martin, F., (1) Hist. de la coutume de la prévôté et vicomté de Paris, 3 vols., 1922–30; (2) Soc. J. Bodin: Liens de Vassalité et les immunités, 1936. Olleris, A., Oeuvres de Gerbert, 1867. Olrik, A., (1) Saga Book of Viking Club, vi, pt 2, 1910; (2) Nord. Geistesleben, 1908. Olsen, M., Farming and Farms of Anc. Norway, 1928. Onslow, Earl of, The Dukes of Normandy, 1947. Ordericus Vitalis, ed. Chibnall and Le Prévost. Orwin, C. S., The Open Fields, 1938. Osborne, J. van Wyck, The Greatest Norman Conquest,

1937. Oschinsy, D., EcHR, xvii, 1947, 52–61. Owst, G. R., *Preaching in Med. England*, 1926.

Packhard, S. R., *Anniversary Essays in Med. Hist. by Students of C. H. Haskins*, 1929, ii, 231–54. Page, W., *Archaeologia*, lxvi, 1915, 61–102. Painter, S., (1) *The Reign of King John*, 1949; (2) *Studies in the Hist. of the Eng. Feudal Barony*, 1943; (3) *Feudalism and Liberty*, 1961; (4) *The Rise of the Feudal Monarchies*, 1951; (5) *William Marshall*, 1933. Panofky, E., *Abbot Suger on the Abbey Church of St Denia*, 1946. Pantin, W. A., MA, iii, 1959, 216–58. Parain, C., AN, ii, 1952, 127. Paterson, D. R., *Early Cardiff*, 1926. Payne, F. G., *Arch. J.*, civ, 1947, 84f. Payne, J. F., *Medicine in AS Times*, 1904. Pertz, G. H., (1) ed. *Encomium Emmae*; (2) *De bello parisiaco of Abbon of St Germain*, 1871. Pettit-Dutaillis, C., (1) *Studies and Notes suppl. to Stubbs' Conct. Hist.*, 1908; (2) *Feudal Monarchs in Fr. and Eng.*, 1936; (3) *Les communes fr.*, 1947. Philippson, E. A., (1) *Die Genealogie der Götter in germ. Relig.*, 1953; Phillpotts, B. S., *Kindred and Clan in the Middle Ages and after*, 1913. Pidal, R. M., *La chanson de Roland*, 1960. Pigeon, E. A., *Hist. de la cathédral de Coutances*, 1876. Pirenne, H., (1) ed. *Galbert De Bruges, Hist. du meutre de Charles le Bon* (2) *Econ. and Social Hist. of Med. Europe*, 1937; (3) *Amer. Hist. Rev.* xix, 1914, 494–515; (4) *Hist. de Belgique*, i, 3rd ed. 1909; (5) *Med. Cities*, 1956. Plucknett, T. F. T., (1) *Legislation of Ed. I.*, 1949 (2) *Med. Bailiff*, 1954, Plummer, C., with Earle, *Two of the Saxon Chronicles*, 1929. Pognon, E., *L'an mille*, 1947. Pollock, F., (1) with Maitland, *Hist. of Eng. Law*, 1891; (2) 2nd ed. 1923. Poole, A. L., (1) ed. *Med. England*, 2 vols. (2) *Obligations of Society in the 12th and 13th c.*, 1946; (3) *From DB to Magna Carta*, 2nd ed. 1955; (4) EHR, lv, 1940, 284–95. Poole, R. L., (1) *The Exchequer in 12th c.*, 1912; (2) *Early Correspond. of John of Salisbury*, 1924, (Br. Acad.). Portejoie, I. *Le régime des fiefs d'après la coutume de Poitiers*, 1924. Porter, A. K., *Romanesque Sculpture*, 1923. Post, G., *Studies in Med. Legal Thought*, 1964. Postan, M. M., (1) TRHS, 4th s., xx, 1937, 169–93; (2) EcHR, 2nd s., ii, 1950; (3) Suppl. 2, EHR, 1954, *Famuli*; (4) with Brooke, *Carte Nativorum* (Northants RSS, xx), 1950; (5) EcHR, xiv, 1944; (6) *J. Rylands Lib. Bull*, vi, 1921–2; (7) with Titow, EcHR, xii, n.s. 1959, 392–411. Powicke, M., (1) *Stephen Langton*, 1925; (2) *Loss of Normandy*, 2nd ed. 1961; (3) EHR, xxvi, 1911, 89–93. Powicke, M. R., Spec., xxv, 1950, 457–70. Prawer J., *Hist. of Latin Kingdom of Jerusalem*, 1932. Prentout, H., (1) *Essai sur l'origine et la foundation du duché de Normandie*, 1911; (2) *Intro. à l'hist. de Caen*, 1904; (3) *Hist. de Guillaume le Conquérant*, i, 1936; (4) *Étude critique sur Dudon de Saint Quentin*, 1916; (5) *Le Régime de Richard II*, 1929. Prestwick, J., (1) TRHS, 5th s., iv, 1954, 19–43; (2) PP, no 26, Nov. 1963, 39–57. Prince, A. E., EHR, xlvi, 1931, 355–21. Pryce, T. D., EHR, xx, 1905, 703–11.

Raby, F. J. E., *Secular Latin Poetry*, 2 vols., 1934. Radcliffe-Brown, A. R., *Structure and Function in Prim. Soc.*, 1952. Radley, J., *Med. Arch.*, 1971, 37–57. Raftis, J. A., (1) *The Estates of Ramsey Abbey*, 1957; (2) *Tenure and Mobility*, 1964. Ralph of Coggeshall, *Chron. Anglicanum*, (RS). Randall, H. J., *The Vale of Glamorgan*, 1961. Reid, R., EHR, xxxv, 161–99. Renn, D. F., *Norman Castles in Britain*, 1968. Reynolds, R. L., Spec., xii, 1937, 225–56. Riant, P., *Expéditions et Péleringages des Scandinaves en Terre Sainte*, 1865 Rice, D. T., ed. *The Dark Ages*, 1965. Richards, D. H., *J. Arch. Assn.*, 3rd s., xxiv, 1961, 67–69. Richardson, H. G., (1) with Sayles, *The Governance of Med. Eng. from the Conquest to Magna Carta*, 1963; (2) *English Jewry under the Angevin Kings*, 1960; (3) TRHS, 1941, 129ff; (4) EHR, xliii, 1928, 161–71, 321–40; (5) *History*, xxvi, 1942; (6) with Sayles, *Parliaments and Gt. Councils in*

Med. Eng., 1961. (7) TRHS, 4th s., xi, 137–83; (8) EHR, 1954, 596–611. Richer, *Historia*, ed. R. Latouche 1930, Pugol 1876. Rigold, S. E., *Antiq. J.*, cxv, for 1958, 1960, 264f. Riley, H. T., *Chronicles of Old London*, 1963. Ritchie, R. L. G., (1) *The Normans in Scotland*, 1954; (2) *The Normans in Eng. before the N.C.*, 1948. Robertson, A. J., (1) *The Laws of the Kings of Eng. from Edmund to Henry I*, 1925; (2) *AS Charters*, 1956; (3) *Materials for the Hist. of T. Becket* (RS). Robinson, J. A., (1) *Gilbert Crispin*, 1911; (2) *St. Oswald and the Church of Worcester*, 1919; (3) *J. Theolog. St.*, 1929. Robinson, W. C., EcHR, 2nd s., xii, 1959, 63–76. Rogers, T., *Hist. of Agric. and Prices*, 1866–1902. Roncière, C. de la, *Hist. de la marine fr.*, i, 1899. Rose-Troup, F., *Trans. Devon. Assn.*, lxiii, 1931. Ross, A. S. C., *Terfinnas and Beormas of Ohthere*, 1940. Roth, C., *Hist. of Jews in Eng.*, 1949. Round, J. H., (1) *Feudal Eng.*, 1895; (2) *ib.*, 1909; (3) *Archaeologia*, lviii, 1902; (4) *The King's Sergeants and Officers of State*, 1911; (5) *Arch. J.*, lix, 1902; (6) *Geoffrey de Mandville*, 1892; (7) *Studies in the Peerage and Family Hist.*, 1907; (8) ed. *Calendar of Docs. preserved in France*, 1899; (9) in Dove, 119–21; (10) *The Commune of London*, 1899; (11) *Ancestor*, xi, 153–7; (12) EHR, x, 732. Rousset, P., *Les origines et les caractères de la prem. croisade*, 1945. Roy, J., *L'an mille*, 1885. Runciman, S., *A Hist of the Crusades*, 3 vols., 1965. Ruprecht, A., *Die augehende Wikingerzeit im Licht d. Runeninschr.*, 1958. Russell, J. B., *Dissent and Reform in the Early Middle Ages*, 1965. Russell, J. C., (1) *Trans. Amer. Philos, Soc.*, xlviii, 3, 1958; (2) *Spec.*, iii, 1928, 34–63. Rye, W., *Norfolk Antiq. Misc.*, 1877.

Sacral Kingship contribs. to central theme of viiith internat. congress for Hist. of Religions, Rome, April, 1955: Leiden 1959. Salin E., *Civil mèrovingienne*, iv, 1954. Salter H., *Cartulary of Oseney Abbey*, 1935. Salzmann, L. F., (1) *Med. Byeways*, 1913; (2) *More Med. Byeways*, 1926; (3) *Eng. Life in the Middle Ages*, 1926; (4) *Eng. Industries in the Middle Ages*, 1923. Saltman, *Theobald Archbishop of Canterbury*. Sanders, I. J., (1) *Eng. Baronies*, 1960; (2) *Feudal Military Service in Eng.*, 1956. Sawyer, P. H., (1) *The Age of the Vikings*, 1962; (2) *ib.*, 1971; (3) TRHS, 5th s., xv, 1965, 145–64; (4) PP, xxiv, 1963, 90–5. Sayles, G. O., (1) *The Med. Foundations of Eng.*, 1958; (2) see Richardson; (3) *Select Cases of the Court of the King's Bench under Ed. I*, 1939. Schieffer, T., *Deut. Archiv f. Dess. d. Mitt.*, i, 1937, 323–60. Schlesinger, W., *Beitr. z. deut. Verfass d. Mitt.*, 1963, i. Schmidt. C., *Hist. et doctrines de la secte de Cathars*, 1848. Schoenbeck, ILN Arch. Section 2244, (14 May 1968). Schramm, P. E., *Hist. of Eng. Coronation* (trans. Legg), 1937. Sczaniecki, N., *Essai sur les fiefs-rentes*, 1946. Seaby, P., *Brit. Num., J.*, xxviii, 1955, 111–46. Seagrave, B. G., with Thomas, *Songs of the Minnesingers*, 1970. Searle, E., EcHR, 2nd s., xvi, 1963–4, 290–300. Seaver, E. I., in *Med. St. in Mem. A. K. Porter*, ed. W. Kochler, 1939. Sée, H., (1) *Les classes rurales et le régime domaniale en France*, 1901; (2) *Hist. écon. de la France*, i, 1939. Seebohm, F., *The Eng. Village Community*, 2nd ed. 1890. Seebohm, M. E., *The Evolution of the Eng. Farm*, 1927. Seignobos, C., *Hist. of the French People*, 1933. Sellwood, D. G., *Brit. Num. J.*, xxxi, 1962, 57–65. Sewter, E. R. A., *Alexiad*, 1969. Shannon, E. F., *Spec.*, 1951. Shetelig, H., (1) with Falk, *Scand. Archaeology*, 1937; (2) *Préhistoire de la Norvège*, 1926; (3) see Brøgger. Simpson, J., *Everyday Life in the Viking Age*, 1967. Singer, C., *From Magic to Science*, 1928. Singer, H., *Die Summa Decretorum*, 1902. Sisam, K., *Procs. Brit. Acad.*, xxxix, 1953, 287–346. Sjovold, T., *The Viking Ships*, 1954. Sluach, M., *Spec.*, xiv, 1939, 448–64. Smail, R. C., (1) *Crusading Warfare*, 1956; (2) in A. L. Poole, i, 128–67. Smalley, B., ed. *Trends in Med. Political Thought*, 1965. Smet, J. J. de, *Bull. Acad. roy. de Belgique*, xiv, 2, 1847, 334–60. Smith, A. H., (1) *Eng.*

Place Name Elements; (2) trans. *Heimskringla,* 1932. Smith, J. T., *Antiq. J.,* xcv, for 1958 (1960), 111–49. Snape, R. H., *Eng. Monastic Finances,* 1926. Sohm, R., *Das altkath. Kirchenrecht,* 1918. Southern, R. W., (1) *The Making of the Middle Ages,* 1953; (2) *History,* xlv, 1960, 201–16; (3) *St Anselm and his Biographer,* 1963; (4) *Listener,* 6 April 1967 and 26 Aug. 1965; (5) TRHS 4th s., xvi, 1933, 95–128; (6) *Med. and Renaissance Studies,* iv, 1958, 176–216; (7) *Procs. Brit. Acad,* xlviii, 1962, 127–69; (8) in *Studies . . . to F. M. Powicke,* 1948; (9) EHR, lvii, 1943, 389–91; (10) *Western Society and the Church,* 1970; (11) *Med. Humanism,* 1970. Speakman, E., in Tout (3), 57–75. Steele, R., *Med. Lore from Bartholomew Anglicus,* 1905. Steensberg, *Laos,* i, 1951, 198. Steenstrup, J., *Normandiets Historie mider de syv første Hertuger,* 1925. Stefano, G. de, *Monumenti della Sicilia normanna.* Stein, E., *Untersuch. z. spätbyz. Verfass, etc.,* 1925. Steinberg, S., *La Bibliofila,* xxxix, 1937 (Normans in Sicily). Stenberger, M., *Sweden,* 1963. Stenton, D. M., (1) *Eng. Society in Early Middle Ages,* 1951; (2) *Eng. Justice between the N.C. and the Great Charter,* 1963. Stenton, F. M., (1) *Norman London,* 1934; (2) ed. *Bayeux Tapestry,* 1957, (3) *William the Conqueror,* 1908; (4) *The First Century of Eng. Feudalism,* 1961; (5) *AS Eng.,* 1947; (6) *Procs. Brit. Acad.* (Danes in Eng.), 1927, 203–46; (7) *Bull. Soc. roy. des Lettres de Lund,* 1925–6; (8) *History,* xix, 1935, 298; (9) TRHS, 1944; (10) *ib.* 1945, 1–12; (11) *Facsimile of Early Charters, Northants Colls.* 1930; (12) *Types of Manorial Structure in Northern Danelaw,* 1910; (13) *Early Hist. of Abbey of Abingdon,* 1913; (14) *Latin Charters of the AS Period;* (15) with Mawer, *Place Names of Sussex,* 1929; (16) *K. Humanistika Vetenskampsfunt,* 1925–6, 73ff; (17) *Danelaw Charters,* 1920; (18) EHR, xxxvii, 1922, 225–35; (19) *Oxford Studies in Social and Legal Hist.,* ii, 1910; (20) *History,* xviii, 258. Stephenson, C., (1) with Marcham, *Sources of Eng. Constit. Hist.,* 1937; (2) *Med. Feudalism,* 1942; (3) *Amer. Hist. Rev.,* xlvi, 1940, 778–812; (4) *ib.* xlviii, 1942–3, 245–65; (5) *Borough and Town,* 1933; (6) EHR, lix, 1944, 289–310. Stevenson, J., *Chron. mon. de Abingdon,* (RS), 1858. Stevenson, W. H., EHR, xxviii, 115f. Stokes, W., *Martyrology of Gorman,* 1895. Stone, L., *Sculpture in Britain: the Middle Ages,* 1955. Strayer, J. R., (1) in Hoyt (3) 51–65; (2) in Clagett. Stubbs, W., (1) *Select Charters,* 1921; (2) *De Gestis Regum Anglorum,* 1887; (3) *Hist. Intro. to Rolls Series,* 1902; (4) *Memorials of St Dunstan,* (RS), 1874; (5) *Seventeen Lectures on Med. and Mod. Hist.,* 1886; (6) *Constit. Hist. of Eng.,* 1891; (7) with Haddan, *Councils and Eccles. Docs.* Sturler, J. de, *Relations politiques . . . entre le duché de Brabant et l'Angleterre,* 1936. Stutz, V., (1) *Gesch. des kirchl. Benefizialwesens,* i, 1895; (2) *Gött. Gelehr. Anz.,* 1900 (rev. Imbart 1). Suger, (1) *Vie de Louis VI le Gros,* ed. H. Waquet; (2) *De Vita Lud. Grossi,* ed., Duchesne.

Tait, J., *Med. Eng. Borough,* 1926. Talbot, C. H., ed. *The Life of Christina of Markyate,* 1859. Tardif, J., in *Congrès du Millenaire de la Normandie* i. Tahahashi, H. K., in *Transition.* Tatlock, J., (1) *Spec.,* viii, 1933, 454ff; (2) PMLA, xlviii, 1939, 317ff; (3) *Legendary Hist. of Britain,* 1950. Taylor, A., *The Glory of Regality,* 1820. Taylor, C. S., in Finberg (6). Taylor, E. G. R., *J. of Inst. of Navigation,* 1960, xiii, 1ff. Taylor, H. M., (1) *Arch. J.,* cxxvii, 1970, 211–21; (2) *ib.,* cxxvi, 1969, 101–30 and 192–8; (3) with J. Taylor, *AS Architecture.* Testaert, A., *La confession aux laiques,* 1949. Theoloe, H., *Die Ketzerverfolgungen im 11 u. 12 J.,* 1913. Thirsk, J., (1) PP, xxix, 3–25; (2) PP, xxxiii, 142–7. Thomas, P., *Le droit de propriété des laiques sur l'église etc.,* 1906. Thompson, M. W., (1) MA, v, 1961, 305f; (2) MA, with Jope, 1960, 81–94. Thorndyke, L., (1) *Michael Scot,* 1965; (2) *Spec.,* iii, 1928 (sanitation). Thorne, S. E., *Camb.*

Law J., 1950, 193–209. Thorpe, B., ed. *Chronicon Florence of Worcester*, 1849. Thoseider, E. D., *L'idèa imp. di Roma nella tradizione de Med.*, 1942. Thrupp, S. L., *The Merchant Class of Med.* London, 1948. Tierney, B., (1) *Foundations of Conciliar Theory;* (2) *Med. Poor Law*, 1959. Titow, J. Z., (1) *Agric. Hist. Rev.*, x, 1962, 1–13; (2) PP, xxxii, 86–102. Tikhomorov, M., *The Towns of Ancient Rus*, 1959. Tolkien, J. R. R., *Angles and Britons*, 1963. Tout, T. F., (1) on Hereward DNB; (2) *France and England*, 1922; (3) with J. Tait, *Hist. Essays*, 1907; (4) *Chapters in the admin. Power of Med. Eng.*, i, 1937. *Transition from Freudalism to Capitalism*, 1954 (Arene Publications). Trow-Smith, R., (1) *Eng. Husbandry*, 1951; (2) *Hist. of Brit. Live-Stock Husbandry*, 1957. Turberville, A. S., *Med. Heresy and the Inquisition*, 1920. Turner, G. J., (1) *Select Pleas of the Forest* (Selden Soc. 1888); (2) *Calendar of the Feet of Fines ref. to the County of Huntingdon*, 1913; (3) with Salter, *The Regesta of St Augustine's, Canterbury*, 1924. Turner, R. V., *J. of Brit. Stud.*, vii, 1968, 1–10 (Jury). Turville-Petrie, G., (1) *The Heroic Age of Scand.*, 1951; (2) in Clemoes (2) 104–21; (3) *Myth and Religion of the North*, 1964.

Ullman, W., (1) *Med. Papalism;* (2) ed. Lea's *Hist. of Inquisition*, 1963; (3) *Carolingian Renaissance and Idea of Kingship*, 1969. Unwin, G., *Industrial Organization in 16th and 17th c.*, 1904. Urry, W., (1) *The Normans in Canterbury*, 1959; (2) AN, viii, 1958, 119–38; (3) *Canterbury under the Angevin Kings*, 1967. Utterström, G., *Scand. Econ. Hist. Rev.*, iii, 1955, 3–47.

Valin, L., *Le duc de Normandie et sa cour*, 1910. Vasiliev, A., *Ann. Inst. Kondakov*, ix, 1937, 39–70. Vercauteren, F., (1) *Actes des comtes de Flandres*, 1938; (2) *Les civitates de la Belgique seconde*, 1934. Vergruggen, J. F., *Krijgskunst in West-Europe in den Middel*, 1954. Verhein, K., *Deut. Archiv f. Erforsch. d. Mitt.*, x, 1943–4, 352–5. Verlinden, C., (1) *Robert le Frisson*, 1935; (2) TRHS, 5th s., iv, 1954, 1–18. Vermeesch, A., *Essai sur les origines . . . de la commune dans le N. de la France*, 1866. Vigneron, B., *Rev. hist. du droit*, 1959, 17–47. Vinogradoff, P., (1) *Growth of the Manor*, 1911; (2) *Villeinage in Eng.*, 1892; (3) *Eng. Society in the 11 c.*, 1908; (4) *Roman Law in Med. Europe*, 2nd ed. 1929. *Vita Wulfstani*, ed. R. R. Darlington. Vogel, W., (1) *Die Normannen und das fränk. Reich*, 1906; (2) *Hansische Geschichtsblätte*, 1912, 239ff. Voss, L., *Heinrich von Blois*, 1932. Vries, J. de, *Saeculum*, vii, 1906, 289–309.

Waddell, H., (1) *The Wandering Scholars*, 1927; (2) *Med. Latin Lyrics*, 1952. Wagner, A. R., in A. L. Poole (1), 338–81. Waitz, G. ed., *Annales Bertiniani*, 1883. Wallace-Hadrill, J. M., (1) *The Long-Haired King*, 1962; (2) in Smalley, 22–40; (3) *Early Germanic Kingship*, 1971. Walle, A. van de, MA, v, 1961, 123–136. Walsh, A., *Scand. Rels. with Ireland during the Viking Period*, 1922. Waquet, H., ed. Abbo, *Siege of Paris* (see Pertz) 1942. Ward, P. L., *Spec.*, xiv, 160–78. Waters, G. R., *The Anglo-Norman Voyages of St Brendan*, 1928. Watkins, O. D., *Hist. of Penance*, 1920. Weaver, *Chron. of John of Worcester*. Weber, M., (1) *Die protest. Ethik*, 1904–5; (2) *Gesamm. Aufsätze z. Relig.* i, 1940, 49f. Weiswiler, H., (1) *Recherches de théologie anc. et méd.*, iv, 237–68, 371–91; (2) *ib.*, v, 1933, 245–75. Welcher, C., *The Churchwardens' Accounts of Allhallows*, London Wall, 1912. Wells, C. M., *The German Policy of Augustus*, 1972. Welsford, E., *The Fool*, 1968. Wheeler, R. E. M., *London and the Vikings*, 1927. White, G. H., TRHS, 4th s., xxx, 1948. White, L. T., *Latin Monasticism in Norman Sicily*, 1938. White Lynn (1) *Spec.*, xv, 1940, 141–59; (2) in Hoyt (3), 85–100; (3) *Med. Techology and Social Change*, 1962; (4) *Amer. Hist. Rev.*, lxv, 1960. White, T. H., *The Book of Beasts*. Whitelock,

D., (1) *The Beginnings of Eng. Society*, 1952; (2) with Douglas and Tucker, *Peterborough Chronicle*, 1961; (3) *Eng. Hist. Docs*, 1955; (4) *AS Wills*, 1930; (5) in Clemoes, 70–88; (5) *The Will of Aildgifu*, 1968; (6) *The audience of Beowulf*, 1951. Wightman, W. F., AN, xi, 1961, 267–77. Wilks, M., *The Problem of Sovereignty in the later Middle Ages*, 1963. William of Apulia, *Gesta Rob. Wiscardi* (MGH Scriptores ix), see Mathieu. William of Malmesbury, (1) *Gesta Regum Anglorum*, MPL, clxxix; (2) MGH Scriptores, x and xiii; (3) see Stubbs (RS). William of Newburgh, HRA, ed. R. Howlett, 1884. William of Poitiers, see Foreville and Giles (2). Williams, G. H., ed. *The Norman Anon. of 1100 A.D.*, 1951. Williamson, D. M., *Lincoln. Archit. and Arch. Soc. Reports*, 1953, 19–26. Williamson, H. R., *The Arrow and the Sword*, 1947. Willis, R., *Hist. of Monastery of Christ Church, Canterbury*. Wilson, D., (1) *The Anglo-Saxons*, 1960; (2) *The Vikings*, 1970; (3) with P. G. Foote, *The Viking Achievement*, 1970. Wilson, E. M. *Lost Lit. of Med. Eng.* Wilson, R. M., *Early Middle English Lit.*, 1939. Winter, J. M., van, *Acta Neerlandica*, i, 1966. Wood, M., *Arch. J.*, cxii, for 1935 (1936) pt, 2, 167–242. Wormald, F., (1) *Procs. Brit. Acad.*, xxx, 1944; (2) in F. M. Stenton (2); (3) *Archaelogia*, xci, 107–31.

Young, J. I., *History*, n.s., xxxv, 1950, 11–33. Yver, J., (1) *Travaux de la semaine d'hist. du droit normand*, 1927, (1928); (2) AN, viii, 1958, 139–83; (3) *Bull. Soc. Antiq. de Normandie*, liii, 1953.

Zarnecki, G., *Later Eng. Romanesque Sculpture*. Zechlin, E., *Hist. Zeits.*, clii, 1935, 1–47.

NOTES

NOTES

The following abbreviations are used : AN (Annales de Normandie); AS (Anglo-Saxon); Ant. (Antiquity); B (Barlow); Chron. or Chronicle (Anglo-Saxon Chronicle); DB (Domesday Book); D (Douglas); EcHR (Economic History Review); EHR (English History Review); F (Finberg); H (Hollister); H. of H. (Henry of Huntingdon); L (Lennard); Li (Liebermann); LL (L. Lancaster); LW (Lynn White); MA (Medieval Archaeology); N. (Norman); Ord. (Ordericus Vitalis); PP (Past and Present); RS (Rolls Series); Sp. (Speculum); S (Stenton, F.M.); TRHS (Transaction of the Royal Historical Society); W (Whitelock); W. of M. (William of Malmesbury); W. of P. (William of Poitiers).

Apart from the inevitable debt to the older scholars such as Stenton, Haskins, Poole, Cam, and so on, I should like to make special mention of Barlow, Loyn, Sayles, Hollister, Hallam, Harvey, Lennard, Finberg, Hilton, Lynn White, Douglas, and, for the last chapter, Kiernan.

CHAPTER I
THE NORMANS AND THE VIKING AGE

1. Bloch (7) 89; Douglas (15) 12–4. Sweden : Magoun (1) and (2); Chaney, 5. Scandinavian elements in AS society : Brown (4); B (2).

2. Latouche (2), 243ff.
3. Randall 83–6; Paterson; Charles.
4. *Germ.* xiv, viii; Chaney, 8 & 13f; Wells, Woden: H. R. E. Davidson. 72f & 80 (human sacrifices, hanging); Shetelig (1), 415f; Turville-Petrie (3), 190–5; Chadwick (2), 295–303; Höfler; Naumann.
5. Wilson (2), 21f & fig. 5.
6. Waquet, 28–30; Sawyer, 117.
7. *The War of the Gaedhil with the Gaill.*
8. Jansson, 11–15: a useful book for the Runes.
9. Delisle, 17f.
10. Poupardin, pp. xxv–xl.
11. Sawyer, 137f. Leblond, 204f, 241, n 22; *Rec. Hist. des Gaules et de la France*, vii, 231.
12. *Ib.* 138f, 143f.
13. S (14), 40. Cott. Claud. D. xiii, f.49, App. no 5; Haskins (7), 19; *Red. Bk. of Exch.*, 360–2.
14. Graham, 119; Birch, ii, no. 587.
15. Knowles (2), 69f.
16. W (3), 273f; Sawyer, 140.
17. W (3), 818; Sawyer, 141f.
18. Lestocquoy (1), 4; Lot (2); Flodoard; Sawyer, 139. Verse; Copley, 130; Magoun (1) and (2): cf. genealogies.
19. Vogel, 76f, 85f; Nithard, 122f.
20. W (3), 190f; Dhont (1), 28n; Sawyer, 144.
21. B (4), xiii–iv; G. Henderson (1), ch.v.
22. *Olaf Tryg. Saga*, xx.
23. Simpson, 152. Heriot: Li. (2), 500–2.
24. W (1), 29–31 and 35. There was a popular tale of how the followers of the Danish Hnaef avenged their lord against great odds: *Wanderer*, lines 92f; Lo (1), 280. Cross on '*ubi sunt*'.
25. Simpson, 147.
26. H (2), 171.
27. W (3), 188.
28. S (12), 74f.
29. *Olaf Tryg.* lviii; also *St Olaf*, liii and lx, cf. lxiv. *Olaf Tryg.* appendix i (Laing, 101). Harald wants to settle: *Olaf Tryg.* viii. Euvind: *St Olaf*, lx and lxiii. Gudleif: lxiv at Novgorod.
30. Sawyer, 198 and 97–9.
31. Latouche (3), 253f; rights often called *vicaria*. In general: *Capitul, de Pîtres.* Lords call themselves comtes, vicomtes, châtelains. Dorestead at Rhine mouth controlled by Rorik who ruled Lowlands, 9th c. *Annals of St Bertin* on attacks. Trade: Dunning; Levison, 6; Crawford; Magoun. Amsterdam: van de Walle (Norse burn it 836, but it revives). *Liber Tradit.* of St Peter's Ghent for the marquisate. Quentovic: Grierson.
32. *St Olaf*, lxxii. 300 retainers, but they counted in long hundreds, each 120.
33. Baker, 2.
34. *Alodarius*, proprietor bound to king or lord by commendation, a personal tie not affecting his legal title to the land: Dubled, Dudo, 169; Lo (3) ch. 1; Musset (2); Boüard; Gautries.
35. B (4), 4, *Avta Sanct.* Aug. iv, 829; Musset (8), 132f.
36. Gautries, 264 and 265–70; Musset 330–9; Beaurepaire; D (4); Sawyer 165f. Rollo: *St Olaf*, xix.

37. S (16).
38. Baker, 6.
39. Li. i, 94; Attenborough i, 40f; Lot (3), i, 99; Sawyer, 120, 125f.
40. Lestocquoy (1), 5; Flodoard, 127; Vercauteren (2), 257; Richer (2), ii, 87–96. Cf. small towers etc. of Montreuil-sur-Mer.
41. *St Olaf*, xi–xii (castle perhaps where the Tower was later); xiii for Thing-men, free men entitled to appear at a Thing, as udal–born to land; they hired themselves out as retainers or hired-men. Also vi for operations in Sweden. Musset (9), 46–9.
42. Wheeler.
43. Olrik, 212ff.
44. C. L. Kingsford in Stow, *Survey*, ii, 373.
45. W. of M., II, xii.
46. Jansson, 51–53. See E. G. Bowen, *Britain and the western seaways* (1972) for continuity; Christensen in *Hist. of Seafaring based on underwater arch.*, ed. G. Bass (1972).

CHAPTER II
A CLOSER LOOK AT THE VIKINGS

1. Klind-Jensen (1) and (2); Hagen; Kivikovski; Shetelig; Stenberger; D. Wilson (2) and (3); Kendrick; Arbman; Brønsted; Jones; Turville-Petrie (1); Sawyer (1) and (3), to which I owe much. For norse god Njord and the Nerthus of Tacitus and the bog-sacrifices, P.V. Glob. Ideal landlord: *Olaf Tryg.*, xxi–xxii.
2. *Olaf Tryg.*, ix; D. Wilson (3), 143f, 147. *Rigsmal; C. P. Boreal* i, 236–40.
3. *Gisli*, G. Johnston, 1963; handclasp seals all bargains.
4. Phillpotts, ch. iv (problem still existed in 17th c.); oath of compurgation, 99f; saga wergilds, 13–22. Also chs. ii–iii.
5. Wilson (3), 42. Pagan themes into Christian art, 44.
6. Simpson, 153, fig. 93, cf. fig. 92.
7. *Grettir*, ii. Not till well into 12th c. that even the great pagan temple at Uppsala was destroyed.
8. *Olaf Tryg.*, xxiv.
9. *Olaf Tryg.*, lxv, 'the bonders changed the Thing-token into a War-token', lxxii, cf. xvii, liii; combat, xxxiv, holm-gang, as the fighters went to a holm or uninhabited isle. The quarrel here is over a girl. Marking battle field with hazel boughs, Archery: *St Olaf*, xx.
10. *Bor.*, i, 265f. Heroes are Woden's Oak; 'the javelin sought out the life of a man', etc.; blood is 'the wave of the sword'. *Bor*, i, 268–70.
11. *Olaf Tryg.*, xxx–xxxi; Njal, xxx and lxi. Stream of wolf: stream of blood. The warrior is the wolf-leader, the breaker of the raven's fast. Grappling-iron: *Olaf Tryg.*, cxiii, cxvi. Forecastle: *Grettir*. Use of cable: *St Olaf*, xxviii (pulley and lever); liv, throws tiller. Walk round ship-rails, juggle with three daggers: *Olaf Tryg.*, xcii. Ships: *karfi* for coastal waters, *langskip* for war voyages, *hafskip* for a seagoer, at times a trader, *kaupskip*. For Raven: Chaney, 132–4; *Chronicle*, 878; Krappe (2), 408–11; J. Anderson, 210; *Enc. Emmae*, ii, 9; Turville-Petrie (3) 57–60; Lukman, 133; W. (3), 687 8; Helm II, i, 161; Colgrave, 116–8, (a raven, as well as boar, stag, wolf, horse, troubled St. Guthlac, ch. 36). The AS raven may go back to days of the Woden cult.

12. *Flateyjarbok* i, ch. 63; N. K. Chadwick (1), 28–31. Davidson, 112ff; Shetelig (1), 166, 280f, 430 etc.; Wilson (2), 47f, and link of Vanir cult and Odin, 119f. Boatgrave in AS England on Snape Common, Suffolk, c. 500: R. A. Smith, *VCH of Suffolk*, i.

13. Jansson, 85ff; Legge (1), 8–13; G. R. Waters, lines 268–70.

14. Young; Walsh; Marcus (Faroes); AN, 1958, 407–14 etc.; Gathorne-Hardy; Zechlin; Bronsted 80, 103–8, Greenland: Norlund. Iceland: Gjesset. Eskimos: Oleson. Glyn Daniel, *Ant*. no 184, 288–92.

15. Sawyer, 200, n18.

16. Hodgkin, ii, 487f; Brøgger, ch. 4; Shetelig (2), ch. 8; Olsen; Sawyer 200, 166f. Jarlshof: Hamilton.

17. Sawyer, 30; N. Chadwick (1), 14. Kendrick, 96f. Sea level; Jansson, 26.

18. N. Chadwick (1), 14f. Kiev conquered and refounded by Oleg. In general, M. Rostovtzev, *Iranians and Greeks in S. Russia*, 1922, 210ff; Vernadsky, *Ancient Russia*, 1943, and *Byzantion* xiv, also *The Origins of Russia*, 1939 179; M. Tikhomirov.

19. Jansson, 19ff.

20. Shetelig, 352; Salten fiord: *Olaf Tryg.*, lxxxvi.

21. Riant, 97–129.

22. Jansson, 26ff.

23. *Olaf Tryg.*, v, also vi. Tavastland linked with personal name Tafaeistr.

24. Jansson, 36.

25. Vogel (3), 982, and (1) 16f.

26. For Sigtuna scales-box: Jansson 33f; Wilson (2), fig. 32. Swedes like little isles in lakes, but the sites changed: Lillo 7th (c.), Birka (9th c.), Sigtuna (11th c.), Stockholm (13th c.). Lopez (4) gives Birka 35 acres, Paris was smaller (some 20 acres), expanding from the Ile north and south in suburbs. But much inside Birka seems unbuilt on.

27. Sawyer, 84f, 178: silver, important in the arts of the Viking period.

28. Schoenbeck.

29. Hodgkin, ii, 646; Hübener, 39; Malone (1) holds that O. told his tale not later than 871. Also Geidel; Malone (1) (2) and (3); S. H. Cross; Ross.

30. Jansson, 50ff; for others, 61ff.

31. W. of M., II, xii.

32. Crossley-Holland, 30f.

33. Sawyer (2), 171–3. Pre-Scandanavian sokes: R. H. C. Davis (4) pp. xliii–vii; Vinogradoff (1), 303. Li. i, 358 (II Cn. 71, 3); Robertson (1), 210; Maitland, 139; Stephenson (6), 305–8. See also ch. 3. & 7 here. Coins: Sawyer (1), 93f & (3); Seaby; Dolley. Assessment of personal names is difficult, because after a while through intermarriage both people used the same names; but it is still significant that in DB 60 per cent of peasants in Lincolnshire have Danish names, 40 per cent in East Anglia. See Clemoes (1) for Cameron on Scand. settlement (A. S. villages possibly annexed by Danes); Brooks on military obligations of 8–9 cs; Loyn, later Saxon town-developments; Page on Scand. language in England. Also E. Okasha, *Hand-list A. S. Non-Runic Inscriptions* (1971).

34. *Liber Eliensis*, 148; S (20); Cam (1), 9f. Silver coins struck from Edward (Martyr) to 1066 show Cambridge's trading reputation.

35. Latouche, 256; Shetelig (1), 357; Sawyer 60, 66–82, 200f; Bronsted, 130–7; Wilson (2), 35f, 85–91. Warriors getting together for voyage: *Njal*, xxix. Lagouëlle, 85–8 and 230–50; Prentout (4), 207–49; Musset (12), 606; Carabie, 230–9.

36. *Olaf Tryg.*, xcv. See lxxiv for the Crane, a *snaekke*, a longship probably framed for speed; xx for clash of two vikings (fifteen benches).
37. Also Shetelig (1), 352; *Olaf Tryg.*, lxxxii on three men in a boat–note hanging of rudder, butter-kits, bread-chest, big ale keg. Carving: C. E. Gibson, *The Story of the Ship*, 1948, 87, pl. 9. Needham (3), IV, 3, 608.
38. *Olaf Tryg.*, xxv, also lxxxv for dog.
39. Wilson (2), 91.
40. *St. Olaf*, lxiv and lxxvii.
41. Shetelig (1), 348ff.
42. *Olaf Tryg.*, xlvii, song of Sigvald the scald; xxix, Halfred Vandraedaskald on Olaf's white-winged ocean-horses. Ships are skates that skim on the sea-belt; *Njal* xc; W. of M., II, xii. Olaf on his serpent's quarter-deck, cxiv; binding the stems together, cxiii.
43. Sawyer (1), 126–8.
44. Maréchal 270f; Bouard (5); great Mercian earthworks by Offa against the Welsh; the Dane-Dicke in Yorkshire. Denmark: *Olaf Tryg.*, xxiv, xxvi. In 1160 Valdemar the Great added a brick wall with battlements.
45. Jom or Jomsborg: a fortified town on east side of isle of Wollin off the mouths of the Oder.
46. Sawyer (1), 129–35 and (2) 132, 249, n5. *Illustrated London News* archaeological section, 2105, (6 Oct. 1962).
47. D. Wilson (2), 60f; Ekekorp, 61f; Pertz (2) lines 156f, 213f, 360–6. No credit to tale of Paris in 886 despite inventive powers of barbarians (Anon: *De Rebus Bell.*, LW (1), 150.

CHAPTER III
NORMAN DUKES AND ENGLISH KINGS

1. Complaint: J. Lair, *Étude sur la Complainte*; Lauer; Becker; Leblond, 173–5; continuity of tenure: Musset (8), 1025; Dudo (Lair), 221; Adhémar ed. Chavanon, 148.
2. Rollo's descent was said to be from Fornjot, king of Finland, through Gorr (settled in Lofoten Islands), Sveithi the Sea-king, Halfdan earl of the Uplands, Eystein Glumra. Sources: Dudo of St Quentin; William of Jumièges; Flodoard of Rheims; Richer; Ralph Glaber; Widukind the German; Chronicles of Rouen and of St Vaast; Benedict of St More; etc., with Haskins; Musset.
3. Postan in Hallam (1) p. vii–viii. Olaf, lix; Leblond, 57. Scandinavian element in Dudo: Prentout (5), 83; Borges; also Dudo, iii, 53f, iv, 68 and 81; Steenstrup, 302f; Musset (9), 45ff.
4. Dudo 154; Benedict, lines 3299–3303; Loyn (3), 23.
5. Sawyer (1); Li. i, 228; Robertson, 64.
6. Robertson (2), no. xl; S (11), 505; Sawyer 151f.
7. S (11), 504, for more examples.
8. S (16), 74f; 82–4 for charters of monastries with grants of land by peasants. Sokeman in Kent and Surrey, 1066, but such sporadic cases south of Thames only stresses the distinctive aspect of Danelaw: S (11), 509ff.
9. Hoyt, 192–204; R. H. C. Davis, pp. xliii–xlvii; Sawyer, 164, 238; homines liberi, L. 225f. Against Danish hypotheses for sokeman tenures: Davis (2), S(12), 21–39; F (1), 148f.
10. B (1), 57.

11. H. A. Ellis; Davidson, 126–30. Andreas stone: 128. Weland: Ellis, 234. Rasmund stone in Sweden with Sigurd theme, dragon as ornamental border.
12. B (2), 172 and (4) 1f; *Olaf Tryg.*, xi. W. of M. says that William near the end of his life sent men to Nicaea to bring back his father's body, but in Apulia they heard of his death and buried the body there.
13. Aelgifu in charge of Danelaw or Scandinavia? She was ultimately a regent in Norway; her father was once earl of Northumbria and owned much land in Northants. *Chronicle* 1037 on Bruges. Also W. H. Stevenson. Harald's nickname Harefoot probably contemporary.
14. H. M. Chadwick (2), 237f; Chaney, 26f.
15. Bede HE., ii, 5 and i, 27; Asser, *Alfred*, xvii; Frazer, *Lectures on Early History of Kingship*, 1905, 243f.
16. Chadwick (2), 102–10; Chaney, 27, n 79, for custom among the Warni, a tribe closely connected with Angles. Simeon of Durham on maternal as well as paternal descent of King Oswald: Arnold, 18; Bede, ii, 6.
17. *Chronicle* E; C & D add that the enemy went up into Wilts; the gnomic saying echoes Alcuin (Plummer).
18. Ritchie (2), 14f; the bishop was pluralist of Crediton and Cornwall.
19. Fécamp and Mont St M.: Prentout (5), 90; *Gall. Chr.*, xi, 202f; PL, cxxxvii; Will. Jum., v, 4.
20. Prentout (4), 46f; Plummer-Earle, ii, p. cx–cxii.
21. Malm. *Pont. Angl.*, v, (PL clxxix 1667); Osbern, *Transl. St. Elph.*, x, (PL cxlix); Plummer, ii, 223; Loth, 176. MSS style: Malm. *Life St Wulfstan*, 738f; Martin 358.
22. Bezzola, 194; Grierson (2), 89ff; Barlow (2), 17, cult of St Oswald, 176.
23. Grierson, 95, n3; van Lokeren, no 124.
24. Ritchie (2), 5f.

CHAPTER IV
EDWARD, HAROLD, AND WILLIAM

1. W. of M., II, xiii; A. Campbell (2), pp. xliii, xlvi, 32 (IIxvi); Freeman, i, 735–7. Alfred: Plummer, ii, 211–5. Emma's marriage-gifts: Campbell, p. xliv. Roger of Wendover says she turned to Flanders as William was still too young to get order in Normandy.
2. *Formanna Sögur*, iii, 63f; B (1), 58; S (5), 421. Ralf the Staller: G. H. White, *Complete Peerage*, ix, 560–71. S (5), 419f, 561, 553.
3. W. of M., II, xiii; Baker, 72.
4. B (4), 55.
5. *Vita Aedwardi*, i; W. of M., l.c., year 1065.
6. M. Bloch (11), 43–9; Southern (9); B(3), 61f, 123; Delaborde; Chaney, 73.
7. Greg. Tours, HF, IX, xxi (Dalton, 1927, ii, 395); Chaney, 73f. The invocation of King Guntram drove out evil spirits and he made *blot* to cure a plague affecting the groin.
8. Ritchie (1), 39f.
9. B (1), 39f.
10. T. D. Hardy, I, i, 381; *Enc. Emmae*, ii, 16; S (5), 420.
11. Grierson, 103, n2.
12. *Vita Aed.* (402–4) on Baldwin and Godwin as former allies. *Chron. C.* has 'Frenchmen'. Harold: *Chron.* D and S (5) 564f.

13. *Chron.* D & C. Harold seems to have been behind the outlawing of Aelfgar (1053); but after the fighting he reinstated him in E. Anglia; and when Leofric died, he let him become Earl of Mercia, though insisting that E. Anglia should then go to Gyrth.

14. B (4), 36. Gilbert was grandson of Richard I; he was murdered at the instigation of kinsman Ralph de Gacé, son of Archbishop Robert of Rouen.

15. Loyn (3), 36.

16. His sister Adelaide, after the count of Ponthieu was killed at Arques, 1053, married Lambert a count in Artois and younger brother of Eustace II of Boulogne, who may have been married to Godgifu, daughter of Emma and Aethelred, some time after 1035 when her first husband died.

17. See later, end of ch. xiv.

18. Runciman, i, 85f; Mansi, xix, 89f and xix, 2671; Hefele-Leclercq, iv, pt. 2, 1409; Glaber in Bouquet, RHF, x, 27f; Pfister, p. lx. Odo: *Miracles de Saint Benoît*, ed. de Certain, 182.

19. In general Bouard (4). Mansi, *Concilia*, xix, 483–8; MGH, vii, 474 and viii, 103. A link with Verdun synod 1016 through bishop of Soissons.

20. Schieffer (1); Pfister, 172. The basis has been taken as being the survivals of Roman law in S. France: Huberti (2), 34–51. More likely the movement emerged through the lack of kingly power there: M. Bloch (6), 202.

21. Dauphin, 26off; Bouard, 169f.

22. N. legislation against feud (*faida*): Yver (1) and (2). Truce: Tardif, 596, n5 (Richard, not Odilon of Cluny). *Ignis*: Du Cange sv; Laporte, 48; Bouard 171. H. E. J. Cowdrey, PP no 46, *ignis*; also for rapidly widening gap, early 11 c., between *milites* and *pauperes*, with burdens falling on peasants; and on the Truce working out ultimately to strengthen papacy; after 1066 helping ducal power over church and nobles.

23. Fulbert, *Miracula S. Audoeni*, 1087–92. In late 1046 William faced a big rising in lower Normandy, so he had no time then.

24. Church militia: Ord refers to Gacé as *princeps* of the *militia* of the Normans. Marx, 159. Texts: Bouard, 176ff. For N. bishops: AN, viii, 1958, 87–102.

25. Excommunications were imprecise before the 13th c.; MS of Douai gives text of imprecation: Huberti (1), 337. The movement was strong where kingly authority was weak: MGH, vii, 74; Lenariginier. Council of Toulonge 1050 recommends additions: Mansi, xix, 1042.

26. Mansi, xix, 827–32.

27. Already Clovis, 481–511, had done his best to make it easy for a man to cut loose from his kindred, etc.

28. Runciman, i, 86f; *Alexiad*, x, 9, 5f (B. Leib ii, 218, 222). Eastern church had a stronger anti-war tradition, e.g. Basil, PG, xxxii, 681.

29. Blair, 297.

30. D (11); Foreville; Loyn (3), 56. I find no likelihood in the thesis that the terms of Godwin's return involved accepting William as heir. S (5), 557f accepts the tale of William's visit.

31. Urry, 11f; Dodswell (2), 59.

32. Edwards, 296; Ord., iii, 189; Dodswell, 550.

33. Baker, 374, 276; Wormald (2), style and design; Digby, techniques.

34. S (2); Janssen; Bertrand; Chefneux; Dodswell etc.

35. R. F. Paris, 100; Dodswell 534 n33.

36. Eadmer HN I vi–viii.

37. W. of M., II, xiii; Freeman, iii, 671ff; H. of H., vi (year 1063).
38. Grierson (3), 90–7. S. Fest argues that the Aetheling's wife was daughter of Stephen king of Hungary and Gisela, niece of emperor Henry II; see also Freeman, i, 483 (Aelfgiva as the woman who deceived Christ, bearing a son by a priest, another by a shoemaker).
39. B (4), 60; Aelfgiva is associated with phallic figure in border; for various identifications, even as a witch: Freeman, iii, 696–9 (William's daughter or Harold's sister).
40. Holmes. Harold and light horse go to Dol via sands, the heavier-armed inland via Rennes.
41. Loyn (3), 58; Douglas and Foreville.

CHAPTER V
NORMANS IN THE SOUTH

1. Runciman, I (ii 1); Boissonade, 6–32; Hatem, 43–63; Fliche, 551–3; Rousset, 31–5; Vellay, 71. Baudri: Ord., iii, 248; D (2), ii, 289.
2. D (15), 41f; Joransen; Norwich (1); Chalandon, i, 42–57; Amatus, i, chs. 17–20; Leo of Ostia (redaction Peter Deacon); Ord, ii, 53f; Will of Apulia, i, lines 10–45.
3. See also Mon. Germ. Hist., SS, vii, 652, note a; Adhémar, ed. Chevanon, 178; Glaber, ed. Pron, 52f. Adhémar completed his work before 1034; Glaber apparently before 1044, may have got information from Odilo abbot of Cluny who was on pilgrimage to Monte Cassino c. 1023. For Rodolf: D (15), 219 n37; D (17), 110f.
4. Amatus, I, i, 2; Cahen; Chalandoni, i, 81f.
5. Norwich, 70; Anna, Alex. i, 10 (Dawes). Amatus, iii, ch. 7; Malaterra i, ch. 16; Will. of Apulia, ii, vv. 320–43; Alex. i, 200, 10f; Ord, ii, 54.
6. Jamison, 247f.
7. Norwich, 82.
8. D (15), 58 and 129–32; Will. of Apulia 384ff. If put to it, the papacy would have appealed to its basic weapon, the forged Donation of Constantine.
9. Mal., ii, 53.
10. Jamison, 243f; Lair, 137; Marx (Interpolation), 163; D (15), 102.
11. Jamison, 244. Ord. vol. ii, lib. iii, 27.
12. Jamison, 244; Ord. l.c. 56f, 87, 109; Jamison, 279, nn35–37, sources 245. Many MSS of books from S. Italy in monastic libraries.
13. Jamison, 248f; Chronicles of Reign of Stephen etc., iii, 186; Historia Anglorum, 261f.
14. Ord. Marx, 1968; St Martin de Sées, Bibl. nat. MS Fran. 18, 953f, ix. Caen: Lehmann-Brockhaus, ii, 593, nos 4484f; Musset (3), 286f.
15. D (15), 91–103.

CHAPTER VI
THE NORMAN SYSTEM

1. B (1), 7.
2. Bouquet, Recueil, x, 463; Ganshof (2), 76.

3. Green, 40.
4. Loyn (3), 16.
5. Guilhiermoz.
6. S (4), 12f.
7. *Ib.* 14.
8. *Service d'host* (*servicia debita*) and *arrière ban* affected all free tenants, but especially the more prosperous, men with knights' fees and vavasours with more than 50 acres: H (1), 81. Before 1066 there is no proof the dukes could impose fixed quotas of war service on all tenants, though they probably did so on the great monastries (always big landowners), and perhaps on bishops. As the church was better organized, it was perhaps easier to force the dues on them. Baronial obligations were generally lighter than later in England.
9. Duby (1) 13–5; Genicot, 16; van Winter, 174; Beech, 94; Dhont, 545; Harvey, 27. More south, the knights were earlier drawn from noble families. Ganshof (2); M. Bloch (10).
10. Harvey, 27, n104.
11. Strayer (1), 56f. And Fauroux, nos 196, 13, 16, 107 and pp. 58–64; Lemarignier (5); Duby (2), 154f; Werner, 186; Halphen (3), 109.
12. Bloch (7), 177, 332; Round (7), i, 108f; Guilhiermoz, 184–6; Harvey 28, n105; H (2), 79.
13. Vinogradoff (3), 66, finds that drengs usually held about 1 hide.
14. B (4), 37f, 48. Robert was kinsman of the abbey's founder. Also Dodswell, 557; Faral, 275f: archbishop Turpin.
15. Phillpotts, 193; Viollet, *Hist. du droit civil*, 2nd ed., 435. For fourth degree: *Law of Northumbrian Priests* (c. 1020–30?), 61, 1. Six degrees: laws VI Aethelred and I Cnut.
16. Yver (2) in general, also for past history. Vicomte: Genestal (2); Haskins (7), 46; Koch, 448 & n66. Revolts: Prentout (3), 19ff. Concessions: Haskins (7), 30–4. Lemarignier (2), 74ff, 156ff. Yver (2), 157, for abbey of Préaux in 1050: grant of jurisdiction in cases of arson, rape, etc. It is suggested they inherited from the Frankish kings a tradition of the use of *missi dominici* (Carolingian) and of the sworn investigation. Hereditary: Holt (3),7f and 40. *Alodarius* in *Domesday*: Maitland (1),153f
17. Baker, 25.
18. Musset (3), 285, (4), (5) and (6), 120. Burgundy: Vigneron.
19. Musset (3), for refs.
20. Le Patourel (2); Baker 28f, Caen, Gallo-Roman: AN, viii (3), 295–8. Development of lower Brittany: Lemarignier. Herrings were salted at Dieppe, 1030.
21. Legras 36. Then in documents 1032–5 and c. 1040; with 12th c. references are more numerous.
22. Boussard (5), 430–2. Latouche (1); Legras in general. List of terms: Boussard, 426.
23. Boussard, 433.
24. Bateson (1), (2); Hemmeon; Ballard (2); Stephenson (5); Tait. Breteuil customs were inspired by those of Cormeilles, which existed before 1079 when they were transmitted to Aufay: Bateson 76f, 304f, 754–7.
25. Boussard, 434–8.
26. AS pilgrims: W. J. Moore; Green, 12of; Hodgkin, 448–51, English school 450, 636f.
27. F. P. Paris, 180–2; Holmes, 182; Erdmann, 181–3, thinks no gonfalon is shown.

28. Dodswell, 549; W of M., iii, year 1066.
29. B (4), 41.
30. He got the papal legates to give correct form to his deposition of
    Mauger; got the pope to accept the transference of Bishop John
    from Avranches to Rouen etc. Guernsey: *Times*, Dec. 23 1971, on sale
    of the charter dated *c.* 1060.
31. Theobald, later in Canterbury see, was trained at Bec. Further: Freeman
    iii, 102f; Will. of P., 125; Lanfranc, 287. Leblond ch. ix; Garnier, ed.
    L. Musset; Dudo, Gall. Chr. xi, app. 284; Prentout (4), 48, 171, 370, 414;
    Musset (9), 64, n.1.
32. Money: L. Musset (3): contrast Burgundy, Duby (3) 348ff.
33. Haskins (5), 62f. Fulk Rechin: Halphen (1) 235-7.
34. D (15), 77; *Alex.* iii, ch. 8., v, ch. 4.

CHAPTER VII
ANGLO-SAXON ENGLAND

1. Hilton (1), 12; F (1), 8f; de Coulanges (1), 265f; Vinogradoff (1), 223;
   Chronicle shows the main links with Franks and road to Rome in 9th c.,
   no Scandinavian place-names.
2. Sayles, 129f.
3. Robersson (1), 12 (III, Edmand 1). Egfrith: Schramm, 15; S (5), 217.
4. Stubbs (6), i, 198-206; Pollock (2), i, 44f.
5. Chaney, 205f; Attenborough, 5.
6. Chaney, 206f for more details; German parallels, Pollock (2), i, 51, n2.
7. Attenborough 65; Robertson 87, 103, 205 (triple ordeal).
8. Chaney, 28-35; W (3), 12, n11; Philippson (1); Sisam; Hauck. Seaxnet:
   Turville-Petrie (3), 100 (rel. to Frey or Njordr) and Philippson (2), 117f.
   Woden and harvest, Wednesday: Chaney, 35; Olrik (2), 41; Chantepie,
   226f. Sceaf: Chadwick (2), ch. xi, (256-67, 272-6); R. W. Chambers (2),
   68-86, 314-22; Sisam, 315, on Bedwig. Theocratic: P. S. Lewis, *Later
   Med. France*, 1968, 81-4. Beli (?Bilwis, hypostasis of Woden), Bilwis a
   Germanic ruler of underworld: Krappe, 18, 26. Howel: Wade-Evans,
   ed. Nennius, *Hist.*, 102; J. Williams ab Ithel, *Annales Camb.* (RS), xx,
   1860 p,x., n1; N. Chadwick (2), 132, 196 (Belenus). Bible: Magoun (3).
9. W (1), 28; Chaney, 208f; *Germania*, xii; Pollock, 51f.
10. W (1) 31f; Bede, II, 9.
11. *Chron.* A. E, under 755 (757). Magoun (4); H. M. Chadwick (4), 363f.
    Note length and detail: an often told tale or theme of song: S (5), 208,
    n3. Lord as well as kindred got compensation money for death of his
    man. Bede on King Raedwald and Edwin, II 12. Cf. *Finnesburh* fragment.
12. Attenborough, 65; in general Lea. MGH *Epist.* iv, no 231. Torhtmund
    was in company of archbishop of Canterbury as he passed through
    Charles's territory. Writer: Napier, 3.
13. W (1), 37f, 32 and (3), 856f.
14. Chaney 248, 257-9, 252; Stubbs (4), 356. 796: W (3), 771; Stubbs (7),
    iii, 454, 447.
15. Schramm, 19-22. Witness: *Vita S. Oswaldi* (*Historians of Church of
    York*, RS) i, 436-8. Influence of Dunstan: S (5), 363.
16. Estates, e.g. Aldermaston, Ealdormannestum.
17. Sayles, 146f.
18. Dobb (1), 1f.

19. Hilton (1). Slaves, 9th–10th cs., M. Bloch (8) and (9); G. Roupnel, *Histoire de la campagne française*, 270.
20. Postan (3). Most extant AS wills order the freeing of some or all slaves on estates. Kent: S (5), 300f (*laets*).
21. Li. i, 27; H. Hecht 35 (1.2), 41 (32), 45 (24), 213 (13).
22. Laws of Ine 3, 2, 67. From earliest time peasant land had obligation to pay rent, so the village on the landlord's soil must have been the rule, Li., ii, 298.
23. Li., ii, 506; Stephenson (6), 291.
24. LL, 261 (II, Cnut, 79), see law of Aethelred given at Wantage, 978–1008: W (3), 403.
25. F (1).
26. Aston, 14f.
27. All land, unless exempted, had folk burdens, especially the need to contribute to upkeep of king, court, and officials. Exemption by charter or writ also gave the owner right to will the land away from their kindred, first to religious houses, then to lay heirs.
28. Aston, 28–32; also for effects of land grants to followers. Disintegration of demesne before 1066 by leasing to large groups (often all the manor's villeins).
29. F (1), 158–60. *Regia villa*: S (5), 474f. Laws of Alfred, I 2. Coins were struck under Aethelred II at places like Reading, Bedwyn and Warminster.
30. E. John.
31. Sayles (1), 8. II, Cnut, 78; 77
32. F (1), 131–43. Dependent tenures had evolved in 10th–11th cs., mainly known from leases showing reorganization of estates by Bishop Oswald at Worcester, under Edgar, with the aim of ensuring services, sometimes military, in return for dependent tenures normally for three lives. Services: hunting, escort, bridge-building. But military service still essentially a matter of status, not tenure.
33. King, lords, church, held estates that consisted mainly in rents paid by reeves, rent-farmers and lessees. Latter got in lords' rents and customs due from town, village, and other agricultural groupings (units called manors by Ns.) and took their own profit from the result. Lord also had vassals or under-tenants who rendered him services and at times also rent for land – though terms of contract between lord and under-tenant, reeve, etc. often varied in details.
34. LL, 376, 373; Athelstan, VIII, 2 (London district).
35. LL, 472; Ewen. A paternal kinsman is made child's protector, Hlothhere and Eadric's law 6; Alfred's (30), if a man without paternal kin kills a man, maternal kin pay a third of wergild; Athelstan's (11) at Grateley keeps proportion of two to one for man demanding payment for skilled kinsman (three oath-givers, two paternal, one maternal). Sister's son important in Irish legend; in literature Christ is Our Sister's Son.
36. Charles-Edwards (1) and (2)
37. Bede, HE, i, 25, ii, 9, iii, 4 and 24; Ine, Lieb., i, 118–21 and 104–6; HA, xi (Plummer, 375f); Kent: Charles-Edwards, 12–4, and three *munds*. 12f, plough 14f; Irish evidence, *ib.* 15–20 and Z. f. celt. Phil., xiv, 1923, 372 (par. 34); *ib.* 21, against Lancaster and Kroeschell; see also Leyser and Schlesinger, 289–96.
38. Charles-Edwards (2) and Tac., *Germ.*, xx. In general Radcliffe-Brown, 15ff, 97ff; also C. H. Bell and Farnsworth.

39. Charles-Edwards (1), 30 esp. n51. A. H. Smith prefers to see as group under a lord, but surely kindreds would tend to gather under a particular lord.

40. Ine, xlii; vi, Athelstan, viii, 2, (Lieb., i, 178); *Symeonis . . . opera* (RS), i, 218f.

41. Charles-Edwards (1) 31; *Chron.* E under 449; gegildan, Lieb. (3) sv Genossenschaft.

42. Treasury had charge of heregeld. Development: Robertson (2), 136; Loyn (3), 74. Continuity: S (5), 389f; Barlow (1), 46.

43. Edward was still the biggest landowner despite the earls; William strengthened this position, by DB held nearly a quarter of landed wealth. B (1) 45. Change to title deeds: Barraclough (1), 211–3. Writ: Clemoes, 102; Harmer. E. John on charters as depositive, not evidential. King did not keep copies of writs; archives small, in chapel with his relics. Harmer for writs.

44. AS poem, *The Arts of Man*: 'One can in the council of sages devise a decree for the people, where the Witan is gathered together.' Witan under Ns. determined by territorial status. In general Oleson (2).

45. Earlier laws or codes consist of kingly dooms distinguished from ancient customary law or *aew*: usually judgments on doubtful points or administrative edicts for better enforcement. Perhaps Aethelbert's laws arose from problem of how far to apply the system of *bots* to Christian clergy; Ine's from similiar issues regarding newly conquered *Wealas*. Perhaps embryonic sense of law-making as such in preamble to Alfred's laws.

46. Hodgkin, ii, 607.

47. B (1), 51f. Thegns: EHR, 1926, 33f; Cam (1), 42. Case: Kemble, no 755; Robertson (2), ho lxxxviii. Note stone, suggesting sacral tree or stone as tribal meeting-place.

48. Later hundreds neatly designed, imposed; smaller ones attached administratively to royal town, showing original setting. Yorkshire Ridings, Anglo-Danish *thrithings*.

49. King's income from *feorm*, profits of justice, control of coinage, tolls and other windfalls; kings and magnates had been converting the right to provisions for twenty-four hours into rents.

50. Wessex and Mercia assessed by hides; in East Anglia a less territorialized method a township paid a proportion of the tax amount laid on the leet (ancient subdivision of shire): B (1), 50f; S (5), 638f; Maitland, 455–7; D (6), 191–204 and (10) pp. cli-clxxi. Geld: Robertson, *Northants Geld Rolls* in (2), 230–7; Round (11), hundreds. Carucate: S (12), 87–9; Foster pp. xi–xiv; S (17), pp. lxiii–lxx, etc. Hides, sulungs and carucates in assessments had become fiscal entities, not much related to actual holdings.

51. The slow working out of the principle under Henry I & II, which ultimately produced common law; an important stage under Edward the Elder with special wites by which failures or corruptions of justice could be corrected. Pleas of the crown: under Cnut seven capital crimes (murder or hidden homicide, treason, arson, wounding, mayhem, rape).

52. Hodgkin, ii, 605f.

53. LL, 374, 234; *Widsith*. Models: Duly (6) and (7). For *Wer*: Charles-Edwards (1), 23–5; *Leis W.*, ix, i; vi, Aethelred, xii; Cnut, ii, 51 and 70, 1. Tac., *Germ.*, xxi, shows that he thought the feud extended past the limited family.

54. LL, 374; III, Ath., 6; IV, 3; VI, 8, 2f. Phillpotts, 215f; Norse influence under Edgar, 219f. Whitelock (6), 13–9; Lieb, i, 186–90 (Edmund).

55. LL, 375.

56. *Vita Wulf.* 38; LL, 375 refs.; Loyn (1), 353, 295f; Leges H. 68, 1; 70, 7a; 76, 2, cf. 70, 2; Loyn, 322.

57. J. Rivière; Green, 105; Abelard, *Expos. in Rom.*, iii, 23–6, PL, clxxviii, 833–6. Army: Alfred's division of fyrd; *Chron.* year 893; churchmen fight: Hodgkin, ii, 594. Ch. 37 of Alfred's laws seems aimed at stopping men escaping service by slippng from one district to another in quest of a lord. A freeman joining a fyrd seems to do so under a lord. The warrior seems distinct from the freeman in Alfred's words, 'A king must have men of prayer, *fyrdmen* (men of war), and *weocmen* (workmen).' H. M. Chadwick (2), 158–62; (4) 311–8, 346ff.

58. By Edmund's reign over thirty-five monasteries, lords following the royal example. Bretons: (4), 29. Lotharingian influence via Ghent; Cluniac via Fleury-sur-Loire. Odha, head of English church, while Dunstan was at Glastonbury, was a monk of Fleury. The anti-reform clerics were high-born and high-living; one tried to poison Aethelwold: *Vita Oswaldi* 411; *Liber Vitae . . . Hyde Abbey, Winchester*, ed. W. de Gray Birch, 7.

59. Blair, 90, 207f; when we speak of Benedictine we mean the tradition of the Benedictine rule modified and applied locally over the centuries.

60. Even most moral offences were dealt with by folk courts; king's courts covered both lay and cleric.

61. Frankish craftsmen learned to make such organs after one was sent as a gift to Pepin and Charlemagne from Byzantion with technicians to teach its use. In the east they were secular (in circus and at palatial entertainments), but in the west only monks could muster the craft resources to build and use them, so they became religious, in opposition to the papal view. The Sistine chapel still allows no organs; and Thomas Aquinas denounced them as a Judaizing force. The W. organ survived the great fire of 1202: JL (1) 328f and (2), 112, 270.

62. Anti-monastic reaction: D. J. V. Fisher, 443f; S. J. Crawford; Robinson (2) and (3).

63. Barraclough (3), i, 68; (4) p.i. No special court for pleas of clergy, which were heard in shire court, where the bishops sat with sheriff and earl, or in that of the hundred. There were ecclesiastical jurisdictions exercised according to secular procedures.

64. Thomas.

65. Stutz (1), 29, n19.

66. Council of Coblenz 922 insisted that monks with churches should 'obey their bishop in everything'.

67. L (1), 323.

68. B (2), 199–204. Lances and cross-bows: Sawyer (4), 93f; Mann (2), 67. This detail suggests an early date for the Tapestry. The cross-piece might easily injure the forehead of a rider's horse; so it is more common in the hands of footmen.

69. Hartridge, 11–4. Fleury: Thomas, 77. Village-church: Ault (2).

70. Speakman, 65; Freeman (3), 33.

71. B (2), 184, 198f, 191.

72. 'The old minister to which obedience is due': Lib, i, 264; Robertson, 118f etc. L, 299, for compilation of N. date with same classification.

73. Burgesses at Lincoln objected that a monk had illegally given a church there to the abbot of Peterborough, as no one could grant their possessions outside the city without the king's consent. Churches here are hereditary like any other property. A Thegn's church was sometimes called after him: an important part of his capital equipment and social status.

74. Goscelin, *Mirac. S. Yvonis; Chron. Ramsey*, pp. lxx–lxxi; B (1), 206f, 142. Much homiletic literature in 10th-11th cs., without parallel in Europe. Saint and relics: LW (2), 98–1000; J. Lindsay (1), 173–7, 191f, 221f, 263–7, 308.

75. Combinations of bishoprics correspond to enlarged earldoms. No great interest in canon law. Stigand as outstanding example of pluralist: *Liber Eliensis* condemned this but admitted his generosity. Ealdred of York another example. Few hints of diocesan synods; bishops at times held their own courts to discipline clergy.

76. L (3), 80f; Sayles, 194; B (1), 34f; B (3), 300, Dunstan; 301, cases reserved for pope. Peter's Pence is paralleled by payments from Scotland and Poland.

77. L (1), 12 f; S (15), 1.

78. L (1), 15; Ely, 18; East Anglia, 19; also Danby (3).

79. Plots in rotation, so that each man shared good and bad; same strips were kept normally year after year. In open fields of Mercia and central Wessex the typical family-holding was a virgate or yardland (nominally 30 acres: called after measurement unit for the strip-width, landyard or rod, 15 to 21 feet). But generally the unit was the area that could be worked by the plough team: different terms in different regions. B (1). 17f; S (5), 467, 309f; Ine, 64–6; Lipson (1) & (2) etc. F (1), 181–5; Maitland, 478–80. Teams: L (4); F (5).

80. H. Hall, 36. Cattle and fodder: Curwen, 83f.

81. Kent: B (1), 17f. Mercia and Shropshire: F (1), 66–82, esp. 77f. Welshry: Randall.

82. Carsten. Duly (4) for increased productivity. Flanders: Pirenne (4), i, 149ff; Bloch (9); *Cart. Dunois de Marmoutier*; Green, 58f.

83. LW (1), 143f, 152f for refs, and (3), ch. 2., ii; Criticism: Hilton (10) and Sawyer (4).

84. LW (3), ch. 2, ii. *Hames* Haudricourt.

85. LW (3), 63. Above here ch. 2, n27, and Ross 20.

86. Bloch (5), 545; LW (1), 155 and (3), ch. 2, i; Gille (1), 2f; Hodgen; Latouche (1), 313; L(1), 278–80; MA, ii, 1958, 154 (with three wheels at Old Windsor, 9th c.). Tamworth: Hammond.

87. LW (3), ch. 2, i; Delisle; Lees 131, 135; H. Salter no 692; Ambroise, *L'Estoire de la guerre sainte*, ed. G. Paris, 1897, 3227–9. Pope: P. Jaffré, *Regesta* 1888 no 17. Normandy: Delisle (6), 406; Gille (1) and (2) ii, 1951, 34.

88. LW (3), 63f; S (2), fig. 12 & pp. 11, 33. Gerona date: LW (3), 63; Ord., HE, ix, 3 (iii p. 471); Sarton, i, 758 and ii, 696. Kiev: LW (3), 63; Novgorod (12th) c.), PP, v, 1954, 5. *Liber Niger*: Trow-Smith (2), 91. 1167: A. L. Poole (3), 52. Smithfield: W. Fitzstephen (1), 574. Durham: Greenwell, 8, 9, 17. *Records of Templars in England: Inquest of 1185*, ii, 1935, 8, and p. cxviii. Bury: R. H. C. Davis (4), 119, 127f. Ramsey: Raftis, 314. 13th c., Richardson (5), 288.

89. LW's theory cannot stand up against Hilton (19), but he has much useful information, which needs to be sorted and tested.

90. Asser, ch. 91; Tait, 15f, 19, n1; Lobel. Burghal hidage: Robertson (2), 246–9.
91. Hassall Oxford: *VCH Berks*, ii, 1906, 313, 337; Jope (8th c. monastery founded by St Frideswide, with traders coming to gates) etc. Burhs: R. A. Brown (1), 140; Armitage (1) 22; Birch, ii, 222. Pevensey: Rigold in MA, xiii, 294.
92. B (1), 24–6.
93. Loyn (3), 72. Reforms: Metcalf (2), 153; *Fornvannen*, 1915, 53–116, 189, 246. Number of coins: Metcalf (1); C. S. S. Lyon; Sellwood. Viking hoards: Metcalf (1), 479f; hoard in Sicily, Dolley (2).
94. *Historians of the Church of York*, (RS), i, 454.
95. S (1), 15.
96. *Ib.*, 16.
97. 13–5. Portsoken: the ward had a unique position, the lord of the soke being *ex officio* alderman: S (1), 12; H. W. C. Davis, *Essays . . . to T. F. Tout*, 48. Four benches: Round, EHR, x, 732
98. W (4), 82. Urki: S (4), 122; Thorpe, *Diplomaterium*, 605–8. Exeter may go back to Athelstan: B (2), 197, n1.
99. B (2) 196–8.
100. Fifth part of Cambridge alms to Ely. Women: name Atheleove (Woodbury I) may be feminine; Godgith (Exmouth) could be either sex.
101. Phillpotts, 125–34: C. Harm, *Vermischte Aufsätze*, 1833, 75, 77.

CHAPTER VIII
THE CONQUEST

1. Tales of early quarrels between Harold and Tostig (plus prophecies by Edward) seem to have been inventions after the event.
2. *Vita Aed*, 31f, 37f.
3. W (1), 33. We have no reliable testimony as to what Harold did swear.
4. Foreville (2), 232. *Gregarii*: Guilhiermoz, 145–7, 336–41.
5. Bridgenorth: Ord., iv, 175. Haimo: W. of P., 216ff; Ord., ii, 187; Prestwich (1), 25f.
6. W of M., iii, year 1060; Pidal, 271; Wace, 131, 49–55. Omens: W. of M. on William slipping as he lands, cf. Caesar and Rollo etc. Further: Dodswell, 558, for omens in Tapestry and *chansons*.
7. Pidal, 340–3; Frappier, 160, 185; Bédier, ii, 432; *Chanson de Roland*, 1093. *Chanson de R*: D (15), 97–100.
8. Dodswell, 559; Warnke for AS origin, pp. xlvi–vii, 327f.
9. Phillpotts, 198–200; *Roland esp.* 3905f; Girard 53; *Renaus de Montauban*, 16f, 30; *Chev. Ogier*, 388f.
10. W. of P., 222; Loyn (3), 51.
11. Musset (3), 294. A writ issued before 1069 is to 'Normans, Flemish, and English'; Bretons not mentioned.
12. Wace, 8689ff.
13. W. of M., ii, 478; Wace, 6271ff; Haskins (7), 11; Wace, 6305. Wace says that Harold cries at Hastings, *'li quens di Flandres m'a trahi'*, 797ff. Tostig probably passed through Flanders *c.* 1061 in pilgrimage.
14. Ord., Marx 192; Brown (2), 82, n5.
15. Loyn (3), 90; an Irish (Norse) king also killed.

R

16. Giles (2), 127f; Round (2), 331. He is called kinsman of both William and Edward.
17. *Chron.* D & E.
18. Li, i, 603; Dutaillis, ii, 176; H (2), 218, n2. Men with sticks and clubs are not angry peasants roused by the harrying (S, (5), 575), but are poorly armed soldiers under Harold (W. of P.). For early date of *Carmen*: C. Morton.
19. S (2), 176; Drögereit, 283f.
20. H (2), 219. W. of M. (near end of II) as against W. of P., who says Harold had large levies from all over England plus Danish auxiliaries. Levies: S (5), 575, and (4) 116f; Maitland, 156ff; Glover, 10, n1. Tactics: D (15), 79.
21. Glover, 6f; Chambers (1), 303–5; Freeman, iii, (2nd ed.), 370, n2. Battle: Lemmon (1), and (2).
22. Freeman, ii, 389, n1; Stubbs (2), 279; Larsen (1), opp. 88.
23. B (4), 85.
24. W. of P. 238. Ord. on castles: Le P., ii, 184; Chibnall, 218f.
25. H (2), 251, 255. Tinchebrai: H. W. C. Davis (3) with EHR., xxv, 1910, 295f.
26. H. of H., vi, near end; Coulton (4), 23.
27. B (4), 108f; W. of M., ii, 320; *Vita Wulf.*, 55; Florence, ii, 18; *Chron. Abingdon*, ii, 11; H. of H., of H., 207; C. Verlinden, 110; S (5), 608f, and (4), 149–51 and 150, note citing Aegelnoth.

CHAPTER IX
WILLIAM RUFUS TO HENRY II

1. Accounts of death by monk of Caen and by Ord.; William's ashes were scattered in religious wars of 16th c.; a thighbone survived till French Revolution.
2. H (2), 219f, 61.
3. Stephen of Blois could compare William's bounty only with that of the Byzantine emperor.
4. Rufus may have been too easy to magnates who helped him to power, e.g. the Clares: Southern (5), 117. Magnates and monasteries: DB, i, 120b (Exeter church), Sym of Durham, ii, 231; *History of Abingdon*, (RS), ii, 43.
5. Ord. says Ranulf was from the Vessin. Treasury: Li. (2), 153. Abacus: Haskins (8), 105f; Yeldham, chs. 3 & 5. 1198: Wightman, 226. Hindu Arabic numerals not popularized till late 12th c. Needham (3), iii,, 15, 146; E. G. R. Taylor, *J. Institute Navigation*, 1960, xiii 1. Roll of N. Exchequer, 1198, shows lands of a single lord in both Normandy and England treated as owning an essential unity.
6. H (2), 232 and (1) 43f; Flor., ii, 35; H. of H., 217; *Chron.*, year 1094; DB, i,56b – cf. John, 1201 & 1205: Roger of Howden, *Chronica*, iv, 163; Ralph de Coggeshall, *Chron. Angl.*, 153.
7. McIlwain. After Henry II, neither Richard nor John issued such a charter; Henry III returned to the traditional coronation oath of English kings. Richardson (3); Schramm; Legg; Taylor; Ward; and *Bull. Instit. Hist. Research*, xiii 124–45, xiv 1–9, 145–8, xv 94–9, xvi 1–11. For law under William: Sayles, 235–8.

8. W. of M., V, year 1119; H. of H., beginning VIII. Suger (2), iv, 308.
W. of M. mentions a chamberlain of a 'plebeian father', keeper of
the treasures, who conspired, confessed, was blinded and castrated.

9. B (1), 176 (? Ranulf in secret agreement with Henry). Treaty of Dover:
Ganshof (8), for details, e.g. French king, 249; Henry's obligations, 251;
the earlier treaty, 250. Robert of Bellême: W. of M. year 1102.

10. Stubbs (1), 118f; Ord., iv, 1764, 173f; Flor., ii, 49 (gregarii), Harvey (1),
26f; Hoyt (1), 53; Eadmer, ch. 172.

11. H (2), 185f; Prestwich (1), 37–42. Henry II also tried to crown his son
while he himself was still alive; no one tried again.

12. H (2), 92ff, 206, 68; Joliffe (1), 156ff. Also H (2), 250–4, and Round (5),
380; date prob. between Dec. 1148 and Dec. 1153. Perhaps about this
time the English term of two months' service was reduced to the forty
days usual in Normandy and on the continent.

13. Sayles (1), 342f; ch. xxi for summary.

CHAPTER X
MORE ON THE NORMANS IN THE SOUTH

1. Grégoire (1); Dante, Paradiso, xviii, 46–8. Anna Comnena and tale of
Jerusalem, Holingshed has the same of Henry IV in 1413: Norwich (1),
745f. Chanson de Roland: D (15), 98f; Pidal, 269–470, 500f; Bédier, iii,
183–455; W. T. Holmes: D (17). Varangians: Bréhier; Vasiliev; Anna
Comnena, viii, i; x, 3; ii, 9; A. S. S. Bull., May 6, 406, etc.

2. D (15), 104–9. Yet Roger entered Sicily as ally of Moslem emir of
Syracuse; he made a solemn treaty to their mutual advantage against
the Sultan of Mehden who was trying to regain Sicily, etc.

3. Eadmer, ch. 97f. Abolition of feud rights in S. Italy: Norwich (1),
321.

4. Legge (1), 85–96; Eadmer, chs. 179–81. The master had grown up
at Bec 'to man's estate' under Anselm. Ipomedon appears in the alliterate
poem, The Parlement of the Thre Ages; see also Kölbing.

5. Chalandon, i, 146; Ménager, Quellen u. Forsch., xxxix, 39 and Messina,
306.

6. D (15), 171, 182, 179 for refs.

7. D (15), 173, 180 for refs.

8. Jamison, 40ff; Chalandon, ii, 644–50 and i, 348.

9. Chalandon, ii, 530; Cusa, ii, 541; Garufi, 21–3 and 7; Ménager, Messina;
33, Cahen, 36.

10. D (15), 180 for refs; 177; 181f.

11. Runciman, i, 153f. In 1149 Roger II of Sicily convinced Louis of France
that a crusade should be launched against Byzantion; St Bernard agreed,
but Conrad of Germany obstructed. For Edgar; Runciman, 227f, 255.

12. Feudal incidents earlier in England than in Italy, Sicily, or Antioch.

13. For Jerusalem: Runciman, ii, book 4, ch. 1; Munro; The Kingdoms of
the Crusades. M. Grandclaude, Mélanges P. Fournier, 1929; La Monte;
Riant; Prawer.

CHAPTER XI

TENURES, FIEFS AND MILITARY ORGANIZATION

1. *Acta Sanct.*, May, IV, 1688, 410.
2. J. W. F. Hill, 48; Finn, 32. In general S (9); Loyn (1), 316f. Aelfwine: *VCH Hereford*, i, 275. London: D (17), 62f; Eadmoth, Loyn (3), 172. From about 1179 thegns and drengs are subject to incidents of feudal type and the trend to commutation: Harvey, 28.
3. Finn, 33; DB, 199bi, 196b2. Finn, 33–5 for Ely; for DB as accepting usurpations, 35f.
4. Harvey, 6, n12.
5. Loyn (3), 120f; Barlow (4), 115; D (2), ii, 22. Flemings in army 1066: Eustace of Boulogne prominent; under him was Arnold of Andres who had followed his father; later his brother Gonfrid was called in by William and rewarded with Arnold: George, 84f; MGH, xxiv, 612–5, 620; Round (1), 462ff. Later, various nobles: Gilbert of Ghent, Walter Bec, Dreux of Beuvrière, but exactly when they came is obscure. We find Gilbert in York garrison 1069. Probably Gerbod the Fleming was also there early: Freeman (2), 680; Stapledon *Arch. J.*, iii, 1846, 16ff. In 1070 William gave him the city and county of Chester, but he seems to have been so harrassed that he was glad to get back to Flanders: Ord. ii, 219; George, 87, n26. For evidence about others we must wait till 1084 and also DB: George, 85ff for details of Flemish holdings, especially of Eustace.
6. Valin, 29–33; Dudo, 250. Demesne: Hoyt, 5ff; H (2), 278.
7. Harvey, 6 nn8–10; H (2), 175, nn5–6. Fighting bishops: H. of H., year 1142.
8. Haimo: Harvey, 7f; Matthew, 108ff; G. J. Turner, ii, 462; H (2), 50. Continuity of commendation: H (2), 67f; S (18); Stephenson (6); D (6), 124–7 and app. 1 no 14. Ban: H (2), 68, n4. Heriot: H (2), 67, n2; forfeitures, 86, n2. Danegeld: Bloch, *Soc. feodale*, ii, 230.
9. Oth: Holt (3), 32, 37; S (5), 483f. The need to collect Danegeld had helped fiscal development.
10. B (4), 110f; H (2), 134, 50; D (12); *Chron. Mon. de Abingdon*, ii, 6. In 1208 Henry I gave a barony of Marshwood to the younger son of the previous holder as 'the better knight', S (3), 38.
11. Harvey, 4f, see further details 11f. Strayer, 60–3, on rise of knights in 11 c. Normandy till they witness charters; fragmentation of political power etc., with refs.
12. Joliffe (1), 77ff; H (2), 49–54, 62–6; S (4), 154; Galbraith (2); D (12), 245–7; Holt (3), 32.
13. S (4), 161f for charters under Henry II still lacking clause of warranty, and forgery adding it under Henry III. Horse: *ib.* 163f. Prestwich (1), 32; Ord., i, 325; Li., i, 554; Holt, 36, n167 (loanlands). See Holt further for the way the crisis worked out.
14. H. Hall (2), i, 413; Harvey, 9; H (2), 55. Nigel: CRR, ii, 76; Poole (2), 40; *Rot. Lit. Claus.*, i, 123a (Ramsey). Clusiacs, Cistercians, and Regular Canons of 12th c. never held by military tenure; but sub-enfeoffments, once made, stayed fast.
15. Halphen, 178ff; CRR, vi, 54; viii, 365; Poole (2), 34.
16. *Chron.* Land 1095; H (2), 172f; Knowles (2), 175.
17. H (2), 174; D (18), p. cviii.
18. Harvey, 12f; DB, ii, 372; D (8), for just who they were.

19. *Red Book*, i, 230, 442. Harvey, 15ff, for details, 18 for DB *homines*.
20. Harvey, 19f. Early Bury charter seems to refer to four types and conditions of royal and abbatial services
21. H (2), 167–90. English forces: 170, n2.
22. H (1), 16–9; Poole (2), 52. *Dextarius* in late period cost no less than 10 marks. Mercenaries used by vassals in revolt (1074–5): Lanfranc *Opera* (Giles), i, 57. Tale of Robert: H (2), 179.
23. Rufus: H (2), 180–3; Ord., iv, 172–5; Prestwich (1), 28; W. of M., GR, ii, 540, and HN (Potter) 17.
24. Eadmer, ch. 184; *Gesta Norm. Ducum*, 297; Sym. of D., ii, 281; Weaver, 18; *Chron.* 1125 (1124).
25. *Dial de Scacc.* 2; Boussard (1), 189–224; Grundmann (1); Lyon (1), 198ff; H (2), 273 n6; M. Powicke (2), 218, 223; Sanders (2), 29f; A. L. Poole (2), 52; Joliffe (3); Barrow (3), 19, Scotland; Lot (4), ii, 517ff, Europe.
26. Poole (2), 94–6; examples of £15 and £75, 95. Mesne tenant: S (4), 162f.
27. Also sergeantry-tenures: Poole (2), 97–102.
28. 11th c. knight and AS warrior of 5 hides: Glover; Denham-Young 108; H (2), 161; Harvey, 20, n64. Also H (2), 157–60, 211–3; Richardson and Sayles, 87.
29. Harvey 21; S (4), 136; Galbraith (2), 364–8, on possible link of land grants for life, Feudal grants, demesne land *de vestitu et victu*. Harvey, 22, on Knightwick and Worcester.
30. Harvey, 22–4. Money-fief: Lyon (1), 11, 99f.
31. Harvey 24f; relation of such grants to services, 25. Li, i, 634–7; *Dialogie*, 56; Tallage, etc., Harvey, 25f. Generally manor (unlike villein lands) paid little or no geld – through royal concession or the lord pushing the geld due from the manor on to villein holdings; knightly land also at first had exceptions.
32. Rates under Henry II: Harvey, 29.
33. Hoyt, 34, 13; Thorne; Colvin; Genicot (2), 16 and (3).
34. Harvey 32.
35. Prestwich (1), 21; Harvey, 32f. Fragmentation: Poole (2), 45f; CRR, vii, 156; Hatton, MS no 528 (*Book of Seals*); Dugdale, *Antiq. of Warwickshire* 467; Poole, 46; case of sharing 42–5. 'For ½ of a fief of a hauberk,' Harvey, 34. Scutage and use of mercenaries facilitated the dropping out of vavasour-knight.
36. *Dialogue*, 112, 11; Harvey, 34f, 41 (assize).
37. Harvey, 36, for details; Fines: Poole (2), 41f, 52; EHR, xxxvi, 1921 45; Morris, i; Chew, 49. Fine common after 1194; may have been used 1172.
38. H (2), 190, 192f, 15f, 212, 195 (more examples): esp. 1110 (marriage) and loan of Rufus to bro. for Crusade.
39. Distraint: M. Powicke, 457–65; H (2), 196–9, 203. Profits: Poole (2), 41. There may have been attempts, later given up, to bring fyrd soldiers under scutage: which would have been profitable to tenants-in-chief and might have happened in later 11th c. when conditions of subinfeudations were still blurred. Scutage was late in establishing itself in the marches.
40. Barons seek to escape all military commitments. Poole (2), 41–3; Harvey, 42; H (2), 207ff, 108f, 215; Chew (2) and (3). By 1180 the crown gave up trying to get scutage on new enfeoffments uncovered in 1166. Occasionally a lord increased a tenant's fee from his own land: S (4), 159.
41. Raftis, 56–85.
42. H (2), 157, 212–5.

43. Stubbs, 255; Roger of Hov., iii, 265.
44. Poole (4); T. Rogers, i, 342ff; Gras (2), 186ff; Beveridge, 163. Prices vary for young cattle and pigs; goats at 8d (1185), 6d (1186, 1188, 1195), broodmares 3s 6d (1184, 1195), 4s (1196), hives of bees 8d (1166, 1172), 1s (1167, 1195, 1196).
45. Chew, 89f; Denholm-Young (1), 114f; Smail, 106f (horse).
46. Chew; Denholm-Young l.c. Inflation: Farmer. Rise of money economy: Postan (5). Population: Duby (5), 120; W.C. Robinson; Hollingworth 113f, 117–9. 129, 375–88; Postan (7).
47. H (2), 181, n3, 186–90; Hilton (1), 15f. Rise in costs in 13th c.; Denholm-Young. Population figures are largely conjectural but give some relative idea.
48. Poole (3), 401–12; Harvey, 41, n170. 1181: M. Powicke, 459, 465. H (2), 273, 258–60; Postan (5), 130.
49. Poole (2), 53–6: buzones, 56. Also EHR, xvii, 1932, 177, 545. By 14th c. we meet liveried retainers, though the idea of liveries goes back a century or so: 1218, a north-country robber buys 100 marks' worth of cloth to clothe his fifteen men 'as if he had been a baron or an earl'. Eyre of York, (Seldon Soc.) 424; but Cambridge Parliament 1388 is first to legislate on subject: Cam (1), 213.
50. Harvey, 42f.
51. PL, cxcix, 600, cf. Piers Plowman B Prol., 112ff; vi, 25ff; Peter, Epistolae, xciv; Coulton (4), 281f.
52. Denholm-Young (1), 113f.
53. Juvenes: Duby (3) Tournaments: Painter (6); P. Meyer, lines 2471–5094; Denholm-Young (2); Green 306; B (1), 255f, 320; D. M. Stenton, 78ff; Gautier, 681, 683 (popes); Cooper in Henry III's prohibitions (1234, 1236, 1251) at Cambridge.
54. H (2), ch. iv; arrière ban 77, 230. Inquest of Bayeux 1133. The ban embraced all free tenants but laid trees on more prosperous land owners, i.e. holders of knights' fees and vavasours with estates of more than 50 acres. Length of service: H (2), 89ff; Poole (2), 38–40; Chew (1), 4f. 1130: H (2), 92. Anselm's poor soldiers: Eadmer, ch. 78. Skilled English knights: H. of H., 263. More on ban: Verbruggen, 264; Ord., iii, 415; Boutaric, 198ff.
55. H (2), 100ff, later examples of more than forty days; contracts 102ff; duty of rear vassal 109f; details 111ff, 116ff. Church barons seem normally to pay scutage and not go overseas.
56. Poole (2), 61f; Book of Fees pp. 1278, 1202; Cal. Inq. Misc., i, no 501.
57. Translation of serviens: H (2), 130f. AS links, 132.
58. H (2), 128, nn1–2; Poole (2), 37; Smail (2), 140f.
59. Infantry: Verbruggen, 110f, 250ff, 281–4, 291ff, 298ff; H (2), 218f; policing, example at Yarmouth 1104–7: H (2), 229. 1072: Chron., 1075; Clor., ii, 11; Lanfranc, Op., i, 56.. 1088: H (2), 223f; Chron., 1087 (8); Flor., ii, 22f; W. of M., ii, 362; Steenstrup, iv, 27; Larson (2), 160, 165f; join rebels, Flor., ii, 24f; Ord., iii, 271. Select fyrd: H (2), 217, 224, 248ff; definition, 14f.
60. H (2), 227f, 230, 234–40, 246. Esp.: Richard of Hexham, Historia, iii, 161; Aelred, Relation, iii, 192. I accept Hollister's differentiation of general and select fyrds though we must not think of precise definitions at the time; rather of practical modifications of a general principle according to circumstances.

61. H (2), 236ff (Peterborough etc.), 246f, 2of; D (10), p. lxxxix; F (4), 62f; S (3), 237; H (1), 478, 481. Scotland saw a similar process. Before 1066 the typical 5-hide warrior was a thegn: H (1), Hollings.

62. H (2), 260, 258f (assize): note identity of arms in first and second, showing the process that broke down the system of private feudal tenures; we noted 13th c. efforts of crown to force all tenants with land of certain value (generally £20) to become knights: Poole (2), 35f.

63. Hope-Taylor (1); M. W. Thompson (1) and (2); *Antiq. J.*, xxxix, 1959, 219–73; Davison (1); Bloch. *Feudal Soc.*, 301, 'While masonry work called for specialist workers, the tenants, a permanent source of compulsory labour, were almost all to some extent carpenters as well as wood-cutters.' Round and Armitage stress the communal aspect of the *burh* against G. T. Clark who saw *burhs* as mottes. Native chiefs in west parts of the British Isles fortified residences long before the Ns. The Rhineland shows how motte and bailey castle might some times get final form as the end of long process of structural alterations: Herrnbrodt and Müller-Wille. In Ireland, the motte might be built astride or inside an earlier enclosure that then became the bailey: *Ulster J. of Arch.*, xx, 1959, xxvi, 1963. Castle Neroche, Somerset, has a motte added to previous structure: MA, viii, 258, vi–vii, 323. The Motte at S. Mimms is designed to prop up a great timber tower: suggests development from motte tower to tower keep. Penmaen: Davison, 207; also timber gate-houses known in 10th c. and early 11th c. on the continent; timber-towers may have been a common accompaniment of earthwork fortifications c. 1066.

We know the names of some military architects, for they appear in accounts. They were strictly designers of military engines and of the defence-works to withstand them. Ailnoth, *ingeniator*, appears as surveyor of the king's buildings at Westminster and the Tower in 1157: eighteen years before William of Sens turned up at Canterbury, the first cathedral-builder in England who is more than a name. Ailnoth, whose name sounds English, built, embellished, and demolished castles in the 1160–70s. Gandolf built Rochester Keep. Other architects, one called *prudens architectus*, appear after that in the service of the king or the magnates. A few scholars knew the work of Vitruvius from the ancient world; but the builders were not affected. Their notions of proportion and structure came from other spheres, partly from the whole traditional world of craft, with a steady movement into a fuller grasp of the relevant construction problems, and partly from the general cultural situation which was absorbed in a hundred ways and which affected them through the attitudes of patrons. But the exact way in which ideas and methods were developed and sifted out is lost to us.

64. *Chron.*, 1066, 1086–7, 1067 (8), 1092, 1097, 1114; Flor., ii, 2; H. of H., 230; Ord., ii, 153, 166f, 179–81, 182–4, 198f; Sym. of D., ii, 199f; *Brut Y Tywysogion*, 54f, 6of, 82; H (2), 137f. Poitou: Painter (3), 23ff, 127; H (2), 138, n1. Matilda: *Gesta Stephani* (Potter), 92; S (4), 203, the castle on the church must be a watch-tower. List of *burhs*: Brooks; D. Hill. See H. L. Turner, *Town Defences in England and Wales* (1973) pre-Conquest system of defences in form of tenurial responsibility lasted through 12th c; murage grants, 32ff. Also Renn.

Note the origin of Russian towns in 11th–13th cs. as 'a feudal castle, the medieval West-European burg, and not a stone castle . . . but a wooden one situated on a high bank. Inside were the prince, his *druzhina*, and the tribal elders.' S. Y. Yushkov, *Essays on the History of Feudalism in Kiev Rus (in Russian,)* 1939, 20–4; Tikhomirov, 57f, adding how important the urban *posads* were.

65. Castle at peace: S (4), 160f; building of castle wall for confirmation of hereditary fee from new lord. Castles in general. Painter, W. Anderson; Pryce; R. A. Brown; H. Brown; etc. N (2), 139; relation to Normandy, 140f; scutage, 152; host service, 144–6; relation of castleguard to training (? forty days). S (4), 170–7, 192–5, 205–16; Round (4) and (10). Barons under John: H (2), 149; garrison sergeants S (4), 207 and app. no 43; tenants, 209. Castle service in military tenures quickly decayed.

66. North frontier of old Mercia: Loyn (3), 123; S (4), 195ff, scattered holdings 64–6, 97–101. Commutation: Poole (2), 49; H (2), 149–61.

67. Swein: Ord., ii, 191. In general: Beeler (1), 590–601; H (2), 161–6; Powicke (2), 196–8; R. A. Brown (2), 192; Harvey, 3; Painter (3), 127f, 133f.

68. Duby (3).

CHAPTER XII
STATE AND CHURCH

1. Finn (3), 33; Baker, 169–71; *Liber Eliensis*, i, 267–9; Sayles (1), 235–30, 248, 182.

2. L (1), 145; Barlow (1), 191.

3. Cam (3), 188–94 and (1) 60, 65.

4. Baker, 175.

5. L (1) 266f. Under English kings: W (1), 65, 85, 99, 91, 103, 208, 172. D. M. Stenton: forests 98–110, 116. Old *loan* leases still used in dioceses. King as god: D (2), 154, 249f, 261f; D (15), 106–8, 167f; Kantorowicz, 61–78; H. Bloch.

6. B (1), 131f.

7. Richardson (6), 9, 11–3; (7).

8. B (1), 189; Sayles (1), 172–9; Richardson (6), 11, end of office of Justiciar in relation to advent of Parliament. For detailed analysis of *Court. D. R.*, see Richardson (8); increase under Henry I, 601f; tendency to specialize, 604.

9. R. A. Brown (4), 55 and n195, note Hugh de Segillo.

10. Haskins (6), 648–51; *duana*, 652–5; N. elements in S. Italian feudalism, 661f; Brown and others, 438ff.

11. S (5), 503, 642–4.

12. B (4), 131. Perhaps under Lanfranc there begins a sort of division of church from state business; at Christmas court 1085, when DB decided, the prelates held a more private meeting for three days.

13. Harvey, 15, for knights.

14. J. P. C. Kent, 193f, in *Essays on Roman Coinage*, ed. R. A. G. Carson and Sutherland, 1956. Leontius: *Vita S. John. Eleem.*, 41. *Descriptio* used in Merovingian and Carolingian times for assessment and enrolment for public taxation; also in relation to tax collection: Ducange; Dopsch 292, 377; Ralph of Diceto on 1173. *Descriptio generalis* by royal exactors to supply army: Prestwich (1), 26. In general: Darby; Finn; Galbraith (6); Dove etc.

15. M. Bloch (3), 59–61; DB, ii, folio 290, 30v.

16. Poole (2), 88f.

17. Poole (2), 83f; EHR, 1901, xvi, 730; Baker, 176; Green, 227, 230–2.

18. Lanfranc used forged papal documents; the discovery of their character in 1125 helped to get the decision reversed. William did appoint some men of high standing to sees (Osmund, Robert Losinga, Gundolf).

19. Several unions of sees despite denunciations of simony; Herbert of Losinga; Source of Simony; W. of M., iv, 1, year 1100; M. D. Anderson, 36f.

20. Eadmer, chs. 149–5, for the measures at 1102 Council under Anselm. Failure of steps against marriage: L (1), 332. D (15), 167f.

21. B (4), 156f.

22. Baker, 209f.

23. Eadmer, chs. 26f, cf. 74f, 49f, 186 (Henry II). Anger: P. L., ccvii, 978.

24. Southern (2), 213f. Henry of Blois: C. Brooke (1), 148f. Some works of art survive, e.g. books: St Swithin psalter and Winchester bible.

25. Morrison (2); B (4) 140, disputes on boundaries.

26. Ailred: Waites. Eadmer, ch. 15, on Rochester. No monasteries north of Trent though a college of clerics guarded the bones of St Cuthbert at Durham. North: Baker, 204f. Work: Coulton (6), 78–81. Before Lanfranc's death the number of monks doubled: from one or two dozen in a house to sixty or even a hundred; the land that the barons had taken was made up for by new grants.

27. Eadmer, ch. 19.

28. Knowles (2); Galbraith (3); Waites monastery lay-out, no fixed system. Knowles (1), 181.

29. Knowles in his various books; D. Seward, *The Monks of War*.

30. Baths: Green, 19–24, also diseases; R. Willis, 159; St John Hope. Kings: G. H. White, 147; Tout (4), 84 n; Cheney, 166f. Towns: Sulzman, 273; Thrupp, 167; G. A. Williams, 85; John D. M. Stenton, 25f; Hardy (2), 115, 137, 170, 159, 120; H. Cole, 231–69.

31. B (1), 132; *Chron.* 1087. Often in monasteries on account of the dates. For seal-tags and tablet-woven braids: Henshall. Clerks: Peter of Blois, letters 14, 150; Girald Lamb, *De jure et statu Menev. Eccl* (*Opera*, iii, 302); Cartul, *Rievallense*, 66 (Sutees Soc.).

32. PL, cliii, 200. Cistercians: Hartridge, 16f, Whitby, 18f. Darley: BM, MSS. Cotton Titus, cix, 132 (fol. 154). 1102: Wilkins *Concilia*, i, 383, 22; Pope Alexander; Hartridge 19f. John of Salisbury: PL, cxlix, 678.

33. Hartridge, 20f. Already 1175 in a provincial enactment is a ref. to a perpetual vicar. Struggles: Hartridge, 27f, 40f. Tithes to monasteries, L(1), 316f; incumbents, 317–9. Ministers: L(1), 300f; S(5), 156.

34. L (2). *Hospites*: Delisle (4), 12; Latouche (1), 317, 252 etc.

35. L (1), ch. x, 68; Boehmer.

36. L (1); free land in East Anglia, 323f; *pro elemosina*, 324–7; priests with courier service, 331. Aisculf: *Hist. Coll. for Staffs*, 1916, Survey A, 222f.

37. Owst, 8, 20, 48–51; Wilkins, *Concilia*, ii, 1737, 54. Coulton (4), 264. Priests in 1102 told not to booze or drink by the peg; St Dunstan was said to have introduced pegs into drinking cups so that when the cup went round a man might tell when he had drunk his share: Stubbs (3), 24f; W. of M., i, 166.

38. Farrer, i, no 1233; iii, no 1895.

39. L (1), 334f; *Vita*, I, i, 4 (written within thirty years of death).

40. Clark, 9. Plays: Darwin, 12. False ancre: *ib.* 27f. *Ancren Riwle*: Arch. J., xi, 1854, 53. Gossip: Ailred: Darwin 22f; servants 13f. For Scilly hermit and saga-relations: *Arch. J.* cxxi for 1964, 40–69.

41. Southern (2), 215f; Talbot.
42. Eader, ch. 135; Peter, *Sent*, lv, xxvi, 6, 7; xxvii, 2, 3; xxviii, 2; Green, 183; Le Bras (2).

CHAPTER XIII
COUNTRY, TOWN, TRADE

1. L (1), 373f.
2. L (1), 230f, 236, 210–2. Monks: Prestwich, (1) 35, n 1. Some sokes seem to have come about, or to have fallen under a lord, through a royal grant of a wapentake and its courts, or of the king's rights over all the unattached free men in a given wapentake. But many sokemen seem to have been dependent on a lord through having commended themselves and thus been brought under the manor where the lord exercised his rights. (Farm at Wicken Bonhant, Essex, c. 800; more than a dozen rectangular buildings, 2 walls; a later Saxon-Norman hall. *Times*, 22 Nov. 1972.)
3. Sayles, 244–7; L (1), ch. IX; peasant obligations, 368f.
4. Instability of prices with local variations in markets helped to weaken value of slavework. By the 13th c. the shift from services to wages. Loyn (1), 326; Round, VCH Essex, i, 360f; Sayles, 241.
5. W. of M., III, xiii; Greg., *Registrum Epist.*, v. 59 (*MGH epist*. i. 371); O. Lottin, 206; Green, 34.
6. Aquinas: ST, I, ii, 94, 5, iii; Gratian, *decret.*, xii, 2, 39; PL, xcix, 913c; Coulton (4), 377ff; Eadmer, ch. 143; Barlow (1), 14–6, 20f, 120f, 438; S (5), 310, 469, 472, 507 (Danelaw).
7. L (1), 147–59. Firmarius could utilize far more than customary services, 197.
8. L (1), 195, 197–9, monasteries, 207–9.
9. L (1), ch. viii. *Liber homo*, 225f. Slump: Postan (5); Prestwich (1), 21 f. (I owe much to Lennard and Hallam for this chapter.)
10. Hallam 119–21; tides 124ff.
11. *Ib.*, 132ff; royal interference in 1253, 135; field systems, ch. vii.
12. *Ib.*, 166, 222; division 167, 169, fen-reeves 168.
13. *Ib.*, 201ff for figures.
14. *Ib.*, 207–9, 215 villein holdings, 217.
15. *Ib.*, 220–2.
16. Steele, 105–7.
17. B (1), 276f. Children drink the whey. Crops: Hilton (16), 98f.
18. L (1), 260–5, 266f. Largest number of cows in Exon. DB at Stafort in Dorset. Horses: Hilton (10), 99f; L (5), 201; Gaydon, p. xxviii (Beds).
19. L (1), 242–8 and 248–52. Hodgen, 266. Oxen: *Hist. Mon. de Abingdon*, ii, 150; Sym. of D., ii, 356f and 260. In general: D. M. Stenton, 253–7.
20. Clay, vii, 55f (no 4), cf. *Reg. Worcester priory* (Camden Soc. 1865), 32a; L (1), 281; DB has 5624 for some 3000 communities, but there were probably more mills: B: Gille in Daumas, i, 467f; LW (3), 83f; L (1), 282–7.
21. *VCH Derbyshire*, i, 316; Pipe Roll of 1130; L (1), 241f. At Green's Norton (Northants) smiths under Edward rendered £7 out of a manor-value of £12. Blast furnaces in 13th c. at Liège and Styria; papermill at Jativa, Spain, and Fabriano, Italy, in 13th c.; at Troyes 1338; Nuremberg 1390.

22. B (1), 121; Vinagradoff (3), 21f; A. R. Lewis, 467–72; Prestwich (1), 20f; Postan (5) – expansion from 1180; Sayles, 185–7. Note pattern of hill-top villages (B. Cunliffe, *Med. Arch.* xvi 1–12, Hants: 35–450 large nucleated settlements, 450–900, villages, often hilltop, 900–1100 shift of population (often in valley bottoms) with some original villages still occupied; 1100–1400 expansion of village-lands with new farms in later years colonising waste.
23. Coulton (6), 53–5 and (4),, 513; M. Bateson (3), 41 (commission of 1253). The earl is Robert I (d. 1118). Rules of ordeal, Pollock (1), ii, ch. 9, par. 4.
24. S (1), 10, 7, n 1; Stubbs, 991; Li., i, 48; Tait, *Hist.*, xiii, 279f; W. of P. (Giles), 147. The dual terms in William's speech show that he addressed both bishop and citizens.
25. Stubbs; GR (RS), 1889, ii, 576.
26. Round (5), 116; S (1), 23f.
27. EHR, xvii, 720 (Bateson); S (1), 23f.
28. Beresford, charters 209f.
29. Coulton (4), 514f; C. Gross 33, 36.
30. EHR, xvii, 499; pottery found at Dowgate, MA, iii, 1959, 77.
31. Herteig, for settlements and wharves.
32. Round (7), nos 109, 1375, 1352. A hythe for ships above bridge. Embargoes: Prestwich (1), 31f; Pipe Roll, 3, Henry I, 77; Pirenne (1), 152; W. of M., GP, 191, 308; Prestwich (1), 35f. Travelling artisans etc.: Haskins (1), 198f; Pirenne (4), 333; Müller, 493, 557.
33. S (1), 21f, 19–22.
34. Vogel (2); Pirenne (3), 504–6.
35. C. A. J. Armstrong in R. W. Hunt, esp. 444–54.
36. Haskins (1), 95; Leach, 89–95; Ord., ii, 89–91; Matt., *Paris Chron. Maj.*; St Nicholas, A.K., Porter nos 224f, and Coffman. Cathedral schools: Haskins (1), 96f.
37. Foreign relations, Henry II: Stubbs (5), chs. 6f and intro. to Roger of Hov., ii, p. xcii; Haskins (3); Porter.
38. Urry, 136f; *Acta Sanct.*, May IV, 401f; *Vita S. Wulf.*, ii, 19 (ii 20); see *Vita* for other rivalries with saints. Lundy, p. li of Miracles. Wales: Y Cymm., xi, 128; Charles 26–9, 52ff. Wrecks: Plunknett, 136f; *Chron. Monast. de Bello*, 66; Prestwich (1), 36.
39. Green, 80–2; PL, xxv, 176; Hrab. Maur. cviii, 934; cxcviii, 1256.
40. GR, iv, 317; Sayles (3), iii, cxv. Coulton (10), 348. Heresy: Matt. *Paris Chr. Maj.*, iii, 520; *Acta Sanct.*, xxiv, 309 and xxviii, 442; Auvray, no 392; Haskins (1), 199. Inquisition: Coulton (12); Turbeville; Ullmann; Guirard; Maissoneuve.
41. J. Jacobs. Jurnet: Adler, 23f; Richardson (2), 32–4; W. Rye, 338f; Pipe Roll, 33, Henry II, 44; 2, Richard I, 94; Issac, W. Cade, and Sheriff William of Chesnay: Richardson (5), 609f.
42. Richardson (2), 50–66; Roth 14f, 17; M. D. Anderson (2), 53f.
43. Richardson (2), 135ff and (5); Cramer.
44. Blumenkranz; W. of M., IV, i, year 1096; Eadmer, chs. 100f.
45. Jenkinson (2); Richardson (8) 605ff, his holding of the farm at Dover.
46. LW (3), 83, 89, also Carus-Wilson (3) for haubergier cloth, and (2) in general; L (6).
47. LW (3), 89; Carus-Wilson (2); L (7); Hocking.
48. Southern (2), 209f; Darlington (2); Crombie, i, 10, 19–24, 26f. Lanfranc: Powicke (8), 27–48.

Further note on Norsemen and the Heavy Plough. A key implement in bringing about the agricultural advances on which the medieval west reposed was a new kind of plough, a wheeled plough with mouldboard. Plinius shows that wheeled ploughs, doubtless Celtic in origin, were known in the Po valley in his time; but the new implement had many important new features. It could move easily from field to field, and was made of three main elements (coulter fixed to beam, which struck vertically into the earth; flat share, perpendicular to coulter, which cut through roots; mouldboard turning soil to left or right and driving a furrow that allowed drainage and could free mineral substances in the undersoil). This plough begot the long field (contrasted with the square field which comes from cross-ploughing with a lighter plough). It could work rich alluvial soils, and needed greater traction-power: yokes of four pairs of oxen, not a pair. So peasants had to pool their oxen and the long strip led to cooperative methods and the openfield system.

Where did the new plough originate? Already in the last century B.C. the Belgic tribesmen had a plough turning the furrow-slice to the right, so that the farmer ploughed in 'lands' or ridges. The origins perhaps go further back to the struggles of farmers on the north German plain, when the change from a dry sub-boreal phase to a wet cold sub-Atlantic one came about, with a lessening of available open ground and an increase of heather: see Curwen, 66f; Hilton (10); Payne, 97; Haudricourt (2).

Attempts have been made to trace the advent of the plough proper by taking *aratrum* and *carruca* as scratch-plough and heavy plough – which they are not. Nor can we take O.E. *sulh* as scratch-plough with small team; for Kentish *sulung*, derived from *sulh*, meant a unit for ploughing subdivided into four yokes, each of two oxen. The origin of our plough is unsure. Latin *plovum* appears among Lombards in N. Italy in 643; in England *ploh* is not found before 1100, certainly derived from O. Norse *plogr*. Slavs had twenty-six terms, with key-word *plug*, which is not Slavonic, Germanic, Celtic or Roman; the Slavs got their word-complex by the end of 6th c. (before their dispersal): LW (3), 49ff.

It has been suggested that the openfield system did not exist in early AS times and was brought in from Scandinavia; cap. 42 of Ine's laws of late 7th c. is taken as a revision of text in Alfredian rescension. But no, the laws not only mention strips and common pasture, but also refer to mixed ownership of parcels in arable and meadow, and to the joint responsibility of villagers for fencing crops to keep animals out till harvest: a matter often dealt with in later manorial records. Also the term *yardland* proves the earlier existence of openfields. In the 7th c. 'the yard of land undoubtedly had its primitive meaning of a tenement formed by detaching one rood – a strip of arable one rod or *geard* in width – from every acre in a hide. The use of the term is itself proof of the existence of openfields in 7th c. Wessex' (S (5), 309; Hilton (10), 97f).

In Scandinavia the unit was the *bol*, divided into 8 *attingar*; 2 *attingar* made up a mark: typical estate of a middle peasant. They were equivalent to a pair of oxen. No texts indeed cite the *bol* before 1085, but it is claimed that traces of it appear in Norman communities towards 900. England shows no sign of the Norse system; but it is argued that the *oxgang* corresponds to it, with no relation to the *hide*, the AS basis. The Normans on arrival found a system they could recognize as akin to their own; they used the Latinized term *carruca* for the basic unit, which was divided into 8 parts or *bovates*, the latter in turn grouped to form 4 *virgates* in each carrucate. This system depended on the eight ox plough, unlike the hide: LW (3), 52ff; contrast Bouard (6) on Norman openfields in 13th c.

But in fact the virgate or yardland was a subdivision of the hide; and the hide was used in Danelaw till the start of the 11th c., and there is no evidence of ploughland as a unit in Scandinavia till the 13th c. The change in England from hide to ploughland may well be part of general reorganization under Aethelred in his last years, when the Midland shires were created: Sawyer (2), 172, also on the duodecimal system as a sign of Norse influence; Mercia: C. S. Taylor. We must then drop the thesis that the Danes brought the heavy plough and openfields into England; but they may well at an earlier date have played their part in evolving that plough. We saw how in Alfred's day the horse was being used in the far north; the Norsemen may have adopted or developed advanced methods found in the Danelaw. (Sawyer (4) demolishes LW on stirrups.)

For a ridge-and-furrow field system in Wales (Hen Domen, Montgomery-shire) see *Med. Arch.* xv, 1971. It lies round and under a castle of the Conquest period. Normally the field – outfield system was followed (with one common field permanently cultivated, and supplemented by outfields, temporary culti-vations of waste. This system operated in neighbouring Shropshire till early 13th c. But through lowland regions of central Wales some form of openfield agriculture was widespread in the Middle Ages. The hamlet linked with Hen Domen probably belong to thegns Sewar, Oslac, and Azor in 1066).

CHAPTER XIV
PORTENTS AND PROPHECIES

1. Bede, ed. Jones, 202; Bonner; Kinnard, 30f, 18f. Wulfstan sees O.T. events in terms of his own barbarian invasions.
2. Pognon; Focillon, 50; Roy, 188ff. Abbon: PL, cxxxix, 461ff. Adso in 954: Roy,186f; PL, ci 1289ff. Arnulf; Olleris; Amman, 518.
3. Glaber (year 1000 and 1032–4): Focillon, 55; Roy, 188. *Historia,* iii, 3; Pognon, 87f; Roy, 204f; PL, cxlii, 675f. Jerusalem: Roy, 180. Comet of 1022: *Rec. des hist. de Gaules et de la France,* x, letter of King Robert to half-brother, abbot of St Benoît-sur-Loire. Gerbert: Focillon, 108, 135ff. Sky-prodigies abound, eg. H. of H., for 1118; for 1132, Bagley, 39f.
4. Ritchie (2), 112, also 54, 128; Ingulph, *Chron. Croyland,* 258. Omens for 1065 in W. of M., with a symbol of England and Normandy (Siamese twins).
5. W. of M., year 1100; Higden; *Polychron.* vii 11; Ord., 102; Ritchie (2), 112; *Brut,* EETS, 1906, zu 138; Coulton (4), 275; Murray, 129; Freeman, app. SS. In 1950s occurred the outbreak of the Democratie Patavia at Milan.
6. Murray; Williamson; Dunstan prophecies, W. of M., II, xiii, under year 1065; Murray, 115. I cannot accept Murray's idea that Lucca = Loki, but the oath is an oddity. Prophecies about Edgar: Chaney, 155; Crow and Edwin, 134.
7. MS. Lamb, 51, fol. 23a; Coulton (4), 218ff.
8. General account in Cohn; Tubeville; Coulton (12); Williamson; Heaskins (1); Green 163–7. Beghards or Beguines in Germany etc.
9. B (2), 262ff; Oakley; le Bras; Fournier (2); Watkins; Fehr.
10. Brittain; Legge, 254–6, 259f. H. M. Taylor (1); R. M. Clay. For a late

growth of the local parish feast of St Giles (near Oxford) into a great popular fair: S. Alexander.

11. Bleddri: Loomis, 193–5; J. L. Weston, *From Ritual to Romance*, 1922, and Ezio Levi take the count to be W.VIII. Ailsi: Coulton (4), 218–21. *Leechbooks;* Hodgkin, ii, 466f; Cockayne; J. F. Payne: Grendon; Singer, ch. iv.

12. In general, Chaney, Murray, Chambers, *The Medieval Stage*, etc.; B (2), 141ff. Thorkill: *Chron. Ramsey*, 129–34; *Chron. Evesham*, 42. Only much later did the church feel strong enough to grapple directly with witchcraft. Stags: Chaney, 131f; Turville-Petrie (3), 2041. Owst, 336; hell mouth, Add. MSS 37049ff 17 and 74; Linc. Cath. Libr. C, 4, 6ff, 34 and 120; Owst 338ff. 'Drede': MS Roy, 18, B, xxiii, f 169. Ale-houses L (1), app. v. Will. of N. (c. 1136–1198) rejected Trojan descent of Brit.

13. W. of M., II, xiii, citing Pope Gregory's *Dialogues* for similar tales, and the end of Charles Martel who had looted monasteries to pay soldiers; following with tale of man who put a ring at Rome on a statue of Venus and fell into the goddess's power. Vision under 1065 (*Vit. Aed*, 75) another tale of a monk who tried to fly with wings and broke his leg. For effeminacy: Wulfstan, *Vita* 23. For the witch: *Alphabet of Tales* (EETS 1904), 487. Abbot Suger (Waquet, 98) said the prophecy about Henry I came true. Dreams not always taken seriously, e.g. Thomas's *Horn*, 4644–64. For a pre-1066 Latin dreambook: Harrison, 49–52. Swein, Cnut's father, was said to have been killed by St Edmund in a vision (dream): W. of M., GP, ii, 136b. Mockers: Green, 162; Berengar, *de sacra coena* (W. H. Beikenkamp, 1941); A. J. Macdonald. William of Newburgh: HRA, ed. R. Howlett (RS) 1884, 85f.

14. Southern (2), 212f; H. Farmer; Legge, 8–18.

15. Southern (2), 211f; Legge, 187–91; Kjellman.

16. See Eadmer, ch. 135; Peter *Sent*, lv, xxvi, 6, 7; xxvii, 2, 3; xxviii, 2; Green, 183; le Bras (2).

17. Legge, 42f; Love C. S. Lewis, 13ff. Troubadors: J. Lindsay (3). Women: D. M. Stenton, 151f; Coulton (4), section xii.

18. Legge (1), 7–18.

19. Frank: *Rhein. Landesmus.*, Bonn; Barraclough (3), 41.

20. Eamer, chs. 48f, 167f, 214, 143f; W. of M., GR, IV, i, year 1093; NH i, year 1128. Shoes: Ord., 682; H. of H., vii, year 120 (Arnold, 242–4); Ord., iii, 290. For 1102: Mansi, *Sacr. Concil.* coll. xx, 1152; (Nablus) xxi, 261f; Anselm, *Op.*, 169f. White Ship: also Gervase, *Chron.* (Stubbs RS), ii, 92; PL, cxlv, 159–90; Brittan (ed. F. M. Nicholls, 1865) i, 41f.

21. I am unable to treat art here; for AS churches, H. M. Taylor, Fisher etc; minor medieval sculpture, Butler; Baldwin Brown; Clapham etc.

CHAPTER XV

RESISTANCES AND RECONCILIATIONS

1. B(4), 113f; Eadmer, chs. 192, 121f.

2. Rolls of the Justices in Eyre for Warwickshire (Selden Soc., lix).

3. *Chron. Ramsey*, 212; *Cart. Ram.* ii, 62; *Chron. Abingdon*, ii, 81f; *Regesta*, ii, nos 716, 856, 1799, cf. *Leis Willelme*, c. 30. Abbey of Revesby was founded in Lincolnshire 1142; when ground was cleared, the earl gave rustici of R. and two near villages the choice of getting more land from

him or going free. Thirty-one went off, seven chose to stay on his estate with a year free from all services. (William de Roumara, earl of Lincoln, appears as an aggressive baron under Stephen.) D. M. Stenton, 148f; S (18), iv, 1–7; Waites, 651f, on depopulation. W. of P., 264. Spoliation of churches, 1170: Wilkins, *concilia*, i, 366.

4. Keen, 38. Richard I was first king after 1066 to become a popular figure. *Murdrum*: Li., i, 487; Coulton (4), 25f; Stubbs (1), 201.

5. Knowles (1), 114f; Trevisa, Higden, vii, 299; Flor., ii, 117. Turold was a warrior-abbot who led his mercenaries against Hereward (a Peterborough landholder before 1066), and it was these men who got the sixty-two fees on the abbey-lands (Walter of Whittesley in Chron. of Hugh Candidus, 84, n4). Turold built a castle near the abbey (*ib.*, 85n and 197; Mellows (2), 200); he showed no concern for abbey demesne and assumed hereditary tenure. Finn, 37f; H (2), 173, n6. W. of M., *de ant. Glast. eccl,.* in Hearne, i, 113–6. Gallery: Clapham (2), 91; Baldwin Brown, ii, 170, 147, 152.

6. *Liber confortatorius*, 77, 83; B (2), 28f; Baker, 203; B (4), 143; the exchange as showing sympathy.

7. W. of M., RG, ii, start of ch. 6, tale of Anlaf as harper. Tale of Edwin's drowning by being set afloat in a 'narrow sea' flowing between Wissant and Dover. Londoner: S (1), 10.

8. Waltheof: Ritchie (2), 111, 137f. Aethelwold: PL, cxxxvii, 102f. Dunstan was also soon treated as saint. Adelard's *Life* (1006–11) was written in the form of a series of lections, showing that the cult was celebrated liturgically by time of bishop Aelfheah: Gilbert, 205f. Cult of Edgar at Glastonbury: B (2), 28.

9. Ashdown; F. J. Child, v. 14, 21; Liestøl; den Hoed, 99–110; Freeman, iii, ch. xv, and note QQ. A 13th c. Icelander might well know of Canterbury, but could not know that at the time of DB 'a certain concubine of Herald' (sic) held house property there. Connection with Lewes seems based on confusion of names: T. W. Horsfield, *History . . . of Lewes*, 1824, 273–6. Other heroes who will return: Nero (still in medieval legend), Richard II, James II of Flodden Field, Charlemagne, Barbarossa, Henry the Fowler – merging with the Grail King, the Seven Sleepers, the Wild Hunt. Also Ogier the Dane changed into Holger Dansk, William Tell sleeping in triple form near Vierwaldstätterses.

10. Cf. with Haveloc, Hamlet in Saxon Grammaticus. For Viking relations, Legge (1), 96–107; Hall. Anglo-Norman *Horn* by a Thomas who may have had links with Poitou.

11. J. Lindsay (6), for Beowulf as a bear, Hereward: Grierson, 102; Gaimar, *Gesta Herwardi*, i, 353f; an impossible ref. to Gilbert of Ghent, 343; Smet is of little value; Round takes the whole thing as legend. For Robert: Huizinga.

12. M. Cassino: Norwich (1), 72. Warenne: Ord., ii, 221. Host at Ely: Gaimar, ii, 83ff; H (2), 116, 248, and (11) 7f; Flor., ii, 19; H (1), 18; *Chron.* 1071. For Hereward and Outlaws in general: Keen. Note three different ends for Hereward: lives on in peace, is killed in own home, is killed in quarrel with son-in-law, Hugh de Ewermouthe.

13. Flowers: Keen, 30. Wild: Ritchie (1), 31. Eadric: Walter Map, *Courtiers' Trifles* (end of 12 c.); Keen 29. For ordinary fugitives from the law, often taking to woods: D. M. Stenton, 147f.

14. Keen, chs. 4–5; Legge, 171–5. Castle of Whittington and *Brutt*: Keen, 41.

15. Faral (2), ii, 9; Chambers (1), 21, 95–9; Legge, 32. The tree symbol is

used, without the dream of Edward, in the verse *Life of Edward the Confessor* by a man of Barking: written early in the reign of *Henry II*, with stress on the Norman origin of the king's mother. Ailred's *Latin Life* is dated 1163. The nun goes back to Alfred the Great; and we may note that Marie de France (who prob. wrote later for Henry II's court) attributed to Alfred the fables she professed to be translating.

16. Compare the star battles in Sibylline Books and Nonnos' *Dionysiaka*: J. Lindsay (4), (5). Merovingians: Le Goff.

17. Chambers, 28. Note abbot Suger expounded the passage on Henry I in *Life of Louis the Fat* (written before 1152), by John of Cornwall in his hexameter version of the *Prophecies* (dedicated about 1155 to bishop of Exeter); and c. 1167–83 the Doctor Universalis, Alain de Lille, published a long commentary (printed 1603 as *Prophetia Anglica*).

18. Chambers, 18,, 249; PL, clvi, 983. W. of M. (before 1125) referred to Arthur as a man 'of whom the Britons tell so many tales, even to the present day', adding 'he long upheld the sinking state and roused the broken spirits of his countrymen'. Gervase: Chambers, 221f; Lombard documents: Loomis (1), 179, 198–214. O. Pächt on illustrations of Arthurian material; Lejeune on *Roland* shows that it first clearly deals with the legend in S. France.

19. Bec: Parry, 5. Espec: Legge (1), 28, Wace, 30f, Crestien, 31. Gaimar: Legge, 28–36, 277ff; Parry, 72–93; Bell, 56. Ralph: D. M. Williamson. Becher, 39, thinks it is David Bishop of Bangor writing in Latin. *AS Chronicle*: Darlington (2), 6. *Haveloc*: Bell (2), (3), and Fahnestock. *Bruts*: Legge, 280ff. Thomas: *ib.* 58. Wace: *ib.* 45, 50. Bestiaries, *ib.* 22ff.

20. H. M. Chadwick (1), 110.

21. Baker, ch. 10. Tradition: R. W. Chambers (4). Heiresses: Stubbs (1), 374, no 6.

22. Galbraith (1), 122f. Norman French, variant of central French, which evolved into Anglo-Norman, was even more provincial by 13th c., and the court looked to the French of Paris as more fashionable. Loan words show the English folk in inferior position: French provides abstract nouns, words connected with government, law, war, church. Not many place-names affected, though monasteries, for example, often called themselves after parent houses: Orr, 11.

23. R. W. Chambers (5), 139; Galbraith (1), 124f.

CHAPTER XVI
A WIDER PERSPECTIVE

1. Maitland; H (2), 269. Feudalism: H (2), 278; Galbraith (5), 177; Barlow (1), 440; Strayer (1), 51f; Dobb; Hilton. Also Cronne (3); Coulborn; Ganshof (1), (2); H (5), (6); Holt (1); D (5). See discussion H (2), ch. i, Sayles (1), 199f, 211f; M. Hollings, etc.

2. Tribal society reveals a large number of stages or levels, which have never been fully or correctly analysed and related: J.L. (3) and (7).

3. I owe much here to Dobb and Hilton.

4. Cam (1), 63; relation to manor, ch. v; link of grant of hundred with royal manor, 69f; in-hundred, out-hundred, 74.

5. Germany: Barraclough (1), 136ff. Note election of Henry the Fowler duke of Saxony as German ruler in 919; reduction of power of English earls by election of the greatest one, Harold, as king. Also effort by

Frederick Barbarossa in 12th c. to widen the class of counts and dukes who ruled locally (some 300 of them) by getting their sons and daughters to intermarry with his *ministrales*, while the latter in turn became landowners; he hoped thus to bind large areas (N. Italy, Burgundy, Germany), but was drawn into clash with duke of Saxony, Henry the Lion, and the link of emperor and princes could not be made as strong as that of vassal and local lord.

6. Verlinden (2). Germanic settlement of Belgium and establishment of the linguistic frontier came later, the result of colonizing activity in the framework of the Merovingian state, then the Carolingian. Gaul, 6–7 c., P. Demolon, *La village mérov. de Brebières* (1972). Sporadic eastern contacts: Indian elephants (via Italy) in Gaul, 801; African dromedaries, mid-9th c. (via Spain) on Rhine banks; 986, two-humped Asiatic camel at Quedlinburg, Saxony: M. Lombard, *Espaces et roseaux du haut m.a.*

7. Loyn (3), 195.

8. LL, 375; W (3), 557.

9. GR (RS), ii, 399. Fawtier says by 13th c. a sort of feudal nationality emerging. Galbraith (1), 114f; Green, 12. Peasants: P. Lindsay, 20. Tithing: L (2), 269f; Maitland; Pollock, i, 526, 569; we must not forget also the ale-house or tavern as club centre. Note effect of *nationes* in universities.

10. Phillpotts, etc. Lyon (1), 297; *gegaldan* paid to a substitute kindred when a true kindred was lacking – such formations helped the idea of associations for other purposes. Painter (3), 195–219 (Family in 12th c.).

11. Ganshof, *Byzantion*, iv, 658–60; Maeri, 73, 89 etc. Early Venetian trade: PL, cxxxiii, 658. The emperor Frederick II granted Jewish artisans in Sicily the monopoly of silk manufacture and dyeing in Sicily and Apulia. Li i, 173, 675; Attenborough, 156ff; S (1), 6. Writs: Robinson, 137; S (4), 85–90 on *baro*; *Hist. MSS Comm.*, 14th, app, pt. viii, 216.

12. Bréhier, 386.

13. Kiernan, 22f: I owe much to his suggestive essay.

14. A. P. d'Entrèves, *Dante as Political Thinker*, 1952, 57; in general, Gierke; Lagarde; Theseider; Ullmann (EHR, 1949) etc. Bettenson for Gregory. Moslems: Kiernan, 32; Letter, Marx to Engels, 2 June 1853. Europeans: Green, 2; Hay.

15. Kiernan, 25f.

16. Hilton (9), 71.

17. Pirenne (3), 507; A. Guesnon, *Livre de la Vintaine d'Arras*, on traders there 1222.

18. Pirenne, 509, 511: man of Cahors.

19. Hilton (10), 25. There are no records of amount and character of wage labour used by peasants and smaller (usually lay) landlords; yet in late 13th c. this was probably larger in extent and decisive in determining the direction. Carlo Cipolla for way relatively backward areas catch up with late developers; England among late developers, with peasants gaining spending power and stirring up industrial production. For effects Trade and Finance: M. M. Postan, *Essays on Med. Agriculture* etc. T. H. Lloyd, *Movement of Wool Prices in Med. Eng.* for failure of wool prices to get landowners to shift from corn before 1450s.

20. Hilton (9), 71f.

21. J. Mackinnon, *Luther and Reformation* 1925–9, iii, 161ff.

22. Dobb (1), 171, (2); Tahahashi 43–8; in general Unwin and Max Weber, etc.

INDEX